GENERAL MOTORS

PONTIAC MID-SIZE
1974-83 REPAIR MANUAL

SSF

D1474392

CHILTON'S

President	Dean F. Morgantini, S.A.E.
Vice President–Finance	Barry L. Beck
Vice President–Sales	Glenn D. Potere
Managing Editor	Kevin M. G. Maher
Production Manager	Ben Greisler, S.A.E.
Project Managers	Michael Abraham, Will Kessler, A.S.E., Richard Schwartz
Editor	Christine L. Nuckowski, S.A.E.

CHILTON™ Automotive Books
PUBLISHED BY W. G. NICHOLS, INC.

Manufactured in USA
© 1997 W. G. Nichols
Chilton Way, Radnor, PA 19089
ISBN 0-8019-9074-2
Library of Congress Catalog Card No. 97-67989
1234567890 6543210987

Contents

1 GENERAL INFORMATION AND MAINTENANCE

1-2	HOW TO USE THIS BOOK
1-3	TOOLS AND EQUIPMENT
1-7	SERVICING YOUR VEHICLE SAFELY
1-8	FASTENERS, MEASUREMENTS AND CONVERSIONS
1-14	SERIAL NUMBER IDENTIFICATION
1-19	ROUTINE MAINTENANCE
1-42	FLUIDS AND LUBRICANTS
1-58	TRAILER TOWING
1-59	JUMP STARTING A DEAD BATTERY
1-60	JACKING
1-62	HOW TO BUY A USED VEHICLE

2 ENGINE PERFORMANCE AND TUNE-UP

2-2	TUNE-UP PROCEDURES
2-8	FIRING ORDERS
2-9	POINT TYPE IGNITION
2-12	HIGH ENERGY IGNITION (HEI) SYSTEM
2-20	IGNITION TIMING
2-21	DIESEL INJECTION TIMING
2-21	VALVE LASH
2-22	IDLE SPEED AND MIXTURE ADJUSTMENTS

3 ENGINE AND ENGINE REBUILDING

3-2	ENGINE ELECTRICAL
3-22	ENGINE MECHANICAL
3-90	EXHAUST SYSTEM

4 EMISSION CONTROLS

4-2	AIR POLLUTION
4-3	AUTOMOTIVE EMISSIONS
4-5	EVAPORATIVE EMISSION CONTROLS
4-9	EXHAUST EMISSION CONTROLS
4-31	DIESEL ENGINE EMISSIONS CONTROLS
4-34	VACUUM DIAGRAMS

5 FUEL SYSTEM

5-2	BASIC FUEL SYSTEM DIAGNOSIS
5-2	CARBURETED FUEL SYSTEM
5-25	DIESEL ENGINE FUEL SYSTEM
5-29	FUEL TANK

6 CHASSIS ELECTRICAL

6-2	UNDERSTANDING AND TROUBLESHOOTING ELECTRICAL SYSTEMS
6-12	HEATER
6-20	RADIO
6-24	WINDSHIELD WIPERS
6-27	INSTRUMENTS AND SWITCHES
6-32	LIGHTING
6-39	TRAILER WIRING
6-39	CIRCUIT PROTECTION
6-44	WIRING DIAGRAMS

Contents

7-2 MANUAL TRANSMISSION   **7-23** DRIVELINE
7-7 CLUTCH   **7-26** REAR AXLE
7-12 AUTOMATIC TRANSMISSION

DRIVE TRAIN   7

8-2 WHEELS   **8-13** REAR SUSPENSION
8-2 FRONT SUSPENSION   **8-20** STEERING

SUSPENSION AND STEERING   8

9-2 BRAKE OPERATING SYSTEM   **9-24** REAR DRUM BRAKES
9-12 FRONT DISC BRAKES   **9-29** PARKING BRAKE

BRAKES   9

10-2 EXTERIOR   **10-10** INTERIOR

BODY   10

10-27 GLOSSARY

GLOSSARY

10-31 MASTER INDEX

MASTER INDEX

SAFETY NOTICE

Proper service and repair procedures are vital to the safe, reliable operation of all motor vehicles, as well as the personal safety of those performing repairs. This manual outlines procedures for servicing and repairing vehicles using safe, effective methods. The procedures contain many NOTES, CAUTIONS and WARNINGS which should be followed along with standard procedures to eliminate the possibility of personal injury or improper service which could damage the vehicle or compromise its safety.

It is important to note that the repair procedures and techniques, tools and parts for servicing motor vehicles, as well as the skill and experience of the individual performing the work vary widely. It is not possible to anticipate all of the conceivable ways or conditions under which vehicles may be serviced, or to provide cautions as to all of the possible hazards that may result. Standard and accepted safety precautions and equipment should be used when handling toxic or flammable fluids, and safety goggles or other protection should be used during cutting, grinding, chiseling, prying, or any other process that can cause material removal or projectiles.

Some procedures require the use of tools specially designed for a specific purpose. Before substituting another tool or procedure, you must be completely satisfied that neither your personal safety, nor the performance of the vehicle will be endangered.

Although information in this manual is based on industry sources and is complete as possible at the time of publication, the possibility exists that some vehicle manufacturers made later changes which could not be included here. While striving for total accuracy, W. G. Nichols. Inc. cannot assume responsibility for any errors, changes or omissions that may occur in the compilation of this data.

PART NUMBERS

Part numbers listed in this reference are not recommendations by Chilton for any product by brand name. They are references that can be used with interchange manuals and aftermarket supplier catalogs to locate each brand supplier's discrete part number.

SPECIAL TOOLS

Special tools are recommended by the vehicle manufacturer to perform their specific job. Use has been kept to a minimum, but where absolutely necessary, they are referred to in the text by the part number of the tool manufacturer. These tools can be purchased, under the appropriate part number, from your local dealer or regional distributor, or an equivalent tool can be purchased locally from a tool supplier or parts outlet. Before substituting any tool for the one recommended, read the SAFETY NOTICE at the top of this page.

ACKNOWLEDGMENTS

Portions of the materials contained herein have been reprinted with the permission of General Motors Corporation, Service Technology Group.

HOW TO USE THIS BOOK 1-2
WHERE TO BEGIN 1-2
AVOIDING TROUBLE 1-2
MAINTENANCE OR REPAIR? 1-2
AVOIDING THE MOST COMMON
  MISTAKES 1-2
TOOLS AND EQUIPMENT 1-3
SPECIAL TOOLS 1-6
SERVICING YOUR VEHICLE SAFELY 1-7
DO'S 1-7
DON'TS 1-8
**FASTENERS, MEASUREMENTS AND
  CONVERSIONS 1-8**
BOLTS, NUTS AND OTHER THREADED
  RETAINERS 1-8
TORQUE 1-9
  TORQUE WRENCHES 1-11
  TORQUE ANGLE METERS 1-12
STANDARD AND METRIC
  MEASUREMENTS 1-12
SERIAL NUMBER IDENTIFICATION 1-14
VEHICLE 1-14
  ENGINE 1-15
TRANSMISSION 1-17
  MANUAL TRANSMISSIONS 1-17
  AUTOMATIC TRANSMISSIONS 1-17
VEHICLE EMISSION CONTROL INFORMATION
  LABEL 1-17
ROUTINE MAINTENANCE 1-19
AIR CLEANER 1-20
  REMOVAL & INSTALLATION 1-20
POSITIVE CRANKCASE VENTILATION (PCV)
  VALVE 1-20
  REMOVAL & INSTALLATION 1-21
CRANKCASE DEPRESSION REGULATOR AND
  FLOW CONTROL VALVE 1-21
  SERVICING 1-21
EVAPORATIVE CANISTER 1-22
  SERVICING 1-22
FUEL FILTER 1-22
  REMOVAL & INSTALLATION 1-22
BATTERY 1-24
  GENERAL MAINTENANCE 1-24
  BATTERY FLUID 1-24
  CABLES 1-26
  CHARGING 1-27
  REPLACEMENT 1-27
BELTS 1-27
  INSPECTION 1-27
  CHECKING TENSION & ADJUSTING 1-28
  REMOVAL & INSTALLATION 1-29
HOSES 1-30
  INSPECTION 1-30
  REMOVAL & INSTALLATION 1-30
AIR CONDITIONING 1-31
  SAFETY PRECAUTIONS 1-31
  GENERAL SERVICING PROCEDURES 1-32
  SYSTEM INSPECTION 1-33
  DISCHARGING, EVACUATING &
    CHARGING 1-33
WINDSHIELD WIPERS 1-34
  ELEMENT (REFILL) CARE &
    REPLACEMENT 1-34
TIRES AND WHEELS 1-38
  TIRE ROTATION 1-38
  TIRE DESIGN 1-39
  TIRE STORAGE 1-39
  INFLATION & INSPECTION 1-39
  CARE OF SPECIAL WHEELS 1-41
FLUIDS AND LUBRICANTS 1-42
FLUID DISPOSAL 1-42
ENGINE OIL AND FUEL
  RECOMMENDATIONS 1-42
  OIL 1-43
  SYNTHETIC OIL 1-44

FUEL 1-44
ENGINE 1-45
  LEVEL CHECK 1-45
  OIL & FILTER CHANGE 1-46
MANUAL TRANSMISSION 1-48
  FLUID RECOMMENDATIONS 1-48
  LEVEL CHECK 1-48
  DRAIN & REFILL 1-48
AUTOMATIC TRANSMISSION 1-48
  LEVEL CHECK & FLUID
    RECOMMENDATIONS 1-48
  DRAIN, REFILL & FILTER SERVICE 1-49
REAR AXLE 1-49
  LEVEL CHECK & FLUID
    RECOMMENDATIONS 1-49
  DRAIN & REFILL 1-50
COOLING SYSTEM 1-50
  LEVEL CHECK & FLUID
    RECOMMENDATIONS 1-50
  DRAINING, FLUSHING & TESTING THE
    COOLING SYSTEM 1-52
  CHECK THE RADIATOR CAP 1-53
  CLEAN THE RADIATOR OF DEBRIS 1-53
BRAKE MASTER CYLINDER 1-54
  LEVEL CHECK & FLUID
    RECOMMENDATIONS 1-54
POWER STEERING PUMP 1-54
  LEVEL CHECK & FLUID
    RECOMMENDATIONS 1-54
CHASSIS GREASING 1-55
  FRONT SUSPENSION 1-55
  STEERING LINKAGE 1-56
  PARKING BRAKE LINKAGE 1-56
  AUTOMATIC TRANSMISSION LINKAGE 1-57
BODY LUBRICATION 1-57
  HOOD LATCH & HINGES 1-57
  DOOR HINGES 1-57
WHEEL BEARINGS 1-58
  REMOVAL, PACKING & INSTALLATION 1-58
TRAILER TOWING 1-58
GENERAL RECOMMENDATIONS 1-58
TRAILER WEIGHT 1-58
HITCH (TONGUE) WEIGHT 1-58
COOLING 1-58
  ENGINE 1-58
  TRANSMISSION 1-59
HANDLING A TRAILER 1-59
JUMP STARTING A DEAD BATTERY 1-59
JUMP STARTING PRECAUTIONS 1-59
JUMP STARTING PROCEDURE 1-60
JACKING 1-60
JACKING PRECAUTIONS 1-62
HOW TO BUY A USED VEHICLE 1-62
TIPS 1-62
  USED VEHICLE CHECKLIST 1-62
  ROAD TEST CHECKLIST 1-63
COMPONENT LOCATIONS
MAINTENANCE COMPONENT LOCATIONS—231
V6 1-19
SPECIFICATION CHARTS
STANDARD TORQUE SPECIFICATIONS AND
  FASTENER MARKINGS 1-10
ENGINE IDENTIFICATION CODES 1-16
RECOMMENDED LUBRICANTS 1-43
1974–76 MAINTENANCE INTERVALS—
  GASOLINE-ENGINED CARS 1-64
1977 AND LATER MAINTENANCE INTERVALS—
  GASOLINE-ENGINED CARS 1-65
DIESEL MAINTENANCE INTERVALS 1-66
CAPACITIES CHART 1-67
ENGLISH TO METRIC CONVERSION
  CHARTS 1-70

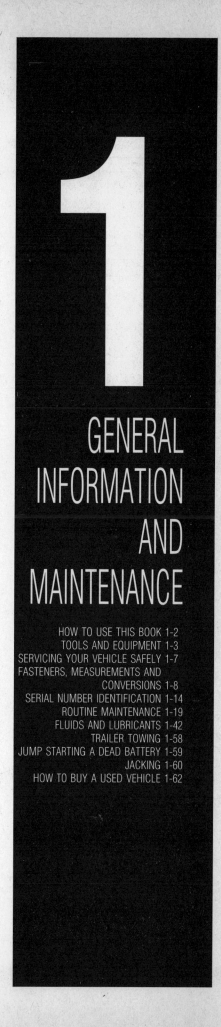

1

GENERAL INFORMATION AND MAINTENANCE

HOW TO USE THIS BOOK 1-2
TOOLS AND EQUIPMENT 1-3
SERVICING YOUR VEHICLE SAFELY 1-7
FASTENERS, MEASUREMENTS AND
  CONVERSIONS 1-8
SERIAL NUMBER IDENTIFICATION 1-14
ROUTINE MAINTENANCE 1-19
FLUIDS AND LUBRICANTS 1-42
TRAILER TOWING 1-58
JUMP STARTING A DEAD BATTERY 1-59
JACKING 1-60
HOW TO BUY A USED VEHICLE 1-62

HOW TO USE THIS BOOK

Chilton's Total Car Care manual is intended to help you learn more about the inner workings of your vehicle while saving you money on its upkeep and operation.

The beginning of the book will likely be referred to the most, since that is where you will find information for maintenance and tune-up. The other sections deal with the more complex systems of your vehicle. Operating systems from engine through brakes are covered to the extent that the average do-it-yourselfer becomes mechanically involved. This book will not explain such things as rebuilding a differential for the simple reason that the expertise required and the investment in special tools make this task uneconomical. It will, however, give you detailed instructions to help you change your own brake pads and shoes, replace spark plugs, and perform many more jobs that can save you money, give you personal satisfaction and help you avoid expensive problems.

A secondary purpose of this book is a reference for owners who want to understand their vehicle and/or their mechanics better. In this case, no tools at all are required.

Where to Begin

Before removing any bolts, read through the entire procedure. This will give you the overall view of what tools and supplies will be required. There is nothing more frustrating than having to walk to the bus stop on Monday morning because you were short one bolt on Sunday afternoon. So read ahead and plan ahead. Each operation should be approached logically and all procedures thoroughly understood before attempting any work.

All sections contain adjustments, maintenance, removal and installation procedures, and in some cases, repair or overhaul procedures. When repair is not considered practical, we tell you how to remove the part and then how to install the new or rebuilt replacement. In this way, you at least save the labor costs. Backyard repair of some components is just not practical.

Avoiding Trouble

Many procedures in this book require you to "label and disconnect . . ." a group of lines, hoses or wires. Don't be lulled into thinking you can remember where everything goes—you won't. If you hook up vacuum or fuel lines incorrectly, the vehicle will run poorly, if at all. If you hook up electrical wiring incorrectly, you may instantly learn a very expensive lesson.

You don't need to know the official or engineering name for each hose or line. A piece of masking tape on the hose and a piece on its fitting will allow you to assign your own label such as the letter A or a short name. As long as you remember your own code, the lines can be reconnected by matching similar letters or names. Do remember that tape will dissolve in gasoline or other fluids; if a component is to be washed or cleaned, use another method of identification. A permanent felt-tipped marker can be very handy for marking metal parts. Remove any tape or paper labels after assembly.

Maintenance or Repair?

It's necessary to mention the difference between maintenance and repair. Maintenance includes routine inspections, adjustments, and replacement of parts which show signs of normal wear. Maintenance compensates for wear or deterioration. Repair implies that something has broken or is not working. A need for repair is often caused by lack of maintenance. Example: draining and refilling the automatic transmission fluid is maintenance recommended by the manufacturer at specific mileage intervals. Failure to do this can ruin the transmission/transaxle, requiring very expensive repairs. While no maintenance program can prevent items from breaking or wearing out, a general rule can be stated: MAINTENANCE IS CHEAPER THAN REPAIR.

Two basic mechanic's rules should be mentioned here. First, whenever the left side of the vehicle or engine is referred to, it is meant to specify the driver's side. Conversely, the right side of the vehicle means the passenger's side. Second, most screws and bolts are removed by turning counterclockwise, and tightened by turning clockwise.

Safety is always the most important rule. Constantly be aware of the dangers involved in working on an automobile and take the proper precautions. See the information in this section regarding SERVICING YOUR VEHICLE SAFELY and the SAFETY NOTICE on the acknowledgment page.

Avoiding the Most Common Mistakes

Pay attention to the instructions provided. There are 3 common mistakes in mechanical work:

1. **Incorrect order of assembly, disassembly or adjustment.** When taking something apart or putting it together, performing steps in the wrong order usually just costs you extra time; however, it CAN break something. Read the entire procedure before beginning disassembly. Perform everything in the order in which the instructions say you should, even if you can't immediately see a reason for it. When you're taking apart something that is very intricate, you might want to draw a picture of how it looks when assembled at one point in order to make sure you get everything back in its proper position. We will supply exploded views whenever possible. When making adjustments, perform them in the proper order; often, one adjustment affects another, and you cannot expect even satisfactory results unless each adjustment is made only when it cannot be changed by any other.

2. **Overtorquing (or undertorquing).** While it is more common for overtorquing to cause damage, undertorquing may allow a fastener to vibrate loose causing serious damage. Especially when dealing with aluminum parts, pay attention to torque specifications and utilize a torque wrench in assembly. If a torque figure is not available, remember that if you are using the right tool to perform the job, you will probably not have to strain yourself to get a fastener tight enough. The pitch of most threads is so slight that the tension you put on the wrench will be multiplied many times in actual force on what you are tightening. A good example of how critical torque is can be seen in the case of spark plug in-

stallation, especially where you are putting the plug into an aluminum cylinder head. Too little torque can fail to crush the gasket, causing leakage of combustion gases and consequent overheating of the plug and engine parts. Too much torque can damage the threads or distort the plug, changing the spark gap.

There are many commercial products available for ensuring that fasteners won't come loose, even if they are not torqued just right (a very common brand is Loctite®). If you're worried about getting something together tight enough to hold, but loose enough to avoid mechanical damage during assembly, one of these products might offer substantial insurance. Before choosing a threadlocking compound, read the label on the package and make sure the product is compatible with the materials, fluids, etc. involved.

3. **Crossthreading.** This occurs when a part such as a bolt is screwed into a nut or casting at the wrong angle and forced. Crossthreading is more likely to occur if access is difficult. It helps to clean and lubricate fasteners, then to start threading with the part to be installed positioned straight in. Then, start the bolt, spark plug, etc. with your fingers. If you encounter resistance, unscrew the part and start over again at a different angle until it can be inserted and turned several times without much effort. Keep in mind that many parts, especially spark plugs, have tapered threads, so that gentle turning will automatically bring the part you're threading to the proper angle, but only if you don't force it or resist a change in angle. Don't put a wrench on the part until it's been tightened a couple of turns by hand. If you suddenly encounter resistance, and the part has not seated fully, don't force it. Pull it back out to make sure it's clean and threading properly.

Always take your time and be patient; once you have some experience, working on your vehicle may well become an enjoyable hobby.

TOOLS AND EQUIPMENT

Naturally, without the proper tools and equipment it is impossible to properly service your vehicle. It would also be virtually impossible to catalog every tool that you would need to perform all of the operations in this book. Of course, It would be unwise for the amateur to rush out and buy an expensive set of tools on the theory that he/she may need one or more of them at some time.

The best approach is to proceed slowly, gathering a good quality set of those tools that are used most frequently. Don't be misled by the low cost of bargain tools. It is far better to spend a little more for better quality. Forged wrenches, 6 or 12-point sockets and fine tooth ratchets are by far preferable to their less expensive counterparts. As any good mechanic can tell you, there are few worse experiences than trying to work on a vehicle with bad tools. Your monetary savings will be far outweighed by frustration and mangled knuckles.

Begin accumulating those tools that are used most frequently: those associated with routine maintenance and tune-up. In addition to the normal assortment of screwdrivers and pliers, you should have the following tools:

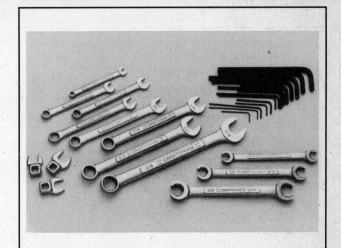

In addition to ratchets, a good set of wrenches and hex keys will be necessary

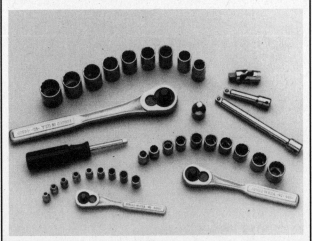

All but the most basic procedures will require an assortment of ratchets and sockets

A hydraulic floor jack and a set of jackstands are essential for lifting and supporting the vehicle

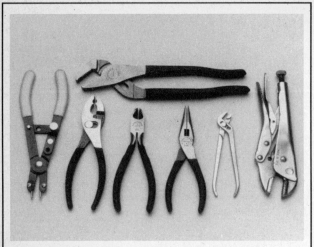

An assortment of pliers, grippers and cutters will be handy for old rusted parts and stripped bolt heads

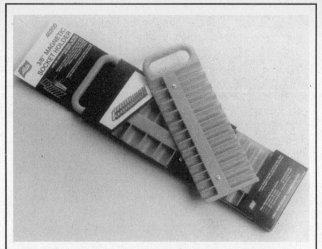

Tools from specialty manufacturers such as Lisle® are designed to make your job easier . . .

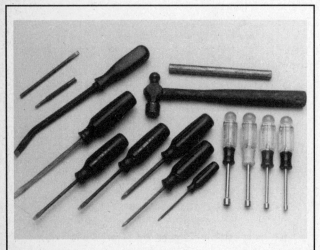

Various drivers, chisels and prybars are great tools to have in your toolbox

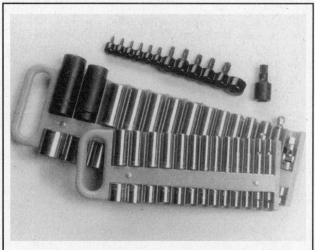

. . . these Torx® drivers and magnetic socket holders are just 2 examples of their handy products

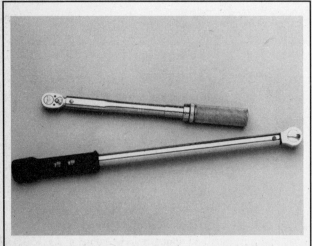

Many repairs will require the use of a torque wrench to assure the components are properly fastened

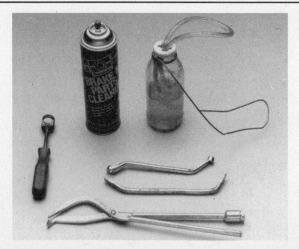

Although not always necessary, using specialized brake tools will save time

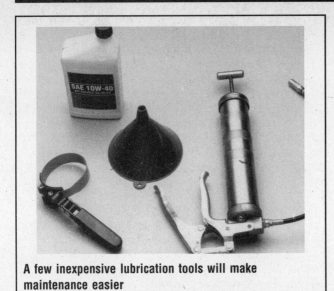

A few inexpensive lubrication tools will make maintenance easier

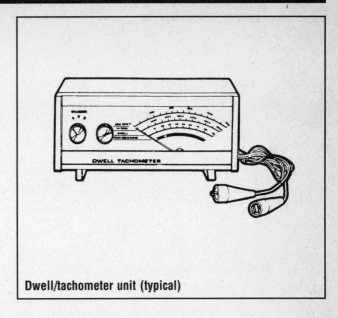

Dwell/tachometer unit (typical)

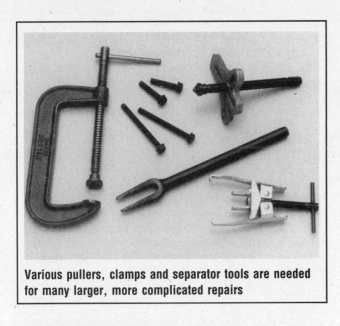

Various pullers, clamps and separator tools are needed for many larger, more complicated repairs

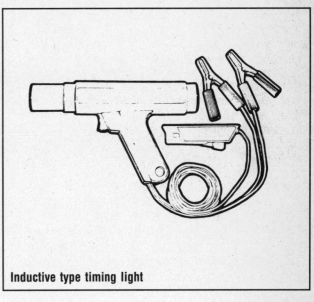

Inductive type timing light

A variety of tools and gauges should be used for spark plug gapping and installation

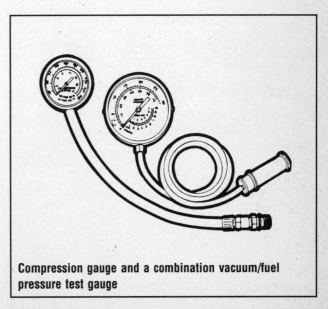

Compression gauge and a combination vacuum/fuel pressure test gauge

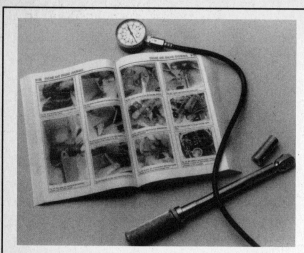

Proper information is vital, so always have a Chilton Total Car Care manual handy

• Wrenches/sockets and combination open end/box end wrenches in sizes from 1/8–3/4 in. or 3mm–19mm (depending on whether your vehicle uses standard or metric fasteners) and a 13/16 in. or 5/8 in. spark plug socket (depending on plug type).

➡**If possible, buy various length socket drive extensions. Universal-joint and wobble extensions can be extremely useful, but be careful when using them, as they can change the amount of torque applied to the socket.**

• Jackstands for support.
• Oil filter wrench.
• Spout or funnel for pouring fluids.
• Grease gun for chassis lubrication (unless your vehicle is not equipped with any grease fittings—for details, please refer to information on Fluids and Lubricants found later in this section).
• Hydrometer for checking the battery (unless equipped with a sealed, maintenance-free battery).
• A container for draining oil and other fluids.
• Rags for wiping up the inevitable mess.

In addition to the above items there are several others that are not absolutely necessary, but handy to have around. These include Oil Dry® (or an equivalent oil absorbent gravel—such as cat litter) and the usual supply of lubricants, antifreeze and fluids, although these can be purchased as needed. This is a basic list for routine maintenance, but only your personal needs and desire can accurately determine your list of tools.

After performing a few projects on the vehicle, you'll be amazed at the other tools and non-tools on your workbench. Some useful household items are: a large turkey baster or siphon, empty coffee cans and ice trays (to store parts), ball of twine, electrical tape for wiring, small rolls of colored tape for tagging lines or hoses, markers and pens, a note pad, golf tees (for plugging vacuum lines), metal coat hangers or a roll of mechanics's wire (to hold things out of the way), dental pick or similar long, pointed probe, a strong magnet, and a small mirror (to see into recesses and under manifolds).

A more advanced set of tools, suitable for tune-up work, can be drawn up easily. While the tools are slightly more sophisticated, they need not be outrageously expensive. There are several inexpensive tach/dwell meters on the market that are every bit as good for the average mechanic as a professional model. Just be sure that it goes to a least 1200–1500 rpm on the tach scale and that it works on 4, 6 and 8-cylinder engines. (If you own one or more vehicles with a diesel engine, a special tachometer is required since diesels don't use spark plug ignition systems). The key to these purchases is to make them with an eye towards adaptability and wide range. A basic list of tune-up tools could include:

• Tach/dwell meter.
• Spark plug wrench and gapping tool.
• Feeler gauges for valve or point adjustment. (Even if your vehicle does not use points or require valve adjustments, a feeler gauge is helpful for many repair/overhaul procedures).

A tachometer/dwell meter will ensure accurate tune-up work on vehicles without electronic ignition. The choice of a timing light should be made carefully. A light which works on the DC current supplied by the vehicle's battery is the best choice; it should have a xenon tube for brightness. On any vehicle with an electronic ignition system, a timing light with an inductive pickup that clamps around the No. 1 spark plug cable is preferred.

In addition to these basic tools, there are several other tools and gauges you may find useful. These include:

• Compression gauge. The screw-in type is slower to use, but eliminates the possibility of a faulty reading due to escaping pressure.
• Manifold vacuum gauge.
• 12V test light.
• A combination volt/ohmmeter
• Induction Ammeter. This is used for determining whether or not there is current in a wire. These are handy for use if a wire is broken somewhere in a wiring harness.

As a final note, you will probably find a torque wrench necessary for all but the most basic work. The beam type models are perfectly adequate, although the newer click types (breakaway) are easier to use. The click type torque wrenches tend to be more expensive. Also keep in mind that all types of torque wrenches should be periodically checked and/or recalibrated. You will have to decide for yourself which better fits your purpose.

Special Tools

Normally, the use of special factory tools is avoided for repair procedures, since these are not readily available for the do-it-yourself mechanic. When it is possible to perform the job with more commonly available tools, it will be pointed out, but occasionally, a special tool was designed to perform a specific function and should be used. Before substituting another tool, you should be convinced that neither your safety nor the performance of the vehicle will be compromised.

Special tools can usually be purchased from an automotive parts store or from your dealer. In some cases special tools may be available directly from the tool manufacturer.

SERVICING YOUR VEHICLE SAFELY

It is virtually impossible to anticipate all of the hazards involved with automotive maintenance and service, but care and common sense will prevent most accidents.

The rules of safety for mechanics range from "don't smoke around gasoline," to "use the proper tool(s) for the job." The trick to avoiding injuries is to develop safe work habits and to take every possible precaution.

Do's

• Do keep a fire extinguisher and first aid kit handy.

• Do wear safety glasses or goggles when cutting, drilling, grinding or prying, even if you have 20–20 vision. If you wear glasses for the sake of vision, wear safety goggles over your regular glasses.

• Do shield your eyes whenever you work around the battery. Batteries contain sulfuric acid. In case of contact with the eyes or

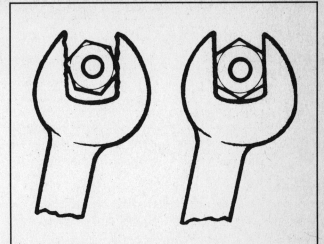

Using the correct size wrench will help prevent the possibility of rounding off a nut

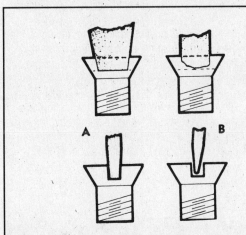

Screwdrivers should be kept in good condition to prevent injury or damage which could result if the blade slips from the screw

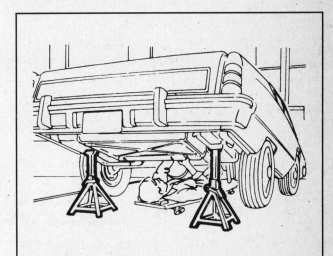

NEVER work under a vehicle unless it is supported using safety stands (jackstands)

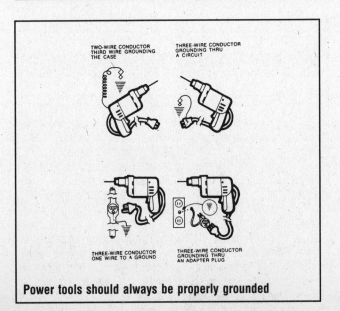

Power tools should always be properly grounded

skin, flush the area with water or a mixture of water and baking soda, then seek immediate medical attention.

• Do use safety stands (jackstands) for any undervehicle service. Jacks are for raising vehicles; jackstands are for making sure the vehicle stays raised until you want it to come down. Whenever the vehicle is raised, block the wheels remaining on the ground and set the parking brake.

• Do use adequate ventilation when working with any chemicals or hazardous materials. Like carbon monoxide, the asbestos dust resulting from some brake lining wear can be hazardous in sufficient quantities.

• Do disconnect the negative battery cable when working on the electrical system. The secondary ignition system contains EXTREMELY HIGH VOLTAGE. In some cases it can even exceed 50,000 volts.

• Do follow manufacturer's directions whenever working with potentially hazardous materials. Most chemicals and fluids are poisonous if taken internally.

• Do properly maintain your tools. Loose hammerheads, mushroomed punches and chisels, frayed or poorly grounded electrical cords, excessively worn screwdrivers, spread wrenches (open end), cracked sockets, slipping ratchets, or faulty droplight sockets can cause accidents.

• Likewise, keep your tools clean; a greasy wrench can slip off a bolt head, ruining the bolt and often harming your knuckles in the process.

• Do use the proper size and type of tool for the job at hand. Do select a wrench or socket that fits the nut or bolt. The wrench or socket should sit straight, not cocked.

• Do, when possible, pull on a wrench handle rather than push on it, and adjust your stance to prevent a fall.

• Do be sure that adjustable wrenches are tightly closed on the nut or bolt and pulled so that the force is on the side of the fixed jaw.

• Do strike squarely with a hammer; avoid glancing blows.

• Do set the parking brake and block the drive wheels if the work requires a running engine.

Don'ts

• Don't run the engine in a garage or anywhere else without proper ventilation—EVER! Carbon monoxide is poisonous; it takes a long time to leave the human body and you can build up a deadly supply of it in your system by simply breathing in a little every day. You may not realize you are slowly poisoning yourself. Always use power vents, windows, fans and/or open the garage door.

• Don't work around moving parts while wearing loose clothing. Short sleeves are much safer than long, loose sleeves. Hard-toed shoes with neoprene soles protect your toes and give a better grip on slippery surfaces. Jewelry such as watches, fancy belt buckles, beads or body adornment of any kind is not safe working around a vehicle. Long hair should be tied back under a hat or cap.

• Don't use pockets for toolboxes. A fall or bump can drive a screwdriver deep into your body. Even a rag hanging from your back pocket can wrap around a spinning shaft or fan.

• Don't smoke when working around gasoline, cleaning solvent or other flammable material.

• Don't smoke when working around the battery. When the battery is being charged, it gives off explosive hydrogen gas.

• Don't use gasoline to wash your hands; there are excellent soaps available. Gasoline contains dangerous additives which can enter the body through a cut or through your pores. Gasoline also removes all the natural oils from the skin so that bone dry hands will suck up oil and grease.

• Don't service the air conditioning system unless you are equipped with the necessary tools and training. When liquid or compressed gas refrigerant is released to atmospheric pressure it will absorb heat from whatever it contacts. This will chill or freeze anything it touches. Although refrigerant is normally non-toxic, R-12 becomes a deadly poisonous gas in the presence of an open flame. One good whiff of the vapors from burning refrigerant can be fatal.

• Don't use screwdrivers for anything other than driving screws! A screwdriver used as an prying tool can snap when you least expect it, causing injuries. At the very least, you'll ruin a good screwdriver.

• Don't use a bumper or emergency jack (that little ratchet, scissors, or pantograph jack supplied with the vehicle) for anything other than changing a flat! These jacks are only intended for emergency use out on the road; they are NOT designed as a maintenance tool. If you are serious about maintaining your vehicle yourself, invest in a hydraulic floor jack of at least a 1½ ton capacity, and at least two sturdy jackstands.

FASTENERS, MEASUREMENTS AND CONVERSIONS

Bolts, Nuts and Other Threaded Retainers

Although there are a great variety of fasteners found in the modern car or truck, the most commonly used retainer is the threaded fastener (nuts, bolts, screws, studs, etc). Most threaded retainers may be reused, provided that they are not damaged in use or during the repair. Some retainers (such as stretch bolts or torque prevailing nuts) are designed to deform when tightened or in use and should not be reinstalled.

Whenever possible, we will note any special retainers which should be replaced during a procedure. But you should always inspect the condition of a retainer when it is removed and replace any that show signs of damage. Check all threads for rust or corrosion which can increase the torque necessary to achieve the desired clamp load for which that fastener was originally selected. Additionally, be sure that the driver surface of the fastener has not been compromised by rounding or other damage. In some cases a driver surface may become only partially rounded, allowing the driver to catch in only one direction. In many of these occurrences, a fastener may be installed and tightened, but the driver would not be able to grip and loosen the fastener again. (This could lead to frustration down the line should that component ever need to be disassembled again).

If you must replace a fastener, whether due to design or damage, you must ALWAYS be sure to use the proper replacement. In all cases, a retainer of the same design, material and strength should be used. Markings on the heads of most bolts will help determine the proper strength of the fastener. The same material, thread and pitch must be selected to assure proper installation and safe operation of the vehicle afterwards.

Thread gauges are available to help measure a bolt or stud's thread. Most automotive and hardware stores keep gauges available to help you select the proper size. In a pinch, you can use another nut or bolt for a thread gauge. If the bolt you are replacing is not too badly damaged, you can select a match by finding another bolt which will thread in its place. If you find a nut which threads properly onto the damaged bolt, then use that nut to help select the replacement bolt. If however, the bolt you are replacing is so badly damaged (broken or drilled out) that its threads cannot be used as a gauge, you might start by looking for another bolt (from the same assembly or a similar location on your vehicle) which will thread into the damaged bolt's mounting. If so, the other bolt can be used to select a nut; the nut can then be used to select the replacement bolt.

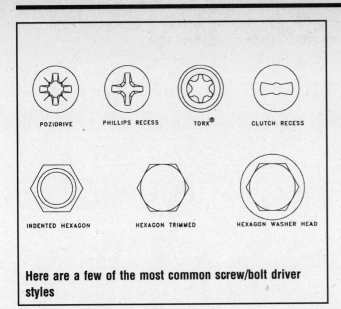

Here are a few of the most common screw/bolt driver styles

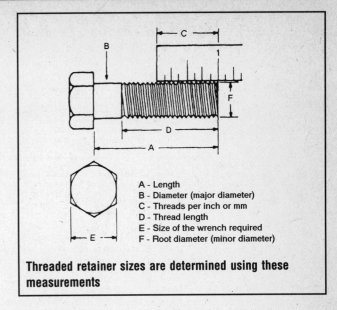

A - Length
B - Diameter (major diameter)
C - Threads per inch or mm
D - Thread length
E - Size of the wrench required
F - Root diameter (minor diameter)

Threaded retainer sizes are determined using these measurements

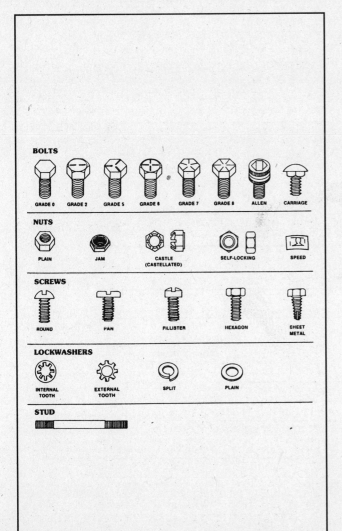

There are many different types of threaded retainers found on vehicles

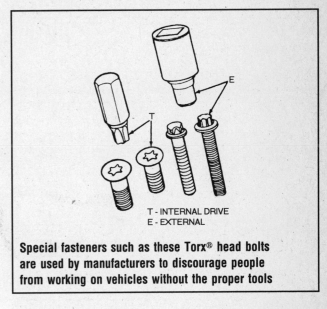

T - INTERNAL DRIVE
E - EXTERNAL

Special fasteners such as these Torx® head bolts are used by manufacturers to discourage people from working on vehicles without the proper tools

In all cases, be absolutely sure you have selected the proper replacement. Don't be shy, you can always ask the store clerk for help.

✳✳ WARNING

Be aware that when you find a bolt with damaged threads, you may also find the nut or drilled hole it was threaded into has also been damaged. If this is the case, you may have to drill and tap the hole, replace the nut or otherwise repair the threads. NEVER try to force a replacement bolt to fit into the damaged threads.

Torque

Torque is defined as the measurement of resistance to turning or rotating. It tends to twist a body about an axis of rotation. A common example of this would be tightening a threaded retainer such as a nut, bolt or screw. Measuring torque is one of the most

Standard Torque Specifications and Fastener Markings

In the absence of specific torques, the following chart can be used as a guide to the maximum safe torque of a particular size/grade of fastener.

- There is no torque difference for fine or coarse threads.
- Torque values are based on clean, dry threads. Reduce the value by 10% if threads are oiled prior to assembly.
- The torque required for aluminum components or fasteners is considerably less.

U.S. Bolts

SAE Grade Number	1 or 2			5			6 or 7		
Number of lines always 2 less than the grade number.									
Bolt Size (Inches)—(Thread)	Maximum Torque			Maximum Torque			Maximum Torque		
	Ft./Lbs.	Kgm	Nm	Ft./Lbs.	Kgm	Nm	Ft./Lbs.	Kgm	Nm
¼ —20	5	0.7	6.8	8	1.1	10.8	10	1.4	13.5
—28	6	0.8	8.1	10	1.4	13.6			
5/16 —18	11	1.5	14.9	17	2.3	23.0	19	2.6	25.8
—24	13	1.8	17.6	19	2.6	25.7			
⅜ —16	18	2.5	24.4	31	4.3	42.0	34	4.7	46.0
—24	20	2.75	27.1	35	4.8	47.5			
7/16 —14	28	3.8	37.0	49	6.8	66.4	55	7.6	74.5
—20	30	4.2	40.7	55	7.6	74.5			
½ —13	39	5.4	52.8	75	10.4	101.7	85	11.75	115.2
—20	41	5.7	55.6	85	11.7	115.2			
9/16 —12	51	7.0	69.2	110	15.2	149.1	120	16.6	162.7
—18	55	7.6	74.5	120	16.6	162.7			
⅝ —11	83	11.5	112.5	150	20.7	203.3	167	23.0	226.5
—18	95	13.1	128.8	170	23.5	230.5			
¾ —10	105	14.5	142.3	270	37.3	366.0	280	38.7	379.6
—16	115	15.9	155.9	295	40.8	400.0			
⅞ — 9	160	22.1	216.9	395	54.6	535.5	440	60.9	596.5
—14	175	24.2	237.2	435	60.1	589.7			
1 — 8	236	32.5	318.6	590	81.6	799.9	660	91.3	894.8
—14	250	34.6	338.9	660	91.3	849.8			

Metric Bolts

Relative Strength Marking	4.6, 4.8			8.8		
Bolt Markings						
Bolt Size Thread Size x Pitch (mm)	Maximum Torque			Maximum Torque		
	Ft./Lbs.	Kgm	Nm	Ft./Lbs.	Kgm	Nm
6 x 1.0	2–3	.2–.4	3–4	3–6	4–.8	5–8
8 x 1.25	6–8	.8–1	8–12	9–14	1.2–1.9	13–19
10 x 1.25	12–17	1.5–2.3	16–23	20–29	2.7–4.0	27–39
12 x 1.25	21–32	2.9–4.4	29–43	35–53	4.8–7.3	47–72
14 x 1.5	35–52	4.8–7.1	48–70	57–85	7.8–11.7	77–110
16 x 1.5	51–77	7.0–10.6	67–100	90–120	12.4–16.5	130–160
18 x 1.5	74–110	10.2–15.1	100–150	130–170	17.9–23.4	180–230
20 x 1.5	110–140	15.1–19.3	150–190	190–240	26.2–46.9	160–320
22 x 1.5	150–190	22.0–26.2	200–260	250–320	34.5–44.1	340–430
24 x 1.5	190–240	26.2–46.9	260–320	310–410	42.7–56.5	420–550

Standard and metric bolt torque specifications based on bolt strengths—WARNING: use only as a guide

common ways to help assure that a threaded retainer has been properly fastened.

When tightening a threaded fastener, torque is applied in three distinct areas, the head, the bearing surface and the clamp load. About 50 percent of the measured torque is used in overcoming bearing friction. This is the friction between the bearing surface of the bolt head, screw head or nut face and the base material or washer (the surface on which the fastener is rotating). Approximately 40 percent of the applied torque is used in overcoming thread friction. This leaves only about 10 percent of the applied torque to develop a useful clamp load (the force which holds a joint together). This means that friction can account for as much as 90 percent of the applied torque on a fastener.

TORQUE WRENCHES

In most applications, a torque wrench can be used to assure proper installation of a fastener. Torque wrenches come in various designs and most automotive supply stores will carry a variety to suit your needs. A torque wrench should be used any time we supply a specific torque value for a fastener. A torque wrench can also be used if you are following the general guidelines in the accompanying charts. Keep in mind that because there is no worldwide standardization of fasteners, the charts are a general guideline and should be used with caution. Again, the general rule of "if you are using the right tool for the job, you should not have to strain to tighten a fastener" applies here.

Beam Type

The beam type torque wrench is one of the most popular types. It consists of a pointer attached to the head that runs the length of the flexible beam (shaft) to a scale located near the handle. As the wrench is pulled, the beam bends and the pointer indicates the torque using the scale.

Click (Breakaway) Type

Another popular design of torque wrench is the click type. To use the click type wrench you pre-adjust it to a torque setting. Once the torque is reached, the wrench has a reflex signalling fea-

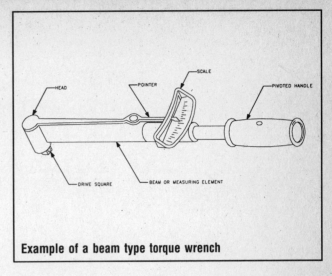

Example of a beam type torque wrench

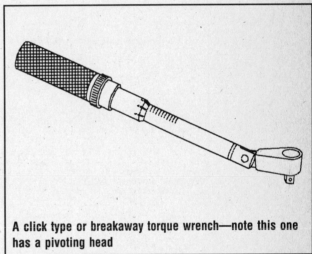

A click type or breakaway torque wrench—note this one has a pivoting head

ture that causes a momentary breakaway of the torque wrench body, sending an impulse to the operator's hand.

Pivot Head Type

Some torque wrenches (usually of the click type) may be equipped with a pivot head which can allow it to be used in areas of limited access. BUT, it must be used properly. To hold a pivot head wrench, grasp the handle lightly, and as you pull on the handle, it should be floated on the pivot point. If the handle comes in contact with the yoke extension during the process of pulling, there is a very good chance the torque readings will be inaccurate because this could alter the wrench loading point. The design of the handle is usually such as to make it inconvenient to deliberately misuse the wrench.

➡️ It should be mentioned that the use of any U-joint, wobble or extension will have an effect on the torque readings, no matter what type of wrench you are using. For the most accurate readings, install the socket directly on the wrench driver. If necessary, straight extensions (which hold a socket directly under the wrench driver) will have the least effect on the torque reading. Avoid any extension that alters the length of the wrench from the handle to the head/driving point (such as a crow's foot). U-joint or Wobble extensions can greatly affect the readings; avoid their use at all times.

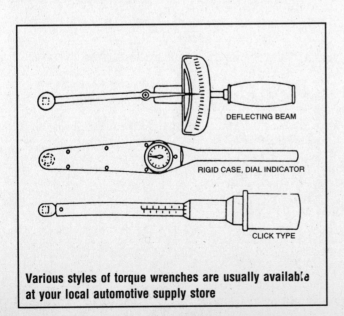

Various styles of torque wrenches are usually available at your local automotive supply store

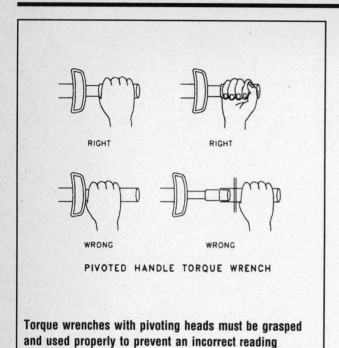

Torque wrenches with pivoting heads must be grasped and used properly to prevent an incorrect reading

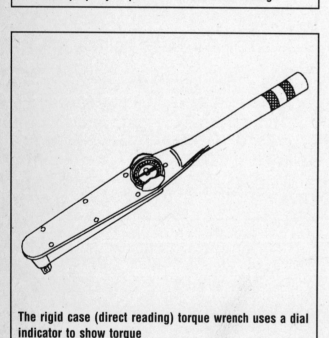

The rigid case (direct reading) torque wrench uses a dial indicator to show torque

Rigid Case (Direct Reading)

A rigid case or direct reading torque wrench is equipped with a dial indicator to show torque values. One advantage of these wrenches is that they can be held at any position on the wrench without affecting accuracy. These wrenches are often preferred because they tend to be compact, easy to read and have a great degree of accuracy.

TORQUE ANGLE METERS

Because the frictional characteristics of each fastener or threaded hole will vary, clamp loads which are based strictly on

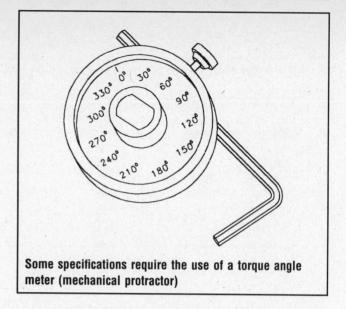

Some specifications require the use of a torque angle meter (mechanical protractor)

torque will vary as well. In most applications, this variance is not significant enough to cause worry. But, in certain applications, a manufacturer's engineers may determine that more precise clamp loads are necessary (such is the case with many aluminum cylinder heads). In these cases, a torque angle method of installation would be specified. When installing fasteners which are torque angle tightened, a predetermined seating torque and standard torque wrench are usually used first to remove any compliance from the joint. The fastener is then tightened the specified additional portion of a turn measured in degrees. A torque angle gauge (mechanical protractor) is used for these applications.

Standard and Metric Measurements

Throughout this manual, specifications are given to help you determine the condition of various components on your vehicle, or to assist you in their installation. Some of the most common measurements include length (in. or cm/mm), torque (ft. lbs., inch lbs. or Nm) and pressure (psi, in. Hg, kPa or mm Hg). In most cases, we strive to provide the proper measurement as determined by the manufacturer's engineers.

Though, in some cases, that value may not be conveniently measured with what is available in your toolbox. Luckily, many of the measuring devices which are available today will have two scales so the Standard or Metric measurements may easily be taken. If any of the various measuring tools which are available to you do not contain the same scale as listed in the specifications, use the accompanying conversion factors to determine the proper value.

The conversion factor chart is used by taking the given specification and multiplying it by the necessary conversion factor. For instance, looking at the first line, if you have a measurement in inches such as "free-play should be 2 in." but your ruler reads only in millimeters, multiply 2 in. by the conversion factor of 25.4 to get the metric equivalent of 50.8mm. Likewise, if the specification was given only in a Metric measurement, for example in Newton Meters (Nm), then look at the center column first. If the measurement is 100 Nm, multiply it by the conversion factor of 0.738 to get 73.8 ft. lbs.

CONVERSION FACTORS

LENGTH–DISTANCE

Inches (in.)	x 25.4	= Millimeters (mm)	x .0394	= Inches
Feet (ft.)	x .305	= Meters (m)	x 3.281	= Feet
Miles	x 1.609	= Kilometers (km)	x .0621	= Miles

VOLUME

Cubic Inches (in3)	x 16.387	= Cubic Centimeters	x .061	= in3
IMP Pints (IMP pt.)	x .568	= Liters (L)	x 1.76	= IMP pt.
IMP Quarts (IMP qt.)	x 1.137	= Liters (L)	x .88	= IMP qt.
IMP Gallons (IMP gal.)	x 4.546	= Liters (L)	x .22	= IMP gal.
IMP Quarts (IMP qt.)	x 1.201	= US Quarts (US qt.)	x .833	= IMP qt.
IMP Gallons (IMP gal.)	x 1.201	= US Gallons (US gal.)	x .833	= IMP gal.
Fl. Ounces	x 29.573	= Milliliters	x .034	= Ounces
US Pints (US pt.)	x .473	= Liters (L)	x 2.113	= Pints
US Quarts (US qt.)	x .946	= Liters (L)	x 1.057	= Quarts
US Gallons (US gal.)	x 3.785	= Liters (L)	x .264	= Gallons

MASS–WEIGHT

Ounces (oz.)	x 28.35	= Grams (g)	x .035	= Ounces
Pounds (lb.)	x .454	= Kilograms (kg)	x 2.205	= Pounds

PRESSURE

Pounds Per Sq. In. (psi)	x 6.895	= Kilopascals (kPa)	x .145	= psi
Inches of Mercury (Hg)	x .4912	= psi	x 2.036	= Hg
Inches of Mercury (Hg)	x 3.377	= Kilopascals (kPa)	x .2961	= Hg
Inches of Water (H_2O)	x .07355	= Inches of Mercury	x 13.783	= H_2O
Inches of Water (H_2O)	x .03613	= psi	x 27.684	= H_2O
Inches of Water (H_2O)	x .248	= Kilopascals (kPa)	x 4.026	= H_2O

TORQUE

Pounds–Force Inches (in–lb)	x .113	= Newton Meters (N·m)	x 8.85	= in–lb
Pounds–Force Feet (ft–lb)	x 1.356	= Newton Meters (N·m)	x .738	= ft–lb

VELOCITY

Miles Per Hour (MPH)	x 1.609	= Kilometers Per Hour (KPH)	x .621	= MPH

POWER

Horsepower (Hp)	x .745	= Kilowatts	x 1.34	= Horsepower

FUEL CONSUMPTION*

Miles Per Gallon IMP (MPG)	x .354	= Kilometers Per Liter (Km/L)
Kilometers Per Liter (Km/L)	x 2.352	= IMP MPG
Miles Per Gallon US (MPG)	x .425	= Kilometers Per Liter (Km/L)
Kilometers Per Liter (Km/L)	x 2.352	= US MPG

*It is common to covert from miles per gallon (mpg) to liters/100 kilometers (1/100 km), where mpg (IMP) x 1/100 km = 282 and mpg (US) x 1/100 km = 235.

TEMPERATURE

Degree Fahrenheit (°F)   = (°C x 1.8) + 32
Degree Celsius (°C)   = (°F – 32) x .56

Standard and metric conversion factors chart

SERIAL NUMBER IDENTIFICATION

Vehicle

♦ **See Figure 1 and 2**

The Vehicle Identification Number (VIN) is important for ordering parts and for servicing. The VIN is a thirteen digit (1974–1980) or seventeen digit (1981 and later) sequence of numbers and letters visible on a plate fastened to the upper left instrument panel area.

➡**Model years appear in the VIN as the last digit of each particular year (6 is 1976, 8 is 1978, etc.), until 1980 (which is A). This is the final year under the thirteen digit code. The seventeen digit VIN begins with 1981(B) and continues 1982(C), 1983(D), etc.**

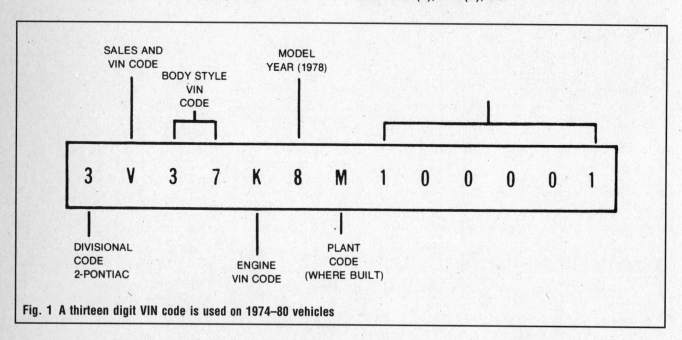

Fig. 1 A thirteen digit VIN code is used on 1974–80 vehicles

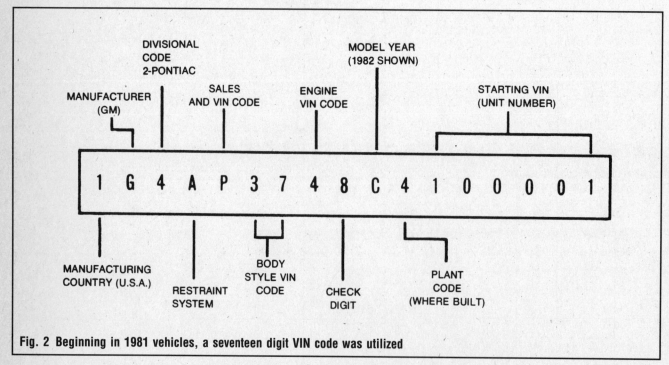

Fig. 2 Beginning in 1981 vehicles, a seventeen digit VIN code was utilized

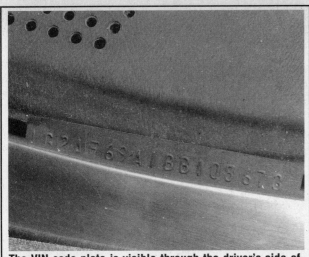

The VIN code plate is visible through the driver's side of the windshield

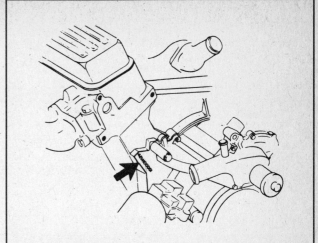

Fig. 4 Location of the early model V6 engine ID number location—1977 vehicle shown

ENGINE

◆ See Figures 3, 4, 5, 6 and 7

The engine identification number may be located in one of a few different locations, depending on engine. Please refer to the accompanying illustrations for specifics.

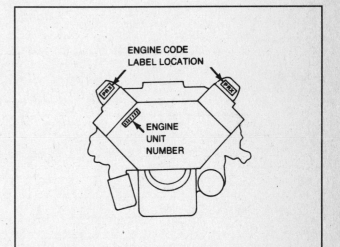

Fig. 5 Engine VIN locations—265, 301, 305 and code L 350 engines

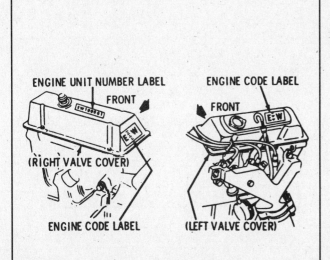

Fig. 3 Engine identification number label locations—231 and 250 cu. in. V6 engines shown

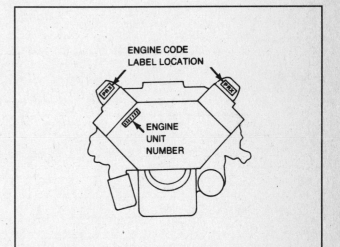

Fig. 6 Engine identification number locations—VIN code F, N, R and K engines. The Pontiac and Olds built engine number is stamped on the oil filler tube

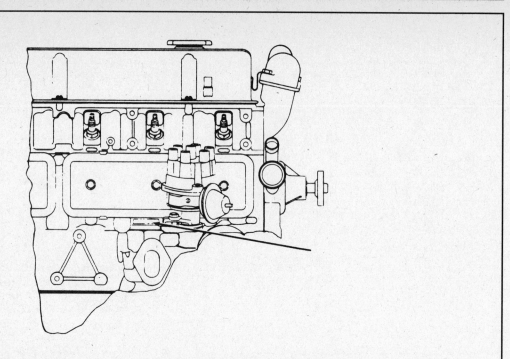

Fig. 7 Location of the engine identification numbers—151 4-cylinder and 250 6-cylinder engines

Engine Identification Codes

Engine	Eng. Mfg.	Bbl.	'74	'75	'76	'77	'78	'79	'80	'81	'82	'83
4-151	Pont.	2				V, 1	V, 1	V, 1				
V6-231	Buick	2			C	C	A	A	A	A	A	A
6-250	Chev.	1	D	D	D							
V6-252	Buick	4									4	4
V8-260	Olds.	2		F	F							
V8-265	Pont.	2							S	S		
V8-301	Pont.	2				Y	Y					
V8-301	Pont.	4						W	W	W	W	
V8-305	Chev.	2				U	U	G				
V8-305	Chev.	4						H	H			
V8-350	Pont.	2	M①	M	M							
V8-350	Pont.	4	J②	E	E							
V8-350	Buick	2		H	H							
V8-350	Buick	4			J	J	X	X				
V8-350	Olds.	4				R	R	R				
V8-350	Chev.	4				L	L	L				
V8-350	Olds.	Diesel						N	N	N	N	N
V8-400	Pont.	2	R	R								
V8-400	Pont.	4	S	S	S	Z	Z					
V8-403	Olds.	4				K	K					
V8-455	Pont.	4		W	W							

① N code w/dual exhaust
② K code w/dual exhaust

Transmission

MANUAL TRANSMISSIONS

▶ **See Figure 8**

The Pontiac mid-size models covered in this guide have been equipped, through the years, with various types of manual transmissions. A three-speed Saginaw-built transmission (both floor and column shift versions) was available from 1974 through 1976 in 250 six-cylinder, 260 V8 and 350 V8 (LeMans only) cars. A three-speed Muncie has also been available from 1974 through 1981. Both Saginaw and Muncie-built four-speed transmissions have been offered through 1979, and a five-speed Muncie was available from 1977 through 1978.

All manual transmissions covered here can be identified by checking the markings on the right side of the gearbox case. The numbers stamped on the case should always be used when ordering replacement parts or inquiring about service.

AUTOMATIC TRANSMISSIONS

Various GM Turbo Hydra-Matic (THM) automatic transmissions are used in the models covered in this guide. Transmission identification numbers are found on either side of the transmission case, depending on model. Some models also have I.D. numbers stamped on the governor cover.

The 1974 through 1976 automatics were designated either M-38 or M-40; the M-38 models were used on all six-cylinder through 350 V8-equipped cars, and the M-40 transmissions were used behind the big 400 and 455 V8s. From 1977 through 1983, the automatic transmissions available in Pontiac mid-size cars have been the THM 200, THM 350 and THM 400. Generally, the 200 series are available in four-cylinder, 231 V6, 301 V8 and 305 V8-equipped cars; the THM 350s are found in 231 V6 through 403 V8 cars; and the THM 400s are found behind various small-block (301) through big-block (455) V8s. However, always check the transmission I.D. numbers, as many different engine/transmission combinations have been used.

A quick way to visually identify the transmissions is to look at the shapes of the pans. The M-38 and THM-350 have a squareish pan with the right rear corner cut off. The THM 200 pan is similar but more rectangular. The pans of the M-40 and THM 400 transmissions are irregular-shaped. See Chapter 7 for pan illustrations.

The 200 model transmission was first used in 1977 and is the first all-metric unit built by GM in the U.S. This transmission sometimes has the word METRIC stamped on the pan.

Vehicle Emission Control Information Label

▶ **See Figure 9**

The Vehicle Emission Control Information Label is located in the engine compartment (fan shroud, radiator support, hood underside, etc.) of every vehicle produced by General Motors. The label contains important emission specifications and setting procedures, as well as a vacuum hose schematic with various emissions components identified.

When servicing your Pontiac, this label should always be checked for up-to-date information pertaining specifically to your car.

➡**Always follow the timing procedures on this label when adjusting ignition timing.**

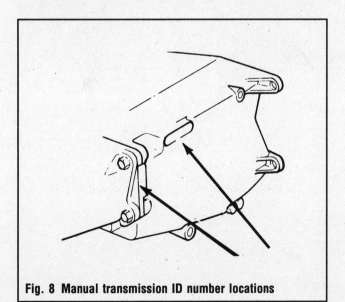

Fig. 8 Manual transmission ID number locations

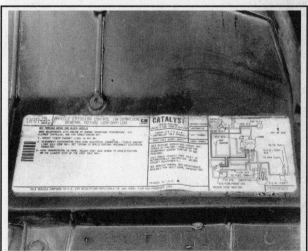

The VECI label is usually located on the radiator or fan shroud

BF	3.8L *940E2LU 9B3-4	VEHICLE EMISSION CONTROL INFORMATION GENERAL MOTORS CORPORATION	GM

SET PARKING BRAKE AND BLOCK WHEELS

MAKE ADJUSTMENTS WITH ENGINE AT NORMAL OPERATING TEMPERATURE, CHOKE OPEN, AIR CLEANER ON, AND WHERE APPLICABLE, AIR CONDITIONING OFF. PLUG DISCONNECTED VACUUM FITTINGS AND/OR HOSES.

1. DISCONNECT AND PLUG DISTRIBUTOR VACUUM HOSE, EGR HOSE TO EGR VALVE AND EVAPORATIVE PURGE HOSE TO VAPOR CANISTER.
2. SET TIMING AT SPECIFIED RPM. DISCONNECT THROTTLE SOLENOID WIRE (WHERE APPLICABLE). RECONNECT DISTRIBUTOR VACUUM ADVANCE HOSE.
3. ADJUST CARBURETOR SPEED SCREW TO SPECIFIED RPM.
4. RECONNECT SOLENOID WIRE. MANUALLY EXTEND SOLENOID SCREW AND ADJUST TO SPECIFIED RPM. (WHERE APPLICABLE).
5. WITH TRANSMISSION IN PARK OR NEUTRAL, SET FAST IDLE TO SPECIFIED SPEED ON HIGHEST CAM STEP.
6. RECONNECT CANISTER AND EGR VALVE HOSES.

SEE SERVICE MANUAL AND MAINTENANCE SCHEDULE II FOR ADDITIONAL INFORMATION.

THIS VEHICLE CONFORMS TO U.S. EPA AND CALIFORNIA REGULATIONS APPLICABLE TO 1979 MODEL YEAR NEW PASSENGER CARS.

CATALYST
EGR-EFE-RAIR
LOW ALTITUDE CERTIFICATION

	TRANSMISSION
	AUTOMATIC
TIMING (°B.T.D.C. @ RPM)	15° @ 600
SPARK PLUG — TYPE	R45TSX/R46TSX
SPARK PLUG — GAP	.060 IN.
CARBURETOR SCREW (RPM)	600 (DRIVE)
FAST IDLE SCREW (RPM)	2200 (PARK)

IDLE MIXTURE SCREWS ARE PRESET AND SEALED AT FACTORY. PROVISION FOR ADJUSTMENT DURING TUNE-UP IS NOT PROVIDED.

FOR MAJOR REPAIR, ADJUSTING MIXTURE SETTING BY OTHER THAN APPROVED SERVICE MANUAL PROCEDURE MAY VIOLATE FEDERAL AND/OR CALIFORNIA OR OTHER STATE LAWS.

1264991
9BOB2

Fig. 9 Typical Vehicle Emission Control Information (VECI) label—1979 231 V6 engine shown

ROUTINE MAINTENANCE

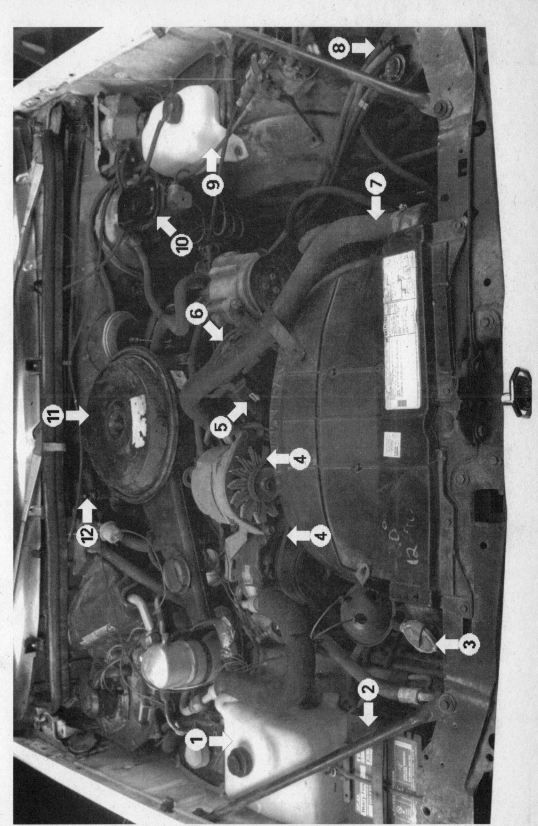

MAINTENANCE COMPONENT LOCATIONS—231 V6

1. Coolant recovery reservoir
2. Battery
3. Radiator cap
4. Accessory drive belts
5. Distributor cap
6. Spark plug wire
7. Upper radiator hose
8. Evaporative canister
9. Windshield washer fluid reservoir
10. Brake master cylinder
11. Air cleaner assembly
12. Automatic transmission fluid dipstick

Air Cleaner

All engines are equipped with dry type air cleaners with replaceable air filter elements. The Positive Crankcase Ventilation (PCV) system air filter element on gasoline engines is also found in the air filter housing (usually mounted on the inside of the housing rim). Both of these filter elements should be replaced at 30,000 mile or 1½ year intervals on all models, except in extremely dusty or smoggy conditions where replacement should be much more frequent.

✳✳ WARNING

Never remove the air cleaner from a diesel with the engine running. The intake vacuum is very great, and dirt, wingnuts, etc. will be sucked directly into the combustion chambers, causing major engine damage.

REMOVAL & INSTALLATION

Air Cleaner Element and PCV Filter

1. Remove the wingnut(s) from the top of the air cleaner assembly and lay it aside.
2. Remove the air cleaner cover and gently lift the air cleaner element out of the housing without knocking any dirt into the carburetor.
3. Pull the PCV filter out of the retainer.
4. Wipe the inside of the air cleaner housing with a paper towel or clean rag.
5. Clean the inside of the PCV filter retainer and install a new PCV filter element.
6. Install a new air cleaner element.
7. Replace the air cleaner cover and install the wing nut(s).

To remove the air cleaner element, remove the wingnut . . .

. . . then remove the air cleaner assembly cover

Now, remove the air cleaner element from the housing

Positive Crankcase Ventilation (PCV) Valve

▶ **See Figures 10 and 11**

All gasoline engines covered in this guide are equipped with a closed crankcase emission control system (see Chapter 4) featuring a vacuum-operated Positive Crankcase Ventilation (PCV) valve. A faulty PCV valve or clogged hoses to and from the valve can cause a rough idle, oil leaks, or excessive oil sludging. Check the system at least once a year and replace the valve at least every 30 months or 30,000 miles. A general test is to remove the PCV valve from the valve cover and shake it. If a rattle is heard, the valve is usually OK.

A more positive test is:

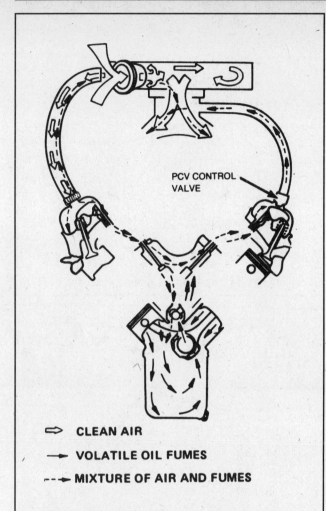

⇨ **CLEAN AIR**

⟶ **VOLATILE OIL FUMES**

--⟶ **MIXTURE OF AIR AND FUMES**

Fig. 10 Typical Positive Crankcase Ventilation (PCV) system flow

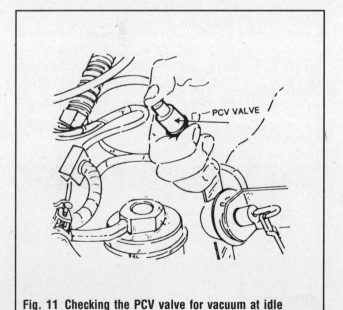

Fig. 11 Checking the PCV valve for vacuum at idle

1. Remove the PCV valve from the rocker arm cover or intake manifold.

2. Connect a tachometer to the engine and run the engine at idle.

3. Check the tachometer reading, then place your thumb over the end of the valve. You should feel a suction.

4. Check the tachometer again. The engine speed should have dropped at least 50 rpm. It should return to a normal idle when you remove your thumb from the end of the valve.

5. If the engine does not change speed or if the change is less than 50 rpm, the hose is clogged or the valve defective. Check the hose first—if it is not clogged, replace the PCV valve. Test the new valve in the same way.

REMOVAL & INSTALLATION

The PCV valve is located in the rubber grommet in the valve cover, connected to the air cleaner housing by a rubber hose. To replace the valve:

1. Pull the valve (with the hose attached) or the hose from the rubber grommet in the valve cover.

2. Remove the PCV valve from the hose.

To install:

3. Install a new PCV valve into the hose.

4. Press the valve or hose back into the rubber grommet in the valve cover.

Crankcase Depression Regulator and Flow Control Valve

▶ **See Figures 12 and 13**

The Crankcase Depression Regulator (CDR), found on 1981 and later diesels, and the flow control valve, used in 1980, are designed to scavenge crankcase vapors in basically the same manner as the PCV valve on gasoline engines. The valves are located either on the left rear corner of the intake manifold (CDR), or on the rear of the intake crossover pipe (flow control valve). On each system there are two ventilation filters, one per valve cover.

SERVICING

The filter assemblies should be cleaned every 15,000 miles by simply prying them carefully from the valve covers (be aware of the grommets underneath), and washing them out in solvent. The ventilation pipes and tubes should also be cleaned. Both the CDR and flow control valves should also be cleaned every 30,000 miles (the cover can be removed from the CDR; the flow control valve can simply be flushed with solvent). Dry each valve, filter, and hose with compressed air before installation.

➡ **Do not attempt to test the crankcase controls on these diesels. Instead, clean the valve cover filter assembly and vent pipes and check the vent pipes.**

Replace the breather cap assembly every 30,000 miles. Replace all rubber fittings as required every 15,000 miles.

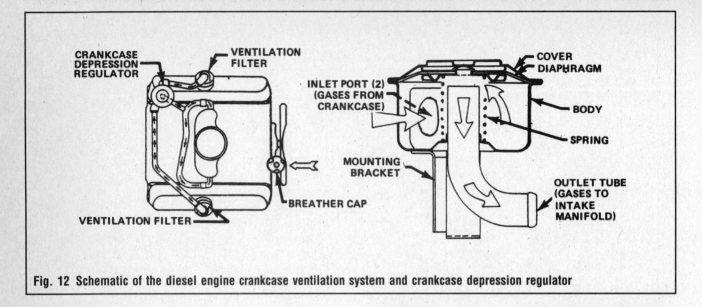

Fig. 12 Schematic of the diesel engine crankcase ventilation system and crankcase depression regulator

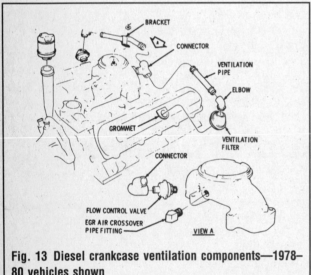

Fig. 13 Diesel crankcase ventilation components—1978–80 vehicles shown

You should label the evaporative canister vacuum hoses before disconnecting them

Evaporative Canister

The evaporative canister, sometimes referred to as a charcoal canister, is mounted inside the engine compartment. The canister and its filter are part of the evaporative emissions system (see Chapter 4) and work to eliminate the release of unburned fuel vapor into the atmosphere. The vapor is absorbed by the carbon in the canister and stored until manifold vacuum, when the engine is running, draws the vapors into the engine for burning.

The filter in the bottom of the canister must be changed every two years or 24,000 miles, or more often under extremely dusty or smoggy conditions.

SERVICING

1. Tag and disconnect all hoses connected to the evaporative canister.

2. Loosen the retaining clamps and then lift out the canister.
3. Grasp the filter element in the bottom of the canister with your fingers and pull it out. Replace it with a new element.
4. Replace the canister in the clamps and reconnect all hoses. If any of the hoses are brittle or cracked, replace them *only with fuel-resistant replacement hose marked "EVAP."*

Fuel Filter

REMOVAL & INSTALLATION

Gasoline Engines

The carburetor inlet fuel filter should be replaced every year or 15,000 miles, or more often if necessary. This paper-element filter is located behind the large fuel line inlet nut on the carburetor. Some cars may also have an inline fuel filter located between the

To remove the fuel filter, use a back-up wrench and loosen the nut and the inlet line . . .

. . . then remove the fuel filter assembly

Remove the fuel filter element from the inlet

fuel pump and carburetor. This filter should be changed at the same time as the inlet-type filter; in both cases filters should only be changed when the engine is cold.

To replace the inlet (carburetor body) fuel filter:

1. Place some absorbent rags under the fuel fittings to catch the gasoline which will spill out when the lines are loosened.

2. Disconnect the fuel line connection at the intake fuel filter nut. Plug the opening to prevent loss of fuel.

3. Remove the intake fuel filter nut from the carburetor with a box wrench or socket.

4. Remove the filter element and spring.

5. The filter element can be cleaned in solvent and blown dry. However, for the low cost of a new filter it is more advisable to simply install a new element.

To install:

6. Install the element spring, then the filter element in the carburetor.

7. Install a new gasket on the intake fuel nut, then install the nut in the carburetor body and tighten securely.

8. Install the fuel line and tighten the connector. Check for leaks at all fittings with the engine idling.

Some models have an inline fuel filter in addition to the inlet filter in the carburetor. This filter is cylindrical and located in the fuel line between the pump and the carburetor. It may be made of either metal or plastic.

To replace the in-line filter:

1. Place some absorbent rags under the filter, remembering that it will be full of gasoline when removed.

2. Use a pair of pliers to expand the clamp on one end of the filter, then slide the clamp down past the point to which the filter pipe extends in the rubber hose. Do the same with the other clamp.

3. Gently twist and pull the hoses free of the filter pipes. Remove and discard the old filter.

4. Install the new filter into the hoses, slide the clamps back into place, and check for leaks with the engine idling.

Diesel Engines

♦ See Figures 14 and 15

The diesel fuel filter is mounted on the rear of the intake manifold, and is larger than that on a gasoline engine because diesel

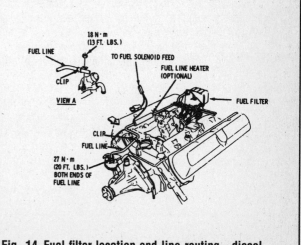

Fig. 14 Fuel filter location and line routing—diesel engines

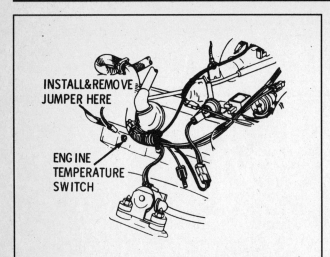

INSTALL & REMOVE
JUMPER HERE

ENGINE
TEMPERATURE
SWITCH

Fig. 15 After changing the diesel fuel filter, you must activate the Housing Pressure Cold Advance (HPCA)

fuel generally is "dirtier" (has more suspended particles) than gasoline.

The diesel fuel filter should be changed every 30,000 miles or two years.

To install a new filter:

1. With the engine cool, place absorbent rags underneath the fuel line fittings at the filter.
2. Disconnect the fuel lines from the filter.
3. Unbolt the filter from its bracket.
4. Install the new filter. Start the engine and check for leaks. Run the engine for about two minutes, then shut the engine off for the same amount of time to allow any trapped air in the injection system to bleed off.

The GM diesel cars also have a fuel filter inside the fuel tank which is maintenance-free.

➡️**If the filter element ever becomes clogged, the engine will stop. This stoppage is usually preceded by a hesitation or sluggish running. General Motors recommends that after changing the diesel fuel filter, the Housing Pressure Cold Advance (HPCA) be activated manually, if the engine temperature is above 125°F. Activating the HPCA will reduce engine cranking time.**

To activate the H.P.C.A. solenoid, disconnect the two lead connector at the engine temperature switch and bridge the connector with a jumper. After the engine is running, remove the jumper and reconnect the connector to the engine temperature switch. When the new filter element is installed, start the engine and check for leaks.

Battery

GENERAL MAINTENANCE

All batteries, regardless of type, should be carefully secured by a battery hold-down device. If this is not done, the battery terminals or casing may crack from stress applied to the battery during vehicle operation. A battery which is not secured may allow acid to leak out, making it discharge faster; such leaking corrosive acid can also eat away components under the hood. A battery that is not sealed must be checked periodically for electrolyte level. You cannot add water to a sealed maintenance-free battery (though not all maintenance-free batteries are sealed), but a sealed battery must also be checked for proper electrolyte level as indicated by the color of the built-in hydrometer "eye."

Keep the top of the battery clean, as a film of dirt can help completely discharge a battery that is not used for long periods. A solution of baking soda and water may be used for cleaning, but be careful to flush this off with clear water. DO NOT let any of the solution into the filler holes. Baking soda neutralizes battery acid and will de-activate a battery cell.

✳️ CAUTION

Always use caution when working on or near the battery. Never allow a tool to bridge the gap between the negative and positive battery terminals. Also, be careful not to allow a tool to provide a ground between the positive cable/terminal and any metal component on the vehicle. Either of these conditions will cause a short circuit leading to sparks and possible personal injury.

Batteries in vehicles which are not operated on a regular basis can fall victim to parasitic loads (small current drains which are constantly drawing current from the battery). Normal parasitic loads may drain a battery on a vehicle that is in storage and not used for 6–8 weeks. Vehicles that have additional accessories such as a cellular phone, an alarm system or other devices that increase parasitic load may discharge a battery sooner. If the vehicle is to be stored for 6–8 weeks in a secure area and the alarm system, if present, is not necessary, the negative battery cable should be disconnected at the onset of storage to protect the battery charge.

Remember that constantly discharging and recharging will shorten battery life. Take care not to allow a battery to be needlessly discharged.

BATTERY FLUID

✳️ CAUTION

Battery electrolyte contains sulfuric acid. If you should splash any on your skin or in your eyes, flush the affected area with plenty of clear water. If it lands in your eyes, get medical help immediately.

The fluid (sulfuric acid solution) contained in the battery cells will tell you many things about the condition of the battery. Because the cell plates must be kept submerged below the fluid level in order to operate, maintaining the fluid level is extremely important. And, because the specific gravity of the acid is an indication of electrical charge, testing the fluid can be an aid in determining if the battery must be replaced. A battery in a vehicle with a properly operating charging system should require little maintenance, but careful, periodic inspection should reveal problems before they leave you stranded.

Fluid Level

Check the battery electrolyte level at least once a month, or more often in hot weather or during periods of extended vehicle operation. On non-sealed batteries, the level can be checked either through the case on translucent batteries or by removing the cell caps on opaque-cased types. The electrolyte level in each cell should be kept filled to the split ring inside each cell, or the line marked on the outside of the case.

If the level is low, add only distilled water through the opening until the level is correct. Each cell is separate from the others, so each must be checked and filled individually. Distilled water should be used, because the chemicals and minerals found in most drinking water are harmful to the battery and could significantly shorten its life.

If water is added in freezing weather, the vehicle should be driven several miles to allow the water to mix with the electrolyte. Otherwise, the battery could freeze.

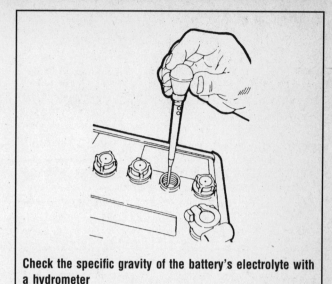

Check the specific gravity of the battery's electrolyte with a hydrometer

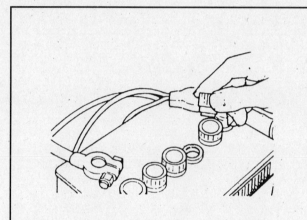

On non-maintenance free batteries, the level can be checked through the case on translucent batteries; the cell caps must be removed on other models

Although some maintenance-free batteries have removable cell caps for access to the electrolyte, the electrolyte condition and level on all sealed maintenance-free batteries must be checked using the built-in hydrometer "eye." The exact type of eye varies between battery manufacturers, but most apply a sticker to the battery itself explaining the possible readings. When in doubt, refer to the battery manufacturer's instructions to interpret battery condition using the built-in hydrometer.

➡**Although the readings from built-in hydrometers found in sealed batteries may vary, a green eye usually indicates a properly charged battery with sufficient fluid level. A dark eye is normally an indicator of a battery with sufficient fluid, but one which may be low in charge. And a light or yellow eye is usually an indication that electrolyte supply has dropped below the necessary level for battery (and hydrometer) operation. In this last case, sealed batteries with an insufficient electrolyte level must usually be discarded.**

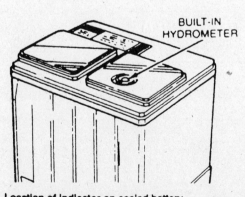

Location of indicator on sealed battery

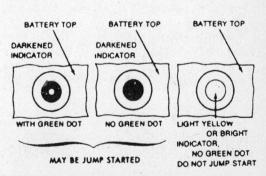

Check the appearance of the charge indicator on top of the battery before attempting a jump start; if it's not green or dark, do not jump start the car

A typical sealed (maintenance-free) battery with a built-in hydrometer—NOTE that the hydrometer eye may vary between battery manufacturers; always refer to the battery's label

Specific Gravity

As stated earlier, the specific gravity of a battery's electrolyte level can be used as an indication of battery charge. At least once a year, check the specific gravity of the battery. It should be between 1.20 and 1.26 on the gravity scale. Most auto supply stores carry a variety of inexpensive battery testing hydrometers. These can be used on any non-sealed battery to test the specific gravity in each cell.

The battery testing hydrometer has a squeeze bulb at one end and a nozzle at the other. Battery electrolyte is sucked into the hydrometer until the float is lifted from its seat. The specific gravity is then read by noting the position of the float. If gravity is low in one or more cells, the battery should be slowly charged and checked again to see if the gravity has come up. Generally, if after charging, the specific gravity between any two cells varies more than 50 points (0.50), the battery should be replaced as it can no longer produce sufficient voltage to guarantee proper operation.

On sealed batteries, the built-in hydrometer is the only way of checking specific gravity. Again, check with your battery's manufacturer for proper interpretation of its built-in hydrometer readings.

CABLES

Once a year (or as necessary), the battery terminals and the cable clamps should be cleaned. Loosen the clamps and remove the cables, negative cable first. On batteries with posts on top, the use of a puller specially made for this purpose is recommended. These are inexpensive and available in most auto parts stores. Side terminal battery cables are secured with a small bolt.

Clean the cable clamps and the battery terminal with a wire brush, until all corrosion, grease, etc., is removed and the metal is shiny. It is especially important to clean the inside of the clamp (an old knife is useful here) thoroughly, since a small deposit of foreign material or oxidation there will prevent a sound electrical connection and inhibit either starting or charging. Special tools are available for cleaning these parts, one type for conventional top post batteries and another type for side terminal batteries.

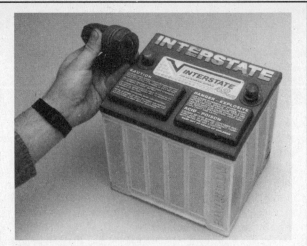

The underside of this special battery tool has a wire brush to clean post terminals

Place the tool over the terminals and twist to clean the post

Maintenance is performed with household items and with special tools like this post cleaner

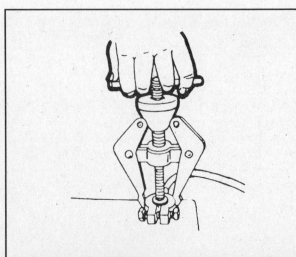

A special tool is available to pull the clamp from the post

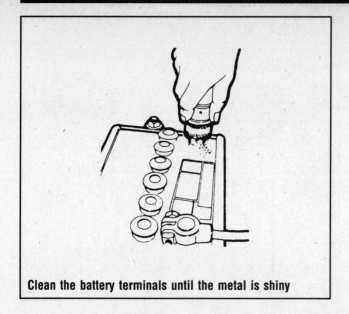

Clean the battery terminals until the metal is shiny

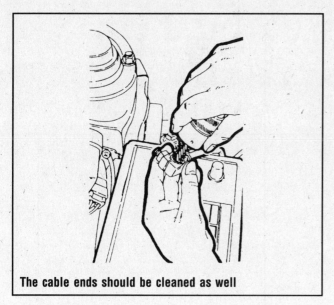

The cable ends should be cleaned as well

Before installing the cables, loosen the battery hold-down clamp or strap, remove the battery and check the battery tray. Clear it of any debris, and check it for soundness (the battery tray can be cleaned with a baking soda and water solution). Rust should be wire brushed away, and the metal given a couple coats of anti-rust paint. Install the battery and tighten the hold-down clamp or strap securely. Do not overtighten, as this can crack the battery case.

After the clamps and terminals are clean, reinstall the cables, negative cable last; DO NOT hammer the clamps onto post batteries. Tighten the clamps securely, but do not distort them. Give the clamps and terminals a thin external coating of grease after installation, to retard corrosion.

Check the cables at the same time that the terminals are cleaned. If the cable insulation is cracked or broken, or if the ends are frayed, the cable should be replaced with a new cable of the same length and gauge.

CHARGING

✳✳ CAUTION

The chemical reaction which takes place in all batteries generates explosive hydrogen gas. A spark can cause the battery to explode and splash acid. To avoid serious personal injury, be sure there is proper ventilation and take appropriate fire safety precautions when connecting, disconnecting, or charging a battery and when using jumper cables.

A battery should be charged at a slow rate to keep the plates inside from getting too hot. However, if some maintenance-free batteries are allowed to discharge until they are almost "dead," they may have to be charged at a high rate to bring them back to "life." Always follow the charger manufacturer's instructions on charging the battery.

REPLACEMENT

When it becomes necessary to replace the battery, select one with a rating equal to or greater than the battery originally installed. Deterioration and just plain aging of the battery cables, starter motor, and associated wires makes the battery's job harder in successive years. The slow increase in electrical resistance over time makes it prudent to install a new battery with a greater capacity than the old.

Belts

INSPECTION

Inspect the belts for signs of glazing or cracking. A glazed belt will be perfectly smooth from slippage, while a good belt will

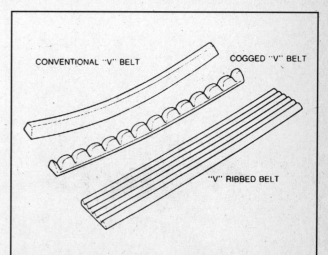

There are typically 3 types of accessory drive belts found on vehicles today

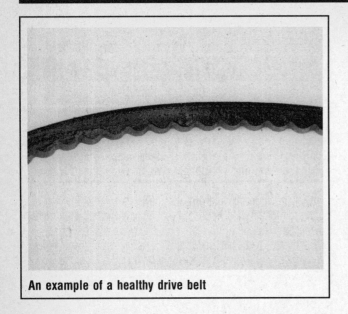

An example of a healthy drive belt

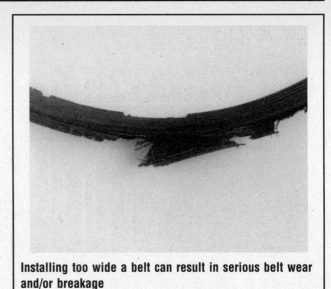

Installing too wide a belt can result in serious belt wear and/or breakage

Deep cracks in this belt will cause flex, building up heat that will eventually lead to belt failure

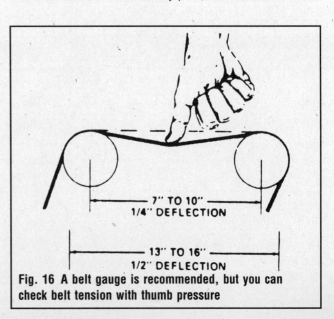

The cover of this belt is worn, exposing the critical reinforcing cords to excessive wear

have a slight texture of fabric visible. Cracks will usually start at the inner edge of the belt and run outward. All worn or damaged drive belts should be replaced immediately. It is best to replace all drive belts at one time, as a preventive maintenance measure, during this service operation.

CHECKING TENSION & ADJUSTING

▶ See Figures 16 and 17

Inspect your car's drive belts every 7,500 miles or six months. Replace the belts at a maximum of 30,000 miles, even if they still look acceptable.

You can determine belt tension at a point halfway between the pulleys by pressing on the belt with moderate thumb pressure. The amount of deflection should be in proportion to the length of the belt between pulleys (measured from the center of each pulley). For example, a belt stretched 13–16 in. between pulleys should deflect ½ in. at the halfway point; a belt stretched 7–10

Fig. 16 A belt gauge is recommended, but you can check belt tension with thumb pressure

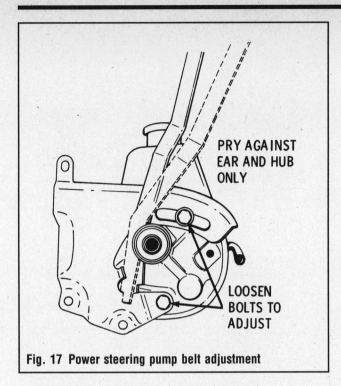

Fig. 17 Power steering pump belt adjustment

in. should deflect ¼ in., etc. If the deflection is found to be too little or too tight, an adjustment must be made.

Before adjusting any of your engine's drive belts, clean all mounting bolts on the component being adjusted and apply penetrating oil if necessary on those bolts which are hard to reach—which may be many if your car has a V8 with lots of power options. Loosen the mounting and adjusting bolts of whichever component (alternator, air pump, air conditioner compressor, power steering pump, etc.) you are adjusting. Pull outward, away from the engine, on the component until the belt seems tight. Temporarily snug up on the adjusting bolt and check belt deflection; if it is OK, tighten the mounting bolts and adjusting bolt.

➡Avoid using a metal prybar when adjusting belt tension of any component; a sawed-off broom handle or large wooden dowel rod works fine. Excessive force on any of the component housings (which are usually aluminum) will damage the housings.

REMOVAL & INSTALLATION

◆ **See Figures 18, 19, 20 and 21**

1. Loosen the drive accessory's pivot and mounting bolts.
2. Move the accessory toward the engine until enough slack is created to remove the belt from the pulley.
3. Place the new belt over the pulley and move the accessory away from the engine until the tension is correct. You can use a wooden hammer handle, or broomstick, as a lever, but do not use anything metallic, such as a prybar.

➡It is better to have belts too loose than too tight, because overtight belts will lead to bearing failure, particularly in the water pump and alternator. However, loose belts place an extremely high impact load on the driven component due to the whipping action of the belt.

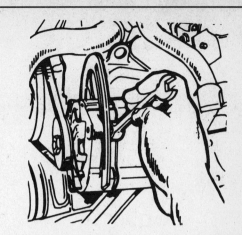

Fig. 18 To adjust belt tension, or to change belts, first loosen the component's mounting and adjusting bolts slightly

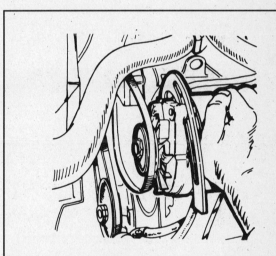

Fig. 19 Push the component toward the engine and slip the belt off

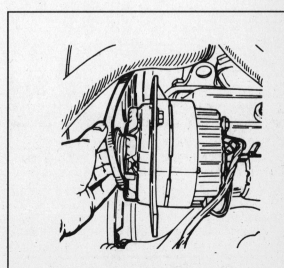

Fig. 20 Slip the new belt over the pulley

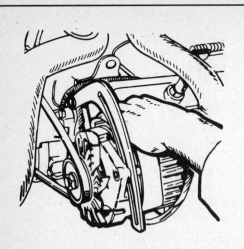

Fig. 21 Pull outward on the component and tighten the mounting bolts

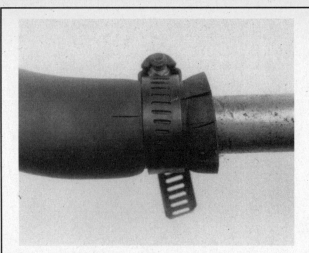

The cracks developing along this hose are a result of age-related hardening

4. Tighten the bolts and recheck the tension. If new belts have been installed, run the engine for a few minutes, then recheck and readjust as necessary.

Hoses

INSPECTION

Upper and lower radiator hoses along with the heater hoses should be checked for deterioration, leaks and loose hose clamps at least every 15,000 miles (24,000 km). It is also wise to check the hoses periodically in early spring and at the beginning of the fall or winter when you are performing other maintenance. A quick visual inspection could discover a weakened hose which might have left you stranded if it had remained unrepaired.

Whenever you are checking the hoses, make sure the engine and cooling system are cold. Visually inspect for cracking, rotting or collapsed hoses, and replace as necessary. Run your hand along the length of the hose. If a weak or swollen spot is noted when squeezing the hose wall, the hose should be replaced.

A hose clamp that is too tight can cause older hoses to separate and tear on either side of the clamp

REMOVAL & INSTALLATION

1. Remove the radiator pressure cap.

✳✳ CAUTION

Never remove the pressure cap while the engine is running, or personal injury from scalding hot coolant or steam may result. If possible, wait until the engine has cooled to remove the pressure cap. If this is not possible, wrap a thick cloth around the pressure cap and turn it slowly to the stop. Step back while the pressure is released from the cooling system. When you are sure all the pressure has been released, use the cloth to turn and remove the cap.

2. Position a clean container under the radiator and/or engine draincock or plug, then open the drain and allow the cooling sys-

A soft spongy hose (identifiable by the swollen section) will eventually burst and should be replaced

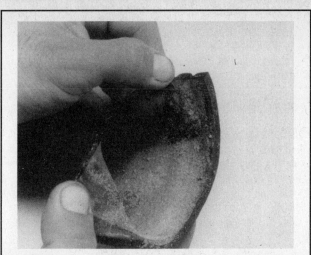

Hoses are likely to deteriorate from the inside if the cooling system is not periodically flushed

tem to drain to an appropriate level. For some upper hoses, only a little coolant must be drained. To remove hoses positioned lower on the engine, such as a lower radiator hose, the entire cooling system must be emptied.

✳✳ CAUTION

When draining coolant, keep in mind that cats and dogs are attracted by ethylene glycol antifreeze, and are quite likely to drink any that is left in an uncovered container or in puddles on the ground. This will prove fatal in sufficient quantity. Always drain coolant into a sealable container. Coolant may be reused unless it is contaminated or several years old.

3. Loosen the hose clamps at each end of the hose requiring replacement. Clamps are usually either of the spring tension type (which require pliers to squeeze the tabs and loosen) or of the screw tension type (which require screw or hex drivers to loosen). Pull the clamps back on the hose away from the connection.

4. Twist, pull and slide the hose off the fitting, taking care not to damage the neck of the component from which the hose is being removed.

➡**If the hose is stuck at the connection, do not try to insert a screwdriver or other sharp tool under the hose end in an effort to free it, as the connection and/or hose may become damaged. Heater connections especially may be easily damaged by such a procedure. If the hose is to be replaced, use a single-edged razor blade to make a slice along the portion of the hose which is stuck on the connection, perpendicular to the end of the hose. Do not cut deep so as to prevent damaging the connection. The hose can then be peeled from the connection and discarded.**

5. Clean both hose mounting connections. Inspect the condition of the hose clamps and replace them, if necessary.

To install:

6. Dip the ends of the new hose into clean engine coolant to ease installation.

7. Slide the clamps over the replacement hose, then slide the hose ends over the connections into position.

8. Position and secure the clamps at least ¼ in. (6.35mm) from the ends of the hose. Make sure they are located beyond the raised bead of the connector.

9. Close the radiator or engine drains and properly refill the cooling system with the clean drained engine coolant or a suitable mixture of ethylene glycol coolant and water.

10. If available, install a pressure tester and check for leaks. If a pressure tester is not available, run the engine until normal operating temperature is reached (allowing the system to naturally pressurize), then check for leaks.

✳✳ CAUTION

If you are checking for leaks with the system at normal operating temperature, BE EXTREMELY CAREFUL not to touch any moving or hot engine parts. Once temperature has been reached, shut the engine OFF, and check for leaks around the hose fittings and connections which were removed earlier.

Air Conditioning

➡**Be sure to consult the laws in your area before servicing the air conditioning system. In most areas, it is illegal to perform repairs involving refrigerant unless the work is done by a certified technician. Also, it is quite likely that you will not be able to purchase refrigerant without proof of certification.**

SAFETY PRECAUTIONS

There are two major hazards associated with air conditioning systems and they both relate to the refrigerant gas. First, the refrigerant gas (R-12) is an extremely cold substance. When exposed to air, it will instantly freeze any surface it comes in contact with, including your eyes. The other hazard relates to fire. Although normally non-toxic, the R-12 gas becomes highly poisonous in the presence of an open flame. One good whiff of the vapor formed by burning R-12 can be fatal. Keep all forms of fire (including cigarettes) well clear of the air conditioning system.

Because of the inherent dangers involved with working on air conditioning systems and R-12 refrigerant, these safety precautions must be strictly followed.

• Avoid contact with a charged refrigeration system, even when working on another part of the air conditioning system or vehicle. If a heavy tool comes into contact with a section of tubing or a heat exchanger, it can easily cause the relatively soft material to rupture.

• When it is necessary to apply force to a fitting which contains refrigerant, as when checking that all system couplings are securely tightened, use a wrench on both parts of the fitting involved, if possible. This will avoid putting torque on refrigerant tubing. (It is also advisable to use tube or line wrenches when tightening these flare nut fittings.)

➡**R-12 refrigerant is a chlorofluorocarbon which, when released into the atmosphere, can contribute to the depletion of the ozone layer in the upper atmosphere. Ozone filters out harmful radiation from the sun.**

• Do not attempt to discharge the system without the proper tools. Precise control is possible only when using the service gauges and a proper A/C refrigerant recovery station. Wear protective gloves when connecting or disconnecting service gauge hoses.

• Discharge the system only in a well ventilated area, as high concentrations of the gas which might accidentally escape can exclude oxygen and act as an anesthetic. When leak testing or soldering, this is particularly important, as toxic gas is formed when R-12 contacts any flame.

• Never start a system without first verifying that both service valves are properly installed, and that all fittings throughout the system are snugly connected.

• Avoid applying heat to any refrigerant line or storage vessel. Charging may be aided by using water heated to less than 125°F (50°C) to warm the refrigerant container. Never allow a refrigerant storage container to sit out in the sun, or near any other source of heat, such as a radiator or heater.

• Always wear goggles to protect your eyes when working on a system. If refrigerant contacts the eyes, it is advisable in all cases to consult a physician immediately.

• Frostbite from liquid refrigerant should be treated by first gradually warming the area with cool water, and then gently applying petroleum jelly. A physician should be consulted.

• Always keep refrigerant drum fittings capped when not in use. If the container is equipped with a safety cap to protect the valve, make sure the cap is in place when the can is not being used. Avoid sudden shock to the drum, which might occur from dropping it, or from banging a heavy tool against it. Never carry a drum in the passenger compartment of a vehicle.

• Always completely discharge the system into a suitable recovery unit before painting the vehicle (if the paint is to be baked on), or before welding anywhere near refrigerant lines.

• When servicing the system, minimize the time that any refrigerant line or fitting is open to the air in order to prevent moisture or dirt from entering the system. Contaminants such as moisture or dirt can damage internal system components. Always replace O-rings on lines or fittings which are disconnected. Prior to installation coat, but do not soak, replacement O-rings with suitable compressor oil.

GENERAL SERVICING PROCEDURES

➡It is recommended, and possibly required by law, that a qualified technician perform the following services.

The most important aspect of air conditioning service is the maintenance of a pure and adequate charge of refrigerant in the system. A refrigeration system cannot function properly if a significant percentage of the charge is lost. Leaks are common because the severe vibration encountered underhood in an automobile can easily cause a sufficient cracking or loosening of the air conditioning fittings; allowing, the extreme operating pressures of the system to force refrigerant out.

The problem can be understood by considering what happens to the system as it is operated with a continuous leak. Because the expansion valve regulates the flow of refrigerant to the evaporator, the level of refrigerant there is fairly constant. The receiver/drier stores any excess refrigerant, and so a loss will first appear there as a reduction in the level of liquid. As this level nears the bottom of the vessel, some refrigerant vapor bubbles will begin to

appear in the stream of liquid supplied to the expansion valve. This vapor decreases the capacity of the expansion valve very little as the valve opens to compensate for its presence. As the quantity of liquid in the condenser decreases, the operating pressure will drop there and throughout the high side of the system. As the R-12 continues to be expelled, the pressure available to force the liquid through the expansion valve will continue to decrease, and, eventually, the valve's orifice will prove to be too much of a restriction for adequate flow even with the needle fully withdrawn.

At this point, low side pressure will start to drop, and a severe reduction in cooling capacity, marked by freeze-up of the evaporator coil, will result. Eventually, the operating pressure of the evaporator will be lower than the pressure of the atmosphere surrounding it, and air will be drawn into the system wherever there are leaks in the low side.

Because all atmospheric air contains at least some moisture, water will enter the system and mix with the R-12 and the oil. Trace amounts of moisture will cause sludging of the oil, and corrosion of the system. Saturation and clogging of the filter/drier, and freezing of the expansion valve orifice will eventually result. As air fills the system to a greater and greater extent, it will interfere more and more with the normal flows of refrigerant and heat.

From this description, it should be obvious that much of the repairman's focus in on detecting leaks, repairing them, and then restoring the purity and quantity of the refrigerant charge. A list of general rules should be followed in addition to all safety precautions:

• Keep all tools as clean and dry as possible.

• Thoroughly purge the service gauges/hoses of air and moisture before connecting them to the system. Keep them capped when not in use.

• Thoroughly clean any refrigerant fitting before disconnecting it, in order to minimize the entrance of dirt into the system.

• Plan any operation that requires opening the system beforehand, in order to minimize the length of time it will be exposed to open air. Cap or seal the open ends to minimize the entrance of foreign material.

• When adding oil, pour it through an extremely clean and dry tube or funnel. Keep the oil capped whenever possible. Do not use oil that has not been kept tightly sealed.

• Use only R-12 refrigerant. Purchase refrigerant intended for use only in automatic air conditioning systems.

• Completely evacuate any system that has been opened for service, or that has leaked sufficiently to draw in moisture and air. This requires evacuating air and moisture with a good vacuum pump for at least one hour. If a system has been open for a considerable length of time it may be advisable to evacuate the system for up to 12 hours (overnight).

• Use a wrench on both halves of a fitting that is to be disconnected, so as to avoid placing torque on any of the refrigerant lines.

• When overhauling a compressor, pour some of the oil into a clean glass and inspect it. If there is evidence of dirt, metal particles, or both, flush all refrigerant components with clean refrigerant before evacuating and recharging the system. In addition, if metal particles are present, the compressor should be replaced.

• Schrader valves may leak only when under full operating pressure. Therefore, if leakage is suspected but cannot be located, operate the system with a full charge of refrigerant and look for leaks from all Schrader valves. Replace any faulty valves.

Additional Preventive Maintenance

USING THE SYSTEM

The easiest and most important preventive maintenance for your A/C system is to be sure that it is used on a regular basis. Running the system for five minutes each month (no matter what the season) will help assure that the seals and all internal components remain lubricated.

ANTIFREEZE

In order to prevent heater core freeze-up during A/C operation, it is necessary to maintain a proper antifreeze protection. Use a hand-held antifreeze tester (hydrometer) to periodically check the condition of the antifreeze in your engine's cooling system.

➡**Antifreeze should not be used longer than the manufacturer specifies.**

RADIATOR CAP

For efficient operation of an air conditioned vehicle's cooling system, the radiator cap should have a holding pressure which meets manufacturer's specifications. A cap which fails to hold these pressures should be replaced.

CONDENSER

Any obstruction of or damage to the condenser configuration will restrict the air flow which is essential to its efficient operation. It is therefore a good rule to keep this unit clean and in proper physical shape.

➡**Bug screens which are mounted in front of the condenser, (unless they are original equipment), are regarded as obstructions.**

CONDENSATION DRAIN TUBE

This single molded drain tube expels the condensation, which accumulates on the bottom of the evaporator housing, into the engine compartment. If this tube is obstructed, the air conditioning performance can be restricted and condensation buildup can spill over onto the vehicle's floor.

SYSTEM INSPECTION

➡**R-12 refrigerant is a chlorofluorocarbon which, when released into the atmosphere, can contribute to the depletion of the ozone layer in the upper atmosphere. Ozone filters out harmful radiation from the sun.**

The easiest and often most important check for the air conditioning system consists of a visual inspection of the system components. Visually inspect the air conditioning system for refrigerant leaks, damaged compressor clutch, compressor drive belt tension and condition, plugged evaporator drain tube, blocked condenser fins, disconnected or broken wires, blown fuses, corroded connections and poor insulation.

A refrigerant leak will usually appear as an oily residue at the leakage point in the system. The oily residue soon picks up dust or dirt particles from the surrounding air and appears greasy. Through time, this will build up and appear to be a heavy dirt impregnated grease. Most leaks are caused by damaged or missing O-ring seals at the component connections, damaged charging valve cores or missing service gauge port caps.

An antifreeze tester can be used to determine the freezing and boiling levels of the coolant

For a thorough visual and operational inspection, check the following:

1. Check the surface of the radiator and condenser for dirt, leaves or other material which might block air flow.
2. Check for kinks in hoses and lines. Check the system for leaks.
3. Make sure the drive belt is under the proper tension. When the air conditioning is operating, make sure the drive belt is free of noise or slippage.
4. Make sure the blower motor operates at all appropriate positions, then check for distribution of the air from all outlets with the blower on **HIGH**.

➡**Keep in mind that under conditions of high humidity, air discharged from the A/C vents may not feel as cold as expected, even if the system is working properly. This is because the vaporized moisture in humid air retains heat more effectively than does dry air, making the humid air more difficult to cool.**

Make sure the air passage selection lever is operating correctly. Start the engine and warm it to normal operating temperature, then make sure the hot/cold selection lever is operating correctly.

DISCHARGING, EVACUATING & CHARGING

Discharging, evacuating and charging the air conditioning system must be performed by a properly trained and certified mechanic in a facility equipped with refrigerant recovery/recycling equipment that meets SAE standards for the type of system to be serviced.

If you don't have access to the necessary equipment, we recommend that you take your vehicle to a reputable service station to have the work done. If you still wish to perform repairs on the vehicle, have them discharge the system, then take your vehicle home and perform the necessary work. When you are finished, return the vehicle to the station for evacuation and charging. Just be sure to cap ALL A/C system fittings immediately after opening them and keep them protected until the system is recharged.

Windshield Wipers

ELEMENT (REFILL) CARE & REPLACEMENT

For maximum effectiveness and longest element life, the windshield and wiper blades should be kept clean. Dirt, tree sap, road tar and so on will cause streaking, smearing and blade deterioration if left on the glass. It is advisable to wash the windshield carefully with a commercial glass cleaner at least once a month. Wipe off the rubber blades with the wet rag afterwards. Do not attempt to move wipers across the windshield by hand; damage to the motor and drive mechanism will result.

To inspect and/or replace the wiper blade elements, place the wiper switch in the **LOW** speed position and the ignition switch in the **ACC** position. When the wiper blades are approximately vertical on the windshield, turn the ignition switch to **OFF.**

Examine the wiper blade elements. If they are found to be cracked, broken or torn, they should be replaced immediately. Replacement intervals will vary with usage, although ozone deterioration usually limits element life to about one year. If the wiper pattern is smeared or streaked, or if the blade chatters across the glass, the elements should be replaced. It is easiest and most sensible to replace the elements in pairs.

If your vehicle is equipped with aftermarket blades, there are several different types of refills and your vehicle might have any kind. Aftermarket blades and arms rarely use the exact same type blade or refill as the original equipment. Here are some typical aftermarket blades; not all may be available for your vehicle:

The Anco® type uses a release button that is pushed down to allow the refill to slide out of the yoke jaws. The new refill slides back into the frame and locks in place.

Some Trico® refills are removed by locating where the metal backing strip or the refill is wider. Insert a small screwdriver blade between the frame and metal backing strip. Press down to release the refill from the retaining tab.

Other types of Trico® refills have two metal tabs which are unlocked by squeezing them together. The rubber filler can then be withdrawn from the frame jaws. A new refill is installed by in-

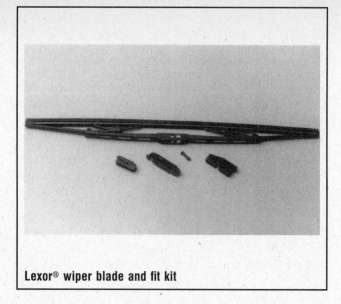

Lexor® wiper blade and fit kit

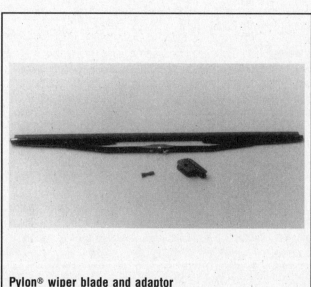

Pylon® wiper blade and adaptor

Bosch® wiper blade and fit kit

Trico® wiper blade and fit kit

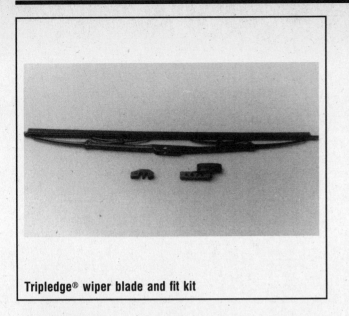

Tripledge® wiper blade and fit kit

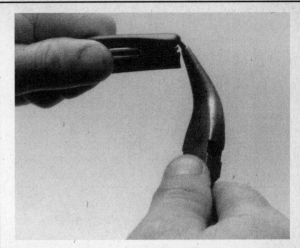

On Trico® wiper blades, the tab at the end of the blade must be turned up . . .

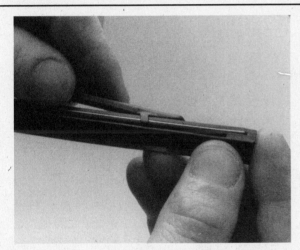

To remove and install a Lexor® wiper blade refill, slip out the old insert and slide in a new one

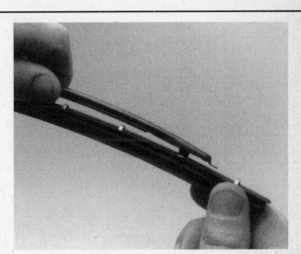

. . . then the insert can be removed. After installing the replacement insert, bend the tab back

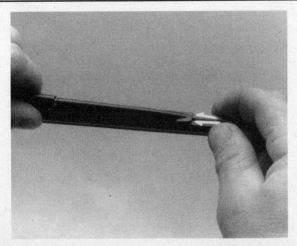

On Pylon® inserts, the clip at the end has to be removed prior to sliding the insert off

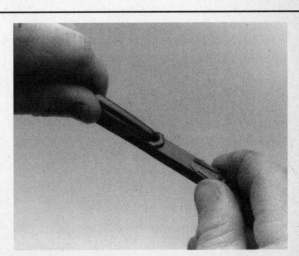

The Tripledge® wiper blade insert is removed and installed using a securing clip

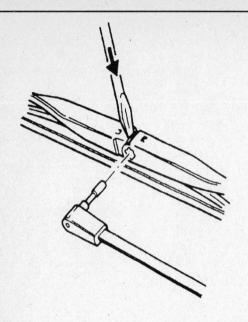

BLADE REPLACEMENT

1. CYCLE ARM AND BLADE ASSEMBLY TO UP POSITION-
ON THE WINDSHIELD WHERE REMOVAL OF BLADE
ASSEMBLY CAN BE PERFORMED WITHOUT
DIFFICULTY. TURN IGNITION KEY OFF AT DESIRED
POSITION.

2. TO REMOVE BLADE ASSEMBLY, INSERT
SCREWDRIVER IN SLOT, PUSH DOWN ON SPRING
LOCK AND PULL BLADE ASSEMBLY FROM PIN (VIEW
A)

3. TO INSTALL, PUSH THE BLADE ASSEMBLY ON THE
PIN SO THAT THE SPRING LOCK ENGAGES THE PIN
(VIEW A). BE SURE THE BLADE ASSEMBLY IS
SECURELY ATTACHED TO PIN

VIEW A

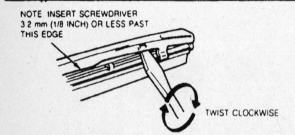

NOTE INSERT SCREWDRIVER
3 2 mm (1/8 INCH) OR LESS PAST
THIS EDGE

TWIST CLOCKWISE

ELEMENT REPLACEMENT

1 INSERT SCREWDRIVER BETWEEN THE EDGE OF THE
SUPER STRUCTURE AND THE BLADE BACKING DRIP
(VIEW B) TWIST SCREWDRIVER SLOWLY UNTIL
ELEMENT CLEARS ONE SIDE OF THE SUPER STRUC-
TURE CLAW

2 SLIDE THE ELEMENT INTO THE SUPER
STRUCTURE CLAWS

VIEW B

4 INSERT ELEMENT INTO ONE SIDE OF THE END
CLAWS (VIEW D) AND WITH A ROCKING MOTION
PUSH ELEMENT UPWARD UNTIL IT SNAPS IN (VIEW
E)

VIEW D

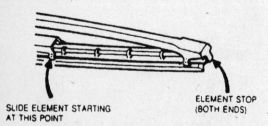

SLIDE ELEMENT STARTING
AT THIS POINT

ELEMENT STOP
(BOTH ENDS)

3. SLIDE THE ELEMENT INTO THE SUPER STRUCTURE
CLAWS, STARTING WITH SECOND SET FROM EITHER
END (VIEW C) AND CONTINUE TO SLIDE THE BLADE
ELEMENT INTO ALL THE SUPER STRUCTURE CLAWS
TO THE ELEMENT STOP (VIEW C)

VIEW C

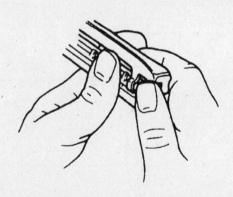

VIEW E

Trico® wiper blade insert (element) replacement

BLADE REPLACEMENT

1. Cycle arm and blade assembly to a position on the windshield where removal of blade assembly can be performed without difficulty. Turn ignition key off at desired position.
2. To remove blade assembly from wiper arm, pull up on spring lock and pull blade assembly from pin (View A). Be sure spring lock is not pulled excessively or it will become distorted.
3. To install, push the blade assembly onto the pin so that the spring lock engages the pin (View A). Be sure the blade assembly is securely attached to pin.

ELEMENT REPLACEMENT

1. In the plastic backing strip which is part of the rubber blade assembly, there is an 11.11mm (7/16 inch) long notch located approximately one inch from either end. Locate either notch.
2. Place the frame of the wiper blade assembly on a firm surface with either notched end of the backing strip visible.
3. Grasp the frame portion of the wiper blade assembly and push down until the blade assembly is tightly bowed.
4. With the blade assembly in the bowed position, grasp the tip of the backing strip firmly, pulling up and twisting C.C.W. at the same time. The backing strip will then snap out of the retaining tab on the end of the frame.
5. Lift the wiper blade assembly from the surface and slide the backing strip down the frame until the notch lines up with the next retaining tab, twist slightly, and the backing strip will snap out. Continue this operation with the remaining tabs until the blade element is completely detached from the frame.
6. To install blade element, reverse the above procedure, making sure all six (6) tabs are locked to the backing strip before installing blade to wiper arm.

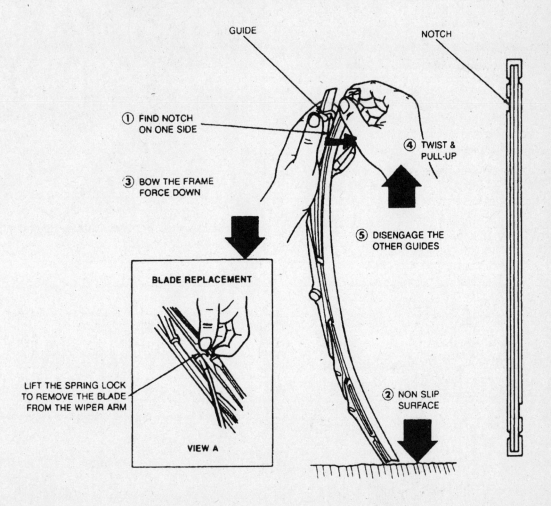

Tridon® wiper blade insert (element) replacement

serting the refill into the front frame jaws and sliding it rearward to engage the remaining frame jaws. There are usually four jaws; be certain when installing that the refill is engaged in all of them. At the end of its travel, the tabs will lock into place on the front jaws of the wiper blade frame.

Another type of refill is made from polycarbonate. The refill has a simple locking device at one end which flexes downward out of the groove into which the jaws of the holder fit, allowing easy release. By sliding the new refill through all the jaws and pushing through the slight resistance when it reaches the end of its travel, the refill will lock into position.

To replace the Tridon® refill, it is necessary to remove the wiper blade. This refill has a plastic backing strip with a notch about 1 in. (25mm) from the end. Hold the blade (frame) on a hard surface so that the frame is tightly bowed. Grip the tip of the backing strip and pull up while twisting counterclockwise. The backing strip will snap out of the retaining tab. Do this for the remaining tabs until the refill is free of the blade. The length of these refills is molded into the end and they should be replaced with identical types.

Regardless of the type of refill used, be sure to follow the part manufacturer's instructions closely. Make sure that all of the frame jaws are engaged as the refill is pushed into place and locked. If the metal blade holder and frame are allowed to touch the glass during wiper operation, the glass will be scratched.

Tires and Wheels

Common sense and good driving habits will afford maximum tire life. Fast starts, sudden stops and hard cornering are hard on tires and will shorten their useful life span. Make sure that you don't overload the vehicle or run with incorrect pressure in the tires. Both of these practices will increase tread wear.

➡For optimum tire life, keep the tires properly inflated, rotate them often and have the wheel alignment checked periodically.

Inspect your tires frequently. Be especially careful to watch for bubbles in the tread or sidewall, deep cuts or underinflation. Replace any tires with bubbles in the sidewall. If cuts are so deep that they penetrate to the cords, discard the tire. Any cut in the sidewall of a radial tire renders it unsafe. Also look for uneven tread wear patterns that may indicate the front end is out of alignment or that the tires are out of balance.

TIRE ROTATION

Tires must be rotated periodically to equalize wear patterns that vary with a tire's position on the vehicle. Tires will also wear in an uneven way as the front steering/suspension system wears to the point where the alignment should be reset.

Rotating the tires will ensure maximum life for the tires as a set, so you will not have to discard a tire early due to wear on only part of the tread. Regular rotation is required to equalize wear.

When rotating "unidirectional tires," make sure that they always roll in the same direction. This means that a tire used on the left side of the vehicle must not be switched to the right side and

Unidirectional tires are identifiable by sidewall arrows and/or the word "rotation"

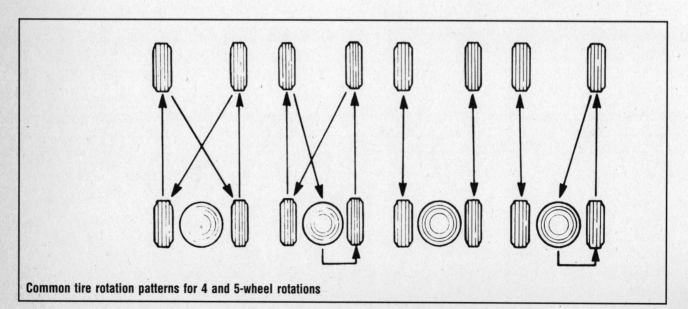

Common tire rotation patterns for 4 and 5-wheel rotations

vice-versa. Such tires should only be rotated front-to-rear or rear-to-front, while always remaining on the same side of the vehicle. These tires are marked on the sidewall as to the direction of rotation; observe the marks when reinstalling the tire(s).

Some styled or "mag" wheels may have different offsets front to rear. In these cases, the rear wheels must not be used up front and vice-versa. Furthermore, if these wheels are equipped with uni-directional tires, they cannot be rotated unless the tire is re-mounted for the proper direction of rotation.

➡**The compact or space-saver spare is strictly for emergency use. It must never be included in the tire rotation or placed on the vehicle for everyday use.**

TIRE DESIGN

For maximum satisfaction, tires should be used in sets of four. Mixing of different types (radial, bias-belted, fiberglass belted) must be avoided. In most cases, the vehicle manufacturer has designated a type of tire on which the vehicle will perform best. Your first choice when replacing tires should be to use the same type of tire that the manufacturer recommends.

When radial tires are used, tire sizes and wheel diameters should be selected to maintain ground clearance and tire load capacity equivalent to the original specified tire. Radial tires should always be used in sets of four.

✳✳ CAUTION

Radial tires should never be used on only the front axle.

When selecting tires, pay attention to the original size as marked on the tire. Most tires are described using an industry size code sometimes referred to as P-Metric. This allows the exact identification of the tire specifications, regardless of the manufacturer. If selecting a different tire size or brand, remember to check the installed tire for any sign of interference with the body or suspension while the vehicle is stopping, turning sharply or heavily loaded.

Snow Tires

Good radial tires can produce a big advantage in slippery weather, but in snow, a street radial tire does not have sufficient tread to provide traction and control. The small grooves of a street tire quickly pack with snow and the tire behaves like a billiard ball on a marble floor. The more open, chunky tread of a snow tire will self-clean as the tire turns, providing much better grip on snowy surfaces.

To satisfy municipalities requiring snow tires during weather emergencies, most snow tires carry either an M + S designation after the tire size stamped on the sidewall, or the designation "all-season." In general, no change in tire size is necessary when buying snow tires.

Most manufacturers strongly recommend the use of 4 snow tires on their vehicles for reasons of stability. If snow tires are fitted only to the drive wheels, the opposite end of the vehicle may become very unstable when braking or turning on slippery surfaces. This instability can lead to unpleasant endings if the driver can't counteract the slide in time.

Note that snow tires, whether 2 or 4, will affect vehicle handling in all non-snow situations. The stiffer, heavier snow tires

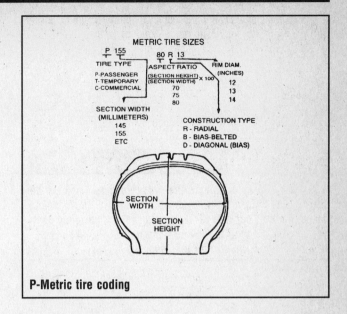

P-Metric tire coding

will noticeably change the turning and braking characteristics of the vehicle. Once the snow tires are installed, you must re-learn the behavior of the vehicle and drive accordingly.

➡**Consider buying extra wheels on which to mount the snow tires. Once done, the "snow wheels" can be installed and removed as needed. This eliminates the potential damage to tires or wheels from seasonal removal and installation. Even if your vehicle has styled wheels, see if inexpensive steel wheels are available. Although the look of the vehicle will change, the expensive wheels will be protected from salt, curb hits and pothole damage.**

TIRE STORAGE

If they are mounted on wheels, store the tires at proper inflation pressure. All tires should be kept in a cool, dry place. If they are stored in the garage or basement, do not let them stand on a concrete floor; set them on strips of wood, a mat or a large stack of newspaper. Keeping them away from direct moisture is of paramount importance. Tires should not be stored upright, but in a flat position.

INFLATION & INSPECTION

The importance of proper tire inflation cannot be overemphasized. A tire employs air as part of its structure. It is designed around the supporting strength of the air at a specified pressure. For this reason, improper inflation drastically reduces the tires's ability to perform as intended. A tire will lose some air in day-to-day use; having to add a few pounds of air periodically is not necessarily a sign of a leaking tire.

Two items should be a permanent fixture in every glove compartment: an accurate tire pressure gauge and a tread depth gauge. Check the tire pressure (including the spare) regularly with a pocket type gauge. Too often, the gauge on the end of the air hose at your corner garage is not accurate because it suffers too much abuse. Always check tire pressure when the tires are cold, as pressure increases with temperature. If you must move the vehicle to check the tire inflation, do not drive more than a mile before checking. A cold tire is generally one that has not been driven for more than three hours.

A plate or sticker is normally provided somewhere in the vehicle (door post, hood, tailgate or trunk lid) which shows the proper pressure for the tires. Never counteract excessive pressure build-up by bleeding off air pressure (letting some air out). This will cause the tire to run hotter and wear quicker.

✳✳ CAUTION

Never exceed the maximum tire pressure embossed on the tire! This is the pressure to be used when the tire is at maximum loading, but it is rarely the correct pressure for everyday driving. Consult the owner's manual or the tire pressure sticker for the correct tire pressure.

Once you've maintained the correct tire pressures for several weeks, you'll be familiar with the vehicle's braking and handling personality. Slight adjustments in tire pressures can fine-tune these characteristics, but never change the cold pressure specification by more than 2 psi. A slightly softer tire pressure will give a softer ride but also yield lower fuel mileage. A slightly harder tire will give crisper dry road handling but can cause skidding on wet surfaces. Unless you're fully attuned to the vehicle, stick to the recommended inflation pressures.

All tires made since 1968 have built-in tread wear indicator bars that show up as ½ in. (13mm) wide smooth bands across the tire when ¹⁄₁₆ in. (1.5mm) of tread remains. The appearance of tread wear indicators means that the tires should be replaced. In fact, many states have laws prohibiting the use of tires with less than this amount of tread.

You can check your own tread depth with an inexpensive gauge or by using a Lincoln head penny. Slip the Lincoln penny (with Lincoln's head upside-down) into several tread grooves. If you can see the top of Lincoln's head in 2 adjacent grooves, the tire has less than ¹⁄₁₆ in. (1.5mm) tread left and should be replaced. You can measure snow tires in the same manner by using the "tails" side of the Lincoln penny. If you can see the top of the Lincoln memorial, it's time to replace the snow tire(s).

Tires with deep cuts, or cuts which show bulging should be replaced immediately

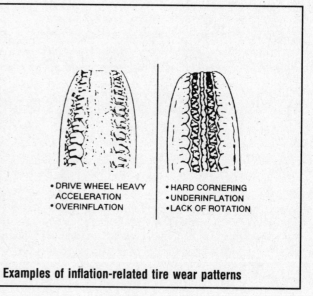
Examples of inflation-related tire wear patterns

• DRIVE WHEEL HEAVY ACCELERATION
• OVERINFLATION

• HARD CORNERING
• UNDERINFLATION
• LACK OF ROTATION

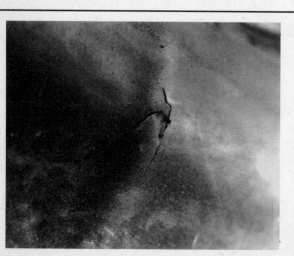
Tires should be checked frequently for any sign of puncture or damage

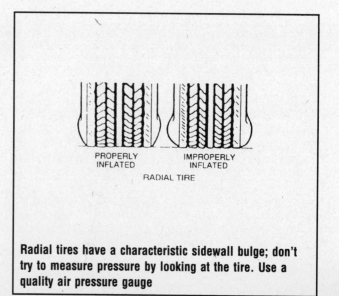
PROPERLY INFLATED   IMPROPERLY INFLATED
RADIAL TIRE

Radial tires have a characteristic sidewall bulge; don't try to measure pressure by looking at the tire. Use a quality air pressure gauge

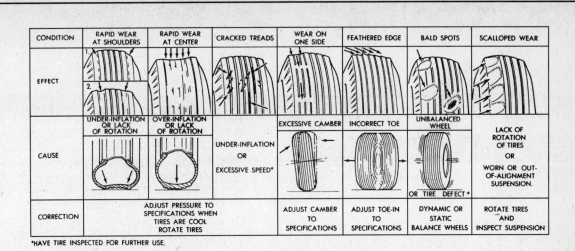

CONDITION	RAPID WEAR AT SHOULDERS	RAPID WEAR AT CENTER	CRACKED TREADS	WEAR ON ONE SIDE	FEATHERED EDGE	BALD SPOTS	SCALLOPED WEAR
EFFECT	1. / 2.						
CAUSE	UNDER-INFLATION OR LACK OF ROTATION	OVER-INFLATION OR LACK OF ROTATION	UNDER-INFLATION OR EXCESSIVE SPEED*	EXCESSIVE CAMBER	INCORRECT TOE	UNBALANCED WHEEL OR TIRE DEFECT*	LACK OF ROTATION OF TIRES OR WORN OR OUT-OF-ALIGNMENT SUSPENSION.
CORRECTION		ADJUST PRESSURE TO SPECIFICATIONS WHEN TIRES ARE COOL ROTATE TIRES		ADJUST CAMBER TO SPECIFICATIONS	ADJUST TOE-IN TO SPECIFICATIONS	DYNAMIC OR STATIC BALANCE WHEELS	ROTATE TIRES AND INSPECT SUSPENSION

*HAVE TIRE INSPECTED FOR FURTHER USE.

Common tire wear patterns and causes

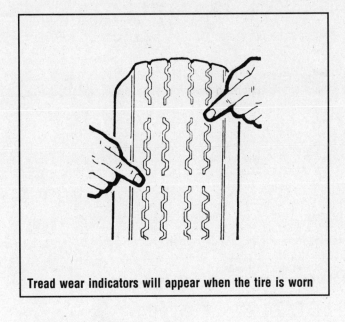

Tread wear indicators will appear when the tire is worn

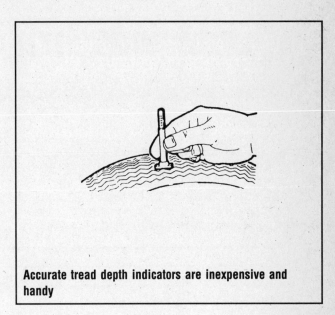

Accurate tread depth indicators are inexpensive and handy

CARE OF SPECIAL WHEELS

If you have invested money in magnesium, aluminum alloy or sport wheels, special precautions should be taken to make sure your investment is not wasted and that your special wheels look good for the life of the vehicle.

Special wheels are easily damaged and/or scratched. Occasionally check the rims for cracking, impact damage or air leaks. If any of these are found, replace the wheel. But in order to prevent this type of damage and the costly replacement of a special wheel, observe the following precautions:

• Use extra care not to damage the wheels during removal, installation, balancing, etc. After removal of the wheels from the vehicle, place them on a mat or other protective surface. If they are to be stored for any length of time, support them on strips of wood. Never store tires and wheels upright; the tread may develop flat spots.

• When driving, watch for hazards; it doesn't take much to crack a wheel.

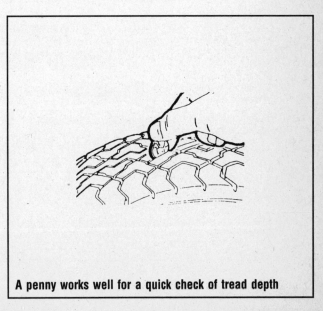

A penny works well for a quick check of tread depth

• When washing, use a mild soap or non-abrasive dish detergent (keeping in mind that detergent tends to remove wax). Avoid cleansers with abrasives or the use of hard brushes. There are many cleaners and polishes for special wheels.

• If possible, remove the wheels during the winter. Salt and sand used for snow removal can severely damage the finish of a wheel.

• Make certain the recommended lug nut torque is never exceeded or the wheel may crack. Never use snow chains on special wheels; severe scratching will occur.

FLUIDS AND LUBRICANTS

Fluid Disposal

Used fluids such as engine oil, transmission fluid, antifreeze and brake fluid are hazardous wastes and must be disposed of properly. Before draining any fluids, consult with the local authorities; in many areas, waste oil, etc. is being accepted as a part of recycling programs. A number of service stations and auto parts stores are also accepting waste fluids for recycling.

Be sure of the recycling center's policies before draining any fluids, as many will not accept different fluids that have been mixed together, such as oil and antifreeze.

Engine Oil and Fuel Recommendations

▶ **See Figures 22 and 23**

When adding oil to the crankcase or changing the oil or filter, it is important that oil of an equal quality to original equipment be used in your car. The use of inferior oils may void the warranty, damage your engine, or both.

The SAE (Society of Automotive Engineers) grade number of oil indicates the viscosity of the oil (its ability to lubricate at a given temperature). The lower the SAE number, the lighter the oil; the lower the viscosity, the easier it is to crank the engine in cold weather but the less the oil will lubricate and protect the engine at high temperatures. This number is marked on every oil container.

Oil viscosities should be chosen from those oils recommended for the *lowest anticipated temperatures during the oil change interval*. Due to the need for an oil that embodies both good lubrication at high temperatures and easy cranking in cold weather, multigrade oils have been developed. Basically, a multigrade oil is thinner at low temperatures and thicker at high temperatures. For example, a 10W-40 oil (the W stands for winter) exhibits the characteristics of a 10 weight (SAE 10) oil when the car is first started and the oil is cold. Its lighter weight allows it to travel to the lubricating surfaces quicker and offer less resistance to starter motor cranking than, say, a straight 30 weight (SAE 30) oil. But after the engine reaches operating temperature, the 10W-40 oil begins acting like straight 40 weight (SAE 40) oil, its heavier weight providing greater lubrication with less chance of foaming than a straight 30 weight oil.

➡**Single-grade ("straight weight") oils such as SAE 30 are more satisfactory than multi-viscosity oils for highway driving in diesel engines.**

The API (American Petroleum Institute) designation, also found on the oil container, indicates the classification of engine oil used under certain given operating conditions. Only oils designated for use "Service SE", or "SF heavy duty detergent" should be used in your Pontiac. Oils of the SE and SF type perform many functions inside the engine besides their basic lubrication. Through a balanced system of metallic detergents and polymeric dispersants,

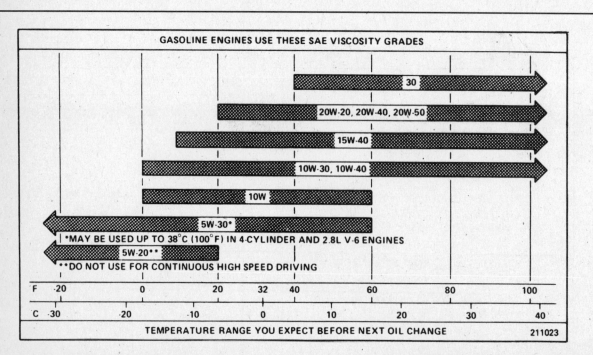

Fig. 22 Gasoline engine oil viscosity chart

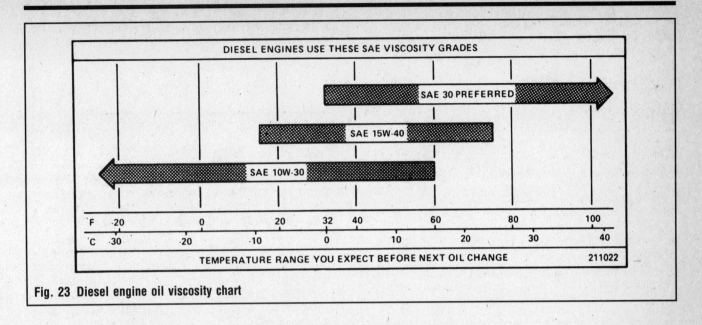

Fig. 23 Diesel engine oil viscosity chart

Recommended Lubricants

Item	Lubricant
Engine Oil	API "SE" or "SF," "SF/CC" or "SF/CD" (gasoline engine) API "SF/CC," "SF/CD" or "SE/CC" (diesel)
Automatic Transmission	DEXRON® or DEXRON® II ATF
Rear Axle-Standard	SAE 80W GL-5 or SAE 80W/90 GL-5
Positraction/Limited Slip	GM Part #1052271 or 1052272
Power Steering Reservoir	DEXRON® ATF—1975–76 Power Steering Fluid—1977 and later
Brake Fluid	DOT 3
Antifreeze	Ethylene Glycol
Front Wheel Bearings	GM Wheel Bearing Grease
Clutch Linkage	Engine Oil
Hood and Door Hinges	Engine Oil
Chassis Lubrication	NLGI #1 or NLGI #2
Lock Cylinders	WD-40 or Powdered Graphite

the oil prevents high and low temperature deposits and also keeps sludge and dirt particles in suspension. Acids, particularly sulphuric acid, as well as other byproducts of engine combustion are neutralized by the oil. If these acids are allowed to concentrate, they can cause corrosion and rapid wear of the internal engine parts.

✳✳ CAUTION

Non-detergent or "straight" mineral oils should not be used in your GM gasoline engine.

OIL

Under the American Petroleum Institute (API) classifications, gasoline engine oil codes begin with an "S". This first letter designation is followed by a second letter code which explains what type of service (heavy, moderate, light) the oil is meant for. For example, a typical oil bottle will include: "API SERVICES SC, SD, SE, CA, CB, CC." This means the oil in the bottle is a good, moderate-to-heavy duty engine oil when used in a gasoline engine (the "C" ratings are for diesel engines, and follow the same designations).

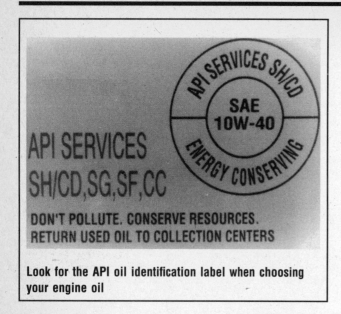

Look for the API oil identification label when choosing your engine oil

It should be noted here that the farther down the alphabet the second letter of the API classification is, the greater the oil's protective qualities (SH is the severest duty gasoline engine oil, SA is the lightest duty oil, etc.). Consult the owner's manual for recommended specs on diesel oil.

SYNTHETIC OIL

There are excellent synthetic and fuel-efficient oils available that, under the right circumstances, can help provide better fuel mileage and better engine protection. However, these advantages come at a price, which can be three or four times the price per quart of conventional motor oils.

Before pouring any synthetic oils into your car's engine, you should consider the condition of the engine and the type of driving you do. Also, check the car's warranty conditions regarding the use of synthetics.

Generally, it is best to avoid the use of synthetic oil in both brand new and older, high mileage engines. New engines require a proper break-in, and the synthetics are so "slippery" that they can prevent this; most manufacturers recommend that you wait at least 5,000 miles before switching to a synthetic oil. Conversely, older engines are looser and tend to "use" more oil; synthetics will slip past worn parts more readily than regular oil, and will be used up faster. If your car already leaks and/or "uses" oil (due to worn parts and bad seals or gaskets), it will leak and use more with a slippery synthetic inside.

Consider your type of driving. If most of your accumulated mileage is on the highway at higher, steadier speeds, a synthetic oil will reduce friction and probably help deliver better fuel mileage. Under such ideal highway conditions, the oil change interval can be extended, as long as the oil filter will operate effectively for the extended life of the oil. If the filter can't do its job for this extended period, dirt and sludge will build up in your engine's crankcase, sump, oil pump and lines, no matter what type of oil is used. If using synthetic oil in this manner, you should continue to change the oil filter at the recommended intervals.

Cars used under harder, stop-and-go, short hop circumstances should always be serviced more frequently, and for these cars synthetic oil may not be a wise investment. Because of the necessary shorter change interval needed for this type of driving, you cannot take advantage of the long recommended change interval of most synthetic oils.

FUEL

▶ **See Figure 24**

Gasoline

It is important that you use fuel of the proper gasoline octane rating in your car. Octane rating is based on the quantity of anti-knock compounds added to the fuel and it determines the speed at which the gasoline will burn. The lower the octane, the faster the gas burns. The higher the octane, the slower the fuel burns and a greater percentage of compounds in the fuel prevent spark ping (knock), detonation and preignition, and postignition (dieseling).

All 1975 and later models covered in this guide will perform happily on the unleaded regular gasoline. All 1974 models do not have catalytic converters, and thus run fine on leaded regular, or leaded premium (if you can find it). Since many factors such as altitude, terrain, air temperature, and humidity affect operating efficiency, knocking may result even though the recommended fuel grade is being used. If persistent knocking occurs, it may be necessary to switch to a higher grade of fuel. Continuous or heavy knocking may result in engine damage.

➡**Your engine's fuel requirement can change with time, mainly due to carbon buildup, which will in turn change the compression ratio. If your engine pings, knocks, or diesels (runs with the ignition off) switch to a higher grade of fuel. Sometimes just changing brands will cure the problem. If it becomes necessary to retard the timing from the specifications, don't change it more than a few degrees. Retarded timing will reduce power output and fuel mileage, in addition to making the engine run hotter.**

Diesel Fuel

Fuel makers produce two grades of diesel fuel, No. 1 and No. 2, for use in automotive diesel engines. Generally speaking, No. 2

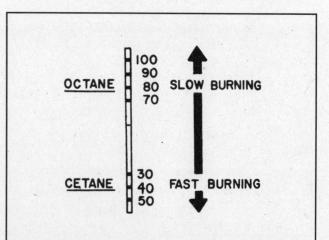

Fig. 24 Diesel engine cetane versus gasoline engine octane ratings. The higher the cetane number, the faster the fuel burns

fuel is recommended over No. 1 for driving in temperatures above 20°F. In fact, in many areas, No. 2 diesel is the only fuel available. By comparison, No. 2 diesel fuel is less volatile than No. 1 fuel, and gives better fuel economy. No. 2 fuel is also a better injection pump lubricant.

Two important characteristics of diesel fuel are its cetane number and its viscosity.

The cetane number of a diesel fuel refers to the ease with which a diesel fuel ignites. High cetane numbers mean that the fuel will ignite with relative ease or that it ignites well at low temperatures. Naturally, the lower the cetane number, the higher the temperature must be to ignite the fuel. Most commercial fuels have cetane numbers that range from 35 to 65. No. 1 diesel fuel generally has a higher cetane rating than No. 2 fuel.

Viscosity is the ability of a liquid, in this case diesel fuel, to flow. Using straight No. 2 diesel fuel below 20°F can cause problems, because this fuel tends to become cloudy, meaning wax crystals begin forming in the fuel (20°F is often called the "cloud point" for No. 2 fuel). In extreme cold weather, No. 2 fuel can stop flowing altogether. In either case, fuel flow is restricted, which can result in a "no start" condition or poor engine performance. Fuel manufacturers often "winterize" No. 2 diesel fuel by using various fuel additives and blends (No. 1 diesel fuel, kerosene, etc.) to lower its winter-time viscosity. Generally speaking, though, No. 1 diesel fuel is more satisfactory in extremely cold weather.

➡**No. 1 and No. 2 diesel fuels will mix and burn with no ill effects, although the engine manufacturer will undoubtedly recommend one or the other. Consult the owner's manual for information.**

Depending on local climate, most fuel manufacturers make winterized No. 2 fuel available seasonally.

Many automobile manufacturers (Oldsmobile, for example) publish pamphlets giving the locations of diesel fuel stations nationwide. Contact the local dealer for information.

Do not substitute home heating oil for automotive diesel fuel. While in some cases, home heating oil refinement levels equal those of diesel fuel, many times they are far below diesel engine requirements. The result of using "dirty" home heating oil will be a clogged fuel system, in which case the entire system may have to be dismantled and cleaned.

One more word on diesel fuels. Don't thin diesel fuel with gasoline in cold weather. The lighter gasoline, which is more explosive, will cause rough running at the very least, and may cause extensive damage if enough is used.

Engine

LEVEL CHECK

Every time you stop for fuel, check the engine oil as follows:
1. Make sure the car is parked on level ground.
2. When checking the oil level it is best for the engine to be at normal operating temperature, although checking the oil immediately after stopping will lead to a false reading. Wait a few minutes after turning off the engine to allow the oil to drain back into the crankcase.

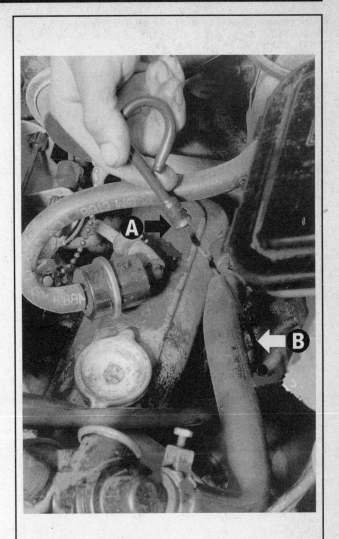

To check the engine oil level, remove the dipstick (A) from the tube (B), then wipe on a clean cloth

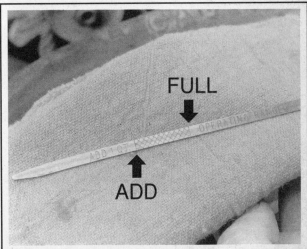

Check the oil level and compare with the marks on the dipstick

If oil addition is necessary, remove the cap from the valve cover . . .

The best way to loosen the oil pan drain plug is to use the proper size socket . . .

. . . then add the specified amount of oil and recheck the level

. . . then quickly withdraw the plug and allow the oil to completely drain into a suitable pan

3. Open the hood and locate the dipstick which will be on either the right or left side depending upon your particular engine. Pull the dipstick from its tube, wipe it clean and then reinsert it.

4. Pull the dipstick out again and, holding it horizontally, read the oil level. The oil should be between the "FULL" and "ADD" marks on the dipstick. If the oil is below the "ADD" mark, add oil of the proper viscosity through the capped opening in the top of the valve cover. See the "Oil and Fuel Recommendations" chart in this chapter for the proper viscosity and rating of oil to use.

5. Replace the dipstick and check the oil level again after adding any oil. Be careful not to overfill the crankcase. Approximately one quart of oil will raise the level from the "ADD" mark to the "FULL" mark. Excess oil will generally be consumed at a faster rate.

OIL & FILTER CHANGE

The oil in the engine of your Pontiac should be changed every six months or 7,500 miles, whichever comes first (Diesels should

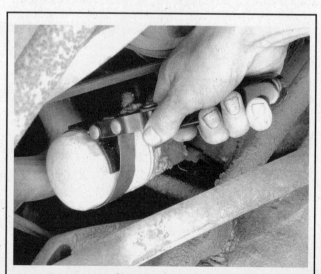

Use a strap wrench to loosen the oil filter

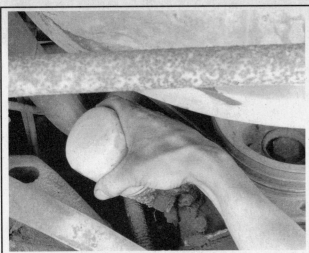

Always install the oil filter by hand, never use a wrench to tighten the filter

be changed every 5,000 miles). If you live in an extremely dusty or smoggy area, change your car's oil more frequently. A new filter should be installed with every oil change, and the used oil put into a suitable container and taken to a collection or reclamation point for recycling (many garages and gas stations have storage tanks for this purpose).

The oil should always be changed while hot, so the dirt and particles will still be suspended in the oil when it drains out of the engine. To change the oil and filter:

1. Run the engine until it reaches normal operating temperature.

2. Put the transmission in "Park," set the parking brake, and jack up the front of the car. Support the front end with jackstands.

3. Slide a drain pan of at least 6 quarts capacity under the engine oil pan.

4. Loosen the drain plug. Turn the plug out slowly by hand, keeping an inward pressure on the plug as you unscrew it so the hot oil will not escape until the plug is completely removed.

✳✳ CAUTION

When you are ready to release the plug, pull it away from the drain hole quickly, to avoid being burned by the hot oil.

5. Allow the oil to drain completely and then install the drain plug. DO NOT OVERTIGHTEN the plug, or you will strip the threads in the drain hole and you'll have to buy a new pan or a "trick" replacement plug.

6. Using an oil filter strap wrench, remove the oil filter. Keep in mind that it's holding about a quart of dirty, hot oil.

7. As soon as you remove the oil filter, hold it upright until you can empty it into the drain pan. Dispose of the filter.

✳✳ CAUTION

Prolonged and repeated skin contact with used engine oil, with no effort to remove the oil, may be harmful. Follow these simple precautions when handling used motor oil.
1. **Avoid prolonged skin contact with used motor oil.**
2. **Remove oil from skin by washing thoroughly with soap and water or waterless hand cleaner. Do not use gasoline, thinners or solvents.**

8. Using a clean rag, wipe off the filter mounting adaptor on the engine block. Be sure that the rag doesn't leave any lint which could clog an oil passage.

9. Wipe a coating of clean engine oil on the rubber gasket of the new filter. Spin it onto the engine *by hand—do not use the strap wrench.* When the gasket starts to snug up against the adaptor surface, give it another ½–¾ turn *by hand.* Don't turn it any more, or you'll squash the gasket and the filter will leak.

10. Refill the engine with the correct amount of fresh oil through the valve cover cap, or breather tube (diesels). See the "Capacities" chart in this chapter.

11. Check the oil level on the dipstick. It is normal for the oil level to be slightly above the full mark right after an oil change. Start the engine and allow it to idle for a few minutes.

After filling the crankcase with the proper amount of oil, check the level to be sure it is correct

Before installing a new oil filter, lightly coat the rubber gasket with clean oil

✳✳ CAUTION

Do not run the engine above idle speed until the oil pressure light (usually red) goes out, indicating the engine has built up oil pressure.

12. Shut off the engine and allow the oil to drain back down for a few minutes before checking the dipstick again. Check for oil leaks around the filter and drain plug.

Manual Transmission

FLUID RECOMMENDATIONS

In all manual transmissions, use only standard GL-5 hypoid gear oil, SAE 80W or SAE 80W/90.

LEVEL CHECK

1. Raise and safely support the vehicle with jackstands, preferably in a level altitude. Remove the filler plug from the side of the transmission housing.

2. If the lubricant begins to trickle out of the hole, there is enough and you need not go any further. Otherwise, carefully insert your finger (watch out for sharp threads) and check to see if the oil is up to the edge of the hole.

3. If the oil is not up to the edge of the hole, add oil through the hole until the level is at the edge of the hole. Most gear lubricants come in a plastic squeeze bottle with a nozzle, making additions simple. You can also use a common kitchen baster to add fluid. Use only standard GL-5 hypoid gear oil, SAE 80W or SAE 80W/90.

4. Replace the filler plug, then carefully lower the vehicle.

5. Take the vehicle for a test drive, then check for leaks.

DRAIN & REFILL

There is no recommended interval for the manual transmission, but it is always a good idea to change the fluid if you have purchased the car used or if it has been driven in water high enough to reach the axles.

1. The oil must be hot before it is drained. Drive the car until the engine reaches normal operating temperature.

2. Raise and safely support the vehicle with jackstands. Remove the filler plug to provide a vent.

3. Place a large container underneath the transmission and then remove the drain plug.

4. Allow the oil to drain completely. Clean off the drain plug and replace it; tighten it until it is just snug.

5. Fill the transmission with the proper lubricant, as detailed earlier in this section. Refer to the Capacities chart for the correct amount of lubricant.

6. when the oil level is up to the edge of the filler hole, replace the filler plug and lower the vehicle. Drive the car for a few minutes, then stop and check for any leaks.

Automatic Transmission

LEVEL CHECK & FLUID RECOMMENDATIONS

▶ **See Figure 25**

Check the automatic transmission fluid level at least every 7,500 miles. The dipstick can be found in the rear of the engine compartment. The fluid level should be checked only when the transmission is hot (normal operating temperature). The transmission is considered hot after about 20 miles of highway driving.

1. Park the car on a level surface with the engine idling. Shift the transmission into Neutral and set the parking brake.

2. Remove the dipstick, wipe it clean and then reinsert it firmly. Be sure that it has been pushed all the way in. Remove the dipstick

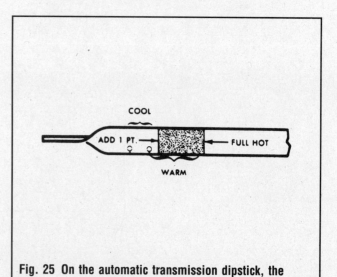

Fig. 25 On the automatic transmission dipstick, the proper level is within the shaded area

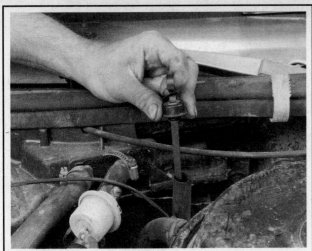

To check the A/T fluid level, pull the dipstick from the tube located at the rear of the engine . . .

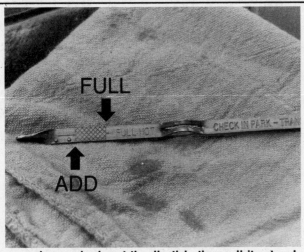

FULL

ADD

. . . clean and reinsert the dipstick, then pull it out and check the level while holding it horizontal

If necessary, add the proper amount of automatic transmission fluid

again and check the fluid level while holding it horizontally. With the engine running, the fluid level should be between the second notch and the "FULL HOT" line. If the fluid must be checked when it is cool, the level should be between the first and second notches.

3. If the fluid level is below the second notch (engine hot) or the first notch (engine cold), add DEXRON® (1974–75) or DEXRON® II (1976 and later) automatic transmission fluid through the dipstick tube. This is easily done with the aid of a funnel. Check the level often as you are filling the transmission. Be extremely careful not to overfill it. Overfilling will cause slippage, seal damage and overheating. Approximately one pint of ATF will raise the fluid level from one notch/line to the other.

➡**Always use DEXRON® or DEXRON® II ATF. The use of ATF Type F or any other fluid will cause severe damage to the transmission.**

The fluid on the dipstick should always be a bright red color. If it is discolored (brown or black), or smells burnt, serious transmission troubles, probably due to overheating, should be suspected. The transmission should be inspected by a qualified technician to locate the cause of the burnt fluid.

DRAIN, REFILL & FILTER SERVICE

The procedures for automatic transmission fluid drain and refill, filter change and band adjustment are all detailed in Chapter 7.

Rear Axle

LEVEL CHECK & FLUID RECOMMENDATIONS

♦ **See Figure 26**

The oil in the differential should be checked at least every 7,500 miles.

1. Park the car on a level surface and remove the filler plug from the front side of the differential.

2. If the oil begins to trickle out of the hole when the plug is

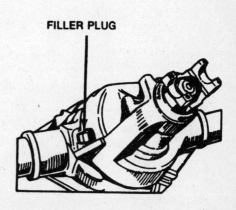

FILLER PLUG

Fig. 26 Remove the filler plug to check the lubrication level in the rear axle

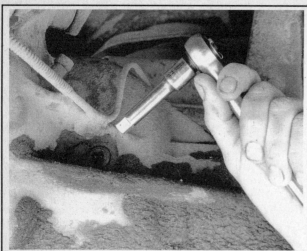

To check the rear axle fluid, use a socket and ratchet combination to loosen . . .

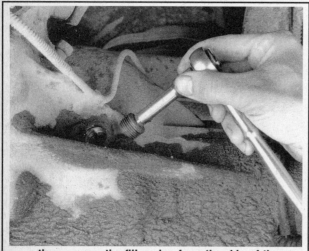

. . . then remove the filler plug from the side of the differential

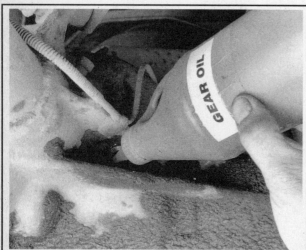

If the level is low, add fluid through the hole until the level is at the edge of the hole

removed, the differential is full. If no lubricant trickles out, carefully insert your finger (watch out for sharp threads) into the hole and check that the oil is up to the bottom edge of the filler hole.

3. If not, add oil through the hole until the level is at the edge of the hole. Most gear oils come in a plastic squeeze bottle with a nozzle end, which makes adding lubricant simple. You can also use a common turkey baster for this job. Use only standard GL-5 hypoid-type gear oil—SAE 80W or SAE 80W/90.

➡ **On all models equipped with a positraction/limited slip differential, GM recommends that you use only special GM lubricant available at your local Pontiac parts department.**

DRAIN & REFILL

There is no recommended change interval for the rear axle lubricant, but it is always a good idea to change the lube if you have purchased the car used or if it has been driven in water high enough to reach the axle.

1. Park the car on a level surface and set the parking brake.
2. Remove the rear axle filler plug on the front side of the differential housing.
3. Place a large drain pan underneath the rear axle.
4. Unscrew the retaining bolts and remove the rear axle cover. The axle lubricant will now be able to drain into the container.
5. Using a new cover gasket and sealant, install the axle cover. Tighten the retaining bolts in a crisscross pattern.
6. Refill the axle with the proper quantity (see "Capacities" chart in this chapter) of SAE 80W or SAE 80W-90 GL-5 gear lubricant. Replace the filler plug, take the car for a short ride and check for any leaks around the plug or rear cover.

Cooling System

LEVEL CHECK & FLUID RECOMMENDATIONS

◗ **See Figure 27**

➡ **The coolant recovery tank is the only accurate place to check the coolant level; however, coolant can be added to either the tank or directly to the radiator.**

It is best to check the coolant level when the engine and radiator are cool. Pontiac cars covered in this guide are equipped with coolant recovery tanks connected by hoses to the radiator and mounted on the inner fender skirt. If the coolant level is at or near the "FULL COLD" (engine cold) or the "FULL HOT" (engine hot) lines on the tank, the level is satisfactory.

✳ CAUTION

Never add coolant to a hot engine unless it is running; if it is not running, you risk cracking the engine block.

If you find the coolant level low, add a 50/50 mixture of ethylene glycol-based antifreeze and clean water. Do not add straight water unless you are out on the road and in emergency circumstances; if this is the case, drain the radiator and replenish the cooling system with an ethylene glycol mix at the next opportunity. Modern ethylene glycol antifreezes are special blends of anti-

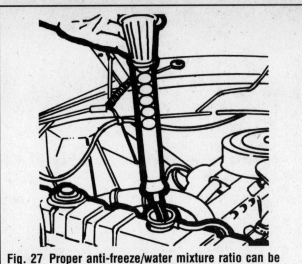

Fig. 27 Proper anti-freeze/water mixture ratio can be checked with an inexpensive tester

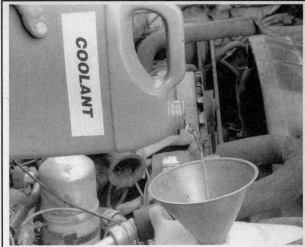

If the level is low, add coolant to the recovery reservoir, located on the fender skirt

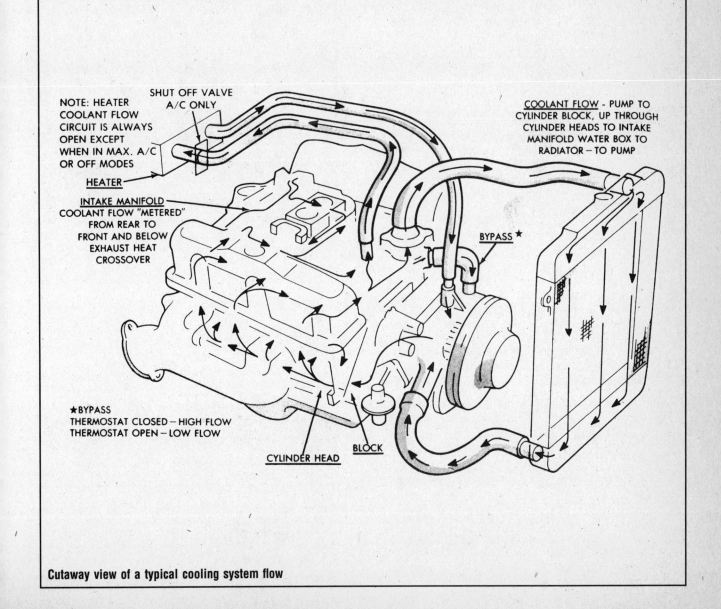

NOTE: HEATER COOLANT FLOW CIRCUIT IS ALWAYS OPEN EXCEPT WHEN IN MAX. A/C OR OFF MODES

SHUT OFF VALVE A/C ONLY

HEATER

INTAKE MANIFOLD COOLANT FLOW "METERED" FROM REAR TO FRONT AND BELOW EXHAUST HEAT CROSSOVER

COOLANT FLOW - PUMP TO CYLINDER BLOCK, UP THROUGH CYLINDER HEADS TO INTAKE MANIFOLD WATER BOX TO RADIATOR — TO PUMP

BYPASS ★

★BYPASS
THERMOSTAT CLOSED — HIGH FLOW
THERMOSTAT OPEN — LOW FLOW

CYLINDER HEAD

BLOCK

Cutaway view of a typical cooling system flow

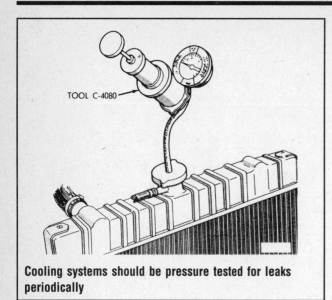

Cooling systems should be pressure tested for leaks periodically

The radiator draincock is located at the bottom corner of the radiator

corrosive additives and lubricants that help keep the cooling system clean and help lubricate water pump bearings, which is why they are recommended by the manufacturers.

DRAINING, FLUSHING & TESTING THE COOLING SYSTEM

The cooling system in your car accumulates some internal rust and corrosion in its normal operation. A simple method of keeping the system clean is known as "flushing" the system. It is performed by circulating a can of radiator flush through the system, and then draining and refilling the system with the normal coolant. Radiator flush is marketed by several different manufacturers, and is available in cans at auto departments, parts stores, and many hardware stores. This operation should be performed every 30,000 miles or once a year.

To flush the cooling system:

1. Drain the existing anti-freeze and coolant. Open the radiator and engine drain petcocks (located near the bottom of the radiator and engine block, respectively), or disconnect the bottom radiator hose at the radiator outlet.

➡Before opening the radiator petcock, spray it with some penetrating oil. Be aware that if the engine has been run up to operating temperature, the coolant emptied will be HOT.

2. Close the petcock or re-connect the lower hose and fill the system with water—hot water if the system has just been run.

3. Add a can of quality radiator flush to the radiator or recovery tank, following any special instructions on the can.

4. Idle the engine as long as specified on the can of flush, or until the upper radiator hose gets hot.

5. Drain the system again. There should be quite a bit of scale and rust in the drained water.

6. Repeat this process until the drained water is mostly clear.

7. Close all petcocks and connect all hoses.

8. Flush the coolant recovery reservoir with water and leave empty.

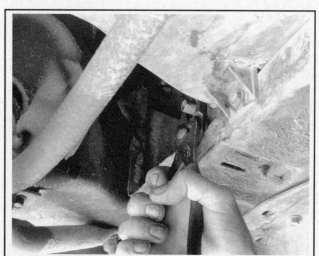

To drain the radiator, use a pair of pliers to open the draincock . . .

. . . then allow the coolant to drain into a suitable container

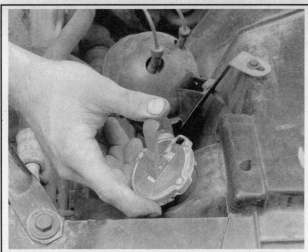

Make sure the engine is cool, then remove the radiator cap

Add the proper amount of coolant and water, then check the level and add more if necessary

9. Determine the capacity of your car's cooling system (see "Capacities" specifications in this guide). Add a 50/50 mix of ethylene glycol antifreeze and water to provide the desired protection.

10. Run the engine to operating temperature, then stop the engine and check for leaks. Check the coolant level and top up if necessary.

11. Check the protection level of your antifreeze mix with an antifreeze tester (a small, inexpensive syringe-type device available at any auto parts store). The tester has five or six small colored balls inside, each of which signify a certain temperature rating. Insert the tester in the recovery tank and suck just enough coolant into the syringe to float as many individual balls as you can (without sucking in too much coolant and floating all the balls at once). A table supplied with the tester will explain how many floating balls equal protection down to a certain temperature

(three floating balls might mean the coolant will protect your engine down to 5°F, for example).

CHECK THE RADIATOR CAP

Anytime you check the coolant level, check the radiator cap as well. A worn or cracked gasket can mean improper sealing, which can cause lost coolant, lost pressure, and engine overheating (the cooling system is pressurized and the radiator cap has a pressure rating above the pressure of the system).

A worn cap should be replaced with a new one. Make sure

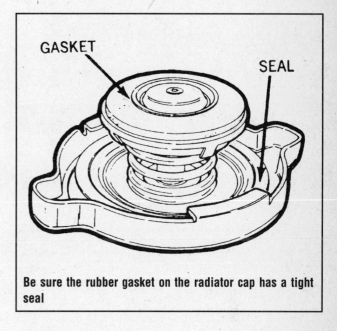

Be sure the rubber gasket on the radiator cap has a tight seal

the new cap has the proper pressure rating for your car's system; this is usually marked on the standard factory cap. You may want to go a few pounds per-square-inch over this rating, but never buy a cap having a rating *less* than the pressure of your car's system.

CLEAN THE RADIATOR OF DEBRIS

The efficiency of the radiator can be seriously impaired by blockage of the radiator fins. Leaves, insects, road dirt, paper—all are common obstacles to fresh air entering your radiator and doing its job.

Large pieces of debris, leaves and large insects can be removed from the fins by hand. The smaller pieces can be washed out with water pressure from a garden hose. This is often a neglected area of auto maintenance, so do a thorough job.

Bent radiator fins can be straightened carefully with a pair of needle-nose pliers. The fins are soft, so don't wiggle them—move them once.

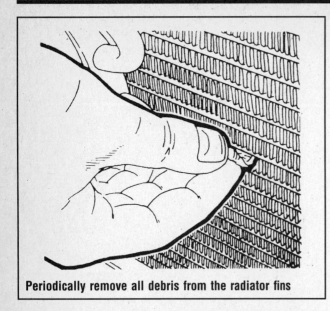

Periodically remove all debris from the radiator fins

. . . then check the level and add fresh DOT 3 brake fluid, if necessary

Brake Master Cylinder

LEVEL CHECK & FLUID RECOMMENDATIONS

The brake master cylinder is located under the hood, in the left rear section of the engine compartment. It is divided into two sections (reservoirs) and the fluid must be kept within 1/4 in. of the top edge of both reservoirs. The level should be checked at least every 7,500 miles.

➡️**Any sudden decrease in the level of fluid indicates a possible leak in the system and should be checked out immediately.**

To check the fluid level, simply pry off the retaining bar (if necessary) and then lift off the top cover of the master cylinder. When making additions of brake fluid, use only fresh, uncontami-

nated brake fluid which meets or exceeds DOT 3 standards (as stated on the container). *Be careful not to spill any brake fluid on painted surfaces, as it eats paint.* Do not allow the brake fluid container or the master cylinder reservoir to remain open any longer than necessary; brake fluid absorbs moisture from the air, reducing its effectiveness and causing corrosion in the lines.

➡️**The reservoir cover on some later models (1978–83) may be without a retaining bail. If so, simply pry the cover off with your fingers.**

Power Steering Pump

LEVEL CHECK & FLUID RECOMMENDATIONS

⬥ See Figure 28

Power steering fluid level should be checked at least every 7,500 miles. The power steering pump is belt driven and has the dipstick built into the filler cap. To prevent possible over-filling,

A. Minimum level mark

To check the brake fluid level on some later model vehicles, remove the master cylinder lid . . .

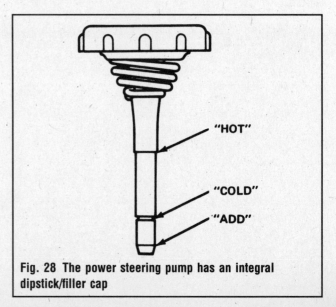

"HOT"

"COLD"

"ADD"

Fig. 28 The power steering pump has an integral dipstick/filler cap

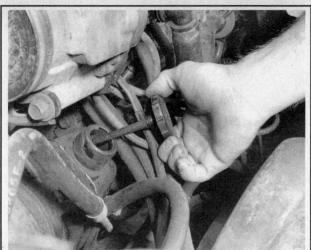

To check the power steering fluid level, remove the integral reservoir cap/dipstick

If the fluid level is low, add to the reservoir using a funnel and tube to prevent a mess

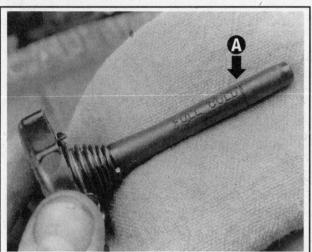

The power steering dipstick is marked with a FULL COLD mark (A) on one side

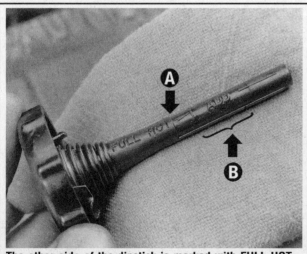

The other side of the dipstick is marked with FULL HOT (A) and ADD (B) marks

check the fluid level only when the fluid has warmed up to operating temperature and with the front wheels turned straight ahead. If the level is low, fill the pump reservoir with DEXRON® Automatic Transmission Fluid on 1974–76 cars. 1977 and later models require GM power steering fluid (or its equivalent), available at any Buick, Olds, Pontiac or Chevrolet dealer. Fill the reservoir until the fluid level measures "full" on the reservoir dipstick. When the fluid level is low, there is usually a moaning sound coming from the pump as the front wheels are turned, especially when standing still or parking. The steering wheel will also be difficult to turn when fluid level in the pump reservoir gets low.

Chassis Greasing

FRONT SUSPENSION

Every year or 7,500 miles the front suspension ball joints, both upper and lower on each side of the car, must be greased. Most cars covered in this guide should be equipped with grease nipples on the ball joints, although some may have plugs which must be removed and nipples fitted.

Jack up the front end of the car and safely support it with jackstands. Block the rear wheels and firmly apply the parking brake. If the car has been parked in temperatures below 20°F for any length of time, park it in a heated garage for an hour or so until the ball joints loosen up enough to accept the grease.

Depending on which front wheel you work on first, turn the wheel and tire outward, either full-lock right or full-lock left. You now have the ends of the upper and lower suspension control arms in front of you; the grease nipples are visible pointing up (top ball joint) and down (lower ball joint) through the end of each control arm. If the nipples are not accessible enough, remove the wheel and tire. Wipe all dirt and crud from the nipples or from around the plugs (if installed). If plugs are on the car, remove them and install grease nipples in the holes (nipples are available in various thread sizes at most auto parts stores). Using a hand-operated, low pressure grease gun loaded with a quality chassis grease, grease the ball joint only until the rubber joint boot begins to swell out.

➡**Do not pump so much grease into the ball joint that excess grease squeezes out of the rubber boot. This destroys the water-tight seal.**

STEERING LINKAGE

▶ **See Figure 29**

The steering linkage should be greased at the same interval as the ball joints. Grease nipples are installed on the steering tie rod ends on most models. Wipe all dirt and crud from around the nipples at each tie rod end. Using a hand-operated, low pressure grease gun loaded with a suitable chassis grease, grease the linkage until the old grease begins to squeeze out around the tie rod ends. Wipe off the nipples and any excess grease. Also grease the nipples on the steering idler arms.

PARKING BRAKE LINKAGE

▶ **See Figure 30**

Use chassis grease on the parking brake cable where it contacts the cable guides, levers and linkage.

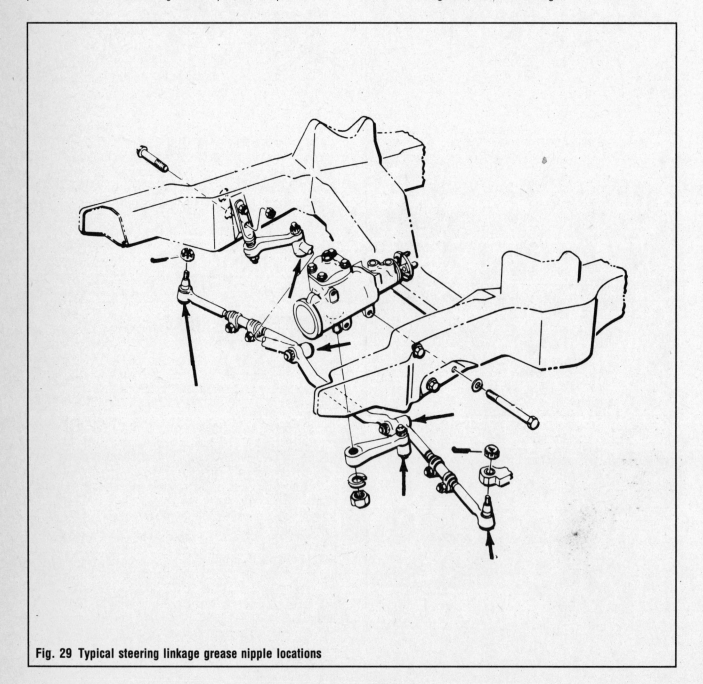

Fig. 29 Typical steering linkage grease nipple locations

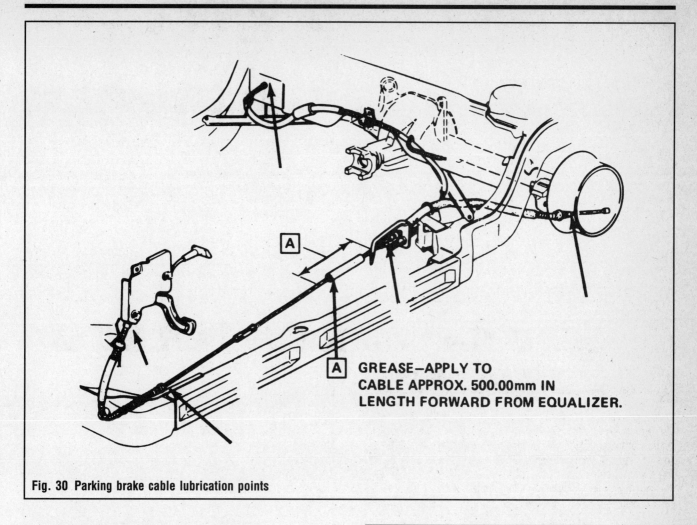

Fig. 30 Parking brake cable lubrication points

GREASE—APPLY TO
CABLE APPROX. 500.00mm IN
LENGTH FORWARD FROM EQUALIZER.

AUTOMATIC TRANSMISSION LINKAGE

Apply a small amount of clean engine oil to the kickdown and shift linkage points at 7,500 mile intervals.

Body Lubrication

HOOD LATCH & HINGES

Clean the latch surfaces and apply clean engine oil to the latch pilot bolts and the spring anchor. Also lubricate the hood hinges with engine oil. Use a chassis grease to lubricate all the pivot points in the latch release mechanism.

DOOR HINGES

▶ **See Figures 31 and 32**

The gas tank filler door, car doors, and trunk lid hinges should be wiped clean and lubricated with clean engine oil once a year.

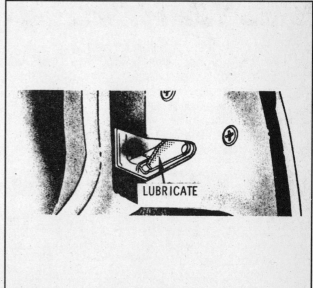

Fig. 31 Use a graphite lubricant on the door lock fork bolts

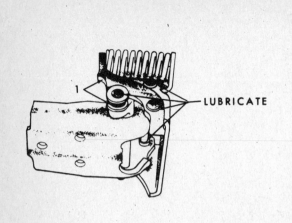

Fig. 32 For the front door hinge, use a spray lubricant

Use engine oil to lubricate the trunk lock mechanism and the lock-bolt striker. The door lock cylinders and latch mechanisms should be lubricated periodically with a few drops of graphite lock lubricant or a few shots of silicone spray.

Wheel Bearings

REMOVAL, PACKING & INSTALLATION

Refer to Chapter 9 for removal, installation, adjustment and re-packing procedures.

TRAILER TOWING

General Recommendations

Your vehicle was primarily designed to carry passengers and cargo. It is important to remember that towing a trailer will place additional loads on your vehicles engine, drivetrain, steering, braking and other systems. However, if you decide to tow a trailer, using the prior equipment is a must.

Local laws may require specific equipment such as trailer brakes or fender mounted mirrors. Check your local laws.

Trailer Weight

The weight of the trailer is the most important factor. A good weight-to-horsepower ratio is about 35:1, 35 lbs. of Gross Combined Weight (GCW) for every horsepower your engine develops. Multiply the engine's rated horsepower by 35 and subtract the weight of the vehicle passengers and luggage. The number remaining is the approximate ideal maximum weight you should tow, although a numerically higher axle ratio can help compensate for heavier weight.

Hitch (Tongue) Weight

Calculate the hitch weight in order to select a proper hitch. The weight of the hitch is usually 9–11% of the trailer gross weight and should be measured with the trailer loaded. Hitches fall into various categories: those that mount on the frame and rear bumper, the bolt-on type, or the weld-on distribution type used for larger trailers. Axle mounted or clamp-on bumper hitches should never be used.

Check the gross weight rating of your trailer. Tongue weight is usually figured as 10% of gross trailer weight. Therefore, a trailer with a maximum gross weight of 2000 lbs. will have a maximum tongue weight of 200 lbs. Class I trailers fall into this category. Class II trailers are those with a gross weight rating of 2000–3000 lbs., while Class III trailers fall into the 3500–6000 lbs. cate-

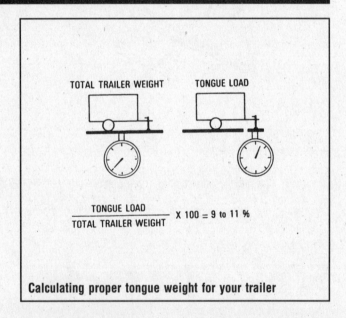

$$\frac{\text{TONGUE LOAD}}{\text{TOTAL TRAILER WEIGHT}} \times 100 = 9 \text{ to } 11\ \%$$

Calculating proper tongue weight for your trailer

gory. Class IV trailers are those over 6000 lbs. and are for use with fifth wheel trucks, only.

When you've determined the hitch that you'll need, follow the manufacturer's installation instructions, exactly, especially when it comes to fastener torques. The hitch will subjected to a lot of stress and good hitches come with hardened bolts. Never substitute an inferior bolt for a hardened bolt.

Cooling

ENGINE

Overflow Tank

One of the most common, if not THE most common, problems associated with trailer towing is engine overheating. If you have a cooling system without an expansion tank, you'll definitely need to get an aftermarket expansion tank kit, preferably one with at least a 2 quart capacity. These kits are easily installed on the radiator's overflow hose, and come with a pressure cap designed for expansion tanks.

Flex Fan

Another helpful accessory for vehicles using a belt-driven radiator fan is a flex fan. These fans are large diameter units designed to provide more airflow at low speeds, by using fan blades that have deeply cupped surfaces. The blades then flex, or flatten out, at high speed, when less cooling air is needed. These fans are far lighter in weight than stock fans, requiring less horsepower to drive them. Also, they are far quieter than stock fans. If you do decide to replace your stock fan with a flex fan, note that if your vehicle has a fan clutch, a spacer will be needed between the flex fan and water pump hub.

Oil Cooler

Aftermarket engine oil coolers are helpful for prolonging engine oil life and reducing overall engine temperatures. Both of these factors increase engine life. While not absolutely necessary in towing Class I and some Class II trailers, they are recommended for heavier Class II and all Class III towing. Engine oil cooler systems usually consist of an adapter, screwed on in place of the oil filter, a remote filter mounting and a multi-tube, finned heat exchanger, which is mounted in front of the radiator or air conditioning condenser.

TRANSMISSION

An automatic transmission is usually recommended for trailer towing. Modern automatics have proven reliable and, of course,

easy to operate, in trailer towing. The increased load of a trailer, however, causes an increase in the temperature of the automatic transmission fluid. Heat is the worst enemy of an automatic transmission. As the temperature of the fluid increases, the life of the fluid decreases.

It is essential, therefore, that you install an automatic transmission cooler. The cooler, which consists of a multi-tube, finned heat exchanger, is usually installed in front of the radiator or air conditioning compressor, and hooked in-line with the transmission cooler tank inlet line. Follow the cooler manufacturer's installation instructions.

Select a cooler of at least adequate capacity, based upon the combined gross weights of the vehicle and trailer.

Cooler manufacturers recommend that you use an aftermarket cooler in addition to, and not instead of, the present cooling tank in your radiator. If you do want to use it in place of the radiator cooling tank, get a cooler at least two sizes larger than normally necessary.

➡**A transmission cooler can, sometimes, cause slow or harsh shifting in the transmission during cold weather, until the fluid has a chance to come up to normal operating temperature. Some coolers can be purchased with or retrofitted with a temperature bypass valve which will allow fluid flow through the cooler only when the fluid has reached above a certain operating temperature.**

Handling A Trailer

Towing a trailer with ease and safety requires a certain amount of experience. It's a good idea to learn the feel of a trailer by practicing turning, stopping and backing in an open area such as an empty parking lot.

JUMP STARTING A DEAD BATTERY

Whenever a vehicle is jump started, precautions must be followed in order to prevent the possibility of personal injury. Remember that batteries contain a small amount of explosive hydrogen gas which is a by-product of battery charging. Sparks should always be avoided when working around batteries, especially when attaching jumper cables. To minimize the possibility of accidental sparks, follow the procedure carefully.

✳✳ CAUTION

NEVER hook the batteries up in a series circuit or the entire electrical system will go up in smoke, including the starter!

Vehicles equipped with a diesel engine may utilize two 12 volt batteries. If so, the batteries are connected in a parallel circuit (positive terminal to positive terminal, negative terminal to negative terminal). Hooking the batteries up in parallel circuit increases battery cranking power without increasing total battery voltage output. Output remains at 12 volts. On the other hand, hooking two 12 volt batteries up in a series circuit (positive termi-

nal to negative terminal, positive terminal to negative terminal) increases total battery output to 24 volts (12 volts plus 12 volts).

Jump Starting Precautions

• Be sure that both batteries are of the same voltage. Vehicles covered by this manual and most vehicles on the road today utilize a 12 volt charging system.

• Be sure that both batteries are of the same polarity (have the same terminal, in most cases NEGATIVE grounded).

• Be sure that the vehicles are not touching or a short could occur.

• On serviceable batteries, be sure the vent cap holes are not obstructed.

• Do not smoke or allow sparks anywhere near the batteries.

• In cold weather, make sure the battery electrolyte is not frozen. This can occur more readily in a battery that has been in a state of discharge.

• Do not allow electrolyte to contact your skin or clothing.

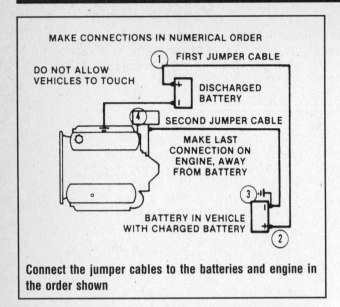

MAKE CONNECTIONS IN NUMERICAL ORDER

FIRST JUMPER CABLE

DO NOT ALLOW VEHICLES TO TOUCH

DISCHARGED BATTERY

SECOND JUMPER CABLE

MAKE LAST CONNECTION ON ENGINE, AWAY FROM BATTERY

BATTERY IN VEHICLE WITH CHARGED BATTERY

Connect the jumper cables to the batteries and engine in the order shown

Jump Starting Procedure

1. Make sure that the voltages of the 2 batteries are the same. Most batteries and charging systems are of the 12 volt variety.

2. Pull the jumping vehicle (with the good battery) into a position so the jumper cables can reach the dead battery and that vehicle's engine. Make sure that the vehicles do NOT touch.

3. Place the transmissions/transaxles of both vehicles in **Neutral** (MT) or **P** (AT), as applicable, then firmly set their parking brakes.

➡**If necessary for safety reasons, the hazard lights on both vehicles may be operated throughout the entire procedure without significantly increasing the difficulty of jumping the dead battery.**

4. Turn all lights and accessories OFF on both vehicles. Make sure the ignition switches on both vehicles are turned to the **OFF** position.

5. Cover the battery cell caps with a rag, but do not cover the terminals.

6. Make sure the terminals on both batteries are clean and free of corrosion or proper electrical connection will be impeded. If necessary, clean the battery terminals before proceeding.

7. Identify the positive (+) and negative (−) terminals on both batteries.

8. Connect the first jumper cable to the positive (+) terminal of the dead battery, then connect the other end of that cable to the positive (+) terminal of the booster (good) battery.

9. Connect one end of the other jumper cable to the negative (−) terminal on the booster battery and the final cable clamp to an engine bolt head, alternator bracket or other solid, metallic point on the engine with the dead battery. Try to pick a ground on the engine that is positioned away from the battery in order to minimize the possibility of the 2 clamps touching should one loosen during the procedure. DO NOT connect this clamp to the negative (−) terminal of the bad battery.

✳✳ CAUTION

Be very careful to keep the jumper cables away from moving parts (cooling fan, belts, etc.) on both engines.

10. Check to make sure that the cables are routed away from any moving parts, then start the donor vehicle's engine. Run the engine at moderate speed for several minutes to allow the dead battery a chance to receive some initial charge.

11. With the donor vehicle's engine still running slightly above idle, try to start the vehicle with the dead battery. Crank the engine for no more than 10 seconds at a time and let the starter cool for at least 20 seconds between tries. If the vehicle does not start in 3 tries, it is likely that something else is also wrong or that the battery needs additional time to charge.

12. Once the vehicle is started, allow it to run at idle for a few seconds to make sure that it is operating properly.

13. Turn ON the headlights, heater blower and, if equipped, the rear defroster of both vehicles in order to reduce the severity of voltage spikes and subsequent risk of damage to the vehicles' electrical systems when the cables are disconnected. This step is especially important to any vehicle equipped with computer control modules.

14. Carefully disconnect the cables in the reverse order of connection. Start with the negative cable that is attached to the engine ground, then the negative cable on the donor battery. Disconnect the positive cable from the donor battery and finally, disconnect the positive cable from the formerly dead battery. Be careful when disconnecting the cables from the positive terminals not to allow the alligator clips to touch any metal on either vehicle or a short and sparks will occur.

JACKING

▶ **See Figures 33 and 34**

Your vehicle was supplied with a jack for emergency road repairs. This jack is fine for changing a flat tire or other short term procedures not requiring you to go beneath the vehicle. If it is used in an emergency situation, carefully follow the instructions provided either with the jack or in your owner's manual. Do not attempt to use the jack on any portions of the vehicle other than specified by the vehicle manufacturer. Always block the diagonally opposite wheel when using a jack.

A more convenient way of jacking is the use of a garage or floor jack.

Never place the jack under the radiator, engine or transmission components. Severe and expensive damage will result when the jack is raised. Additionally, never jack under the floorpan or bodywork; the metal will deform.

Whenever you plan to work under the vehicle, you must support it on jackstands or ramps. Never use cinder blocks or stacks of wood to support the vehicle, even if you're only going to be un-

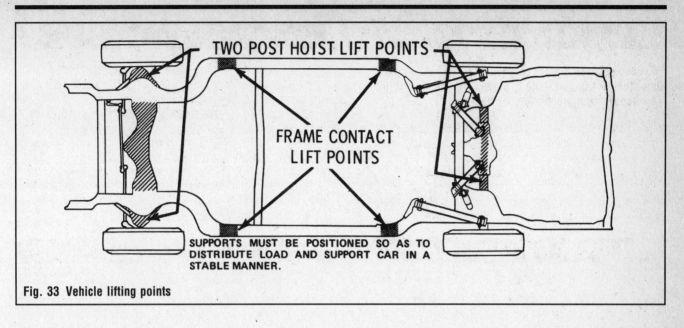

TWO POST HOIST LIFT POINTS

FRAME CONTACT LIFT POINTS

SUPPORTS MUST BE POSITIONED SO AS TO DISTRIBUTE LOAD AND SUPPORT CAR IN A STABLE MANNER.

Fig. 33 Vehicle lifting points

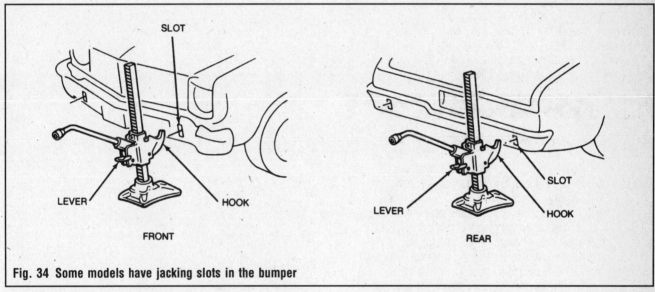

SLOT

LEVER   HOOK

FRONT

SLOT

LEVER   HOOK

REAR

Fig. 34 Some models have jacking slots in the bumper

Jacking point and jackstand location for the front of the vehicle

Location of the jackstand and jacking point for the rear of the vehicle

der it for a few minutes. Never crawl under the vehicle when it is supported only by the tire-changing jack or other floor jack.

➡**Always position a block of wood or small rubber pad on top of the jack or jackstand to protect the lifting point's finish when lifting or supporting the vehicle.**

Small hydraulic, screw, or scissors jacks are satisfactory for raising the vehicle. Drive-on trestles or ramps are also a handy and safe way to both raise and support the vehicle. Be careful though, some ramps may be too steep to drive your vehicle onto without scraping the front bottom panels. Never support the vehicle on any suspension member (unless specifically instructed to do so by a repair manual) or by an underbody panel.

HOW TO BUY A USED VEHICLE

Many people believe that a two or three year old used car or truck is a better buy than a new vehicle. This may be true as most new vehicles suffer the heaviest depreciation in the first two years and, at three years old, a vehicle is usually not old enough to present a lot of costly repair problems. But keep in mind, when buying a non-warranted automobile, there are no guarantees. Whatever the age of the used vehicle you might want to purchase, this section and a little patience should increase your chances of selecting one that is safe and dependable.

Tips

1. First decide what model you want, and how much you want to spend.
2. Check the used car lots and your local newspaper ads. Privately owned vehicles are usually less expensive, however, you may not get a warranty that, in many cases, comes with a used vehicle purchased from a lot. Of course, some aftermarket warranties may not be worth the extra money, so this is a point you will have to debate and consider based on your priorities.
3. Never shop at night. The glare of the lights make it easy to miss faults on the body caused by accident or rust repair.
4. Try to get the name and phone number of the previous owner. Contact him/her and ask about the vehicle. If the owner of a lot refuses this information, look for a vehicle somewhere else.

A private seller can tell you about the vehicle and maintenance. But remember, there's no law requiring honesty from private citizens selling used vehicles. There is a law that forbids tampering with or turning back the odometer mileage. This includes both the private citizen and the lot owner. The law also requires that the seller or anyone transferring ownership of the vehicle must provide the buyer with a signed statement indicating the mileage on the odometer at the time of transfer.

5. You may wish to contact the National Highway Traffic Safety Administration (NHTSA) to find out if the vehicle has ever been included in a manufacturer's recall. Write down the year, model and serial number before you buy the vehicle, then contact NHTSA (there should be a 1-800 number that your phone company's information line can supply). If the vehicle was listed for a recall, make sure the needed repairs were made.
6. Refer to the Used Vehicle Checklist in this section and check all the items on the vehicle you are considering. Some items are more important than others. Only you know how much money you can afford for repairs, and depending on the price of

Jacking Precautions

The following safety points cannot be overemphasized:
• Always block the opposite wheel or wheels to keep the vehicle from rolling off the jack.
• When raising the front of the vehicle, firmly apply the parking brake.
• When the drive wheels are to remain on the ground, leave the vehicle in gear to help prevent it from rolling.
• Always use jackstands to support the vehicle when you are working underneath. Place the stands beneath the vehicle's jacking brackets. Before climbing underneath, rock the vehicle a bit to make sure it is firmly supported.

the vehicle, may consider performing any needed work yourself. Beware, however, of trouble in areas that will affect operation, safety or emission. Problems in the Used Vehicle Checklist break down as follows:
• Numbers 1–8: Two or more problems in these areas indicate a lack of maintenance. You should beware.
• Numbers 9–13: Problems here tend to indicate a lack of proper care, however, these can usually be corrected with a tune-up or relatively simple parts replacement.
• Numbers 14–17: Problems in the engine or transmission can be very expensive. Unless you are looking for a project, walk away from any vehicle with problems in 2 or more of these areas.
7. If you are satisfied with the apparent condition of the vehicle, take it to an independent diagnostic center or mechanic for a complete check. If you have a state inspection program, have it inspected immediately before purchase, or specify on the bill of sale that the sale is conditional on passing state inspection.
8. Road test the vehicle—refer to the Road Test Checklist in this section. If your original evaluation and the road test agree—the rest is up to you.

USED VEHICLE CHECKLIST

➡**The numbers on the illustrations refer to the numbers on this checklist.**

1. Mileage: Average mileage is about 12,000–15,000 miles per year. More than average mileage may indicate hard usage or could indicate many highway miles (which could be less detrimental than half as many tough around town miles).
2. Paint: Check around the tailpipe, molding and windows for overspray indicating that the vehicle has been repainted.
3. Rust: Check fenders, doors, rocker panels, window moldings, wheelwells, floorboards, under floormats, and in the trunk for signs of rust. Any rust at all will be a problem. There is no way to permanently stop the spread of rust, except to replace the part or panel.

➡**If rust repair is suspected, try using a magnet to check for body filler. A magnet should stick to the sheet metal parts of the body, but will not adhere to areas with large amounts of filler.**

4. Body appearance: Check the moldings, bumpers, grille, vinyl roof, glass, doors, trunk lid and body panels for general over-

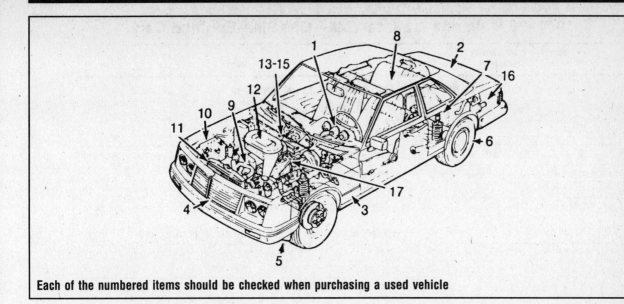

Each of the numbered items should be checked when purchasing a used vehicle

all condition. Check for misalignment, loose hold-down clips, ripples, scratches in glass, welding in the trunk, severe misalignment of body panels or ripples, any of which may indicate crash work.

5. Leaks: Get down and look under the vehicle. There are no normal leaks, other than water from the air conditioner evaporator.

6. Tires: Check the tire air pressure. One old trick is to pump the tire pressure up to make the vehicle roll easier. Check the tread wear, then open the trunk and check the spare too. Uneven wear is a clue that the front end may need an alignment.

7. Shock absorbers: Check the shock absorbers by forcing downward sharply on each corner of the vehicle. Good shocks will not allow the vehicle to bounce more than once after you let go.

8. Interior: Check the entire interior. You're looking for an interior condition that agrees with the overall condition of the vehicle. Reasonable wear is expected, but be suspicious of new seat covers on sagging seats, new pedal pads, and worn armrests. These indicate an attempt to cover up hard use. Pull back the carpets and look for evidence of water leaks or flooding. Look for missing hardware, door handles, control knobs, etc. Check lights and signal operations. Make sure all accessories (air conditioner, heater, radio, etc.) work. Check windshield wiper operation.

9. Belts and Hoses: Open the hood, then check all belts and hoses for wear, cracks or weak spots.

10. Battery: Low electrolyte level, corroded terminals and/or cracked case indicate a lack of maintenance.

11. Radiator: Look for corrosion or rust in the coolant indicating a lack of maintenance.

12. Air filter: A severely dirty air filter would indicate a lack of maintenance.

13. Ignition wires: Check the ignition wires for cracks, burned spots, or wear. Worn wires will have to be replaced.

14. Oil level: If the oil level is low, chances are the engine uses oil or leaks. Beware of water in the oil (there is probably a cracked block or bad head gasket), excessively thick oil (which is often used to quiet a noisy engine), or thin, dirty oil with a distinct gasoline smell (this may indicate internal engine problems).

15. Automatic Transmission: Pull the transmission dipstick out when the engine is running. The level should read FULL, and the fluid should be clear or bright red. Dark brown or black fluid that has distinct burnt odor, indicates a transmission in need of repair or overhaul.

16. Exhaust: Check the color of the exhaust smoke. Blue smoke indicates, among other problems, worn rings. Black smoke can indicate burnt valves or carburetor problems. Check the exhaust system for leaks; it can be expensive to replace.

17. Spark Plugs: Remove one or all of the spark plugs (the most accessible will do, though all are preferable). An engine in good condition will show plugs with a light tan or gray deposit on the firing tip.

ROAD TEST CHECKLIST

1. Engine Performance: The vehicle should be peppy whether cold or warm, with adequate power and good pickup. It should respond smoothly through the gears.

2. Brakes: They should provide quick, firm stops with no noise, pulling or brake fade.

3. Steering: Sure control with no binding harshness, or looseness and no shimmy in the wheel should be expected. Noise or vibration from the steering wheel when turning the vehicle means trouble.

4. Clutch (Manual Transmission/Transaxle): Clutch action should give quick, smooth response with easy shifting. The clutch pedal should have free-play before it disengages the clutch. Start the engine, set the parking brake, put the transmission in first gear and slowly release the clutch pedal. The engine should begin to stall when the pedal is $1/2$–$3/4$ of the way up.

5. Automatic Transmission/Transaxle: The transmission should shift rapidly and smoothly, with no noise, hesitation, or slipping.

6. Differential: No noise or thumps should be present. Differentials have no normal leaks.

7. Driveshaft/Universal Joints: Vibration and noise could mean driveshaft problems. Clicking at low speed or coast conditions means worn U-joints.

8. Suspension: Try hitting bumps at different speeds. A vehicle that bounces excessively has weak shock absorbers or struts. Clunks mean worn bushings or ball joints.

9. Frame/Body: Wet the tires and drive in a straight line. Tracks should show two straight lines, not four. Four tire tracks indicate a frame/body bent by collision damage. If the tires can't be wet for this purpose, have a friend drive along behind you and see if the vehicle appears to be traveling in a straight line.

1974–76 Maintenance Intervals—Gasoline-Engined Cars

Interval At Which Services Are To Be Performed	Service
LUBRICATION AND GENERAL MAINTENANCE	
Every 6 months or 7,500 miles	*CHASSIS-Lubricate ●*FLUID LEVELS-Check *ENGINE OIL-Change·
At first oil change-then every 2nd	*ENGINE OIL FILTER-Replace (V-6 Replace each oil change)
See Explanation of Maintenance Schedule	TIRES-Rotate DIFFERENTIAL
Every 12 months	AIR CONDITIONING SYSTEM-Check charge & hose condition. TEMPMATIC AIR FILTER-Replace every other year.
Every 12 months or 15,000 miles	*COOLING SYSTEM-See Explanation of Maintenance Schedule
Every 30,000 miles	WHEEL BEARINGS-Clean and repack WHEEL BEARINGS-Clean & repack FINAL DRIVE AXLE BOOTS & OUTPUT SHAFT SEAL-Check Cond. *AUTOMATIC TRANS.-Change fluid and service filter MANUAL STEERING GEAR-Check seals CLUTCH CROSS SHAFT-Lubricate
SAFETY MAINTENANCE	
Every 6 months or 7,500 miles	TIRES AND WHEELS-Check condition *EXHAUST SYSTEM-Check condition of system *DRIVE BELTS-Ck. cond. & adjustment. Replace every 30,000 miles FRONT AND REAR SUSPENSION & STEERING SYSTEM-Ck. cond. BRAKES AND POWER STEERING-Check all lines and hoses
Every 12 months or 15,000 miles	DRUM BRAKES AND PARKING BRAKE-Check condition of linings; adjust parking brake THROTTLE LINKAGE-Check operation and condition UNDERBODY-Flush and check condition BUMPERS-Check condition
EMISSION CONTROL MAINTENANCE	
At 1st 6 months or 7,500 miles-then at 18 month/22,500 mile intervals there after	THERMOSTATICALLY CONTROLLED AIR CLEANER-Check operation CARBURETOR CHOKE-Check operation ENGINE IDLE SPEED ADJUSTMENT EFE VALVE-Check operation CARBURETOR-Torque attaching bolts or nuts to manifold
Every 12 months or 15,000 miles	CARBURETOR FUEL INLET FILTER-Replace VACUUM ADVANCE SYSTEM AND HOSES-Check oper. PCV SYSTEMS-See Explanation of Maintenance Schedule
Every 18 months or 22,500 miles	IDLE STOP SOLENOID OR DASHPOT-Check operation SPARK PLUG AND IGNITION COIL WIRES-Inspect and clean
Every 22,500 miles	SPARK PLUGS-Replace ENGINE TIMING ADJUSTMENT & DISTRIBUTOR CHECK
Every 24 months or 30,000 miles	ECS SYSTEM-See Explanation of Maintenance Schedule FUEL CAP, TANK AND LINES-Check condition
Every 30,000 miles	AIR CLEANER ELEMENT-Replace

*Also Required Emission Control Maintenance
● Also a Safety Service

1977 and Later Maintenance Intervals—Gasoline-Engined Cars

When to Perform Services (Months or Miles, Whichever Occurs First)	Services
LUBRICATION AND GENERAL MAINTENANCE	
Every 12 months or 7,500 miles (12 000 km)	● CHASSIS-Lubricate ● FLUID LEVELS-Check CLUTCH PEDAL FREE TRAVEL-Check/Adjust
See Explanation of Maintenance Schedule	*ENGINE OIL-Change *ENGINE OIL FILTER-Replace TIRES-Rotation (Radial Tires) REAR AXLE OR FINAL DRIVE-Check lube
Every 12 months or 15,000 miles (24 000 km)	*COOLING SYSTEM-See Explanation of Maintenance Schedule
Every 30,000 miles (48 000 km)	WHEEL BEARINGS-Repack CLUTCH CROSS SHAFT-Lubricate
See Explanation	AUTOMATIC TRANSMISSION-Change fluid and service filter
SAFETY MAINTENANCE	
Every 12 months or 7,500 miles (12 000 km)	TIRES, WHEELS AND DISC BRAKES-Check condition *EXHAUST SYSTEM-Check condition SUSPENSION & STEERING SYSTEM-Check condition BRAKES AND POWER STEERING-Check all lines and hoses
Every 12 months or 15,000 miles (24 000 km)	*DRIVE BELTS-Check condition and adjustment (1) DRUM BRAKES AND PARKING BRAKE-Check condition of linings; adjust parking brake THROTTLE LINKAGE-Check operation and condition BUMPERS-Check condition *FUEL CAP, TANK AND LINES-Check
EMISSION CONTROL MAINTENANCE	
At first 6 Months or 7,500 Miles (12 000 km)–Then at 24-Month/30,000 Mile (48 000 km) Intervals as Indicated in Log, Except Choke Which Requires Service at 45,000 Miles (72 000 km)	CARBURETOR CHOKE & HOSES-Check (2) ENGINE IDLE SPEED-Check adjustment (2) EFE SYSTEM-Check operation (if so equipped) CARBURETOR-Torque attaching bolts or nuts to manifold (2)
Every 30,000 miles (48 000 km)	THERMOSTATICALLY CONTROLLED AIR CLEANER-Check operation VACUUM ADVANCE SYSTEM AND HOSES-Check (3) SPARK PLUG WIRES-Check IDLE STOP SOLENOID AND/OR DASH POT OR ISC-Check operation SPARK PLUGS-Replace (2) ENGINE TIMING ADJUSTMENT AND DISTRIBUTOR-Check AIR CLEANER AND PCV FILTER ELEMENT-Replace (2) PCV VALVE-Replace EGR VALVE-Service

● Also a Safety Service
* Also an Emission Control Service
(1) In California, a separately driven air pump belt check is recommended but not required at 15,000 miles (24 000 km) and 45,00 miles (72 000 km).
(2) Only these emission control maintenance items are considered to be required maintenace as defined by the California Air Resources Board (ARB) regulation and are, according to such regulation, the minimum maintenance an owner in California must perform to fulfill the minimum requirements of the emission warranty. All other emission maintenance items are recommended maintenance as defined by such regulation. General Motors urges that all emission control maintenance items be performed.
(3) Not applicable on vehicles equipped with electronic spark timing (EST).

Diesel Maintenance Intervals

When to Perform Services (Months or Miles, Whichever Occurs First)	Services
LUBRICATION AND GENERAL MAINTENANCE	
Every 5,000 Miles (8 000 km)	*ENGINE OIL-Change *OIL FILTER-Change ● CHASSIS-Lubricate ● FLUID LEVELS-Check
See Explanation	TIRES-Rotation REAR AXLE OR FINAL DRIVE-Check lube
Every 12 months or 15,000 miles (24 000 km)	*COOLING SYSTEM-Check *CRANKCASE VENTILATION-Service
Every 30,000 miles (48 000 km)	WHEEL BEARINGS-Repack FINAL DRIVE BOOTS AND SEALS-Check
See Explanation	AUTOMATIC TRANSMISSION-Change fluid and filter
SAFETY MAINTENANCE	
At first 5,000 (8 000 km) Then at 15,000/30,000/45,000 miles	*EXHAUST SYSTEM-Check condition
Every 12 months or 10,000 miles (16 000 km)	TIRES, WHEEL AND DISC BRAKE-Check SUSPENSION AND STEERING-Check BRAKES AND POWER STEERING-Check
Every 5,000 Miles (8 000 km)	*DRIVE BELTS-Check condition and adjustment
Every 12 months or 15,000 miles (24 000 km)	DRUM BRAKES AND PARKING BRAKE-Check THROTTLE LINKAGE-Check operation BUMPERS-Check condition
EMISSION CONTROL MAINTENANCE	
At first 5,000 miles (8 000 km) Then at 15,000/30,000/45,000 miles	EXHAUST PRESSURE REGULATOR VALVE
At first 5,000 miles (8 000 km) Then at 30,000 miles (48 000 km)	ENGINE IDLE SPEED-Adjust
Every 30,000 miles (48 000 km)	AIR CLEANER-Replace FUEL FILTER-Replace

● Also a Safety Service
*Also on Emission Control Service

Capacities

Year	Engine No. Cyl. Displacement (Cu. In.)	Engine Crankcase Add 1 Qt For New Filter	Transmission (Pts To Refill After Draining) Automatic	Manual	Drive Axle (pts)	Fuel Tank (gals)	Cooling System (qts) With Heater	With A/C	Heavy Duty Cooling
			LeMans, Grand LeMans, Grand Am						
'74	6-250	4	9.0	3.5①	3.0②	21.8	14.7	14.7	14.7
	8-350	5	9.0	3.5①	3.0②	21.8	21.3	23.6	23.6
	8-400	5	9.0	3.5①	3.0②	21.8	21.3	22.8	22.8
'75	6-250	4	8.0	3.5①	3.0②	21.8	14.7	14.7	14.7
	8-350	5	9.0	3.5①	3.0②	21.8	21.3	23.6	23.6
	8-400	5	9.0	3.5①	3.0②	21.8	21.3	23.6	22.8
	8-455	5	9.0	3.5①	3.0②	21.8	21.3	23.6	22.8
'76	6-250	4	8.0	3.5①	3.0②	21.0③	15.0	15.0	15.0
	6-231	4	8.0	3.5①	3.0	21.0③	15.0	15.0	15.0
	8-260	5	8.0	3.5①	3.0	21.0③	15.0	23.5	23.5
	8-350	5	8.0	3.5①	3.0	21.0③	21.4	22.0	22.0
	8-400	5	9.0	3.5①	3.0	21.0③	21.4	22.0	22.0
	8-455	5	9.0	3.5①	3.0	21.0③	21.6	21.6	—
'77	6-231	4	8.0	3.5	4.3	22.0	15.0	15.0	—
	8-301	5	8.0	3.5	4.3	22.0	20.2	20.2	20.8
	8-350	4	8.0	3.5	4.3	22.0	16.7	16.7	17.5
	8-400	5	8.0	3.5	4.3	22.0	21.4③	22.0	23.9
	8-403	4	8.0	3.5	4.3	22.0	17.9④	17.9④	18.7
'78	6-231	4	⑤	3.5	4.3	22.0	15.0	15.0	—
	8-301	5	⑤	3.5	4.3	22.0	20.2	20.2	20.8
	8-350 Buick	5	⑤	3.5	4.3	22.0	16.7	16.7	17.5
	8-350 Olds.	4	⑤	3.5	4.3	22.0	16.7	16.7	17.5
	8-350 Chev.	4	⑤	3.5	4.3	22.0	16.7	16.7	17.5
	8-400	5	⑤	3.5	4.3	22.0	21.4③	22.0	23.9
	8-403	4	⑤	3.5	4.3	22.0	17.9④	17.9④	18.7
'79	6-231	4	⑤	3.5	4.3	22.0	15.0	15.0	—
	8-301	5	⑤	3.5	4.3	22.0	20.2	20.2	20.8
	8-350 Buick	5	⑤	3.5	4.3	22.0	16.7	16.7	17.5
	8-350 Olds.	4	⑤	3.5	4.3	22.0	16.7	16.7	17.5
	8-350 Chev.	4	⑤	3.5	4.3	22.0	16.7	16.7	17.5
'80	6-231	4	⑤	3.5	4.3	22.0	15.0	15.0	—
	8-265	5	8	3.5	4.3	22.0	20	20	20
	8-301	5	8	3.5	4.3	22.0	20.2	20.2	20.8
	8-305	4	⑤	3.5	4.3	22.0	17.3	17.3	—
'81	6-231	4	⑤	3.5	4.3	22.0	15.0	15.0	—
	8-265	5	8	3.5	4.3	22.0	20	20	20

Capacities (cont.)

Year	Engine No. Cyl. Displacement (Cu. In.)	Engine Crankcase Add 1 Qt For New Filter	Transmission (Pts To Refill After Draining)		Drive Axle (pts)	Fuel Tank (gals)	Cooling System (qts)		Heavy Duty Cooling
			Automatic	Manual			With Heater	With A/C	
				Grand Prix					
'74	8-400	5	9.0	—	3.0②	25.0	21.6	24.0	24.0
'75	8-400	5	9.0	—	3.0②	25.0	21.6	24.0	24.0
	8-455	5	9.0	—	3.0②	25.0	22.2	22.2	—
'76	8-350	5	8.0	—	3.0	25.0	21.6	22.0	22.0
	8-400	5	9.0	—	3.0	25.0	21.4	22.0	22.0
	8-455	5	9.0	—	3.0	25.0	22.2	22.2	—
'77	8-301	5	⑤	—	4.3	25.0	19.4	19.4	20.1
	8-350 Pontiac	4	⑤	—	4.3	25.0	21.6	22.2	24.1
	8-350 Olds.	4	⑤	—	4.3	25.0	17.0	17.0	17.8
	8-400	5	⑤	—	4.3	25.0	21.6	22.1	24.1
	8-403	4	⑤	—	4.3	25.0	18.2⑥	19.0⑥	19.0
'78	6-231	4	⑤	—	3.4	18.2	14.0	14.0	14.3
	8-301	5	⑤	—	3.4	18.2	21.6	22.0	24.1
	8-305	4	⑤	—	3.4	18.2	17.7	17.7	18.1
'79	6-231	4	⑤	—	3.4	18.2	14.0	14.0	14.3
	8-301	5	⑤	—	3.4	18.2	21.6	22.0	24.1
	8-305	4	⑤	—	3.4	18.2	17.7	17.7	18.1
'80	6-231	4	⑤	—	3.4	18.2	12.6	12.6	—
	8-265	4	⑤	—	3.4	18.2	19.2	19.2	19.2
	8-301	5	⑤	—	3.4	18.2	19.2	19.2	19.2
	8-305	4	⑤	—	3.4	18.2	17.2	17.2	17.2
'81	6-231	4	⑤	—	3.4	18.2	13.1	13.1	13.1
	8-265	4	⑤	—	3.4	18.2	13.0	13.1	13.1
	8-350 Diesel	7	⑤	—	3.4	19.1	—	17.0	—
'82	6-231	4⑦	⑤	—	3.4	18.2	13.1	13.1	13.1
	6-252	4⑦	⑤	—	3.4	18.2	13.1	13.1	13.1
	8-350 Diesel	7	⑤	—	3.4	19.1	—	17.0	—
'83	6-231	4③	⑤	—	3.4	17.5	13.1	13.1	13.1
	8-305	4	⑤	—	3.4	18.2	17.2	17.2	17.2
	8-350 Diesel	7	⑤	—	3.4	19.1	—	17.0	—
				Ventura, Phoenix, GTO					
'74	6-250	4	9.0	3.5⑧	3.75	21.5	13.1	13.1	—
	8-350	5	9.0	3.5⑧	3.75	21.5	20.0	20.0	20.0
'75	6-250	4	5.0	3.5⑧	3.75	20.5	13.5	13.5	—
	8-260	4	5.0	3.5⑧	3.75	20.5	18.5	19.5	—
	8-350	4	5.0	3.5⑧	3.75	20.5	18.5	19.5	—
'76	6-250	4	5.0	3.5⑨	3.75	20.5	13.0	13.0	—
	8-260	4	5.0	3.5⑨	3.75	20.5	20.6	21.3	—
	8-350	4	5.0	3.5⑨	3.75	20.5	17.3	18.0	—

Capacities (cont.)

Year	Engine No. Cyl. Displacement (Cu. In.)	Engine Crankcase Add 1 Qt For New Filter	Transmission (Pts To Refill After Draining)		Drive Axle (pts)	Fuel Tank (gals)	Cooling System (qts)		Heavy Duty Cooling
			Automatic	Manual			With Heater	With A/C	
			Ventura, Phoenix, GTO						
'77	4-151	3	6.0	3.5⑨	3.5	21.0	12.4	12.4	—
	6-231	4	6.0	3.5⑨	3.5	21.0	13.8	13.8	—
	8-301	5	6.0	3.5⑨	3.5	21.0	19.6	20.3	—
	8-305	4	6.0	3.5⑨	3.5	21.0	17.3	17.3	—
	8-350	4	6.0	3.5⑨	3.5	21.0	16.6	16.6	16.6
'78	4-151	3	6.0⑤	3.5⑨	3.5	21.0	12.4	12.4	—
	6-231	4	6.0⑤	3.5⑨	3.5	21.0	13.8	13.8	—
	8-301	5	6.0⑤	3.5⑨	3.5	21.0	19.6	20.3	—
	8-305	4	6.0⑤	3.5⑨	3.5	21.0	17.3	17.3	—
	8-350	4	6.0⑤	3.5⑨	3.5	21.0	16.6	16.6	16.6
'79	4-151	3	6.0⑤	3.5⑨	3.5	21.0	12.4	12.4	—
	6-231	4	6.0⑤	3.5⑨	3.5	21.0	13.8	13.8	—
	8-301	5	6.0⑤	3.5⑨	3.5	21.0	19.6	20.3	—
	8-305	4	6.0⑤	3.5⑨	3.5	21.0	17.3	17.3	—
	8-350	4	6.0⑤	3.5⑨	3.5	21.0	16.6	16.6	16.6

① Saginaw; 3-spd. Muncie 2.8; 4-spds. 2.5
② "C"-type axle 4.9
③ Station wagon 22.0
④ Station wagon and California 18.7
⑤ THM 200: 6 pts.; THM 350: 7.5 pts.; THM 400: 7.5
⑥ Except California; California 19.0
⑦ On microfilter-equipped cars, capacity is same with or without filter
⑧ 4 spd.: 2.5 pts.
⑨ 3 spd.; 4 spd. 2.5 pts.; 5 spd. 3.0 pts.

ENGLISH TO METRIC CONVERSION: MASS (WEIGHT)

Current **mass** measurement is expressed in pounds and ounces (lbs. & ozs.). The metric unit of mass (or weight) is the kilogram (kg). Even although this table does not show conversion of masses (weights) larger than 15 lbs, it is easy to calculate larger units by following the data immediately below.

To convert ounces (oz.) to grams (g): multiply th number of ozs. by 28
To convert grams (g) to ounces (oz.): multiply the number of grams by .035

To convert pounds (lbs.) to kilograms (kg): multiply the number of lbs. by .45
To convert kilograms (kg) to pounds (lbs.): multiply the number of kilograms by 2.2

lbs	kg	lbs	kg	oz	kg	oz	kg
0.1	0.04	0.9	0.41	0.1	0.003	0.9	0.024
0.2	0.09	1	0.4	0.2	0.005	1	0.03
0.3	0.14	2	0.9	0.3	0.008	2	0.06
0.4	0.18	3	1.4	0.4	0.011	3	0.08
0.5	0.23	4	1.8	0.5	0.014	4	0.11
0.6	0.27	5	2.3	0.6	0.017	5	0.14
0.7	0.32	10	4.5	0.7	0.020	10	0.28
0.8	0.36	15	6.8	0.8	0.023	15	0.42

ENGLISH TO METRIC CONVERSION: TEMPERATURE

To convert Fahrenheit (°F) to Celsius (°C): take number of °F and subtract 32; multiply result by 5; divide result by 9

To convert Celsius (°C) to Fahrenheit (°F): take number of °C and multiply by 9; divide result by 5; add 32 to total

Fahrenheit (F)	Celsius (C)	Celsius (C)	Fahrenheit	Fahrenheit (F)	Celsius (C)	Celsius (C)	Fahrenheit	Fahrenheit (F)	Celsius (C)	Celsius (C)	Fahrenheit
°F	°C	°C	°F	°F	°C	°C	°F	°F	°C	°C	°F
−40	−40	−38	−36.4	80	26.7	18	64.4	215	101.7	80	176
−35	−37.2	−36	−32.8	85	29.4	20	68	220	104.4	85	185
−30	−34.4	−34	−29.2	90	32.2	22	71.6	225	107.2	90	194
−25	−31.7	−32	−25.6	95	35.0	24	75.2	230	110.0	95	202
−20	−28.9	−30	−22	100	37.8	26	78.8	235	112.8	100	212
−15	−26.1	−28	−18.4	105	40.6	28	82.4	240	115.6	105	221
−10	−23.3	−26	−14.8	110	43.3	30	86	245	118.3	110	230
−5	−20.6	−24	−11.2	115	46.1	32	89.6	250	121.1	115	239
0	−17.8	−22	−7.6	120	48.9	34	93.2	255	123.9	120	248
1	−17.2	−20	−4	125	51.7	36	96.8	260	126.6	125	257
2	−16.7	−18	−0.4	130	54.4	38	100.4	265	129.4	130	266
3	−16.1	−16	3.2	135	57.2	40	104	270	132.2	135	275
4	−15.6	−14	6.8	140	60.0	42	107.6	275	135.0	140	284
5	−15.0	−12	10.4	145	62.8	44	112.2	280	137.8	145	293
10	−12.2	−10	14	150	65.6	46	114.8	285	140.6	150	302
15	−9.4	−8	17.6	155	68.3	48	118.4	290	143.3	155	311
20	−6.7	−6	21.2	160	71.1	50	122	295	146.1	160	320
25	−3.9	−4	24.8	165	73.9	52	125.6	300	148.9	165	329
30	−1.1	−2	28.4	170	76.7	54	129.2	305	151.7	170	338
35	1.7	0	32	175	79.4	56	132.8	310	154.4	175	347
40	4.4	2	35.6	180	82.2	58	136.4	315	157.2	180	356
45	7.2	4	39.2	185	85.0	60	140	320	160.0	185	365
50	10.0	6	42.8	190	87.8	62	143.6	325	162.8	190	374
55	12.8	8	46.4	195	90.6	64	147.2	330	165.6	195	383
60	15.6	10	50	200	93.3	66	150.8	335	168.3	200	392
65	18.3	12	53.6	205	96.1	68	154.4	340	171.1	205	401
70	21.1	14	57.2	210	98.9	70	158	345	173.9	210	410
75	23.9	16	60.8	212	100.0	75	167	350	176.7	215	414

ENGLISH TO METRIC CONVERSION: LENGTH

To convert inches (ins.) to millimeters (mm): multiply number of inches by 25.4

To convert millimeters (mm) to inches (ins.): multiply number of millimeters by .04

Inches	Decimals	Milli-meters	Inches to millimeters inches	mm	Inches	Decimals	Milli-meters	Inches to millimeters inches	mm
1/64	0.051625	0.3969	0.0001	0.00254	33/64	0.515625	13.0969	0.6	15.24
1/32	0.03125	0.7937	0.0002	0.00508	17/32	0.53125	13.4937	0.7	17.78
3/64	0.046875	1.1906	0.0003	0.00762	35/64	0.546875	13.8906	0.8	20.32
1/16	0.0625	1.5875	0.0004	0.01016	9/16	0.5625	14.2875	0.9	22.86
5/64	0.078125	1.9844	0.0005	0.01270	37/64	0.578125	14.6844	1	25.4
3/32	0.09375	2.3812	0.0006	0.01524	19/32	0.59375	15.0812	2	50.8
7/64	0.109375	2.7781	0.0007	0.01778	39/64	0.609375	15.4781	3	76.2
1/8	0.125	3.1750	0.0008	0.02032	5/8	0.625	15.8750	4	101.6
9/64	0.140625	3.5719	0.0009	0.02286	41/64	0.640625	16.2719	5	127.0
5/32	0.15625	3.9687	0.001	0.0254	21/32	0.65625	16.6687	6	152.4
11/64	0.171875	4.3656	0.002	0.0508	43/64	0.671875	17.0656	7	177.8
3/16	0.1875	4.7625	0.003	0.0762	11/16	0.6875	17.4625	8	203.2
13/64	0.203125	5.1594	0.004	0.1016	45/64	0.703125	17.8594	9	228.6
7/32	0.21875	5.5562	0.005	0.1270	23/32	0.71875	18.2562	10	254.0
15/64	0.234375	5.9531	0.006	0.1524	47/64	0.734375	18.6531	11	279.4
1/4	0.25	6.3500	0.007	0.1778	3/4	0.75	19.0500	12	304.8
17/64	0.265625	6.7469	0.008	0.2032	49/64	0.765625	19.4469	13	330.2
9/32	0.28125	7.1437	0.009	0.2286	25/32	0.78125	19.8437	14	355.6
19/64	0.296875	7.5406	0.01	0.254	51/64	0.796875	20.2406	15	381.0
5/16	0.3125	7.9375	0.02	0.508	13/16	0.8125	20.6375	16	406.4
21/64	0.328125	8.3344	0.03	0.762	53/64	0.828125	21.0344	17	431.8
11/32	0.34375	8.7312	0.04	1.016	27/32	0.84375	21.4312	18	457.2
23/64	0.359375	9.1281	0.05	1.270	55/64	0.859375	21.8281	19	482.6
3/8	0.375	9.5250	0.06	1.524	7/8	0.875	22.2250	20	508.0
25/64	0.390625	9.9219	0.07	1.778	57/64	0.890625	22.6219	21	533.4
13/32	0.40625	10.3187	0.08	2.032	29/32	0.90625	23.0187	22	558.8
27/64	0.421875	10.7156	0.09	2.286	59/64	0.921875	23.4156	23	584.2
7/16	0.4375	11.1125	0.1	2.54	15/16	0.9375	23.8125	24	609.6
29/64	0.453125	11.5094	0.2	5.08	61/64	0.953125	24.2094	25	635.0
15/32	0.46875	11.9062	0.3	7.62	31/32	0.96875	24.6062	26	660.4
31/64	0.484375	12.3031	0.4	10.16	63/64	0.984375	25.0031	27	690.6
1/2	0.5	12.7000	0.5	12.70					

ENGLISH TO METRIC CONVERSION: TORQUE

To convert foot-pounds (ft. lbs.) to Newton-meters: multiply the number of ft. lbs. by 1.3

To convert inch-pounds (in. lbs.) to Newton-meters: multiply the number of in. lbs. by .11

in lbs	N-m	in lbs	N-m	in lbs	N-m	in lbs	N-m	in lbs	N-m
0.1	0.01	1	0.11	10	1.13	19	2.15	28	3.16
0.2	0.02	2	0.23	11	1.24	20	2.26	29	3.28
0.3	0.03	3	0.34	12	1.36	21	2.37	30	3.39
0.4	0.04	4	0.45	13	1.47	22	2.49	31	3.50
0.5	0.06	5	0.56	14	1.58	23	2.60	32	3.62
0.6	0.07	6	0.68	15	1.70	24	2.71	33	3.73
0.7	0.08	7	0.78	16	1.81	25	2.82	34	3.84
0.8	0.09	8	0.90	17	1.92	26	2.94	35	3.95
0.9	0.10	9	1.02	18	2.03	27	3.05	36	4.0

ENGLISH TO METRIC CONVERSION: TORQUE

Torque is now expressed as either foot-pounds (ft./lbs.) or inch-pounds (in./lbs.). The metric measurement unit for torque is the Newton-meter (Nm). This unit—the Nm—will be used for all SI metric torque references, both the present ft./lbs. and in./lbs.

ft lbs	N-m	ft lbs	N-m	ft lbs	N-m	ft lbs	N-m
0.1	0.1	33	44.7	74	100.3	115	155.9
0.2	0.3	34	46.1	75	101.7	116	157.3
0.3	0.4	35	47.4	76	103.0	117	158.6
0.4	0.5	36	48.8	77	104.4	118	160.0
0.5	0.7	37	50.7	78	105.8	119	161.3
0.6	0.8	38	51.5	79	107.1	120	162.7
0.7	1.0	39	52.9	80	108.5	121	164.0
0.8	1.1	40	54.2	81	109.8	122	165.4
0.9	1.2	41	55.6	82	111.2	123	166.8
1	1.3	42	56.9	83	112.5	124	168.1
2	2.7	43	58.3	84	113.9	125	169.5
3	4.1	44	59.7	85	115.2	126	170.8
4	5.4	45	61.0	86	116.6	127	172.2
5	6.8	46	62.4	87	118.0	128	173.5
6	8.1	47	63.7	88	119.3	129	174.9
7	9.5	48	65.1	89	120.7	130	176.2
8	10.8	49	66.4	90	122.0	131	177.6
9	12.2	50	67.8	91	123.4	132	179.0
10	13.6	51	69.2	92	124.7	133	180.3
11	14.9	52	70.5	93	126.1	134	181.7
12	16.3	53	71.9	94	127.4	135	183.0
13	17.6	54	73.2	95	128.8	136	184.4
14	18.9	55	74.6	96	130.2	137	185.7
15	20.3	56	75.9	97	131.5	138	187.1
16	21.7	57	77.3	98	132.9	139	188.5
17	23.0	58	78.6	99	134.2	140	189.8
18	24.4	59	80.0	100	135.6	141	191.2
19	25.8	60	81.4	101	136.9	142	192.5
20	27.1	61	82.7	102	138.3	143	193.9
21	28.5	62	84.1	103	139.6	144	195.2
22	29.8	63	85.4	104	141.0	145	196.6
23	31.2	64	86.8	105	142.4	146	198.0
24	32.5	65	88.1	106	143.7	147	199.3
25	33.9	66	89.5	107	145.1	148	200.7
26	35.2	67	90.8	108	146.4	149	202.0
27	36.6	68	92.2	109	147.8	150	203.4
28	38.0	69	93.6	110	149.1	151	204.7
29	39.3	70	94.9	111	150.5	152	206.1
30	40.7	71	96.3	112	151.8	153	207.4
31	42.0	72	97.6	113	153.2	154	208.8
32	43.4	73	99.0	114	154.6	155	210.2

ENGLISH TO METRIC CONVERSION: FORCE

Force is presently measured in pounds (lbs.). This type of measurement is used to measure spring pressure, specifically how many pounds it takes to compress a spring. Our present force unit (the pound) will be replaced in SI metric measurements by the Newton (N). This term will eventually see use in specifications for electric motor brush spring pressures, valve spring pressures, etc.

To convert pounds (lbs.) to Newton (N): multiply the number of lbs. by 4.45

lbs	N	lbs	N	lbs	N	oz	N
0.01	0.04	21	93.4	59	262.4	1	0.3
0.02	0.09	22	97.9	60	266.9	2	0.6
0.03	0.13	23	102.3	61	271.3	3	0.8
0.04	0.18	24	106.8	62	275.8	4	1.1
0.05	0.22	25	111.2	63	280.2	5	1.4
0.06	0.27	26	115.6	64	284.6	6	1.7
0.07	0.31	27	120.1	65	289.1	7	2.0
0.08	0.36	28	124.6	66	293.6	8	2.2
0.09	0.40	29	129.0	67	298.0	9	2.5
0.1	0.4	30	133.4	68	302.5	10	2.8
0.2	0.9	31	137.9	69	306.9	11	3.1
0.3	1.3	32	142.3	70	311.4	12	3.3
0.4	1.8	33	146.8	71	315.8	13	3.6
0.5	2.2	34	151.2	72	320.3	14	3.9
0.6	2.7	35	155.7	73	324.7	15	4.2
0.7	3.1	36	160.1	74	329.2	16	4.4
0.8	3.6	37	164.6	75	333.6	17	4.7
0.9	4.0	38	169.0	76	338.1	18	5.0
1	4.4	39	173.5	77	342.5	19	5.3
2	8.9	40	177.9	78	347.0	20	5.6
3	13.4	41	182.4	79	351.4	21	5.8
4	17.8	42	186.8	80	355.9	22	6.1
5	22.2	43	191.3	81	360.3	23	6.4
6	26.7	44	195.7	82	364.8	24	6.7
7	31.1	45	200.2	83	369.2	25	7.0
8	35.6	46	204.6	84	373.6	26	7.2
9	40.0	47	209.1	85	378.1	27	7.5
10	44.5	48	213.5	86	382.6	28	7.8
11	48.9	49	218.0	87	387.0	29	8.1
12	53.4	50	224.4	88	391.4	30	8.3
13	57.8	51	226.9	89	395.9	31	8.6
14	62.3	52	231.3	90	400.3	32	8.9
15	66.7	53	235.8	91	404.8	33	9.2
16	71.2	54	240.2	92	409.2	34	9.4
17	75.6	55	244.6	93	413.7	35	9.7
18	80.1	56	249.1	94	418.1	36	10.0
19	84.5	57	253.6	95	422.6	37	10.3
20	89.0	58	258.0	96	427.0	38	10.6

ENGLISH TO METRIC CONVERSION: LIQUID CAPACITY

Liquid or fluid capacity is presently expressed as pints, quarts or gallons, or a combination of all of these. In the metric system the liter (l) will become the basic unit. Fractions of a liter would be expressed as deciliters, centiliters, or most frequently (and commonly) as milliliters.

To convert pints (pts.) to liters (l): multiply the number of pints by .47
To convert liters (l) to pints (pts.): multiply the number of liters by 2.1
To convert quarts (qts.) to liters (l): multiply the number of quarts by .95

To convert liters (l) to quarts (qts.): multiply the number of liters by 1.06
To convert gallons (gals.) to liters (l): multiply the number of gallons by 3.8
To convert liters (l) to gallons (gals.): multiply the number of liters by .26

gals	liters	qts	liters	pts	liters
0.1	0.38	0.1	0.10	0.1	0.05
0.2	0.76	0.2	0.19	0.2	0.10
0.3	1.1	0.3	0.28	0.3	0.14
0.4	1.5	0.4	0.38	0.4	0.19
0.5	1.9	0.5	0.47	0.5	0.24
0.6	2.3	0.6	0.57	0.6	0.28
0.7	2.6	0.7	0.66	0.7	0.33
0.8	3.0	0.8	0.76	0.8	0.38
0.9	3.4	0.9	0.85	0.9	0.43
1	3.8	1	1.0	1	0.5
2	7.6	2	1.9	2	1.0
3	11.4	3	2.8	3	1.4
4	15.1	4	3.8	4	1.9
5	18.9	5	4.7	5	2.4
6	22.7	6	5.7	6	2.8
7	26.5	7	6.6	7	3.3
8	30.3	8	7.6	8	3.8
9	34.1	9	8.5	9	4.3
10	37.8	10	9.5	10	4.7
11	41.6	11	10.4	11	5.2
12	45.4	12	11.4	12	5.7
13	49.2	13	12.3	13	6.2
14	53.0	14	13.2	14	6.6
15	56.8	15	14.2	15	7.1
16	60.6	16	15.1	16	7.6
17	64.3	17	16.1	17	8.0
18	68.1	18	17.0	18	8.5
19	71.9	19	18.0	19	9.0
20	75.7	20	18.9	20	9.5
21	79.5	21	19.9	21	9.9
22	83.2	22	20.8	22	10.4
23	87.0	23	21.8	23	10.9
24	90.8	24	22.7	24	11.4
25	94.6	25	23.6	25	11.8
26	98.4	26	24.6	26	12.3
27	102.2	27	25.5	27	12.8
28	106.0	28	26.5	28	13.2
29	110.0	29	27.4	29	13.7
30	113.5	30	28.4	30	14.2

ENGLISH TO METRIC CONVERSION: PRESSURE

The basic unit of pressure measurement used today is expressed as pounds per square inch (psi). The metric unit for psi will be the kilopascal (kPa). This will apply to either fluid pressure or air pressure, and will be frequently seen in tire pressure readings, oil pressure specifications, fuel pump pressure, etc.

To convert pounds per square inch (psi) to kilopascals (kPa): multiply the number of psi by 6.89

Psi	kPa	Psi	kPa	Psi	kPa	Psi	kPa
0.1	0.7	37	255.1	82	565.4	127	875.6
0.2	1.4	38	262.0	83	572.3	128	882.5
0.3	2.1	39	268.9	84	579.2	129	889.4
0.4	2.8	40	275.8	85	586.0	130	896.3
0.5	3.4	41	282.7	86	592.9	131	903.2
0.6	4.1	42	289.6	87	599.8	132	910.1
0.7	4.8	43	296.5	88	606.7	133	917.0
0.8	5.5	44	303.4	89	613.6	134	923.9
0.9	6.2	45	310.3	90	620.5	135	930.8
1	6.9	46	317.2	91	627.4	136	937.7
2	13.8	47	324.0	92	634.3	137	944.6
3	20.7	48	331.0	93	641.2	138	951.5
4	27.6	49	337.8	94	648.1	139	958.4
5	34.5	50	344.7	95	655.0	140	965.2
6	41.4	51	351.6	96	661.9	141	972.2
7	48.3	52	358.5	97	668.8	142	979.0
8	55.2	53	365.4	98	675.7	143	985.9
9	62.1	54	372.3	99	682.6	144	992.8
10	69.0	55	379.2	100	689.5	145	999.7
11	75.8	56	386.1	101	696.4	146	1006.6
12	82.7	57	393.0	102	703.3	147	1013.5
13	89.6	58	399.9	103	710.2	148	1020.4
14	96.5	59	406.8	104	717.0	149	1027.3
15	103.4	60	413.7	105	723.9	150	1034.2
16	110.3	61	420.6	106	730.8	151	1041.1
17	117.2	62	427.5	107	737.7	152	1048.0
18	124.1	63	434.4	108	744.6	153	1054.9
19	131.0	64	441.3	109	751.5	154	1061.8
20	137.9	65	448.2	110	758.4	155	1068.7
21	144.8	66	455.0	111	765.3	156	1075.6
22	151.7	67	461.9	112	772.2	157	1082.5
23	158.6	68	468.8	113	779.1	158	1089.4
24	165.5	69	475.7	114	786.0	159	1096.3
25	172.4	70	482.6	115	792.9	160	1103.2
26	179.3	71	489.5	116	799.8	161	1110.0
27	186.2	72	496.4	117	806.7	162	1116.9
28	193.0	73	503.3	118	813.6	163	1123.8
29	200.0	74	510.2	119	820.5	164	1130.7
30	206.8	75	517.1	120	827.4	165	1137.6
31	213.7	76	524.0	121	834.3	166	1144.5
32	220.6	77	530.9	122	841.2	167	1151.4
33	227.5	78	537.8	123	848.0	168	1158.3
34	234.4	79	544.7	124	854.9	169	1165.2
35	241.3	80	551.6	125	861.8	170	1172.1
36	248.2	81	558.5	126	868.7	171	1179.0

ENGLISH TO METRIC CONVERSION: PRESSURE

The basic unit of pressure measurement used today is expressed as pounds per square inch (psi). The metric unit for psi will be the kilopascal (kPa). This will apply to either fluid pressure or air pressure, and will be frequently seen in tire pressure readings, oil pressure specifications, fuel pump pressure, etc.

To convert pounds per square inch (psi) to kilopascals (kPa): multiply the number of psi by 6.89

Psi	kPa	Psi	kPa	Psi	kPa	Psi	kPa
172	1185.9	216	1489.3	260	1792.6	304	2096.0
173	1192.8	217	1496.2	261	1799.5	305	2102.9
174	1199.7	218	1503.1	262	1806.4	306	2109.8
175	1206.6	219	1510.0	263	1813.3	307	2116.7
176	1213.5	220	1516.8	264	1820.2	308	2123.6
177	1220.4	221	1523.7	265	1827.1	309	2130.5
178	1227.3	222	1530.6	266	1834.0	310	2137.4
179	1234.2	223	1537.5	267	1840.9	311	2144.3
180	1241.0	224	1544.4	268	1847.8	312	2151.2
181	1247.9	225	1551.3	269	1854.7	313	2158.1
182	1254.8	226	1558.2	270	1861.6	314	2164.9
183	1261.7	227	1565.1	271	1868.5	315	2171.8
184	1268.6	228	1572.0	272	1875.4	316	2178.7
185	1275.5	229	1578.9	273	1882.3	317	2185.6
186	1282.4	230	1585.8	274	1889.2	318	2192.5
187	1289.3	231	1592.7	275	1896.1	319	2199.4
188	1296.2	232	1599.6	276	1903.0	320	2206.3
189	1303.1	233	1606.5	277	1909.8	321	2213.2
190	1310.0	234	1613.4	278	1916.7	322	2220.1
191	1316.9	235	1620.3	279	1923.6	323	2227.0
192	1323.8	236	1627.2	280	1930.5	324	2233.9
193	1330.7	237	1634.1	281	1937.4	325	2240.8
194	1337.6	238	1641.0	282	1944.3	326	2247.7
195	1344.5	239	1647.8	283	1951.2	327	2254.6
196	1351.4	240	1654.7	284	1958.1	328	2261.5
197	1358.3	241	1661.6	285	1965.0	329	2268.4
198	1365.2	242	1668.5	286	1971.9	330	2275.3
199	1372.0	243	1675.4	287	1978.8	331	2282.2
200	1378.9	244	1682.3	288	1985.7	332	2289.1
201	1385.8	245	1689.2	289	1992.6	333	2295.9
202	1392.7	246	1696.1	290	1999.5	334	2302.8
203	1399.6	247	1703.0	291	2006.4	335	2309.7
204	1406.5	248	1709.9	292	2013.3	336	2316.6
205	1413.4	249	1716.8	293	2020.2	337	2323.5
206	1420.3	250	1723.7	294	2027.1	338	2330.4
207	1427.2	251	1730.6	295	2034.0	339	2337.3
208	1434.1	252	1737.5	296	2040.8	240	2344.2
209	1441.0	253	1744.4	297	2047.7	341	2351.1
210	1447.9	254	1751.3	298	2054.6	342	2358.0
211	1454.8	255	1758.2	299	2061.5	343	2364.9
212	1461.7	256	1765.1	300	2068.4	344	2371.8
213	1468.7	257	1772.0	301	2075.3	345	2378.7
214	1475.5	258	1778.8	302	2082.2	346	2385.6
215	1482.4	259	1785.7	303	2089.1	347	2392.5

TUNE-UP PROCEDURES 2-2
  DIESEL ENGINE PRECAUTIONS 2-2
  SPARK PLUGS 2-2
    SPARK PLUG HEAT RANGE 2-2
    REMOVAL & INSTALLATION 2-3
    INSPECTION & GAPPING 2-4
    CHECKING & REPLACING SPARK
    PLUG WIRES 2-7
FIRING ORDERS 2-8
POINT TYPE IGNITION 2-9
  BREAKER POINTS AND
    CONDENSER 2-9
  REMOVAL & INSTALLATION 2-9
  DWELL ADJUSTMENT 2-12
HIGH ENERGY IGNITION (HEI)
SYSTEM 2-12
  DESCRIPTION AND OPERATION 2-12
  HEI SYSTEM PRECAUTIONS 2-13
  TROUBLESHOOTING THE HEI
    SYSTEM 2-14
    ENGINE FAILS TO START 2-14
    ENGINE RUNS, BUT RUNS ROUGH
    OR CUTS OUT 2-14
  DISTRIBUTOR COMPONENTS
    TESTING 2-14
  HEI SYSTEM MAINTENANCE 2-15
    COMPONENT REPLACEMENT 2-15
  TACHOMETER HOOKUP 2-19
    GASOLINE ENGINES (HEI
    SYSTEM) 2-19
IGNITION TIMING 2-20
  GASOLINE ENGINES 2-20
    INSPECTION & ADJUSTMENT 2-20
DIESEL INJECTION TIMING 2-21
  DIESEL ENGINES 2-21
VALVE LASH 2-21
IDLE SPEED AND MIXTURE
ADJUSTMENTS 2-22
  GENERAL INFORMATION 2-22
  CARBURETED ENGINES 2-22
    IDLE SPEED & MIXTURE 2-22
    FAST IDLE 2-31
  DIESEL FUEL INJECTION 2-31
    IDLE SPEED ADJUSTMENT 2-31
SPECIFICATION CHARTS
  GASOLINE ENGINE TUNE-UP
    SPECIFICATIONS 2-33
  GRAND PRIX DIESEL TUNE-UP
    SPECIFICATIONS 2-36

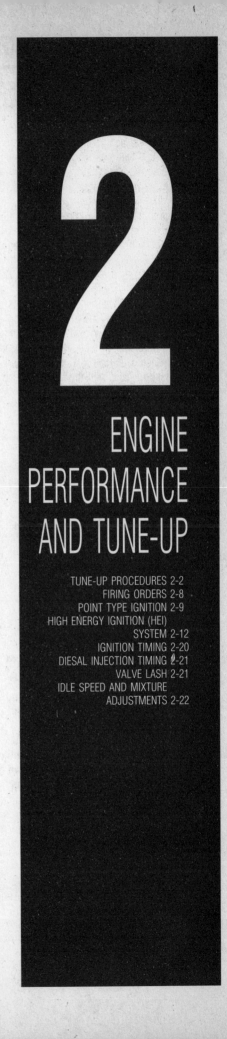

2

ENGINE
PERFORMANCE
AND TUNE-UP

TUNE-UP PROCEDURES 2-2
FIRING ORDERS 2-8
POINT TYPE IGNITION 2-9
HIGH ENERGY IGNITION (HEI)
SYSTEM 2-12
IGNITION TIMING 2-20
DIESAL INJECTION TIMING 2-21
VALVE LASH 2-21
IDLE SPEED AND MIXTURE
ADJUSTMENTS 2-22

TUNE-UP PROCEDURES

The tune-up is a routine maintenance procedure which is essential for the efficient and economical operation of your car's engine. Regular tune-ups will also help prolong the life of the engine.

The interval between tune-ups is a variable factor which depends upon the way you drive your car, the conditions under which you drive it (city versus highway, weather, etc.), and the type of engine installed. A complete tune-up should be performed on your Pontiac *at least every 15,000 miles or one year, whichever comes first.* 1981 and later cars have an increased tune-up interval of 25,000 miles; 1974 cars should have their distributor contact points replaced every 12,000 miles, along with a complete tune up.

This interval should be halved if the car is operated under severe conditions such as trailer towing, prolonged idling (a common occurrence in the city), start and stop driving, or if starting and running problems are noticed. It is assumed here that the routine maintenance described in Chapter 1 has been followed, as this goes hand-in-hand with the recommended tune-up procedures. The end result of a tune-up can only be the sum of all the various steps, so every step applicable to the tune-up should be followed.

If the specifications on the underhood sticker in the engine compartment of your car disagree with the "Tune-Up Specifications" chart in this chapter, the figures on the sticker must be used. The sticker often reflects changes made during the production run, or displays specifications that apply only to your particular engine.

The replaceable parts involved in a tune-up include the spark plugs, ignition points on 1974 models, air filter, distributor cap, rotor, and the spark plug wires. In addition to these parts and the adjustments involved in properly installing them, there are several adjustments of other parts involved in completing the job. These include carburetor idle speed and air/fuel mixture, ignition timing, and valve clearance adjustments.

This chapter gives specific procedures on how to tune-up your Pontiac, and is intended to be as complete and basic as possible.

✳✳ CAUTION

When working with a running engine, make sure that there is proper ventilation. Also make sure that the transmission is in Neutral (unless otherwise specified) and the parking brake is fully applied. Always keep hands, clothing and tools well clear of the hot exhaust manifolds and radiator and especially the belts and fan. Remove any wrist or long neck jewelry or ties before beginning any job, and tuck long hair under a cap. When the engine is running, do not grasp ignition wires, distributor cap or coil wires as a shock in excess of 50,000 volts may result. Whenever working around the distributor, make sure the ignition is "off."

Diesel Engine Precautions

1. Never run the engine with the air cleaner removed: if anything is sucked into the inlet manifold it will go straight to the combustion chambers, or jam behind a valve.

2. *Never wash a diesel engine:* the reaction of a warm fuel injection pump to cold (or even warm) water can ruin the pump.

3. Never operate a diesel engine with one or more fuel injectors removed unless fully familiar with injector testing procedures: some diesel injection pumps spray fuel at up to 1400 psi— enough pressure to allow the fuel to penetrate your skin.

4. Do not skip engine oil and filter changes.

5. Strictly follow the manufacturer's oil and fuel recommendations as given in the owner's manual.

6. Most manufacturers caution against using starting fluids in the automotive diesel engine, as it can cause severe internal engine damage.

7. Do not run a diesel engine with the "Water in Fuel" warning light on in the dashboard. See Chapter 5 for water purging procedure.

8. If removing water from the fuel tank yourself, use the same caution you would use when working around gasoline engine fuel components.

9. Do not allow diesel fuel to come in contact with rubber hoses or components on the engine, as it can damage them.

Spark Plugs

A typical spark plug consists of a metal shell surrounding a ceramic insulator. A metal electrode extends downward through the center of the insulator and protrudes a small distance. Located at the end of the plug and attached to the side of the outer metal shell is the side electrode. The side electrode bends in at a 90° angle so that its tip is just past and parallel to the tip of the center electrode. The distance between these two electrodes (measured in thousandths of an inch or hundredths of a millimeter) is called the spark plug gap.

The spark plug does not produce a spark but instead provides a gap across which the current can arc. The coil produces anywhere from 20,000 to 50,000 volts (depending on the type and application) which travels through the wires to the spark plugs. The current passes along the center electrode and jumps the gap to the side electrode, and in doing so, ignites the air/fuel mixture in the combustion chamber.

SPARK PLUG HEAT RANGE

Spark plug heat range is the ability of the plug to dissipate heat. The longer the insulator (or the farther it extends into the engine), the hotter the plug will operate; the shorter the insulator (the closer the electrode is to the block's cooling passages) the cooler it will operate. A plug that absorbs little heat and remains too cool will quickly accumulate deposits of oil and carbon since it is not hot enough to burn them off. This leads to plug fouling and consequently to misfiring. A plug that absorbs too much heat will have no deposits but, due to the excessive heat, the electrodes will burn away quickly and might possibly lead to preignition or other ignition problems. Preignition takes place when plug tips get so hot that they glow sufficiently to ignite the air/fuel mixture before the actual spark occurs. This early ignition will usually cause a pinging during low speeds and heavy loads.

The general rule of thumb for choosing the correct heat range when picking a spark plug is: if most of your driving is long distance, high speed travel, use a colder plug; if most of your driv-

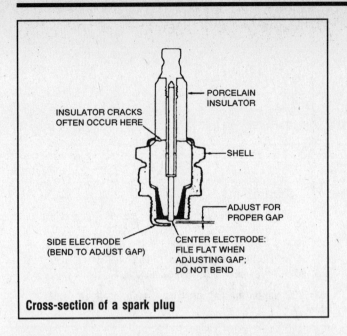

PORCELAIN INSULATOR

INSULATOR CRACKS OFTEN OCCUR HERE

SHELL

ADJUST FOR PROPER GAP

SIDE ELECTRODE (BEND TO ADJUST GAP)

CENTER ELECTRODE: FILE FLAT WHEN ADJUSTING GAP; DO NOT BEND

Cross-section of a spark plug

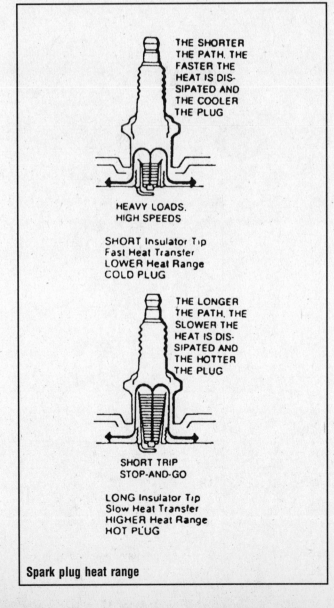

THE SHORTER THE PATH, THE FASTER THE HEAT IS DISSIPATED AND THE COOLER THE PLUG

HEAVY LOADS. HIGH SPEEDS

SHORT Insulator Tip
Fast Heat Transfer
LOWER Heat Range
COLD PLUG

THE LONGER THE PATH, THE SLOWER THE HEAT IS DISSIPATED AND THE HOTTER THE PLUG

SHORT TRIP STOP-AND-GO

LONG Insulator Tip
Slow Heat Transfer
HIGHER Heat Range
HOT PLUG

Spark plug heat range

ing is stop and go, use a hotter plug. Original equipment plugs are generally a good compromise between the 2 styles and most people never have the need to change their plugs from the factory-recommended heat range.

REMOVAL & INSTALLATION

A set of spark plugs usually requires replacement after about 20,000–30,000 miles (32,000–48,000 km), depending on your style of driving. In normal operation plug gap increases about 0.001 in. (0.025mm) for every 2500 miles (4000 km). As the gap increases, the plug's voltage requirement also increases. It requires a greater voltage to jump the wider gap and about two to three times as much voltage to fire the plug at high speeds than at idle. The improved air/fuel ratio control of modern fuel injection combined with the higher voltage output of modern ignition systems will often allow an engine to run significantly longer on a set of standard spark plugs, but keep in mind that efficiency will drop as the gap widdens (along with fuel economy and power).

After detaching the spark plug wire, use the proper sized ratchet and socket extension to loosen . . .

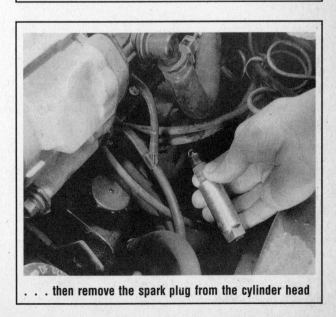

. . . then remove the spark plug from the cylinder head

When you're removing spark plugs, work on one at a time. Don't start by removing the plug wires all at once, because, unless you number them, they may become mixed up. Take a minute before you begin and number the wires with tape.

1. Disconnect the negative battery cable, and if the vehicle has been run recently, allow the engine to thoroughly cool.

2. Carefully twist the spark plug wire boot to loosen it, then pull upward and remove the boot from the plug. Be sure to pull on the boot and not on the wire, otherwise the connector located inside the boot may become separated.

3. Using compressed air, blow any water or debris from the spark plug well to assure that no harmful contaminants are allowed to enter the combustion chamber when the spark plug is removed. If compressed air is not available, use a rag or a brush to clean the area.

➡**Remove the spark plugs when the engine is cold, if possible, to prevent damage to the threads. If removal of the plugs is difficult, apply a few drops of penetrating oil or silicone spray to the area around the base of the plug, and allow it a few minutes to work.**

4. Using a spark plug socket that is equipped with a rubber insert to properly hold the plug, turn the spark plug counterclockwise to loosen and remove the spark plug from the bore.

✳✳ WARNING

Be sure not to use a flexible extension on the socket. Use of a flexible extension may allow a shear force to be applied to the plug. A shear force could break the plug off in the cylinder head, leading to costly and frustrating repairs.

To install:

5. Inspect the spark plug boot for tears or damage. If a damaged boot is found, the spark plug wire must be replaced.

6. Using a wire feeler gauge, check and adjust the spark plug gap. When using a gauge, the proper size should pass between the electrodes with a slight drag. The next larger size should not be able to pass while the next smaller size should pass freely.

7. Carefully thread the plug into the bore by hand. If resistance is felt before the plug is almost completely threaded, back the plug out and begin threading again. In small, hard to reach areas, an old spark plug wire and boot could be used as a threading tool. The boot will hold the plug while you twist the end of the wire and the wire is supple enough to twist before it would allow the plug to crossthread.

✳✳ WARNING

Do not use the spark plug socket to thread the plugs. Always carefully thread the plug by hand or using an old plug wire to prevent the possibility of crossthreading and damaging the cylinder head bore.

8. Carefully tighten the spark plug. If the plug you are installing is equipped with a crush washer, seat the plug, then tighten about ¼ turn to crush the washer. If you are installing a tapered seat plug, tighten the plug to specifications provided by the vehicle or plug manufacturer.

9. Apply a small amount of silicone dielectric compound to the end of the spark plug lead or inside the spark plug boot to prevent sticking, then install the boot to the spark plug and push until it clicks into place. The click may be felt or heard, then gently pull back on the boot to assure proper contact.

INSPECTION & GAPPING

Check the plugs for deposits and wear. If they are not going to be replaced, clean the plugs thoroughly. Remember that any kind of deposit will decrease the efficiency of the plug. Plugs can be cleaned on a spark plug cleaning machine, which can sometimes be found in service stations, or you can do an acceptable job of cleaning with a stiff brush. If the plugs are cleaned, the electrodes must be filed flat. Use an ignition points file, not an emery board or the like, which will leave deposits. The electrodes must be filed perfectly flat with sharp edges; rounded edges reduce the spark plug voltage by as much as 50%.

Check spark plug gap before installation. The ground electrode (the L-shaped one connected to the body of the plug) must be parallel to the center electrode and the specified size wire gauge (please refer to the Tune-Up Specifications chart for details) must pass between the electrodes with a slight drag.

➡**NEVER adjust the gap on a used platinum type spark plug.**

A normally worn spark plug should have light tan or gray deposits on the firing tip

A carbon fouled plug, identified by soft, sooty, black deposits, may indicate an improperly tuned vehicle. Check the air cleaner, ignition components and engine control system

A physically damaged spark plug may be evidence of severe detonation in that cylinder. Watch that cylinder carefully between services, as a continued detonation will not only damage the plug, but could also damage the engine

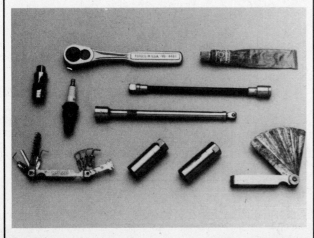

A variety of tools and gauges are needed for spark plug service

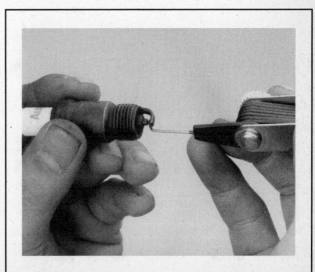

Checking the spark plug gap with a feeler gauge

An oil fouled spark plug indicates an engine with worn piston rings and/or bad valve seals allowing excessive oil to enter the chamber

This spark plug has been left in the engine too long, as evidenced by the extreme gap—Plugs with such an extreme gap can cause misfiring and stumbling accompanied by a noticeable lack of power

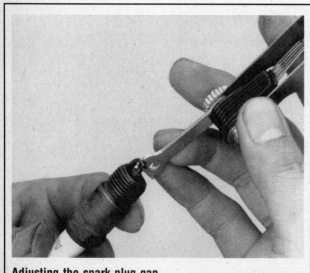

Adjusting the spark plug gap

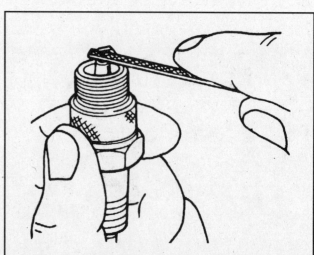

If the standard plug is in good condition, the electrode may be filed flat—CAUTION: do not file platinum plugs

Always check the gap on new plugs as they are not always set correctly at the factory. Do not use a flat feeler gauge when measuring the gap on a used plug, because the reading may be inaccurate. A round-wire type gapping tool is the best way to check the gap. The correct gauge should pass through the electrode gap with a slight drag. If you're in doubt, try one size smaller and one larger. The smaller gauge should go through easily, while the larger one shouldn't go through at all. Wire gapping tools usually have a bending tool attached. Use that to adjust the side electrode until the proper distance is obtained. Absolutely never attempt to bend the center electrode. Also, be careful not to bend the side electrode too far or too often as it may weaken and break off within the engine, requiring removal of the cylinder head to retrieve it.

CHECKING & REPLACING SPARK PLUG WIRES

Every 10,000 miles, inspect the spark plug wires for burns, cuts, or breaks in the insulation. Check the boots and the nipples on the distributor cap. Replace any damaged wiring.

A bridged or almost bridged spark plug, identified by a build-up between the electrodes caused by excessive carbon or oil build-up on the plug

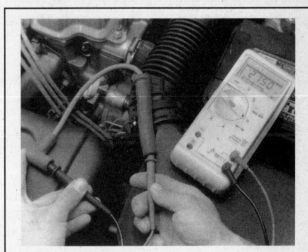

Checking individual plug wire resistance with a digital ohmmeter

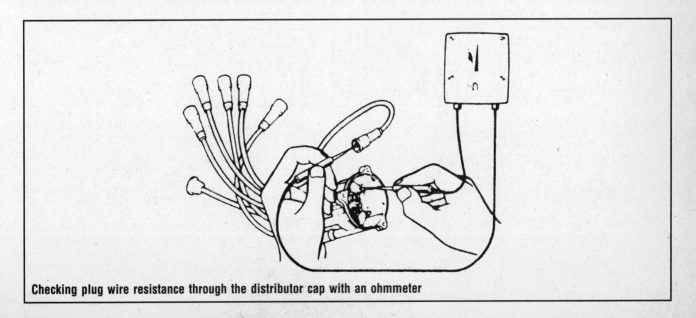

Checking plug wire resistance through the distributor cap with an ohmmeter

Every 30,000 miles or so, the resistance of the wires should be checked with an ohmmeter. Wires with excessive resistance will cause misfiring, and may make the engine difficult to start in damp weather. Generally, the useful life of the cables is 45,000–60,000 miles.

To check resistance, remove the distributor cap, leaving the wires in place. Connect one lead of an ohmmeter to an electrode within the cap; connect the other lead to the corresponding spark plug terminal (remove it from the spark plug for this test). Replace any wire which shows a resistance over 30,000 ohms (see chart). Generally speaking, however, resistance should not be over 25,000 ohms, and 30,000 ohms must be considered the outer limit of acceptability.

It should be remembered that resistance is also a function of length; the longer the wire, the greater the resistance. Thus, if the wires on your car are longer than the factory originals, the resistance will be higher, possibly outside these limits.

When installing new wires, replace them one at a time to avoid mixups. Start by replacing the longest one first. Install the boot firmly over the spark plug. Route the wire over the same path as the original. Insert the nipple firmly onto the tower on the distributor cap, then install the cap cover and latches to secure the wires.

FIRING ORDERS

◆ **See Figure 1 thru 6**

➡**To avoid confusion, remove and tag the wires one at a time.**

If a distributor is not keyed for installation with only one orientation, it could have been removed previously and rewired. The resultant wiring would hold the correct firing order, but could change the relative placement of the plug towers in relation to the engine. For this reason it is imperative that you label all wires before disconnecting any of them. Also, before removal, compare the current wiring with the accompanying illustrations. If the current wiring does not match, make notes in your book to reflect how your engine is wired.

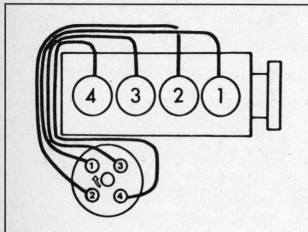

Fig. 1 Pontiac built 151 cu. in. 4-cylinder engine
Firing order: 1–3–4–2
Distributor rotation: Clockwise

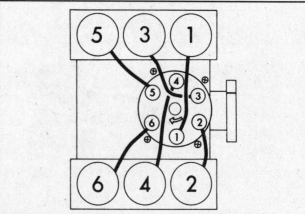

Fig. 3 Buick built 231 cu. in. (3.8L) and 252 cu. in. (4.2L) engines
Firing order: 1–6–5–4–3–2
Distributor rotation: Clockwise

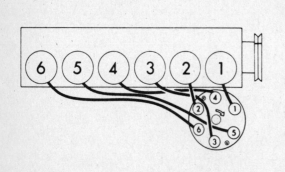

Fig. 2 Chevrolet built 250 cu. in. inline 6-cylinder engine
Firing order: 1–5–3–6–2–4
Distributor rotation: Clockwise

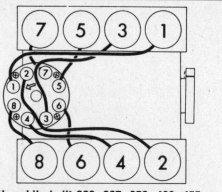

Fig. 4 Oldsmobile built 260, 307, 350, 400, 455 cu. in. and Pontiac built 265, 301, 350, 400, 455 cu. in. V8 engines
Firing order: 1–8–4–3–6–5–7–2
Distributor rotation: Counterclockwise

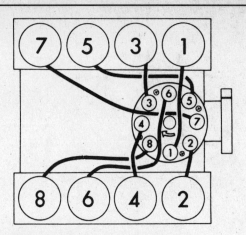

Fig. 5 Buick built 350 cu. in. V8 engine
Firing order: 1–8–4–3–6–5–7–2
Distributor rotation: Clockwise

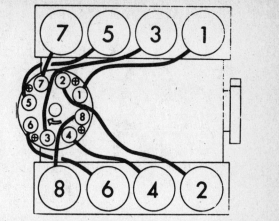

Fig. 6 Chevrolet built 305 and 350 cu. in. V8 engines
Firing order: 1–8–4–3–6–5–7–2
Distributor rotation: Clockwise

POINT TYPE IGNITION

Breaker Points and Condenser

REMOVAL & INSTALLATION

1974 Vehicles
◗ **See Figures 7 thru 15**

The condenser should be replaced each time you replace the points. Every time you adjust or replace the breaker points, the ignition timing must be checked and, if necessary, adjusted. No special equipment other than a feeler gauge is required for point replacement or adjustment, but a dwell meter is strongly advised. A magnetic screwdriver is handy to prevent the small points and condenser screws from falling down into the distributor.

Point sets using the push-in type wiring terminal should be used on those distributors equipped with an Radio Frequency Interference (RFI) shield. Points using a lockscrew-type terminal may short out due to contact between the shield and the screw.

1. Push down on the spring-loaded V8 distributor cap retaining screws and give them a half-turn to release. Unscrew the six-cylinder cap retaining screws. Remove the cap. You might have to unclip or detach some or all of the plug wires to remove the cap. If so, number the wires and the cap before removal.

2. Clean the cap inside and out with a clean rag. Check for cracks and carbon paths. A carbon path shows up as a dark line, usually from one of the cap sockets or inside terminals to a ground. Check the condition of the carbon button inside the center of the cap and the inside terminals. Replace the cap as necessary. Carbon paths cannot usually be successfully scraped off. It is better to replace the cap.

3. Pull the six-cylinder rotor up and off the shaft. Remove the two screws and lift the round V8 rotor off. There is less danger of losing the screws if you just back them out all the way and lift them off with the rotor. Clean off the metal outer tip if it is burned or corroded. *Don't file it.* Replace the rotor as necessary or if one came with your tune-up kit.

4. Remove the radio frequency interference shield if your distributor has one. *Watch out for those little screws!* The factory says that the points don't need to be replaced if they are only slightly rough or pitted. However, experience shows that it is more economical and reliable in the long run to replace the point set while the distributor is open, than to have to do this at a later (and possibly more inconvenient) time.

5. Pull off the two wire terminals from the point assembly. One wire comes from the condenser and the other comes from within the distributor. The terminals are usually held in place by spring tension only. There might be a clamp screw securing the terminals on some older versions. There is also available a one-piece point/condenser assembly for V8s. The radio frequency interference shield isn't needed with this set. Loosen the point set hold-down screw(s). Be very careful not to drop any of these little

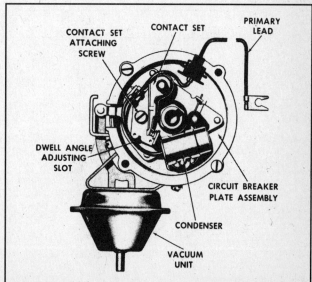

Fig. 7 Top view of a points-type distributor with the cap and rotor removed

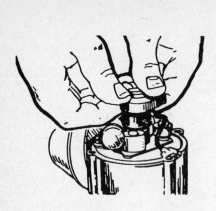

Fig. 8 On the six-cylinder engine, pull the rotor straight up to remove it from the distributor

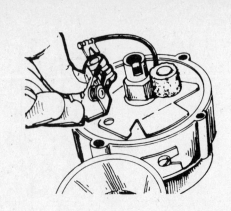

Fig. 11 Install the point set on the breaker plate, then attach the wires

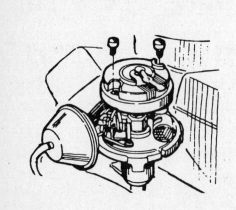

Fig. 9 The rotor on the eight-cylinder engine is retained by two screws

Fig. 12 The condenser is held in place by a screw and a clamp

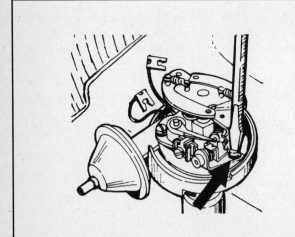

Fig. 10 The points are retained by screws. Use a magnetic screwdriver to avoid dropping them

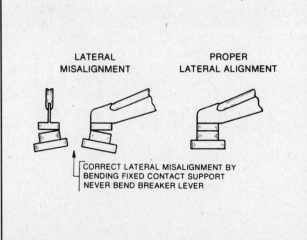

Fig. 13 After installation, check the points for proper alignment

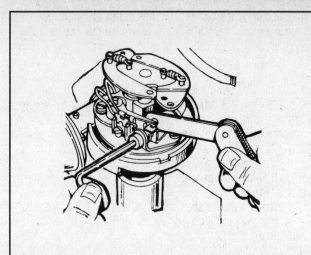

Fig. 14 You will need an Allen wrench to adjust the V8 point gap

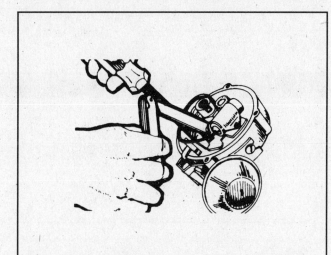

Fig. 15 Use a prytool to carefully lever the points closer together or farther apart on six-cylinder models

screws inside the distributor. If this happens, the distributor will probably have to be removed to get at the screw. If the hold-down screw is lost elsewhere, it must be replaced with one that is no longer than the original to avoid interference with the distributor workings. Remove the point set, even if it is to be reused.

6. If the points are to be reused, clean them with a few strokes of a special point file. This is done with the points *removed* to prevent tiny metal filings getting into the distributor. Don't use sandpaper or emery cloth; they will cause rapid point burning.

7. Loosen the condenser hold-down screw and slide the condenser out of the clamp. This will save you a struggle with the clamp, condenser, and the tiny screw when you install the new one. If you have the type of clamp that is permanently fastened to the condenser, remove the screw and the condenser. Don't lose the screw.

8. Attend to the distributor cam lubricator. If you have the round kind, turn it around on its shaft at the first tune-up and replace it at the second. If you have the long kind, switch ends at the first tune-up, and replace it at the second.

➡**Don't oil or grease the lubricator. The foam is impregnated with a special lubricant.**

If you didn't get any lubricator at all, or if it looks like someone took it off, don't worry. You don't really need it. Just rub a matchhead size dab of grease on the cam lobes.

9. Install the new condenser. If you left the clamp in place, just slide the new condenser into the clamp.

10. Replace the point set and tighten the screws on a V8 engine. Leave the screw slightly loose on the six-cylinder engine. Replace the two wire terminals, making sure that the wires don't interfere with anything. Some V8 distributors have a ground wire that must go under one of the screws.

11. Check that the contacts meet squarely. If they don't, bend the tab supporting the fixed contact.

➡**If you are installing preset points on a V8, go ahead to Step 16. If they are preset, it will say so on the package. It would be a good idea to make a quick check on point gap, anyway. Sometimes those preset points aren't.**

12. Turn the engine until a high point on the cam that opens the points contacts the rubbing block on the point arm. You can turn the engine by hand if you can get a wrench on the crankshaft pulley nut, or you can grasp the fan belt and turn the engine with the spark plugs removed.

✳✳ CAUTION

If you try turning the engine by hand, be very careful not to get your fingers pinched in the pulleys.

Another alternative is to bump the starter switch or use a remote starter switch.

13. On the six cylinder, there is a screwdriver slot near the contacts. Insert a screwdriver and lever the points open or closed until they appear to be at about the gap specified in the "Tune-Up Specifications." On a V8, simply insert a ⅛ in. Allen wrench into the adjustment screw and turn. The wrench sometimes comes with a tune-up kit.

14. Insert the correct size feeler gauge and adjust the gap until you can push the gauge in and out between the contacts with a slight drag, but without disturbing the point arm. This operation takes a bit of experience to obtain the correct feel. Check by trying the gauges 0.001–0.002 larger and smaller than the setting size. The larger one should disturb the point arm, while the smaller one should not drag at all. Tighten the six-cylinder point set hold-down screw. Recheck the gap, because it often changes when the screw is tightened.

15. After all the point adjustments are complete, pull a white index card through (between) the contacts to remove any traces of oil. Oil will cause rapid contact burning.

➡**You can adjust six-cylinder dwell at this point, if you wish. Refer to Step 18.**

16. Replace the radio frequency interference shield, if any. You don't need it if you are installing the one-piece point/condenser set. Push the rotor firmly down into place. It will only go on one way. Tighten the V8 rotor screws. If the rotor is not installed properly, it will probably break when the starter is operated.

17. Replace the distributor cap.

18. If a dwell meter is available, check the dwell.

1975–83 Vehicles

These engines use the electronic, breakerless High Energy Ignition (HEI) system. Since there is no mechanical contact, there is no wear or need for periodic service. There is an item in the distributor that resembles a condenser; it is a radio interference suppression capacitor which requires no service.

DWELL ADJUSTMENT

➡**This hookup may not apply to electronic, capacitive discharge, or other special ignition systems. Some dwell meters won't work at all with such systems.**

Dwell can be checked with the engine running or cranking. Decrease dwell by increasing the point gap; increase by decreasing the gap. Dwell angle is simply the number of degrees of distributor shaft rotation during which the points stay closed. Theoretically, if the point gap is correct, the dwell should also be correct or nearly so. Adjustment with a dwell meter produces more exact, consistent results since it is a dynamic adjustment. If dwell varies more than 3 degrees from idle speed to 1,750 engine rpm, the distributor is worn.

1. To adjust dwell on the six cylinder, trial and error point adjustments are required. On a V8, simply open the metal window on the distributor and insert a ⅛ in. Allen wrench. Turn until the meter shows the correct reading. Be sure to snap the window closed.

2. An approximate dwell adjustment can be made without a meter on a V8. Turn the adjusting screw clockwise until the engine begins to misfire, then back it out ½ turn.

3. If the engine won't start, check:

   a. That all the spark plug wires are in place.

   b. That the rotor has been installed.

   c. That the two (or three) wires inside the distributor are connected.

   d. That the points open and close when the engine turns.

   e. That the gap is correct and the hold-down screw (on a six) is tight.

4. After the first 200 miles or so on a new set of points, the point gap often closes up due to initial rubbing block wear. For best performance, recheck the dwell (or gap) at this time. This quick initial wear is the reason the factory recommends 0.003 in. more gap on new points.

5. Since changing the gap affects the ignition timing, the timing should be checked and adjusted as necessary after each point replacement or adjustment.

HIGH ENERGY IGNITION (HEI) SYSTEM

Description and Operation

♦ **See Figures 16 and 17**

The General Motors HEI system is a pulse-triggered, transistor-controlled, inductive discharge ignition system. Except on inline six-cylinder models through 1977, the entire HEI system is contained within the distributor cap. Inline six-cylinder engines through 1977 have an external coil. Otherwise, the systems are the same.

The distributor, in addition to housing the mechanical and vacuum advance mechanisms (1975 through 1980), contains the igni-

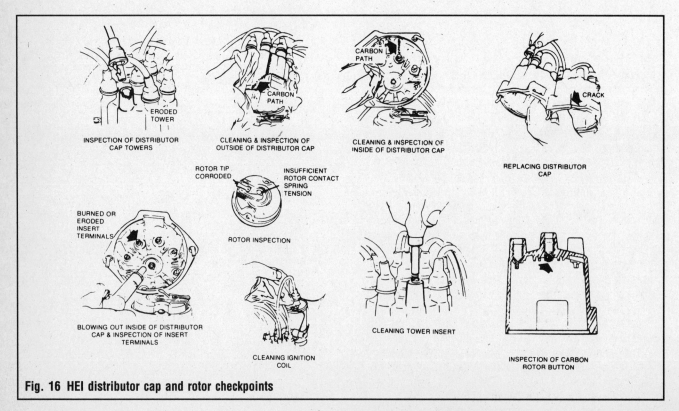

Fig. 16 HEI distributor cap and rotor checkpoints

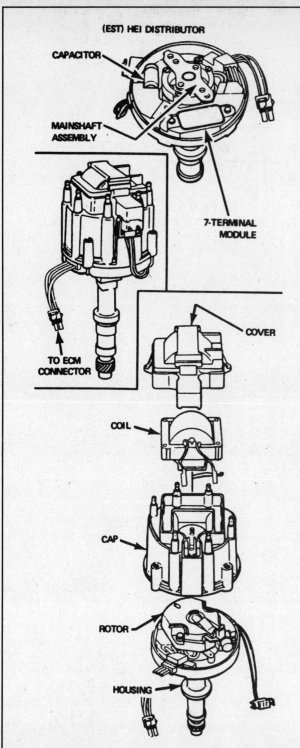

(EST) HEI DISTRIBUTOR

CAPACITOR

MAINSHAFT ASSEMBLY

7-TERMINAL MODULE

TO ECM CONNECTOR

COVER

COIL

CAP

ROTOR

HOUSING

Fig. 17 Exploded view of an HEI distributor. Note that some distributors have a vacuum advance unit mounted on the side

tion coil (except on some inline six engines), the electronic control module, and the magnetic triggering device. The magnetic pick-up assembly contains a permanent magnet, a pole piece with internal "teeth," and a pick-up coil (not to be confused with the ignition coil).

The 1981 and later HEI distributors are equipped with Electronic Spark Control (EST). This system uses a one-piece distributor, with the ignition coil mounted in the distributor cap similar to the 1980 system. For more information on EST, refer to Chapter 4.

All spark timing changes in the 1981 distributors are done electronically by the Electronic Control Module (ECM), which monitors information from various engine sensors, computes the desired spark timing and then signals the distributor to change the timing accordingly. No vacuum or mechanical advance units are used.

In the HEI system, as in other electronic ignition systems, the breaker points have been replaced with an electronic switch—a transistor—which is located *within* the control module. This switching transistor performs the same function the points did in a conventional ignition system; it simply turns coil primary current on and off at the correct time. Essentially then, electronic and conventional ignition systems operate on the same principle.

The module which houses the switching transistor is controlled (turned on and off) by a magnetically generated impulse induced in the pick-up coil. When the teeth of the rotating timer align with the teeth of the pole piece, the induced voltage in the pick-up coil signals the electronic module to open the coil primary circuit. The primary current then decreases, and a high voltage is induced in the ignition coil secondary windings which is then directed through the rotor and high voltage leads (spark plug wires) to fire the spark plugs.

In essence then, the pick-up coil module system simply replaces the conventional breaker points and condenser. The condenser found within the distributor is for radio suppression purposes only and has nothing to do with the ignition process. The module automatically controls the dwell period, increasing it as engine speed increases. Some dwell is automatically controlled, it cannot be adjusted. The module itself is non-adjustable and non-repairable and must be replaced if found defective.

➡ **When experiencing a "no start" situation with the HEI system check the rotor carefully. The HEI system has a tendency to burn a hole through the rotor which will cause a no start situation or cause the engine to stop running when going down the highway.**

It is a good idea to carry a spare rotor and electronic module in your car.

HEI SYSTEM PRECAUTIONS

Before going on to troubleshooting, it might be a good idea to take note of the following precautions:

Timing Light Use

Inductive pick-up timing lights are the best kind to use if your car is equipped with HEI. Timing lights which connect between the spark plug and the spark plug wire occasionally (not always) give false readings.

Spark Plug Wires

The plug wires used with HEI systems are of a different construction than conventional wires. When replacing them, make sure you get the correct wires, since conventional wires won't carry the voltage. Also, handle them carefully to avoid cracking or splitting them and *never* pierce them.

Tachometer Use

Not all tachometers will operate or indicate correctly when used on a HEI system. While some tachometers may give a reading, this does not necessarily mean the reading is correct. In addition, some tachometers hook up differently from others. If you can't figure out whether or not your tachometer will work on your car's engine, check with the tachometer manufacturer. Dwell readings, of course, have no significance at all.

When using a tachometer with the HEI system the following procedure will help save you time.

1. Secure a piece of 14 gauge wire about 8 inches long.
2. Skin both ends back about ½ inch.
3. Place a female spade connector on one end. Make sure this connection is secure by soldering it together.
4. Place a small washer, about ⁷⁄₁₆, on the other end and solder it to the wire.
5. When you hook up your tachometer slide the female connector over the male connector. You can now hook up your tachometer to this connection.

HEI System Testers

Instruments designed specifically for testing HEI systems are available from several tool manufacturers. Some of these will even test the module itself. However, the tests given in the following section will require only an ohmmeter and a voltmeter.

Troubleshooting the HEI System

The symptoms of a defective component within the HEI system are exactly the same as those you would encounter in a conventional system. Some of these symptoms are:

- Hard or no Starting
- Rough Idle
- Poor Fuel Economy
- Engine misses under load or while accelerating

If you suspect a problem in your ignition system, there are certain preliminary checks which you should carry out before you begin to check the electronic portions of the system. First, it is extremely important to make sure the vehicle battery is in a good state of charge. A defective or poorly charged battery will cause the various components of the ignition system to read incorrectly when they are being tested. Second, make sure all wiring connections are clean and tight, not only at the battery, but also at the distributor cap, ignition coil, and at the Electronic Control Module.

Since the only change between electronic and conventional ignition systems is in the distributor component area, it is imperative to check the secondary ignition circuit first. If the secondary circuit checks out properly, then the engine condition is probably not the fault of the ignition system. To check the secondary ignition system, perform a simple spark test. Remove one of the plug wires and insert some sort of extension in the plug socket. An old spark plug with the ground electrode removed makes a good extension. Hold the wire and extension about ¼ in. away from the block and crank the engine. If a normal spark occurs, then the problem is most likely *not* in the ignition system. Check for fuel system problems, or fouled spark plugs.

If, however, there is no spark or a weak spark, then further igni-

tion system testing will have to be done. Troubleshooting techniques fall into two categories, depending on the nature of the problem. The categories are (1) Engine cranks, but won't start or (2) Engine runs, but runs rough or cuts out. To begin with, let's consider the first case.

ENGINE FAILS TO START

If the engine won't start, perform a spark test as described earlier. This will narrow the problem area down considerably. If no spark occurs, check for the presence of normal battery voltage at the battery (BAT) terminal in the distributor cap. The ignition switch must be in the **ON** position for this test. Either a voltmeter or a test light may be used for this test. Connect the test light wire to ground and the probe end to the BAT terminal at the distributor. If the light comes on, you have voltage to the distributor. If the light fails to come on, this indicates an open circuit in the ignition primary wiring leading to the distributor. In this case, you will have to check wiring continuity back to the ignition switch using a test light. If there is battery voltage at the BAT terminal, but no spark at the plugs, then the problem lies within the distributor assembly. Go on to the distributor components test section.

ENGINE RUNS, BUT RUNS ROUGH OR CUTS OUT

1. Make sure the plug wires are in good shape first. There should be no obvious cracks or breaks. You can check the plug wires with an ohmmeter, but *do not* pierce the wires with a probe. Check the chart for the correct plug wire resistance.
2. If the plug wires are OK, remove the cap assembly and check for moisture, cracks, chips, or carbon tracks, or any other high voltage leaks or failures. Replace the cap if any defects are found. Make sure the timer wheel rotates when the engine is cranked. If everything is all right so far, go on to the distributor components test section following.

Distributor Components Testing

▶ **See Figure 18**

If the trouble has been narrowed down to the units within the distributor, the following tests can help pinpoint the defective component. An ohmmeter with both high and low ranges should be used. These tests are made with the cap assembly removed and the battery wire disconnected. If a tachometer is connected to the TACH terminal, disconnect it before making these tests.

1. Connect an ohmmeter between the TACH and BAT terminals in the distributor cap. The primary coil resistance should be less than one ohm.
2. To check the coil secondary resistance, connect an ohmmeter between the rotor button and the BAT terminal. Note the reading. Connect the ohmmeter between the rotor button and the TACH terminal. Note the reading. The resistance in both cases should be between 6,000 and 30,000 ohms. Be sure to test between the rotor button and both the BAT and TACH terminals.
3. Replace the coil *only* if the readings in Step 1 and Step 2 are infinite.

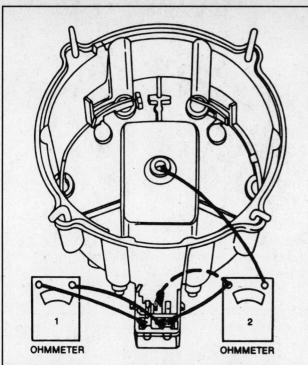

Fig. 18 Ohmmeter 1 shows the primary coil resistance connection. Ohmmeter 2 shows the secondary resistance connection

➡These resistance checks will not disclose shorted coil windings. This condition can only be detected with scope analysis or a suitably designed coil tester. If these instruments are unavailable, replace the coil with a known good coil as a final coil test.

4. To test the pick-up coil, first disconnect the white and green module leads. Set the ohmmeter on the high scale and connect it between a ground and either the white or green lead. Any resistance measurement *less* than infinity requires replacement of the pick-up coil.

5. Pick-up coil continuity is tested by connecting the ohmmeter (on low range) between the white and green leads. Normal resistance is between 650 and 850 ohms, or 500 and 1500 ohms on 1977 and later models. Move the vacuum advance arm while performing this test. This will detect any break in coil continuity. Such a condition can cause intermittent misfiring. Replace the pick-up coil if the reading is outside the specified limits.

6. If no defects have been found at this time, and you still have a problem, then the module will have to be checked. If you do not have access to a module tester, the only possible alternative is a substitution test. If the module fails the substitution test, replace it.

HEI System Maintenance

Except for periodic checks of the spark plug wires, and an occasional check of the distributor cap for cracks (see Steps 1 and 2 under "Engine Runs, But Runs Rough or Cuts Out" for details),

no maintenance is required on the HEI System. No periodic lubrication is necessary; engine oil lubricates the lower bushing, and an oil-filled reservoir lubricates the upper bushing.

COMPONENT REPLACEMENT

Integral Ignition Coil

1. Remove the ignition wire set retainer.
2. Disconnect the feed and module wire terminal connectors from the distributor cap.
3. Remove the 4 coil cover-to-distributor cap screws and the coil cover.
4. Remove the 4 coil-to-distributor cap screws.
5. Using a blunt drift, press the coil wire spade terminals up out of the distributor cap.
6. Lift the coil up out of the distributor cap.

To remove the integral ignition coil, first remove the spark plug wire set retainer

Although not necessary, you can matchmark the ignition coil wire to the terminal . . .

. . . then disconnect the wire from the ignition coil

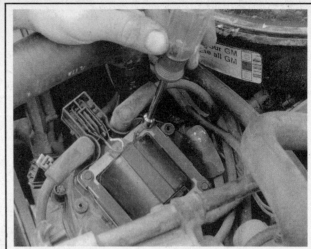

Unfasten the ignition coil-to-distributor retaining screws . . .

Loosen the ignition coil cover bolts . . .

. . . then remove the armrest from the door panel

. . . then remove the cap from the coil

Remove and clean the rubber seal washer . . .

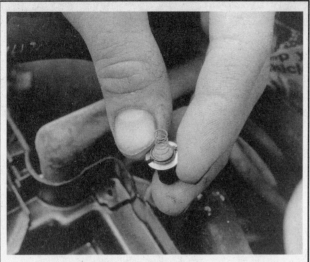

. . . and the ignition coil spring

To remove the distributor cap, first tag all of the wires to avoid confusion during installation

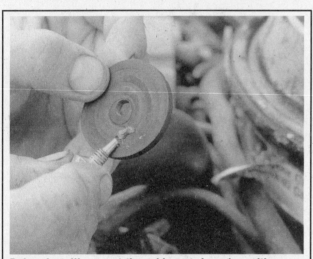

Before installing, coat the rubber seal washer with a suitable silicone dielectric compound

After unlatching the retainers, remove the distributor cap

7. Remove and clean the coil spring, rubber seal washer and coil cavity of the distributor cap.

8. Coat the rubber seal with a dielectric lubricant furnished in the replacement ignition coil package.

9. Installation is the reverse of the removal procedure.

Distributor Cap

1. Remove the feed and module wire terminal connectors from the distributor cap.

2. Remove the retainer and spark plug wires from the cap.

3. Depress and release the 4 distributor cap-to-housing retainers and lift off the cap assembly.

4. Remove the 4 coil cover screws and cover.

5. Using a finger or a blunt drift, push the spade terminals up out of the distributor cap.

6. Remove all 4 coil screws and lift the coil, coil spring and rubber seal washer out of the cap coil cavity.

7. Using a new distributor cap, reverse the removal procedure, being sure to clean and lubricate the rubber seal washer with dielectric lubricant.

Rotor

1. Disconnect the feed and module wire connectors from the distributor.

2. Depress and release the 4 distributor cap-to-housing retainers and lift off the cap assembly.

3. Remove the two rotor attaching screws and rotor.

4. Installation is the reverse of the removal procedure.

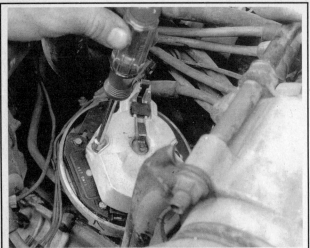

For rotor removal, first remove the distributor cap, then loosen the 2 retaining screws (see arrows) . . .

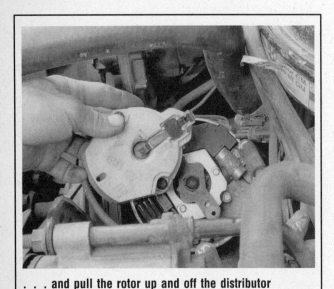

. . . and pull the rotor up and off the distributor

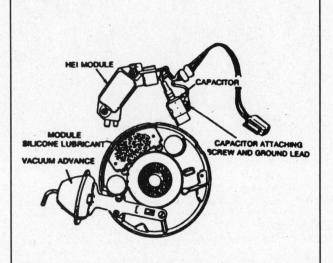

Fig. 19 When replacing the ignition module, be sure to coat the mating surfaces with silicone lubricant

Vacuum Advance (1975–80)

1. Remove the distributor cap and rotor as previously described.
2. Disconnect the vacuum hose from the vacuum advance unit.
3. Remove the two vacuum advance retaining screws, pull the advance unit outward, rotate and disengage the operating rod from its tang.
4. Installation is the reverse of the removal procedure.

Ignition Module
♦ See Figure 19

1. Remove the distributor cap and rotor as previously described.
2. Disconnect the harness connector and pick-up coil spade connectors from the module. Be careful not to damage the wires when removing the connector.

Some distributor components, such as the module (arrow), are accessible once the rotor is removed

To remove the ignition module, detach the electrical connectors

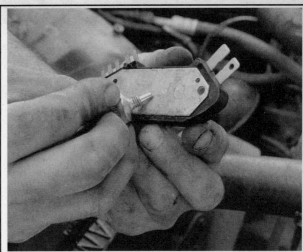

Before installation, coat the bottom of the new module with dielectric silicone lubricant

3. Remove the two screws and module from the distributor housing.

4. Coat the bottom of the new module with dielectric silicone lubricant supplied with the new module. Installation is the reverse of the removal procedure.

➡ **The silicone lubricant supplied with new modules must be applied, as it serves as a heat insulator and aids in module cooling. The module will "cook" itself without the lubricant.**

Tachometer Hookup

GASOLINE ENGINES (HEI SYSTEM)

➡ **See the information on tachometer use, located earlier in this chapter.**

There is a terminal marked TACH on the distributor cap. Connect one tachometer lead to this terminal and the other lead to a ground. On some tachometers, the leads must be connected to the TACH terminal and to the battery positive terminal.

✸✸ WARNING

Never ground the TACH terminal; serious module and ignition coil damage will result. If there is any doubt as to the correct tachometer hookup, check with the tachometer manufacturer.

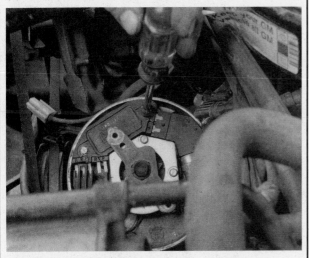

Remove the ignition module retaining screws . . .

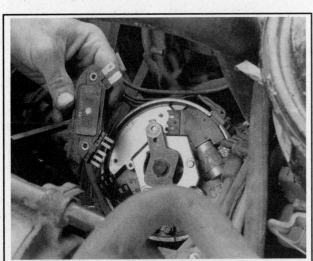

. . . then remove the ignition module from the distributor

IGNITION TIMING

Gasoline Engines

Ignition timing is the measurement, in degrees of crankshaft rotation, of the point at which the spark plugs fire in each of the cylinders. It is measured in degrees before or after Top Dead Center (TDC) of the compression stroke.

Because it takes a fraction of a second for the spark plug to ignite the mixture in the cylinder, the spark plug must fire a little before the piston reaches TDC. Otherwise, the mixture will not be completely ignited as the piston passes TDC and the full power of the explosion will not be used by the engine.

The timing measurement is given in degrees of crankshaft rotation before the piston reaches TDC (BTDC). If the setting for the ignition timing is 5° BTDC, the spark plug must fire 5° before each piston reaches TDC. This only holds true, however, when the engine is at idle speed.

As the engine speed increases, the pistons go faster. The spark plugs have to ignite the fuel even sooner if it is to be completely ignited when the piston reaches TDC. To do this, the distributor has two means to advance the timing of the spark as the engine speed increases. This is accomplished by centrifugal weights within the distributor, and a vacuum diaphragm mounted on the side of the distributor.

If the ignition is set too far advanced (BTDC), the ignition and expansion of the fuel in the cylinder will occur too soon and tend to force the piston down while it is still traveling up. This is one of the causes of engine ping. If the ignition spark is set too far retarded, after TDC (ATDC), the piston will have already passed TDC and started on its way down when the fuel is ignited. This will cause the piston to be forced down for only a portion of its travel. This will result in poor engine performance and lack of power.

Timing marks consist of a notch on the rim of the crankshaft pulley and a scale of degrees attached to the front of the engine. The notch corresponds to the position of the piston in the number 1 cylinder. A stroboscopic (dynamic) timing light is used, which is hooked into the circuit of the No. 1 cylinder spark plug. Every time the spark plug fires, the timing light flashes. By aiming the timing light at the timing marks, the exact position of the piston within the cylinder can be read, since the stroboscopic flash makes the mark on the pulley appear to be standing still. Proper timing is indicated when the notch is aligned with the correct number on the scale.

There are three basic types of timing lights available. The first is a simple neon bulb with two wire connections (one for the spark plug and one for the plug wire, connecting the light in series). This type of light is quite dim, and must be held closely to the marks to be seen, but it is quite inexpensive. The second type of light operates from the car's battery. Two alligator clips connect to the battery terminals, while a third wire connects to the spark plug with an adapter. This type of light is more expensive, but the xenon bulb provides a nice bright flash which can even be seen in sunlight. The third type replaces the battery source with 110 volt house current. Some timing lights have other functions built into them, such as dwell meters, tachometers, or remote starting switches. These are convenient, in that they reduce the tangle of wires under the hood, but may duplicate the functions of the tools you already have.

If your car has electronic ignition, you should use a timing light with an inductive pickup. This pickup simply clamps onto the No. 1 spark plug wire, eliminating the adapter. It is not susceptible to crossfiring or false triggering, which may occur with a conventional light, due to the greater voltages produced by electronic ignition.

INSPECTION & ADJUSTMENT

♦ **See Figure 20**

1. Warm the engine to normal operating temperature. Shut off the engine and connect the timing light to the No. 1 spark plug (left front).

➡**DO NOT, under any circumstances, pierce a spark plug wire to hook up the light. Once the insulation is broken, voltage will jump to the nearest ground, and the spark plug will not fire properly.**

2. Clean off the timing marks and mark the pulley or damper notch and the timing scale with white chalk or paint. The timing notch on the damper or pulley can be elusive. Bump the engine around with the starter or turn the crankshaft with a wrench on the front pulley bolt to get it to an accessible position.

3. Disconnect and plug the vacuum advance hose at the distributor, to prevent any distributor advance. The vacuum line is the rubber hose connected to the metal cone-shaped canister on the side of the distributor. A short screw, pencil, or a golf tee can be used to plug the hose.

➡**1981 and later models with Electronic Spark Timing (EST) have no vacuum advance, therefore you may skip the previous step, but you must disconnect the four terminal EST connector before going on.**

4. Start the engine and adjust the idle speed to that specified in the "Tune-Up Specifications" chart. Some cars require that the timing be set with the transmission in Neutral. You can disconnect the idle solenoid, if any, to get the speed down. Otherwise, adjust the idle speed screw. This is to prevent any centrifugal advance of timing in the distributor.

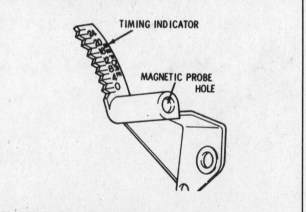

Fig. 20 Typical V8 timing indicator—Oldsmobile built engine shown, others similar. The timing mark is on the harmonic balancer

On 1975–77 HEI systems, the tachometer connects to the TACH terminal on the distributor and to a ground. For 1978 and later models, all tachometer connections are to the TACH terminal. Some tachometers must connect to the TACH terminal and to the positive battery terminal. Some tachometers won't work at all with HEI. Consult the tachometer manufacturer if the instructions supplied with the unit do not give the proper connection.

✳✳ WARNING

Never ground the HEI TACH terminal; serious system damage will result, including module burnout.

5. Aim the timing light at the timing marks. Be careful not to touch the fan, which may appear to be standing still. Keep your clothes and hair, and the light's wires clear of the fan, belts, and pulleys. If the pulley or damper notch isn't aligned with the proper timing mark (see the "Tune-Up Specifications" chart), the timing will have to be adjusted.

➡**TDC or Top Dead Center corresponds to 0 degrees; B, or BTDC, or Before Top Dead Center, may be shown as BE-**FORE; A, or ATDC, or After Top Dead Center, may be shown as AFTER.

6. Loosen the distributor base clamp locknut. You can buy special wrenches which make this task a lot easier on V8s. Turn the distributor slowly to adjust the timing, holding it by the body and not the cap. Turn the distributor in the direction of rotor rotation (found in the "Firing Order" illustration, earlier in this chapter) to retard, and against the direction to advance.

➡**The 231 and 252 V6 engines have two timing marks on the crankshaft pulley. One timing mark is ⅛ in. wide and the other, four inches away, is ¹⁄₁₆ in. wide. The smaller mark is used for setting the timing with a hand-held timing light. The larger mark is used with the magnetic probe and is only of use to a professional mechanic. Make sure you set the timing using the smaller mark.**

7. Tighten the locknut. Check the timing, in case the distributor moved as you tightened it.
8. Replace the distributor vacuum hose, if removed. Correct the idle speed to specifications.
9. Shut off the engine and disconnect the light.

DIESEL INJECTION TIMING

◆ **See Figure 21**

For the engine to be properly timed, the marks on the top of the injection pump adaptor and the flange of the injection pump must be aligned. The engine must be turned off when the timing is set.

DIESEL ENGINES

A magnetic pick-up tachometer is necessary for diesel work because of the lack of an ignition system. The tachometer probe is inserted into the hole in the timing indicator.

➡**A special GM service tool, J-26987, must be used for this adjustment. These are available through most GM car dealers.**

1. Loosen the three pump retaining nuts using special tool J-26987.
2. Align the mark on the injection pump with marks on the adapter and tighten the nuts to 35 ft. lbs.

➡**Use a ¾ in. open end wrench on the nut at the front of the injection pump to aid in rotating the pump to align the marks.**

3. Adjust the throttle linkage if necessary.

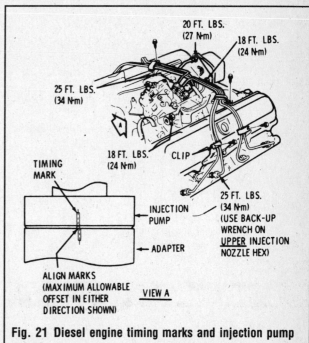

Fig. 21 Diesel engine timing marks and injection pump lines

VALVE LASH

All engines covered in this guide are equipped with hydraulic valve lifters. Engines so equipped operate with zero clearance in the valve train; because of this the rocker arms are non-adjustable. The hydraulic lifters themselves do not require any adjustment as part of the normal tune-up, although they occasionally become noisy (especially on high-mileage engines) and need to be replaced. In the event of cylinder head removal or any operation that requires disturbing or removing the rocker arms, the rocker arms have to be adjusted. Please refer to Chapter 3. Hydraulic lifter service is also covered in Chapter 3.

IDLE SPEED AND MIXTURE ADJUSTMENTS

General Information

This section contains only carburetor adjustments as they normally apply to engine tuneups. Descriptions of the carburetors and complete adjustment procedures can be found in Chapter 5.

When the engine in your Pontiac is running, air/fuel mixture from the carburetor is being drawn into the engine by a partial vacuum which is created by the downward movement of the pistons on the intake stroke of the four-stroke cycle of the engine. The amount of air/fuel mixture that enters the engine is controlled by throttle plates in the bottom of the carburetor. When the engine is not running, the throttle plates are closed, completely blocking off the bottom of the carburetor from the inside of the engine. The throttle plates are connected, through the throttle linkage, to the gas pedal. What you are actually doing when you depress the gas pedal is opening up the throttle plates in the carburetor to admit more of the fuel/air mixture to the engine. The further you open the throttle plates in the carburetor, the higher the engine speed becomes.

As previously stated, when the engine is not running, the throttle plates in the carburetor remain closed. When the engine is idling, it is necessary to open the throttle plates slightly. To prevent having to keep your foot on the gas pedal when the engine is idling, an idle speed adjusting screw was added to the carburetor. This screw has the same effect as keeping your foot slightly depressed on the gas pedal. The idle speed adjusting screw contacts a lever, or, on most late model cars, a solenoid on the outside of the carburetor. When the screw is turned in, it opens the throttle plate or plates on the carburetor, raising the idle speed of the engine. This screw is called the curb idle adjusting screw and the procedures in this section will tell you how to adjust it.

Since it is difficult for the engine to draw the air/fuel mixture from the carburetor with the small amount of throttle plate opening that is present when the engine is idling, an idle mixture passage is provided in the carburetor. This passage delivers air/fuel mixture to the engine from a hole which is located in the bottom of the carburetor below the throttle plates. This idle mixture passage contains an adjusting screw which restricts the amount of air/fuel mixture that enters the engine at idle. The idle mixture screws are capped on late model cars due to emission control regulations.

Carbureted Engines

Idle mixture and idle speed adjustments are critical aspects of engine tune and exhaust emission control. It is important that all tune-up instructions be carefully followed to ensure good engine performance and minimum exhaust pollution. Through the succeeding model years covered in this guide, the different combinations of emissions systems on different engine models have resulted in a wide variety of tune-up specifications. See the "Tune-Up Specifications" chart at the beginning of this chapter. All models covered here have an emissions information sticker placed within easy sight in the engine compartment, giving timing, carburetor adjustment and other important tune-up information. If there is any difference between the specifications listed in this guide and those on your car's emissions sticker, *always follow the specs on the sticker.*

The following carburetor adjustment procedures are listed by year, carburetor type, and engine displacement and code where necessary (consult the "Engine Identification Code" chart in this guide), as many of the carburetors covered are used simultaneously by all four GM divisions. Other carburetor adjustments and maintenance are found in Chapter 5.

➡️**Idle mixture screws have been preset and capped at the factory. The caps should be removed only in the case of major carburetor overhaul, or if all other possible causes of poor idle have been thoroughly checked. If you must adjust the idle mixture, have the carbon monoxide (CO) concentration checked at a professional shop equipped with a CO meter. Mixture adjustments are included only where it is possible for the owner/mechanic to perform them.**

IDLE SPEED & MIXTURE

🔹 **See Figures 22 thru 36 (p. 23–29)**

1974 Models

All model carburetors in 1974 are equipped with idle limiter caps and idle solenoids. Disconnect the fuel tank line from the evaporative canister. The engine must be at running temperature, choke off, parking brake on, and rear wheels blocked. Disconnect the distributor vacuum hose and plug it. After adjustment, reconnect the vacuum and evaporative hoses.

6-250 (1-BBL. ROCHESTER MV)

1. Using the hex nut on the end of the solenoid body, turn the entire solenoid to get 850 rpm for manual transmission models, and 600 rpm for automatic transmissions in Drive.

V8-350 AND 400 (2-BBL.—ROCHESTER 2GC)

1. Turn the air conditioning off, if equipped. Adjust the idle stop solenoid screw for 900 rpm on manual transmission cars, and 600 rpm on automatics (in Drive).
2. De-energize the solenoid and adjust the carburetor idle cam screw (on the low step of the cam) for 400 rpm on automatic models (in Drive), 500 rpm on 350 engines with manual transmissions.

V8-350 AND 400 (4-BBL.—ROCHESTER 4 MC)

1. Turn the air conditioning off, if equipped. Adjust the idle stop solenoid screw for 900 rpm on manual transmission cars, and 600 rpm on automatics (in Drive).
2. Connect the distributor vacuum hose. Position the fast idle cam follower on the top step of the fast idle cam and adjust the fast idle speed to 1300 rpm on manual transmission cars, and 1600 rpm on automatics (in Park).

1975–76 Models

6-250 (1-BBL.—ROCHESTER MV)

1. Idle speed is adjusted with the engine at normal operating temperature, air cleaner on, choke open, and air conditioning off (air conditioning on—1976 automatic transmission models). Hook up a tachometer to the engine.
2. Block the rear wheels and apply the parking brake.

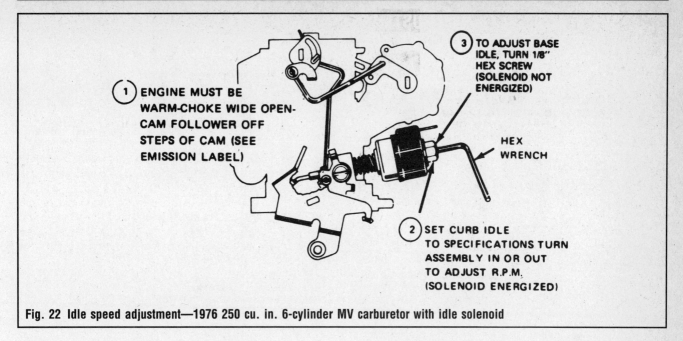

Fig. 22 Idle speed adjustment—1976 250 cu. in. 6-cylinder MV carburetor with idle solenoid

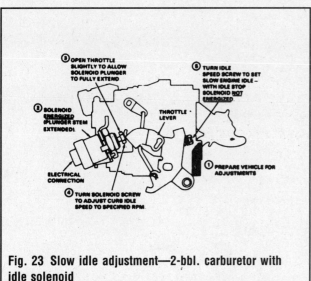

Fig. 23 Slow idle adjustment—2-bbl. carburetor with idle solenoid

3. Disconnect the fuel tank hose from the evaporative canister.

4. Disconnect and plug the distributor vacuum advance hose.

5. Start the engine and check the ignition timing. Adjust if necessary. Reconnect the vacuum hose. To adjust the idle speed, turn the solenoid in or out to obtain the higher of the two specifications listed on the decal. With the automatic transmission in Drive or the manual transmission in Neutral, disconnect the solenoid electrical connector and turn the 1/8 in. allen screw in the end of the solenoid body to the lower idle speed.

6. Place the shift lever in Drive on cars with automatic transmissions and have an assistant apply the brakes. On cars with manual transmissions, put it into Neutral.

7. Cut the tab off the mixture limiter cap, but don't remove the cap. Turn the screw counterclockwise until the highest idle speed is reached.

8. Set the idle speed to the higher of the two listed idle speeds by turning the solenoid in or out.

9. Check the tachometer and turn the mixture screw clockwise until the idle speed is at the lower of the two listed idle speeds.

10. Shut off the engine, remove the tachometer, and reconnect the carbon canister hose.

V8-260 (2-BBL.—ROCHESTER 2MC)

1. Apply the parking brake and block the rear wheels.

2. After making sure the timing is correct, connect a tachometer to the engine and run the engine until it reaches normal operating temperature.

3. Remove the air cleaner and disconnect its vacuum hose from the intake manifold. Plug the manifold fitting. Disconnect and plug the evaporative emission hose at the air cleaner.

4. Make sure the choke is open and the air-conditioner is turned off.

5. Disconnect and plug the vapor canister and EGR vacuum hoses.

6. Leave the distributor vacuum line connected: there is no line on California cars.

7. Adjust the curb idle screw to obtain the specified rpm. On cars equipped with manual transmissions, depress the dashpot and turn it to obtain 0.040 in. clearance between its stem and the throttle lever.

8. On air conditioned cars with automatic transmissions, adjust the idle speed-up solenoid as follows:

9. Turn the air conditioner on.

10. Disconnect the compressor wiring at the compressor.

11. Use the curb idle adjusting screw to adjust the idle speed to 650 rpm.

12. Reconnect the compressor wiring.

13. To adjust the idle mixture, proceed as follows:

➡️ **Idle mixture is preset at the factory and normally does not require adjustment. Adjust the idle mixture only in the case of major overhaul, throttle body removal, or when all other possible causes of poor idle condition have been thoroughly checked. If you find it necessary to adjust the idle mixture, have the CO concentration checked by a dealer or a garage with a CO meter.**

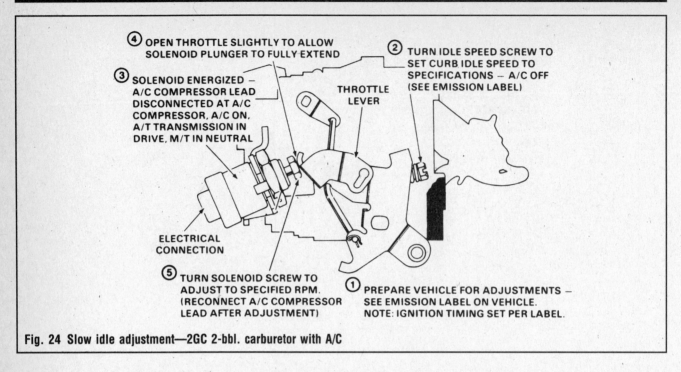

④ OPEN THROTTLE SLIGHTLY TO ALLOW SOLENOID PLUNGER TO FULLY EXTEND

③ SOLENOID ENERGIZED — A/C COMPRESSOR LEAD DISCONNECTED AT A/C COMPRESSOR, A/C ON, A/T TRANSMISSION IN DRIVE, M/T IN NEUTRAL

② TURN IDLE SPEED SCREW TO SET CURB IDLE SPEED TO SPECIFICATIONS — A/C OFF (SEE EMISSION LABEL)

THROTTLE LEVER

ELECTRICAL CONNECTION

⑤ TURN SOLENOID SCREW TO ADJUST TO SPECIFIED RPM. (RECONNECT A/C COMPRESSOR LEAD AFTER ADJUSTMENT)

① PREPARE VEHICLE FOR ADJUSTMENTS — SEE EMISSION LABEL ON VEHICLE. NOTE: IGNITION TIMING SET PER LABEL.

Fig. 24 Slow idle adjustment—2GC 2-bbl. carburetor with A/C

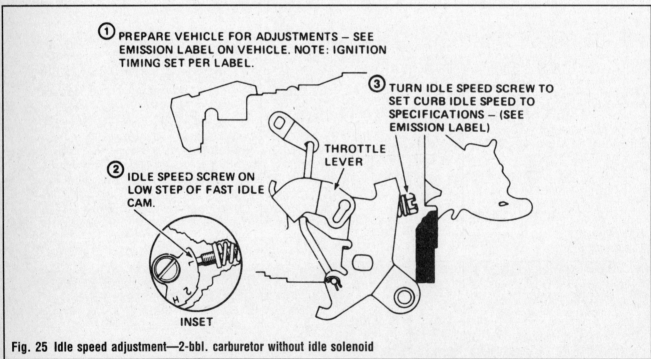

① PREPARE VEHICLE FOR ADJUSTMENTS — SEE EMISSION LABEL ON VEHICLE. NOTE: IGNITION TIMING SET PER LABEL.

③ TURN IDLE SPEED SCREW TO SET CURB IDLE SPEED TO SPECIFICATIONS — (SEE EMISSION LABEL)

THROTTLE LEVER

② IDLE SPEED SCREW ON LOW STEP OF FAST IDLE CAM.

INSET

Fig. 25 Idle speed adjustment—2-bbl. carburetor without idle solenoid

14. The engine should be at operating temperature, the timing should be set, choke open, EGR valve hose and air cleaner vacuum hose disconnected and plugged. Leave the distributor vacuum hose connected.

15. Remove the idle mixture screw caps, and lightly seat the idle mixture screws.

16. On automatic transmission cars, back the screws out five turns. On manual transmission cars, back the screws out six turns.

17. With the idle speed screw, set the idle to the following initial specifications:

• Manual transmission—1075 rpm
• Automatic transmission (in Drive)—610 rpm
• California Automatic (in Drive)—700 rpm

18. Turn each mixture screw ½ turn at a time until the specified curb idle speed is reached.

19. Install the air cleaner and reconnect all hoses.

ROCHESTER 2GC 2-BBL.

1. With the engine at normal operating temperature, remove the air cleaner and disconnect the air cleaner vacuum hose at the intake manifold. Plug the fitting with a clean rag.

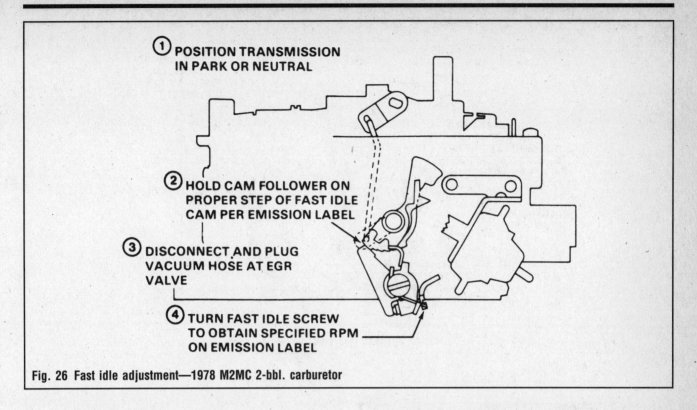

① POSITION TRANSMISSION IN PARK OR NEUTRAL

② HOLD CAM FOLLOWER ON PROPER STEP OF FAST IDLE CAM PER EMISSION LABEL

③ DISCONNECT AND PLUG VACUUM HOSE AT EGR VALVE

④ TURN FAST IDLE SCREW TO OBTAIN SPECIFIED RPM ON EMISSION LABEL

Fig. 26 Fast idle adjustment—1978 M2MC 2-bbl. carburetor

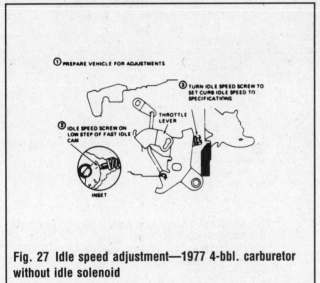

Fig. 27 Idle speed adjustment—1977 4-bbl. carburetor without idle solenoid

2. Make sure the choke plate is open and the air conditioning is off.

3. Set the parking brake and block the drive wheels.

4. Disconnect the evaporative emission hose from the air cleaner.

5. Disconnect the hose from the EGR valve. Plug the hose to the carburetor with a golf tee or pencil.

6. Disconnect the distributor vacuum hose, and plug the hose to the carburetor as above.

7. Connect a tachometer to the engine.

8. With the timing properly adjusted, adjust the carburetor idle solenoid screw (with solenoid energized) so that the engine is turning 650 rpm (or the figure specified on the underhood sticker) or with the transmission in Drive. The solenoid is "energized" when the plunger is fully extended; disconnect the idle and solenoid lead and open the throttle slightly for this to occur.

> ✳✳ **CAUTION**
>
> **Any time the car is tuned with the transmission in gear, you must always have a helper in the car with his or her foot on the brake. The parking brake must be fully applied.**

9. Disconnect the carburetor solenoid. With the transmission again in Drive, adjust the solenoid screw so that the engine turns 550 rpm (or the figure specified on the underhood sticker).

10. Reconnect the distributor vacuum hose, evaporative emission and EGR hoses. Disconnect the tachometer.

ROCHESTER M4MC AND 4MC 4-BBL.

1. Run the engine to normal operating temperature. Remove the air cleaner and disconnect the air cleaner vacuum hose at the intake manifold. Plug the fitting with a clean rag.

2. Make sure the choke plate is open and the air conditioning turned off.

3. Set the parking brake and block the rear wheels. Connect a tachometer to the engine.

4. Disconnect and plug the carburetor hoses from the vapor canister and the EGR valve. Plug the hoses with golf tees or pencils.

5. With the timing adjusted properly, set the slow idle screw to obtain 550 rpm (non-California 350 and 455 cu. in. V8s) or 600 rpm (Calif.) in Drive. Adjust 400 V8s to 650 rpm in Drive. If the sticker specs vary from these, adjust to sticker specifications.

> ✳✳ **CAUTION**
>
> **When adjusting idle speeds with the vehicle in Drive, always have a helper in the car with his or her foot on the brake and the parking brake fully applied.**

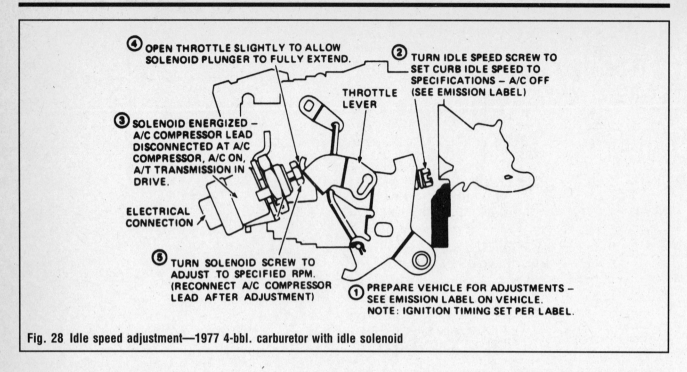

④ OPEN THROTTLE SLIGHTLY TO ALLOW SOLENOID PLUNGER TO FULLY EXTEND.

② TURN IDLE SPEED SCREW TO SET CURB IDLE SPEED TO SPECIFICATIONS – A/C OFF (SEE EMISSION LABEL)

THROTTLE LEVER

③ SOLENOID ENERGIZED – A/C COMPRESSOR LEAD DISCONNECTED AT A/C COMPRESSOR, A/C ON, A/T TRANSMISSION IN DRIVE.

ELECTRICAL CONNECTION

⑤ TURN SOLENOID SCREW TO ADJUST TO SPECIFIED RPM. (RECONNECT A/C COMPRESSOR LEAD AFTER ADJUSTMENT)

① PREPARE VEHICLE FOR ADJUSTMENTS – SEE EMISSION LABEL ON VEHICLE. NOTE: IGNITION TIMING SET PER LABEL.

Fig. 28 Idle speed adjustment—1977 4-bbl. carburetor with idle solenoid

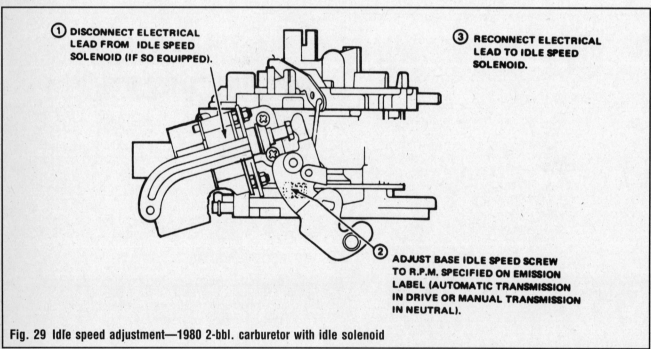

① DISCONNECT ELECTRICAL LEAD FROM IDLE SPEED SOLENOID (IF SO EQUIPPED).

③ RECONNECT ELECTRICAL LEAD TO IDLE SPEED SOLENOID.

② ADJUST BASE IDLE SPEED SCREW TO R.P.M. SPECIFIED ON EMISSION LABEL (AUTOMATIC TRANSMISSION IN DRIVE OR MANUAL TRANSMISSION IN NEUTRAL).

Fig. 29 Idle speed adjustment—1980 2-bbl. carburetor with idle solenoid

6. Adjust the idle speed-up solenoid on 350 and 455 V8s with air conditioning *on* to 650 rpm. The A/C compressor wires must be disconnected at the A/C compressor, and the transmission must be in Drive.

7. Reconnect the compressor wires and reconnect all hoses.

1977 Models

ROCHESTER 2GE AND 2GC 2-BBL.

1. Run the engine to normal operating temperature. Block the rear wheels and firmly set the parking brake.

2. Disconnect and plug the distributor vacuum advance hose, va-

por canister hose, and EGR vacuum hose, using golf tees or pencils.

3. Disconnect the emission hose from the air cleaner. Keep the air cleaner connected.

4. With the timing properly adjusted and the air cleaner attached, make sure the choke plates are open and the air conditioning is off. Connect a tachometer to the engine.

5. Place the transmission in Drive. *Make sure you have a helper inside the car with his or her foot on the brake, and the parking brake fully applied.* Adjust the idle speed screw until the engine is idling at the specified rpm (see underhood sticker or "Tune-Up Specifications" chart in this guide). On cars with an air conditioning idle solenoid (on carburetor), disconnect the air con-

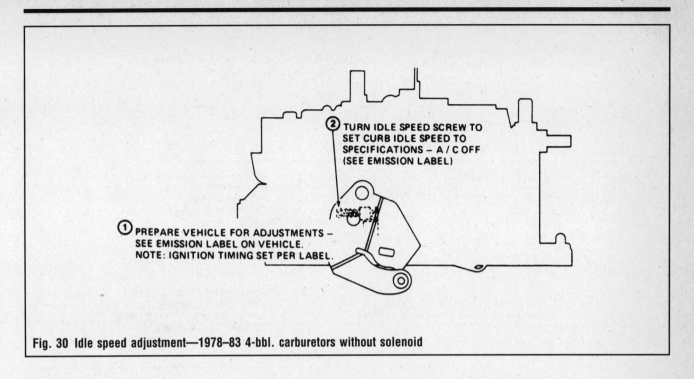

Fig. 30 Idle speed adjustment—1978–83 4-bbl. carburetors without solenoid

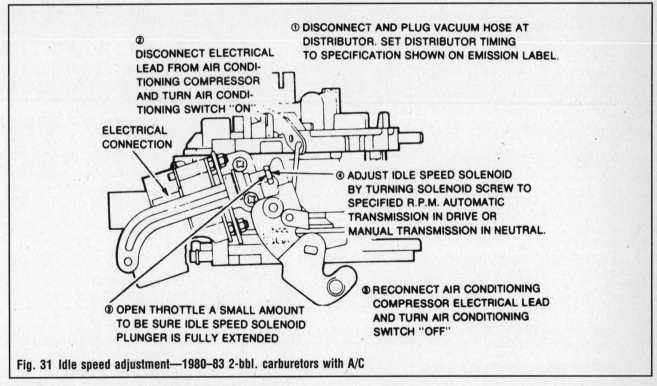

Fig. 31 Idle speed adjustment—1980–83 2-bbl. carburetors with A/C

ditioner compressor clutch wire, and turn the air conditioning on. Adjust the screw on the idle solenoid so the engine idles at the speed specified "solenoid energized" idle speed.

6. Reconnect all hoses, and disconnect the tachometer.

5210-C 2-BBL. (4-151) IDLE SPEED

1. Run the engine up to normal operating temperature. Make sure the choke is fully open and the air conditioning is off. Connect a tachometer to the engine.

2. Set the parking brake and block the rear wheels.

3. Disconnect and plug the PCV hose from the evaporation canister.

4. Disconnect and plug the vacuum advance hose at the distributor.

5. Connect a timing light to the engine. Start the engine and put the transmission in Drive (automatic) or neutral (manual). Check the timing and adjust if necessary.

6. Unplug and reconnect the vacuum advance hose and adjust the idle speed.

7. Disconnect the electrical connection at the A/C override

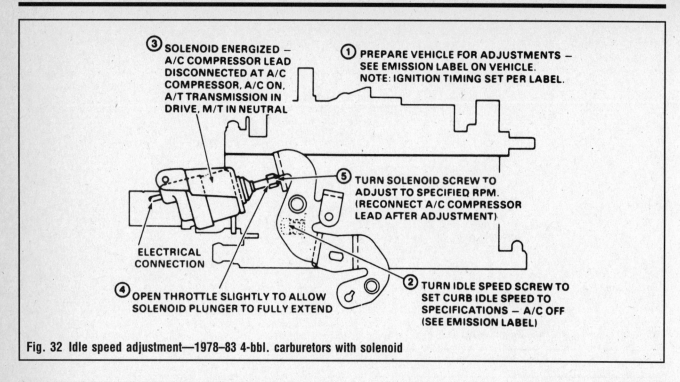

Fig. 32 Idle speed adjustment—1978–83 4-bbl. carburetors with solenoid

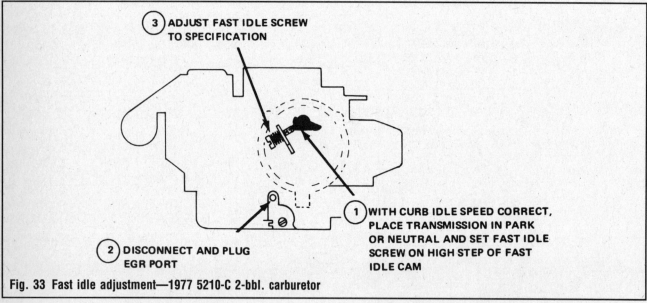

Fig. 33 Fast idle adjustment—1977 5210-C 2-bbl. carburetor

switch, located on the accelerator linkage bracket. Set the A/C to the on position. Momentarily open the throttle to allow the solenoid to fully extend, and adjust the solenoid screw to the specified idle rpm.

8. Reconnect the A/C override switch and turn the A/C off. Place the transmission in neutral or Park.

9. Adjust the fast idle speed as shown in the illustration.

10. Unplug and reconnect the PCV hose at the canister.

11. Shut off the engine and disconnect the tachometer.

M4MC AND M4ME 4-BBL.

1. Run the engine up to normal operating temperature. Make sure the choke is fully open and the air conditioning is off. Connect a tachometer to the engine.

2. Set the parking brake and block the rear wheels.

3. Disconnect and plug the hoses from the EGR valve and evaporation canister.

4. Start the engine and put the transmission in Park (automatic) or neutral (manual).

5. Disconnect the distributor vacuum advance line.

6. Connect a timing light and check the timing at the specified rpm; adjust if necessary.

7. Reconnect the vacuum advance line.

8. Place the transmission in drive (automatic) or neutral (manual). On A/C equipped cars, turn the A/C on and disconnect the electrical connector at the A/C compressor clutch. Momentarily open the throttle to make sure the solenoid plunger is fully extended. Adjust the solenoid screw to the specified rpm depending on engine. On manual transmission cars, adjust the idle stop screw to the specified rpm depending on engine.

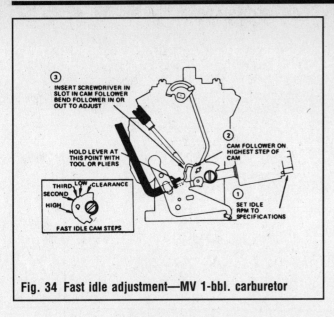

Fig. 34 Fast idle adjustment—MV 1-bbl. carburetor

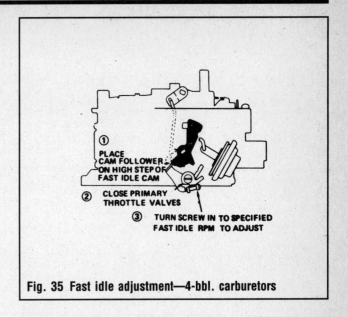

Fig. 35 Fast idle adjustment—4-bbl. carburetors

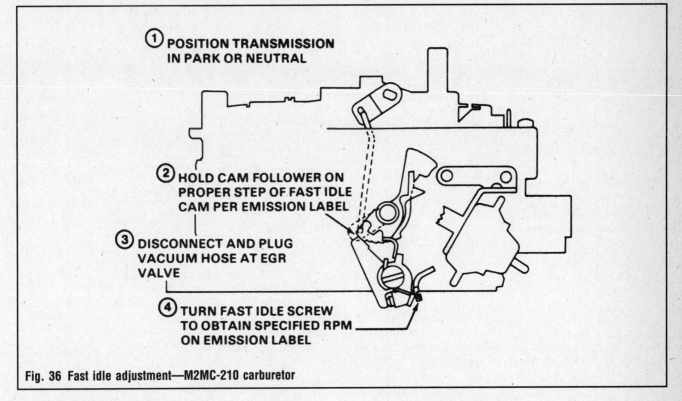

Fig. 36 Fast idle adjustment—M2MC-210 carburetor

9. Reconnect the A/C compressor clutch electrical connector and turn the A/C off. Unplug and reconnect the evaporation canister and EGR hoses. Shut off the engine and remove the tachometer.

1978–80 Models

5210-C 2-BBL. (4-151) IDLE SPEED

Adjustments are the same as those for 1977 models.

6510-C 2-BBL. IDLE SPEED

1. Run the engine to normal operating temperature. Turn the air conditioning off and connect a tachometer and timing light to the engine.

2. Set the parking brake and block the drive wheels.

3. Disconnect and plug the PCV hose at the vapor canister.

4. Disconnect and plug the vacuum advance hose at the distributor.

5. Place the transmission in Drive (AT) or Neutral (MT). Check, and if necessary, adjust the timing.

6. Connect the vacuum advance hose.

7. Manual transmission, without A/C: turn the idle speed screw to obtain the specified rpm. Manual transmission with A/C or automatic transmission with or without A/C: Turn the idle speed screw to obtain the specified rpm. Disconnect the wire at the wide open throttle switch located on the accelerator linkage. Set the A/C to on. Momentarily open the throttle to extend the solenoid plunger.

Adjust the solenoid screw to obtain the solenoid idle speed specified on the underhood sticker.

8. Connect the PCV hose and remove the tachometer and timing light.

2GC AND 2GE 2-BBL. IDLE SPEED

1. Run the engine to normal operating temperature. Make sure that the choke is fully opened, turn the A/C off and connect a tachometer and timing light to the engine according to the manufacturers' instructions.

2. Set the parking brake and block the drive wheels.

3. Disconnect and plug the vacuum hoses at the vapor canister and EGR valve.

4. Place the transmission in Park (AT) or Neutral (MT).

5. Disconnect and plug the vacuum advance hose at the distributor.

6. Check, and if necessary, adjust the timing.

7. Connect the vacuum advance hose.

8. Cars with manual transmission, without A/C: turn the idle speed screw to obtain the specified rpm. Cars with automatic transmission, without A/C: open the throttle momentarily to extend the solenoid plunger. Turn the solenoid screw to adjust the speed to the curb idle rpm listed on the underhood sticker. Turn the idle speed screw to the specified rpm.

Cars with A/C: Turn the idle speed screw to obtain the specified rpm. Disconnect the A/C compressor clutch wire. Turn the A/C on. Open the throttle momentarily to extend the solenoid plunger. Turn the solenoid screw to obtain the rpm specified on the underhood sticker. Connect the compressor clutch wire.

9. Connect all hoses. Remove the tachometer and timing light.

M2MC-210 2-BBL. IDLE SPEED

1. Run the engine to normal operating temperature.

2. Disconnect the A/C compressor clutch wire, turn the A/C off, make sure that the choke is fully opened, place the manual transmission in Neutral, and the automatic transmission in Drive. Set the parking brake and block the drive wheels.

3. Disconnect and plug the vacuum advance hose at the distributor.

4. Check and adjust the timing.

5. Connect the vacuum advance hose.

6. Disconnect the purge hose at the vapor canister.

7. Cars without A/C: turn the idle speed screw to obtain the specified rpm. Cars with A/C: turn the idle speed screw to obtain the specified rpm, turn the A/C on, open throttle momentarily to extend the solenoid plunger and set the solenoid screw to obtain the rpm specified on the underhood sticker. Turn the A/C off.

8. Connect all hoses and remove the tachometer and timing light. Connect the compressor clutch wire.

M4MC 4-BBL. IDLE SPEED

1. Run the engine to normal operating temperature.

2. Make sure that the choke is fully opened, turn the A/C off and connect a tachometer and timing light to the engine according to the manufacturers' instructions. Set the parking brake and block the drive wheels.

3. Disconnect the purge hose at the vapor canister.

4. Disconnect and plug the EGR vacuum hose at the EGR valve. On 350 engines, plug the purge hose at the canister.

5. Place the transmission in Park.

6. Disconnect and plug the vacuum advance line at the distributor.

7. Check and adjust the timing.

8. Connect the vacuum advance line.

9. Place the transmission in Drive.

10. On cars without A/C: adjust the idle speed screw to obtain the specified rpm. On cars with A/C: disconnect the compressor clutch wire. Open the throttle momentarily to extend the solenoid plunger. Turn the A/C on and adjust the solenoid screw to obtain the rpm specified on the underhood sticker. Connect the compressor clutch wire and turn the A/C off.

11. Connect all hoses and remove the tachometer and timing light.

2SE AND E2SE IDLE SPEED

1. Run the engine until it reaches normal operating temperature.

2. Prepare the vehicle for adjustment as indicated on the emission label under the hood.

3. Check the ignition timing and adjust as necessary.

4. Reconnect the vacuum advance line.

5. With the A/C off, turn the idle speed screw to obtain the curb idle as specified on the emission label.

6. With the automatic transmission in Drive or the manual transmission in Neutral, disconnect the A/C compressor wire at the compressor and turn the A/C on.

7. Open the throttle slightly to extend the solenoid plunger.

8. Turn the solenoid screw to obtain the correct rpm.

9. Turn the engine off and reconnect the A/C compressor line and all hoses.

IDLE MIXTURE

Changes in the idle system have made adjustment of the fuel mixture impossible without the aid of a propane enrichment system not available to the general public.

1981–82 E2MC/E2ME or E4MC/E4ME Idle Speed

1. Set the parking brake and block the wheels.

2. Disconnect and plug the hoses listed on the underhood specifications label.

3. Check, and if necessary, adjust the timing.

4. Connect a dwell meter and tachometer to the engine.

5. Start the engine and let it warm at idle until a varying swell is noted. It is absolutely necessary for the engine to be operated for a length of time sufficient for coolant and oxygen sensors to operate.

6. Check the idle speed. If necessary, turn the idle screw to obtain the speed shown on the underhood sticker.

➡ **On models with Idle Speed Control (ISC), no adjustment is possible.**

7. Place the transmission in Drive (AT) or Neutral (MT). Note the dwell reading on the 6-cylinder scale of the dwell meter. It should be varying between the 10°–50° marks. If not, do the following:

a. Shut the engine off. Cover the internal bowl vents and the bleed valve air inlets with masking tape. Cover the air horn with a cloth.

b. Align a ⅛ inch drill bit on the rivet head which holds the idle air bleed valve cover in place and drill only enough to remove the rivet head. Drive the remainder of the rivet out.

c. Remove the cover. Clean out any metal chips from the housing.

d. Remove the tape and cloth. Start the engine and let it

idle in Drive (AT) or Neutral (MT). With the engine at full operating temperature, slowly turn the idle bleed valve until the dwell reading varies within the 25°–35° range on the meter. The valve is very sensitive, so turn it very slowly.

e. If the dwell reading cannot be attained, it will be necessary to adjust the mixture. Special equipment is needed for this procedure, and this is best handled by a professional mechanic.

1981–83 Idle Mixture

➡**This is a very complicated procedure which requires special factory service tools; it is best left to a professional mechanic with the proper equipment.**

FAST IDLE

1974–76 1 MV 1-bbl. (6-250)

1. Adjust the curb idle speed with the idle stop solenoid, according to the underhood decal and the "Idle Speed" adjustment procedure earlier in this chapter.
2. Place the carburetor cam follower (on the throttle lever) on the high step of the fast idle cam.
3. Carefully bend the cam follower tang in or out to adjust to the specified rpm.

✳✳ WARNING

Support the throttle lever when bending the idle tang.

1974–76 2GC 2-bbl.

➡**The fast idle is present on some V8 engines when the slow idle is adjusted.**

1. Place the fast idle cam follower on the low step of the fast idle cam, against the shoulder of the next higher step.
2. Adjust the fast idle screw to obtain the following specified idle speeds: (with transmission in Park):
   • 900 rpm, 350 V8 (non-Calif.)
   • 1000 rpm, 350 V8 (Calif.)
   • 1800 rpm, 400 V8 (where adjustable)

1974–76 4MC and M4MC 4-bbl.

1. On 350 and 455 V8s, place the fast idle cam follower on the lowest step of the fast idle cam against the shoulder of the next highest step. Adjust the fast idle screw to 900 rpm in Park.
2. On 400 cu. in. V8s, place the cam follower on the highest step of the fast idle cam. Adjust the fast idle screw until the engine is turning 1800 rpm in Park.
3. Reconnect all hoses and install the air cleaner. Disconnect the tach.

1977 Models Except 5210-C 2-bbl. (4-151)

No fast idle adjustment is necessary, as the fast idle is automatically adjusted when the curb idle is set.

1977 5210-C 2-bbl. (4-151)

Adjust the fast idle speed according to the accompanying illustration.

1978–80 Vehicles

➡**The fast idle on all 231 V6 and some 305 V8 engines is automatically set when the curb idle adjustment is made. Refer to the emissions sticker under your car's hood for this specific application.**

Prepare the engine and car according to the emissions sticker before proceeding with the steps below.

4-151 (5210-C 2-bbl.)

The fast idle speed is adjusted in the same manner as on 1977 models.

BUICK-BUILT 350 V8

1. Set the cam follower on the specified step of the fast idle cam according to the emissions sticker. Disconnect the vacuum hose at the EGR valve on 2-barrel models and plug this.
2. Turn the fast idle screw out until the butterfly valves in the primary throttle boxes are closed. You can see this by looking down into the carburetor; the butterfly valves are at the bottom of the bores.
3. Turn the fast idle screw in to adjust the idle speed to specifications. On 4-barrel models, turn the fast idle screw in until it just contacts the lever, then turn it in an additional three turns. Adjust to specified rpm.

PONTIAC BUILT V8

1. After making all adjustment preparations according to the emissions sticker, place the transmission in Neutral.
2. Place the cam follower on the specified step of the fast idle cam.
3. Disconnect and plug the EGR vacuum hose, using a golf tee or pencil, at the EGR valve.
4. Adjust the fast idle speed screw to obtain the specified rpm.

OLDSMOBILE BUILT V8

Since the carburetor tuning procedures vary by model and component application, the procedure given on the emissions sticker in the engine compartment should be followed.

1981–83 Vehicles

Carburetor adjustment procedures for 1981–83 models vary by model and component application. Follow the procedure on the underhood emissions sticker, using the diagrams included in this guide as reference.

Diesel Fuel Injection

IDLE SPEED ADJUSTMENT

350 V8 Diesel
◗ **See Figure 37**

A special tachometer with an RPM counter suitable for the 350 V8 diesel is necessary for this adjustment; a standard tach suitable for gasoline engines will not work.

1. Place the transmission in Park, block the rear wheels and firmly set the parking brake.
2. If necessary, adjust the throttle linkage as described in Chapter 7.

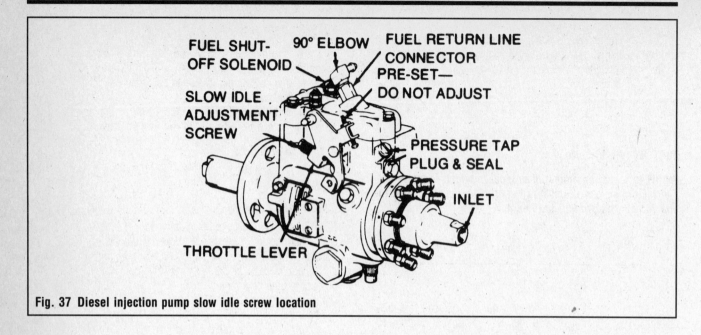

FUEL SHUT-OFF SOLENOID

90° ELBOW

FUEL RETURN LINE CONNECTOR PRE-SET— DO NOT ADJUST

SLOW IDLE ADJUSTMENT SCREW

PRESSURE TAP PLUG & SEAL

INLET

THROTTLE LEVER

Fig. 37 Diesel injection pump slow idle screw location

3. Start the engine and allow it to warm up for 10–15 minutes.

4. Shut off the engine and remove the air cleaner.

5. Clean off any grime from the timing probe holder on the front cover; also clean off the crankshaft balancer rim.

6. Install the magnetic probe end of the tachometer fully into the timing probe holder. Complete the remaining tachometer connections according to the tach manufacturer's instructions.

7. Disconnect the two-lead connector from the generator.

8. Make sure all electrical accessories are off.

➡**At no time should either the steering wheel or the brake pedal be touched.**

9. Start the engine and place the transmission in Drive (after first making sure the parking brake is firmly applied).

10. Check the slow idle speed reading against the one printed on the underhood emissions sticker. Reset if necessary.

11. Unplug the connector from the fast idle cold advance (engine temperature) switch, and install a jumper wire between the connector terminals.

➡**DO NOT allow the jumper to ground.**

12. Check the fast idle speed and reset if necessary according to the specification printed on the underhood emissions sticker.

13. Remove the jumper wire and reconnect it to the temperature switch.

14. Recheck the slow idle speed and reset if necessary.

15. Shut off the engine.

16. Reconnect the leads at the generator and A/C compressor.

17. Disconnect and remove the tachometer.

18. If the car is equipped with cruise control, adjust the servo throttle rod to minimum slack, then put the clip in the first free hole closest to the bellcrank or throttle lever.

19. Install the air cleaner.

Gasoline Engine Tune-Up Specifications

(When analyzing compression test results, look for uniformity among cylinders rather than specific pressures)

Year	Engine V.I.N. Code	Engine Type (No. of cyl- C.I.D.)	Engine Manufac- turer	Spark Plugs Orig. Type	Gap (In.)	Distributor Point Dwell (deg.)	Point Gap (In.)	Ignition Timing (deg. B.T.D.C.) Automatic Trans- mission	Manual Trans- mission	Intake Valve Opens (°B.T.D.C.)	Fuel Pump Pressure (psi)	Idle Speed (rpm) Automatic Trans- mission	Manual Trans- mission
'74	D	6-250	Chev.	R46T	.035	32.5	.019	6B	6B	25	4-5	600	850
	M, N	8-350	Pont.	R46S	.040	30	.019	12B(10B)	10B	26	5.5-6.5	650(625)	900
	J, K	8-350	Pont.	R46S	.040	30	.019	12B(10B)	10B	26	5.5-6.5	650(625)	1000
	R	8-400	Pont.	R46TSX	.040	30	.019	12B(10B)	10B	26	5.5-6.5	650(625)	1000
	S	8-400	Pont.	R45TSX	.040	30	.019	12B(10B)	10B	23①	5.5-6.5	650(625)	1000
'75	D	6-250	Chev.	R46TX	.060	Electronic		10B	10B	25	4-5	550(600)	850
	F	8-260	Olds.	R46SX	.080	Electronic		16B	18B(16)	14	5-6.5	650	750
	M	8-350	Pont.	R46TSX	.060	Electronic		12B	12B	26	3-6	600	800
	E	8-350	Pont.	R45TSX	.060	Electronic		12B	12B	26	3-6	600(650)	800
	H	8-350	Buick	R46TSX	.060	Electronic		12B	12B	19	3-6	600(650)	775
	R	8-400	Pont.	R46TSX	.040	Electronic		12B	12B	26	3-6	650(600)	750(650)
	S	8-400	Pont.	R45TSX	.060	Electronic		12B	16B	23/30	3-6	650(600)	750(650)
	W	8-455	Pont.	R45TSX	.060	Electronic		16B	—	23	3-6	675(650)	—
'76	C	V6-231	Buick	R44SX	.060	Electronic		12B	12B	17	3-6	500③	600(500)②
	D	6-250	Chev.	R46TX	.060	Electronic		10B	6B	14	3-6	650	850
	F	8-260	Olds.	R46SX	.080	Electronic		16B @1100	16B @1100	14	3-6	650	750
	M	8-350	Pont.	R46TSX	.060	Electronic		12B	—	22	3-6	600	—
	E	8-350	Pont.	R46TSX	.060	Electronic		12B	—	26	3-6	600	—
	H	8-350	Buick	R45TSX	.060	Electronic		12B	—	13	3-6	600	—
	J	8-350	Buick	R45TSX	.060	Electronic		16B	16B	13	3-6	550	650
	S	8-400	Pont.	R45TSX	.060	Electronic		16B	12B	23/30	3-6	575	750
	W	8-455	Pont.	R45TSX	.060	Electronic		16B(12B)	—	23	3-6	600④	—

Gasoline Engine Tune-Up Specifications (cont.)

(When analyzing compression test results, look for uniformity among cylinders rather than specific pressures)

Year	Engine V.I.N. Code	Engine Type (No. of cyl- C.I.D.)	Engine Manufacturer	Spark Plugs Orig. Type	Gap (In.)	Distributor Point Dwell (deg.)	Point Gap (In.)	Ignition Timing (deg. B.T.D.C.) Automatic Transmission	Manual Transmission	Intake Valve Opens (°B.T.D.C.)	Fuel Pump Pressure (psi)	Idle Speed (rpm) Automatic Transmission	Manual Transmission
'77	V,1	4-151	Pont.	R44TSX	.060	Electronic		14B	14B	27	4-5.5	500[5]	500[6]
	C	V6-231	Buick	R46TSX	.060	Electronic		12B	12B	17	4-6	500[5]	500[6]
	Y	8-301	Pont.	R46TSX	.060	Electronic		12B @ 550	16B @ 850	31/27	7-8	750[7]	800
	U	8-305	Chev.	R45TS	.060	Electronic		8B	8B	28	7-9	550[6]	700
	R	8-350	Olds.	R46SZ	.060	Electronic		—	20B @ 1100	29	5-6	550[6]	—
	L	8-350	Chev.	R45TS	.045	Electronic		14B	14B	28	7-9	500[6]	700
	Z	8-400	Pont.	R45TSX	.060	Electronic		16B	—	29	7-8	575[8]	—
	K	8-403	Olds.	R46SZ	.060	Electronic		22B	—	16	5-6	550[6]	—
'78	V,1	4-151	Pont.	R43TSX	.060	Electronic		14B	—	28	5-6.5	650[9]	—
	A	V6-231	Buick	R46TSX	.060	Electronic		15B	15B	17	4.5-5.7	600[8]	800
	Y	8-301	Pont.	R46TSX	.060	Electronic		12B	—	27	7-8.5	550[6]	—
	U	8-305	Chev.	R45TS	.045	Electronic		4B	4B	28	7.5-9	500[11]	600[10]
	X	8-350	Buick	R46TSX	.060	Electronic		15B	—	13.5	5.9-7.4	550	—
	R	8-350	Olds.	R46SZ	.060	Electronic		20B @ 1100	—	16	5.5-6.5	550[6]	—
	L	8-350	Chev.	R45TS	.045	Electronic		8B	6B	28	7.5-9	500[11]	700
	Z	8-400	Pont.	R45TSX	.060	Electronic		16B	18B	21	7-8.5	575[6]	775
	K	8-403	Olds.	R46SZ	.060	Electronic		20B	—	16	5.5-6.5	550[6]	—
'79	V,1	4-151	Pont.	R43TSX	.060	Electronic		12B(14B)	13B (14B)	33	5-6.5	600(850)[8]	900(1000)
	A	V6-231	Buick	R46TSX	.060	Electronic		15B	15B	17	4.5-5.7	600	800
	Y	8-301	Pont.	R45TSX	.060	Electronic		12B	—	27	7-8.5	650	—

Year	Code	Engine	Mfr.	Spark Plug	Gap	Distributor						
	G	8-305	Chev.	R45TS	.045	Electronic	4B	4B	28	7-8.5	650	—
	H	8-305	Chev.	R46SZ	.080	Electronic	4B	4B	28	7.5-9	600	⑫
	X	8-350	Buick	R46TSX	.080	Electronic	15B	—	13.5	5.9-7.4	600⑧	—
	R	8-350	Olds.	R45TSX	.060	Electronic	20 @ 1100	—	16	5.5-6.5	600⑧	—
	L	8-350	Chev.	R46SZ	.080	Electronic	15B (20B)⑬	—	28	7.5-9	600	—
'80	A	V6-231	Buick	R45TS	.060	Electronic	⑭	⑭	17	4-5	600	800
	S	8-265	Pont.	R45TSX	.060	Electronic	⑭	⑭	27	7-8.5	600	700
	W	8-301	Pont.	R45TSX	.060	Electronic	12B	—	16	7-8.5	600⑮	—
	H	8-305	Chev.	R45TS	.045	Electronic	4B	⑭	27	7-8.5	600⑮	700
'81	A	V6-231	Buick	R45TS	.060	Electronic	⑭	⑭	17	4-5	600	800
	S	8-265	Pont.	R45TSX	.060	Electronic	10B	⑭	27	7-8.5	600	⑭
	W	8-301	Pont.	R45TSX	.060	Electronic	12B	—	16	7-8.5	600⑮	—
'82	A	V6-231	Buick	R45TS8	.080	Electronic	⑭	⑭	16	4-5.75	⑭	⑭
	A	V6-252	Buick	R45TS8	.080	Electronic	⑭	⑭	16	4-5.75	⑭	⑭
	W	8-301	Pont.	R45TSX	.060	Electronic	⑭	⑭	16	7-8.5	⑭	⑭
'83	A	V6-231	Buick	R45TS8	.080	Electronic	⑭	⑭	16	4-5.75	⑭	⑭
	A	V6-252	Buick	R45TS8	.080	Electronic	⑭	⑭	16	4-5.75	⑭	⑭
	W	8-301	Pont.	R45TSX	.060	Electronic	⑭	⑭	16	7-8.5	⑭	⑭

NOTE: Figures in parentheses for California engines (if different from 49 states models)
① Manual transmission; 30° automatic transmission
② 800 rpm with A/C on, 49 states; 1000 rpm in Neutral with A/C on Calif.
③ 650 rpm with A/C on, 49 states and Calif.
④ 550 rpm High Altitude
⑤ 1000 rpm with A/C on
⑥ 650 rpm with A/C on
⑦ 875 rpm with A/C on
⑧ 675 rpm with A/C on
⑨ 850 rpm with A/C on
⑩ 700 rpm with A/C on
⑪ 600 rpm with A/C on
⑫ 500 rpm High Altitude
⑬ High Altitude 8° BTDC
⑭ See Underhood Decal
⑮ 675 rpm with A/C on, 49 states; 700 rpm with A/C on Calif.

Grand Prix Diesel Tune-Up Specifications

Year	Eng V.I.N. Code	Engine No. Cyl. Displacement (Cu. In.)	Eng. Mfg.	Fuel Pump Pressure (psi)	Compression (lbs) ▲	Ignition Timing (deg) Auto. Trans.	Intake Valve Opens (deg)	Idle Speed● (rpm)
'79	N	8-350	Olds.	5.5–6.5	275 min.	①	16	650/675
'80	N	8-350	Olds.	5.5–6.5	275 min.	5B ②	16	750/600
'81	N	8-350	Olds.	5.5–6.5	275 min.	①	16	①
'82	N	8-350	Olds.	5.5–6.5	275 min.	①	16	①
'83	N	8-350	Olds.	5.5–6.5	275 min.	①	16	①

NOTE: The underhood specifications sticker often reflects changes made in production. Sticker figures must be used if they disagree with those in this chart.

① See underhood specifications sticker.

② Static

● Where two idle speed figures appear separated by a slash, the first is idle speed with solenoid energized; the second is with solenoid disconnected.

▲ The lowest cylinder reading should not be less than 70% of the highest cylinder reading.

ENGINE ELECTRICAL 3-2
UNDERSTANDING ELECTRICITY 3-2
  BASIC CIRCUITS 3-2
  TROUBLESHOOTING 3-3
BATTERY, STARTING AND CHARGING
  SYSTEMS 3-4
  BASIC OPERATING PRINCIPLES 3-4
DISTRIBUTOR 3-5
  REMOVAL & INSTALLATION 3-5
ALTERNATOR 3-10
  ALTERNATOR PRECAUTIONS 3-10
  REMOVAL & INSTALLATION 3-11
  TESTING 3-13
VOLTAGE REGULATOR 3-14
STARTER 3-14
  REMOVAL & INSTALLATION 3-14
  SHIMMING THE STARTER 3-16
  STARTER OVERHAUL 3-17
BATTERY 3-19
  REMOVAL & INSTALLATION 3-19
ENGINE MECHANICAL 3-22
ENGINE OVERHAUL TIPS 3-22
  TOOLS 3-22
  INSPECTION TECHNIQUES 3-22
  OVERHAUL TIPS 3-22
  REPAIRING DAMAGED THREADS 3-22
CHECKING ENGINE COMPRESSION 3-23
DESIGN 3-24
ENGINE 3-33
  REMOVAL & INSTALLATION 3-33
VALVE COVER 3-35
  REMOVAL & INSTALLATION 3-35
ROCKER ARMS 3-36
  REMOVAL & INSTALLATION 3-36
INTAKE MANIFOLD 3-38
  REMOVAL & INSTALLATION 3-38
EXHAUST MANIFOLD 3-42
  REMOVAL & INSTALLATION 3-42
CYLINDER HEAD 3-43
  REMOVAL & INSTALLATION 3-43
  CLEANING & INSPECTION 3-47
  CHECKING FOR HEAD WARPAGE 3-48
VALVES, SPRINGS AND GUIDES 3-48
  REMOVAL 3-48
  INSPECTION 3-50
  LAPPING THE VALVES 3-51
  VALVE GUIDES 3-52
  VALVE SPRINGS 3-53
  VALVE INSTALLATION 3-53
  VALVE ADJUSTMENT 3-54
VALVE LIFTERS 3-55
  REMOVAL & INSTALLATION 3-55
TIMING CHAIN COVER AND FRONT OIL
  SEAL 3-56
  REMOVAL & INSTALLATION 3-56
TIMING CHAIN 3-61
  REMOVAL & INSTALLATION 3-61
TIMING GEARS 3-64
  REMOVAL & INSTALLATION 3-64
CAMSHAFT 3-64
  REMOVAL & INSTALLATION 3-64
  INSPECTION 3-65
CAMSHAFT BEARINGS 3-66
  REMOVAL & INSTALLATION 3-66
PISTONS AND CONNECTING RODS 3-66
  REMOVAL 3-66
  CLEANING & INSPECTION 3-69

PISTON RING END-GAP 3-71
PISTON RING SIDE CLEARANCE
  CHECK & INSTALLATION 3-71
CONNECTING ROD BEARINGS 3-73
  ASSEMBLY & INSTALLATION 3-74
CRANKSHAFT AND MAIN BEARINGS 3-75
  REMOVAL 3-75
  MAIN BEARING INSPECTION &
    REPLACEMENT 3-76
  CHECKING CLEARANCE 3-76
  MAIN BEARING REPLACEMENT 3-76
  CRANKSHAFT END-PLAY &
    INSTALLATION 3-77
OIL PAN 3-78
  REMOVAL & INSTALLATION 3-78
OIL PUMP 3-78
  REMOVAL & INSTALLATION 3-78
  OVERHAUL 3-79
REAR MAIN OIL SEAL 3-80
  REMOVAL & INSTALLATION 3-80
FLYWHEEL AND RING GEAR 3-83
  REMOVAL & INSTALLATION 3-83
ENGINE CORE PLUGS (FREEZE
  PLUGS) 3-83
  REMOVAL & INSTALLATION 3-83
BLOCK HEATER 3-84
  REMOVAL & INSTALLATION 3-84
WATER PUMP 3-84
  REMOVAL & INSTALLATION 3-84
THERMOSTAT 3-86
  REMOVAL & INSTALLATION 3-86
RADIATOR 3-87
  REMOVAL & INSTALLATION 3-87
EXHAUST SYSTEM 3-90
GENERAL INFORMATION 3-90
  SPECIAL TOOLS 3-91
  COMPONENT REPLACEMENT 3-91
COMPONENT LOCATIONS
HEI DISTRIBUTOR COMPONENTS 3-8
SPECIFICATION CHARTS
BATTERY AND STARTER
  SPECIFICATIONS 3-20
GENERAL ENGINE SPECIFICATIONS 3-25
VALVE SPECIFICATIONS 3-27
CRANKSHAFT AND CONNECTING ROD
  SPECIFICATIONS 3-29
PISTON AND RING SPECIFICATIONS 3-30
TORQUE SPECIFICATIONS 3-31
CAMSHAFT SPECIFICATIONS 3-32
TROUBLESHOOTING CHARTS
ENGINE MECHANICAL PROBLEMS 3-93
ENGINE PERFORMANCE 3-96

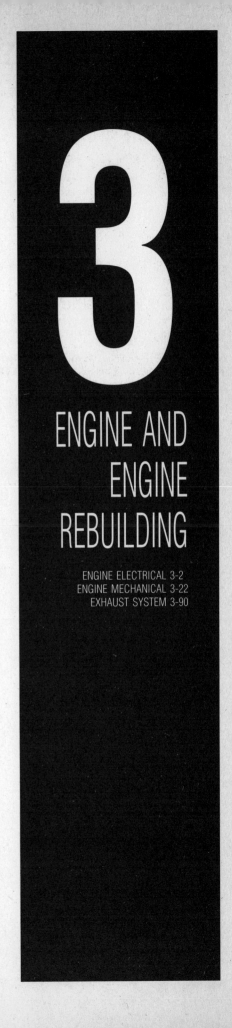

3

ENGINE AND ENGINE REBUILDING

ENGINE ELECTRICAL 3-2
ENGINE MECHANICAL 3-22
EXHAUST SYSTEM 3-90

ENGINE ELECTRICAL

Understanding Electricity

For any electrical system to operate, there must be a complete circuit. This simply means that the power flow from the battery must make a full circle. When an electrical component is operating, power flows from the battery to the components, passes through the component (load) causing it to function, and returns to the battery through the ground path of the circuit. This ground may be either another wire or a metal part of the vehicle (depending upon how the component is designed).

BASIC CIRCUITS

Perhaps the easiest way to visualize a circuit is to think of connecting a light bulb (with two wires attached to it) to the battery. If one of the two wires was attached to the negative post (−) of the battery and the other wire to the positive post (+), the circuit would be complete and the light bulb would illuminate. Electricity could follow a path from the battery to the bulb and back to the battery. It's not hard to see that with longer wires on our light bulb, it could be mounted anywhere on the vehicle. Further, one wire could be fitted with a switch so that the light could be turned on and off. Various other items could be added to our primitive circuit to make the light flash, become brighter or dimmer under certain conditions, or advise the user that it's burned out.

Ground

Some automotive components are grounded through their mounting points. The electrical current runs through the chassis of the vehicle and returns to the battery through the ground (−) cable; if you look, you'll see that the battery ground cable connects between the battery and the body of the vehicle.

Load

Every complete circuit must include a "load" (something to use the electricity coming from the source). If you were to connect a

Damaged insulation can allow wires to break (causing an open circuit) or touch (causing a short circuit)

wire between the two terminals of the battery (DON'T do this, but take our word for it) without the light bulb, the battery would attempt to deliver its entire power supply from one pole to another almost instantly. This is a short circuit. The electricity is taking a short cut to get to ground and is not being used by any load in the circuit. This sudden and uncontrolled electrical flow can cause great damage to other components in the circuit and can develop a tremendous amount of heat. A short in an automotive wiring harness can develop sufficient heat to melt the insulation on all the surrounding wires and reduce a multiple wire cable to one sad lump of plastic and copper. Two common causes of shorts are broken insulation (thereby exposing the wire to contact with surrounding metal surfaces or other wires) or a failed switch (the pins inside the switch come out of place and touch each other).

Switches and Relays

Some electrical components which require a large amount of current to operate also have a relay in their circuit. Since these cir-

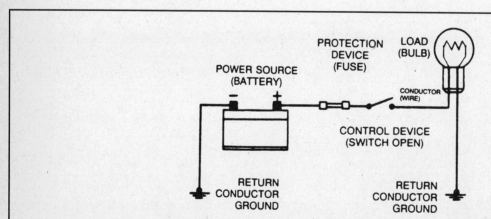

Here is an example of a simple automotive circuit. When the switch is closed, power from the positive battery terminal flows through the fuse, the switch and then the load (light bulb). The light illuminates and the circuit is completed through the return conductor and the vehicle ground. If the light did not work, the tests could be made with a voltmeter or test light at the battery, fuse, switch or bulb socket

cuits carry a large amount of current (amperage or amps), the thickness of the wire in the circuit (wire gauge) is also greater. If this large wire were connected from the load to the control switch on the dash, the switch would have to carry the high amperage load and the dash would be twice as large to accommodate wiring harnesses as thick as your wrist. To prevent these problems, a relay is used. The large wires in the circuit are connected from the battery to one side of the relay and from the opposite side of the relay to the load. The relay is normally open, preventing current from passing through the circuit. An additional, smaller wire is connected from the relay to the control switch for the circuit. When the control switch is turned on, it grounds the smaller wire to the relay and completes its circuit. The main switch inside the relay closes, sending power to the component without routing the main power through the inside of the vehicle. Some common circuits which may use relays are the horn, headlights, starter and rear window defogger systems.

Protective Devices

It is possible for larger surges of current to pass through the electrical system of your vehicle. If this surge of current were to reach the load in the circuit, it could burn it out or severely damage it. To prevent this, fuses, circuit breakers and/or fusible links are connected into the supply wires of the electrical system. These items are nothing more than a built-in weak spot in the system. It's much easier to go to a known location (the fusebox) to see why a circuit is inoperative than to dissect 15 feet of wiring under the dashboard, looking for what happened.

When an electrical current of excessive power passes through the fuse, the fuse blows (the conductor melts) and breaks the circuit, preventing the passage of current and protecting the components.

A circuit breaker is basically a self repairing fuse. It will open the circuit in the same fashion as a fuse, but when either the short is removed or the surge subsides, the circuit breaker resets itself and does not need replacement.

A fuse link (fusible link or main link) is a wire that acts as a fuse. One of these is normally connected between the starter relay and the main wiring harness under the hood. Since the starter is usually the highest electrical draw on the vehicle, an internal short during starting could direct about 130 amps into the wrong places. Consider the damage potential of introducing this current into a system whose wiring is rated at 15 amps and you'll understand the need for protection. Since this link is very early in the electrical path, it's the first place to look if nothing on the vehicle works, but the battery seems to be charged and is properly connected.

TROUBLESHOOTING

Electrical problems generally fall into one of three areas:
• The component that is not functioning is not receiving current.
• The component is receiving power but is not using it or is using it incorrectly (component failure).
• The component is improperly grounded.

The circuit can be can be checked with a test light and a jumper wire. The test light is a device that looks like a pointed screwdriver with a wire on one end and a bulb in its handle. A jumper wire is simply a piece of wire with alligator clips or spe-

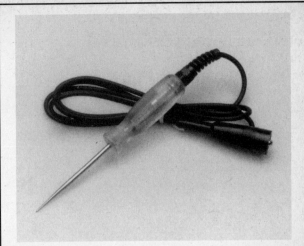

A 12 volt test light is useful when checking parts of a circuit for power

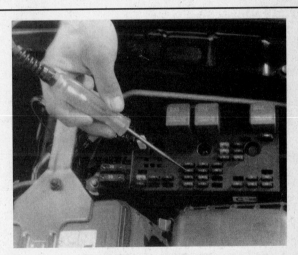

Here, someone is checking a circuit by making sure there is power to the component's fuse

cial terminals on each end. If a component is not working, you must follow a systematic plan to determine which of the three causes is the villain.

1. Turn ON the switch that controls the item not working.

➡Some items only work when the ignition switch is turned ON.

2. Disconnect the power supply wire from the component.
3. Attach the ground wire of a test light or a voltmeter to a good metal ground.
4. Touch the end probe of the test light (or the positive lead of the voltmeter) to the power wire; if there is current in the wire, the light in the test light will come on (or the voltmeter will indicate the amount of voltage). You have now established that current is getting to the component.
5. Turn the ignition or dash switch OFF and reconnect the wire to the component.

If there was no power, then the problem is between the battery and the component. This includes all the switches, fuses, relays and the battery itself. The next place to look is the fusebox; check

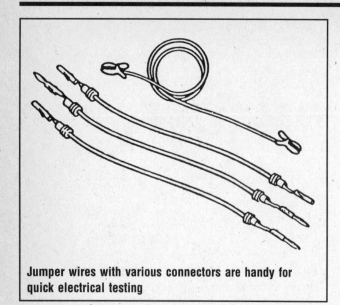

Jumper wires with various connectors are handy for quick electrical testing

carefully either by eye or by using the test light across the fuse clips. The easiest way to check is to simply replace the fuse. If the fuse is blown, and upon replacement, immediately blows again, there is a short between the fuse and the component. This is generally (not always) a sign of an internal short in the component. Disconnect the power wire at the component again and replace the fuse; if the fuse holds, the component is the problem.

❊❊ WARNING

DO NOT test a component by running a jumper wire from the battery UNLESS you are certain that it operates on 12 volts. Many electronic components are designed to operate with less voltage and connecting them to 12 volts could destroy them. Jumper wires are best used to bypass a portion of the circuit (such as a stretch of wire or a switch) that DOES NOT contain a resistor and is suspected to be bad.

If all the fuses are good and the component is not receiving power, find the switch for the circuit. Bypass the switch with the jumper wire. This is done by connecting one end of the jumper to the power wire coming into the switch and the other end to the wire leaving the switch. If the component comes to life, the switch has failed.

❊❊ WARNING

Never substitute the jumper for the component. The circuit needs the electrical load of the component. If you bypass it, you will cause a short circuit.

Checking the ground for any circuit can mean tracing wires to the body, cleaning connections or tightening mounting bolts for the component itself. If the jumper wire can be connected to the case of the component or the ground connector, you can ground the other end to a piece of clean, solid metal on the vehicle. Again, if the component starts working, you've found the problem.

A systematic search through the fuse, connectors, switches and the component itself will almost always yield an answer. Loose and/or corroded connectors, particularly in ground circuits, are becoming a larger problem in modern vehicles. The computers and on-board electronic (solid state) systems are highly sensitive to improper grounds and will change their function drastically if one occurs.

Remember that for any electrical circuit to work, ALL the connections must be clean and tight.

➡ **For more information on Understanding and Troubleshooting Electrical Systems, please refer to Section 6 of this manual.**

Battery, Starting and Charging Systems

BASIC OPERATING PRINCIPLES

Battery

The battery is the first link in the chain of mechanisms which work together to provide cranking of the automobile engine. In most modern vehicles, the battery is a lead/acid electrochemical device consisting of six 2v subsections (cells) connected in series so the unit is capable of producing approximately 12v of electrical pressure. Each subsection consists of a series of positive and negative plates held a short distance apart in a solution of sulfuric acid and water.

The two types of plates are of dissimilar metals. This sets-up a chemical reaction, and it is this reaction which produces current flow from the battery when its positive and negative terminals are connected to an electrical accessory such as a lamp or motor. The continued transfer of electrons would eventually convert the sulfuric acid to water, and make the two plates identical in chemical composition. As electrical energy is removed from the battery, its voltage output tends to drop. Thus, measuring battery voltage and battery electrolyte composition are two ways of checking the ability of the unit to supply power. During engine cranking, electrical energy is removed from the battery. However, if the charging circuit is in good condition and the operating conditions are normal, the power removed from the battery will be replaced by the alternator which will force electrons back through the battery, reversing the normal flow, and restoring the battery to its original chemical state.

Starting System

The battery and starting motor are linked by very heavy electrical cables designed to minimize resistance to the flow of current. Generally, the major power supply cable that leaves the battery goes directly to the starter, while other electrical system needs are supplied by a smaller cable. During starter operation, power flows from the battery to the starter and is grounded through the vehicle's frame/body or engine and the battery's negative ground strap.

The starter is a specially designed, direct current electric motor capable of producing a great amount of power for its size. One thing that allows the motor to produce a great deal of power is its tremendous rotating speed. It drives the engine through a tiny pinion gear (attached to the starter's armature), which drives the very large flywheel ring gear at a greatly reduced speed. Another factor allowing it to produce so much power is that only intermittent operation is required of it. Thus, little allowance for air circulation is necessary, and the windings can be built into a very small space.

The starter solenoid is a magnetic device which employs the small current supplied by the start circuit of the ignition switch. This magnetic action moves a plunger which mechanically engages the starter and closes the heavy switch connecting it to the battery. The starting switch circuit usually consists of the starting switch contained within the ignition switch, a neutral safety switch or clutch pedal switch, and the wiring necessary to connect these in series with the starter solenoid or relay.

The pinion, a small gear, is mounted to a one way drive clutch. This clutch is splined to the starter armature shaft. When the ignition switch is moved to the **START** position, the solenoid plunger slides the pinion toward the flywheel ring gear via a collar and spring. If the teeth on the pinion and flywheel match properly, the pinion will engage the flywheel immediately. If the gear teeth butt one another, the spring will be compressed and will force the gears to mesh as soon as the starter turns far enough to allow them to do so. As the solenoid plunger reaches the end of its travel, it closes the contacts that connect the battery and starter, then the engine is cranked.

As soon as the engine starts, the flywheel ring gear begins turning fast enough to drive the pinion at an extremely high rate of speed. At this point, the one-way clutch begins allowing the pinion to spin faster than the starter shaft so that the starter will not operate at excessive speed. When the ignition switch is released from the starter position, the solenoid is de-energized, and a spring pulls the gear out of mesh interrupting the current flow to the starter.

Some starters employ a separate relay, mounted away from the starter, to switch the motor and solenoid current on and off. The relay replaces the solenoid electrical switch, but does not eliminate the need for a solenoid mounted on the starter used to mechanically engage the starter drive gears. The relay is used to reduce the amount of current the starting switch must carry.

Charging System

The automobile charging system provides electrical power for operation of the vehicle's ignition system, starting system and all electrical accessories. The battery serves as an electrical surge or storage tank, storing (in chemical form) the energy originally produced by the engine driven generator. The system also provides a means of regulating output to protect the battery from being overcharged and to avoid excessive voltage to the accessories.

The storage battery is a chemical device incorporating parallel lead plates in a tank containing a sulfuric acid/water solution. Adjacent plates are slightly dissimilar, and the chemical reaction of the two dissimilar plates produces electrical energy when the battery is connected to a load such as the starter motor. The chemical reaction is reversible, so that when the generator is producing a voltage (electrical pressure) greater than that produced by the battery, electricity is forced into the battery, and the battery is returned to its fully charged state.

Newer automobiles use alternating current generators or alternators, because they are more efficient, can be rotated at higher speeds, and have fewer brush problems. In an alternator, the field usually rotates while all the current produced passes only through the stator winding. The brushes bear against continuous slip rings. This causes the current produced to periodically reverse the direction of its flow. Diodes (electrical one way valves) block the flow of current from traveling in the wrong direction. A series of diodes is wired together to permit the alternating flow of the stator

to be rectified back to 12 volts DC for use by the vehicle's electrical system.

The voltage regulating function is performed by a regulator. The regulator is often built in to the alternator; this system is termed an integrated or internal regulator.

Distributor

REMOVAL & INSTALLATION

1974 Vehicles with Point-type Ignition
◆ See Figures 1 and 2 (p. 7)

1. Remove the distributor cap and position it out of the way.
2. Disconnect the primary coil wire and the vacuum advance hose.
3. Scribe a mark on the distributor body and the engine block showing their relationship. Mark the distributor housing to show the direction in which the rotor is pointing. Note the positioning of the vacuum advance unit.
4. Remove the hold-down bolt and clamp and remove the distributor.

To install:

5. Reinsert the distributor into its opening, aligning the previously made marks on the housing and the engine block.
6. The rotor may have to be turned either way a slight amount to align the rotor-to-housing marks.
7. Install the retaining clamp and bolt. Install the distributor cap, primary wire or electrical connector, and the vacuum hose.
8. Start the engine and check the ignition timing.
To install the distributor with the engine disturbed:
9. Turn the engine to bring No. 1 piston to the top of its compression stroke. This may be determined by placing your finger over the No. 1 spark plug hole and slowly turning the engine over. When the timing mark on the crankshaft pulley aligns with the 0 on the timing scale you will feel pressure against your finger. This is when the No. 1 cylinder is on the compression stroke.

➡**On some 400 and 455 V8 engines there is a punch mark on the distributor drive gear which indicates the rotor position. Thus, the distributor may be installed with the cap in place. Align the punch mark 2° clockwise from the No. 1 cap terminal, then rotate the distributor body ⅛ turn counterclockwise and push the distributor down into the block.**

10. Install the distributor in the engine block so that the vacuum advance unit points in the correct direction.
11. Turn the rotor so that it will point to No. 1 terminal in the cap. *It may be necessary to turn the rotor a little in either direction in order to engage the gears.*
13. Tap the starter a few times to ensure that the oil pump shaft is mated to the distributor shaft.
14. Bring the engine to No. 1 TDC again and check to see that the rotor is indeed pointing toward the No. 1 terminal of the cap.
15. After correct positioning is assured, turn the distributor housing so that the points are just opening. Tighten the retaining clamp.
16. Install the cap and primary wire. Check the ignition timing. Install the vacuum hose.

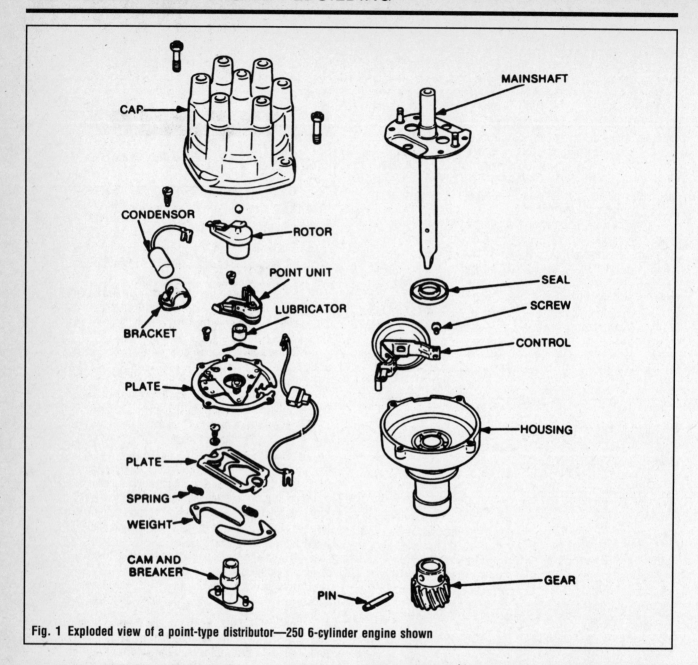

Fig. 1 Exploded view of a point-type distributor—250 6-cylinder engine shown

High Energy Ignition (HEI) Distributor

The Delco-Remy Energy Ignition (HEI) System is a breakerless, pulse triggered, transistor controlled, inductive discharge ignition system available as an option in 1974 and standard in all Pontiacs beginning in 1975.

There are only nine electrical connections in the system; the ignition switch feed wire and the eight spark plug leads. On all models, the ignition coil is located in the distributor cap, connecting directly to the rotor.

The magnetic pick up assembly located inside the distributor contains a permanent magnet, a pole piece with internal teeth, and a pick up coil. When the teeth of the rotating timer core and pole piece align, an induced voltage in the pick-up coil signals the electronic module to open the coil primary circuit. As the primary current decreases, a high voltage is induced in the secondary windings of the ignition coil directing a spark through the rotor and high voltage leads to fire the spark plugs. The dwell period is automatically controlled by the electronic module and is increased with increasing engine rpm. The HEI system features, as do most electronic ignition systems, a longer spark duration which is instrumental in firing today's lean and EGR-diluted fuel/air mixtures (a lean mixture requires a much hotter, longer duration spark to ignite it than does a rich mixture). A capacitor, which looks like the condenser in the old points-type ignition systems, is located within the HEI distributor and is used for noise (static) suppression in conjunction with the car's radio. The capacitor is not a regularly replaced component.

As noted in Chapter 2, 1981 and later models continue to use the HEI distributor, although it now incorporates an Electronic Spark Timing system (for more information on EST, please refer to Chapter 4). With the EST system, all spark timing changes are performed electronically by the Electronic Control Module (ECM) which monitors information from various engine sensors, computes the desired spark timing and then signals the distributor to change the timing accordingly. Because all timing changes are

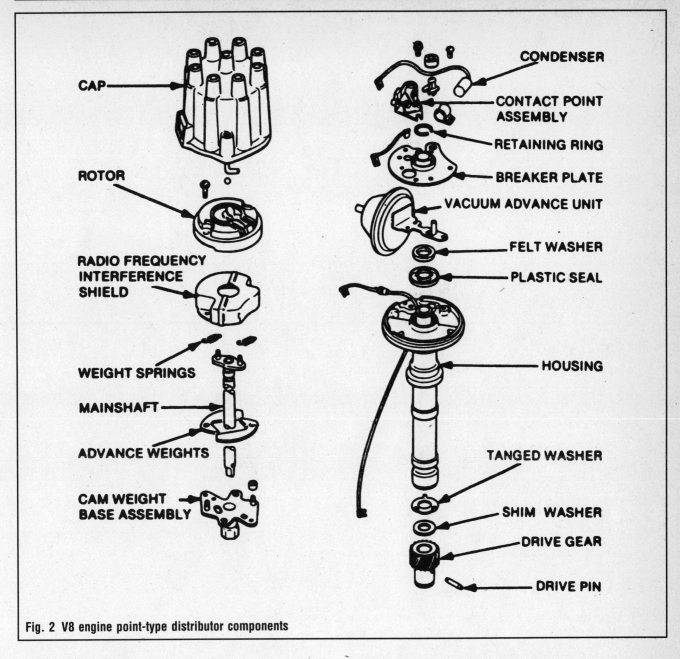

Fig. 2 V8 engine point-type distributor components

controlled electronically, no vacuum or mechanical advance systems are used.

1. Disconnect the ground cable from the battery.

2. Tag and disconnect the feed and module terminal connectors from the distributor cap.

3. On 1975–80 models, disconnect the hose at the vacuum advance unit.

4. Depress and release the 4 distributor cap-to-housing retainers and lift off the cap assembly.

5. Using a magic marker, make locating marks on the rotor and module and on the distributor housing and engine to simplify installation.

➡ The distributor must be installed with the rotor in the correct position.

6. Loosen and remove the distributor clamp bolt and clamp, and lift the distributor out of the engine. Noting the relative posi-

tion of the rotor and module alignment marks, make a second mark on the rotor to align it with the mark on the module.

To install:

7. With a new O-ring on the distributor housing and the second mark on the rotor aligned with the mark on the module, install the distributor, taking care to align the mark on the housing with the one on the engine. It may be necessary to lift the distributor and turn the rotor slightly to align the gears and the oil pump driveshaft.

8. With the respective marks aligned, install the clamp and bolt finger-tight.

9. Install and secure the distributor cap.

10. Connect the feed and module connectors to the distributor cap.

11. Connect a timing light to the engine and plug the vacuum hose.

12. Connect the ground cable to the battery.

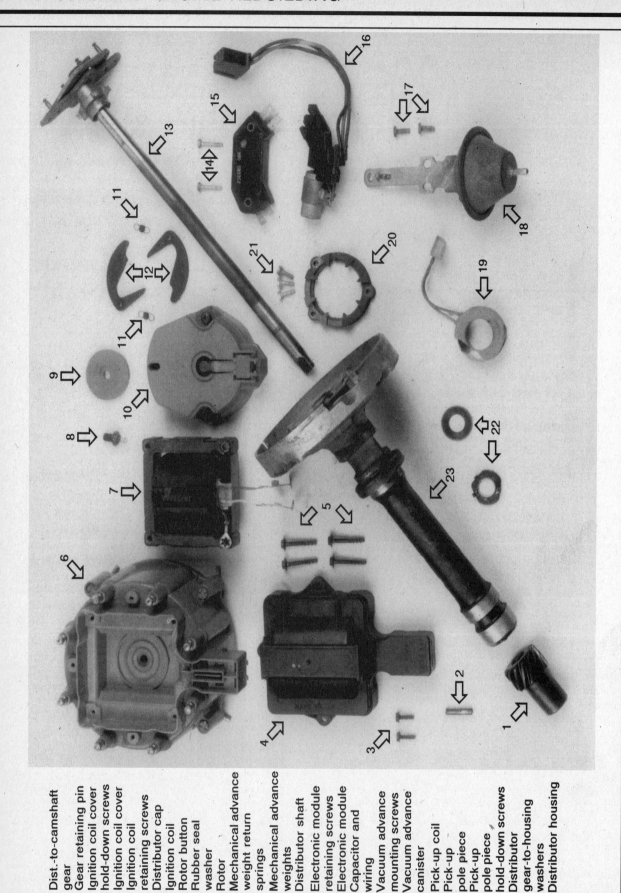

HEI DISTRIBUTOR COMPONENTS

1. Dist.-to-camshaft gear
2. Gear retaining pin
3. Ignition coil cover hold-down screws
4. Ignition coil cover
5. Ignition coil retaining screws
6. Distributor cap
7. Ignition coil
8. Rotor button
9. Rubber seal washer
10. Rotor
11. Mechanical advance weight return springs
12. Mechanical advance weights
13. Distributor shaft
14. Electronic module retaining screws
15. Electronic module
16. Capacitor and wiring
17. Vacuum advance mounting screws
18. Vacuum advance canister
19. Pick-up coil
20. Pick-up pole piece
21. Pick-up pole piece hold-down screws
22. Distributor gear-to-housing washers
23. Distributor housing

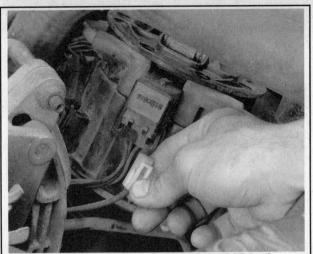

To remove the distributor, disconnect the BAT feed wire . . .

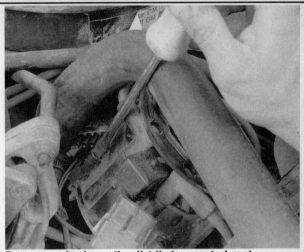

Depress and release the distributor cap-to-housing retainers . . .

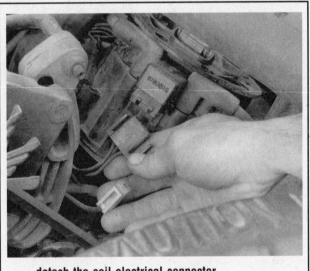

. . . detach the coil electrical connector

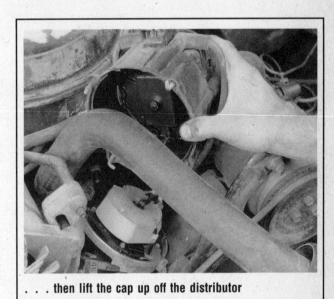

. . . then lift the cap up off the distributor

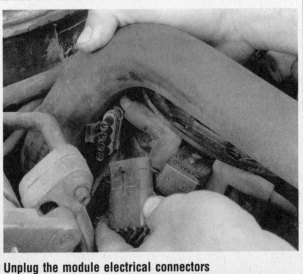

Unplug the module electrical connectors

Use a marker to matchmark the rotor to the distributor housing

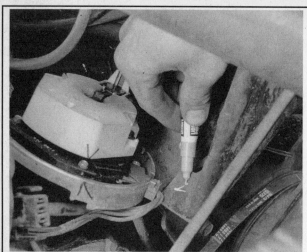

Matchmark the position of the distributor in the engine block

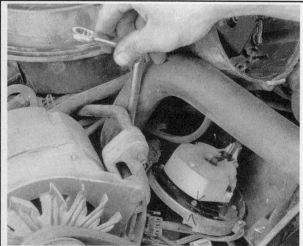

Use a distributor wrench to unfasten the hold-down bolt . . .

. . . then remove the distributor from the engine

13. Start the engine and set the timing.

14. Turn the engine off and tighten the distributor clamp bolt. Disconnect the timing light and unplug and disconnect the hose to the vacuum advance.

Alternator

◆ **See Figures 3 and 4**

The alternating current generator (alternator) supplies a continuous output of electrical energy at all engine speeds. The belt-driven alternator generates electrical energy and recharges the battery by supplying it with electrical current. The alternator consists of four main assemblies: two end frame assemblies, a stator assembly, and a rotor assembly. The rotor assembly is supported in the drive end frame by a ball bearing and at the other end by a roller bearing. These bearings are permanently lubricated and require no maintenance. There are six diodes in the end frame assembly. These diodes are electrical check valves that also change the alternating current developed within the stator windings to direct current (DC) at the output (BAT) terminal. Three of these diodes are negative and are mounted flush with the end frame while the other three are positive and are mounted into a component called a heat sink (which serves as a reservoir for excess heat, thus protecting the alternator). The positive diodes are easily identified as the ones within small cavities or depressions.

No periodic adjustments or maintenance of any kind, except for regular belt adjustments, are required on the entire alternator assembly. Alternator output, in amps, is sometimes stamped on the case of each unit, near the mounting hole. Output ratings of the alternators fitted to engines covered here are 37, 42, 55, 57, 61, 63, 70 and 80 amps. Regulator voltages range between 13.6 and 16 volts at 75°.

ALTERNATOR PRECAUTIONS

To prevent serious damage to the alternator and the rest of the charging system, the following precautions must be observed:

1. When installing a battery, make sure that the *positive cable is connected to the positive terminal and the negative to the negative.*

2. When jump-starting the car with another battery, make sure that like terminals are connected. This also applies when using a battery charger.

3. Never operate the alternator with the battery disconnected or otherwise on the uncontrolled open circuit. Double-check to see that all connections are tight.

4. Do not short across or ground any alternator or regulator terminals.

5. Do not try to polarize the alternator.

6. Do not apply full battery voltage to the field (brown) connector.

7. Always disconnect the battery ground cable before disconnecting the alternator lead.

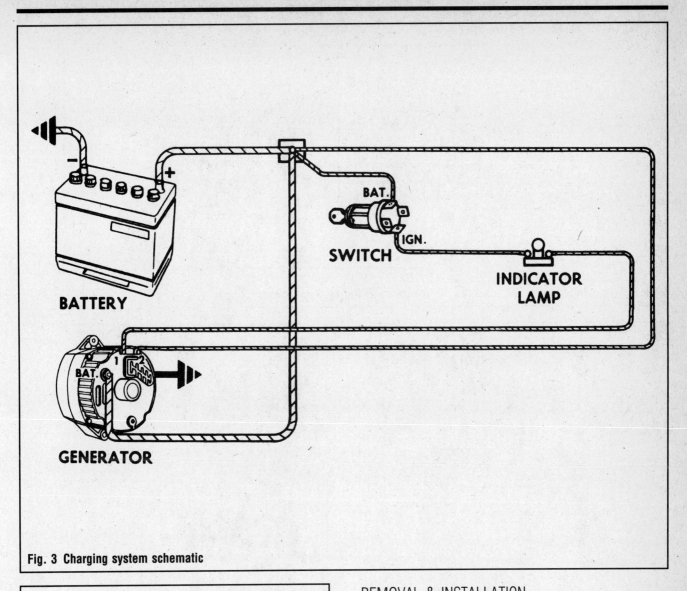

Fig. 3 Charging system schematic

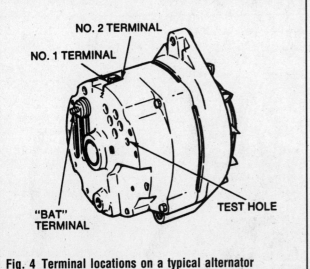

Fig. 4 Terminal locations on a typical alternator (generator)

REMOVAL & INSTALLATION

◆ **See Figure 5**

1. Disconnect the battery ground cable to prevent diode damage.

2. Tag and disconnect the alternator wiring.

3. Remove the alternator brace bolt. If the car is equipped with power steering, loosen the pump brace and mount nuts. Detach the drive belt(s).

4. Support the alternator and remove the mount bolt(s). Remove the unit from the vehicle.

5. To install, reverse the above removal procedure. Alternator belt tension is quite critical. A belt that is too tight may cause alternator bearing failure; one that is too loose will cause a gradual battery discharge. For details on correct belt adjustment, see "Drive Belts" in Chapter One.

➡ **When adjusting alternator belt tension, apply pressure at the center of the alternator unit, NEVER against either end frame.**

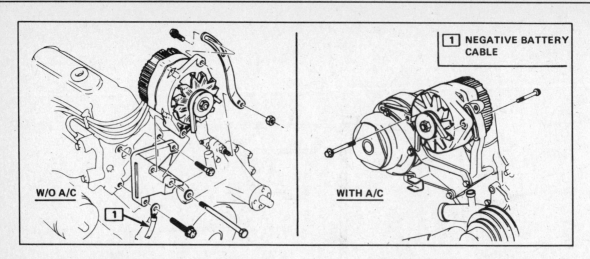

Fig. 5 Generally, all alternators are mounted in basically the same manner

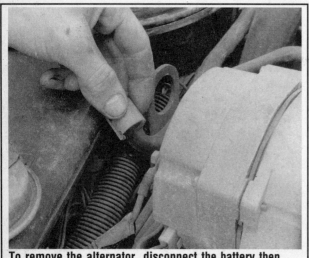

To remove the alternator, disconnect the battery then pull off the terminal cap

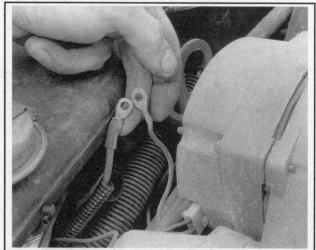

. . . then remove the terminal connectors from the rear of the alternator

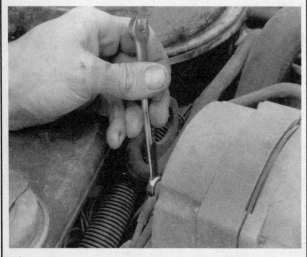

Use a wrench to unfasten the terminal retaining nut . . .

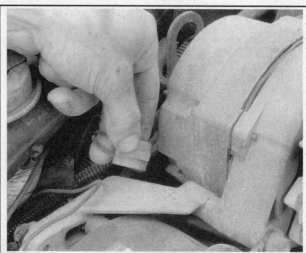

Make sure to unplug all of the alternator electrical connectors

Remove the alternator brace bolt

Use a wrench to loosen . . .

. . . then remove the alternator mounting bolt

Remove the alternator from the vehicle

TESTING

Preliminary Tests

1. If you suspect a defect in your charging system, first perform these general checks before going on to more specific tests.

2. Check the condition of the alternator belt and tighten if necessary.

3. Clean the battery cable connections at the battery. Make sure the connections between the battery wires and the battery clamps are good. Reconnect the negative terminal only and proceed to the next step.

4. With the key **OFF,** insert a test light between the positive terminal on the battery and the disconnected positive battery terminal clamp. If the test light comes on, there is a short in the electrical system of the car. The short must be repaired before proceeding. If the light does not come on, then proceed to the next step.

➡**If the car is equipped with an electric clock, the clock must be disconnected.**

5. Check the charging system wiring for any obvious breaks or shorts.

6. Check the battery to make sure it is fully charged and in good condition.

Operational Test

➡**You will need a current indicator to perform this test. If the current indicator is to give an accurate reading, the battery cables must be the same gauge and length as the original equipment.**

1. With the engine running and all electrical systems turned off, place a current indicator over the positive battery cable.

2. If a charge of roughly five amps is recorded, the charging system is working. If a draw of about five amps is recorded, the system is not working. The needle moves toward the battery when a charge condition is indicated, and away from the battery when a draw condition is indicated.

3. If a draw is indicated, proceed with further testing. If an excessive charge (10–15 amps) is indicated, the regulator may be at fault.

Output Test

1. You will need an ammeter for this test.
2. Disconnect the battery ground cable.
3. Disconnect the wire from the battery terminal on the alternator.
4. Connect the ammeter negative lead to the battery terminal wire removed in step three, and connect the ammeter positive lead to the battery terminal on the alternator.
5. Reconnect the battery ground cable and turn on all electrical accessories. If the battery is fully charged, disconnect the coil wire and bump the starter a few times to partially discharge it.
6. Start the engine and run it until you obtain a maximum current reading on the ammeter.
7. If the current is within ten amps of the rated output of the alternator, the alternator is working properly. If the current is not within ten amps, insert a screwdriver in the test hole in the end frame of the alternator and ground the tab in the test hole against the side of the hole.
8. If the current is now within ten amps of the rated output, remove the alternator and have the voltage regulator replaced. If it is still below ten amps of rated output, have the alternator repaired. See the alternator and regulator output chart in this chapter.

Voltage Regulator

The voltage regulator works with the battery and alternator to comprise the charging system. As its name implies, the voltage regulator regulates the voltage output of the alternator to a safe level (so the alternator does not overcharge the battery). A properly working regulator also prevents excessive voltage from burning out wiring, bulbs and other electrical components. All Pontiac models covered in this guide are equipped with integral regulators, which are built into the alternator case. The regulators are solid state and require no maintenance or adjustment.

Starter

REMOVAL & INSTALLATION

▸ **See Figures 6 and 7**

➡**The starters on some engines require the addition of shims to provide proper clearance between the starter pinion gear and the flywheel. These shims are available in .015 in. sizes from Pontiac dealers. Flat washers can be used if shims are unavailable.**

1. Disconnect the negative battery cable.
2. Jack up the car to a convenient working height and safely support it with jackstands.

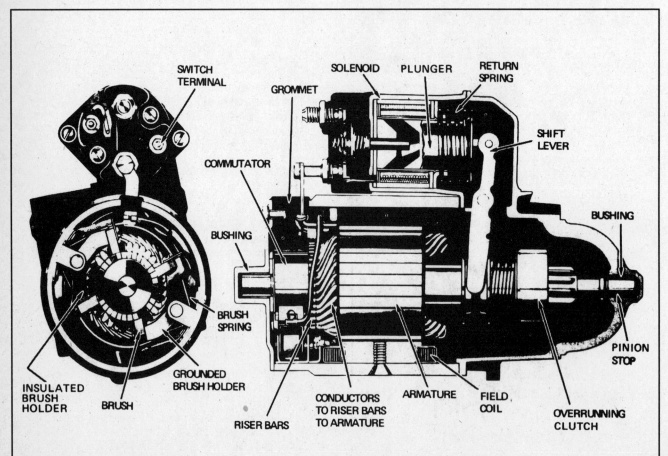

Fig. 6 Cross-sectional view of a starter motor

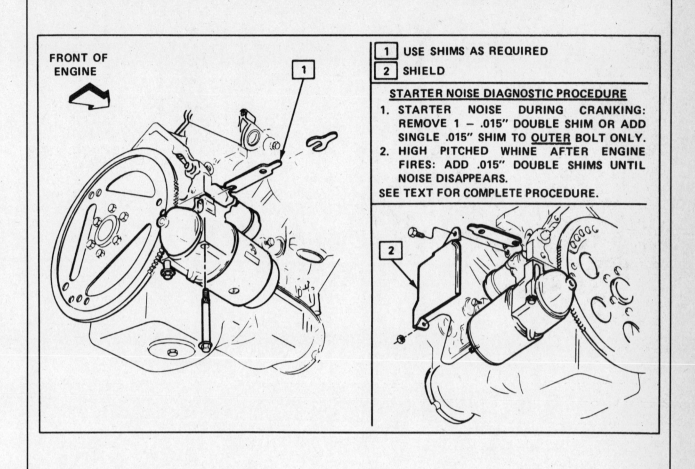

FRONT OF ENGINE

| 1 | USE SHIMS AS REQUIRED |
| 2 | SHIELD |

STARTER NOISE DIAGNOSTIC PROCEDURE

1. STARTER NOISE DURING CRANKING: REMOVE 1 — .015" DOUBLE SHIM OR ADD SINGLE .015" SHIM TO OUTER BOLT ONLY.
2. HIGH PITCHED WHINE AFTER ENGINE FIRES: ADD .015" DOUBLE SHIMS UNTIL NOISE DISAPPEARS.

SEE TEXT FOR COMPLETE PROCEDURE.

Fig. 7 Starter motor mounting—V6 on left, diesel on right, other engines similar

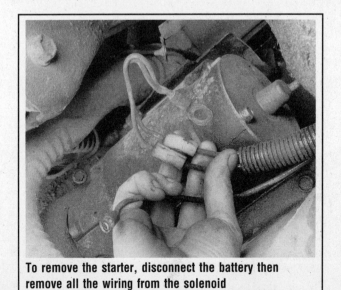

To remove the starter, disconnect the battery then remove all the wiring from the solenoid

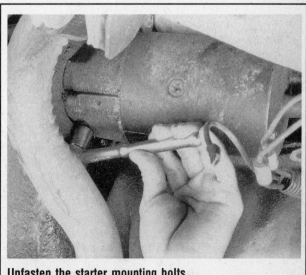

Unfasten the starter mounting bolts . . .

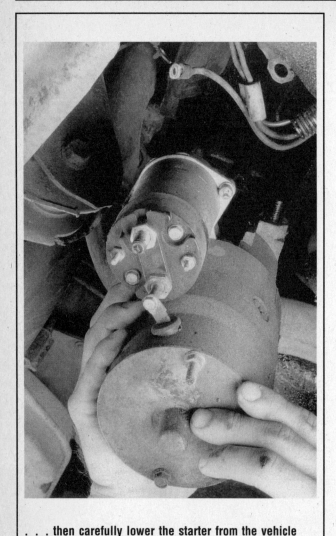

. . . then carefully lower the starter from the vehicle

3. Disconnect all wiring from the starter solenoid. Replace each nut as the connector is removed, as thread sizes differ from connector to connector. Tag the wires for later connection.

4. Remove the flywheel housing cover. On automatic transmission V6s, disconnect the oil cooler lines at the transmission.

5. Starter removal on certain models may necessitate the removal of the frame support. This support runs from the corner of the frame to the front crossmember. To remove:

    a. Loosen the mounting bolt that attaches the support to the corner of the frame.

    b. Loosen and remove the mounting bolt that attaches the support to the front crossmember and then swing the support out of the way.

    c. Installation is in the reverse order of removal.

6. Remove the front bracket from the starter and the two mounting bolts. On engines with a starter solenoid heat shield, remove the front bracket upper bolt and detach the bracket from the starter.

7. Remove the front bracket bolt or nut. Lower the starter front end first, then remove the unit from the car.

8. Reverse the removal procedures to install the starter. Make sure that any shims removed are replaced (see shimming procedure below). Tighten the two mounting bolts to 25–35 ft. lbs.

SHIMMING THE STARTER

◆ See Figures 8 and 9

Starter noise during cranking and after the engine fires is often a result of too much or too little distance between the starter pinion gear and the flywheel. A high pitched whine during cranking (before the engine fires) can be caused by the pinion and flywheel being too far apart. Likewise, a whine after the engine starts (as the key is released) is often a result of the pinion-flywheel relationship being too close. In both cases flywheel damage can occur. Shims are available in .015 in. sizes to properly adjust the starter on its mount. You will also need a flywheel turning tool, available at most auto parts stores or from any auto tool store or salesperson.

If your car's starter emits the above noises, follow the shimming procedure below:

1. Disconnect the negative battery cable.

2. Remove the flywheel inspection cover on the bottom of the bellhousing.

3. Using the flywheel turning tool, turn the flywheel and exam-

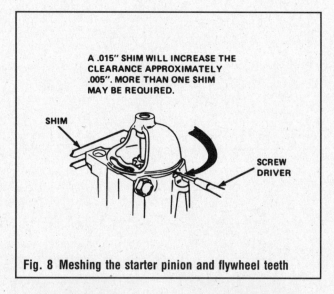

Fig. 8 Meshing the starter pinion and flywheel teeth

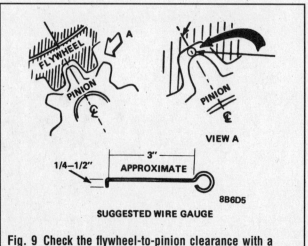

Fig. 9 Check the flywheel-to-pinion clearance with a 0.020 in. wire gauge

ine the flywheel teeth. If damage is evident, the flywheel should be replaced.

4. Insert a screwdriver into the small hole in the bottom of the starter and move the starter pinion and clutch assembly so the pinion and flywheel teeth mesh. If necessary, rotate the flywheel so that a pinion tooth is directly in the center of the two flywheel teeth and on the centerline of the two gears, as shown in the accompanying illustration.

5. Check the pinion-to-flywheel clearance by using a .020 in. wire gauge (a spark plug wire gauge may work here, or you can make your own). Make sure you center the pinion tooth between the flywheel teeth and the gauge—NOT in the corners, as you may get a false reading. If the clearance is *under* this minimum, shim the starter *away* from the flywheel by adding shim(s) one at a time to the starter mount. Check clearance after adding each shim.

6. If the clearance is a good deal *over* .020 in. (in the vicinity of .050 plus), shim the starter *towards* the flywheel. Broken or severely mangled flywheel teeth are also a good indicator that the clearance here is too great. Shimming the starter towards the fly-

wheel is done by adding shims to the outboard starter mounting pad only. Check the clearance after each shim is added. A shim of .015 in. at this location will decrease the clearance about .010 in.

STARTER OVERHAUL

▶ **See Figure 10**

Solenoid Replacement
▶ **See Figure 11**

1. Remove the screw and washer from the field strap terminal.
2. Remove the two solenoid-to-housing retaining screws and the motor terminal bolt.
3. Remove the solenoid by twisting the unit 90°.
4. To replace the solenoid, reverse the above procedure. Make sure the return spring is on the plunger, and rotate the solenoid unit into place on the starter.

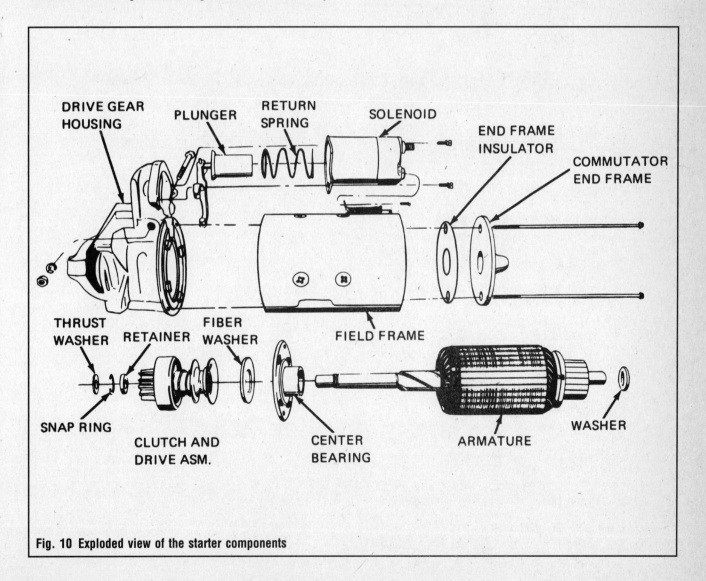

Fig. 10 Exploded view of the starter components

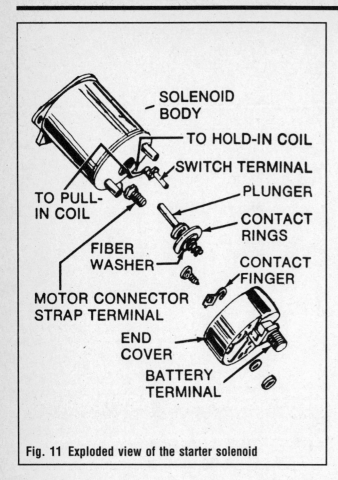

Fig. 11 Exploded view of the starter solenoid

Drive Replacement
♦ **See Figures 12, 13 and 14**

1. Disconnect the field coil straps from the solenoid.
2. Remove the through-bolts (usually 2), and separate the commutator end frame, field frame assembly, drive housing, and armature assembly from each other.

➡**On the diesel starters, remove the insulator from the end frame. The armature on the diesel starter remains in the drive end frame.**

3. On diesel starters, remove the shift lever pivot bolt. On the diesel 25 MT starter only, remove the center bearing screws and remove the drive gear housing from the armature shaft. The shift lever and plunger assembly will now fall away from the starter clutch.
4. Slide the two-piece thrust collar off the end of the armature shaft.
5. Slide a ⅝ in. deep socket, piece of pipe or an old pinion onto the shaft so that the end of the pipe, socket, or pinion butts up against the edge of the pinion retainer.
6. Place the lower end of the armature securely on a soft surface, such as a wooden block or thick piece of foam rubber. Tap the end of the socket, pipe or pinion, driving the retainer towards the armature end of the snapring.
7. Remove the snapring from the groove in the armature shaft with a pair of pliers. If the snapring is distorted, replace it with a new one during reassembly. Slide the retainer and starter drive from the shaft; on diesel starters, remove the fiber washer and the center bearing from the armature shaft. On gasoline engine start-

ers, the shift lever and plunger may be disassembled at this time (if necessary) by removing the roll pin.
To assemble:
8. Lubricate the drive end of the armature shaft with silicone lubricant. On diesel starters, install the center bearing with the bearing *toward the armature winding,* then install the fiber washer on the armature shaft.
9. Slide the starter drive onto the armature shaft *with the pinion facing outward* (away from the armature). Slide the retainer onto the shaft with the cupped surface facing outward.
10. Again support the armature on a soft surface, with the pinion on the upper end. Center the snapring on the top of the shaft (use a new ring if the old one was misshapen or damaged). Gently place a block of wood on top of the snapring so as not to move it from a centered position. Tap the wooden block with a hammer in order to force the snapring around the shaft. Slide the ring down into the snap groove.
11. Lay the armature down flat on your work surface. Slide the retainer close up onto the shaft and position it and the thrust collar next to the snapring. Using two pairs of pliers on opposite ends of the shaft, squeeze the thrust collar and the retainer together until the snapring is forced into the retainer.
12. Lube the drive housing bushing with a silicone lubricant.
13. Engage the shift lever yoke with the clutch. Position the front of the armature shaft into the bushing, then slide the complete drive assembly into the drive gear housing.

➡**On non-diesel starters the shift lever may be installed in the drive gear housing first.**

14. On the 25 MT diesel starter only, install the center bearing screws and the shift lever pivot bolt, and tighten securely.
15. Apply a sealing compound approved for this application onto the drive housing, to the solenoid flange where the field frame contacts it. Position the field frame around the armature shaft and against the drive housing. Work carefully and slowly to prevent damaging the starter brushes.
16. Lubricate the bushing in the commutator end frame with a silicone lubricant, place the leather washer onto the armature shaft, and then slide the commutator end frame over the shaft and into position against the field frame. On diesel starters, install the insulator and then the end frame onto the shaft. Line up the bolt

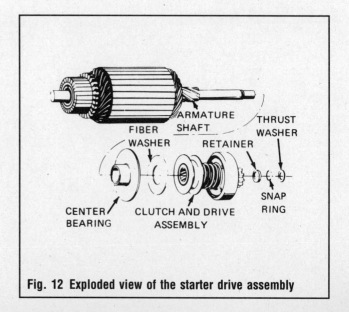

Fig. 12 Exploded view of the starter drive assembly

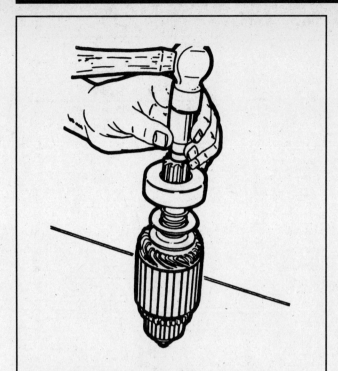

Fig. 13 Use an old socket or piece of pipe to drive the retainer toward the snapring

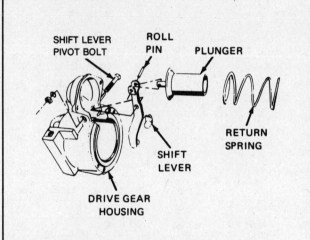

Fig. 14 Remove the shift lever and plunger from the starter

holes, then install and tighten the through-bolts (make sure they pass through the bolt holes in the insulator).

17. Connect the field coil straps to the "motor" terminal of the solenoid.

➡️**If replacement of the starter drive fails to cure improper engagements of the starter pinion to the flywheel, there may be defective parts in the solenoid and/or shift lever. The best procedure is to take the assembly to a shop where a pinion clearance check can be made by energizing the solenoid on a test bench. If the pinion clearance is incorrect, disassemble the solenoid and shift lever, inspect, and replace the worn parts.**

Brush Replacement

1. Disassemble the starter by following steps 1 and 2 of the "Drive Replacement" procedure located earlier in this section.

2. Replace the brushes one at a time to avoid having to mark the wiring. For each brush: remove the brush holding screw; remove the old brush and position the new brush in the same direction (large end toward center of field frame), position the wire connector on top of the brush, line up the holes, and reinstall the screw. Make sure the screw is snug enough to ensure good contact.

3. Reassemble starter according to steps 8–17 above.

Battery

REMOVAL & INSTALLATION

1. Disconnect the battery ground (negative) cable at the battery. Use a battery terminal puller on top-terminal batteries, if you have difficulty, as it is relatively easy to break a terminal off by prying too much. Disconnect the positive cable at the battery.

2. Unfasten the battery hold-down clamps.

3. Remove the battery.

✳✳ CAUTION

Exercise extreme care in and handling the battery—it is filled with a highly corrosive acid.

4. Installation is in the reverse order of removal, following the battery maintenance steps outlined in Chapter 1.

Battery and Starter Specifications

Year	Engine No. Cyl Displacement (cu in.)	Engine VIN Code	Battery Ampere Hour Capacity ②	Battery Volts	Terminal Grounded	Lock Test Amps	Lock Test Volts	Lock Test Torque (ft. lbs.)	No-Load Test Amps	No-Load Test Volts	No-Load Test RPM	Brush Spring Tension (oz) ①
1974	6-250	D	350	12	Neg	Not Recommended			50–80	9	5500–10,500	35
	8-350	M	350	12	Neg	Not Recommended			50–80	9	3500–6000	35
	8-350	J	350	12	Neg	Not Recommended			55–80	9	3500–6000	35
	8-400	R	430	12	Neg	Not Recommended			55–80	9	3500–6000	35
	8-400	S	450	12	Neg	Not Recommended			55–80	9	3500–6000	35
1975	6-250	D	350	12	Neg	Not Recommended			50–80	9	5500–10,500	35
	8-260	F	310	12	Neg	Not Recommended			55–80	9	7000–11,900	35
	8-350	M	350	12	Neg	Not Recommended			55–80	9	3500–6000	35
	8-350	E	350	12	Neg	Not Recommended			55–80	9	3500–6000	35
	8-350	H	350	12	Neg	Not Recommended			55–80	9	3500–6000	35
	8-350	J	310	12	Neg	Not Recommended			55–80	9	3500–6000	35
	8-400	R	430	12	Neg	Not Recommended			55–80	9	3500–6000	35
	8-400	S	450	12	Neg	Not Recommended			55–80	9	3500–6000	35
	8-455	W	420	12	Neg	Not Recommended			45–80	9	4000–6500	35
1976	V6-231	C	350	12	Neg	Not Recommended			50–80	9	5500–10,000	35
	6-250	D	350	12	Neg	Not Recommended			50–80	9	5500–10,500	35
	8-260	F	310	12	Neg	Not Recommended			55–80	9	7000–11,900	35
	8-350	M	350	12	Neg	Not Recommended			55–80	9	3500–6000	35
	8-350	E	350	12	Neg	Not Recommended			55–80	9	3500–6000	35
	8-350	H	350	12	Neg	Not Recommended			55–80	9	3500–6000	35
	8-350	J	350	12	Neg	Not Recommended			55–80	9	3500–6000	35
	8-400	S	450	12	Neg	Not Recommended			55–80	9	3500–6000	35
1977	4-151	V,1	350	12	Neg	Not Recommended			50–75	9	6500–10,500	35
	V6-231	C	350	12	Neg	Not Recommended			50–80	9	5500–10,500	35
	8-301	Y	350	12	Neg	Not Recommended			55–80	9	3500–6000	35
	8-305	U	350	12	Neg	Not Recommended			55–80	9	3500–6000	35
	8-350	R	350	12	Neg	Not Recommended			55–80	9	3500–6000	35
	8-350	L	350	12	Neg	Not Recommended			55–80	9	7500–10,500	35
	8-400	Z	350	12	Neg	Not Recommended			65–95	9	7500–10,500	35
	8-403	K	430	12	Neg	Not Recommended			65–95	9	7500–10,500	35
1978	4-151	V,1	350	12	Neg	Not Recommended			50–75	9	6500–10,500	35
	V6-231	A	350	12	Neg	Not Recommended			60–85	9	6800–10,300	35
	8-301	Y,W	310	12	Neg	Not Recommended			45–70	9	7000–11,900	35
	8-305	U	310	12	Neg	Not Recommended			60–85	9	6800–10,300	35
	8-350	R	310	12	Neg	Not Recommended			65–95	9	7500–10,500	35
	8-350	N	550	12	Neg	Not Recommended			40–140	9	8000–13,000	35
	8-350	L	310	12	Neg	Not Recommended			60–95	9	7500–10,500	35
	8-350	X	310	12	Neg	Not Recommended			60–85	9	6800–10,300	35
	8-400	Z	380	12	Neg	Not Recommended			65–95	9	7500–10,500	35
	8-403	K	430	12	Neg	Not Recommended			65–95	9	7500–10,500	35
1979	4-151	V,1	350	12	Neg	Not Recommended			50–75	9	6500–10,500	35
	V6-231	A	350	12	Neg	Not Recommended			60–85	9	6800–10,300	35

Battery and Starter Specifications

Year	Engine No. Cyl Displacement (cu in.)	Engine VIN Code	Battery			Starter							Brush Spring Tension (oz)①
			Ampere Hour Capacity②	Volts	Terminal Grounded	Lock Test			No-Load Test				
						Amps	Volts	Torque (ft. lbs.)	Amps	Volts	RPM		
1979	8-301	W	350	12	Neg	Not Recommended			45-70	9	7000-11,900		35
	8-305	G	350	12	Neg	Not Recommended			60-85	9	6800-10,300		35
	8-350	R	350	12	Neg	Not Recommended			65-95	9	7500-10,500		35
	8-350	L	350	12	Neg	Not Recommended			65-95	9	7500-10,500		35
	8-350	X	350	12	Neg	Not Recommended			65-95	9	7500-10,500		35
	8-350	N	500	12	Neg	Not Recommended			40-140	9	8000-13,000		35
1980	6-231	A,3	350	12	Neg	Not Recommended			60-85	9	6800-10,300		35
	8-265	S	350	12	Neg	Not Recommended			45-70	9	7000-11,900		35
	8-301	W	350	12	Neg	Not Recommended			45-70	9	7000-11,900		35
	8-305	H	350	12	Neg	Not Recommended			60-85	9	6800-10,300		35
	8-350	N	500	12	Neg	Not Recommended			40-140	9	8000-13,000		35
1981	V6-231	A	350	12	Neg	Not Recommended			60-85	9	6800-10,300		35
	8-265	S	370	12	Neg	Not Recommended			45-70	9	7000-11,900		35
	8-301	W	350	12	Neg	Not Recommended			60-85	9	6800-10,300		35
	8-350	N	500	12	Neg	Not Recommended			40-140	9	8000-13,000		35
1982	V6-231	A	350	12	Neg	Not Recommended			60-85	9	6800-10,300		35
	V6-252	4	370	12	Neg	Not Recommended			65-95	9	7500-10,500		35
	8-301	W	350	12	Neg	Not Recommended			60-85	9	6800-10,300		35
	8-350	N	550	12	Neg	Not Recommended			60-85	9	8000-13,000		35
1983	V6-231	A	350	12	Neg	Not Recommended			60-85	9	6800-10,300		35
	V6-252	4	370	12	Neg	Not Recommended			65-95	9	7500-10,500		35
	8-350	N	550	12	Neg	Not Recommended			160-220	9	4000-5000		35

NOTE: All 350 V8 Diesels use 2 12 volt batteries
① Minimum tension
② Cold Cranking Power in amps @ 0°F

ENGINE MECHANICAL

Engine Overhaul Tips

Most engine overhaul procedures are fairly standard. In addition to specific parts replacement procedures and specifications for your individual engine, this section is also a guide to acceptable rebuilding procedures. Examples of standard rebuilding practice are given and should be used along with specific details concerning your particular engine.

Competent and accurate machine shop services will ensure maximum performance, reliability and engine life. In most instances it is more profitable for the do-it-yourself mechanic to remove, clean and inspect the component, buy the necessary parts and deliver these to a shop for actual machine work.

On the other hand, much of the rebuilding work (crankshaft, block, bearings, piston rods, and other components) is well within the scope of the do-it-yourself mechanic's tools and abilities. You will have to decide for yourself the depth of involvement you desire in an engine repair or rebuild.

TOOLS

The tools required for an engine overhaul or parts replacement will depend on the depth of your involvement. With a few exceptions, they will be the tools found in a mechanic's tool kit (see Section 1 of this manual). More in-depth work will require some or all of the following:
• A dial indicator (reading in thousandths) mounted on a universal base
• Micrometers and telescope gauges
• Jaw and screw-type pullers
• Scraper
• Valve spring compressor
• Ring groove cleaner
• Piston ring expander and compressor
• Ridge reamer
• Cylinder hone or glaze breaker
• Plastigage®
• Engine stand
The use of most of these tools is illustrated in this chapter. Many can be rented for a one-time use from a local parts jobber or tool supply house specializing in automotive work.

Occasionally, the use of special tools is called for. See the information on Special Tools and the Safety Notice in the front of this book before substituting another tool.

INSPECTION TECHNIQUES

Procedures and specifications are given in this chapter for inspecting, cleaning and assessing the wear limits of most major components. Other procedures such as Magnaflux® and Zyglo® can be used to locate material flaws and stress cracks. Magnaflux® is a magnetic process applicable only to ferrous materials. The Zyglo® process coats the material with a fluorescent dye penetrant and can be used on any material.

Checking for suspected surface cracks can be more readily made using spot check dye. The dye is sprayed onto the suspected area, wiped off and the area sprayed with a developer. Cracks will show up brightly.

OVERHAUL TIPS

Aluminum has become extremely popular for use in engines, due to its low weight. Observe the following precautions when handling aluminum parts:
• Never hot tank aluminum parts (the caustic hot tank solution will eat the aluminum.
• Remove all aluminum parts (identification tag, etc.) from engine parts prior to the tanking.
• Always coat threads lightly with engine oil or anti-seize compounds before installation, to prevent seizure.
• Never overtorque bolts or spark plugs especially in aluminum threads.

Stripped threads in any component can be repaired using any of several commercial repair kits (Heli-Coil®, Microdot®, Keenserts®, etc.).

When assembling the engine, any parts that will be exposed to frictional contact must be prelubed to provide lubrication at initial start-up. Any product specifically formulated for this purpose can be used, but engine oil is not recommended as a prelube in most cases.

When semi-permanent (locked, but removable) installation of bolts or nuts is desired, threads should be cleaned and coated with Loctite® or another similar, commercial non-hardening sealant.

REPAIRING DAMAGED THREADS

Several methods of repairing damaged threads are available. Heli-Coil® (shown here), Keenserts® and Microdot® are among the most widely used. All involve basically the same principle—

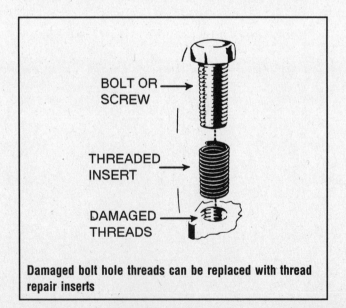

BOLT OR SCREW

THREADED INSERT

DAMAGED THREADS

Damaged bolt hole threads can be replaced with thread repair inserts

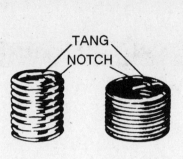

Standard thread repair insert (left), and spark plug thread insert

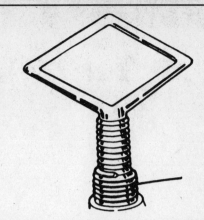

Screw the insert onto the installer tool until the tang engages the slot. Thread the insert into the hole until it is ¼–½ turn below the top surface, then remove the tool and break off the tang using a punch

Drill out the damaged threads with the specified size bit. Be sure to drill completely through the hole or to the bottom of a blind hole

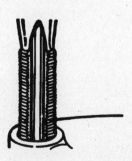

Using the kit, tap the hole in order to receive the thread insert. Keep the tap well oiled and back it out frequently to avoid clogging the threads

drilling out stripped threads, tapping the hole and installing a pre-wound insert—making welding, plugging and oversize fasteners unnecessary.

Two types of thread repair inserts are usually supplied: a standard type for most inch coarse, inch fine, metric course and metric fine thread sizes and a spark lug type to fit most spark plug port sizes. Consult the individual tool manufacturer's catalog to determine exact applications. Typical thread repair kits will contain a selection of prewound threaded inserts, a tap (corresponding to the outside diameter threads of the insert) and an installation tool. Spark plug inserts usually differ because they require a tap equipped with pilot threads and a combined reamer/tap section. Most manufacturers also supply blister-packed thread repair inserts separately in addition to a master kit containing a variety of taps and inserts plus installation tools.

Before attempting to repair a threaded hole, remove any snapped, broken or damaged bolts or studs. Penetrating oil can be used to free frozen threads. The offending item can usually be removed with locking pliers or using a screw/stud extractor. After the hole is clear, the thread can be repaired, as shown in the series of accompanying illustrations and in the kit manufacturer's instructions.

Checking Engine Compression

A noticeable lack of engine power, excessive oil consumption and/or poor fuel mileage measured over an extended period are all indicators of internal engine wear. Worn piston rings, scored and worn cylinder bores, blown head gaskets, sticking or burnt valves and worn valve seats are all possible culprits here. A check of each cylinder's compression will help you locate the problems.

As mentioned in the "Tools and Equipment" section of Chapter 1, a screw-in compression gauge is more accurate than the type you simply hold against the spark plug hole, although it takes slightly longer to use (it's worth it). To check compression:
1. Warm the engine up to operating temperature.
2. Remove all of the spark plugs.
3. Disconnect the high tension wire from the ignition coil.

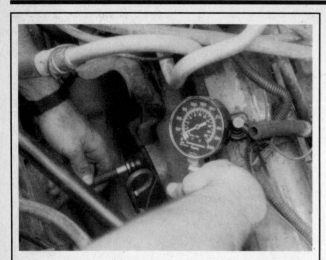

A screw-in type compression gauge is more accurate and easier to use without an assistant

4. Screw the compression gauge into the No. 1 spark plug hole until the fitting is snug. *Be very careful not to crossthread the hole, as the head is aluminum.*

5. Fully open the throttle either by operating the carburetor throttle linkage by hand, or on fuel injected cars having an assistant "floor" the accelerator pedal.

6. Ask the assistant to crank the engine a few times using the ignition switch.

7. Record the highest reading on the gauge.

➡**The variation between or uniformity among cylinders is the important thing to look for when testing engine compression, not necessarily the highest or lowest cylinder readings.**

8. Repeat the procedure for the remaining cylinders, recording each cylinder's compression. The difference between each cylinder should be no more than 14 pounds. If a cylinder is unusually low, pour a tablespoon of clean engine oil into the cylinder through the spark plug hole and repeat the compression test. If the compression comes up after adding the oil, it appears that

that cylinder's piston rings or bore are damaged or worn. If the pressure remains low, the valves may not be seating properly (a valve job is needed) or the head gasket may be blown near that cylinder.

Design

All Pontiac and other GM-built engines covered in this guide—whether inline four, six, V6 or V8—are water-cooled powerplants with pushrod valve actuation. All engines use cast iron cylinder blocks and heads.

The 151 cu. in. inline four and the 250 cu. in. inline six are nearly identical in construction, the four being basically a six with two cylinders removed. Both engines have gear-driven camshafts, hydraulic lifters and pivot-type pressed-steel rocker arms like some of the V8s. The only major variation in these engines is the manifolding on the 151 four. The 1977 and 1978 151 cylinder heads have both their intake and exhaust manifolds mounted on the same side, while the 1979 engines feature a "crossflow" design with the intake and exhaust manifolds mounted on opposite sides of the head; this allows the engine to breathe much more efficiently.

The gasoline V8s are also very similar in construction, and share common design features such as chain-driven camshafts, hydraulic lifters and pressed-steel rocker arms. The Buick-built engines, including V6s, differ in that they have their rockers mounted on shafts. Because of this similarity between engines, many removal and installation procedures given here will simultaneously cover all GM-built engines used in mid-size Pontiacs. Likewise, the 231 and 252 V6 engines are nearly identical to themselves and to the Buick V8s.

The 350 V8 diesel is derived from the 350 cu. in. gasoline engine, except that the cylinder block, crankshaft and main bearings, connecting rods and wrist pins are heavier duty in the diesel (due to the much higher compression ratio). The diesel cylinder heads, intake manifold, ignition and fuel systems are also different from their gasoline engine counterparts. Aircraft-type hydraulic roller valve lifters are used in the diesel.

General Engine Specifications

Year	Engine V.I.N. Code	Engine Type (No. of cyl-C.I.D.)	Engine Manufac-turer	Carb Type	Horsepower @ rpm ①	Torque @ rpm (ft. lbs.) ①	Bore x Stroke (in.)	Compression Ratio	Oil Pressure (psi @ 2000 rpm)
1974	D	6-250	Chev.	1 bbl	100 @ 3600	175 @ 1800	3.88 x 3.53	8.5 : 1	40
	M	8-350	Pont.	2 bbl	155 @ 3600	275 @ 2400	3.88 x 3.75	8.0 : 1	②
	N	8-350	Pont.	2 bbl	170 @ 4000	290 @ 2400	3.88 x 3.75	8.0 : 1	②
	J	8-350	Pont.	4 bbl	170 @ 4000	280 @ 2000	3.88 x 3.75	8.0 : 1	②
	K	8-350	Pont.	4 bbl	200 @ 4400	295 @ 2800	3.88 x 3.75	8.0 : 1	②
	R	8-400	Pont.	2 bbl	175 @ 3600	315 @ 2000	4.12 x 3.75	8.0 : 1	②
	S	8-400	Pont.	4 bbl	225 @ 4000	330 @ 2800	4.12 x 3.75	8.0 : 1	②
1975	D	6-250	Chev.	1 bbl	105 @ 3800	185 @ 1200	3.88 x 3.53	8.25 : 1	40
	F	8-260	Olds.	2 bbl	110 @ 3400	205 @ 1800	3.50 x 3.38	7.5 : 1	40
	M	8-350	Pont.	2 bbl	150 @ 3600	270 @ 2400	3.88 x 3.75	8.0 : 1	②
	E	8-350	Pont.	4 bbl	170 @ 4000	290 @ 2400	3.88 x 3.75	8.0 : 1	②
	H	8-350	Buick	2 bbl	145 @ 3400	240 @ 2000	3.80 x 3.85	8.0 : 1	37 @ 2600
	J	8-350	Buick	4 bbl	165 @ 3800	260 @ 2200	3.80 x 3.85	8.0 : 1	37 @ 2600
	R	8-400	Pont.	2 bbl	170 @ 3600	315 @ 2000	4.12 x 3.75	8.0 : 1	②
	S	8-400	Pont.	4 bbl	185 @ 4000	320 @ 2400	4.12 x 3.75	8.0 : 1	②
	W	8-455	Pont.	4 bbl	200 @ 3600	355 @ 2400	4.15 x 4.21	8.0 : 1	②
1976	C	V6-231	Buick	2 bbl	105 @ 3200	185 @ 2000	3.80 x 3.40	8.0 : 1	37 @ 2600
	D	6-250	Chev.	1 bbl	105 @ 3800	185 @ 1200	3.88 x 3.53	8.25 : 1	40
	F	8-260	Olds.	2 bbl	110 @ 3400	205 @ 1800	3.50 x 3.38	7.5 : 1	40
	M	8-350	Pont.	2 bbl	145 @ 3400	265 @ 2400	3.88 x 3.75	7.6 : 1	②
	E	8-350	Pont.	4 bbl	175 @ 4000	280 @ 2000	3.88 x 3.75	7.6 : 1	②
	H	8-350	Buick	2 bbl	145 @ 3400	240 @ 2000	3.80 x 3.85	8.0 : 1	37 @ 2600
	J	8-350	Buick	4 bbl	155 @ 3400	280 @ 1800	3.80 x 3.85	8.0 : 1	37 @ 2600
	S	8-400	Pont.	4 bbl	185 @ 3600	310 @ 1600	4.12 x 3.75	7.6 : 1	②
	W	8-455	Pont.	4 bbl	200 @ 3500	330 @ 2000	4.15 x 4.21	7.6 : 1	②
1977	V,1	4-151	Pont.	2 bbl	88 @ 4400	128 @ 2400	4.00 x 3.00	8.0 : 1	36 – 41
	C	V6-231	Buick	2 bbl	105 @ 3200	185 @ 2000	3.80 x 3.40	8.0 : 1	37 @ 2400
	Y	8-301	Pont.	2 bbl	135 @ 4000	235 @ 2000	4.00 x 3.00	8.2 : 1	35 – 40 @ 2600
	U	8-305	Chev.	2 bbl	148 @ 3800	245 @ 2400	3.73 x 3.48	8.5 : 1	32 – 40
	R	8-350	Olds.	4 bbl	170 @ 3800	275 @ 2000	4.05 x 3.38	7.6 : 1	30 – 45 @ 1500
	L	8-350	Chev.	4 bbl	170 @ 3800	270 @ 2400	4.00 x 3.48	8.2 : 1	30 – 45 @ 2400
	Z	8-400	Pont.	4 bbl	180 @ 3600	270 @ 2400	4.12 x 3.75	7.7 : 1	35 – 40 @ 2600
	K	8-403	Olds.	4 bbl	185 @ 3600	320 @ 2200	4.35 x 3.38	8.0 : 1	30 – 45 @ 1500
1978	V,1	4-151	Pont.	2 bbl	85 @ 4400	123 @ 2800	4.00 x 3.00	8.0 : 1	36 – 41
	A	V6-231	Buick	2 bbl	105 @ 3200	185 @ 2000	3.80 x 3.40	8.2 : 1	37 @ 2400
	Y	8-301	Pont.	2 bbl	135 @ 4000	250 @ 1600	4.00 x 3.00	8.2 : 1	35 – 40 @ 2600
	U	8-305	Chev.	2 bbl	148 @ 3800	245 @ 2400	3.73 x 3.48	8.5 : 1	32 – 40
	X	8-350	Buick	4 bbl	165 @ 4000	290 @ 1600	3.80 x 3.85	8.0 : 1	37 @ 2600
	R	8-350	Olds.	4 bbl	160 @ 4000	280 @ 1600	4.05 x 3.38	7.9 : 1	30 – 45 @ 1500
	L	8-350	Chev.	4 bbl	170 @ 3800	270 @ 2400	4.00 x 3.48	8.2 : 1	30 – 45 @ 2400
	Z	8-400	Pont.	4 bbl	180 @ 3800	325 @ 1600	4.12 x 3.75	7.7 : 1	35 – 40 @ 2600
	K	8-403	Olds.	4 bbl	180 @ 3400	315 @ 2200	4.35 x 3.38	7.9 : 1	30 – 45 @ 1500
1979	V,1	4-151	Pont.	2 bbl	85 @ 4400	123 @ 2800	4.00 x 3.00	8.0 : 1	36 – 41
	A	V6-231	Buick	2 bbl	115 @ 3800	190 @ 2000	3.80 x 3.40	8.2 : 1	34
	W	8-301	Pont.	4 bbl	150 @ 4000	240 @ 2000	4.00 x 3.00	8.1 : 1	35 – 40
	G	8-305	Chev.	2 bbl	140 @ 3800	270 @ 2400	3.73 x 3.48	8.5 : 1	40
	H	8-305	Chev.	4 bbl	160 @ 3800	235 @ 2400	3.73 x 3.48	8.5 : 1	40
	X	8-350	Buick	4 bbl	155 @ 3400	280 @ 1800	3.80 x 3.85	8.0 : 1	35
	R	8-350	Olds.	4 bbl	170 @ 3800	275 @ 2000	4.05 x 3.38	8.0 : 1	35
	L	8-350	Chev.	4 bbl	160 @ 3800	260 @ 2400	4.00 x 3.48	8.5 : 1	40
	N	8-350	Olds.	Diesel	125 @ 3600	225 @ 1600	4.05 x 3.38	22.5 : 1	40

General Engine Specifications (cont.)

Year	Engine V.I.N. Code	Engine Type (No. of cyl- C.I.D.)	Engine Manufac- turer	Carb Type	Horsepower @ rpm ①	Torque @ rpm (ft. lbs.) ①	Bore x Stroke (in.)	Compression Ratio	Oil Pressure (psi @ 2000 rpm)
1980	A	V6-231	Buick	2 bbl	115 @ 3800	188 @ 2000	3.80 x 3.40	8.0 : 1	37
	S	8-265	Pont.	2 bbl	120 @ 3600	210 @ 1600	3.75 x 3.00	8.0 : 1	40 @ 2600
	W	8-301	Pont.	4 bbl	150 @ 4000	240 @ 2000	4.00 x 3.00	8.2 : 1	40 @ 2600
	H	8-305	Chev.	4 bbl	160 @ 3800	235 @ 2400	3.73 x 3.48	8.5 : 1	40
	N	8-350	Olds.	Diesel	125 @ 3600	225 @ 1600	4.05 x 3.38	22.5 : 1	40
1981	A	V6-231	Buick	2 bbl	115 @ 3800	188 @ 2000	3.80 x 3.40	8.0 : 1	37
	S	8-265	Pont.	2 bbl	120 @ 3600	210 @ 1600	3.75 x 3.00	8.0 : 1	40
	W	8-301	Pont.	4 bbl	150 @ 4000	240 @ 2000	4.00 x 3.00	8.2 : 1	40 @ 2600
	N	8-350	Olds.	Diesel	105 @ 3200	205 @ 1600	4.05 x 3.38	22.5 : 1	40 @ 1500
1982	A	V6-231	Buick	2 bbl	110 @ 3800	190 @ 1600	3.80 x 3.40	8.0 : 1	37
	4	V6-252	Buick	4 bbl	125 @ 4000	205 @ 2000	3.96 x 3.40	8.0 : 1	37
	W	8-301	Pont.	4 bbl	150 @ 4000	240 @ 2000	4.00 x 3.00	8.2 : 1	40 @ 2600
	N	8-350	Olds.	Diesel	105 @ 3200	200 @ 1600	4.05 x 3.38	21.6 : 1	40 @ 1500
1983	A	V6-231	Buick	2 bbl	110 @ 3800	190 @ 1600	3.80 x 3.40	8.0 : 1	37
	4	V6-252	Buick	4 bbl	125 @ 4000	205 @ 2000	3.96 x 3.40	8.0 : 1	37
	H	8-305	Chev.	4 bbl	150 @ 3800	240 @ 2400	3.73 x 3.48	8.6 : 1	45
	N	8-350	Olds.	Diesel	105 @ 3200	200 @ 1600	4.05 x 3.38	21.6 : 1	40 @ 1500

C.I.D.—Cubic Inch Displacement
① Horsepower and torque are SAE net figures. They are measured at the rear of the transmission with all accessories installed and operating. Since the figures vary when a given engine is installed in different models, some are representative rather than exact.
② 55–60 psi above 2600 rpm
③ Manual trans.; automatic 245 @ 2000 rpm

Valve Specifications

Year	Engine No. Cyl. Displacement (cu in.)	Seat Angle (deg)	Face Angle (deg)	Spring Test Pressure (lbs. @ in.)	Spring Installed Height (in.)	Stem to Guide Clearance (in.)		Stem Diameter (in.)	
						Intake	Exhaust	Intake	Exhaust
1974	6-250	46	45	187 @ 1.27	$1\frac{21}{32}$	0.0010–0.0027	0.0010–0.0027	0.3414	0.3414
	8-350	45	44	131 @ 1.18	$1\frac{19}{32}$	0.0016–0.0033	0.0021–0.0038	0.3416	0.3411
	8-400 2 bbl	45	44	139 @ 1.17	$1\frac{9}{16}$	0.0016–0.0033	0.0021–0.0038	0.3416	0.3411
	8-400 4 bbl	30	29	143 @ 1.15	$1\frac{19}{32}$	0.0016–0.0033	0.0021–0.0038	0.3416	0.3411
1975	6-250	46	45	187 @ 1.27	$1\frac{21}{32}$	0.0010–0.0027	0.0010–0.0027	0.3414	0.3414
	8-260	[1]	[2]	187 @ 1.27	$1\frac{43}{64}$	0.0010–0.0027	0.0015–0.0032	0.3429	0.3427
	8-350 Pont.	30	29	131 @ 1.18	$1\frac{19}{32}$	0.0016–0.0033	0.0021–0.0038	0.3416	0.3411
	8-350 Buick	45	45	164 @ 1.34	$1\frac{47}{64}$	0.0015–0.0035	0.0015–0.0032	0.3407	0.3409
	8-400 2 bbl	30	29	186 @ 1.27	$1\frac{9}{16}$	0.0016–0.0033	0.0021–0.0038	0.3416	0.3411
	8-400 4 bbl	30[3]	29[3]	186 @ 1.27	$1\frac{19}{32}$	0.0016–0.0033	0.0021–0.0038	0.3416	0.3411
	8-455	30[3]	29[3]	143 @ 1.15	$1\frac{9}{16}$	0.0016–0.0033	0.0021–0.0038	0.3416	0.3411
1976	V6-231	45	45	164 @ 1.34	$1\frac{47}{64}$	0.0015–0.0035	0.0015–0.0035	0.3400	0.3400
	8-250	46	45	187 @ 1.27	$1\frac{21}{32}$	0.0010–0.0027	0.0010–0.0027	0.3414	0.3414
	8-260	[1]	[2]	187 @ 1.27	$1\frac{43}{64}$	0.0010–0.0027	0.0015–0.0032	0.3429	0.3427
	8-350 Pont.	30	29	131 @ 1.18	$1\frac{19}{32}$	0.0016–0.0033	0.0021–0.0038	0.3416	0.3411
	8-350 Buick	45	45	164 @ 1.34	$1\frac{47}{64}$	0.0015–0.0035	0.0015–0.0032	0.3407	0.3409
	8-400	30[3]	29[3]	186 @ 1.27	$1\frac{19}{32}$	0.0016–0.0033	0.0021–0.0038	0.3416	0.3411
	8-455	30[3]	29[3]	143 @ 1.15	$1\frac{9}{16}$	0.0016–0.0033	0.0021–0.0038	0.3416	0.3411
1977	4-151	46	45	160 @ 1.25	$1\frac{21}{32}$	0.0010–0.0027	0.0010–0.0027[4]	0.3420	0.3420
	V6-231	45	45	164 @ 1.34	$1\frac{47}{64}$	0.0015–0.0035	0.0015–0.0035	0.3405	0.3405
	8-301	46	45	165 @ 1.29	$1\frac{21}{32}$	0.0010–0.0027	0.0010–0.0027	0.3420	0.3420
	8-305	46	45	200 @ 1.16	[5]	0.0010–0.0037	0.0010–0.0037	0.3414	0.3414
	8-350 Olds.	45[6]	44[6]	180 @ 1.34	$1\frac{47}{64}$	0.0010–0.0027	0.0015–0.0032	0.3425	0.3420
	8-350 Chev.	46	45	200 @ 1.16	[5]	0.0010–0.0037	0.0010–0.0037	0.3414	0.3414
	8-400	30	29	135 @ 1.18	$1\frac{19}{32}$	0.0016–0.0033	0.0021–0.0038	0.3417	0.3410
	8-403	45	46	186 @ 1.27	$1\frac{47}{64}$	0.0010–0.0027	0.0015–0.0032	0.3428	0.3423
1978	4-151	46	45	160 @ 1.25	$1\frac{11}{16}$	0.0010–0.0027	0.0010–0.0027[4]	0.3420	0.3420
	V6-231	45	45	168 @ 1.34[7]	$1\frac{47}{64}$	0.0015–0.0032	0.0015–0.0032	0.3408	0.3408
	8-301	46	45	165 @ 1.29	$1\frac{21}{32}$	0.0010–0.0027	0.0010–0.0027	0.3420	0.3420
	8-305	46	45	200 @ 1.16	[5]	0.0010–0.0037	0.0010–0.0037	0.3414	0.3414
	8-350 Buick	45	45	[8]	$1\frac{47}{64}$	0.0015–0.0035	0.0015–0.0032	0.3725	0.3726
	8-350 Olds.	45[6]	44[6]	187 @ 1.27	$1\frac{47}{64}$	0.0010–0.0027	0.0015–0.0032	0.3428	0.3423
	8-350 Chev.	46	45	200 @ 1.16	[5]	0.0010–0.0037	0.0010–0.0037	0.3413	0.3413
	8-400	30	29	135 @ 1.18	$1\frac{19}{32}$	0.0016–0.0033	0.0021–0.0038	0.3417	0.3410
	8-403	45[6]	44[6]	187 @ 1.27	$1\frac{47}{64}$	0.0010–0.0027	0.0015–0.0032	0.3428	0.3423
1979–'81	4-151	46	45	160 @ 1.25	$1\frac{11}{16}$	0.0010–0.0027	0.0010–0.0027[4]	0.3420	0.3420

Valve Specifications

Year	Engine No. Cyl. Displacement (cu in.)	Seat Angle (deg)	Face Angle (deg)	Spring Test Pressure ▲ (lbs. @ in.)	Spring Installed Height (in.)	Stem to Guide Clearance (in.)		Stem Diameter (in.)	
						Intake	Exhaust	Intake	Exhaust
	V6-231	45	45	164 @ 1.34⑦	1⁴⁷/₆₄	0.0015–0.0035	0.0015–0.0032	0.3406	0.3408
	V6-252	45	45	164 @ 1.34⑦	1⁴⁷/₆₄	0.0015–0.0035	0.0015–0.0032	0.3406	0.3408
	8-265	46	45	170 @ 1.29	1⁴³/₆₄	0.0010–0.0027	0.0010–0.0027	0.3425	0.3425
	8-301	46	45	170 @ 1.27	1⁴⁷/₆₄	0.0017–0.0020	0.0017–0.0020	0.3400	0.3400
	8-305	46	45	200 @ 1.25	1²³/₃₂	0.0010–0.0020	0.0010–0.0047	0.3414	0.3414
	8-350 Buick	45	45	⑧	1⁴⁷/₆₄	0.0015–0.0035	0.0015–0.0032	0.3725	0.3726
	8-350 Olds.	45⑥	44⑥	187 @ 1.27	1⁴⁷/₆₄	0.0010–0.0027	0.0015–0.0032	0.3428	0.3423
	8-350 Chev.	46	45	200 @ 1.16	⑤	0.0010–0.0037	0.0010–0.0037	0.3413	0.3413
	8-350 Diesel	45⑥⑨	44⑥⑨	151 @ 1.30⑩	1⁴⁷/₆₄	0.0010–0.0037	0.0015–0.0032	0.3428	0.3423
1982–'83	V6-231	45	45	164 @ 1.34⑦	1⁴⁷/₆₄	0.0015–0.0035	0.0015–0.0032	0.3406	0.3408
	V6-252	45	45	164 @ 1.34⑦	1⁴⁷/₆₄	0.0015–0.0035	0.0015–0.0032	0.3406	0.3408
	8-301	46	45	170 @ 1.27	1⁴⁷/₆₄	0.0017–0.0020	0.0017–0.0020	0.3400	0.3400
	8-305	46	45	200 @ 1.25	1²³/₃₂	0.0010–0.0020	0.0010–0.0037	0.3414	0.3414
	8-350 Diesel	45⑥⑨	44⑥⑨	210 @ 1.22	1⁴³/₆₄	0.0010–0.0027	0.0015–0.0032	0.3429	0.3429

① Intake 45°, exhaust 31°
② Intake 44°, exhaust 30°
③ Intake; exhaust 45° seat, 44° face
④ Figure given is measured at the top of the guide; 0.0020–.0037 is measured at bottom of guide
⑤ Intake: 1²³/₃₂
  Exhaust: 1¹⁹/₃₂
⑥ Exhaust valve seat angle—31°, exhaust valve face angle—30°
⑦ Exhaust: 182 @ 1.34
⑧ Intake: 180 @ 1.34
  Exhaust: 177 @ 1.45
⑨ 1981 Seat: Intake—45°, exhaust—59°
    Face: Intake—46°, exhaust—60°
⑩ 1981: 210 @ 1.23

Crankshaft and Connecting Rod Specifications

Year	Engine Displacement (cu in.)	Crankshaft				Connecting Rod		
		Main Brg. Journal Dia	Main Brg. Oil Clearance	Shaft End-Play	Thrust on No.	Journal Diameter	Oil Clearance	Side Clearance
1974	6-250	2.3004	.0003–.0029	.002–.006	7	1.999–2.000	.0007–.0027	.007–.016
	8-350	3.00	.0002–.0017	.0035–.0085	4	2.25	.0005–.0026①	.012–.017②
	8-400	3.00	.0002–.0017	.0035–.0085	4	2.25	.0005–.0026①	.012–.017②
1975	6-250	2.30	.0003–.0029	.002–.006	7	2.000	.0007–.0027	.007–.0016
	8-260	2.4990③	.0005–.0021④	.004–.008	3	2.1238–2.1248	.0004–.0033	.006–.020
	8-350 Pont.	3.00	.0002–.0017	.0035–.0085	4	2.25	.0005–.0026①	.012–.017②
	8-350 Buick	2.9995	.0004–.0015	.002–.006	3	1.9995	.0005–.0026	.006–.026
	8-400	3.00	.0002–.0017	.0035–.0085	4	2.25	.0005–.0026①	.012–.017②
	8-455	3.25	.0005–.0021⑤	.0035–.0085	4	2.25	.0010–.0031	.012–.017②
1976	V6-231	2.4995	.0004–.0015	.004–.008	2	2.000	.0005–.0026	.006–.027
	6-250	2.30	.0003–.0029	.002–.006	7	2.000	.0007–.0027	.007–.0016
	8-260	2.4990③	.0005–.0021④	.004–.008	3	2.1238–2.1248	.0004–.0033	.006–.020
	8-350 Pont.	3.00	.0002–.0017	.0035–.0085	4	3.000	.0005–.0026①	.012–.017②
	8-350 Buick	2.9995	.0004–.0015	.002–.006	3	1.9995	.0005–.0026	.006–.026
	8-400	3.00	.0002–.0017	.0035–.0085	4	2.25	.0005–.0026①	.012–.017②
	8-455	3.25	.0005–.0021⑤	.0035–.0085	4	2.25	.0010–.0031	.012–.017②
1977	4-151	2.30	.0002–.0022	.0035–.0085	5	2.000	.0005–.0026	.006–.022
	V6-231	2.4995	.0004–.0015	.004–.008	2	2.000	.0005–.0026	.006–.020
	8-301	3.000	.0004–.0020	.003–.009	4	2.000	.0005–.0025	.006–.027
	8-305	2.4502⑦	⑧	.002–.007	5	2.100	.0013–.0035	.006–.016
	8-350 Olds.	2.4990	.0005–.0021④	.004–.014	3	2.1243	.0004–.0015	.006–.027
	8-350 Chev.	2.4502⑦	⑧	.002–.007	5	2.0990–2.1000	.0013–.0035	.006–.016
	8-400	3.00	.0002–.0017	.0035–.0085	4	2.25	.0005–.0026	.012–.017②
	8-403	2.50	.0005–.0021④	.0035–.0135	3	2.1238–2.1248	.0004–.0033	.006–.020
1978	4-151	2.30	.0002–.0022	.0035–.0085	5	2.00	.0005–.0026	.006–.022
	V6-231	2.4995	.0003–.0017	.004–.008	2	2.2487–2.2495	.0005–.0026	.006–.027
	8-301	3.00	.0002–.0020	.003–.009	4	2.250⑨	.0005–.0025	.006–.022
	8-305	2.4502⑦	.0010–.0035	.002–.007	5	2.100	.0013–.0035	.006–.016
	8-350 Buick	3.000	.0004–.0015	.003–.009	3	1.9910–2.000	.0005–.0026	.006–.027
	8-350 Olds.	2.4985–2.4995⑪	.0005–.0021④	.0035–.0135	3	2.1238–2.1248	.0004–.0033	.006–.020
	8-350 Chev.	2.4502⑦	.0010–.0035	.002–.007	5	2.100	.0013–.0035	.006–.016
	8-400	3.00	.0002–.0017	.0035–.0085	4	2.25	.0005–.0026	.012–.017②
	8-403	2.50	.0005–.0021④	.0035–.0135	3	2.1238–2.1248	.0004–.0033	.006–.020
1979–'81	4-151	2.30	.0002–.0022	.0035–.0085	5	2.000	.0005–.0026	.006–.022
	V6-231	2.4995	.0004–.0018	.003–.009	2	2.2487–2.2495	.0005–.0026	.006–.023
	8-301	3.00	.0002–.0020	.0035–.0085	2	2.250⑨	.0005–.0025	.006–.022
	8-305	2.4489⑫	.0010–.0035	.002–.007	5	2.100	.0013–.0035	.006–.016
	8-350 Buick	3.000	.0004–.0015	.003–.009	3	1.9910–2.000	.0005–.0026	.006–.027
	8-350 Olds.	2.4985–2.4995⑪	.0005–.0021④	.0035–.0135	3	2.1238–2.1248	.0004–.0033	.006–.020
	8-350 Chev.	2.4502⑦	.0010–.0035	.002–.007	5	2.100	.0013–.0035	.006–.016
	8-350 Diesel	2.9993–3.003	.0005–.0021④	.0035–.0135	3	2.2495–2.2500	.0005–.0026	.006–.020
1982–'83	V6-231	2.4995	.0003–.0018	.003–.009	2	2.2487–2.2495	.0005–.0026	.006–.023
	V6-252	2.4995	.0003–.0018	.003–.009	2	2.2487–2.2495	.0005–.0026	.006–.023
	8-301	3.00	.0002–.0020	.0035–.0085	2	2.250⑨	.0005–.0025	.006–.022
	8-350 Diesel	2.9993–3.003	.0005–.0021①	.0035–.0135	3	2.2495–2.2500	.0005–.0026	.006–.020

① .0005–.0025 in. on Moraine 100-A bearings (350 and 400 V8 w/ 2 bbl carb.)
② Total for two
③ No. 1—2.4993 in.
④ No. 5—.0015–.0031 in.
⑤ Clearance .00035–.00195 in. on #1
⑥ No. 1: 2.4484–2.4493; 2, 3, 4: 2.4481–2.4490; 5: 2.4479–2.4488
⑦ No. 5: 2.4508
⑧ No. 1: .0008–.0020; 2, 3, 4: .0011–.0023; 5: .0017–.0033
⑨ No. 1: .0020 Max.
⑩ Diameter may also be 2.240 in.
⑪ No. 1: 2.4988–2.4998
⑫ No. 5: 2.4484

Piston and Ring Specifications

| Year | Engine | Piston-Bore Clearance | Ring Side Clearance | | | Ring Gap | | |
			Top Compression	Bottom Compression	Oil Control	Top Compression	Bottom Compression	Oil Control
1976–'83	V6-231	.0013–.0035	.0030–.0050	.0030–.0050	0–.0035	.010–.020①	.010–.020①	.015–.035
1974–'76	6-250	.0025 Max.	.0012–.0027	.0012–.0032	0–.0050	.010–.020	.010–.020	.015–.055
1982–'83	V6-252	.0008–.0020②	.003–.005	.003–.005	.0035	.013–.023	.013–.023	.015–.035
1975–'76	8-260	.0010–.0020	.0020–.0040	.0020–.0040	.005–.011	.010–.023	.010–.023	.015–.055
1980–'81	8-265	.0017–.0041③	.0015–.0035	.0015–.0035	.0015–.0035	.010–.022	.010–.028	.010–.055
1977–'82	8-301	.0025–.0033④	.0015–.0035	.0015–.0035	.0015–.0035	.010–.020	.010–.020	.0035
1977–'80	8-305	.0027	.0012–.0042	.0012–.0042	.0020–.0080	.010–.030	.010–.035	.015–.065
1974–'76	8-350 P	.0029–.0037	.0015–.0050	.0015–.0050	.0015–.0050	.010–.020	.010–.020	.015–.035
1975–'77	8-350 B	.0008–.0014	.003–.005	.003–.005	.0035 Max.	.013–.023	.015–.035	.015–.035⑤
1978–'79	8-350 B	.0008–.0020②	.003–.005	.003–.005	.0035	.010–.020	.010–.020	.015–.035
1977–'78	8-350 O	.0010–.0020	.0020–.0040	.0020–.0040	.0015–.0035	.010–.023	.010–.023	.015–.055
1979	8-350 O	.0010–.0027	.0020–.0040	.0020–.0040	.001–.005	.010–.023⑥	.010–.023⑥	.015–.055
1977–'79	8-350 C	.0027 Max.	.0012–.0042	.0012–.0042	.0020–.0080	.010–.030	.010–.035	.015–.056
1979–'83	8-350 OD	.005–.006	.004–.006⑦	.0018–.0038	.001–.005	.015–.025	.015–.025	.015–.055
1974–'76	8-400	.0029–.0037②	.0015–.005⑧	.0015–.005⑧	.0015–.005	.010–.020	.010–.020	.015–.055
1977–'78	8-400	.0025–.0033④	.0015–.0035	.0015–.0035	.0015–.0035	.009–.019	.005–.015	.015–.035
1977–'78	8-403	.0008–.0018⑨	.0020–.0040	.0020–.0040	.001–.005	.010–.020	.010–.020	.015–.055
1975–'76	8-455	.0021–.0029	.0020–.0040⑩	.0020–.0040⑩	.0021–.0031⑩	.010–.023⑪	.010–.023⑪	.015–.055

P—Pontiac-built
O—Oldsmobile-built
B—Buick-built
C—Chevrolet-built
OD—Olds Diesel
① 1979–82: .013–.023
② Measured at skirt top
③ Measured at skirt bottom
④ Measured 1.1 in. from top of piston
⑤ .015–.055 in. 1977
⑥ w/Sealed Power rings—.010–.020 in.
⑦ .005–.007 in. 1981 and later
⑧ .0015–.0035 in. 1976
⑨ Measured ¾ in. below piston centerline
⑩ .0015–.0050 in. 1976
⑪ .010–.030 in. 1976

Torque Specifications

(All readings in ft. lbs.)

Year	Engine	Cylinder Head Bolts	Rod Bearing Bolts	Main Bearing Bolts	Crankshaft Damper or Pulley Bolt	Flywheel to Crankshaft Bolts	Manifold Intake	Manifold Exhaust
1974	6-250	95	35	65	Press Fit	60	25	30
	8-350	95	43	100①	160	95	40	30
	8-400	95	43	100①	160	95	40	30
1975	6-250	95	35	65	Press Fit	60	25	30
	8-260	85②	42	③	310	60	40	30
	8-350 Pont.	95	43	100①	160	95	40	30
	8-350 Buick	80	40	115	140 min.	60	45	45
	8-400	95	43	100①	160	95	40	30
	8-455	95	43④	100①	160	95	40	30
1976	V6-231	85	42	100	150	55	45	25
	6-250	95	35	65	Press Fit	60	25	30
	8-260	85②	42	③	310	60	40	30
	8-350 Pont.	95	43	100①	160	95	40	30
	8-350 Buick	80	40	115	140	60	45	45
	8-400	95	43	100①	160	95	40	30
	8-455	95	43⑨	100①	160	95	40	30
1977	4-151	95⑤	30	65	160	55	40⑥	30
	V6-231	80	40	100	175 min.	60	45	25
	8-301	85	30	100	160	95	35	40
	8-305	65	45	70	60	60	30	20
	8-350 Olds	130②	42	80①	200–310	60	40②	25
	8-350 Chev.	65	45	70	60	60	30	20
	8-400	100	40	120	160	95	35	40
	8-403	130②	42	80①	200–310	60	40②	25
1978	4-151	95⑤	30	65	160	55	40⑥	30
	V6-231	80	40	100	225⑦	60	45	25
	8-301	95	30	70	160	95	40	35
	8-305	65	45	70	60	60	30	20
	8-350 Buick	80	40	100	225⑦	60	45	25
	8-350 Olds.	130②	42	80①	255⑦	60	40②	25
	8-350 Chev.	65	45	70	60	60	30	20
	8-400	100	40	120	160	95	35	40
	8-403	130②	42	80①	255⑦	60	40②	25
1979 – '81	4-151	85⑤	32	70	200	50	29	44
	V6-231	80	40	100	225⑦	60	45	25
	8-301	95	30	70	160	95	40	35
	8-305	65	45	70	60	60	30	20
	8-350 Buick	80	40	100	225⑦	60	45	25
	8-350 Olds.	130②	42	80①	255⑦	60	40②	25
	8-350 Chev.	65	45	70	60	60	30	20
	8-350 Diesel	130②	42	120	200–310⑦	60	40②	25

Torque Specifications (cont.)
(All readings in ft. lbs.)

Year	Engine	Cylinder Head Bolts	Rod Bearing Bolts	Main Bearing Bolts	Crankshaft Damper or Pulley Bolt	Flywheel to Crankshaft Bolts	Manifold	
							Intake	Exhaust
1982–'83	V6-231	80	40	100	225	60	40	25
	V6-252	80	40	100	225	60	40	25
	8-301	95	30	70	160	95	40	35
	8-350 Diesel	130②	42	③	200–310	60	40②	25

① Rear main cap bolts—120 ft. lbs.
② Dip bolt in oil before torquing
③ 80 ft. lbs. on Nos. 1–4, 120 ft. lbs. on No. 5
④ 63 ft. lbs. on 455 Super Duty engines
⑤ Requires thread sealer
⑥ Intake-to-exhaust manifold bolt—40 ft. lbs.
⑦ Fan pulley-to-balancer—20 ft. lbs.
⑧ Rear main cap bolts—100 ft. lbs.

Camshaft Specifications
(All measurements in inches)

Year	Engine	Journal Diameter	Lobe Lift		Camshaft End Play
			Intake	Exhaust	
1977–'79	4-151	1.869	.406	.406	.0015–.0050
1976–'83	V6-231	1.785–1.786	.383	.366	.011–.077①
1974–'76	6-250	1.8682–1.8692	.388	.388	.009–.013
1975–'76	8-260	②	—	—	.011–.077
1977–'82	8-301	—	.364	.364	—
1977–'80	8-305	1.8682–1.8692	.2485③	.2733④	—
1974–'76	8-350 Pontiac	—	.396	.400	—
1975–'76	8-350 Buick	1.785–1.786	—	—	—
1978–'79	8-350 Buick	1.785–1.786	—	—	—
1977–'79	8-350 Olds.	⑥	—	—	.011–.077
1977–'79	8-350 Chev.	1.8682–1.8692	.2600⑤	.2733	—
1979–'83	8-350 Olds Diesel	⑥	—	—	.011–.077
1974–'78	8-400	—	.374	.407	—
1977–'78	8-403	⑥	—	—	.011–.077
1975–'76	8-455	—	.403	.406	—

① 1983 spec
② No. 1—2.0365–2.0357 in.; No. 2—2.0165–2.0157 in.; No. 3—1.9965–1.9957 in.; No. 4—1.9765–1.9757 in.;
   No. 5—1.9565–1.9557 in.
③ .2484 in 1979–80
④ .2600 in 1979; .2667 in 1980
⑤ .2667 in 1978–79
⑥ No. 1—2.0357–2.0365 in.; No. 2—2.0157–2.0165 in.; No. 3—1.9957–1.9965 in.; No. 4—1.9757–1.9765 in.;
   No. 5—1.9557–1.9565 in.

Engine

REMOVAL & INSTALLATION

◆ **See Figures 15 and 16**

151 Four and 250 Six-Cylinder Engines

1. Disconnect the negative battery cable.
2. Remove the air cleaner assembly and its connecting hoses.

3. Scribe the outline of the hood hinges on the underside of the hood for later alignment during assembly. Remove the hood.
4. Drain the cooling system and remove the radiator hoses.
5. Disconnect the engine ground strap from the cylinder head.
6. Remove the fan shroud.
7. Remove the positive battery cable at the starter. Tag and disconnect the primary coil wire at the coil.
8. Disconnect the throttle linkage at the carburetor. Tag and disconnect the automatic transmission kick-down linkage, if equipped.

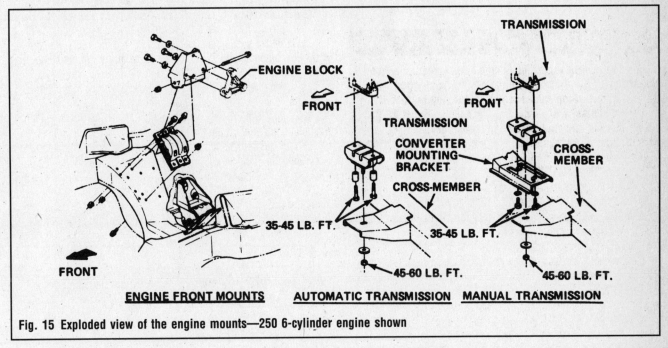

Fig. 15 Exploded view of the engine mounts—250 6-cylinder engine shown

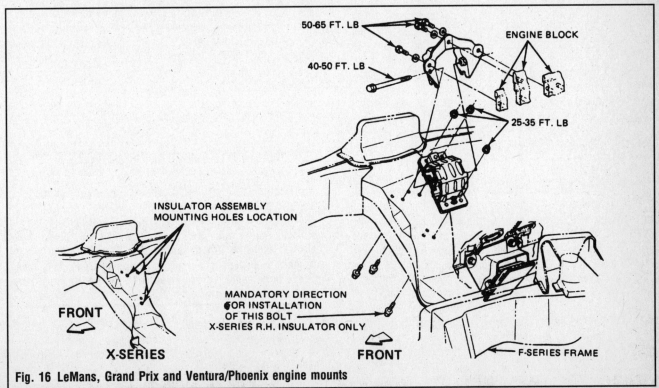

Fig. 16 LeMans, Grand Prix and Ventura/Phoenix engine mounts

9. Disconnect the fuel line from the fuel pump. *Be careful not to strip the threads on the fitting.*

10. Tag and remove the alternator wiring and the heater hoses from the engine.

11. Tag and disconnect the vacuum lines and hoses from the engine. If the car has an automatic transmission, remove the cooler lines from the radiator.

12. If the car is equipped with power steering, remove the power steering pump from the engine with the hoses attached.

13. If the car is equipped with air conditioning, remove the compressor from the engine without disconnecting the compressor lines.

✳✳ CAUTION

Under no circumstances should you disconnect the air-conditioner lines. The air conditioning system is charged with R-12, a gas that when released will freeze any surface it comes in contact with, including your eyes. The R-12 gas also becomes poisonous in the presence of flame. All air conditioning discharging and charging should be handled by a qualified air conditioning mechanic.

14. Remove the radiator.

15. Jack up the car and safely support it with jackstands.

16. Disconnect the exhaust pipe from the exhaust manifold. Remove the starter from the engine.

17. If the car is equipped with a manual transmission, remove the clutch equalizer bar from the engine block.

18. If the car is equipped with an automatic transmission, remove the torque converter cover. Mark the converter and flywheel with a scribe or colored marker to ensure proper reassembly. Turn the crankshaft pulley to gain access to the three bolts which attach the converter to the flywheel, and remove the bolts.

19. If the car is equipped with a manual transmission, remove the bolts which attach the transmission to the bellhousing. On automatic transmission cars, remove the bolts which attach the transmission and raise the transmission slightly.

20. Remove the motor mount through bolts.

21. Attach a chain hoist or other lifting device to the engine, taking all safety precautions.

22. Remove the engine from the car. If the car is equipped with an automatic transmission, make sure the torque converter stays in the transmission; this can be done by attaching the proper size C-clamp to the transmission housing in such a way that the clamp prevents the converter from slipping out.

To install:

23. Lower the engine carefully into the engine compartment. *The engine will have to be hanging from the hoist with the rear of the engine on a downward angle.* Raise the transmission slightly, using the floor jack.

24. If equipped with an automatic transmission, start the converter pilot shaft into the crankshaft pilot bearing. If equipped with a manual transmission, start the transmission mainshaft into the clutch disc. *Both the engine and transmission have to be on the same angle to accomplish this.* This operation will most likely entail a considerable bit of maneuvering of the engine and transmission. If the engine hangs up after the shaft enters on manual transmission cars, slowly turn the crankshaft (with the transmission in gear) until the splines mesh.

25. Make sure the exhaust pipe aligns with the manifold as you lower the engine into the engine compartment. Make sure the engine mounts line up.

26. After the engine is down in the engine compartment on its mounts, install the nuts on the engine mount bolts and tighten the motor mount-to-cylinder blockbolts to 33 ft. lbs.

27. Install the bellhousing-to-transmission attaching bolts on manual transmission cars. On automatic transmission cars, bolt the transmission to the engine block.

28. On automatic transmission-equipped cars, install the torque converter-to-flywheel attaching bolts. *Make sure the marks made during removal are lined up, as this is critical to the balance of the entire assembly.* Turn the crankshaft pulley with the crank pulley bolt (using a socket wrench) to line up the holes.

29. Install the starter and exhaust pipe.

30. On manual transmission cars, install the clutch equalizer bar. On automatic transmission cars, install the torque converter cover.

31. Install the fuel line, vacuum hoses, wiring, heater hoses, throttle linkage and engine ground strap.

32. Install the radiator and radiator hoses. Install the coolant lines on automatic transmission cars.

33. If the car was equipped with air conditioning, install the compressor. Install the power steering pump, if equipped.

34. Lower the car. Install the hood, lining up the scribe marks. Fill the cooling system and connect the battery cables. Give the engine compartment one final, thorough check to make sure all hoses and wiring are properly connected, and that all assemblies are tightened. Start the car and check throttle and transmission linkage for smooth operation.

231 and 252 V6 Engines

1. Scribe marks around the hood hinges and hinge bracket, so the hood can be installed easily. Remove the hood.

2. Disconnect both battery cables.

3. Drain the coolant into a suitable container; it can be reused if in "fresh" condition.

4. Remove the air cleaner.

5. Disconnect the radiator and heater hoses and position them out of the way.

6. On air-conditioned cars, disconnect the A/C compressor ground wire from the mounting bracket. Remove the electrical connector from the compressor clutch, remove the compressor-to-mounting bracket attaching bolts and position the compressor out of the way.

✳✳ CAUTION

If the compressor refrigerant lines do not have enough slack to position the compressor out of the way without discharging the refrigerant lines, the air conditioning system will have to be removed by a trained air conditioning specialist. Under no circumstances should an untrained person attempt to disconnect the air conditioning refrigerant lines. These lines contain pressurized R-12 refrigerant, which can be extremely dangerous.

7. Remove the fan blade, pulleys and belts.

8. Remove the fan shroud assembly.

9. Remove the power steering pump-to-mounting bracket bolts and position the pump out of the way.

10. Tag, remove and plug the fuel pump hoses.

11. Tag and disconnect the vacuum lines from the engine to parts not attached to the engine.

12. Disconnect and tag the throttle cable, downshift cable and/ or throttle valve cable at the carburetor.

13. Disconnect the transmission oil cooler lines at the transmission. Disconnect the oil and coolant sending unit switch connections at the engine.

14. Disconnect the engine-to-body ground strap at the engine.

15. Jack up and support the front end of the car. Disconnect the starter cables and the cable shield from the engine.

16. Disconnect the exhaust pipes from the exhaust manifolds and support the exhaust system.

17. Remove the flywheel cover pan. Remove the flywheel-to-torque converter bolts. Using a scribe or felt tip marker, matchmark the flywheel-to-torque converter relationship for later assembly.

18. Remove the transmission-to-engine attaching bolts from the transmission bell housing.

19. Remove the cruise control bracket, if so equipped.

20. Remove the motor mount bolts.

21. Lower the car and support the transmission with a floor jack.

22. Check to make sure that all wiring and hoses have been disconnected. Attach a lifting device to the engine and raise the engine just enough so that the engine mount through-bolts can be removed.

23. Raise the engine and transmission alternately until the engine can be disengaged and removed.

24. Installation is the reverse of the removal procedure. It may be necessary to alternately raise and lower the transmission to fit the motor mount through-bolts into position. Tighten the through-bolt nuts to 35 ft. lbs. Tighten the automatic transmission-to-engine bolts to 35 ft. lbs.

V8 Engines

1. Drain the cooling system.

2. Scribe the hinge outline on the underside of the hood. Remove the hood attaching bolts and remove the hood.

3. Disconnect the battery cables.

4. Remove the radiator and heater hoses and remove the air cleaner.

5. Disconnect the transmission oil cooler lines. Remove the fan shroud, fan belts, and pulleys.

6. Disconnect the battery ground cable from the engine. Remove the radiator.

7. Disconnect the exhaust pipe or pipes from the exhaust manifold/s.

8. Disconnect the vacuum line from the power brake unit.

9. Disconnect the accelerator-to-carburetor linkage.

10. Disconnect and label all the engine component wiring that would interfere with the engine removal, such as alternator wires, gauge sending unit wires, primary ignition wires, engine-to-body ground strap, etc.

11. Disconnect and plug the gas line at the fuel pump.

12. Detach the power steering pump and position to the left. Do not disconnect the hoses.

13. Detach the air conditioner compressor at the bracket and position to the right. *Do not disconnect the hoses.*

✳✳ CAUTION

If the compressor refrigerant lines do not have enough slack to position the compressor out of the way without disconnecting the refrigerant lines, the air conditioning system will have to be removed by a trained air conditioning specialist. Under no conditions should an untrained person attempt to disconnect the air conditioning refrigerant lines. These lines contain pressurized R-12 gas which can be extremely dangerous.

14. Disconnect the start cable and remove the cable shield.

15. Remove the flywheel cover pan. Remove the flywheel-to-torque converter bolts. Matchmark the flywheel and torque converter for reassembly.

16. Separate the engine from the transmission at the bell housing.

17. Remove the cruise control bracket, if so equipped.

18. Support the transmission with a floor jack.

19. Attach a lifting device to the engine and raise the engine slightly so the engine mount through-bolts can be removed.

20. Check to make sure all of the wiring and hoses have been disconnected. Raise the engine enough to clear the motor mounts.

21. Raise the engine and transmission alternately until the engine can be disengaged and removed.

22. Install by reversing the procedure. When installing an engine, the front mounting pad to frame bolts should be the last mounting bolts to be tightened. Note that there are dowel pins in the block that have matching holes in the bellhousing. These pins must be in almost perfect alignment before the engine will go together with the transmission. Tighten the through-bolt nuts to 35 ft. lbs. Tighten the automatic transmission-to-engine bolts to 35 ft. lbs.

Valve Cover

REMOVAL & INSTALLATION

▶ **See Figure 17**

1. Remove air cleaner.

2. Disconnect and reposition as necessary any vacuum or PCV hoses that obstruct the valve covers.

3. Disconnect electrical wire(s) (spark plug, etc.) from the valve cover clips.

4. Unbolt and remove the valve cover(s).

➡**Do not pry the covers off if they seem stuck. Instead, gently tap around each cover with a rubber mallet until the old gasket or sealer breaks loose.**

To install:

5. Use a new valve cover gasket or RTV (or any equivalent) sealer. If using sealer, follow directions on the tube. Install valve cover and tighten cover bolts to 3 ft. lbs.

6. Connect and reposition all vacuum and PCV hoses, and reconnect electrical and/or spark plug wires at the cover clips. Install the air cleaner.

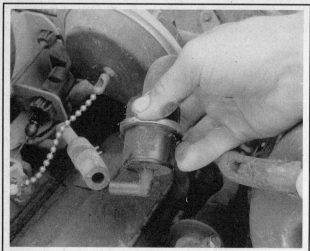

To remove the valve cover, disconnect the vacuum hose from the power brake booster

Remove and discard the valve cover gasket

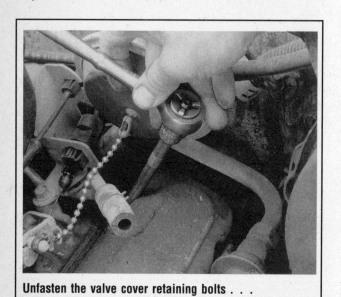

Unfasten the valve cover retaining bolts . . .

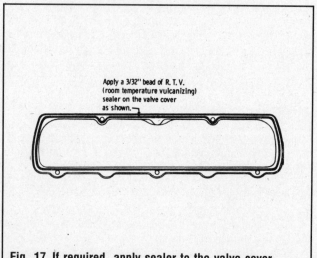

Apply a 3/32'' bead of R. T. V. (room temperature vulcanizing) sealer on the valve cover as shown.

Fig. 17 If required, apply sealer to the valve cover before installation

Rocker Arms

REMOVAL & INSTALLATION

V6 Engines and Buick Built 350 (VINS H, J & X) Engines

1. Remove the valve covers.
2. Remove the rocker arm shaft assembly bolts.
3. Remove the rocker arm shaft assembly and place it on a clean surface.
4. To remove the rocker arms from the shaft, you must first remove the nylon arm retainers. These can be removed with locking jaw pliers, by prying them out, or by breaking them by hitting them below the head with a chisel.
5. Remove the rocker arms from the shaft. Make sure you keep them in order. Also note that the external rib on each arm points *away* from the rocker arm shaft bolt located between each pair of rocker arms.
6. If you are installing new rocker arms, note that the replace-

. . . then remove the valve cover from the cylinder head

After removing the valve cover, you can access the rocker arm shaft (1) and the rocker arms (2)

To remove the rocker arms, remove the rocker arm shaft assembly bolts . . .

. . . then remove the rocker arm shaft assembly and place on a clean workbench

ment rocker arms are marked "R" and "L" for right and left side installation. *Do not* interchange them.

7. Install the rocker arms on the shaft and lubricate them with oil.

➡Install the rocker arms for each cylinder only when the lifters are off the cam lobe and both valves are closed.

8. Center each arm on the ¼ in. hole in the shaft. Install new nylon rocker arm retainers in the holes using a ½ in. drift.

9. Locate the pushrods in the rocker arm "cups" and insert the shaft bolts. Tighten the bolts a little at a time to 30 ft. lbs.

10. Install the valve covers using sealer or new gaskets.

4 Cylinder, Inline 6 Cylinder and V8 Engines

EXCEPT DIESEL ENGINES

◆ See Figure 18

1. Remove the valve cover.
2. Remove the rocker arm flanged bolts, and remove the rocker pivots.
3. Remove the rocker arms.

➡Remove each set of rocker arms (one set per cylinder) as a unit.

To install:

4. Position a set of rocker arms (for one cylinder) in the proper location.

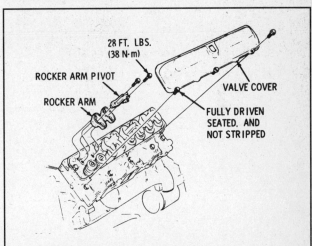

Fig. 18 Exploded view of the valve cover and rocker arms—except Buick built V6 and V8 engines

➡Install the rocker arms for each cylinder only when the lifters are off the cam lobe and both valves are closed.

5. Coat the replacement rocker arm and pivot with SAE 90 gear oil and install the pivots.

6. Install the flanged bolts and tighten alternately. Tighten the bolts to 25 ft. lbs.

DIESEL ENGINES

➡When the diesel engine rocker arms are removed or loosened, the lifters must be bled down to prevent oil pressure buildup inside each lifter, which could cause it to raise up higher than normal and bring the valves within striking distance of the pistons.

1. Remove the valve cover.

2. Remove the rocker arm pivot bolts, the bridged pivot and rocker arms.

3. Remove each rocker set as a unit.

To install:

4. Lubricate the pivot wear points and position each set of rocker arms in its proper location. Do not tighten the pivot bolts for fear of bending the valves when the engine is turned.

5. The lifters can be bled down for six cylinders at once with the crankshaft in either of the following two positions:

   a. For cylinders number 3, 5, 7, 2, 4 and 8, turn the crankshaft so the saw slot on the harmonic balancer is at 0° on the timing indicator.

   b. For cylinders 1, 3, 7, 2, 4 and 6, turn the crankshaft so the saw slot on the harmonic balancer is at 4 o'clock.

6. Tighten the rocker arm pivot bolts VERY SLOWLY to 28 ft. lbs. It will take 45 minutes to completely bleed down the lifters in this position. If additional lifters must be bled, rotate the engine to the other position, tighten the rocker arm pivot bolts, and again wait 45 minutes before rotating the crankshaft. *Excess torque here can bend the pushrods, so be careful!*

7. Assemble the remaining components in the reverse of disassembly. The rocker covers do not use gaskets, but are sealed with a bead of RTV (Room Temperature Vulcanizing) silicone sealer.

Intake Manifold

REMOVAL & INSTALLATION

151 Four and 250 Inline Six Cylinder Engines

♦ **See Figures 19 and 20**

1975 and 1976 250 6-cylinder engines are equipped with an intake manifold which is integrally cast with the cylinder head and cannot be removed. The 1974 250 6-cylinder uses a combined intake and exhaust manifold; both are removed together. Likewise, the 1977 and 1978 151 4-cylinder intake and exhaust manifolds are combined and are removed together. The 1979 151 manifolds

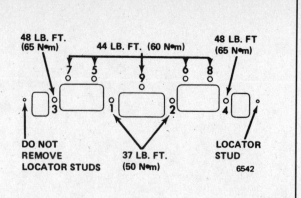

Fig. 20 Intake manifold mounting and bolt tightening sequence—1979 151 4-cylinder engine with separate manifolds

are bolted to opposite sides of the head; 1979 4-cylinder exhaust manifold removal and installation is covered under "Exhaust Manifold."

1. Remove the air cleaner assembly and air ducts.

2. On 1979 151 fours, drain the cooling system.

3. Tag and disconnect the throttle linkage at the carburetor. Tag and disconnect the fuel line, vacuum lines, hoses, and electrical connections.

4. Disconnect the transmission downshift linkage (if equipped), and remove the PCV valve from the rocker cover. On models equipped with air injection, disconnect the air supply hose from the check valve on the air injection manifold.

5. Remove the carburetor, with spacer and heat shield (if equipped).

6. Spray the nuts and bolts connecting the exhaust manifold to the exhaust pipe with a rust penetrant, as these are usually quite difficult to remove. Unbolt the exhaust manifold from the pipe.

➡**It may be necessary to remove the generator rear bracket and/or A/C bracket on some models.**

7. Unbolt the manifold bolts and clamps, and remove the manifold assembly. On 1979 151 fours, remove the intake manifold.

8. If you intend to separate the manifolds, remove the single bolt and two nuts at the center of the 250 six manifold assembly. On 1977 and 1978 151 fours, disconnect the EGR pipe and remove the four bolts at the center of the manifold.

9. Installation is the reverse of removal. When assembling the manifolds, install the connecting bolts loosely first. Place the manifolds on a straight, flat surface and hold them securely during tightening—this assures the proper mating of surfaces when the manifold assembly is fastened to the head. *Stress cracking could occur if the manifolds are not assembled first in this manner.* On the 1977 and '78 151 four, be sure the insulator gasket is in place between the early fuel evaporation (EFE) bracket and the manifold. On all manifolds, always use new gaskets between the manifolds and cylinder head. Tighten the manifold bolts in the patterns illustrated.

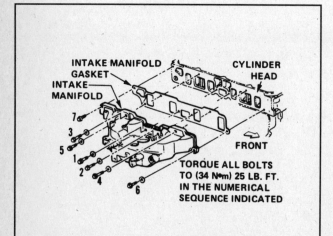

Fig. 19 Combination manifold bolt tightening sequence—1977–78 151 4-cylinder engine

V6 Engine and V8 Engine

EXCEPT DIESEL

▶ See Figures 21, 22, 23, 24 and 25

1. Drain the cooling system.
2. Remove the air cleaner assembly.
3. Remove the thermostat housing and the bypass hose. It is not necessary to remove the top radiator hose from the thermostat housing.
4. Disconnect the heater hose at the rear of the manifold.
5. Disconnect all electrical connections and vacuum lines from the manifold. Remove the EGR valve if necessary.
6. On vehicles equipped with power brakes remove the vacuum line from the vacuum booster to the manifold.

7. Remove the distributor (if necessary).
8. Remove the fuel line to the carburetor.
9. Remove the carburetor linkage.
10. Remove the carburetor.
11. Remove the intake manifold bolts. Remove the manifold and the gaskets. Remember to reinstall the O-ring seal between the intake manifold and timing chain cover during assembly, if so equipped.
12. Installation is the reverse of removal. Use plastic gasket retainers to prevent the manifold gasket from slipping out of place, if so equipped.

➡Before installing the intake manifold, be sure that the gasket surfaces are thoroughly clean.

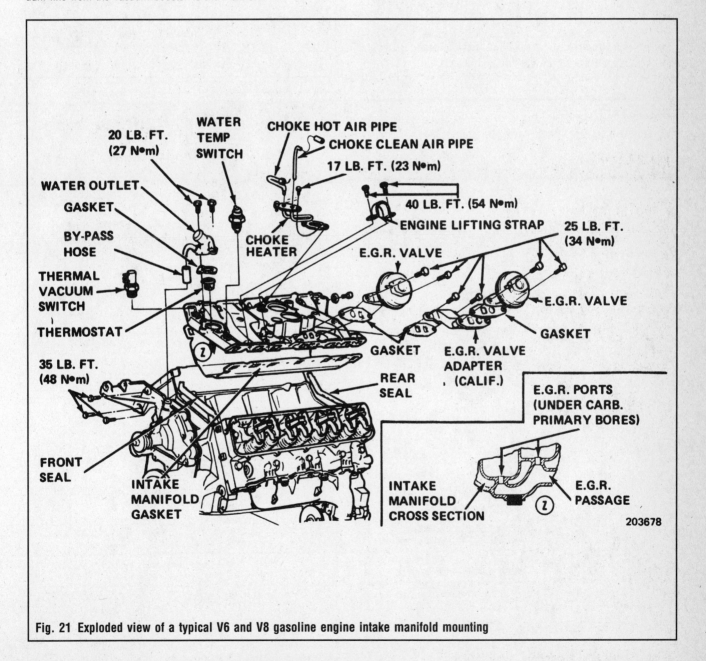

Fig. 21 Exploded view of a typical V6 and V8 gasoline engine intake manifold mounting

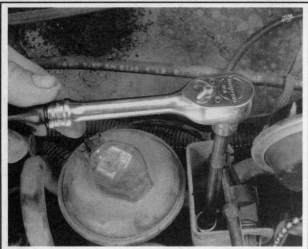

When removing the intake manifold, unfasten the retainers and remove the carburetor linkage

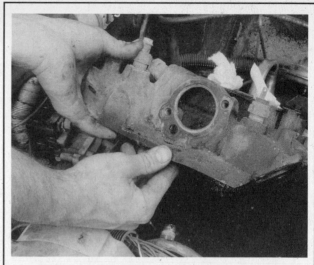

. . . then remove the intake manifold from the engine

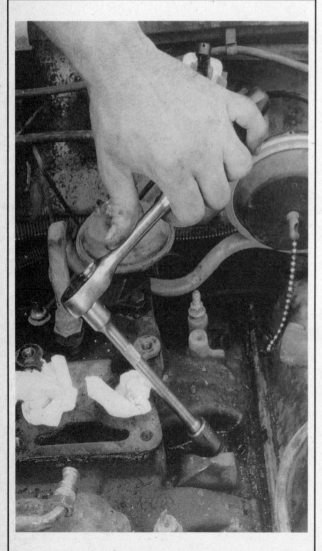

Unfasten the intake manifold retaining bolts . . .

Remove and discard the intake manifold gasket

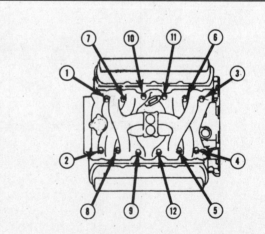

Fig. 22 Intake manifold bolt tightening sequence— Oldsmobile built V8 gasoline and diesel engines

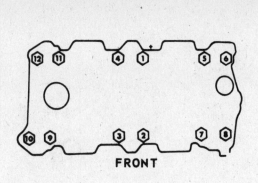

Fig. 23 Chevrolet built 305 and 350 V8 engine intake manifold bolt tightening sequence

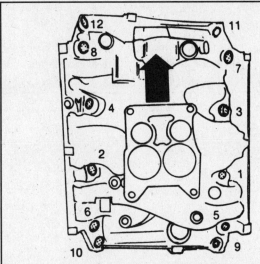

Fig. 24 Intake manifold bolt tightening sequence (arrow points to the front)—Buick built 350 and 455 engines

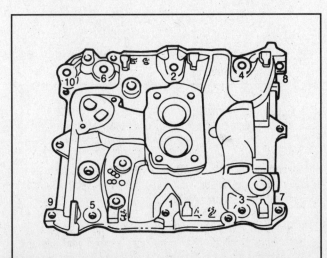

Fig. 25 231 and 252 V6 engine intake manifold bolt tightening sequence

350 DIESEL

▶ **See Figures 22, 26 and 27**

1. Remove the air cleaner.
2. Drain the radiator. Loosen the upper bypass hose clamp, remove the thermostat housing bolts, and remove the housing and the thermostat from the intake manifold.
3. Remove the breather pipes from the rocker covers and the air crossover. Remove the air crossover.
4. Disconnect the throttle rod and the return spring. If equipped with cruise control, remove the servo.
5. Remove the hairpin clip at the bellcrank and disconnect the cables. Remove the throttle cable from the bracket on the manifold; position the cable away from the engine. Disconnect and label any wiring as necessary.
6. Remove the alternator bracket if necessary. If equipped with air conditioning, remove the compressor mounting bolts and move the compressor aside, without disconnecting any of the hoses. Remove the compressor mounting bracket from the intake manifold.

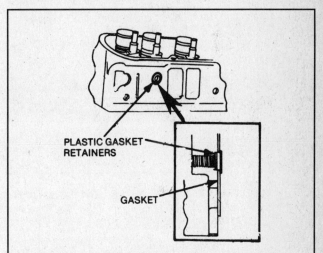

Fig. 26 Some intake manifold gaskets can be held in place by using plastic retainers, available at your local dealer or parts store

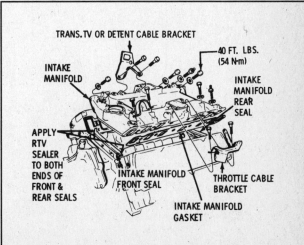

Fig. 27 Diesel engine intake manifold mounting and gasket locations

7. Disconnect the fuel line from the pump and the fuel filter. Remove the fuel filter and bracket.

8. Remove the fuel injection pump and lines. See Chapter 5, "Fuel System," for procedures.

9. Disconnect and remove the vacuum pump or oil pump drive assembly from the rear of the engine.

10. Remove the intake manifold drain tube.

11. Remove the intake manifold bolts and remove the manifold. Remove the adapter seal. Remove the injection pump adapter.

12. Clean the mating surfaces of the cylinder heads and the intake manifold using a putty knife.

13. Coat both sides of the gasket surface that seal the intake manifold to the cylinder heads with G.M. sealer #1050026 or the equivalent. Position the intake manifold gaskets on the cylinder heads. Install the end seals, making sure that the ends are positioned under the cylinder heads.

14. Carefully lower the intake manifold into place on the engine.

15. Clean the intake manifold bolts thoroughly, then dip them in clean engine oil. Install the bolts and tighten to 15 ft. lbs. in the sequence shown. Next, tighten all the bolts to 30 ft. lbs., in sequence, and finally tighten to 40 ft. lbs. in sequence.

16. Install the intake manifold drain tube and clamp.

17. Install injection pump adapter. See Chapter 4. If a new adapter is not being used, skip steps 4 and 9.

Exhaust Manifold

REMOVAL & INSTALLATION

➡1974 250 six and 1977–78 151 four-cylinder exhaust manifold removal and installation is covered under the "Intake Manifold" procedure (both manifolds are a unit).

1979 151 Four Cylinder Engine
◆ See Figure 28

1. Disconnect and remove the air cleaner assembly, including the carburetor, pre-heat tube.

2. Disconnect the exhaust pipe at the exhaust manifold. You will probably have to use a liquid rust penetrant to free the bolts.

3. Remove the engine oil dipstick bracket bolt.

4. Remove the exhaust manifold bolts and remove the manifold.

5. To install, mount the manifold on the cylinder head and start all bolts.

6. Tighten the bolts to specification using the torque sequence illustrated. Complete the installation by reversing the removal procedure.

All V6 and V8 Engines
◆ See Figure 29

Tab locks are used on the front and rear pairs of bolts on each exhaust manifold. When removing the bolts, straighten the tabs from beneath the car using a suitable tool. When installing the tab locks, bend the tabs against the sides of the bolt, not over the top of the bolt.

1. Remove the air cleaner.

2. Remove the hot air shroud, (if so equipped).

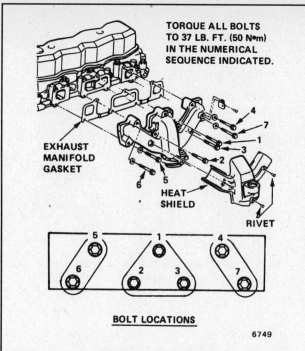

Fig. 28 Exhaust manifold mounting and bolt tightening sequence—1979 151 4-cylinder engine with separate manifolds

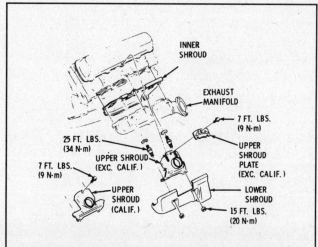

Fig. 29 Typical V6 or V8 exhaust manifold mounting and hot air shroud mounting

3. Loosen the alternator and remove its lower bracket.

4. Jack up your car and support it with jack stands.

5. Disconnect the crossover pipe from both manifolds.

➡On models with air conditioning it may be necessary to remove the compressor, and tie it out of the way. Do not disconnect the compressor lines.

6. Remove the manifold bolts and remove the manifold(s). Some models have lock tabs on the front and rear manifold bolts which must be removed before removing the bolts. These tabs can be bent with a drift pin.

7. Installation is the reverse of the removal procedure.

To remove the exhaust manifold, disconnect the exhaust crossover pipes from the manifolds

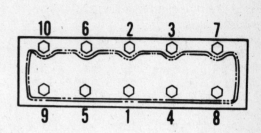

Fig. 30 Cylinder head bolt tightening sequence—151 4-cylinder engine

Fig. 31 250 inline 6-cylinder engine cylinder head bolt tightening sequence

Cylinder Head

REMOVAL & INSTALLATION

151 Four and 250 Inline Six Cylinder Engine
▶ See Figures 30 and 31

1. Drain the cooling system and remove the air cleaner assembly. Disconnect the PCV hose.

2. Tag and disconnect the throttle linkage at the carburetor. Tag and disconnect the fuel line, vacuum lines, and any electrical connections at the carburetor.

3. Remove the top radiator hose, and the battery ground strap. Disconnect the wires from the temperature sending unit, leaving the harness clear of the clips on the rocker cover.

4. On the 250 six, disconnect the coil wires after tagging them, and remove the coil. Tag and disconnect the spark plug wires from the plugs.

5. Remove the intake and exhaust manifolds.

6. Remove the rocker arm cover. Back off the rocker arm nuts, and pivot the rocker arms so the pushrods will clear.

7. Take a piece of heavy cardboard and cut 8 or 12 holes (depending on whether you are working on a four or six cylinder) in

it the same diameter as the pushrod stem. Number the holes in relation to the pushrods being removed. This cardboard holder will keep the pushrods in order (and hopefully out of harms way) while they are out of the engine. Remove the pushrods one at a time.

➡**Pushrods MUST be returned to their original locations.**

8. Remove the cylinder head bolts one at a time, and mark them or keep them in order, as they should go back in their original locations. You may need a flex bar on your socket, or a piece of pipe on your ratchet, as the bolts are under a lot of torque.

9. Remove the cylinder head, along with the gasket. If the head seems tuck to the block, gently tap around the edge of the head with a rubber mallet until the joint breaks. NEVER pry between the head and block as you may gouge one or the other. Often it is necessary to carefully scrape the top of the engine block and the cylinder head to completely remove the gasket.

10. Clean the bottom of the head and top of block thoroughly before reinstalling the head. Place a new gasket over the dowel pins in the top of the block.

➡**Different types of head gaskets are available. If you are using a steel-asbestos composition gasket, do not use gasket sealer.**

11. Lower the cylinder head carefully onto the block, over the dowel pins and gasket.

12. Coat the heads and threads of the cylinder head bolts with sealing compound. GM part No. 1052080 or equivalent, and install finger-tight.

13. Tighten the head bolts gradually in three stages, following the sequence illustrated, to the specification listed under "Torque Specifications."

14. Install the pushrods in the exact location from which they were removed. Make sure they are seated in their lifter sockets.

15. Swing the rocker arms over into their correct position. Tighten the rocker arms until all pushrod play is taken up.

16. Install the manifold assembly (or separate manifolds on the 1979 151 four), using new gaskets. Tighten the manifold(s) to the specified torque.

17. Reverse the remainder of the removal procedure for installation. Adjust the valves, following the procedure in this chapter. Use a new gasket or high-temperature sealer when installing the rocker arm cover.

V6 and V8 Engines

EXCEPT DIESEL ENGINES

◆ See Figures 32, 33, 34, 35 and 36 (p. 46)

1. Disconnect the battery.

2. Drain the coolant and save it if still fresh.

3. Remove the air cleaner.

4. Remove the air conditioning compressor, *but do not disconnect any A/C lines.* Secure the compressor to one side.

5. Disconnect the AIR hose at the check valve.

6. Remove the intake manifold.

7. When removing the right cylinder head, loosen the alternator belt, disconnect the wiring and remove the alternator.

8. When removing the left cylinder head, remove the dipstick, power steering pump and air pump if so equipped.

9. Label the spark plug wires and disconnect them.

10. Disconnect the exhaust manifold from the head being removed.

11. Remove the valve cover. Scribe the rocker arms with an identifying mark for reassembly; it is important that the rocker assembly is reinstalled in the same position as it was removed. Remove the rocker arm bolts, rocker arms and pivots.

12. Take a piece of heavy cardboard and cut 16 holes (or 8 holes if you are only removing one head) in it the same diameter as the pushrod stem. Number the holes in relation to the pushrods being removed. This cardboard holder will keep the pushrods in order (and hopefully out of harm's way) while they are out of the engine. Remove the pushrods.

➡**Pushrods MUST be returned to their original locations.**

13. On models equipped with power brakes, it is necessary to disconnect the brake booster and turn it sideways to remove the No. 7 pushrod.

14. Remove the cylinder head bolts, and remove the cylinder head and gasket. If the head seems stuck to the block, gently tap around the edge of the head with a rubber mallet until the joint breaks.

When removing the cylinder head, remove the valve cover, rocker arms and the pushrods . . .

. . . place the pushrods in a suitable holder since they must be installed in their original positions

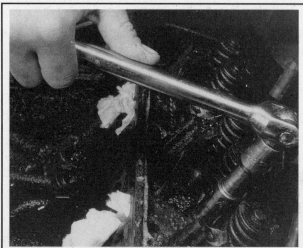
Loosen the cylinder head bolts in stages, in the reverse order of the tightening sequence

Remove the cylinder head from the engine block

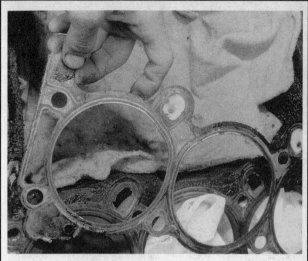

Remove and discard the old cylinder head gasket

Use a gasket scraper to carefully clean the mating surfaces

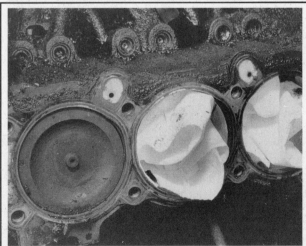

Place paper towels or shop rags in the cylinder bores to avoid getting any debris in them

Be sure to tighten all bolts to specifications and follow the proper torque sequence

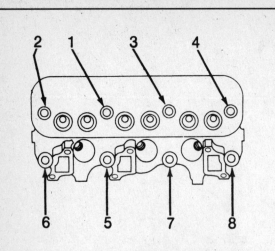

Fig. 32 Cylinder head bolt tightening sequence—Buick built V6 engines

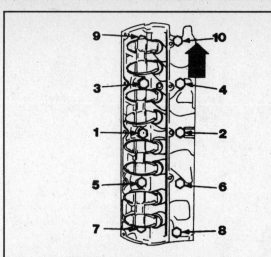

Fig. 35 Cylinder head bolt torque sequence—260, 307, 350 and 403 Oldsmobile built engines

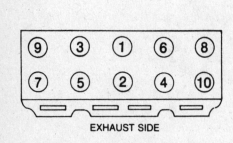

EXHAUST SIDE

Fig. 33 Buick built 350 and 455 V8 engines cylinder head bolt torque sequence

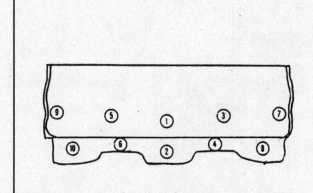

Fig. 36 Pontiac built 265, 301, 350, 400 and 455 V8 engine cylinder head bolt tightening sequence

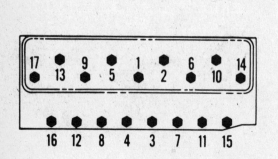

Fig. 34 Chevrolet built 305 and 350 V8 engine cylinder head bolt tightening sequence

15. Install in the reverse order of removal. NEW head gasket(s) should be used. Gaskets on the 260 V8 gaskets do not have a stripe. *On the 265 and 301 engines, coat all rocker stud lower threads, the cylinder head bolt threads, and the underside of the bolt head with thread sealer.* On all engines, the head bolts should be dipped in clean oil before installing. Tighten all head bolts in sequence to 60–70 ft. lbs., then again in sequence to the specified torque (see Torque Specifications chart in this chapter). Re-tighten the bolts after the engine is warmed up.

➡When installing the intake manifold remember to use new gaskets and O-ring seal, if so equipped.

DIESEL ENGINES
◗ See Figure 37

1. Remove the intake manifold, using the procedure outlined earlier in this section.
2. Remove the rocker arm cover(s), after removing any accessory brackets which interfere with cover removal.

Fig. 37 Oldsmobile built 350 diesel engine cylinder head bolt tightening sequence

3. Disconnect and label the glow plug wiring.

4. If the right cylinder head is being removed, remove the ground strap from the head.

5. Remove the rocker arm bolts, the bridged pivots, the rocker arms, and the pushrods, keeping all the parts in order so that they can be returned to their original positions. It is a good practice to number or mark the parts to avoid interchanging them.

6. Remove the fuel return lines from the nozzles.

7. Remove the exhaust manifold(s), using the procedure outlined above.

8. Remove the engine block drain plug on the side of the engine from which the cylinder head is being removed.

9. Remove the head bolts. Remove the cylinder head.

To install:

10. Clean the mating surfaces thoroughly. Install new head gaskets on the engine block. Do NOT coat the gaskets with any sealer. The gaskets have a special coating that eliminates the need for sealer. *The use of sealer will interfere with this coating and cause leaks.* Install the cylinder head onto the block.

11. Clean the head bolts thoroughly. Dip the bolts in clean engine oil and install into the cylinder block until the heads of the bolts lightly contact the cylinder head.

12. Tighten the bolts, in the sequence illustrated, to 100 ft. lbs. When all bolts have been tightened to this figure, begin the tightening sequence again, and torque all bolts to 130 ft. lbs.

13. Install the engine block drain plugs, the exhaust manifolds, the fuel return lines, the glow plug wiring, and the ground strap for the right cylinder head.

14. Install the valve train assembly. Refer to the "Diesel Engine Rocker Arm Replacement" in this chapter for the valve lifter bleeding procedures.

15. Install the intake manifold.

16. Install the valve covers. These are sealed with RTV (Room Temperature Vulcanizing) silicone sealer instead of a gasket. Use GM # 1052434 or an equivalent. Install the cover to the head within 10 minutes, while the sealer is still wet.

CLEANING & INSPECTION

Gasoline Engines

➡**Any diesel cylinder head work should be handled by a reputable machine shop familiar with diesel engines. Disassembly, valve lapping, and assembly can be completed by following the gasoline engine procedures.**

Once the complete valve train has been removed from the cylinder head(s), the head itself can be inspected, cleaned and machined (if necessary). Set the head(s) on a clean work space, so the combustion chambers are facing up. Begin cleaning the chambers and ports with a hardwood chisel or other non-metallic tool (to avoid nicking or gouging the chamber, ports, and especially the valve seats). Chip away the major carbon deposits, then remove the remainder of carbon with a wire brush fitted to an electric drill.

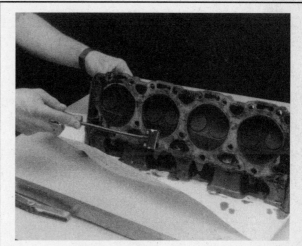

Use a gasket scraper to remove the bulk of the old head gasket from the mating surface

An electric drill equipped with a wire wheel will expedite complete gasket removal

A wire wheel may be used to clean the combustion chambers of carbon deposits

Be sure to check for warpage across the cylinder head at both diagonals

➥Be sure that the carbon is actually removed, rather than just burnished.

After decarbonizing is completed, take the head(s) to a machine shop and have the head "hot tanked." In this process, the head is lowered into a hot chemical bath that very effectively cleans all grease, corrosion, and scale from all internal and external head surfaces. Also, have the machinist check the valve seats and re-cut them if necessary. When you bring the clean head(s) home, place them on a clean surface. Completely clean the entire valve train with solvent.

CHECKING FOR HEAD WARPAGE

Lay the head down with the combustion chambers facing up. Place a straight-edge across the gasket surface of the head, both diagonally and straight across the center. Using a flat feeler gauge, determine the clearance at the center of the straight-edge. If warpage exceeds .003 in. in a 6 in. span, or .006 in. over the total length, the cylinder head must be resurfaced (which is akin

to planing a piece of wood). Resurfacing can be performed at most machine shops.

➥When resurfacing the cylinder head(s) of V6 or V8 engines, the intake manifold mounting position is altered, and must be corrected by machining a proportionate amount from the intake manifold flange.

Valves, Springs and Guides

REMOVAL

◆ See Figure 38

1. Remove the head(s), and place on a clean surface.
2. Using a suitable spring compressor (for pushrod-type over-head valve engines), compress the valve spring and remove the valve spring cap key. Release the spring compressor and remove the valve spring and cap (and valve rotator on some engines).

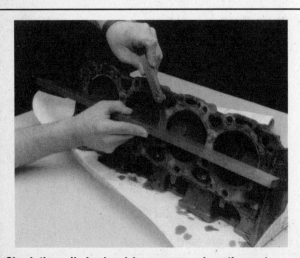

Check the cylinder head for warpage along the center using a straightedge and a feeler gauge

Use a valve spring compressor tool to relieve spring tension from the valve caps

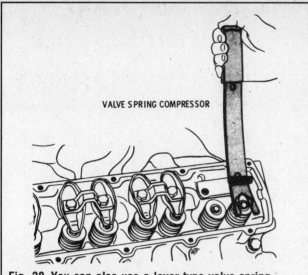

Fig. 38 You can also use a lever type valve spring compressor tool

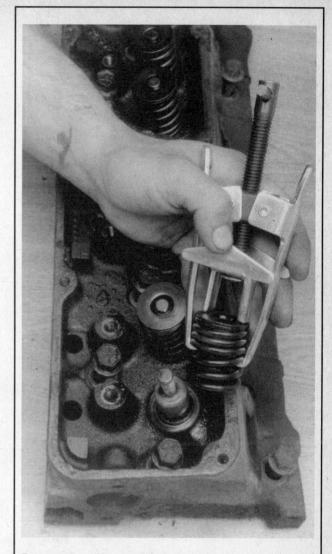

Remove the spring from the valve stem in order to access the seal

Be careful not to lose the valve keepers

A small magnet will help in removal of the valve keepers

Once the spring has been removed, the O-ring may be removed from the valve stem

Remove the valve stem seal from the cylinder head

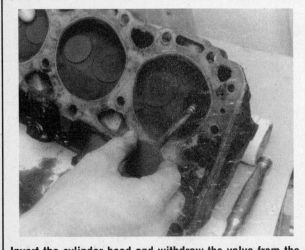

Invert the cylinder head and withdraw the valve from the cylinder head bore

➡**Use care in removing the keys; they are easily lost.**

3. Remove the valve seals from the intake valve guides. Throw these old seals away, as you'll be installing new seals during reassembly.

4. Slide the valves out of the head from the combustion chamber side.

5. Make a holder for the valves out of a piece of wood or cardboard, as outlined for the pushrods in "Cylinder Head Removal." Make sure you number each hole in the cardboard to keep the valves in proper order. Slide the valves out of the head from the combustion chamber side; they MUST be installed as they were removed.

INSPECTION

◆ **See Figures 39 and 40**

Inspect the valve faces and seats (in the head) for pits, burned spots and other evidence of poor seating. If a valve face is in such bad shape that the head of the valve must be ground in order to true up the face, discard the valve because the sharp edge will run too hot. The correct angle for valve faces is 45 degrees. We recommend the re-facing be done at a reputable machine shop.

Check the valve stem for scoring and burned spots. If not noticeably scored or damaged, clean the valve stem with solvent to remove all gum and varnish. Clean the valve guides using solvent and an expanding wire-type valve guide cleaner. If you have ac-

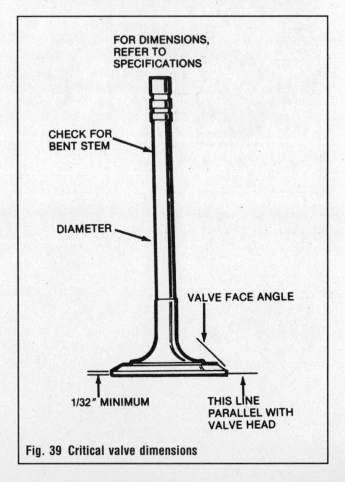

Fig. 39 Critical valve dimensions

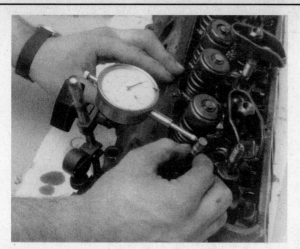

A dial gauge may be used to check valve stem-to-guide clearance

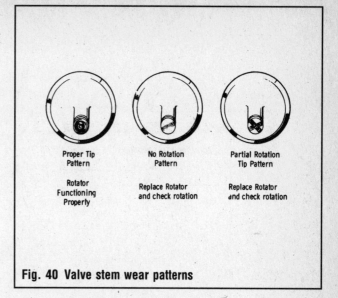

Fig. 40 Valve stem wear patterns

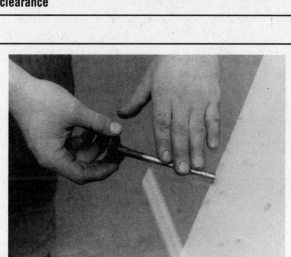

Valve stems may be rolled on a flat surface to check for bends

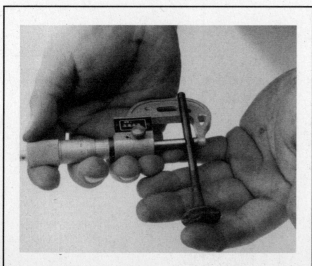

Use a micrometer to check the valve stem diameter

cess to a dial indicator for measuring valve stem-to-guide clearance, mount it so that the stem of the indicator is at 90° to the valve stem, and as close to the valve guide as possible. Move the valve off its seat, and measure the valve guide-to-stem clearance by rocking the stem back and forth to actuate the dial indicator. Measure the valve stems using a micrometer, and compare to specifications to determine whether stem or guide wear is responsible for the excess clearance. If a dial indicator and micrometer are not available to you, take your cylinder head and valves to a reputable machine shop for inspection.

Some of the engines covered in this guide are equipped with valve rotators, which double as valve spring caps. In normal operation the rotators put a certain degree of wear on the tip of the valve stem; this wear appears as concentric rings on the stem tip. However, if the rotator is not working properly, the wear may appear as straight notches or "X" patterns across the valve stem tip. Whenever the valves are removed from the cylinder head, the tips should be inspected for improper pattern, which could indicate valve rotator problems. Valve stem tips will have to be ground flat if rotator patterns are severe.

LAPPING THE VALVES

▶ See Figures 41 and 42

After machine work has been performed on the valves, it may be necessary to lap the valve to assure proper contact. For this, you should first contact your machine shop to determine if lapping is necessary. Some machine shops will perform this for you as part of the service, but the precision machining which is available today often makes lapping unnecessary. Additionally, the hardened valves/seats used in modern automobiles may make lapping difficult or impossible. If your machine shop recommends that you lap the valves, proceed as follows:

1. Invert the cylinder head so that the combustion chambers are facing up.
2. Lightly lubricate the valve stems with clean oil, and coat the valve seats with valve grinding compound. Install the valves in the head as numbered.

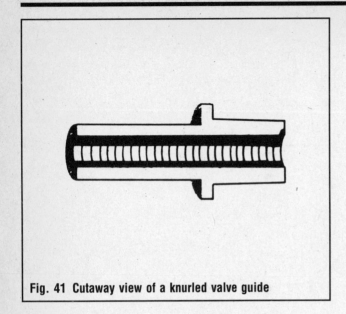

Fig. 41 Cutaway view of a knurled valve guide

Fig. 42 If valve lapping is necessary, you can fabricate a home-made lapping tool

3. Attach the suction cup of a valve lapping tool to a valve head. *You'll probably have to moisten the cup to securely attach the tool to the valve.*

4. Rotate the tool between the palms, changing position and lifting the tool often to prevent grooving. Lap the valve until a smooth, polished seat is evident (you may have to add a bit more compound after some lapping is done).

5. Remove the valve and tool, and remove ALL traces of grinding compound with solvent-soaked rag, or rinse the head with solvent.

➡**Valve lapping can also be done by fastening a suction cup to a piece of drill rod in a hand "eggbeater" type drill. Proceed as above, using the drill as a lapping tool. Due to the higher speeds involved when using the hand drill, care must be exercised to avoid grooving the seat. Lift the tool and change direction of rotation often.**

VALVE GUIDES

▶ **See Figure 43**

The engines covered in this guide use integral valve guides; that is, they are a part of the cylinder head and cannot be replaced. The guides can, however, be reamed oversize if they are found to be worn past an acceptable limit. Occasionally, a valve guide bore will be oversize as manufactured. These are marked on the inboard side of the cylinder heads on the machined surface just above the intake manifold.

If the guides must be reamed (this service is available at most machine shops), then valves with oversize stems must be fitted. Valves are usually available in 0.001, 0.003 and 0.005 in. stem oversizes. Valve guides which are not excessively worn or distorted may, in some cases, be knurled rather than reamed. Knurling is a process in which the metal on the valve guide bore is displaced and raised, thereby reducing clearance. Knurling also provides excellent oil control. The option of knurling rather than reaming valve guides should be discussed with a reputable machinist or engine specialist.

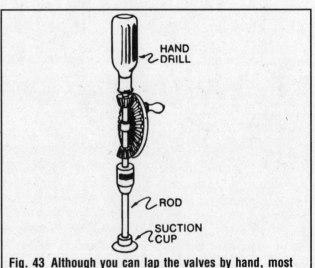

Fig. 43 Although you can lap the valves by hand, most materials used today make lapping obsolete

VALVE SPRINGS

Height and Pressure Check
▶ **See Figure 44**

1. Place the valve spring on a flat, clean surface next to a square.

2. Measure the height of the spring, and rotate it against the edge of the square to measure distortion (out-of-roundness). If spring height varies between springs by more than 1/16 in. or if the distortion exceeds 1/16 in. replace the spring.

A valve spring tester is needed to test spring test pressure, so the valve springs must usually be taken to a professional machine shop for this test. Spring pressure at the installed and compressed heights is checked, and a tolerance of plus or minus 5 lbs. (plus or minus 1 lb. on the 231 V6) is permissible on the springs covered in this guide.

VALVE INSTALLATION

▶ **See Figure 45**

New valve seals must be installed when the valve train is put back together. Certain seals slip over the valve stem and guide boss, while others require that the boss be machined. In some applications, Teflon guide seals are available. Check with a machin-

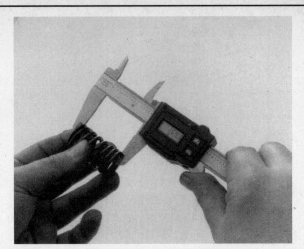

Use a caliper gauge to check the valve spring free-length

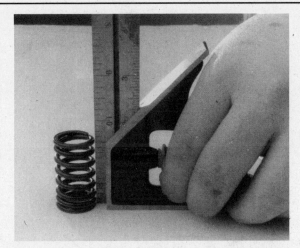

Check the valve spring for squareness on a flat service; a carpenter's square can be used

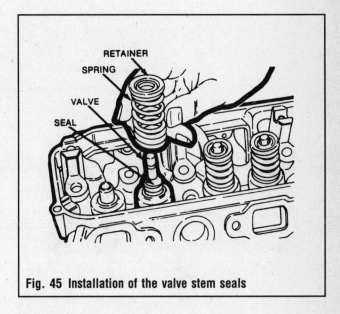

Fig. 45 Installation of the valve stem seals

ist and/or automotive parts store for a suggestion on the proper seals to use.

➡ **Remember that when installing valve seals, a small amount of oil is able to pass the seal to lubricate the valve guides; otherwise, excessive wear will result.**

To install the valves and rocker assembly:
1. Lubricate the valve stems with clean engine oil.
2. Install the valves in the cylinder head, one at a time, as numbered.
3. Lubricate and position the seals and valve springs, again a valve at a time.
4. Install the spring retainers, and compress the springs.
5. With the valve key groove exposed above the compressed valve spring, wipe some wheel bearing grease around the groove. This will retain the keys as you release the spring compressor.
6. Using needlenose pliers (or your fingers), place the keys in the key grooves. The grease should hold the keys in place. Slowly release the spring compressor; the valve cap or rotator will raise up as the compressor is released, retaining the keys.
7. Install the rocker assembly, and install the cylinder head(s).

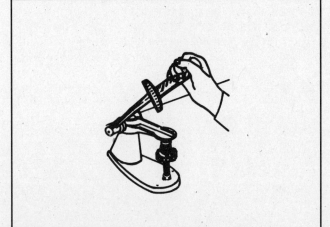

Fig. 44 Have the valve spring pressure checked professionally

VALVE ADJUSTMENT

▶ **See Figures 46, 47, 48 and 49**

All engines in this guide use hydraulic valve lifters, which require no periodic maintenance or adjustment. However, in the event of cylinder head removal or any operation that requires disturbing or removing the rocker arms, the rocker arms have to be adjusted.

151 Four and 250 Inline Six Cylinder Engines

PRELIMINARY ADJUSTMENT

1. After rocker arm or cylinder head disassembly, proceed as follows:

2. Remove the valve cover if it is not already removed.

3. Remove the distributor cap and crank the engine until the rotor points at number one plug terminal in the cap. It is easier to do this if you mark the location of number one plug wire before

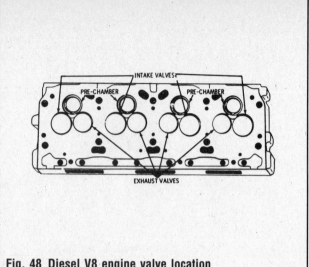

Fig. 48 Diesel V8 engine valve location

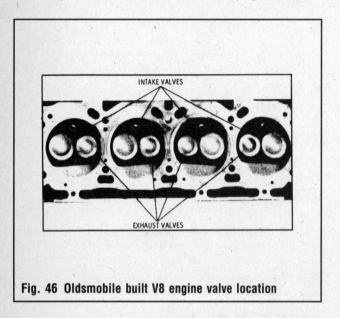

Fig. 46 Oldsmobile built V8 engine valve location

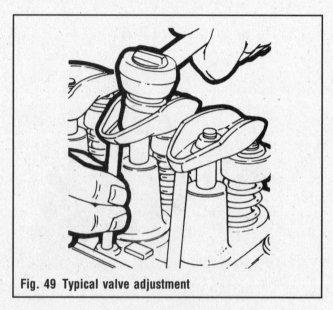

Fig. 49 Typical valve adjustment

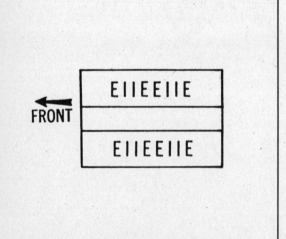

Fig. 47 Location of the intake and exhaust valves—Chevrolet built 305 and 350 V8 engines

you remove the cap. The points should be open (1974 250 six) and timing marks should be aligned. (the 0° mark on the timing tab). Number one cylinder should now be at TDC.

4. With the number one cylinder of the 250 six in this position, adjust: Intake valves 1,2,4, and exhaust valves 1,3,5 (numbered from the front of the engine). On the 151 four cylinder, adjust valves 1,2,3 and 5 (counting from the front of the engine). The adjustment is performed as follows: Turn the adjusting nut until all lash is removed from this particular valve train. This is determined by checking pushrod sideplay while turning the adjusting nut. When all play has been removed, turn the adjusting nut *one more turn*. This will place the lifter plunger in the center of its travel.

5. Crank the 250 six engine over through one complete revolution until number six cylinder is in the firing (TDC, timing pointer at 0°) position. Crank the 151 four through one complete revolution until number four cylinder is in the firing position. At this point, you can adjust the following valves on the 250 six: Intake

valves 3,5, and 6; exhaust valves 2,4 and 6. On the 151 four, adjust valves 4,6,7 and 8 in the same manner.

6. After the engine is running, readjust the valves following the procedure under "Engine Running." Install the valve covers using new gaskets or sealer.

ENGINE RUNNING ADJUSTMENT

1. Run the engine until normal operating temperature is attained. Remove the valve cover. To prevent oil splashing, install oil deflector clips, which are available at auto supply stores.

2. With the engine at idle, back off the rocker arm nut until the rocker arm begins to clatter.

3. Slowly tighten the rocker arm nut until the clatter just stops. This is zero lash.

4. Tighten the nut another quarter turn and then wait about ten seconds until the engine is running smoothly. Tighten the nut another quarter turn and wait another ten seconds. Repeat the procedure until the nut has been turned down one full turn from zero lash.

➡️**Pausing ten seconds each time allows the lifter to adjust itself. Failing to pause might cause interference between the intake valve and the piston top causing internal damage and bent pushrods.**

5. Adjust the remaining valves in the same manner.
6. Replace the valve cover.

V8 and V6 Engines

1. Remove the valve covers and crank the engine until the mark on the damper aligns with the TDC or 0° mark on the timing tab and the engine is in the No. 1 firing position. This can be determined by placing the fingers on the No. 1 cylinder valves as the marks align. If the valves do not move, it is in the No. 1 firing position. If the valves move, it is in the No. 6 firing position (No. 4 on V6) and the crankshaft should be rotated one more revolution to the No. 1 firing position.

2. Back out the adjusting nut until lash is felt at the pushrod, then turn the adjusting nut in until all lash is removed. This can be determined by checking pushrod end-play while turning the adjusting nut. When all play has been removed, turn the adjusting nut in 1 full turn.

3. With the engine in the No. 1 firing position, the following valves can be adjusted:
- V8-Exhaust—1,3,4,8
- V8-Intake—1,2,5,7
- V6-Exhaust—1,5,6
- V6-Intake—1,2,3

4. Crank the engine 1 full revolution until the marks are again in alignment. This is the No. 6 (No. 4 on V6) firing position. The following valves can now be adjusted:
- V8-Exhaust—2,5,6,7
- V8-Intake—3,4,6,8
- V6-Exhaust—2,3,4
- V6-Intake—4,5,6

5. Install the valve covers using new gaskets or sealer as required.

Valve Lifters

REMOVAL & INSTALLATION

151 Four and 250 Inline Six Cylinder Engines

1. Remove the rocker arm cover.
2. Loosen the rocker arm until you can rotate it away from the pushrod, giving clearance to the top of the pushrod.
3. Remove the pushrod. If you are replacing all of the lifters, it is wise to make a pushrod holder as mentioned under "Cylinder Head Removal." This will help keep the pushrods in order, as they MUST go back in their original positions.
4. Remove the pushrod covers on the side of the block.
5. Remove the lifter(s). A hydraulic lifter removal tool (GM part #J-3049 or equivalent) is available at dealers and most parts stores, and is quite handy for this procedure.
6. Before installing new lifters, all sealer coating must be removed from the inside. This can be done with kerosene or carburetor cleaning solvent. Also, the new lifters *must* be primed before installation, as *dry lifters will seize when the engine is started.* Submerge the lifters in clean engine oil and work the lifter plunger up and down.
7. Install the lifter(s) and pushrod(s) into the cylinder block in their original positions.
8. Pivot the rocker arm back into its original position. With the lifter on the base circle of the camshaft (valve closed), tighten the rocker arm nut to 20 ft. lbs. Do not over torque. You will have to rotate the crankshaft to do the individual valves.
9. Replace the pushrod covers using new gaskets. Replace the rocker arm cover, using a new gasket or sealer.

V6 and V8 Engines
▶ See Figure 50

➡️**Valve lifters and pushrods should be kept in order so they can be reinstalled in their original position. Some engines will have both standard size and .010 in. oversize valve lifters as original equipment. The oversize lifters are etched with an "O" on their sides; the cylinder block will also be marked with an "O" if the oversize lifter is used.**

1. Remove the intake manifold and gasket.
2. Remove the valve covers, rocker arm assemblies and pushrods.
3. If the lifters are coated with varnish, apply carburetor cleaning solvent to the lifter body. The solvent should dissolve the varnish in about 10 minutes.
4. Remove the lifters. On diesels, remove the lifter retainer guide bolts, and remove the guides. A special tool for removing lifters is available, and is helpful for this procedure.
5. New lifter MUST be primed before installation, *as dry lifters will seize when the engine is started.* Submerge the lifters in clean engine oil and work the lifter plunger up and down.
6. Install the lifters and pushrods into the cylinder block in their original order. On diesels, install the lifter retainer guide.

A magnet is useful in removing lifters from their bores

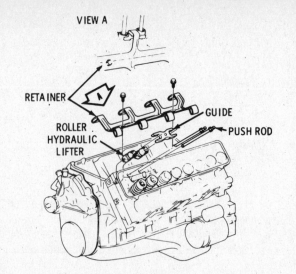

Fig. 50 Exploded view of the diesel valve lifter guide and retainer

Stuck lifters must be freed using a slide hammer type lifter removal tool

7. Install the intake manifold gaskets and manifold.

8. Position the rocker arms, pivots and bolts on the cylinder head.

9. Install the valve covers, connect the spark plug wires and install the air cleaner.

Timing Chain Cover and Front Oil Seal

REMOVAL & INSTALLATION

151 Four and 250 Inline Six Cylinder Engines
▶ **See Figures 51, 52 and 53**

1. Drain the engine coolant, remove the radiator hoses, and remove the radiator.

2. Remove the fan belt and any accessory belts. Remove the fan pulley.

3. A harmonic balancer puller is necessary to pull the balancer. Install the puller and remove the balancer.

4. Remove the two screws which attach the oil pan to the front cover. Remove the screws which attach the front cover to the block. Do not remove the cover yet.

5. Before the front cover is removed, it is necessary to cut the oil pan front seal. Pull the cover forward slightly.

6. Using a sharp knife or razor knife, cut the oil pan front seal flush with the cylinder block on both sides of the cover.

7. Remove the front cover and the attached portion of oil pan front seal. Remove the front cover gasket from the block.

To install:

8. Obtain an oil pan front seal. Cut the tabs from the new seal.

9. Install the seal in the front cover, pressing the tips into the holes provided in the cover. Coat the mating area of the front cover with a Room Temperature Vulcanizing (RTV) sealer first.

10. Coat the new front cover gasket with sealer and install it on the cover.

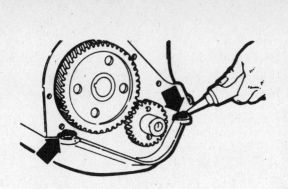

Fig. 51 Apply sealer to the front cover mounting points as shown—151 4-cylinder and 250 inline 6-cylinder engines

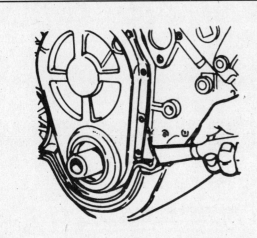

Fig. 52 Cut the oil pan seal flush with the front of the block

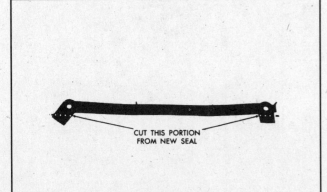

CUT THIS PORTION
FROM NEW SEAL

Fig. 53 You must modify the oil pan front seal by cutting the tabs off, as shown

11. Apply a ⅛ in. bead of RTV sealer to the joint formed at the oil pan and cylinder block.

12. Install the front cover.

13. Install the harmonic balancer. Make sure the front cover seal is positioned evenly around the balancer. If you do not have access to a balancer installation tool (and you probably don't), you can either fabricate one using the illustration as a guide, or you can tap the balancer on using a brass or plastic mallet. If you use the last method, *make sure the balancer goes on evenly.*

14. The rest of the installation is in the reverse order of removal.

V6 and V8 Engines
▶ **See Figures 54 thru 60 (pp. 58–60)**

BUICK ENGINES

1. Drain the cooling system.

2. Remove the radiator, fan, pulley and belt.

3. Remove the fuel pump and alternator, if necessary to remove cover.

4. Remove the distributor. If the timing chain and sprockets will not be disturbed, note the position of the distributor for installation in the same position.

5. Remove the thermostat bypass hose.

6. Remove the harmonic balancer.

7. Remove the timing chain-to-crankcase bolts.

8. Remove the oil pan-to-timing chain cover bolts and remove the timing chain cover.

9. Using a punch, drive out the old seal and the shedder toward the rear of the seal.

10. Coil the new packing around the opening so the ends are at the top. Drive in the shedder using a punch. Properly size the packing by rotating a hammer handle around the packing until the balancer hub can be inserted through the opening.

PONTIAC ENGINES

1. Drain the radiator and the cylinder block.

2. Loosen the alternator adjusting bolts.

3. Remove the fan, fan pulley, accessory drive belts, and water pump.

4. Disconnect the radiator hoses.

5. Remove the fuel pump.

6. Remove the harmonic balancer bolt and washer.

7. Remove harmonic balancer.

➡ **Do not pry on rubber-mounted balancers. If only the seal is to be replaced, proceed to Step 12.**

8. Remove the front four oil pan to timing cover bolts.

9. Remove the timing cover bolts and nuts and cover to intake manifold bolt.

10. Pull the cover forward and remove.

11. Remove the O-ring from the recess in the intake manifold, then clean all the gasket surfaces.

12. To replace the seal, pry it out of the cover using a suitable prytool. Install the new seal with the lip inward.

➡ **The seal can be replaced with the cover installed.**

13. To install, reverse the removal procedure, making sure all gaskets are replaced. Tighten the four oil pan bolts to 12 ft. lbs., and the fan pulley bolts to 20 ft. lbs.

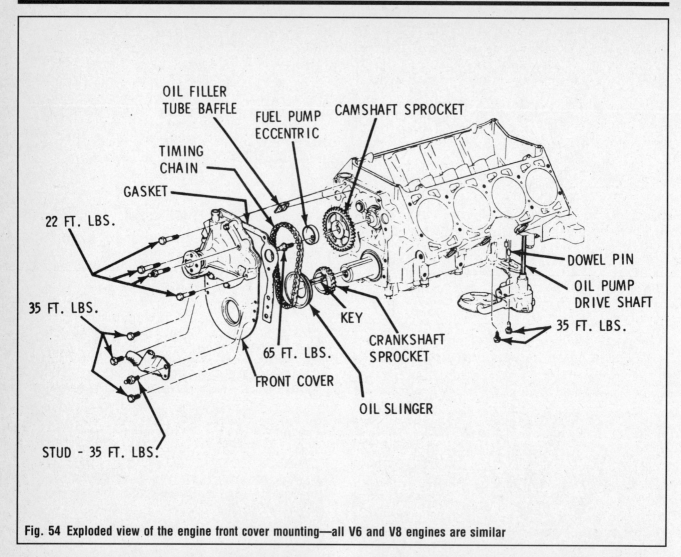

OIL FILLER
TUBE BAFFLE

FUEL PUMP
ECCENTRIC

CAMSHAFT SPROCKET

TIMING
CHAIN

GASKET

22 FT. LBS.

35 FT. LBS.

STUD - 35 FT. LBS.

65 FT. LBS.

FRONT COVER

KEY

CRANKSHAFT
SPROCKET

OIL SLINGER

DOWEL PIN

OIL PUMP
DRIVE SHAFT

35 FT. LBS.

Fig. 54 Exploded view of the engine front cover mounting—all V6 and V8 engines are similar

To remove the timing chain cover, unfasten the pulley retaining bolts . . .

. . . then remove the pulley

Remove the harmonic balancer bolt and washer

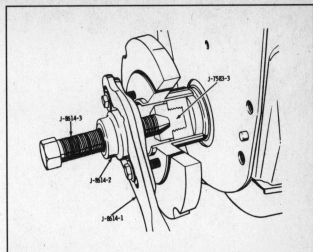

Fig. 55 Some pullers secure the crankshaft to prevent it from turning

Attach a suitable puller to the harmonic balancer . . .

Unfasten the lower timing chain cover retaining bolts

. . . then remove the harmonic balancer from the crankshaft

Remove the upper timing chain cover retaining bolts . . .

. . . then remove the timing chain front cover from the engine

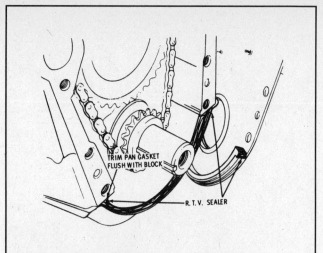

Fig. 58 Sealer application points—Chevrolet and Oldsmobile built engines

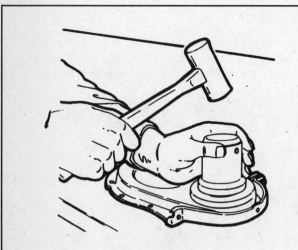

Fig. 56 Install a new front cover seal using a seal installation tool and a rubber mallet

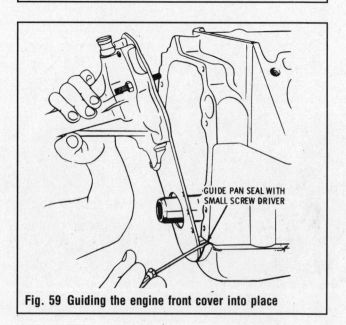

Fig. 59 Guiding the engine front cover into place

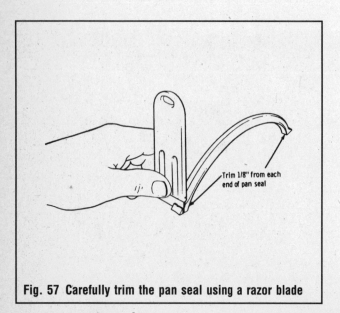

Fig. 57 Carefully trim the pan seal using a razor blade

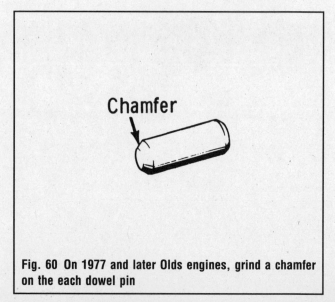

Fig. 60 On 1977 and later Olds engines, grind a chamfer on the each dowel pin

OLDSMOBILE GASOLINE ENGINES

1. Drain the coolant. Disconnect the radiator hose and the by-pass hose. Remove the fan, belts and pulley.

2. Remove the vibration damper and crankshaft pulley.

3. Drain the oil and remove the oil pan.

4. Remove the front cover attaching bolts and remove the cover, timing indicator and water pump from the front of the engine.

5. On 1977 and later models, grind a chamfer on the end of each dowel pin as illustrated. When installing the dowel pins, they must be inserted chamfered end first. Trim about 1/8" from each end of the new front pan seal and trim any excess material from the front edge of the oil pan gasket. Be sure all mating surfaces are clean.

6. Install in the reverse order of removal using a new gasket with sealing compound. Tighten self-tapping water pump attaching screws to 13 ft. lbs., 5/16 in. front cover attaching bolts to 25 ft. lbs. and the four bottom bolts (cover plate) to 35 ft. lbs. Tighten the pulley hub bolt to 310 ft. lbs.

CHEVROLET ENGINES

1. Drain the cooling system.

2. Remove the crankshaft pulley. Remove the water pump. Remove the screws holding the timing case cover to the block and remove the cover and gaskets.

3. Use a suitable tool to pry the old seal out of the front face of the cover.

4. Install the new seal so that open end is toward the inside of the cover.

➡ **Coat the lip of the new seal with oil prior to installation.**

5. Check that the timing chain oil slinger is in place against the crankshaft sprocket.

6. Install the cover carefully onto the locating dowels.

7. Tighten the attaching screws to 6–8 ft. lbs.

DIESEL ENGINE

1. Drain the cooling system and disconnect the radiator hoses.

2. Remove all belts, fan and pulley, crankshaft pulley and balancer, using a balancer puller.

✳✳ CAUTION

The use of any other type of puller, such as a universal claw type which pulls on the outside of the hub, can destroy the balancer. The outside ring of the balancer is bonded in rubber to the hub. Pulling on the outside will break the bond. The timing mark is on the outside ring. If it is suspected that the bond is broken, check that the center of the keyway is 16° from the center of the timing slot. In addition, there are chiseled aligning marks between the weight and the hub.

3. Unbolt and remove the cover, timing indicator and water pump.

4. It may be necessary to grind a flat on the cover for gripping purposes.

5. Grind a chamfer on one end of each dowel pin.

6. Cut the excess material from the front end of the oil pan gasket on each side of the block.

7. Clean the block, oil pan and front cover mating surfaces with solvent.

8. Trim about 1/8 in. off each end of a new front pan seal.

9. Install a new front cover gasket on the block and a new seal in the front cover.

10. Apply sealer to the gasket around the coolant holes.

11. Apply sealer to the block at the junction of the pan and front cover.

12. Place the cover on the block and press down to compress the seal. Rotate the cover left and right and guide the pan seal into the cavity using a small screwdriver. Oil the bolt threads and install two bolts to hold the cover in place. Install both dowel pins (chamfered end first), then install the remaining front cover bolts.

13. Apply a lubricant, compatible with rubber, on the balancer seal surface.

14. Install the balancer and bolt. Tighten the bolt to 200–300 ft. lbs.

15. Install the other parts in the reverse order of removal.

Timing Chain

REMOVAL & INSTALLATION

▶ **See Figures 61 and 62 (pp. 62–63)**

Buick V6 and V8 Engines

1. Remove the timing chain front cover, as outlined earlier in this section.

2. Align the timing marks on the sprockets.

3. Remove the camshaft sprocket bolt without changing the position of the sprocket. On the V6 and 455, remove the oil pan.

4. Remove the front crankshaft oil slinger.

5. On the 350, remove the crankshaft distributor drive gear retaining bolt and washer. Remove the drive gear and the fuel pump eccentric. On the V6 and the 455, remove the camshaft sprocket bolts.

6. Using two large prytools, carefully pry the camshaft sprocket and the crankshaft sprocket forward until they are free. Remove the sprockets and the chain.

To remove the timing chain, first remove the cover, then remove the crankshaft oil slinger

If necessary, remove the camshaft thrust button and spring

Pull the camshaft sprocket and timing chain off the cam. It may be necessary to pry them off

Use a rachet, extension and socket combination to remove the camshaft sprocket bolts

If not already done, remove the crankshaft sprocket

The timing marks on the camshaft and crankshaft (see arrows) must be aligned

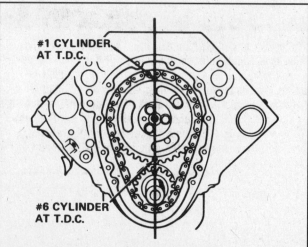

#1 CYLINDER AT T.D.C.

#6 CYLINDER AT T.D.C.

Fig. 61 Timing sprocket alignment marks—Oldsmobile, Chevrolet and Buick (including V6) engines

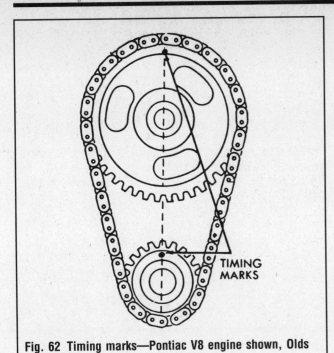

Fig. 62 Timing marks—Pontiac V8 engine shown, Olds 400 similar

To install:

7. Make sure, with sprockets temporarily installed, that No. 1 piston is at top dead center and the camshaft sprocket O-mark is straight down and on the centerline of both shafts.

8. Remove the camshaft sprocket and assemble the timing chain on both sprockets. Then slide the sprockets-and-chain assembly on the shafts with the O-marks in their closest together position and on a centerline with the sprocket hubs.

9. Assemble the slinger on the crankshaft with I.D. against the sprocket, (concave side toward the front of engine). Install the oil pan, if removed.

10. On the 350, slide the fuel pump eccentric on the camshaft and the Woodruff key with the oil groove forward. On the six cylinder and the 455, install the camshaft sprocket bolts.

11. Install the distributor drive gear.

12. Install the drive gear and eccentric bolt and retaining washer. Torque to 40–55 ft. lbs.

13. Install the timing case cover. Install a new seal by lightly tapping it in place. The lip of the seal faces inward. Pay particular attention to the following points.

   a. Remove the oil pump cover and pack the space around the oil pump gears completely full of petroleum jelly. There must be no air space left inside the pump. Reinstall the pump cover using a new gasket.

   b. The gasket surface of the block and timing chain cover must be clean and smooth. Use a new gasket correctly positioned.

   c. Install the chain cover being certain the dowel pins engage the dowel pin holes before starting the attaching bolts.

   d. Lube the bolt threads before installation and install them.

   e. If the car has power steering the front pump bracket should be installed at this time.

   f. Lube the O.D. of the harmonic balancer hub before installation to prevent damage to the seal when starting the engine.

➡ The V6 engine has two timing marks on the harmonic balancer. A one inch long, thin scribe mark is used for strobe light timing. Another mark, four inches back, has a wider slot and is about one-half inch long. This mark is used for magnetic pick-up timing.

Pontiac Engines

1. Remove the timing chain cover.

2. Remove the camshaft bolt, fuel pump eccentric and bushing.

3. Align the timing marks to simplify proper positioning of the sprockets during reassembly.

4. Slide the timing chain and camshaft gear off at the same time.

➡ If you intend to remove the gear on the crankshaft you will need a puller to do so.

5. Install the new timing chain and or sprockets, making sure the marks on both sprockets are exactly on a straight line passing through the shaft centers. The camshaft should extend through the sprocket so that the hole in the fuel pump eccentric will locate on the shaft.

6. Install the fuel pump eccentric and bushing. Install the retainer bolt and tighten it to 40 ft. lbs.

7. Reinstall the timing gear cover, water pump, and harmonic balancer. Remember to install a new O-ring in the water passage.

➡ When reassembling the timing case cover, extra care should be taken to make sure that the oil seal between the bottom of the timing case cover and the front of the oil pan is still good. Gasket cement should be used at the joint to prevent oil leaks.

Oldsmobile Engines

1. Remove the timing case cover and take off the camshaft gear.

➡ The fuel pump operating cam is bolted to the front of the camshaft sprocket and the sprocket is located on the camshaft by means of a dowel.

2. Remove the oil slinger, timing chain, and the camshaft sprocket. If the crankshaft sprocket is to be replaced, remove it also at this time. Remove the crankshaft key before using the puller. If the key can not be removed, align the puller so it does not overlap the end of the key, as the keyway is only machined part of the way into the crankshaft gear.

3. Reinstall the crankshaft sprocket being careful to start it with the keyway in perfect alignment since it is rather difficult to correct for misalignment after the gear has been started on the shaft. Turn the timing mark on the crankshaft gear until it points directly toward the center of the camshaft. Mount the timing chain over the camshaft gear and start the camshaft gear up on to its shaft with the timing marks as close as possible to each other and in line between the shaft centers. Rotate the camshaft to align the shaft with the new gear.

4. Install the fuel pump eccentric with the flat side toward the rear.

5. Drive the key in with a hammer until it bottoms.

6. Install the oil slinger.

➡**Any time the timing chain and gears are replaced on the diesel engine it will be necessary to retime the engine. Refer to the paragraph on Diesel Engine Injection Timing in Chapter 5.**

Chevrolet Engines

To replace the chain, remove the radiator core, water pump, the harmonic balancer and the crankcase front cover. This will allow access to the timing chain. Crank the engine until the timing marks on both sprockets are nearest each other and in line between the shaft centers. Then take out the three bolts that hold the camshaft gear to the camshaft. This gear is a light press fit on the camshaft and will come off easily. It is located by a dowel.

The chain comes off with the camshaft gear.

A gear puller will be required to remove the crankshaft gear.

Without disturbing the position of the engine, mount the new crankshaft gear on the shaft, and mount the chain over the camshaft gear. Arrange the camshaft gear in such a way that the timing marks will line up between the shaft centers and the camshaft locating dowel will enter the dowel hole in the cam sprocket.

Place the cam sprocket, with its chain mounted over it, in position on the front of the car and pull up with the three bolts that hold it to the camshaft.

After the gears are in place, turn the engine two full revolutions to make certain that the timing marks are in correct alignment between the shaft centers.

End-play of the camshaft is zero.

Timing Gears

REMOVAL & INSTALLATION

151 Four and 250 Inline Six Cylinder Engines

The camshaft in these engines is gear-driven, unlike the chain-driven cams in V6s and V8s. The removal of the timing gear requires removal of the camshaft.

1. After the cam is removed, place the camshaft and gear in an arbor press and remove the gear from the cam. Many well-equipped machine shops have this piece of equipment if you need the gear pressed off.

2. Installation is in the reverse order of removal. The clearance between the camshaft and the thrust plate should be 0.001–0.005 in. on both engines. If less than 0.0015 in. clearance exists, the spacer ring should be replaced. If more than 0.005 in. clearance, the thrust plate should be replaced.

Camshaft

REMOVAL & INSTALLATION

151 Four and 250 Inline Six Cylinder Engines

1. Remove the grille. Remove the radiator hoses and remove the radiator.
2. Remove the timing gear cover.
3. Remove the valve cover and gasket, loosen all the rocket arm nuts, and pivot the rocker arms clear of the pushrods.

4. Remove the distributor and the fuel pump.
5. Remove the pushrods. Remove the coil and then remove the side cover. Remove the valve lifters.
6. Remove the two camshaft thrust plate retaining screws by working through the holes in the camshaft gear.
7. Remove the camshaft and gear assembly by pulling it out through the front of the block.
8. If either the camshaft or the camshaft gear is being renewed, the gear must be pressed off the camshaft. The replacement parts must be assembled in the same way. When placing the gear on the camshaft, press the gear onto the shaft until it bottoms against the gear spacer ring. The end clearance of the thrust plate should be .001 to .005 in.
9. Pre-lube the camshaft lobes with either engine oil or a product such as STP, and then install the camshaft assembly in the engine. Be careful not to damage the bearings.
10. Turn the crankshaft and the camshaft gears so that the timing marks align. Push the camshaft into position and install and tighten the thrust plate bolts to 7 ft. lbs.
11. Check camshaft and crankshaft gear runout with a dial indicator. Camshaft gear runout should not exceed .004 in. and crankshaft gear run-out should not be above .003 in.
12. Using a dial indicator, check the backlash at several points between the camshaft and crankshaft gear teeth. Backlash should be .004–.006 in.
13. Install the timing gear cover. Install the harmonic balancer.
14. Install the valve lifters and the pushrods. Install the side cover. Install the coil and the fuel pump.
15. Install the distributor and set the timing. Pivot the rocker arms over the pushrods and adjust the valves.
16. Install the radiator, hoses and grille.

V6 Engines

1. Remove intake manifold.
2. Remove valve covers.
3. Remove rocker arm and shaft assemblies, pushrods and valve lifters. Mark parts as necessary and keep pushrods in order for later assembly.
4. Remove timing chain cover, timing chain and sprocket.
5. Carefully slide camshaft forward, out of the bearing bores. *Working slowly to avoid marring the bearing surfaces.* Remove camshaft.
6. To install, liberally coat the entire cam with a heavy engine oil or a lubricant specially formulated for engine rebuilding. Slowly slide the camshaft into the engine block, *exercising extreme care not to damage the cam bearings.*
7. Reassemble the engine in the reverse order of removal.

V8 Engines

GASOLINE ENGINES

1. Disconnect the battery.
2. Drain and remove the radiator.
3. Disconnect the fuel line at the fuel pump. Remove the pump on 1978 and later models.
4. Disconnect the throttle cable and the air cleaner.
5. Remove the alternator belt, loosen the alternator bolts and move the alternator to one side.
6. Remove the power steering pump from its brackets and move it out of the way.
7. Remove the air conditioning compressor from its brackets

and move the compressor out of the way without disconnecting the lines.

8. Disconnect the hoses from the water pump.

9. Disconnect the electrical and vacuum connections.

10. Mark the distributor as to location in the block. Remove the distributor.

On 1977 and later model Olds engines, remove the crankshaft pulley and the hub attaching bolt. Remove the crankshaft hub. Proceed to Step 19.

11. Raise the car and drain the oil pan.

12. Remove the exhaust crossover pipe and starter motor.

13. Disconnect the exhaust pipe at the manifold.

14. Remove the harmonic balancer and pulley.

15. Support the engine and remove the front motor mounts.

16. Remove the flywheel inspection cover.

17. Remove the engine oil pan.

18. Support the engine by placing wooden blocks between the exhaust manifolds and the front crossmember.

19. Remove the engine front cover.

20. Remove the valve covers.

21. Remove the intake manifold, oil filler pipe, and temperature sending switch.

22. Mark the lifters, pushrods, and rocker arms as to location so that they may be installed in the same position. Remove these parts.

23. If the car is equipped with air conditioning, discharge the A/C system and remove the condenser.

24. Remove the fuel pump eccentric, camshaft gear, oil slinger, and timing chain. Remove the camshaft thrust plate (on front of camshaft) if equipped.

25. Carefully remove the camshaft from the engine.

26. Inspect the shaft for signs of excessive wear or damage.

27. Liberally coat camshaft and bearings with heavy engine oil or engine assembly lubricant and insert the cam into the engine.

28. Align the timing marks on the camshaft and crankshaft gears. See Timing Chain Replacement and Valve Timing for details.

29. Install the distributor using the locating marks made during removal. If any problems are encountered, see "Distributor Installation."

30. To install, reverse the removal procedure but pay attention to the following points:

   a. Install the timing indicator before installing the power steering pump bracket.

   b. Install the flywheel inspection cover after installing the starter.

   c. Replace the engine oil and radiator coolant.

DIESEL ENGINES

➡If equipped with air conditioning, the system must be discharged by an air conditioning specialist before the camshaft is removed. The condenser must also be removed from the car.

Removal of the camshaft also requires removal of the injection pump drive and driven gears, removal of the intake manifold, disassembly of the valve lifters, and retiming of the injection pump.

1. Disconnect the negative battery cables.

2. Remove the intake manifold and gasket and the front and rear intake manifold seals. Refer to the intake manifold removal and installation procedure.

3. Remove the balancer pulley and the balancer. See "Cau-

tion" under diesel engine front cover removal and installation, above. Remove the engine front cover using the appropriate procedure.

4. Remove the valve covers. Remove the rocker arms, pushrods and valve lifters; see the procedure earlier in this section. Be sure to keep the parts in order so that they may be returned to their original positions.

5. Remove the camshaft sprocket retaining bolt, and remove the timing chain and sprockets, using the procedure outlined earlier.

6. Position the camshaft dowel pin at the 3 o'clock position on the V8.

7. On V8s, push the camshaft rearward and hold it there, being careful not to dislodge the oil gallery plug at the rear of the engine. Remove the fuel injection pump drive gear by sliding it from the camshaft while rocking the pump driven gear.

8. To remove the fuel injection pump driven gear, remove the pump adapter, the snapring, and remove the selective washer. Remove the driven gear and spring.

9. Remove the camshaft by sliding it out the front of the engine. Be extremely careful not to allow the cam lobes to contact any of the bearings, or the journals to dislodge the bearings during camshaft removal. Do not force the camshaft, or bearing damage will result.

10. If either the injection pump drive or driven gears are to be replaced, replace both gears.

11. Coat the camshaft and the cam bearings with a heavyweight engine oil, GM lubricant # 1052365 or the equivalent.

12. Carefully slide the camshaft into position in the engine.

13. Fit the crankshaft and camshaft sprockets, aligning the timing marks as shown in the timing chain removal and installation procedure, above. Remove the sprockets without disturbing the timing.

14. Install the injection pump driven gear, spring, shim, and snapring. Check the gear end-play. If the end-play is not within 0.002–0.006 in. on V8s through 1979, and .002 to .015 in. on 1980 and later, replace the shim to obtain the specified clearance. Shims are available in 0.003 in. increments, from 0.080 to 0.115 in.

15. Position the camshaft dowel pin at the 3 o'clock position. Align the zero marks on the pump drive gear and pump driven gear. Hold the camshaft in the rearward position and slide the pump drive gear onto the camshaft. Install the camshaft bearing retainer.

16. Install the timing chain and sprockets, making sure the timing marks are aligned.

17. Install the lifters, pushrods and rocker arms. See "Rocker Arm Replacement, Diesel Engine" for lifter bleed down procedures. *Failure to bleed down the lifters could bend valves when the engine is turned over.*

18. Install the injection pump adapter and injection pump. See the appropriate sections under "Fuel System" above for procedures.

19. Install the remaining components in the reverse order of removal.

INSPECTION

Completely clean the camshaft with solvent, paying special attention to cleaning the oil holes. Visually inspect the cam lobes and bearing journals for excessive wear. If a lobe is questionable, have the cam checked at a reputable machine shop; if a journal or lobe is worn, the camshaft must be reground or replaced. Also have the camshaft checked for straightness on a dial indicator.

➡️If a cam journal is worn, there is a good chance that the bushings are worn.

Camshaft Bearings

REMOVAL & INSTALLATION

◆ **See Figures 63 and 64**

If excessive camshaft wear is found, or if the engine is being completely rebuilt, the camshaft bearings should be replaced.

➡️The front and rear bearings should be removed last, and installed first. Those bearings act as guides for the other bearings and pilot.

1. Drive the camshaft rear plug from the block.
2. Assemble the removal puller with its shoulder on the bear-

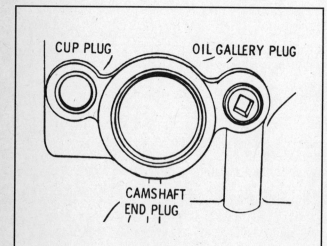

Fig. 63 There are camshaft and oil gallery plugs located at the rear of the engine block

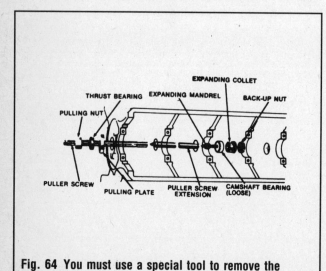

Fig. 64 You must use a special tool to remove the camshaft bearings

ing to be removed. Gradually tighten the puller nut until the bearing is removed.

3. Remove the remaining bearings, leaving the front and rear for last. To remove these, reverse the position of the puller, so as to pull the bearings towards the center of the block. Leave the tool in this position, pilot the new front and rear bearings on the installer, and pull them into position.

4. Return the puller to its original position and pull the remaining bearings into position.

➡️Ensure that the oil holes align when installing the bearings. This is very important!

5. Replace the camshaft rear plug, and stake it into position.

Pistons and Connecting Rods

REMOVAL

◆ **See Figures 65 thru 74 (pp. 67–69)**

Before removing the pistons, the top of the cylinder bore must be examined for a ridge. A ridge at the top of the bore is the result of normal cylinder wear, caused by the piston rings only travelling so far up the bore in the course of the piston stroke. The ridge can be felt by hand; it must be removed before the pistons are removed.

A ridge reamer is necessary for this operation. Place the piston at the bottom of its stroke, and cover it with a rag. Cut the ridge away with the ridge reamer, using extreme care to avoid cutting too deeply. Remove the rag, and remove the cuttings that remain on the piston with a magnet and a rag soaked in clean oil. *Make sure the piston top and cylinder bore are absolutely clean before moving the piston.*

1. Remove intake manifold and cylinder head or heads.
2. Remove oil pan.
3. Remove oil pump assembly if necessary.
4. Match mark the connecting rod cap to the connecting rod with a scribe; each cap must be reinstalled on its proper rod in the proper direction. Remove the connecting rod bearing cap and

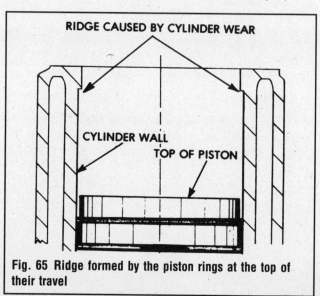

Fig. 65 Ridge formed by the piston rings at the top of their travel

Place rubber hose over the connecting rod studs to protect the crank and bores from damage

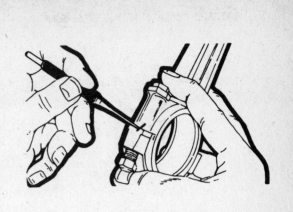

Fig. 66 Matchmark the connecting rods to their caps with a scribe mark . . .

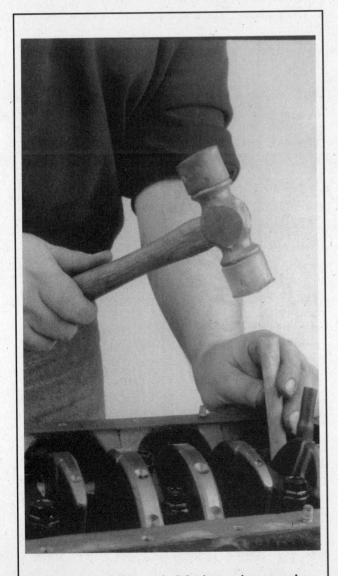

Carefully tap the piston out of the bore using a wooden dowel

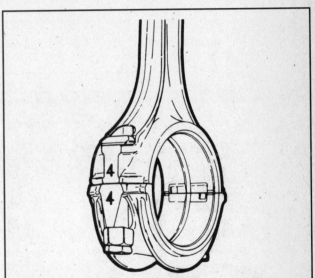

Fig. 67 . . . or use a number stamp to match the connecting rods to their cylinders

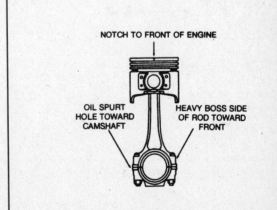

Fig. 68 Piston and connecting rod positioning—151 4-cylinder and 250 inline 6-cylinder engine

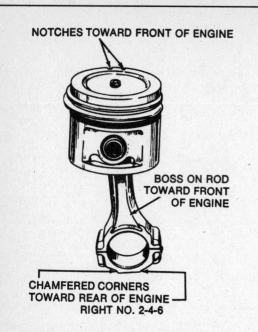

Fig. 69 Right bank piston and rod assembly—231 and 252 V6 engines

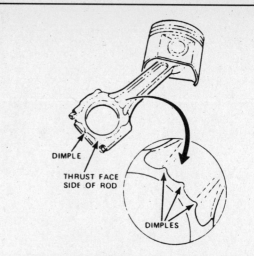

Fig. 71 The dimples identify the connecting rod thrust faces on some Pontiac V8s. Notches on the rod face rearward on the 301, forward on the right bank and rearward on the left bank on the 350 and 400 engines

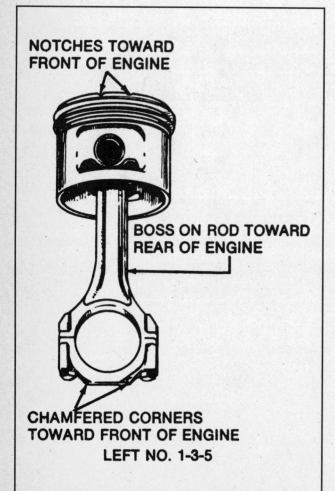

Fig. 70 Left bank piston and rod assembly—231 and 252 V6 engines

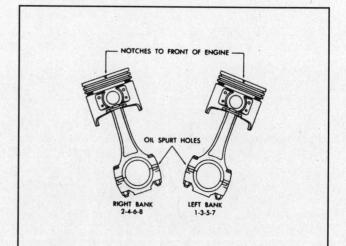

Fig. 72 Pontiac V8 piston and connecting rod assemblies

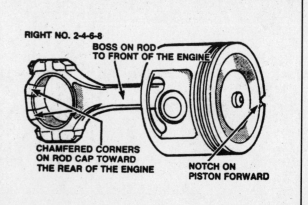

Fig. 73 Buick V8 engine piston and rod assembly—right bank shown

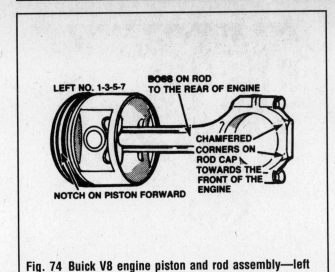

Fig. 74 Buick V8 engine piston and rod assembly—left bank shown

the rod bearing. Number the top of each piston with silver paint or a felt-tip pen for later assembly.

5. Cut lengths of ⅜ in. diameter hose to use as rod bolt guides. Install the hose over the threads of the rod bolts, to prevent the bolt threads from damaging the crankshaft journals and cylinder walls when the piston is removed.

6. Squirt some clean engine oil onto the cylinder wall from above, until the wall is coated. Carefully push the piston and rod assembly up and out of the cylinder by tapping on the bottom of the connecting rod with a wooden hammer handle.

7. Place the rod bearing and cap back on the connecting rod, and install the nuts temporarily. Using a number stamp or punch, stamp the cylinder number on the side of the connecting rod and cap; this will help keep the proper piston and rod assembly on the proper cylinder.

➡On V6 engines, starting at the front the cylinders are numbered 2-4-6 on the right bank and 1-3-5 on the left. On all V8s, starting at the front the right bank cylinders are 2-4-6-8 and the left bank 1-3-5-7.

8. Remove remaining pistons in similar manner.

On all engines, the notch on the piston will face the front of the engine for assembly. The chamfered corners of the bearing caps should face toward the front of the left bank and toward the rear of the right bank, and the boss on the connecting rod should face toward the front of the engine for the right bank and to the rear of the engine on the left bank. On some Pontiac-built engines, the rods have three dimples on one side of the rod and a single dimple on the rod cap. The dimples must face to the rear on the right bank and forward on the left.

On various engines, the piston compression rings are marked with a dimple, a letter "T", a letter "O," "GM" or the word "TOP" to identify the side of the ring which must face toward the top of the piston.

CLEANING & INSPECTION

▶ **See Figures 75 and 76**

Some of the engines covered in this guide utilize pistons with pressed-in wrist pins; these must be removed by a special press designed for this purpose. Other pistons have their wrist pins secured by snaprings, which are easily removed with snapring pliers. Separate the piston from the connecting rod.

A piston ring expander is necessary for removing piston rings without damaging them; any other method (screwdriver blades, pliers, etc.) usually results in the rings being bent, scratched or distorted, or the piston itself being damaged. When the rings are removed, clean the ring grooves using an appropriate ring groove cleaning tool, using care not to cut too deeply. Thoroughly clean all carbon and varnish from the piston with solvent.

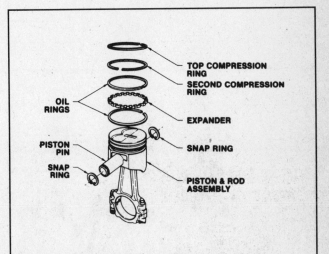

Fig. 75 Exploded view of the piston and related components

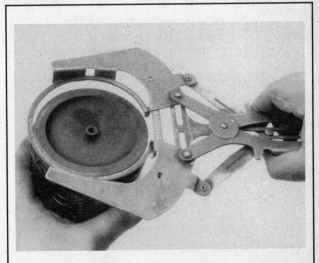

Use a ring expander tool to remove the piston rings

Clean the piston grooves using a ring groove cleaner

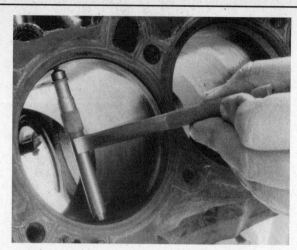

A telescoping gauge may be used to measure the cylinder bore diameter

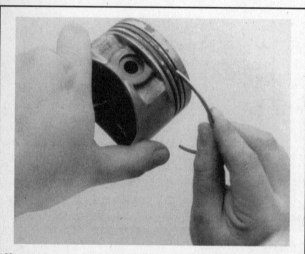

You can use a piece of an old ring to clean the piston grooves, BUT be careful, the ring is sharp

Measure the piston's outer diameter using a micrometer

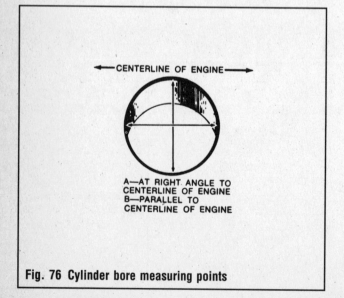

Fig. 76 Cylinder bore measuring points

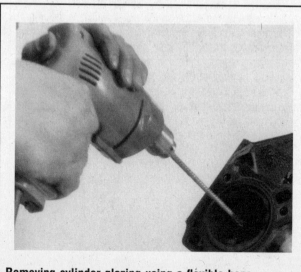

Removing cylinder glazing using a flexible hone

A properly cross-hatched cylinder bore

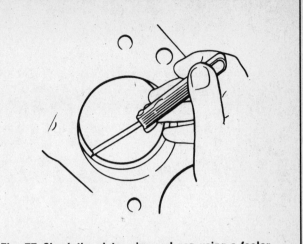

Fig. 77 Check the piston ring end-gap using a feeler gauge

✳✳ WARNING

Do not use a wire brush or caustic solvent (acids, etc.) on pistons.

Inspect the pistons for scuffing, scoring, cracks, pitting, or excessive ring groove wear. If these are evident, the piston must be replaced.

The piston should also be checked in relation to the cylinder diameter. Using a telescoping gauge and micrometer, or a dial gauge, measure the cylinder bore diameter perpendicular (90%) to the piston pin, 2½ in. below the cylinder block deck (surface where the block mates with the heads). Then, with the micrometer, measure the piston perpendicular to its wrist pin on the skirt. The difference between the two measurements is the piston clearance. If the clearance is within specifications or slightly below (after the cylinders have been bored or honed), finish honing is all that is necessary. If the clearance is excessive, try to obtain a slightly larger piston to bring clearance to within specifications. If this is not possible, obtain the first oversize piston and hone (or if necessary, bore) the cylinder to size. Generally, if the cylinder bore is tapered .005 in. or more or is out-of-round .003 in. or more, it is advisable to rebore for the smallest possible oversize piston and rings.

After measuring, mark pistons with a felt-tip pen for reference and for assembly.

➡**Cylinder honing and/or boring should be performed by a reputable, professional mechanic with the proper equipment. In some cases, "clean-up" honing can be done with the cylinder block in the car, but most excessive honing and all cylinder boring must be done with the block stripped and removed from the car.**

PISTON RING END-GAP

◆ **See Figure 77**

Piston ring end-gap should be checked while the rings are removed from the pistons. Incorrect end-gap indicates that the wrong size rings are being used; *ring breakage could occur.*

Compress the piston rings to be used in a cylinder, one at a time, into that cylinder. Squirt clean oil into the cylinder, so that the rings and the top 2 inches of cylinder wall are coated. Using an inverted piston, press the rings apprxoimately 1 in. below the deck of the block (on diesels, measure ring gap clearance with the ring positioned at the *bottom* of ring travel in the bore). Measure the ring end-gap with a feeler gauge, and compare to the "Ring Gap" chart in this chapter. Carefully pull the ring out of the cylinder and file the ends squarely with a fine file to obtain the proper clearance.

PISTON RING SIDE CLEARANCE CHECK & INSTALLATION

◆ **See Figures 78 and 79**

Check the pistons to see that the ring grooves and oil return holes have been properly cleaned. Slide a piston ring into its groove, and check the side clearance with a feeler gauge. On gasoline engines, make sure you insert the gauge between the ring and its lower land (lower edge of the groove), because any wear that occurs forms a step at the inner portion of the lower land. On diesels, insert the gauge between the ring and the *upper* land. If the piston grooves have worn to the extent that relatively high steps exist on the lower land, the piston grooves have worn to the extent that relatively high steps exist on the lower land, the piston should be replaced, because these will interfere with the operation of the new rings and ring clearances will be excessive. Piston rings are not furnished in oversize widths to compensate for ring groove wear.

Install the rings on the piston, *lowest ring first*, using a piston ring expander. There is a high risk of breaking or distorting the rings, or scratching the piston, of the rings are installed by hand or other means.

Position the rings on the piston as illustrated; *spacing of the various piston ring gaps is crucial to proper oil retention and even cylinder wear.* When installing new rings, refer to the installation diagram furnished with the new parts.

Checking the ring-to-ring groove clearance

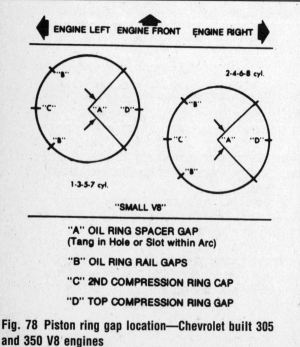

ENGINE LEFT ENGINE FRONT ENGINE RIGHT

2-4-6-8 cyl.

1-3-5-7 cyl.

"SMALL V8"

"A" OIL RING SPACER GAP
(Tang in Hole or Slot within Arc)

"B" OIL RING RAIL GAPS

"C" 2ND COMPRESSION RING CAP

"D" TOP COMPRESSION RING GAP

Fig. 78 Piston ring gap location—Chevrolet built 305 and 350 V8 engines

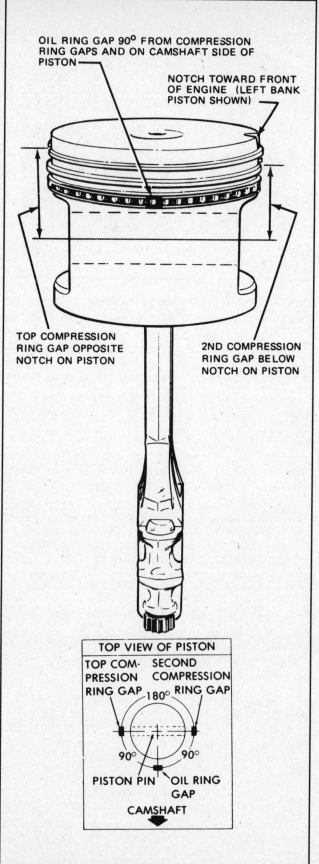

OIL RING GAP 90° FROM COMPRESSION RING GAPS AND ON CAMSHAFT SIDE OF PISTON

NOTCH TOWARD FRONT OF ENGINE (LEFT BANK PISTON SHOWN)

TOP COMPRESSION RING GAP OPPOSITE NOTCH ON PISTON

2ND COMPRESSION RING GAP BELOW NOTCH ON PISTON

TOP VIEW OF PISTON

TOP COM-PRESSION RING GAP

SECOND COMPRESSION RING GAP

180°

90°   90°

PISTON PIN   OIL RING GAP

CAMSHAFT

Fig. 79 Piston ring gap location—Buick built V6 and V8 engines

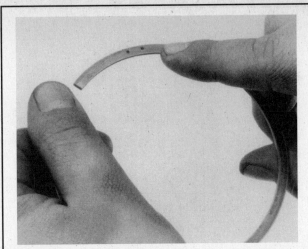

Most rings are marked to show which side should face upward

CONNECTING ROD BEARINGS

Connecting rod bearings for the engines covered in this guide consist of two halves or shells which are interchangeable in the rod and cap. When the shells are placed in position, the ends extend slightly beyond the rod and cap surfaces so that when the rod bolts are tightened, the shells will be clamped tightly in place to insure positive seating and to prevent turning. A tang holds the shells in place.

➡ **The ends of the bearing shells must never be filed flush with the mating surface of the rod and cap.**

If a rod bearing becomes noisy or is worn so that its clearance on the crank journal is sloppy, a new bearing of the correct undersize must be selected and installed since there is a provision for adjustment.

❋❋ WARNING

Under no circumstances should the rod end or cap be filed to adjust the bearing clearance, nor should shims of any kind be used.

Inspect the rod bearings while the rod assemblies are out of the engine. If the shells are scored or show flaking, they should be replaced. If they are in good shape check for proper clearance on the crank journal (see below). Any scoring or ridges on the crank journal means the crankshaft must be replaced, or reground and fitted with undersized bearings.

➡ **Make sure connecting rods and their caps are kept together, and that the caps are installed in the proper direction. On some engines like the Buick-built 350 V8, the caps can only be installed one way.**

Replacement bearings are available in standard size, and in undersizes for reground crankshafts. Connecting rod-to-crankshaft bearing clearance is checked using Plastigage® at either the top or bottom of each crank journal. The Plastigage® has a range of .001 to .003 in.

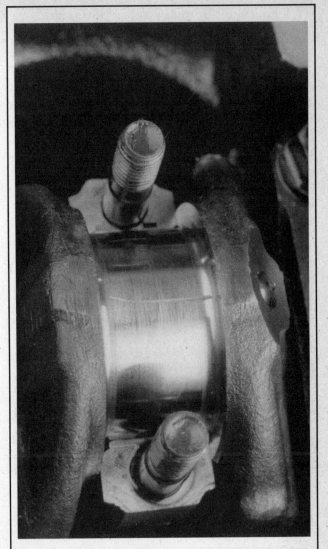

Apply a strip of gauging material to the bearing journal, then install and torque the cap

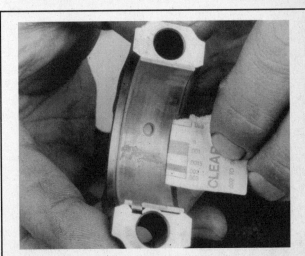

After the cap is removed again, use the scale supplied with the gauge material to check clearances

1. Remove the rod cap with the bearing shell. Completely clean the bearing shell and the crank journal, and blow any oil from the oil hole in the crankshaft; Plastigage® is soluble in oil.

2. Place a piece of Plastigage® lengthwise along the bottom center of the lower bearing shell, then install the cap with shell and tighten the bolt or nuts to specification. DO NOT turn the crankshaft with Plastigage® in the bearing.

3. Remove the bearing cap with the shell. The flattened Plastigage® will be found sticking to either the bearing shell or crank journal. *Do not remove it yet.*

4. Use the scale printed on the Plastigage® envelope to measure the flattened material at its widest point. The number within the scale which most closely corresponds to the width of the Plastigage® indicates bearing clearance in thousandths of an inch.

5. Check the specifications chart in this chapter for the desired clearance. It is advisable to install a new bearing if clearance exceeds .003 in.; however, if the bearing is in good condition and is not being checked because of bearing noise, bearing replacement is not necessary.

6. If you are installing new bearings, try a standard size, then each undersize in order until one is found that is within the specified limits when checked for clearance with Plastigage®. Each undersize shell has its size stamped on it.

7. When the proper size shell is found, clean off the Plastigage®, oil the bearing thoroughly, reinstall the cap with its shell and tighten the rod bolt nuts to specification.

➡ **With the proper bearing selected and the nuts torqued, it should be possible to move the connecting rod back, and forth freely on the crank journal as allowed by the specified connecting rod end clearance. If the rod cannot be moved, either the rod bearing is too far undersize or the rod is misaligned.**

ASSEMBLY & INSTALLATION

♦ **See Figures 80 and 81**

Install the connecting rod to the piston, making sure piston installation notches and any marks on the rod are in proper relation to one another. Lubricate the wrist pin with clean engine oil, and install the pin into the rod and piston assembly, either by hand or by using a wrist pin press as required. Install snaprings if equipped, and rotate them in their grooves to make sure they are seated. To install the piston and connecting rod assembly:

1. Make sure connecting rod big-end bearings (including end cap) are of the correct size and properly installed.

2. Fit rubber hoses over the connecting rod bolts to protect the crankshaft journals, as in the "Piston Removal" procedure. Coat the rod bearings with clean oil.

3. Using the proper ring compressor, insert the piston assembly into the cylinder so that the notch in the top of the piston faces the front of the engine (this assumes that the dimple(s) or other markings on the connecting rods are in correct relation to the piston notch(es)).

4. From beneath the engine, coat each crank journal with clean oil. Pull the connecting rod, with the bearing shell in place, into position against the crank journal.

5. Remove the rubber hoses. Install the bearing cap and cap nuts and torque to specification.

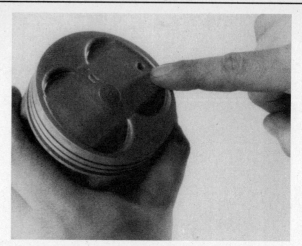

Most pistons are marked to indicate positioning in the engine (usually a mark means the side facing front)

Installing the piston into the block using a ring compressor and the handle of a hammer

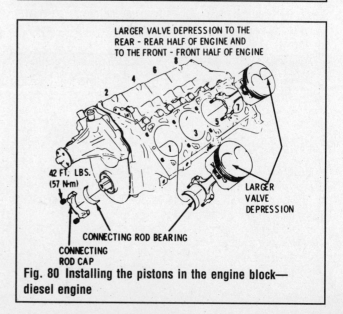

Fig. 80 Installing the pistons in the engine block—diesel engine

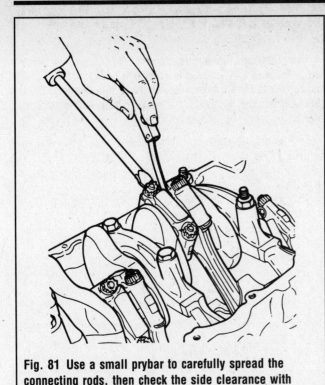

Fig. 81 Use a small prybar to carefully spread the connecting rods, then check the side clearance with feeler gauges

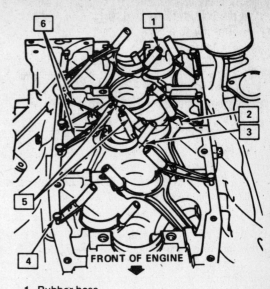

1. Rubber hose
2. #4 rod
3. #3 rod
4. Oil pan bolt
5. Note overlap of adjacent rods
6. Rubber bands

Fig. 82 Install pieces of rubber hose over the connecting rod bolts and hold them with rubber bands to prevent the crank journals from being during crankshaft removal

→When more than one rod and piston assembly is being installed, the connecting rod cap attaching nuts should only be tightened enough to keep each rod in position until all have been installed. This will ease the installation of the remaining piston assemblies.

6. Check the clearance between the sides of the connecting rods and the crankshaft using a feeler gauge. Spread the rods slightly with a suitable prytool to insert the gauge. If clearance is below the minimum tolerance, the rod may be machined to provide adequate clearance. If clearance is excessive, substitute an unworn rod, and recheck. If clearance is still outside specifications, the crankshaft must be welded and reground, or replaced.

7. Replace the oil pump if removed and the oil pan.
8. Install the cylinder head(s) and intake manifold.

Crankshaft and Main Bearings

REMOVAL

♦ **See Figures 82 and 83**

1. Drain the engine oil and remove the engine from the car. Mount the engine on a work stand in a suitable working area. Invert the engine, so the oil pan is facing up.
2. Remove the engine front (timing) cover.
3. Remove the timing chain and gears.
4. Remove the oil pan.
5. Remove the oil pump.
6. Stamp the cylinder number on the machined surfaces of the bolt bosses of the connecting rods and caps for identification when reinstalling. If the pistons are to be removed eventually from the connecting rod, mark the cylinder number on the pistons with

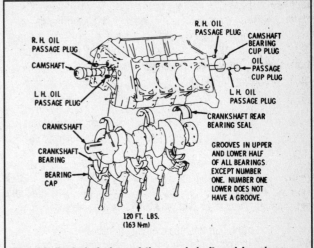

Fig. 83 Exploded view of the crankshaft and bearings—diesel engine shown

silver paint or felt-tip pen for proper cylinder identification and cap-to-rod location.

7. Remove the connecting rod caps. Install lengths of rubber hose on each of the connecting rod bolts, to protect the crank journals when the crank is removed.
8. Mark the main bearing caps with a number punch or punch so that they can be reinstalled in their original positions.
9. Remove all main bearing caps.
10. Note the position of the keyway in the crankshaft so it can be installed in the same position.

11. Install rubber bands between a bolt on each connecting rod and oil pan bolts that have been reinstalled in the block (see illustration). This will keep the rods from banging on the block when the crank is removed.

12. Carefully lift the crankshaft out of the block. The rods will pivot to the center of the engine when the crank is removed.

MAIN BEARING INSPECTION & REPLACEMENT

Like connecting rod big-end bearings, the crankshaft main bearings are shell-type inserts that do not utilize shims and cannot be adjusted. The bearings are available in various standard and undersizes; if main bearing clearance is found to be too sloppy, a new bearing (both upper and lower halves) is required.

➥**Factory-undersized crankshafts are marked, sometimes with a "9" and/or a large spot of light green paint; the bearing caps also will have the paint on each side of the undersized journal.**

Generally, the lower half of the bearing shell (except No. 1 bearing) shows greater wear and fatigue. If the lower half only shows the effects of normal wear (no heavy scoring or discoloration), it can usually be assumed that the upper half is also in good shape; conversely, if the lower half is heavily worn or damaged, both halves should be replaced. *Never replace one bearing half without replacing the other.*

CHECKING CLEARANCE

Main bearing clearance can be checked both with the crankshaft in the car and with the engine out of the car. If the engine block is still in the car, the crankshaft should be supported both front and rear (by the damper and to remove clearance from the upper bearing.) Total clearance can then be measured between the lower bearing and journal. If the block has been removed from the car, and is inverted, the crank will rest on the upper bearings and the total clearance can be measured between the lower bearing and journal. Clearance is checked in the same manner as the connecting rod bearings, with Plastigage®.

➥**Crankshaft bearing caps and bearing shells should NEVER be filed flush with the cap-to-block mating surface to adjust for wear in the old bearings. Always install new bearings.**

1. If the crankshaft has been removed, install it (block removed from car). If the block is still in the car, remove the oil pan and oil pump. Starting with the rear bearing cap, remove the cap and wipe all oil from the crank journal and bearing cap.

2. Place a strip of Plastigage® the full width of the bearing (parallel to the crankshaft), on the journal.

✳✳ WARNING

Do not rotate the crankshaft while the gaging material is between the bearing and the journal.

3. Install the bearing cap and evenly tighten the cap bolts to specification.

4. Remove the bearing cap. The flattened Plastigage® will be sticking to either the bearing shell or the crank journal.

5. Use the graduated scale on the Plastigage® envelope to measure the material at its widest point.

➥**If the flattened Plastigage® tapers towards the middle or ends, there is a difference in clearance indicating the bearing or journal has a taper, low spot or other irregularity. If this is indicated, measure the crank journal with a micrometer.**

6. If bearing clearance is within specifications, the bearing insert is in good shape. Replace the insert if the clearance is not within specifications. *Always replace both upper and lower inserts as a unit.*

7. Standard, .001 in. or .002 in. undersize bearings should produce the proper clearance. If these sizes still produce too sloppy a fit, the crankshaft must be reground for use with the next undersize bearing. Recheck all clearances after installing new bearings.

8. Replace the rest of the bearings in the same manner. After all bearings have been checked, rotate the crankshaft to make sure there is no excessive drag. When checking the No. 1 main bearing, loosen the accessory drive belts (engine in car) to prevent a tapered reading with the Plastigage®.

MAIN BEARING REPLACEMENT

Engine Removed

1. Remove and inspect the crankshaft.

2. Remove the main bearings from the bearing saddles in the cylinder block and main bearing caps.

3. Coat the bearing surfaces of the new, correct size main bearings with clean engine oil and install them in the bearing saddles in the block and in the main bearing caps.

4. Install the crankshaft. See "Crankshaft Installation."

Engine in Vehicle

◗ **See Figure 84**

1. With the oil pan, oil pump and spark plugs removed, remove the cap from the main bearing needing replacement and remove the bearing from the cap.

2. Make a bearing roll-out pin, using a bent cotter pin as

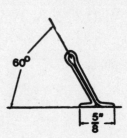

Fig. 84 Fabricate a home-made bearing roll-out pin to remove the main bearing when the engine is in the vehicle

shown in the illustration. Install the end of the pin in the oil hole in the crankshaft journal.

3. Rotate the crankshaft clockwise as viewed from the front of the engine. This will roll the upper bearing out of the block.

4. Lube the new upper bearing with clean engine oil and insert the plain (unnotched) end between the crankshaft and the indented or notched side of the block. Roll the bearing into place, making sure that the oil holes are aligned. Remove the roll pin from the oil hole.

5. Lube the new lower bearing and install the main bearing cap. Install the main bearing cap, making sure it is positioned in proper direction with the matchmarks in alignment.

6. Tighten the main bearing cap bolts to specification.

➡See "Crankshaft Installation" for thrust bearing alignment.

CRANKSHAFT END-PLAY & INSTALLATION

♦ See Figure 85

When main bearing clearance has been checked, bearings examined and/or replaced, the crankshaft can be installed. Thoroughly clean the upper and lower bearing surfaces, and lube them with clean engine oil. Install the crankshaft and main bearing caps.

Dip all main bearing cap bolts in clean oil, and torque all main bearing caps, excluding the thrust bearing cap, to specifications (see the "Crankshaft and Connecting Rod" chart in this chapter to determine which bearing is the thrust bearing). Tighten the thrust bearing bolts finger-tight. To align the thrust bearing, pry the crankshaft the extent of its axial travel several times, holding the last movement toward the front of the engine. Add thrust washers if required for proper alignment. Tighten the thrust bearing cap to specifications.

To check crankshaft end-play, pry the crankshaft to the extreme rear of its axial travel, then to the extreme front of its travel. Using a feeler gauge, measure the end-play at the front of the rear main bearing. End-play may also be measured at the thrust bearing. Install a new rear main bearing oil seal in the cylinder block and main bearing cap. Continue to reassemble the engine.

Mounting a dial gauge to read crankshaft run-out

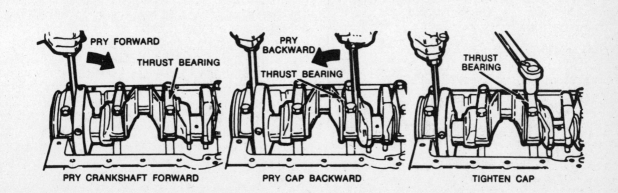

Fig. 85 Aligning the crankshaft thrust bearing

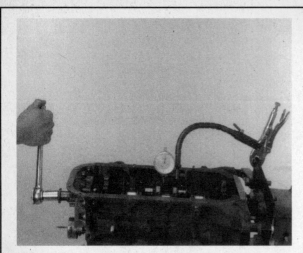

Turn the crankshaft slowly by hand while checking the gauge

Oil Pan

REMOVAL & INSTALLATION

♦ See Figure 86

Gasoline Engines

➡**Pan removal may be easier if the engine is turned to No. 1 cylinder firing position. This positions the crankshaft in the path of least resistance for pan removal.**

1. Disconnect the negative battery terminal.
2. Remove the fan shroud-to-radiator tie bar screws.
3. Remove the air cleaner and disconnect the throttle linkage.
4. Raise the car and support it on jackstands.
5. Drain the oil.
6. Remove the lower flywheel housing, remove the shift link-

age attaching bolt and swing it out of the way, and disconnect the exhaust crossover pipe at the engine.

7. Remove the front engine mounting bolts.
8. Raise the engine by placing a jack under the crankshaft pulley mounting.

❊❊ WARNING

On air conditioned cars, place a support under the right-side of the transmission before raising the engine. If you don't do this, the engine and transmission will cock to the right due to the weight of the air conditioning equipment.

9. Remove the oil pan bolts and remove the pan.
10. Installation is the reverse of removal. Use gasket sealer and new gaskets (if gaskets are used). Tighten the pan bolts to 14 ft. lbs.

Diesel Engines

1. Remove the vacuum pump and drive (with A/C) or the oil pump drive (without A/C).
2. Disconnect the batteries and remove the dipstick.
3. Remove the upper radiator support and fan shroud.
4. Raise and support the car. Drain the oil.
5. Remove the flywheel cover.
6. Disconnect the exhaust and crossover pipes.
7. Remove the oil cooler lines at the filter base.
8. Remove the starter assembly. Support the engine with a jack.
9. Remove the engine mounts from the block.
10. Raise the front of the engine and remove the oil pan.
11. Installation is the reverse of removal.

Oil Pump

REMOVAL & INSTALLATION

The oil pump is mounted to the bottom of the block and is accessible only by removing the oil pan.

On all engines, including diesel, remove the oil pan, then unbolt and remove the oil pump and screen as an assembly. On the 151 four and 250 six, remove the flange mounting bolts and nut from the elongated number 6 main bearing cap bolt, then remove the pump.

To install, align the oil pump drive shaft on 151 four 250 six cylinder engines to match with the distributor tang and position the pump flange over the distributor lower bushing. Install the pump mounting bolts. On V8 engines, insert the drive shaft extension through the opening in the main bearing cap until the shaft mates with the distributor drive gear. *You may have to turn the drive shaft extension* one way or the other to get the two to mesh. Position the pump on the cap and install the attaching bolts. Install the oil pans on all engines.

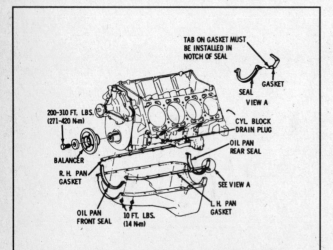

Fig. 86 Exploded view of the oil pan mounting. Gaskets and seals may differ slightly among engines

OVERHAUL

♦ **See Figures 87 and 88**

151 Four and 250 Inline Six Cylinder Engines

1. With the pump removed from the block, remove the 4 cover attaching screws, the cover, idler gear and drive gear and shaft.
2. Remove the pressure regulator valve and related valve parts.

✳✳ WARNING

Do not disturb the oil pickup pipe on the screen or body.

3. Inspect the pump body for excessive wear or cracks, and inspect the pump gears for excessive wear, cracks or damage. Check the shaft for looseness in the housing; it should not be a sloppy fit. Check the inside of the cover for wear that would permit oil to leak past the ends of the gears. Remove any debris from the surface of the screen, and check the screen for damage.

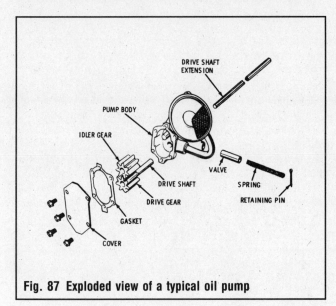

Fig. 87 Exploded view of a typical oil pump

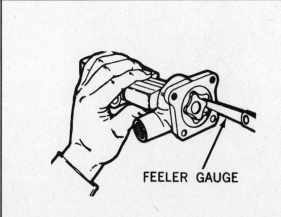

Fig. 88 Use feeler gauges to measure the oil pump side clearance

Check the pressure regulator valve plunger for fit in the pump body.
4. Assemble the pump as previously described. When tightening the cover screws (6 ft. lbs. on the 250 six, 8 ft. lbs. On the 151 four), check to make sure the shaft turns freely.

V6 Engines

The oil pump is located in the timing chain cover and is connected by a drilled passage to the oil screen housing and pipe assembly in the oil pan. All oil is discharged from the pump to the oil pump cover assembly, on which the oil filter is mounted.

1. To remove the oil pump cover and gears, first remove the oil filter.
2. Remove the screws which attach the oil pump cover assembly to the timing chain cover.
3. Remove the cover assembly and slide out the oil pump gears. Clean the gears and inspect them for any obvious defects such as chipping or scoring.
4. Remove the oil pressure relief valve cap, spring and valve. Clean them and inspect them for wear or scoring. Check the relief valve spring to see that it is not worn on its side or collapsed. Replace the spring if it seems questionable.
5. Check the relief valve for a correct fit in its bore. It should be an easy slip fit and no more. If any perceptible shake can be felt, the valve and/or the cover should be replaced.
6. Install the oil pump gears (if removed) and the shaft in the oil pump body section of the timing chain cover to check the gear end clearance and gear side clearance. Check gear end clearance and gear side clearance. Check gear end clearance by placing a straight edge over the gears and measure the clearance between the straight edge and the gasket surface. Clearance should be between .002 in. and .006 in. Check gear side clearance by inserting the feeler gauge between the gear teeth and the side wall of the pump body. Clearance should be between .002 in. and .005 in.
7. Check the pump cover flatness by placing a straight edge across the cover face, with a feeler gauge between the straight edge and the cover. If clearance is .002 in. or more, replace the cover.
6. To install, lubricate the pressure relief valve and spring and place them in the cover. Install the cap and the gasket. Tighten the cap to 35 ft. lbs.
7. Pack the oil pump gear cavity full of petroleum jelly. *Do not use gear lube.* Reinstall the oil pump gears so that the petroleum jelly is forced into every cavity of the gear pocket, and between the gear teeth. There must be no air spaces. *This step is very important.*

✳✳ WARNING

Unless the pump is primed this way, it won't produce any oil pressure when the engine is started.

8. Install the cover assembly using a new gasket and sealer. Tighten the screws to 10 ft. lbs.
9. Install the oil filter.

V8 Engines (Including Diesel)

1. Remove the oil pump drive shaft extension.
2. Remove the cotter pin, spring and the pressure regulator valve.

➡**Place your thumb over the pressure regulator bore before removing the cotter pin, as the spring is under pressure.**

3. Remove the oil pump cover attaching screws and remove the oil pump cover and gasket. Clean the pump in solvent or kerosene, and wash out the pick-up screen.

4. Remove the drive gear and idler gear from the pump body.

5. Check the gears for scoring and other damage. Install the gears if in good condition, or replace them if damaged. Check gear end clearance by placing a straight edge over the gears and measure the clearance between the straight edge and the gasket surface with a feeler gauge. End clearance for the diesel is .0005 in. to .0075 in.; 350 (R) and 403 (K) is .0015 in. to .0085 in.; and other V8s is .002 in. to .0065 in. If end clearance is excessive, check for scores in the cover that would bring the total clearance over the specs.

6. Check gear side clearance by inserting the feeler gauge between the gear teeth and the side wall of the pump body. Clearance should be between .002 in. and .005 in.

7. Pack the inside of the pump completely with petroleum jelly. DO NOT use engine oil. The pump MUST be primed this way or it won't produce any oil pressure when the engine is started.

8. Install the cover screws and tighten alternately and evenly to 8 ft. lbs.

9. Position the pressure regulator valve into the pump cover, closed end first, then install the spring and retaining pin.

➡**When assembling the drive shaft extension to the drive shaft, the end of the extension nearest the washers must be inserted into the drive shaft.**

10. Insert the drive shaft extension through the opening in the main bearing cap and block until the shaft mates into the distributor drive gear.

11. Install the pump onto the rear main bearing cap and install the attaching bolts. Tighten the bolts to 35 ft. lbs.

12. Install the oil pan.

Rear Main Oil Seal

REMOVAL & INSTALLATION

1977–78 151 Four Cylinder Engines and All 250 Six Cylinder Engines

◆ **See Figure 89**

The rear main bearing oil seal, both halves, can be removed without removal of the crankshaft. *Always replace the upper and lower halves together.*

1. Remove the oil pan.

2. Remove the rear main bearing cap.

3. Remove the old oil seal from its groove in the cap, carefully prying from the bottom using a small prytool.

4. Coat a new seal-half completely with clean engine oil, and insert it into the bearing cap groove. Keep oil off of the parting line surface, as this surface is treated with glue. Gradually push the seal with a hammer handle until the seal is rolled into place.

5. To remove the upper half of the old seal, use a small hammer and a soft, blunt punch to tap one end of the oil seal out until it protrudes far enough to be removed with needle-nose pliers. Push the new seal into place with the lip toward the front of the engine.

6. On the 250 six engine, install the bearing cap and tighten the bolts to a loose fit—*do not final torque.* With the cap fitted loosely, move the crankshaft first to the rear and then to the front with a rubber mallet. This will properly position the thrust bear-

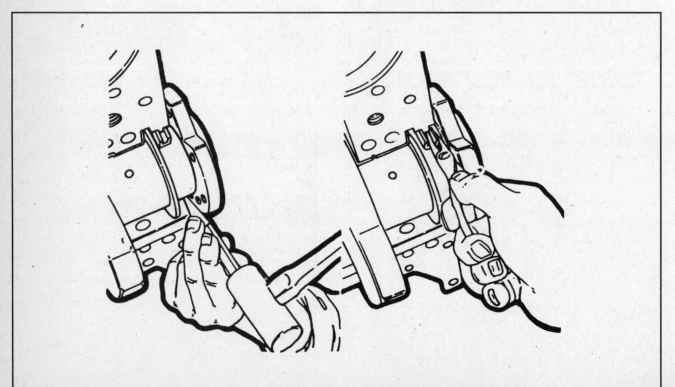

Fig. 89 Remove the upper half of the rear main oil seal with a small hammer and soft, blunt punch

ing. Tighten the bearing cap to a final torque of 65 ft. lbs. Install the oil pan.

7. Install the bearing cap on the 151 four and torque to 65 ft. lbs. Install the oil pan.

1979 151 Four Cylinder Engine

▶ **See Figure 90**

The rear main bearing oil seal in this engine is a one piece unit and is removed and installed without removing the oil pan or crankshaft.

1. Remove the transmission, flywheel bellhousing, and flywheel.

2. Using a small prybar or a suitable prytool, carefully remove the rear main bearing oil seal—*do not scratch the crankshaft!*

3. Thoroughly lubricate a new oil seal with clean engine oil, making sure both the inside and outside diameters are coated. Install the seal onto the rear crankshaft flange, with the helical lip side of the seal facing the engine. Be sure the seal is fitted squarely in place.

4. Install the flywheel, bellhousing and transmission in the reverse order of removal.

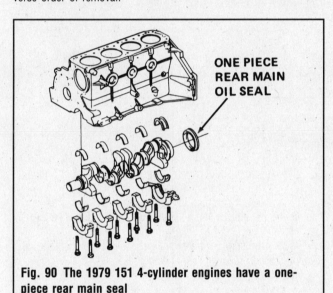

Fig. 90 The 1979 151 4-cylinder engines have a one-piece rear main seal

Oldsmobile Gasoline and Diesel Engines

▶ **See Figures 91 and 92**

The crankshaft need not be removed to replace the rear main bearing upper oil seal. The lower seal is installed in the bearing cap.

1. Drain the crankcase oil and remove the oil pan and rear main bearing cap.

2. Using a special main seal tool or a tool that can be made from a dowel (see illustration), drive the upper seal into its groove on each side until it is tightly packed. This is usually ¼–¾ in.

3. Measure the amount the seal was driven up on one side; add ¹⁄₁₆ in., then cut this length from the old seal that was removed from the main bearing cap. Use a single-edge razor blade. Measure the amount the seal was driven up on the other side; add ¹⁄₁₆ in. and cut another length from the old seal. Use the main bearing cap as a holding fixture when cutting the seal as illustrated. Carefully trim protruding seal.

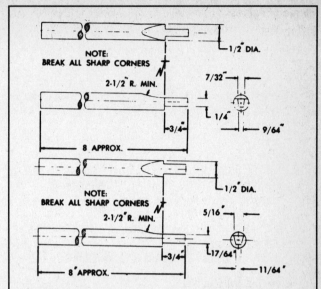

Fig. 91 Make a rear bearing seal packing tool from a wooden dowel. The upper tool dimensions are for engines up to 400 cu. in. The bottom dimensions are for 455 cu. in. engines

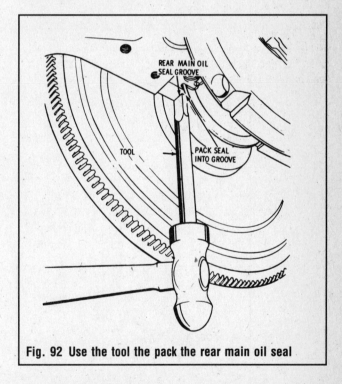

Fig. 92 Use the tool the pack the rear main oil seal

4. Work these two pieces of seal up into the cylinder block on each side with two nailsets or small prytools. Using the packing tool again, pack these pieces into the block, then trim them flush with a razor blade or hobby knife as shown. *Do not scratch the bearing surface with the razor.*

5. Install a new seal in the rear main bearing cap. Run a ¹⁄₁₆ in. bead of sealer onto the outer mating surface of the bearing cap. Assemble the cap to the block and torque to specifications.

Pontiac Engines

▶ **See Figures 91 and 92**

1. Remove the oil pan, baffle, and oil pump.
2. Remove the rear main bearing cap.
3. Obtain an oil seal tool, or construct one from a dowel as illustrated. Insert the tool against one end of the oil seal in the block and drive the seal gently into the groove about ¾ in. Repeat on the other end of the seal.
4. Using the bearing cap as a holder, form a new upper bearing seal in the cap. Cut four ⅜ in. long pieces from this seal.
5. Work two of the pieces into each of the gaps which have been made at the end of the seal in the cylinder block. *Do not cut off any material to make the pieces fit.*
6. Press a new seal into the bearing cap.
7. Apply a ¹⁄₁₆ in. bead of sealer across the outer mating surface of the bearing cap.
8. Reassemble the cap and torque to specifications.

Buick V6 and V8 Engines

▶ **See Figure 93**

On the Buick-built engines, the factory recommends removing the crankshaft to replace the upper seal, but the seal can be replaced using the method below.

1. Remove the oil pan and the rear main bearing cap.
2. Loosen the rest of the crankshaft main bearings slightly and allow the crankshaft to drop about ¹⁄₁₆ in., *no more.*
3. Remove the old upper half of the oil seal.
4. Wrap some soft copper wire around the end of the new seal and leave about 12 in. on the end. Lubricate the new seal generously with clean oil.
5. Slip the free end of the copper wire into the oil seal groove and around the crankshaft. Pull the wire until the seal protrudes an equal amount on each side. Rotate the crankshaft as the seal is pulled into place.
6. Remove the wire. Push any excess seal that may be protruding back into the groove.
7. Before tightening the crankshaft bearing caps, visually check the bearings to make sure they are in place. Tighten the bearing cap bolts to specification. Make sure there is no oil on the mating surfaces.

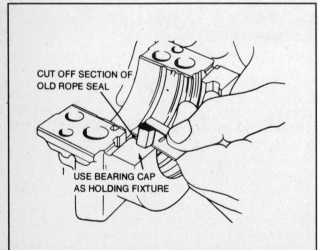

CUT OFF SECTION OF OLD ROPE SEAL

USE BEARING CAP AS HOLDING FIXTURE

Fig. 93 Carefully cut off the lower seal ends, using a razor blade

8. To replace the seal in the main bearing cap, remove the old seal and place a new seal in the groove with both ends projecting above the mating surface of the cap.
9. Force the seal into the cap groove by rubbing down on it with a hammer handle or other smooth round tool, until the seal projects above the groove not more than ¹⁄₁₆ in. Using a razor blade, cut the ends off flush with the surface of the cap.
10. On the V6s and Buick-built 350 V8, place new neoprene seals in the grooves in the sides of the bearing caps after soaking the seals in kerosene for two minutes.

➡ **The neoprene seals will swell up once exposed to the oil and heat. It is normal for the seals to leak for a short time, until they become properly seated. The seals must NOT be cut to fit.**

11. Reverse the above procedure for installation. Use a small bead of sealer on the outer edge of the bearing cap mating surface.
12. Install the oil pan. Run the engine at low rpm for the first few minutes of operation.

Chevrolet V8 Engines

The rear main bearing seal on these engines can also be replaced without removing the crankshaft. Extreme care should be exercised when installing the seal to protect the sealing bead (located in the channel on the outside diameter of the seal). Use of a seal installation tool, as described in the above procedures, is recommended.

1. Remove the oil pan, oil pump and rear main bearing cap.
2. Remove the old oil seal from the cap by carefully prying from the bottom with a small prybar.
3. Using a small hammer and brass pin punch, tap on one end of the oil upper seal until it protrudes far enough on the other side to be removed with needle nose pliers.
4. Clean all sealant and foreign material from the bearing cap, crankshaft journal and all mating surfaces using a solvent. Inspect the components for nicks, scratches and burrs.
5. Coat the lips of the new upper seal with clean engine oil, keeping the oil off of the seal mating ends.
6. Position the tip of the oil seal mating tool between the crank journal and the seal seat in the cylinder block. Position the new seal between the crankshaft and the tip of the tool so that the seal bead contacts the tip of the tool.

➡ **Make sure the oil seal lip is positioned toward the front of the engine.**

7. Rotate the seal around the crank journal, using the tool as a "shoehorn" to protect the seal bead from the sharp corner of the seal seat surface in the cylinder block.

➡ **Keep the installation tool in position until the seal is properly positioned with both ends flush with the block.**

8. Remove the tool, being careful not to withdraw the seal.
9. Thoroughly lubricate the new lower seal-half (for the bearing cap) with clean engine oil. Install the seal into the cap, feeding the seal in with thumb and finger.
10. Install the bearing cap onto the cylinder block, using sealant applied to the cap-to-block mating surfaces. Be careful to keep the sealant off the seal split line.
11. Install the bearing cap bolts and torque to 70 ft. lbs. Install the oil pump and oil pan in the reverse order of removal.

Flywheel and Ring Gear

REMOVAL & INSTALLATION

The ring gear is an integral part of the flywheel and is not replaceable.

1. Remove the transmission.
2. Remove the six bolts attaching the flywheel to the crankshaft flange. Remove the flywheel.
3. Inspect the flywheel for cracks, and inspect the ring gear for burrs or worn teeth. Replace the flywheel if any damage is apparent. Remove burrs with a mill file.
4. Install the flywheel. The flywheel will only attach to the crankshaft in one position, as the bolt holes are unevenly spaced. Install the bolts and torque to specification.

Check across the flywheel surface, it should be flat

If necessary, lock the flywheel in place and remove the retaining bolts . . .

. . . then remove the flywheel from the crankshaft in order replace it or have it machined

Upon installation, it is usually a good idea to apply a thread-locking compound to the flywheel bolts

Engine Core Plugs (Freeze Plugs)

REMOVAL & INSTALLATION

1. Disconnect the negative battery cable.
2. Drain the cooling system.

✲✲ CAUTION

When draining the coolant, keep in mind that cats and dogs are attracted by ethylene glycol antifreeze, and are quite likely to drink any that is left in an uncovered container or in puddles on the ground. This will prove fatal in sufficient quantity. Always drain the coolant into a sealable container. Coolant should be reused unless it is contaminated or several years old.

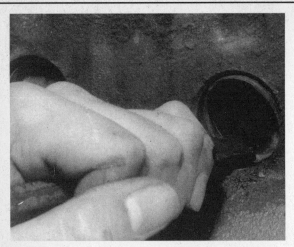

Using a punch and hammer, the freeze plug can be loosened in the block

Once the freeze plug has been loosened, it can be removed from the block

3. If equipped with drain plugs on the engine remove them. They would be located at the bottom of the block near the oil pan.

4. Remove any components that restrict access to the freeze plugs, like the starter or motor mounts.

5. Wearing proper eye protection, tap the bottom edge of the freeze plug with a punch and hammer. This should tilt the freeze plug, not cut it. Then use pliers to pull the freeze or pry the freeze plug from its bore. Another method is to drill the freeze plug and use a slide hammer, but more often there's not enough room to do that.

6. After the plug is removed clean the area completely. Coat the freeze plug and/or bore with gasket sealant.

To install:

7. Install the freeze plug into the hole, it must go in evenly or it will keep popping back out as you tap on it. Using a plug installer or socket that fits the edge of the plug can help keep it straight as you tap it in place.

8. Fill the engine with coolant, connect the battery cable. Start engine and check for leaks.

Block Heater

REMOVAL & INSTALLATION

Factory block heaters are not installed on these models. If an aftermarket heater has been installed the following procedure will most likely work. There are two basic types, one for the oil and one for the coolant. The oil heater usually just slips into the dipstick tube or replaces the oil drain plug. The following procedure is for the coolant type.

1. Remove the negative battery cable.
2. Drain the cooling system.

✳✳ CAUTION

When draining the coolant, keep in mind that cats and dogs are attracted by ethylene glycol antifreeze, and are quite likely to drink any that is left in an uncovered container or in puddles on the ground. This will prove fatal in sufficient quantity. Always drain the coolant into a sealable container. Coolant should be reused unless it is contaminated or several years old.

3. Remove the block heater in the same way as the freeze plugs. Some heater units have a bolt that must be loosened or a V-Clamp that must be removed to remove the heating element.

4. Disconnect the heater connector and remove the heater element.

To install:

5. Coat the new heater with sealant, then install as removed.

6. Fill the engine with coolant, connect the battery cable. Start engine and check for leaks.

Water Pump

REMOVAL & INSTALLATION

1. Disconnect the battery.
2. Drain the radiator.
3. Use a prybar to hold the fan in place, then unfasten the fan and remove the fan from the pulley.
4. Loosen the alternator and other accessories at their adjusting points, and remove the fan belts from the fan pulley.
5. Remove the fan pulley.
6. Remove any accessory brackets that might interfere with water pump removal.
7. Disconnect the hose from the water pump inlet and the heater hose from the nipple on the pump. Remove the bolts, pump assembly and old gasket from the timing chain cover. On 151 four and 250 six engines, remove the pump by pulling it straight out of the block.
8. Check the pump shaft bearings for end-play or roughness in operation. Water pump bearings usually emit a squealing sound with the engine running when the bearings need to be replaced. Replace the pump if the bearings are not in good shape or have been noisy.

To remove the water pump, hold the fan in place with a prybar, then remove the retaining nuts

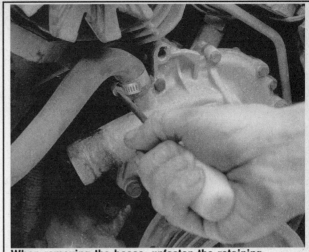

When removing the hoses, unfasten the retaining clamp . . .

Remove the fan assembly from the pulley

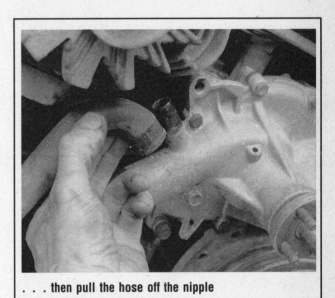

. . . then pull the hose off the nipple

Remove the pulley from the hub by pulling it straight off

Unfasten the water pump retaining bolts . . .

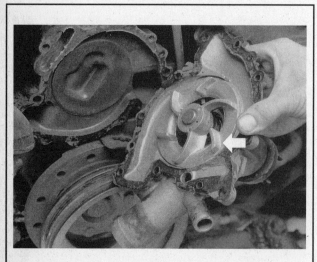

. . . then remove the water pump from the vehicle

Rear view of the water pump splines (see arrow)

To install:

9. To install, make sure the gasket surfaces on the pump and timing chain cover are clean. Install the pump assembly with a new gasket. Tighten the bolts uniformly. Coat the threaded area of the 151 and 250 bolts with sealer.

10. The remainder of installation is the reverse of removal. Fill the cooling system and check for leaks at the pump and hose joints. Make sure all of the accessory belts are properly tensioned.

Thermostat

REMOVAL & INSTALLATION

◆ **See Figure 94**

1. Drain the radiator until the level is below the thermostat level (below the level of the intake manifold on V6 and V8s, below the level of the outlet elbow on inline four and six).

2. Remove the water outlet elbow assembly from the engine. Remove the thermostat from inside the elbow.

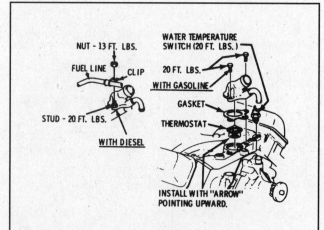

Fig. 94 Typical thermostat installation—V6 and V8 engines

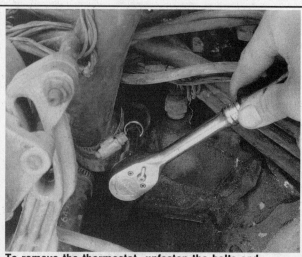

To remove the thermostat, unfasten the bolts and remove the water outlet elbow

Carefully clean the mating surfaces, using a gasket scraper

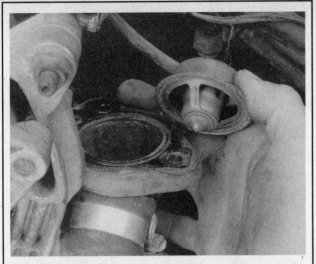

Remove the thermostat from the elbow by lifting it out

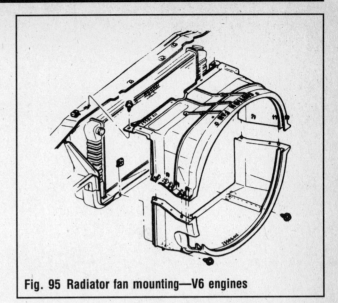

Fig. 95 Radiator fan mounting—V6 engines

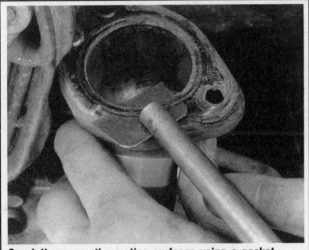

Carefully scrape the mating surfaces using a gasket scraper

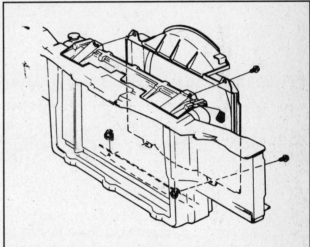

Fig. 96 Diesel sedan and wagon radiator fan shroud mounting

3. Install new thermostat in the reverse order of removal, making sure the spring side is inserted into the elbow. Clean the gasket surfaces on the water outlet elbow and the intake manifold. Use a new gasket when installing the elbow to the manifold. Refill the radiator to approximately 2½ inches below the filler neck.

Radiator

REMOVAL & INSTALLATION

▶ See Figures 95, 96, 97 and 98

1. Drain the cooling system.
2. Disconnect the radiator upper and lower hoses and, if applicable, the transmission coolant lines. Remove the coolant recovery system line, if so equipped.

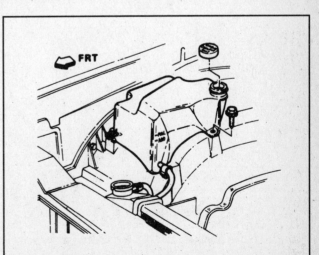

Fig. 97 On some vehicles, you must remove the coolant recovery reservoir, which is mounted on the inner fender

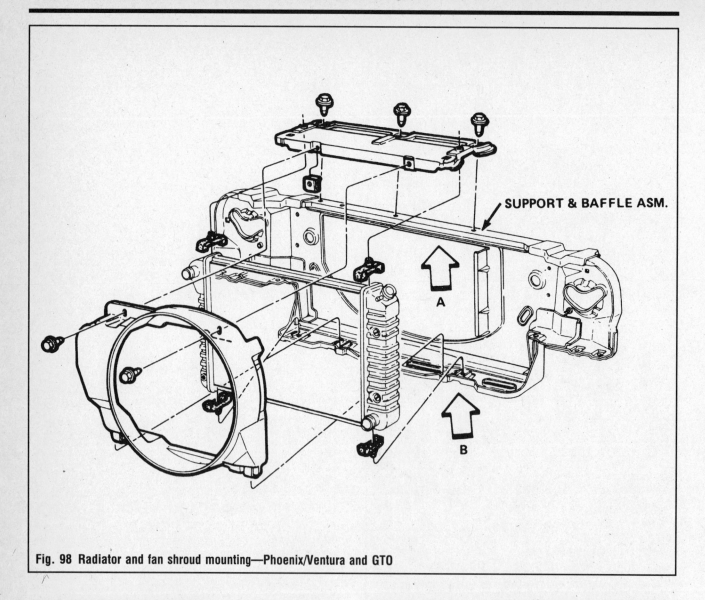

SUPPORT & BAFFLE ASM.

A

B

Fig. 98 Radiator and fan shroud mounting—Phoenix/Ventura and GTO

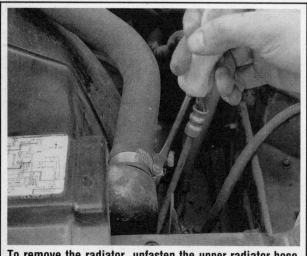

To remove the radiator, unfasten the upper radiator hose clamp . . .

. . . then disconnect the upper radiator hose

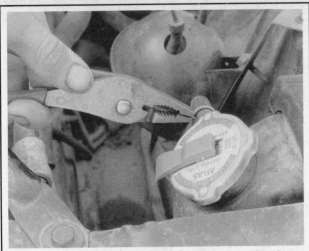

Use a pair of pliers to unhook the radiator overflow hose clamp

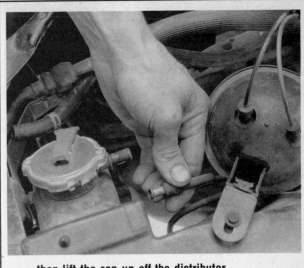

. . . then lift the cap up off the distributor

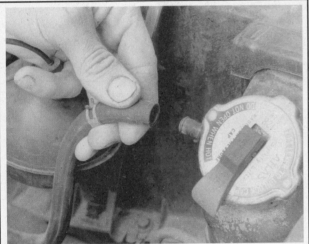

Disconnect the overflow hose from the nipple on the radiator

Use a ratchet and socket to loosen . . .

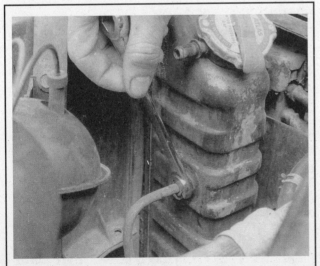

Use a flare nut wrench to loosen . . .

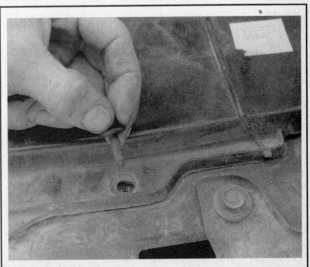

. . . then remove the front fan shroud retaining bolts

Unscrew the side fan shroud retainers

Lift the radiator out of the vehicle

3. Remove the radiator upper panel if so equipped.

4. If there is a radiator shroud in front of the radiator, the radiator and shroud are removed as an assembly.

5. If there is a fan shroud, remove the shroud attaching screws and let the shroud hang on the fan.

6. Remove the radiator attaching bolts and remove the radiator.

7. Installation is the reverse of the removal procedure.

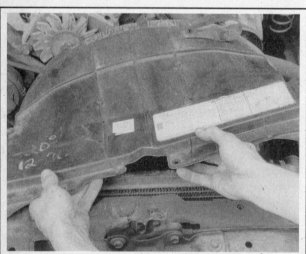

After removing all the retainers, lift the shroud up and off the radiator and fan

EXHAUST SYSTEM

General Information

➡Safety glasses should be worn at all times when working on or near the exhaust system. Older exhaust systems will almost always be covered with loose rust particles which will shower you when disturbed. These particles are more than a nuisance and could injure your eye.

Whenever working on the exhaust system always keep the following in mind:

• Check the complete exhaust system for open seams, holes loose connections, or other deterioration which could permit exhaust fumes to seep into the passenger compartment.

• The exhaust system is usually supported by free-hanging rubber mountings which permit some movement of the exhaust system, but does not permit transfer of noise and vibration into the passenger compartment. Do not replace the rubber mounts with solid ones.

• Before removing any component of the exhaust system, ALWAYS squirt a liquid rust dissolving agent onto the fasteners for ease of removal. A lot of knuckle skin will be saved by following this rule. It may even be wise to spray the fasteners and allow them to sit overnight.

✳✳ CAUTION

Allow the exhaust system to cool sufficiently before spraying a solvent exhaust fasteners. Some solvents are highly flammable and could ignite when sprayed on hot exhaust components.

• Annoying rattles and noise vibrations in the exhaust system are usually caused by misalignment of the parts. When aligning the system, leave all bolts and nuts loose until all parts are properly aligned, then tighten, working from front to rear.

• When installing exhaust system parts, make sure there is

enough clearance between the hot exhaust parts and pipes and hoses that would be adversely affected by excessive heat. Also make sure there is adequate clearance from the floor pan to avoid possible overheating of the floor.

SPECIAL TOOLS

A number of special exhaust system tools can be rented from auto supply houses or local tores that rent special equipment. A common one is a tail pipe expander, designed to enable you to join pipes of identical diameter.

It may also be quite helpful to use solvents designed to loosen rusted bolts or flanges. Soaking rusted parts the night before you do the job can speed the work of freeing rusted parts considerably. Remember that these solvents are often flammable. Apply only to parts after they are cool!

COMPONENT REPLACEMENT

System components may be welded or clamped together. The system consists of a head pipe, catalytic converter (depending upon vehicle year), intermediate pipe, muffler and tail pipe, in that order from the engine to the back of the car.

The head pipe is bolted to the exhaust manifold. Various hangers suspend the system from the floor pan. When assembling exhaust system parts, the relative clearances around all system parts is extremely critical. Observe all clearances during assembly. In the event that the system is welded, the various parts will have to be cut apart for removal. In these cases, the cut parts may not be reused. To cut the parts, a hacksaw is the best choice. An oxyacetylene cutting torch may be faster but the sparks are DANGEROUS near the fuel tank, and, at the very least, accidents could happen, resulting in damage to other under-car parts, not to mention yourself!

The following replacement steps relate to clamped parts:

1. Raise and support the car on jackstands. It's much easier on you if you can get the car up on 4 stands. Some pipes need lots of clearance for removal and installation. If the system has been in the car for a long time, spray the clamped joints with a rust dissolving solution such as WD-40® or Liquid Wrench®, and let it set according to the instructions on the can.

2. Remove the nuts from the U-bolts; don't be surprised if the U-bolts break while removing the nuts. Age and rust account for this. Besides, you shouldn't reuse old U-bolts. When unbolting the headpipe from the exhaust manifold, make sure that the bolts are free before trying to remove them. If you snap a stud in the exhaust manifold, the stud will have to be removed with a bolt ex-

tractor, which often necessitates the removal of the manifold itself.

3. After the clamps are removed from the joints, first twist the parts at the joints to break loose rust and scale, then pull the components apart with a twisting motion. If the parts twist freely but won't pull apart, check the joint. The clamp may have been installed so tightly that it has caused a slight crushing of the joint. In this event, the best thing to do is secure a chisel designed for the purpose and, using the chisel and a hammer, peel back the female pipe end until the parts are freed.

4. Once the parts are freed, check the condition of the pipes which you had intended keeping. If their condition is at all in doubt, replace them too. You went to a lot of work to get one or more components out. You don't want to have to go through that again in the near future. If you are retaining a pipe, check the pipe end. If it was crushed by a clamp, it can be restored to its original diameter using a pipe expander, which can be rented at most good auto parts stores. Check, also, the condition of the exhaust system hangers. If ANY deterioration is noted, replace them. Oh, and one note about parts: use only parts designed for your car. Don't use fits-all parts or flex pipes. The fits-all parts never fit and the flex pipes don't last very long.

5. When installing the new parts, coat the pipe ends with exhaust system lubricant. It makes fitting the parts much easier. It's also a good idea to assemble all the parts in position before clamping them. This will ensure a good fit, detect any problems and allow you to check all clearances between the parts and surrounding frame and floor members.

6. When you are satisfied with all fits and clearances, install the clamps. If the studs were rusty, wire-brush them clean and spray them with WD-40® or Liquid Wrench®. This will ensure a proper torque reading. Position the clamps on the slip points as illustrated. The slits in the female pipe ends should be under the U-bolts, not under the clamp end. Tighten the U-bolt nuts securely, without crushing the pipe. The pipe fit should be tight, so that you can't swivel the pipe by hand. Don't forget: always use new clamps. When the system is tight, recheck all clearances. Start the engine and check the joints for leaks. A leak can be felt by hand. MAKE CERTAIN THAT THE CAR IS SECURE ON THE JACKSTANDS BEFORE GETTING UNDER IT WITH THE ENGINE RUNNING!! If any leaks are detected, tighten the clamp until the leak stops. If the pipe starts to deform before the leak stops, reposition the clamp and tighten it. If that still doesn't stop the leak, it may be that you don't have enough overlap on the pipe fit. Shut off the engine, let it cool, and try pushing the pipe together further. Be careful, the pipe gets hot quickly.

7. When everything is tight and secure, lower the car and take it for a road test. Make sure there are no unusual sounds or vibration. Most new pipes are coated with a preservative, so the system will be pretty smelly for a day or two while the coating burns off.

USING A VACUUM GAUGE

White needle = steady needle   *Dark needle = drifting needle*

The vacuum gauge is one of the most useful and easy-to-use diagnostic tools. It is inexpensive, easy to hook up, and provides valuable information about the condition of your engine.

Indication: Normal engine in good condition

Gauge reading: Steady, from 17–22 in./Hg.

Indication: Sticking valve or ignition miss

Gauge reading: Needle fluctuates from 15–20 in./Hg. at idle

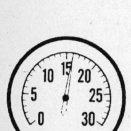

Indication: Late ignition or valve timing, low compression, stuck throttle valve, leaking carburetor or manifold gasket.

Gauge reading: Low (15–20 in./Hg.) but steady

Indication: Improper carburetor adjustment, or minor intake leak at carburetor or manifold

NOTE: Bad fuel injector O-rings may also cause this reading.

Gauge reading: Drifting needle

Indication: Weak valve springs, worn valve stem guides, or leaky cylinder head gasket (vibrating excessively at all speeds).

NOTE: A plugged catalytic converter may also cause this reading.

Gauge reading: Needle fluctuates as engine speed increases

Indication: Burnt valve or improper valve clearance. The needle will drop when the defective valve operates.

Gauge reading: Steady needle, but drops regularly

Indication: Choked muffler or obstruction in system. Speed up the engine. Choked muffler will exhibit a slow drop of vacuum to zero.

Gauge reading: Gradual drop in reading at idle

Indication: Worn valve guides

Gauge reading: Needle vibrates excessively at idle, but steadies as engine speed increases

Troubleshooting Engine Mechanical Problems

Problem	Cause	Solution
External oil leaks	• Cylinder head cover RTV sealant broken or improperly seated	• Replace sealant; inspect cylinder head cover sealant flange and cylinder head sealant surface for distortion and cracks
	• Oil filler cap leaking or missing	• Replace cap
	• Oil filter gasket broken or improperly seated	• Replace oil filter
	• Oil pan side gasket broken, improperly seated or opening in RTV sealant	• Replace gasket or repair opening in sealant; inspect oil pan gasket flange for distortion
	• Oil pan front oil seal broken or improperly seated	• Replace seal; inspect timing case cover and oil pan seal flange for distortion
	• Oil pan rear oil seal broken or improperly seated	• Replace seal; inspect oil pan rear oil seal flange; inspect rear main bearing cap for cracks, plugged oil return channels, or distortion in seal groove
	• Timing case cover oil seal broken or improperly seated	• Replace seal
	• Excess oil pressure because of restricted PCV valve	• Replace PCV valve
	• Oil pan drain plug loose or has stripped threads	• Repair as necessary and tighten
	• Rear oil gallery plug loose	• Use appropriate sealant on gallery plug and tighten
	• Rear camshaft plug loose or improperly seated	• Seat camshaft plug or replace and seal, as necessary
Excessive oil consumption	• Oil level too high	• Drain oil to specified level
	• Oil with wrong viscosity being used	• Replace with specified oil
	• PCV valve stuck closed	• Replace PCV valve
	• Valve stem oil deflectors (or seals) are damaged, missing, or incorrect type	• Replace valve stem oil deflectors
	• Valve stems or valve guides worn	• Measure stem-to-guide clearance and repair as necessary
	• Poorly fitted or missing valve cover baffles	• Replace valve cover
	• Piston rings broken or missing	• Replace broken or missing rings
	• Scuffed piston	• Replace piston
	• Incorrect piston ring gap	• Measure ring gap, repair as necessary
	• Piston rings sticking or excessively loose in grooves	• Measure ring side clearance, repair as necessary
	• Compression rings installed upside down	• Repair as necessary
	• Cylinder walls worn, scored, or glazed	• Repair as necessary

Troubleshooting Engine Mechanical Problems

Problem	Cause	Solution
Excessive oil consumption (cont.)	• Piston ring gaps not properly staggered	• Repair as necessary
	• Excessive main or connecting rod bearing clearance	• Measure bearing clearance, repair as necessary
No oil pressure	• Low oil level	• Add oil to correct level
	• Oil pressure gauge, warning lamp or sending unit inaccurate	• Replace oil pressure gauge or warning lamp
	• Oil pump malfunction	• Replace oil pump
	• Oil pressure relief valve sticking	• Remove and inspect oil pressure relief valve assembly
	• Oil passages on pressure side of pump obstructed	• Inspect oil passages for obstruction
	• Oil pickup screen or tube obstructed	• Inspect oil pickup for obstruction
	• Loose oil inlet tube	• Tighten or seal inlet tube
Low oil pressure	• Low oil level	• Add oil to correct level
	• Inaccurate gauge, warning lamp or sending unit	• Replace oil pressure gauge or warning lamp
	• Oil excessively thin because of dilution, poor quality, or improper grade	• Drain and refill crankcase with recommended oil
	• Excessive oil temperature	• Correct cause of overheating engine
	• Oil pressure relief spring weak or sticking	• Remove and inspect oil pressure relief valve assembly
	• Oil inlet tube and screen assembly has restriction or air leak	• Remove and inspect oil inlet tube and screen assembly. (Fill inlet tube with lacquer thinner to locate leaks.)
	• Excessive oil pump clearance	• Measure clearances
	• Excessive main, rod, or camshaft bearing clearance	• Measure bearing clearances, repair as necessary
High oil pressure	• Improper oil viscosity	• Drain and refill crankcase with correct viscosity oil
	• Oil pressure gauge or sending unit inaccurate	• Replace oil pressure gauge
	• Oil pressure relief valve sticking closed	• Remove and inspect oil pressure relief valve assembly
Main bearing noise	• Insufficient oil supply	• Inspect for low oil level and low oil pressure
	• Main bearing clearance excessive	• Measure main bearing clearance, repair as necessary
	• Bearing insert missing	• Replace missing insert
	• Crankshaft end-play excessive	• Measure end-play, repair as necessary
	• Improperly tightened main bearing cap bolts	• Tighten bolts with specified torque
	• Loose flywheel or drive plate	• Tighten flywheel or drive plate attaching bolts
	• Loose or damaged vibration damper	• Repair as necessary

Troubleshooting Engine Mechanical Problems

Problem	Cause	Solution
Connecting rod bearing noise	• Insufficient oil supply	• Inspect for low oil level and low oil pressure
	• Carbon build-up on piston	• Remove carbon from piston crown
	• Bearing clearance excessive or bearing missing	• Measure clearance, repair as necessary
	• Crankshaft connecting rod journal out-of-round	• Measure journal dimensions, repair or replace as necessary
	• Misaligned connecting rod or cap	• Repair as necessary
	• Connecting rod bolts tightened improperly	• Tighten bolts with specified torque
Piston noise	• Piston-to-cylinder wall clearance excessive (scuffed piston)	• Measure clearance and examine piston
	• Cylinder walls excessively tapered or out-of-round	• Measure cylinder wall dimensions, rebore cylinder
	• Piston ring broken	• Replace all rings on piston
	• Loose or seized piston pin	• Measure piston-to-pin clearance, repair as necessary
	• Connecting rods misaligned	• Measure rod alignment, straighten or replace
	• Piston ring side clearance excessively loose or tight	• Measure ring side clearance, repair as necessary
	• Carbon build-up on piston is excessive	• Remove carbon from piston
Valve actuating component noise	• Insufficient oil supply	• Check for: (a) Low oil level (b) Low oil pressure (c) Wrong hydraulic tappets (d) Restricted oil gallery (e) Excessive tappet to bore clearance
	• Rocker arms or pivots worn	• Replace worn rocker arms or pivots
	• Foreign objects or chips in hydraulic tappets	• Clean tappets
	• Excessive tappet leak-down	• Replace valve tappet
	• Tappet face worn	• Replace tappet; inspect corresponding cam lobe for wear
	• Broken or cocked valve springs	• Properly seat cocked springs; replace broken springs
	• Stem-to-guide clearance excessive	• Measure stem-to-guide clearance, repair as required
	• Valve bent	• Replace valve
	• Loose rocker arms	• Check and repair as necessary
	• Valve seat runout excessive	• Regrind valve seat/valves
	• Missing valve lock	• Install valve lock
	• Excessive engine oil	• Correct oil level

Troubleshooting Engine Performance

Problem	Cause	Solution
Hard starting (engine cranks normally)	• Faulty engine control system component	• Repair or replace as necessary
	• Faulty fuel pump	• Replace fuel pump
	• Faulty fuel system component	• Repair or replace as necessary
	• Faulty ignition coil	• Test and replace as necessary
	• Improper spark plug gap	• Adjust gap
	• Incorrect ignition timing	• Adjust timing
	• Incorrect valve timing	• Check valve timing; repair as necessary
Rough idle or stalling	• Incorrect curb or fast idle speed	• Adjust curb or fast idle speed (If possible)
	• Incorrect ignition timing	• Adjust timing to specification
	• Improper feedback system operation	• Refer to Chapter 4
	• Faulty EGR valve operation	• Test EGR system and replace as necessary
	• Faulty PCV valve air flow	• Test PCV valve and replace as necessary
	• Faulty TAC vacuum motor or valve	• Repair as necessary
	• Air leak into manifold vacuum	• Inspect manifold vacuum connections and repair as necessary
	• Faulty distributor rotor or cap	• Replace rotor or cap (Distributor systems only)
	• Improperly seated valves	• Test cylinder compression, repair as necessary
	• Incorrect ignition wiring	• Inspect wiring and correct as necessary
	• Faulty ignition coil	• Test coil and replace as necessary
	• Restricted air vent or idle passages	• Clean passages
	• Restricted air cleaner	• Clean or replace air cleaner filter element
Faulty low-speed operation	• Restricted idle air vents and passages	• Clean air vents and passages
	• Restricted air cleaner	• Clean or replace air cleaner filter element
	• Faulty spark plugs	• Clean or replace spark plugs
	• Dirty, corroded, or loose ignition secondary circuit wire connections	• Clean or tighten secondary circuit wire connections
	• Improper feedback system operation	• Refer to Chapter 4
	• Faulty ignition coil high voltage wire	• Replace ignition coil high voltage wire (Distributor systems only)
	• Faulty distributor cap	• Replace cap (Distributor systems only)
Faulty acceleration	• Incorrect ignition timing	• Adjust timing
	• Faulty fuel system component	• Repair or replace as necessary
	• Faulty spark plug(s)	• Clean or replace spark plug(s)
	• Improperly seated valves	• Test cylinder compression, repair as necessary
	• Faulty ignition coil	• Test coil and replace as necessary

Troubleshooting Engine Performance

Problem	Cause	Solution
Faulty acceleration (cont.)	• Improper feedback system operation	• Refer to Chapter 4
Faulty high speed operation	• Incorrect ignition timing • Faulty advance mechanism	• Adjust timing (if possible) • Check advance mechanism and repair as necessary (Distributor systems only)
	• Low fuel pump volume • Wrong spark plug air gap or wrong plug • Partially restricted exhaust manifold, exhaust pipe, catalytic converter, muffler, or tailpipe • Restricted vacuum passages • Restricted air cleaner	• Replace fuel pump • Adjust air gap or install correct plug • Eliminate restriction • Clean passages • Cleaner or replace filter element as necessary
	• Faulty distributor rotor or cap	• Replace rotor or cap (Distributor systems only)
	• Faulty ignition coil • Improperly seated valve(s)	• Test coil and replace as necessary • Test cylinder compression, repair as necessary
	• Faulty valve spring(s)	• Inspect and test valve spring tension, replace as necessary
	• Incorrect valve timing	• Check valve timing and repair as necessary
	• Intake manifold restricted	• Remove restriction or replace manifold
	• Worn distributor shaft	• Replace shaft (Distributor systems only)
	• Improper feedback system operation	• Refer to Chapter 4
Misfire at all speeds	• Faulty spark plug(s) • Faulty spark plug wire(s) • Faulty distributor cap or rotor	• Clean or relace spark plug(s) • Replace as necessary • Replace cap or rotor (Distributor systems only)
	• Faulty ignition coil • Primary ignition circuit shorted or open intermittently • Improperly seated valve(s)	• Test coil and replace as necessary • Troubleshoot primary circuit and repair as necessary • Test cylinder compression, repair as necessary
	• Faulty hydraulic tappet(s) • Improper feedback system operation • Faulty valve spring(s)	• Clean or replace tappet(s) • Refer to Chapter 4 • Inspect and test valve spring tension, repair as necessary
	• Worn camshaft lobes • Air leak into manifold	• Replace camshaft • Check manifold vacuum and repair as necessary
	• Fuel pump volume or pressure low • Blown cylinder head gasket • Intake or exhaust manifold passage(s) restricted	• Replace fuel pump • Replace gasket • Pass chain through passage(s) and repair as necessary
Power not up to normal	• Incorrect ignition timing • Faulty distributor rotor	• Adjust timing • Replace rotor (Distributor systems only)

Troubleshooting Engine Performance

Problem	Cause	Solution
Power not up to normal (cont.)	• Incorrect spark plug gap	• Adjust gap
	• Faulty fuel pump	• Replace fuel pump
	• Faulty fuel pump	• Replace fuel pump
	• Incorrect valve timing	• Check valve timing and repair as necessary
	• Faulty ignition coil	• Test coil and replace as necessary
	• Faulty ignition wires	• Test wires and replace as necessary
	• Improperly seated valves	• Test cylinder compression and repair as necessary
	• Blown cylinder head gasket	• Replace gasket
	• Leaking piston rings	• Test compression and repair as necessary
	• Improper feedback system operation	• Refer to Chapter 4
Intake backfire	• Improper ignition timing	• Adjust timing
	• Defective EGR component	• Repair as necessary
	• Defective TAC vacuum motor or valve	• Repair as necessary
Exhaust backfire	• Air leak into manifold vacuum	• Check manifold vacuum and repair as necessary
	• Faulty air injection diverter valve	• Test diverter valve and replace as necessary
	• Exhaust leak	• Locate and eliminate leak
Ping or spark knock	• Incorrect ignition timing	• Adjust timing
	• Distributor advance malfunction	• Inspect advance mechanism and repair as necessary (Distributor systems only)
	• Excessive combustion chamber deposits	• Remove with combustion chamber cleaner
	• Air leak into manifold vacuum	• Check manifold vacuum and repair as necessary
	• Excessively high compression	• Test compression and repair as necessary
	• Fuel octane rating excessively low	• Try alternate fuel source
	• Sharp edges in combustion chamber	• Grind smooth
	• EGR valve not functioning properly	• Test EGR system and replace as necessary
Surging (at cruising to top speeds)	• Low fuel pump pressure or volume	• Replace fuel pump
	• Improper PCV valve air flow	• Test PCV valve and replace as necessary
	• Air leak into manifold vacuum	• Check manifold vacuum and repair as necessary
	• Incorrect spark advance	• Test and replace as necessary
	• Restricted fuel filter	• Replace fuel filter
	• Restricted air cleaner	• Clean or replace air cleaner filter element
	• EGR valve not functioning properly	• Test EGR system and replace as necessary
	• Improper feedback system operation	• Refer to Chapter 4

Troubleshooting the Serpentine Drive Belt

Problem	Cause	Solution
Tension sheeting fabric failure (woven fabric on outside circumference of belt has cracked or separated from body of belt)	• Grooved or backside idler pulley diameters are less than minimum recommended • Tension sheeting contacting (rubbing) stationary object • Excessive heat causing woven fabric to age • Tension sheeting splice has fractured	• Replace pulley(s) not conforming to specification • Correct rubbing condition • Replace belt • Replace belt
Noise (objectional squeal, squeak, or rumble is heard or felt while drive belt is in operation)	• Belt slippage • Bearing noise • Belt misalignment • Belt-to-pulley mismatch • Driven component inducing vibration • System resonant frequency inducing vibration	• Adjust belt • Locate and repair • Align belt/pulley(s) • Install correct belt • Locate defective driven component and repair • Vary belt tension within specifications. Replace belt.
Rib chunking (one or more ribs has separated from belt body)	• Foreign objects imbedded in pulley grooves • Installation damage • Drive loads in excess of design specifications • Insufficient internal belt adhesion	• Remove foreign objects from pulley grooves • Replace belt • Adjust belt tension • Replace belt
Rib or belt wear (belt ribs contact bottom of pulley grooves)	• Pulley(s) misaligned • Mismatch of belt and pulley groove widths • Abrasive environment • Rusted pulley(s) • Sharp or jagged pulley groove tips • Rubber deteriorated	• Align pulley(s) • Replace belt • Replace belt • Clean rust from pulley(s) • Replace pulley • Replace belt
Longitudinal belt cracking (cracks between two ribs)	• Belt has mistracked from pulley groove • Pulley groove tip has worn away rubber-to-tensile member	• Replace belt • Replace belt
Belt slips	• Belt slipping because of insufficient tension • Belt or pulley subjected to substance (belt dressing, oil, ethylene glycol) that has reduced friction • Driven component bearing failure • Belt glazed and hardened from heat and excessive slippage	• Adjust tension • Replace belt and clean pulleys • Replace faulty component bearing • Replace belt
"Groove jumping" (belt does not maintain correct position on pulley, or turns over and/or runs off pulleys)	• Insufficient belt tension • Pulley(s) not within design tolerance • Foreign object(s) in grooves	• Adjust belt tension • Replace pulley(s) • Remove foreign objects from grooves

Troubleshooting the Serpentine Drive Belt

Problem	Cause	Solution
"Groove jumping" (belt does not maintain correct position on pulley, or turns over and/or runs off pulleys)	• Excessive belt speed • Pulley misalignment • Belt-to-pulley profile mismatched • Belt cordline is distorted	• Avoid excessive engine acceleration • Align pulley(s) • Install correct belt • Replace belt
Belt broken (Note: identify and correct problem before replacement belt is installed)	• Excessive tension • Tensile members damaged during belt installation • Belt turnover • Severe pulley misalignment • Bracket, pulley, or bearing failure	• Replace belt and adjust tension to specification • Replace belt • Replace belt • Align pulley(s) • Replace defective component and belt
Cord edge failure (tensile member exposed at edges of belt or separated from belt body)	• Excessive tension • Drive pulley misalignment • Belt contacting stationary object • Pulley irregularities • Improper pulley construction • Insufficient adhesion between tensile member and rubber matrix	• Adjust belt tension • Align pulley • Correct as necessary • Replace pulley • Replace pulley • Replace belt and adjust tension to specifications
Sporadic rib cracking (multiple cracks in belt ribs at random intervals)	• Ribbed pulley(s) diameter less than minimum specification • Backside bend flat pulley(s) diameter less than minimum • Excessive heat condition causing rubber to harden • Excessive belt thickness • Belt overcured • Excessive tension	• Replace pulley(s) • Replace pulley(s) • Correct heat condition as necessary • Replace belt • Replace belt • Adjust belt tension

AIR POLLUTION 4-2
 NATURAL POLLUTANTS 4-2
 INDUSTRIAL POLLUTANTS 4-2
 AUTOMOTIVE POLLUTANTS 4-2
  TEMPERATURE INVERSION 4-2
  HEAT TRANSFER 4-3
AUTOMOTIVE EMISSIONS 4-3
 EXHAUST GASES 4-3
  HYDROCARBONS 4-3
  CARBON MONOXIDE 4-4
  NITROGEN 4-4
  OXIDES OF SULFUR 4-4
  PARTICULATE MATTER 4-4
 CRANKCASE EMISSIONS 4-5
 EVAPORATIVE EMISSIONS 4-5
**EVAPORATIVE EMISSION
 CONTROLS 4-5**
 POSITIVE CRANKCASE VENTILATION
  SYSTEM 4-6
  OPERATION 4-6
  PCV VALVE SERVICE 4-6
  REMOVAL & INSTALLATION 4-7
 EVAPORATIVE EMISSION CONTROL
  SYSTEM 4-7
  OPERATION 4-7
  SERVICE 4-9
**EXHAUST EMISSION
 CONTROLS 4-9**
 THERMOSTATIC AIR CLEANER
  (THERMAC) 4-9
  OPERATION 4-9
  SYSTEM CHECKS 4-10
 AIR INJECTION REACTOR (AIR)
  SYSTEM 4-10
  OPERATION 4-10
  SERVICE 4-12
  COMPONENT REMOVAL &
   INSTALLATION 4-12
 AIR MANAGEMENT SYSTEM 4-13
  OPERATION 4-13
  REMOVAL & INSTALLATION 4-14
 ANTI-DIESELING SOLENOID 4-14
  OPERATION 4-14
 EARLY FUEL EVAPORATION (EFE)
  SYSTEM 4-14
  OPERATION 4-14
  REMOVAL & INSTALLATION 4-15
 EXHAUST GAS RECIRCULATION (EGR)
  SYSTEM 4-16
  OPERATION 4-16
  REMOVAL & INSTALLATION 4-16
  EGR VALVE CLEANING 4-18
 CONTROLLED COMBUSTION
  SYSTEM 4-18
  OPERATION 4-18
  SERVICE 4-19
 COMPUTER CONTROLLED CATALYTIC
  CONVERTER (C-4) SYSTEM 4-19
  OPERATION 4-19
 COMPUTER COMMAND CONTROL
  (CCC) SYSTEM 4-20

 BASIC TROUBLESHOOTING 4-23
  ACTIVATING THE TROUBLE
   CODE 4-25
 MIXTURE CONTROL SOLENOID
 (M/C) 4-26
 THROTTLE POSITION SENSOR
  (TPS) 4-27
 IDLE SPEED CONTROL (ISC) 4-27
  V6 ENGINES 4-27
 ELECTRONIC SPARK TIMING
  (EST) 4-27
 ELECTRONIC SPARK CONTROL
  (ESC) 4-27
 TRANSMISSION CONVERTER CLUTCH
  (TCC) 4-28
 CATALYTIC CONVERTER 4-28
  OPERATION 4-28
  PRECAUTIONS 4-29
  CATALYST TESTING 4-29
 OXYGEN SENSOR 4-29
  OPERATION 4-29
  REMOVAL & INSTALLATION 4-30
**DIESEL ENGINE EMISSIONS
 CONTROLS 4-31**
 CRANKCASE VENTILATION 4-31
  OPERATION 4-31
 EXHAUST GAS RECIRCULATION (EGR)
  SYSTEM 4-32
  OPERATION 3-32
  FUNCTIONAL TESTS OF
   COMPONENTS 4-32
 ENGINE TEMPERATURE SENSOR
  (ETS) 4-34
  OPERATION 4-34
VACUUM DIAGRAMS 4-34
SPECIFICATION CHARTS
 EGR SYSTEM DIAGNOSIS—DIESEL
  ENGINE 4-32
TROUBLESHOOTING CHARTS
 TROUBLE CODE IDENTIFICATION
  CHART 4-24

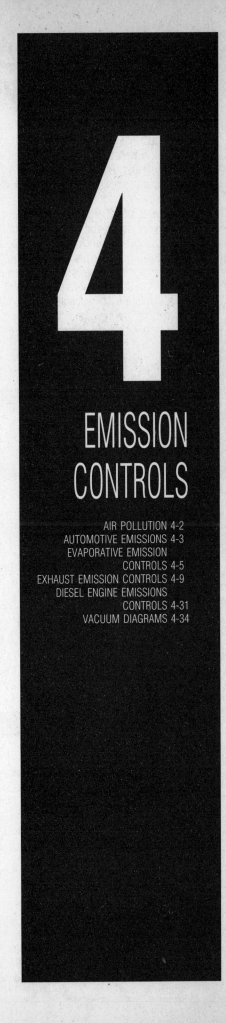

4

EMISSION CONTROLS

AIR POLLUTION 4-2
AUTOMOTIVE EMISSIONS 4-3
EVAPORATIVE EMISSION
CONTROLS 4-5
EXHAUST EMISSION CONTROLS 4-9
DIESEL ENGINE EMISSIONS
CONTROLS 4-31
VACUUM DIAGRAMS 4-34

AIR POLLUTION

The earth's atmosphere, at or near sea level, consists approximately of 78 percent nitrogen, 21 percent oxygen and 1 percent other gases. If it were possible to remain in this state, 100 percent clean air would result. However, many varied sources allow other gases and particulates to mix with the clean air, causing our atmosphere to become unclean or polluted.

Some of these pollutants are visible while others are invisible, with each having the capability of causing distress to the eyes, ears, throat, skin and respiratory system. Should these pollutants become concentrated in a specific area and under certain conditions, death could result due to the displacement or chemical change of the oxygen content in the air. These pollutants can also cause great damage to the environment and to the many man made objects that are exposed to the elements.

To better understand the causes of air pollution, the pollutants can be categorized into 3 separate types, natural, industrial and automotive.

Natural Pollutants

Natural pollution has been present on earth since before man appeared and continues to be a factor when discussing air pollution, although it causes only a small percentage of the overall pollution problem. It is the direct result of decaying organic matter, wind born smoke and particulates from such natural events as plain and forest fires (ignited by heat or lightning), volcanic ash, sand and dust which can spread over a large area of the countryside.

Such a phenomenon of natural pollution has been seen in the form of volcanic eruptions, with the resulting plume of smoke, steam and volcanic ash blotting out the sun's rays as it spreads and rises higher into the atmosphere. As it travels into the atmosphere the upper air currents catch and carry the smoke and ash, while condensing the steam back into water vapor. As the water vapor, smoke and ash travel on their journey, the smoke dissipates into the atmosphere while the ash and moisture settle back to earth in a trail hundreds of miles long. In some cases, lives are lost and millions of dollars of property damage result.

Industrial Pollutants

Industrial pollution is caused primarily by industrial processes, the burning of coal, oil and natural gas, which in turn produce smoke and fumes. Because the burning fuels contain large amounts of sulfur, the principal ingredients of smoke and fumes are sulfur dioxide and particulate matter. This type of pollutant occurs most severely during still, damp and cool weather, such as at night. Even in its less severe form, this pollutant is not confined to just cities. Because of air movements, the pollutants move for miles over the surrounding countryside, leaving in its path a barren and unhealthy environment for all living things.

Working with Federal, State and Local mandated regulations and by carefully monitoring emissions, big business has greatly reduced the amount of pollutant introduced from its industrial sources, striving to obtain an acceptable level. Because of the mandated industrial emission clean up, many land areas and streams in and around the cities that were formerly barren of vege-

tation and life, have now begun to move back in the direction of nature's intended balance.

Automotive Pollutants

The third major source of air pollution is automotive emissions. The emissions from the internal combustion engines were not an appreciable problem years ago because of the small number of registered vehicles and the nation's small highway system. However, during the early 1950's, the trend of the American people was to move from the cities to the surrounding suburbs. This caused an immediate problem in transportation because the majority of suburbs were not afforded mass transit conveniences. This lack of transportation created an attractive market for the automobile manufacturers, which resulted in a dramatic increase in the number of vehicles produced and sold, along with a marked increase in highway construction between cities and the suburbs. Multi-vehicle families emerged with a growing emphasis placed on an individual vehicle per family member. As the increase in vehicle ownership and usage occurred, so did pollutant levels in and around the cities, as suburbanites drove daily to their businesses and employment, returning at the end of the day to their homes in the suburbs.

It was noted that a smoke and fog type haze was being formed and at times, remained in suspension over the cities, taking time to dissipate. At first this "smog," derived from the words "smoke" and "fog," was thought to result from industrial pollution but it was determined that automobile emissions shared the blame. It was discovered that when normal automobile emissions were exposed to sunlight for a period of time, complex chemical reactions would take place.

It is now known that smog is a photo chemical layer which develops when certain oxides of nitrogen (NOx) and unburned hydrocarbons (HC) from automobile emissions are exposed to sunlight. Pollution was more severe when smog would become stagnant over an area in which a warm layer of air settled over the top of the cooler air mass, trapping and holding the cooler mass at ground level. The trapped cooler air would keep the emissions from being dispersed and diluted through normal air flows. This type of air stagnation was given the name "Temperature Inversion."

TEMPERATURE INVERSION

In normal weather situations, surface air is warmed by heat radiating from the earth's surface and the sun's rays. This causes it to rise upward, into the atmosphere. Upon rising it will cool through a convection type heat exchange with the cooler upper air. As warm air rises, the surface pollutants are carried upward and dissipated into the atmosphere.

When a temperature inversion occurs, we find the higher air is no longer cooler, but is warmer than the surface air, causing the cooler surface air to become trapped. This warm air blanket can extend from above ground level to a few hundred or even a few thousand feet into the air. As the surface air is trapped, so are the pollutants, causing a severe smog condition. Should this stagnant air mass extend to a few thousand feet high, enough air movement with the inversion takes place to allow the smog layer to rise above ground level but the pollutants still cannot dissipate. This inversion can remain for days over an area, with the smog level only rising or lowering from ground level to a few hundred feet high. Meanwhile, the pollutant levels increase, causing eye irritation, respiratory problems, reduced visibility, plant damage and in some cases, even disease.

This inversion phenomenon was first noted in the Los Angeles, California area. The city lies in terrain resembling a basin and with certain weather conditions, a cold air mass is held in the basin while a warmer air mass covers it like a lid.

Because this type of condition was first documented as prevalent in the Los Angeles area, this type of trapped pollution was named Los Angeles Smog, although it occurs in other areas where a large concentration of automobiles are used and the air remains stagnant for any length of time.

HEAT TRANSFER

Consider the internal combustion engine as a machine in which raw materials must be placed so a finished product comes out. As in any machine operation, a certain amount of wasted material is formed. When we relate this to the internal combustion engine, we find that through the input of air and fuel, we obtain power during the combustion process to drive the vehicle. The by-product or waste of this power is, in part, heat and exhaust gases with which we must dispose.

The heat from the combustion process can rise to over 4000°F (2204°C). The dissipation of this heat is controlled by a ram air effect, the use of cooling fans to cause air flow and a liquid coolant solution surrounding the combustion area to transfer the heat of combustion through the cylinder walls and into the coolant. The coolant is then directed to a thin-finned, multi-tubed radiator, from which the excess heat is transferred to the atmosphere by 1 of the 3 heat transfer methods, conduction, convection or radiation.

The cooling of the combustion area is an important part in the control of exhaust emissions. To understand the behavior of the combustion and transfer of its heat, consider the air/fuel charge. It is ignited and the flame front burns progressively across the combustion chamber until the burning charge reaches the cylinder walls. Some of the fuel in contact with the walls is not hot enough to burn, thereby snuffing out or quenching the combustion process. This leaves unburned fuel in the combustion chamber. This unburned fuel is then forced out of the cylinder and into the exhaust system, along with the exhaust gases.

Many attempts have been made to minimize the amount of unburned fuel in the combustion chambers due to quenching, by increasing the coolant temperature and lessening the contact area of the coolant around the combustion area. However, design limitations within the combustion chambers prevent the complete burning of the air/fuel charge, so a certain amount of the unburned fuel is still expelled into the exhaust system, regardless of modifications to the engine.

AUTOMOTIVE EMISSIONS

Before emission controls were mandated on internal combustion engines, other sources of engine pollutants were discovered along with the exhaust emissions. It was determined that engine combustion exhaust produced approximately 60 percent of the total emission pollutants, fuel evaporation from the fuel tank and carburetor vents produced 20 percent, with the final 20 percent being produced through the crankcase as a by-product of the combustion process.

Exhaust Gases

The exhaust gases emitted into the atmosphere are a combination of burned and unburned fuel. To understand the exhaust emission and its composition, we must review some basic chemistry.

When the air/fuel mixture is introduced into the engine, we are mixing air, composed of nitrogen (78 percent), oxygen (21 percent) and other gases (1 percent) with the fuel, which is 100 percent hydrocarbons (HC), in a semi-controlled ratio. As the combustion process is accomplished, power is produced to move the vehicle while the heat of combustion is transferred to the cooling system. The exhaust gases are then composed of nitrogen, a diatomic gas (N_2), the same as was introduced in the engine, carbon dioxide (CO_2), the same gas that is used in beverage carbonation, and water vapor (H_2O). The nitrogen (N_2), for the most part, passes through the engine unchanged, while the oxygen (O_2) reacts (burns) with the hydrocarbons (HC) and produces the carbon dioxide (CO_2) and the water vapors (H_2O). If this chemical process would be the only process to take place, the exhaust emissions would be harmless. However, during the combustion pro-

cess, other compounds are formed which are considered dangerous. These pollutants are hydrocarbons (HC), carbon monoxide (CO), oxides of nitrogen (NOx) oxides of sulfur (SOx) and engine particulates.

HYDROCARBONS

Hydrocarbons (HC) are essentially fuel which was not burned during the combustion process or which has escaped into the atmosphere through fuel evaporation. The main sources of incomplete combustion are rich air/fuel mixtures, low engine temperatures and improper spark timing. The main sources of hydrocarbon emission through fuel evaporation on most vehicles used to be the vehicle's fuel tank and carburetor float bowl.

To reduce combustion hydrocarbon emission, engine modifications were made to minimize dead space and surface area in the combustion chamber. In addition, the air/fuel mixture was made more lean through the improved control which feedback carburetion and fuel injection offers and by the addition of external controls to aid in further combustion of the hydrocarbons outside the engine. Two such methods were the addition of air injection systems, to inject fresh air into the exhaust manifolds and the installation of catalytic converters, units that are able to burn traces of hydrocarbons without affecting the internal combustion process or fuel economy.

To control hydrocarbon emissions through fuel evaporation, modifications were made to the fuel tank to allow storage of the fuel vapors during periods of engine shut-down. Modifications were also made to the air intake system so that at specific times during engine operation, these vapors may be purged and burned by blending them with the air/fuel mixture.

CARBON MONOXIDE

Carbon monoxide is formed when not enough oxygen is present during the combustion process to convert carbon (C) to carbon dioxide (CO_2). An increase in the carbon monoxide (CO) emission is normally accompanied by an increase in the hydrocarbon (HC) emission because of the lack of oxygen to completely burn all of the fuel mixture.

Carbon monoxide (CO) also increases the rate at which the photo chemical smog is formed by speeding up the conversion of nitric oxide (NO) to nitrogen dioxide (NO_2). To accomplish this, carbon monoxide (CO) combines with oxygen (O_2) and nitric oxide (NO) to produce carbon dioxide (CO_2) and nitrogen dioxide (NO_2). ($CO + O_2 + NO \ CO_2 + NO_2$).

The dangers of carbon monoxide, which is an odorless and colorless toxic gas are many. When carbon monoxide is inhaled into the lungs and passed into the blood stream, oxygen is replaced by the carbon monoxide in the red blood cells, causing a reduction in the amount of oxygen supplied to the many parts of the body. This lack of oxygen causes headaches, lack of coordination, reduced mental alertness and, should the carbon monoxide concentration be high enough, death could result.

NITROGEN

Normally, nitrogen is an inert gas. When heated to approximately 2500°F (1371°C) through the combustion process, this gas becomes active and causes an increase in the nitric oxide (NO) emission.

Oxides of nitrogen (NOx) are composed of approximately 97–98 percent nitric oxide (NO). Nitric oxide is a colorless gas but when it is passed into the atmosphere, it combines with oxygen and forms nitrogen dioxide (NO_2). The nitrogen dioxide then combines with chemically active hydrocarbons (HC) and when in the presence of sunlight, causes the formation of photo-chemical smog.

Ozone

To further complicate matters, some of the nitrogen dioxide (NO_2) is broken apart by the sunlight to form nitric oxide and oxygen. (NO_2 + sunlight NO + O). This single atom of oxygen then combines with diatomic (meaning 2 atoms) oxygen (O_2) to form ozone (O_3). Ozone is one of the smells associated with smog. It has a pungent and offensive odor, irritates the eyes and lung tissues, affects the growth of plant life and causes rapid deterioration of rubber products. Ozone can be formed by sunlight as well as electrical discharge into the air.

The most common discharge area on the automobile engine is the secondary ignition electrical system, especially when inferior quality spark plug cables are used. As the surge of high voltage is routed through the secondary cable, the circuit builds up an electrical field around the wire, which acts upon the oxygen in the surrounding air to form the ozone. The faint glow along the cable with the engine running that may be visible on a dark night, is called the "corona discharge." It is the result of the electrical field

passing from a high along the cable, to a low in the surrounding air, which forms the ozone gas. The combination of corona and ozone has been a major cause of cable deterioration. Recently, different and better quality insulating materials have lengthened the life of the electrical cables.

Although ozone at ground level can be harmful, ozone is beneficial to the earth's inhabitants. By having a concentrated ozone layer called the "ozonosphere," between 10 and 20 miles (16–32 km) up in the atmosphere, much of the ultra violet radiation from the sun's rays are absorbed and screened. If this ozone layer were not present, much of the earth's surface would be burned, dried and unfit for human life.

OXIDES OF SULFUR

Oxides of sulfur (SOx) were initially ignored in the exhaust system emissions, since the sulfur content of gasoline as a fuel is less than $1/10$ of 1 percent. Because of this small amount, it was felt that it contributed very little to the overall pollution problem. However, because of the difficulty in solving the sulfur emissions in industrial pollutions and the introduction of catalytic converter to the automobile exhaust systems, a change was mandated. The automobile exhaust system, when equipped with a catalytic converter, changes the sulfur dioxide (SO_2) into sulfur trioxide (SO_3).

When this combines with water vapors (H_2O), a sulfuric acid mist (H_2SO_4) is formed and is a very difficult pollutant to handle since it is extremely corrosive. This sulfuric acid mist that is formed, is the same mist that rises from the vents of an automobile battery when an active chemical reaction takes place within the battery cells.

When a large concentration of vehicles equipped with catalytic converters are operating in an area, this acid mist may rise and be distributed over a large ground area causing land, plant, crop, paint and building damage.

PARTICULATE MATTER

A certain amount of particulate matter is present in the burning of any fuel, with carbon constituting the largest percentage of the particulates. In gasoline, the remaining particulates are the burned remains of the various other compounds used in its manufacture. When a gasoline engine is in good internal condition, the particulate emissions are low but as the engine wears internally, the particulate emissions increase. By visually inspecting the tail pipe emissions, a determination can be made as to where an engine defect may exist. An engine with light gray or blue smoke emitting from the tail pipe normally indicates an increase in the oil consumption through burning due to internal engine wear. Black smoke would indicate a defective fuel delivery system, causing the engine to operate in a rich mode. Regardless of the color of the smoke, the internal part of the engine or the fuel delivery system should be repaired to prevent excess particulate emissions.

Diesel and turbine engines emit a darkened plume of smoke from the exhaust system because of the type of fuel used. Emission control regulations are mandated for this type of emission and more stringent measures are being used to prevent excess emission of the particulate matter. Electronic components are being introduced to control the injection of the fuel at precisely the proper time of piston travel, to achieve the optimum in fuel ignition and fuel usage. Other particulate after-burning components are being tested to achieve a cleaner emission.

Good grades of engine lubricating oils should be used, which meet the manufacturers specification. Cut-rate oils can contribute to the particulate emission problem because of their low flash or ignition temperature point. Such oils burn prematurely during the combustion process causing emission of particulate matter.

The cooling system is an important factor in the reduction of particulate matter. The optimum combustion will occur, with the cooling system operating at a temperature specified by the manufacturer. The cooling system must be maintained in the same manner as the engine oiling system, as each system is required to perform properly in order for the engine to operate efficiently for a long time.

Crankcase Emissions

Crankcase emissions are made up of water, acids, unburned fuel, oil fumes and particulates. These emissions are classified as hydrocarbons (HC) and are formed by the small amount of unburned, compressed air/fuel mixture entering the crankcase from the combustion area (between the cylinder walls and piston rings) during the compression and power strokes. The head of the compression and combustion help to form the remaining crankcase emissions.

Since the first engines, crankcase emissions were allowed into the atmosphere through a road draft tube, mounted on the lower side of the engine block. Fresh air came in through an open oil filler cap or breather. The air passed through the crankcase mixing with blow-by gases. The motion of the vehicle and the air blowing past the open end of the road draft tube caused a low pressure area (vacuum) at the end of the tube. Crankcase emissions were simply drawn out of the road draft tube into the air.

To control the crankcase emission, the road draft tube was deleted. A hose and/or tubing was routed from the crankcase to the intake manifold so the blow-by emission could be burned with the air/fuel mixture. However, it was found that intake manifold vacuum, used to draw the crankcase emissions into the manifold, would vary in strength at the wrong time and not allow the proper emission flow. A regulating valve was needed to control the flow of air through the crankcase.

Testing, showed the removal of the blow-by gases from the crankcase as quickly as possible, was most important to the longevity of the engine. Should large accumulations of blow-by gases remain and condense, dilution of the engine oil would oc-

cur to form water, soots, resins, acids and lead salts, resulting in the formation of sludge and varnishes. This condensation of the blow-by gases occurs more frequently on vehicles used in numerous starting and stopping conditions, excessive idling and when the engine is not allowed to attain normal operating temperature through short runs.

Evaporative Emissions

Gasoline fuel is a major source of pollution, before and after it is burned in the automobile engine. From the time the fuel is refined, stored, pumped and transported, again stored until it is pumped into the fuel tank of the vehicle, the gasoline gives off unburned hydrocarbons (HC) into the atmosphere. Through the redesign of storage areas and venting systems, the pollution factor was diminished, but not eliminated, from the refinery standpoint. However, the automobile still remained the primary source of vaporized, unburned hydrocarbon (HC) emissions.

Fuel pumped from an underground storage tank is cool but when exposed to a warmer ambient temperature, will expand. Before controls were mandated, an owner might fill the fuel tank with fuel from an underground storage tank and park the vehicle for some time in warm area, such as a parking lot. As the fuel would warm, it would expand and should no provisions or area be provided for the expansion, the fuel would spill out of the filler neck and onto the ground, causing hydrocarbon (HC) pollution and creating a severe fire hazard. To correct this condition, the vehicle manufacturers added overflow plumbing and/or gasoline tanks with built in expansion areas or domes.

However, this did not control the fuel vapor emission from the fuel tank. It was determined that most of the fuel evaporation occurred when the vehicle was stationary and the engine not operating. Most vehicles carry 5–25 gallons (19–95 liters) of gasoline. Should a large concentration of vehicles be parked in one area, such as a large parking lot, excessive fuel vapor emissions would take place, increasing as the temperature increases.

To prevent the vapor emission from escaping into the atmosphere, the fuel systems were designed to trap the vapors while the vehicle is stationary, by sealing the system from the atmosphere. A storage system is used to collect and hold the fuel vapors from the carburetor (if equipped) and the fuel tank when the engine is not operating. When the engine is started, the storage system is then purged of the fuel vapors, which are drawn into the engine and burned with the air/fuel mixture.

EVAPORATIVE EMISSION CONTROLS

In its normal operation, the internal combustion engine releases several compounds into the atmosphere. Since most of these compounds are harmful to our health if inhaled or ingested for long periods in sufficient quantity, the Federal Government has placed a limit on the quantities of the three main groups of compounds: unburned hydrocarbons (HC); carbon monoxide (CO); and oxides of nitrogen (NOx).

The emissions systems covered in this chapter are designed to regulate the output of these noxious fumes by your car's engine and fuel system. Three areas of the automobile are covered, each

with its own anti-pollution system or systems: the engine crankcase, which emits unburned hydrocarbons in the form of oil and fuel vapors; the fuel storage system (fuel tank and carburetor), which also emits unburned hydrocarbons in the form of evaporated gasoline; and the engine exhaust. Exhaust emissions comprise the greatest quantity of auto emissions in the forms of unburned hydrocarbons, carbon monoxide, and oxides of nitrogen. Because of this, there are more pollution devices on your car dealing with exhaust emissions than there are dealing with the other two emission types.

Positive Crankcase Ventilation System

OPERATION

♦ **See Figures 1, 2 and 3**

All Pontiac engines covered in this guide are equipped with a Positive Crankcase Ventilation (PCV) system to control crankcase blow-by vapors. The system functions as follows:

When the engine is running, a small portion of the gases which are formed in the combustion chamber leak by the piston rings and enter the crankcase. Since these gases are under pressure, they tend to escape from the crankcase and enter the atmosphere. If these gases are allowed to remain in the crankcase for any period of time, they contaminate the engine oil and cause

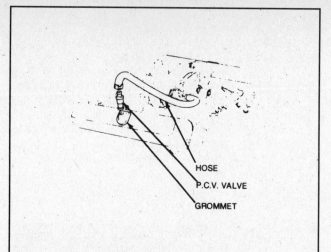

Fig. 3 Location of the Positive Crankcase Ventilation (PCV) valve—V8 engines

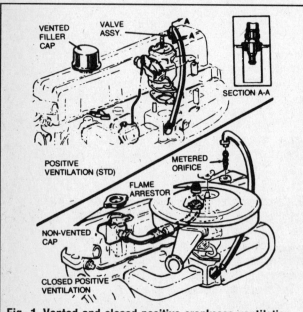

Fig. 1 Vented and closed positive crankcase ventilation systems—4 and 6-cylinder engines

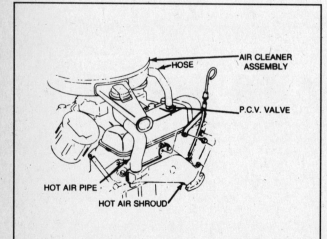

Fig. 2 Positive Crankcase Ventilation (PCV) valve location—V6 engines

sludge to build up in the crankcase. If the gases are allowed to escape into the atmosphere, they pollute the air with unburned hydrocarbons. The job of the crankcase emission control equipment is to recycle these gases back into the engine combustion chamber where they are reburned.

The crankcase (blow-by) gases are recycled in the following way: as the engine is running, clean, filtered air is drawn through the air filter and into the crankcase. As the air passes through the crankcase, it picks up the combustion gases and carries them out of the crankcase, through the oil separator, through the PCV valve, and into the induction system. As they enter the intake manifold, they are drawn into the combustion chamber where they are reburned.

The most critical component in the system is the PCV valve. Located in the valve cover or intake manifold, this valve controls the amount of gases which are recycled into the combustion chamber. At low engine speeds, the valve is partially closed, limiting the flow of the gases into the intake manifold. As engine speed increases, the valve opens to admit greater quantities of the gases into the intake manifold. If the valve should become blocked or plugged, the gases will be prevented from escaping from the crankcase by the normal route. Since these gases are under pressure, they will find their own way out of the crankcase. This alternate route is usually a weak oil seal or gasket in the engine. As the gas escapes by the gasket, it also creates an oil leak. Besides causing oil leaks, a clogged PCV valve also allows these gases to remain in the crankcase for an extended period of time, promoting the formation of sludge in the engine. See chapter one for PCV valve replacement intervals.

PCV VALVE SERVICE

Slow, unstable idling, frequent stalling, oil leaks, and oil in the air cleaner are all signs that the PCV valve may be clogged or faulty. Follow the PCV valve testing procedure in Chapter 1 and replace the valve if necessary. Check the valve at every tune-up. Remove the valve by gently pulling it out of the valve cover or manifold, then open the clamp on the hose end with a pair of pliers. Hold the clamp open while sliding it an inch or two down the hose (away from the valve), and then remove the valve. If the end of the hose is hard or cracked where it holds the valve, it may be feasible to cut the end off if there is plenty of extra hose. Otherwise, replace the hose. Replace the grommet in the valve cover if it is cracked or hard, and replace the clamp if it is broken or weak. In replacing the valve, make sure it is fully inserted in the hose, that the clamp is moved over the ridge on the valve so that the valve will not slip out of the hose, and that the valve is fully inserted into the grommet in the valve cover.

REMOVAL & INSTALLATION

PCV Filter

1. Slide the rubber coupling that joins the tube coming from the valve cover to the filter off the filter nipple. Then, remove the top of the air cleaner. Slide the spring clamp off the filter, and remove the filter. See illustration in Chapter 1.

2. Inspect the rubber grommet in the valve cover and the rubber coupling for brittleness and cracking. Replace parts as necessary.

To remove the PCV filter, use pliers to unfasten the hose clamp

Remove the PCV filter retaining clamp . . .

. . . then remove the PCV filter

3. Insert the new PCV filter through the hole in the air cleaner with the open portion of the filter upward (See illustration in Chapter 1). Make sure that the square portion of filter behind the nipple fits into the (square) hole in the air cleaner.

4. Install a new spring clamp onto the nipple. Make sure the clamp goes under the ridge on the filter nipple all the way around. Then, reconnect the rubber coupling and install the air cleaner cover.

Evaporative Emission Control System

OPERATION

◆ **See Figures 4 and 5**

This system reduces the amount of escaping gasoline vapors. Float bowl emissions are controlled by internal carburetor modifications. Redesigned bowl vents, reduced bowl capacity, heat shields, and improved intake manifold-to-carburetor insulation reduce vapor loss into the atmosphere. The venting of fuel tank vapors into the air has been stopped by means of the carbon canister storage method. This method transfers fuel vapors to an activated carbon storage device which absorbs and stores the vapor that is emitted from the engine's induction system while the engine is not running. When the engine is running, the stored vapor is purged from the carbon storage device by the intake air flow and then consumed in the normal combustion process. As the manifold vacuum reaches a certain point, it opens a purge control valve atop the charcoal storage canister. This allows air to be drawn into the canister, thus forcing the existing fuel vapors back into the engine to be burned normally.

On 1981 and later V6s, the purge function is electronically controlled by a purge solenoid in the line which is itself controlled by the Electronic Control Module (ECM). When the system is in the "Open Loop" mode, the solenoid valve is energized, blocking all vacuum to the purge valve. When the system is in the "Closed Loop" mode, the solenoid is deenergized, thus allowing existing vacuum to operate the purge valve. This releases the trapped fuel vapor and it is forced into the induction system.

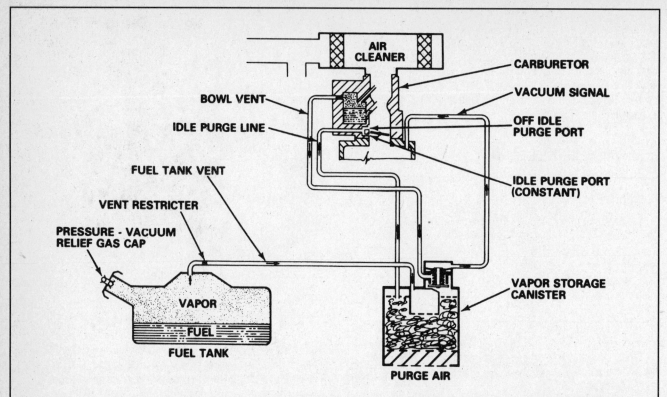

Fig. 4 The open canister Evaporative Emission Control System (EECS), shown here, is more common than the closed system

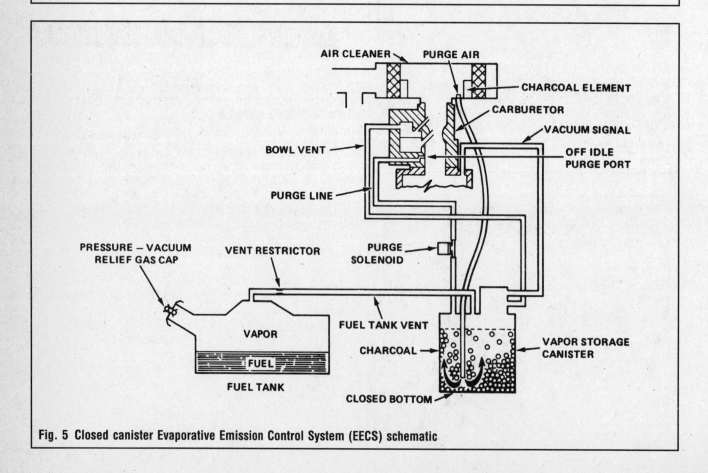

Fig. 5 Closed canister Evaporative Emission Control System (EECS) schematic

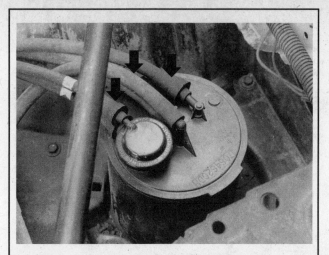

The EVAP canister has several vacuum lines (see arrows) running from it to various components

Most carbon canisters used are of the "Open" design, meaning that air is drawn in through the bottom (filter) of the canister. Some 1981 and later V6 canisters are of the "Closed" design, which means that the incoming air is drawn directly from the air cleaner.

SERVICE

The only service required for the evaporative emissions system is the periodic replacement of the charcoal canister filter. This procedure is covered in Chapter 1. If the fuel tank cap on your car ever requires replacement, make sure that it is of the same type as the original.

EXHAUST EMISSION CONTROLS

Exhaust emission controls comprise the largest body of emission controls installed on your car. Included in this category are: Thermostatic Air Cleaner (THERMAC); Air Injection Reactor System (AIR, 1974–80); Air Management System (1981 and later); Anti-Dieseling Solenoid; Early Fuel Evaporation (EFE) system; Exhaust Gas Recirculation; Controlled Combustion System (CCS); Computer Controlled Catalytic Converter (C-4) system; Computer Command Control (CCC); Mixture Control Solenoid (M/C); Throttle Position Sensor (TPS); Idle Speed Control (ISC); Electronic Spark Timing (EST); Electronic Spark Control (ESC); Transmission Converter Clutch (TCC); Catalytic Converter, Electronic Fuel Control system; and the Oxygen Sensor system. A brief description of each system and any applicable service procedures follows.

Thermostatic Air Cleaner (THERMAC)

OPERATION

◗ **See Figures 6 and 7**

All engines covered in this guide utilize the THERMAC system (in 1978 it was called TAC, but was the same). This system is designed to warm the air entering the carburetor when underhood temperatures are low, and to maintain a controlled air temperature into the carburetor at all times. By allowing preheated air to enter the carburetor, the amount of time the choke is on is reduced, re-

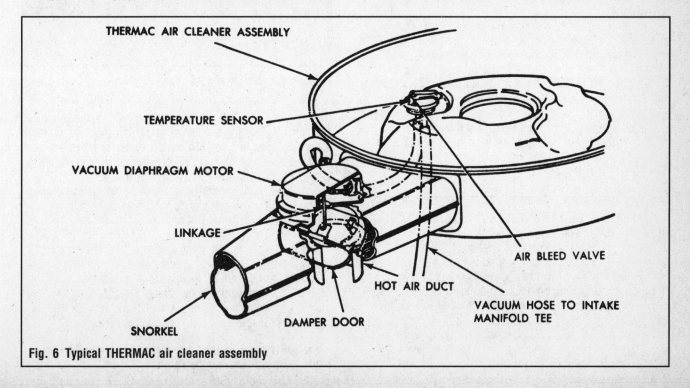

Fig. 6 Typical THERMAC air cleaner assembly

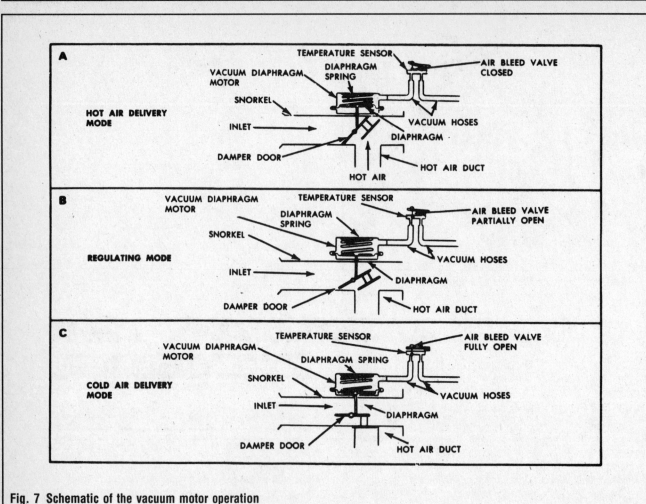

Fig. 7 Schematic of the vacuum motor operation

sulting in better fuel economy and lower emissions. Engine warm-up time is also reduced.

The Thermac system is composed of the air cleaner body, a filter, sensor unit, vacuum diaphragm, damper door, and associated hoses and connections. Heat radiating from the exhaust manifold is trapped by a heat stove and is ducted to the air cleaner to supply heated air to the carburetor. A movable door in the air cleaner case snorkel allows air to be drawn in from the heat stove (cold operation) or from underhood air (warm operation). The door position is controlled by the vacuum motor, which receives intake manifold vacuum as modulated by the temperature sensor.

SYSTEM CHECKS

1. Check the vacuum hoses for leaks, kinks, breaks, or improper connections and correct any defects.
2. With the engine off, check the position of the damper door within the snorkel. A mirror can be used to make this job easier. The damper door should be open to admit outside air.
3. Apply at least 7 in. Hg of vacuum to the damper diaphragm unit. The door should close. If it doesn't, check the diaphragm linkage for binding and correct hookup.
4. With vacuum still applied and the door closed, clamp the tube to trap the vacuum. If the door doesn't remain closed, there is a leak in the diaphragm assembly.

Air Injection Reactor (AIR) System

OPERATION

◆ See Figures 8, 9 and 10

The AIR system injects compressed air into the exhaust system, near enough to the exhaust valves to continue the burning of the normally unburned segment of the exhaust gases. To do this it employs an air injection pump and a system of hoses, valves, tubes, etc., necessary to carry the compressed air from the pump to the exhaust manifolds. Carburetors and distributors for AIR engines have specific modifications to adapt them to the air injection system; those components should not be interchanged with those intended for use on engines that do not have the system.

A diverter valve is used to prevent backfiring. The valve senses sudden increases in manifold vacuum and ceases the injection of air during fuel-rich periods. During coasting, this valve diverts the entire air flow through the pump muffler and during high engine speeds, expels it through a relief valve. Check valves in the system prevent exhaust gases from entering the pump.

➡ The AIR system on the V6 engines is slightly different, but its purpose remains the same.

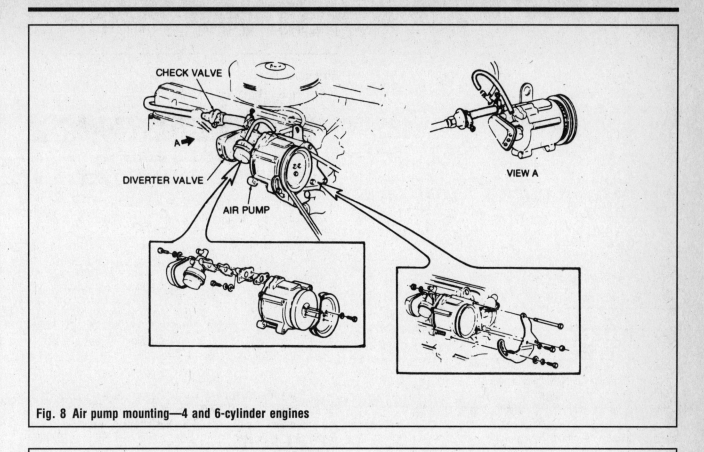

Fig. 8 Air pump mounting—4 and 6-cylinder engines

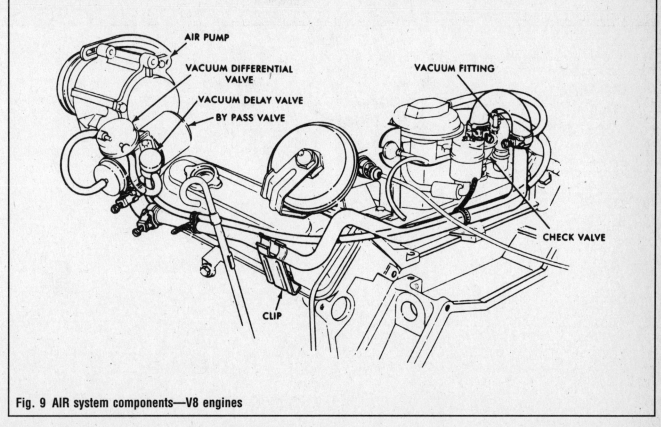

Fig. 9 AIR system components—V8 engines

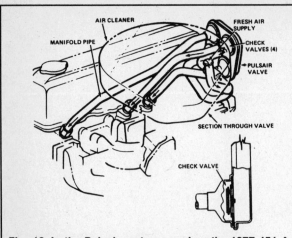

Fig. 10 In the Pulsair system, used on the 1977 151 4-cylinder engine, the engine's exhaust pulses fresh air into the exhaust system

SERVICE

The AIR system's effectiveness depends on correct engine idle speed, ignition timing, and dwell. These settings should be strictly adhered to and checked frequently. All hoses and fittings should be inspected for condition and tightness of connections. Check the drive belt for wear and tension every 12 months or 12,000 miles.

COMPONENT REMOVAL & INSTALLATION

Air Pump
▶ **See Figure 11**

❋❋ WARNING

Do not pry on the pump housing or clamp the pump in a vise: the housing is soft and may become distorted.

1. Disconnect the air hoses at the pump.
2. Hold the pump pulley from turning and loosen the pulley bolts.
3. Loosen the pump mounting bolt and adjustment bracket bolt. Remove the drive belt.
4. Remove the mounting bolts, and then remove the pump.
5. Install the pump using a reverse of the removal procedure.

Pump Filter

1. Remove the drive belt and pump pulley.
2. Using needlenose pliers, pull the fan from the pump hub.

➡**Use care to prevent any dirt or fragments from entering the air intake hole. DO NOT insert a screwdriver between the pump and the filter, and do not attempt to remove the metal hub. It is seldom possible to remove the filter without destroying it.**

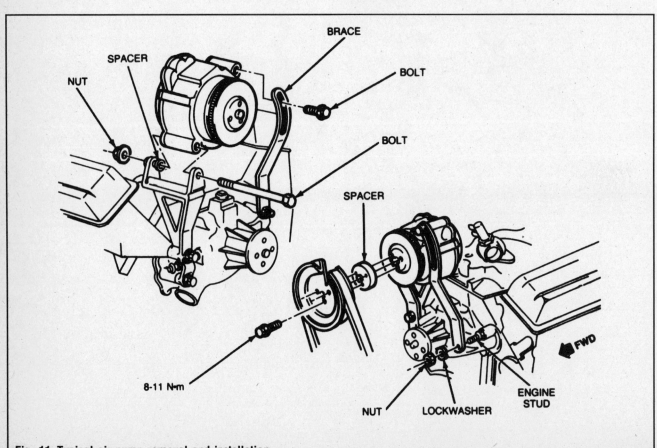

Fig. 11 Typical air pump removal and installation

To install:

3. To install a new filter, draw it on with the pulley and pulley bolts. Do not hammer or press the filter on the pump.

4. Draw the filter down evenly by torquing the bolts alternately. Make sure the outer edge of the filter slips into the housing. A slight amount of interference with the housing bore is normal.

➡**The new filter may squeal initially until the sealing lip on the pump outer diameter has worn in.**

Diverter (Anti-Afterburn) Valve

1. Detach the vacuum sensing line from the valve.
2. Remove the other hose(s) from the valve.
3. Unfasten the diverter valve from the elbow or the pump body.

Installation is performed in the reverse order of removal. Always use a new gasket. Tighten the valve securing bolts to 85 in. lbs.

Air Management System

OPERATION

▸ **See Figures 12 and 13**

The Air Management System is used on 1981 and later to provide additional oxygen to continue the combustion process after the exhaust gases leave the combustion chamber; much the same as the AIR system described earlier in this chapter. Air is injected into either the exhaust port(s), the exhaust manifold(s) or the catalytic converter by an engine driven air pump. The system is in operation at all times and will bypass air only momentarily during deceleration and at high speeds. The bypass function is performed by the Air Management Valve, while the check valve protects the air pump by preventing any backflow of exhaust gases.

The AIR system helps to reduce HC and CO content in the exhaust gases by injecting air into the exhaust ports during cold engine operation. This air injection also helps the catalytic converter to reach the proper temperature quicker during warm-up. When the engine is warm (closed loop), the AIR system injects air into the beds of a three-way converter to lower the HC and CO content in the exhaust.

The Air Management System utilizes the following components:
- An engine driven air pump
- Air management valves (Air Control and Air Switching)
- Air flow and control hoses
- Check valves
- A dual-bed, three-way catalytic converter

The belt driven, vane-type air pump is located at the front of the engine and supplies clean air to the system for purposes al-

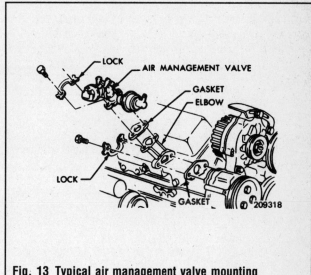

Fig. 13 Typical air management valve mounting

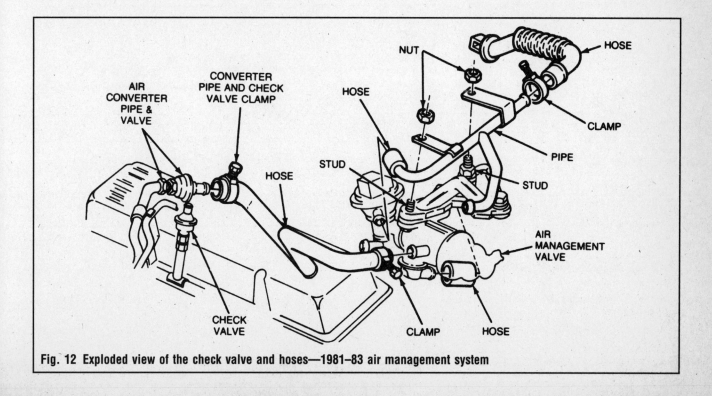

Fig. 12 Exploded view of the check valve and hoses—1981–83 air management system

ready stated. When the engine is cold, the Electronic Control Module (ECM) energizes an air control solenoid. This allows air to flow to the air switching valve. The air switching valve is then energized to direct air into the exhaust ports.

When the engine is warm, the ECM deenergizes the air switching valve, thus directing the air between the beds of the catalytic converter. This then provides additional oxygen for the oxidizing catalyst in the second bed to decrease HC and CO levels, while at the same time keeping oxygen levels low in the first bed, enabling the reducing catalyst to effectively decrease the levels of NOx.

If the air control valve detects a rapid increase in manifold vacuum (deceleration), certain operating modes (wide open throttle, etc.) or if the ECM self-diagnostic system detects any problems in the system, air is diverted to the air cleaner or directly into the atmosphere.

The primary purpose of the ECM's divert mode is to prevent backfiring. Throttle closure at the beginning of deceleration will temporarily create air/fuel mixtures which are too rich to burn completely. These mixtures will become burnable when they reach the exhaust if they are combined with injection air. The next firing of the engine will ignite the mixture causing an exhaust backfire. Momentary diverting of the injection air from the exhaust prevents this.

The Air Management System check valves and hoses should be checked periodically for any leaks, cracks or deterioration.

REMOVAL & INSTALLATION

Air Pump

1. Remove the valves and/or adapter at the air pump.
2. Loosen the air pump adjustment bolt and remove the drive belt.
3. Unscrew the three mounting bolts and then remove the pump pulley.
4. Unscrew the pump mounting bolts and then remove the pump.
5. Installation is in the reverse order of removal. Be sure to adjust the drive belt tension after installing it.

Check Valve

1. Release the clamp and disconnect the air hoses from the valve.
2. Unscrew the check valve from the air injection pipe.
3. Installation is in the reverse order of removal.

Air Management Valve

1. Disconnect the negative battery cable.
2. Remove the air cleaner.
3. Tag and disconnect the vacuum hose from the valve.
4. Tag and disconnect the air outlet hoses from the valve.
5. Bend back the lock tabs and then remove the bolts holding the elbow to the valve.
6. Tag and disconnect any electrical connections at the valve and then remove the valve from the elbow.
7. Installation is in the reverse order of removal.

Anti-Dieseling Solenoid

OPERATION

♦ See Figure 14

Some 1975 models have idle solenoids. Due to the leaner carburetor settings required for emission control, the engine may have a tendency to "diesel" or "run-on" after the ignition is turned **OFF.** The carburetor solenoid, energized when the ignition is **ON,** maintains the normal idle speed. When the ignition is turned **OFF,** the solenoid is de-energized and permits the throttle valves

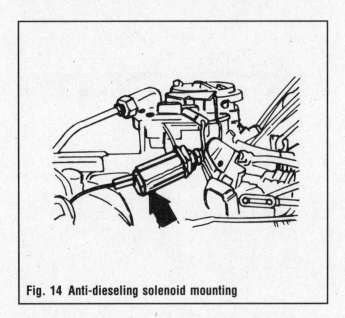

Fig. 14 Anti-dieseling solenoid mounting

to fully close, thus preventing run-on. For adjustment of carburetors with idle solenoids see the section on carburetor adjustments later in this chapter.

Early Fuel Evaporation (EFE) System

OPERATION

♦ See Figures 15, 16 and 17

Two types of EFE have been used on the engines covered in this guide. Both provide quick heat to the induction system, which helps evaporate fuel (reducing emissions) when the engine is cold and aids cold driveability. The Vacuum Servo EFE system uses a valve between the exhaust manifold and exhaust pipe, operated by vacuum and controlled by either a thermal vacuum valve or electric solenoid. The valve causes hot exhaust gas to enter the intake manifold heat riser passages, heating the incoming fuel mixture. The Heated-type EFE uses a ceramic heater plate located under the carburetor, controlled through the ECM. The vacuum-type EFE should be checked for proper operation at every tune-up.

➡On 1981 and later V6 engines, the EFE system is controlled by the ECM.

To check the valve:

1. Locate the EFE valve on the exhaust manifold and note the position of the actuator arm. On some cars, the valve and arm are covered by a two-piece cover which must be removed for access. *Make sure the engine is overnight cold.*

2. Watch the actuator arm when the engine is started. The valve should close when the engine is started cold; the actuator link will be pulled into the diaphragm housing.

3. If the valve does not close, stop the engine. Remove the

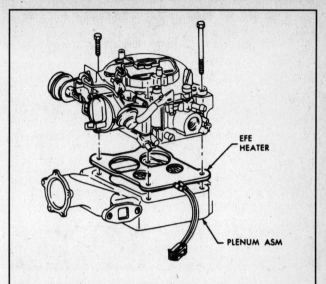

Fig. 17 The electric EFE heater plate is located under the carburetor

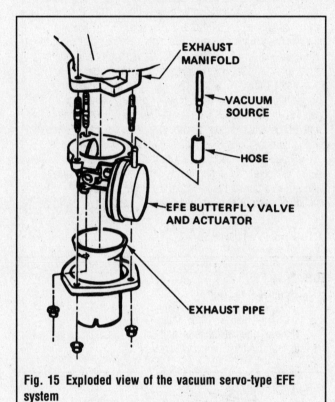

Fig. 15 Exploded view of the vacuum servo-type EFE system

hose from the EFE valve and apply 10 in. of vacuum by hand pump. The valve should close and stay closed for at least 20 seconds (you will hear it close). If the valve opens in less than 20 seconds, replace it. The valve could also be seized if it does not close; lubricate it with spray-type manifold heat valve lube. If the valve does not close when vacuum is applied *and* when it is lubricated, replace the valve.

4. If the valve closes, the problem is not with the valve. Check for loose, cracked, pinched or plugged hoses, and replace as necessary. Test the EFE solenoid (located on the valve cover bracket); if it is working, the solenoid plunger will emit a noise when the current is applied.

5. Warm up the engine to operating temperature.

6. Watch the EFE valve to see if it has opened. It should now be open. If the valve is still closed, replace the solenoid if faulty, and/or check the engine thermostat—the engine coolant may not be reaching normal operating temperature.

REMOVAL & INSTALLATION

EFE Valve Replacement

➡If the car is equipped with an oxygen sensor, it is located near the EFE valve. Use care when removing the EFE valve as not to damage the oxygen sensor.

1. Disconnect the vacuum hose at the EFE valve.

2. Remove the exhaust pipe-to-manifold nuts, and the washers and tension springs if used.

3. Lower the exhaust cross-over pipe. On some models, complete removal of the pipe is not necessary.

4. Remove the EFE valve.

5. To install, reverse the removal procedure. Always install new seals and gaskets.

EFE Solenoid Removal

1. Disconnect the negative battery cable.

2. Remove the air cleaner assembly if necessary.

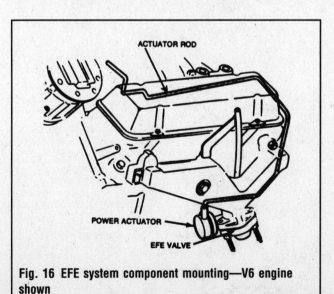

Fig. 16 EFE system component mounting—V6 engine shown

3. Disconnect and tag all electrical and vacuum hoses as required.

4. Remove the screw securing the solenoid to the valve cover bracket and remove the solenoid.

5. Installation is reverse of removal.

Electric-Type EFE

1. Remove the air cleaner.

2. Disconnect all vacuum, electrical and fuel connections from the carburetor.

3. Disconnect the EFE heater electrical connector.

4. Remove the carburetor.

5. Remove the EFE heater insulator (plate) assembly.

6. Installation is the reverse of removal.

Exhaust Gas Recirculation (EGR) System

OPERATION

▶ **See Figure 18**

All engines covered in this guide are equipped with Exhaust Gas Recirculation (EGR). This system consists of a metering valve, a vacuum line to the carburetor, and cast-in exhaust gas passages in the intake manifold. The EGR valve is controlled by carburetor vacuum, and accordingly opens and closes to admit exhaust gases into the fuel/air mixture. The exhaust gases lower the combustion temperature, and reduce the amount of oxides of nitrogen (NO_x) produced. The valve is closed at idle between the two extreme throttle positions.

In most installations, vacuum to the EGR valve is controlled by a Thermal Vacuum Switch (TVS); the switch, which is installed into the engine block, shuts off vacuum to the EGR valve until the engine is hot. This prevents the stalling and lumpy idle which would result if EGR occurred when the engine was cold.

As the car accelerates, the carburetor throttle plate uncovers the vacuum port for the EGR valve. At 3–5 in. Hg, the EGR valve opens and then some of the exhaust gases are allowed to flow into the air/fuel mixture to lower the combustion temperature. At full-throttle the valve closes again.

Some California engines are equipped with a dual diaphragm EGR valve. This valve further limits the exhaust gas opening (compared to the single diaphragm EGR valve) during high intake manifold vacuum periods, such as high-speed cruising, and provides more exhaust gas recirculation during acceleration when manifold vacuum is low. In addition to the hose running to the thermal vacuum switch, a second hose is connected directly to the intake manifold.

For 1977, all California models and cars delivered in areas above 4,000 ft. are equipped with back pressure EGR valves. This valve is also used on all 1978–81 models. The EGR valve receives exhaust back pressure through its hollow shaft. This exerts a force on the bottom of the control valve diaphragm, opposed by a light spring. Under low exhaust pressure (low engine load and partial throttle), the EGR signal is reduced by an air bleed. Under conditions of high exhaust pressure (high engine load and large throttle opening), the air bleed is closed and the EGR valve responds to an unmodified vacuum signal. At wide open throttle, the EGR flow is reduced in proportion to the amount of vacuum signal available.

1979 and later models have a ported signal vacuum EGR valve. The valve opening is controlled by the amount of vacuum obtained from a ported vacuum source on the carburetor and the amount of backpressure in the exhaust system.

REMOVAL & INSTALLATION

EGR Valve
▶ **See Figures 19 and 20**

1. Detach the vacuum lines from the EGR valve.

2. Unfasten the two bolts or bolt and clamp which attach the valve to the manifold. Withdraw the valve.

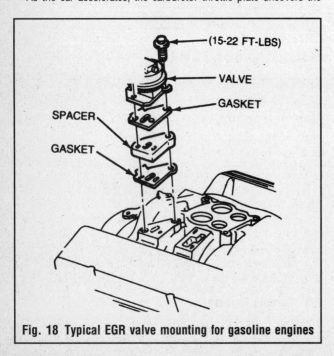

Fig. 18 Typical EGR valve mounting for gasoline engines

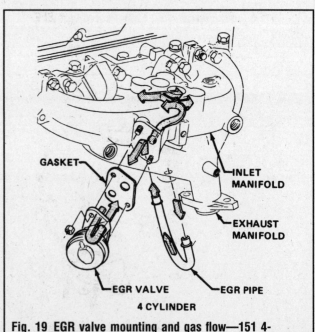

Fig. 19 EGR valve mounting and gas flow—151 4-cylinder engines

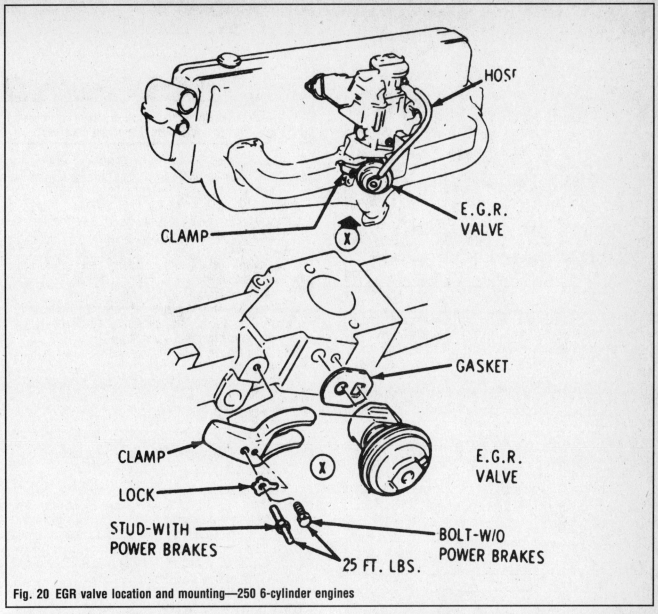

CLAMP

HOSE

E.G.R. VALVE

GASKET

CLAMP

LOCK

STUD-WITH POWER BRAKES

E.G.R. VALVE

BOLT-W/O POWER BRAKES

25 FT. LBS.

Fig. 20 EGR valve location and mounting—250 6-cylinder engines

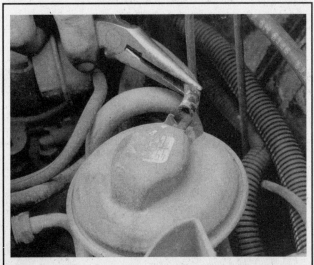

To remove the EGR valve, disconnect the vacuum line

After unfastening the EGR valve retaining bolts, remove the EGR valve

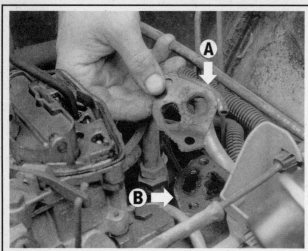

Remove and discard the gasket (A) from the mounting surface (B)

3. Installation is the reverse of removal. Always use a new gasket between the valve and the manifold. On dual diaphragm valves, attach the carburetor vacuum line to the tube at the top of the valve, and the manifold vacuum line to the tube at the center of the valve.

TVS Switch

♦ See Figure 21

1. Drain the radiator.
2. Disconnect the vacuum lines from the switch noting their locations. Remove the switch.
3. Apply sealer to the threaded portion of the new switch, and install it, torquing to 15 ft. lbs.
4. Rotate the head of the switch to a position that will permit easy hookup of vacuum hoses. Then install the vacuum hoses to the proper connectors.

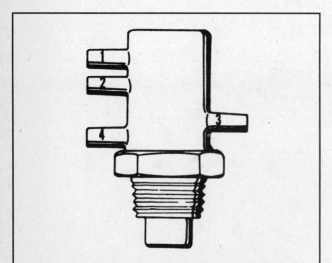

Fig. 21 Thermostatic Vacuum Switch (TVS)—nipple 1 connects to the distributor, nipple 2 to the TCS solenoid, and nipple 4 to the intake manifold

EGR VALVE CLEANING

Valves That Protrude From Mounting Face

❋❋ WARNING

Do not wash the valve assembly in solvents or degreasers; permanent damage to the valve diaphragm may result.

1. Remove the vacuum hose from the EGR valve assembly. Remove the two attaching bolts, remove the EGR valve from the intake manifold and discard the gasket.
2. Holding the valve assembly in hand, tap the valve lightly with a small plastic hammer to remove exhaust deposits from the valve seat. Shake out any loose particles. DO NOT put the valve in a vise.
3. Carefully remove any exhaust deposits from the mounting surface of the valve with a wire wheel or putty knife. Do not damage the mounting surface.
4. Depress the valve diaphragm and inspect the valve seating area through the valve outlet for cleanliness. If the valve and/or seat are not completely clean, repeat Step 2.
5. Look for exhaust deposits in the valve outlet, and remove any deposits with an old screwdriver.
6. Clean the mounting surfaces of the intake manifold and valve assembly. Using a new gasket, install the valve assembly to the intake manifold. Tighten the bolts to 25 ft. lbs. Connect the vacuum hose.

Shielded Valves or Valves That Do Not Protrude

1. Clean the base of the valve with a wire brush or wheel to remove exhaust deposits from the mounting surface.
2. Clean the valve seat and valve in an abrasive-type spark plug cleaning machine or sandblaster. Most machine shops provide this service. Make sure the valve portion is cleaned (blasted) for about 30 seconds, and that the valve is also cleaned with the diaphragm spring fully compressed (valve unseated). The cleaning should be repeated until all deposits are removed.
3. The valve must be blown out with compressed air thoroughly to ensure all abrasive material is removed from the valve.
4. Clean the mounting surface of the intake manifold and valve assembly. Using a new gasket, install the valve assembly to the intake manifold. Tighten the bolts to 25 ft. lbs. Connect the vacuum hose.

Controlled Combustion System

OPERATION

The CCS system relies upon leaner air/fuel mixtures and altered ignition timing to improve combustion efficiency. A special air cleaner with a thermostatically controlled opening is used on most CCS equipped models to ensure that air entering the carburetor is kept at 100°F. This allows leaner carburetor settings and improves engine warm-up. A 15°F higher temperature thermostat is employed on CCS cars to further improve emission control.

SERVICE

Since the only extra component added with a CCS system is the thermostatically controlled air cleaner, there is no additional maintenance required; however, tune-up adjustments such as idle speed, ignition timing, and dwell become much more critical. Care must be taken to ensure that these settings are correct, both for trouble-free operation and a low emission level.

Computer Controlled Catalytic Converter (C-4) System

OPERATION

▶ **See Figure 22**

The C-4 System, installed on certain 1979 and all 1980 cars sold in California, is an electronically controlled exhaust emissions system. The purpose of the system is to maintain the ideal air/fuel ratio at which the catalytic converter is most effective.

Major components of the system include an Electronic Control Module (ECM), an oxygen sensor, an electronically controlled carburetor, and a three-way oxidation reduction catalytic converter. The system also includes a maintenance reminder flag connected to the odometer which becomes visible in the instrument cluster at regular intervals, signaling the need for oxygen sensor replacement.

The oxygen sensor, installed in the exhaust manifold, generates a voltage which varies with exhaust gas oxygen content. Lean mixtures (more oxygen) reduce voltage; rich mixtures (less oxygen) increase voltage. Voltage output is sent to the ECM.

An engine temperature sensor installed in the engine coolant outlet monitors engine coolant temperatures. Vacuum control switches and throttle position sensors also monitor engine conditions and supply signals to the ECM.

The Electronic Control Module receives input signals from all sensors. It processes these signals and generates a control signal sent to the carburetor. The control signal cycles between on (lean command) and off (rich command). The amount of on and off time is a function of the input voltage sent to the ECM by the oxygen sensor.

Rochester Dualjet (2-barrel) E2ME and E4ME carburetors are used with the C-4 System. Basically, an electrically operated mixture control solenoid is installed in the carburetor float bowl. The solenoid controls the air/fuel mixture metered to the idle and main metering systems. Air metering to the idle system is controlled by an idle air bleed valve. It follows the movement of the mixture solenoid to control the amount of air bled into the idle system, enriching or leaning out the mixture as appropriate. Air/fuel mixture enrichment occurs when the fuel valve is open and the air bleed valve is closed. All cycling of this system, which occurs ten times per second, is controlled by the ECM. A throttle position switch informs the ECM of open or closed throttle operation. A number of different switches are used, varying with application. When the ECM receives a signal from the throttle switch, indicating a change of position, it immediately searches its memory for the last set of operating conditions that resulted in an ideal air/fuel ratio, and shifts to that set of conditions. The memory is continually updated during normal operation.

A "Check-Engine" light is included in the C-4 System installation. When a fault develops, the light comes on, and a trouble

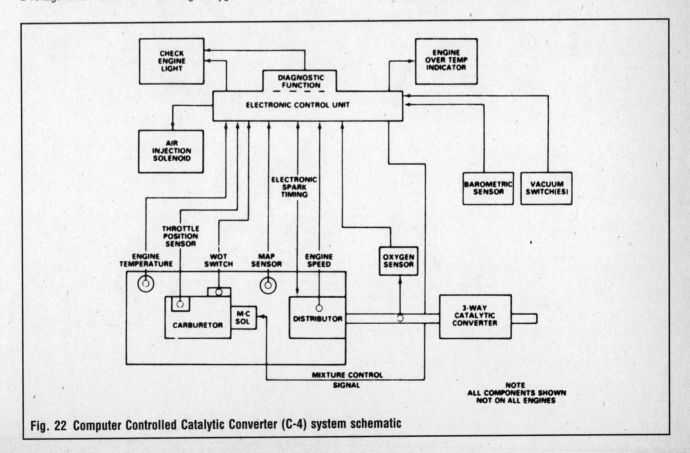

Fig. 22 Computer Controlled Catalytic Converter (C-4) system schematic

code is set into the ECM memory. However, if the fault is intermittent, the light will go out, but the trouble code will remain in the ECM memory as long as the engine is running. The trouble codes are used as a diagnostic aid, and are pre-programmed.

Unless the required tools are available, troubleshooting the C-4 System should be confined to mechanical checks of electrical connectors, vacuum hoses and the like. All diagnosis and repair should be performed by a qualified mechanic.

Computer Command Control (CCC) System

▶ **See Figures 23, 24, 25 and 25a (pp. 22–23)**

The Computer Command Control (CCC) System, installed on all 1981 and later cars, is basically a modified version of the C-4 system. Its main advantage over its predecessor is that it can monitor and control a larger number of interrelated emission control systems.

This new system can monitor up to 15 various engine/vehicle operating conditions and then use this information to control as many as 9 engine related systems. The "System" is thereby making constant adjustments to maintain good vehicle performance under all normal driving conditions while at the same time allowing the catalytic converter to effectively control the emissions of NO$_x$, HC and CO.

In addition, the "System" has a built in diagnostic system that recognizes and identifies possible operational problems and alerts the driver through a "Check Engine" light in the instrument panel. The light will remain ON until the problem is corrected. The "System" also has built in back-up systems that in most cases of an operational problem will allow for the continued operation of the vehicle in a near normal manner until the repairs can be made.

The CCC system has some components in common with the C-4 system, although they are not interchangeable. These components include the Electronic Control Module (ECM), which, as previously stated, controls many more functions than does its predecessor, an oxygen sensor system, an electronically controlled variable-mixture carburetor, a three-way catalytic converter, throttle position and coolant sensors, a Barometric Pressure (BARO) Sensor, Manifold Absolute Pressure (MAP) Sensor and a "Check Engine" light in the instrument panel.

Components unique to the CCC system include the Air Injection Reaction (AIR) management system, a charcoal canister purge solenoid, EGR valve controls, a vehicle speed sensor (in the instrument panel), a transmission converter clutch solenoid (only on models with automatic transmission), idle speed control and Electronic Spark Timing (EST).

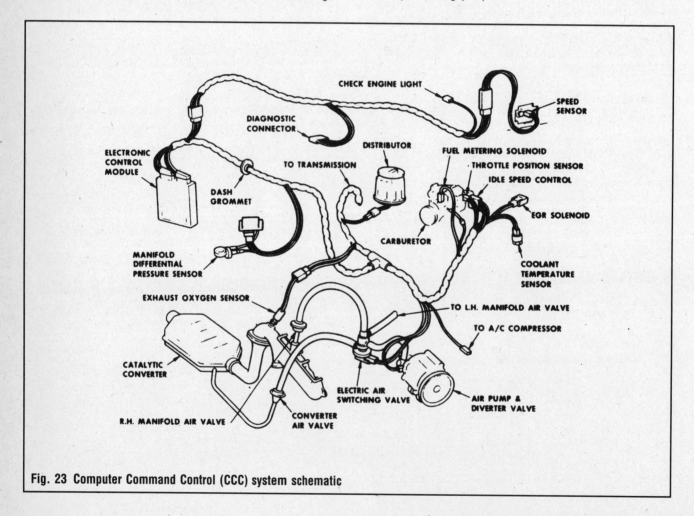

Fig. 23 Computer Command Control (CCC) system schematic

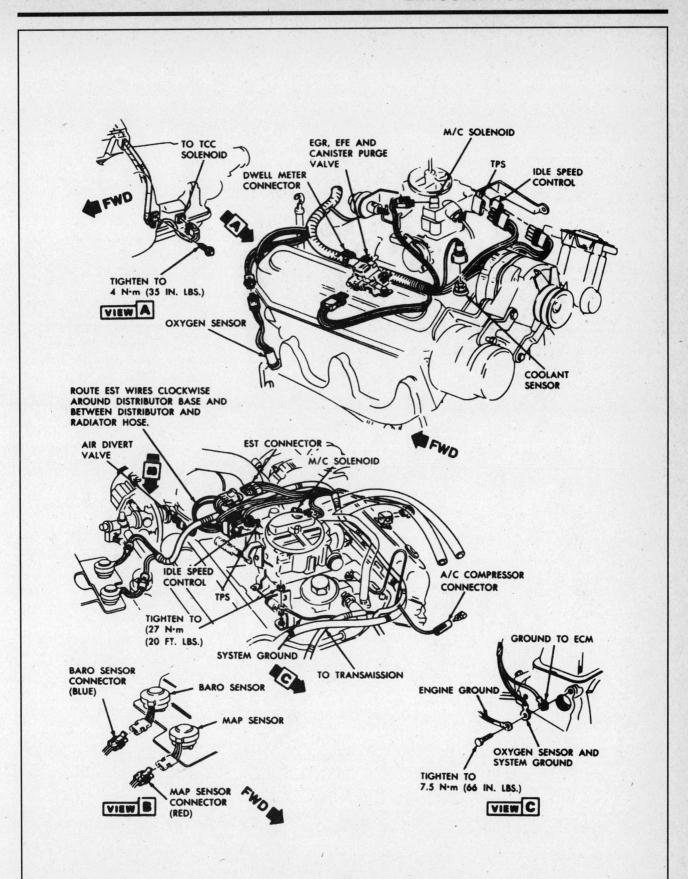

Fig. 24 Computer Command Control (CCC) component location—231 V6 engine

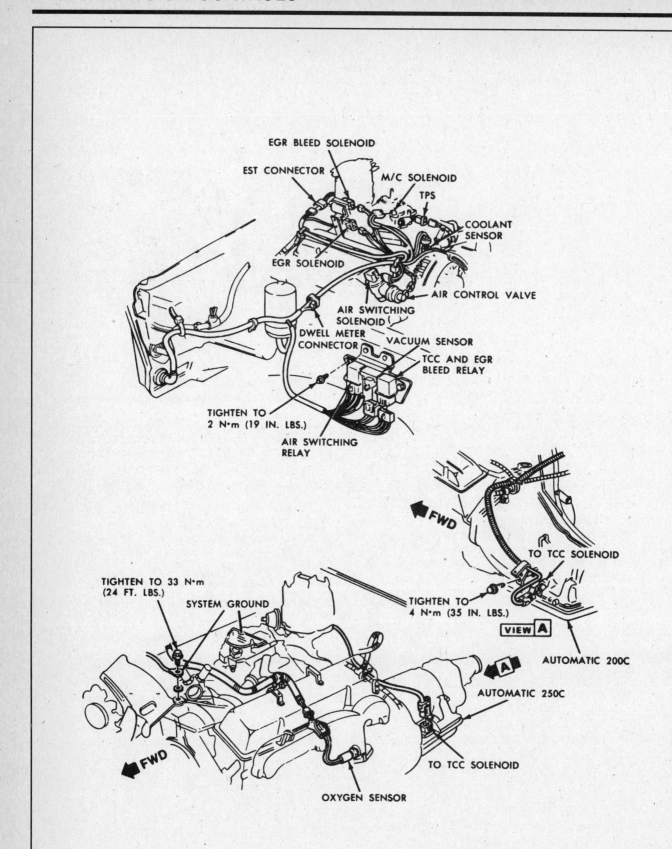

Fig. 25 CCC component location—V8 engines

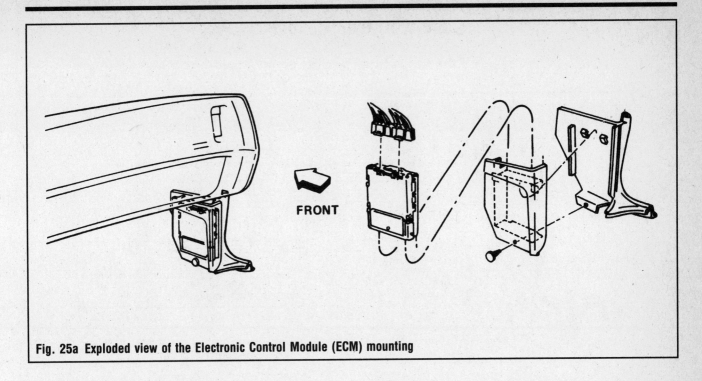

Fig. 25a Exploded view of the Electronic Control Module (ECM) mounting

The ECM, in addition to monitoring sensors and sending out a control signal to the carburetor, also controls the following components or sub-systems: charcoal canister purge control, the AIR system, idle speed, automatic transmission converter lock-up, distributor ignition timing, the EGR valve, and the air conditioner QCONVERTER clutch.

The EGR valve control solenoid is activated by the ECM in a fashion similar to that of the charcoal canister purge solenoid described earlier in this chapter. When the engine is cold, the ECM energizes the solenoid, which blocks the vacuum signal to the EGR valve. When the engine is warm, the ECM de-energizes the solenoid and the vacuum signal is allowed to reach and then activate the EGR valve.

The Transmission Converter Clutch (TCC) lock is controlled by the ECM through an electrical solenoid in the automatic transmission. When the vehicle speed sensor in the dash signals the ECM that the car has attained the pre-determined speed, the ECM energizes the solenoid which then allows the torque converter to mechanically couple the engine to the transmission. When the brake pedal is pushed, or during deceleration or passing, etc., the ECM returns the transmission to fluid drive.

The idle speed control adjusts the idle speed to all particular engine load conditions and will lower the idle under no-load or low-load conditions in order to conserve fuel.

➡**Not all engines use all systems. Control applications may differ.**

BASIC TROUBLESHOOTING

➡**The following explains how to activate the Trouble Code signal light in the instrument cluster. This is not a full fledged C-4 or CCC system troubleshooting and isolation procedure.**

Before suspecting the C-4 or CCC system, or any of its components as being faulty, check the ignition system (distributor, timing, spark plugs and wires). Check the engine compression, the air cleaner and any of the emission control components that are not controlled by the ECM. Also check the intake manifold, the vacuum hoses and hose connectors for any leaks. Check the carburetor mounting bolts for tightness.

The following symptoms could indicate a possible problem area with the C-4 or CCC systems:

1. Detonation;
2. Stalling or rough idling when the engine is cold;
3. Stalling or rough idling when the engine is hot;
4. Missing;
5. Hesitation;
6. Surging;
7. Poor gasoline mileage;
8. Sluggish or spongy performance;
9. Hard starting when engine is cold;
10. Hard starting when the engine is hot;
11. Objectionable exhaust odors;
12. Engine cuts out;
13. Improper idle speed (CCC only).

As a bulb and system check, the "Check Engine" light will come on when the ignition switch is turned to the **ON** position but the engine is not started.

The "Check Engine" light will also produce the trouble code/codes by a series of flashes which translate as follows: When the diagnostic test lead (C-4) or terminal (CCC) under the instrument panel is grounded, with the ignition in the **ON** position and the engine not running, the "Check Engine" light will flash once,

Trouble Code Identification Chart

NOTE: Always ground the test lead/terminal AFTER the engine is running

Trouble Code	Applicable System	Possible Problem Area
12	C-4, CCC	No reference pulses to the ECM. This is not stored in the memory and will only flash when the fault is present (not to be confused with the Code 12 discussed earlier.)
13	C-4, CCC	Oxygen sensor circuit. The engine must run for at least 5 min. (18 min. on the C-4 equipped 231 V6) at part throttle before this code will show.
13 & 14 (at same time)	C-4	See code 43.
13 & 43 (at same time)	C-4	See code 43.
14	C-4, CCC	Shorted coolant sensor circuit. The engine must run 2–5 min. before this code will show.
15	C-4, CCC	Open coolant sensor circuit. The engine must run for at least 5 min. (18 min. on the C-4 equipped 231 V6) before this code will show.
21	C-4	Shorted wide open throttle switch and/or open closed-throttle switch circuit (when used).
	C-4, CCC	Throttle position sensor circuit. The engine must run for at least 10 sec. (25 sec.—CCC) below 800 rpm before this code will show.
21 & 22 (at same time)	C-4	Grounded wide open throttle switch circuit (231 V6).
22	C-4	Grounded closed throttle or wide open throttle switch circuit (231 V6).
23	C-4, CCC	Open or grounded carburetor mixture control (M/C) solenoid circuit.
24	CCC	Vehicle speed sensor circuit. The engine must run for at least 5 min, at normal speed before this code will show.
32	C-4, CCC	Barometric pressure sensor (BARO) circuit output is low.
32 & 55 (at same time)	C-4	Grounded +8V terminal or V(REF) terminal for BARO sensor, or a faulty ECM.
34	C-4	Manifold absolute pressure sensor (MAP) output is high. The engine must run for at least 10 sec. below 800 rpm before this code will show.
	CCC	Manifold absolute pressure sensor (MAP) circuit or vacuum sensor circuit. The engine must run for at least 5 min. below 800 rpm before this code will show.
35	CCC	Idle speed control circuit shorted. The engine must run for at least 2 sec. above ½ throttle before this code will show.
42	CCC	Electronic spark timing (EST) bypass circuit grounded.
43	C-4	Throttle position sensor adjustment. The engine must run for at least 10 sec. before this code will show.
44	C-4, CCC	Lean oxygen sensor indication. The engine must run for at least 5 min. in closed loop (oxygen sensor adjusting carburetor mixture) at part throttle under load (drive car) before this code will show.
44 & 55 (at same time)	C-4, CCC	Faulty oxygen sensor circuit.
45	C-4, CCC	Rich oxygen sensor indication. The engine must run for at least 5 min. before this code will show (see 44 for conditions).
51	C-4, CCC	Faulty calibration unit (PROM) or improper PROM installation in the ECM. It will take at least 30 sec. before this code will show.
52 & 53	C-4	"Check Engine" light off: intermittant ECM problem. "Check Engine" light on: faulty ECM—replace.
52	C-4, CCC	Faulty ECM.
53	CCC	Faulty ECM.

Trouble Code Identification Chart (cont.)

NOTE: Always ground the test lead/terminal AFTER the engine is running

Trouble Code	Applicable System	Possible Problem Area
54	C-4, CCC	Faulty mixture control solenoid circuit and/or faulty ECM.
55	C-4	Faulty throttle position sensor or ECM (all but 231 V6). Faulty oxygen sensor, open MAP sensor or faulty ECM, (231 V6 only).
	CCC	Grounded +8V supply (terminal 19 on ECM connector), grounded 5V reference (terminal 21 on ECM connector), faulty oxygen sensor circuit or faulty ECM.

NOTE: *Not all codes will apply to every model.*

pause, and then flash twice in rapid succession. This is a Code 12, which indicates that the diagnostic system is working. After a long pause, the Code 12 will repeat itself two more times. This whole cycle will then repeat itself until the engine is started or the ignition switch is turned **OFF**.

When the engine is started, the "Check Engine" light will remain on for a few seconds and then turn off. If the "Check Engine" light remains on, the self-diagnostic system has detected a problem. If the test lead (C-4) or test terminal (CCC) is then grounded, the trouble code will flash (3) three times. If more than one problem is found to be in existence, each trouble code will flash (3) three times and then change to the next one. Trouble codes will flash in numerical order (lowest code number to highest). The trouble code series will repeat themselves for as long as the test leads or terminal remains grounded.

A trouble code indicates a problem with a given circuit. For example, trouble code 14 indicates a problem in the cooling sensor circuit. This includes the coolant sensor, its electrical harness and the Electronic Control Module (ECM).

Since the self-diagnostic system cannot diagnose every possible fault in the system, the absence of a trouble code does not necessarily mean that the system is trouble-free. To determine whether or not a problem with the system exists that does not activate a trouble code, a system performance check must be made. This job should be left to a qualified service technician.

In the case of an intermittent fault in the system, the "Check Engine" light will go out when the fault goes away, but the trouble code will remain in the memory of the ECM. Therefore, if a trouble code can be obtained even though the "Check Engine" light is not on, it must still be evaluated. It must be determined if the fault is intermittent or if the engine must be operating under certain conditions (acceleration, deceleration, etc.) before the "Check Engine" light will come on. In some cases, certain trouble codes will not be recorded in the ECM until the engine has been operated at part throttle for at least 5 to 18 minutes.

On the C-4 system, the ECM erases all trouble codes every time that the ignition is turned off. In the case of intermittent faults, a long term memory is desirable. This can be produced by connecting the orange connector/lead from terminal "S" of the ECM directly to the battery (or to a 'hot' fuse panel terminal). This terminal must always be disconnected immediately after diagnosis as it puts an undue strain on the battery.

On the CCC system, a trouble code will be stored until the ter-minal 'R' at the ECM has been disconnected from the battery for at least 10 seconds.

ACTIVATING THE TROUBLE CODE

◗ **See Figures 26, 27, 28 and 29**

On the C-4 system, activate the trouble code by grounding the trouble code test lead. Use the illustrations to help you locate the test lead under the instrument panel (usually a white and black wire with a green connector). Run a jumper wire from the lead to a suitable ground.

On the CCC system, locate the test terminal under the instrument panel (see illustration). Use a jumper wire and ground only the lead.

➡**Ground the test lead/terminal according to the instructions given previously in the "Basic Troubleshooting" section.**

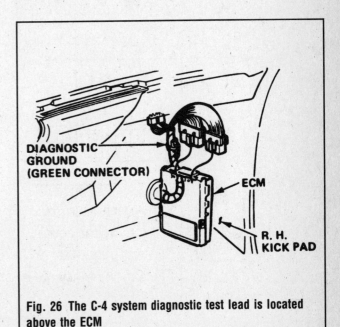

Fig. 26 The C-4 system diagnostic test lead is located above the ECM

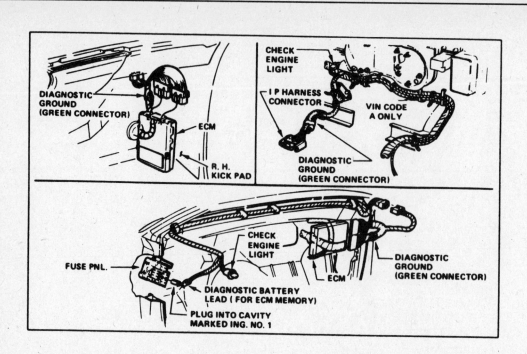

Fig. 27 Typical C-4 system harness layouts. The location of the test lead will depend on the position of the ECM

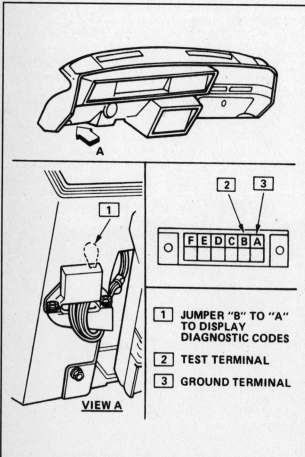

1 JUMPER "B" TO "A" TO DISPLAY DIAGNOSTIC CODES

2 TEST TERMINAL

3 GROUND TERMINAL

VIEW A

Fig. 28 Location of the under-dash terminal used on some vehicles

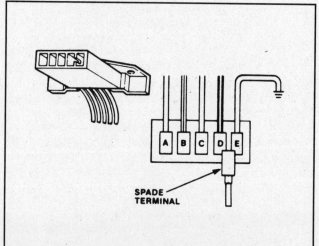

SPADE TERMINAL

Fig. 29 The CCC system diagnostic test terminal is located underneath the left side of the instrument panel

Mixture Control Solenoid (M/C)

The fuel flow through the carburetor idle main metering circuits is controlled by a mixture control (M/C) solenoid located in the carburetor. The M/C solenoid changes the air/fuel mixture to the engine by controlling the fuel flow through the carburetor. The ECM controls the solenoid by providing a ground. When the solenoid is energized, the fuel flow through the carburetor is reduced, providing a leaner mixture. When the ECM removes the ground, the solenoid is de-energized, increasing the fuel flow and providing a richer mixture. The M/C solenoid is energized and de-energized at a rate of 10 times per second.

Throttle Position Sensor (TPS)

◗ See Figure 30

➡A Throttle Position Sensor (TPS) was used on 1980–83 vehicles.

The Throttle Position Sensor (TPS) is mounted in the carburetor body and is used to supply throttle position information to the ECM. The ECM memory stores an average of operating conditions with the ideal air/fuel ratios for each of those conditions. When the ECM receives a signal that indicates throttle position change, it immediately shifts to the last remembered set of operating conditions that resulted in an ideal air/fuel ratio control. The memory is continually being updated during normal operations.

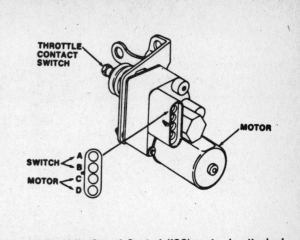

Fig. 31 The Idle Speed Control (ISC) motor is attached to the carburetor

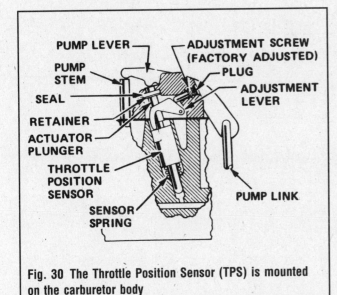

Fig. 30 The Throttle Position Sensor (TPS) is mounted on the carburetor body

Idle Speed Control (ISC)

◗ See Figure 31

V6 ENGINES

The idle speed control does just what its name implies—it controls the idle. The ISC is used to maintain low engine speeds while at the same time preventing stalling due to engine load changes. The system consists of a motor assembly mounted on the carburetor which moves the throttle lever so as to open or close the throttle blades.

The whole operation is controlled by the ECM. The ECM monitors engine load to determine the proper idle speed. To prevent stalling, it monitors the air conditioning compressor switch, the transmission, the park/neutral switch and the ISC throttle switch. The ECM processes all this information and then uses it to control the ISC motor which in turn will vary the idle speed as necessary.

Electronic Spark Timing (EST)

◗ See Figure 32

All 1980 models with the 231 V6 engine and all 1981 and later models use EST. The EST distributor, as described in an earlier chapter, contains no vacuum or centrifugal advance mechanism and uses a seven terminal HEI module. It has four wires going to a four terminal connector in addition to the connectors normally found on HEI distributors. A reference pulse, indicating engine rpm is sent to the ECM. The ECM determines the proper spark advance for the engine operating conditions and then sends an 'EST' pulse back to the distributor.

Under most normal operating conditions, the ECM will control the spark advance. However, under certain operating conditions such as cranking or when setting base timing, the distributor is capable of operating without ECM control. This condition is called BYPASS and is determined by the BYPASS lead which runs from the ECM to the distributor. When the BYPASS lead is at the proper voltage (5), the ECM will control the spark. If the lead is grounded or open circuited, the HEI module itself will control the spark. Disconnecting the 4-terminal EST connector will also cause the engine to operate in the BYPASS mode.

Electronic Spark Control (ESC)

➡This system was only used on 252 cu. in. V6 engines.

The Electronic Spark Control (ESC) system is a closed loop system that controls engine detonation by adjusting the spark timing. There are two basic components in this system, the controller and the detonation sensor.

The controller processes the sensor signal and remodifies the EST signal to the distributor to adjust the spark timing. The process is continuous so that the presence of detonation is monitored and controlled. The controller is not capable of memory storage.

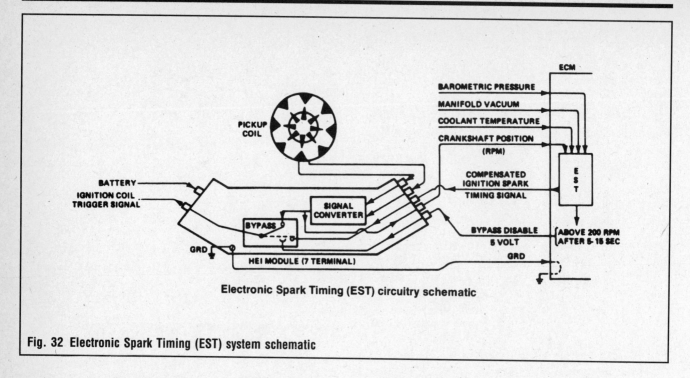

PICKUP COIL

BATTERY
IGNITION COIL
TRIGGER SIGNAL

BYPASS

GRD

HEI MODULE (7 TERMINAL)

SIGNAL CONVERTER

ECM

BAROMETRIC PRESSURE
MANIFOLD VACUUM
COOLANT TEMPERATURE
CRANKSHAFT POSITION
(RPM)

COMPENSATED
IGNITION SPARK
TIMING SIGNAL

BYPASS DISABLE
5 VOLT

GRD

EST

ABOVE 200 RPM
AFTER 5-15 SEC

Electronic Spark Timing (EST) circuitry schematic

Fig. 32 Electronic Spark Timing (EST) system schematic

The sensor is a magnetorestrictive device, mounted in the engine block that detects the presence, or absence, and intensity of detonation according to the vibration characteristics of the engine. The output is an electrical signal which is sent to the controller.

Transmission Converter Clutch (TCC)

All 1981 and later models with an automatic transmission use TCC. The ECM controls the converter by means of a solenoid mounted in the transmission. When the vehicle speed reaches a certain level, the ECM energizes the solenoid and allows the torque converter to mechanically couple the transmission to the engine. When the operating conditions indicate that the transmission should operate as a normal fluid coupled transmission, the ECM will de-energize the solenoid. Depressing the brake will also return the transmission to normal automatic operation.

Catalytic Converter

OPERATION

▶ **See Figures 33, 34 and 35**

The catalytic converter is a muffler-like container built into the exhaust system to aid in the reduction of exhaust emissions. The catalyst element consists of individual pellets or a honeycomb monolithic substrate coated with a metal such as platinum, palladium, rhodium or a combination. When the exhaust gases come into contact with the catalyst, a chemical reaction occurs which will reduce the pollutants into harmless substances like water and carbon dioxide.

There are essentially two types of catalytic converters: an oxidizing type is used on all 1975–80 models with the exception of those 1980 models built for Calif. It requires the addition of oxygen to epur the catalyst into reducing the engine's HC and CO emissions into H_2O and CO_2. Because of this need for oxygen, the AIR system is used with all these models.

The oxidizing catalytic converter, while effectively reducing HC and CO emissions, does little, if anything in the way of reducing NO_x emissions. Thus, the three-way catalytic converter.

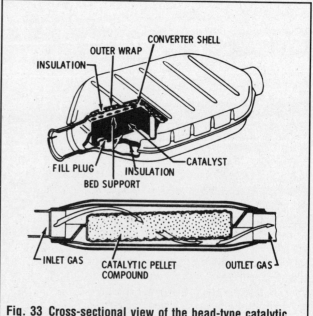

CONVERTER SHELL
OUTER WRAP
INSULATION
FILL PLUG
BED SUPPORT
INSULATION
CATALYST

INLET GAS
CATALYTIC PELLET
COMPOUND
OUTLET GAS

Fig. 33 Cross-sectional view of the bead-type catalytic converter

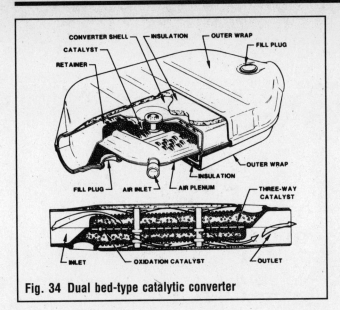

Fig. 34 Dual bed-type catalytic converter

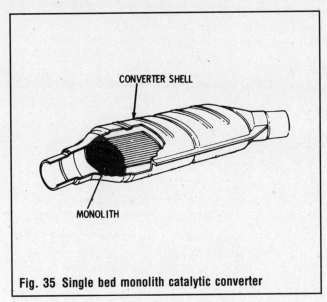

Fig. 35 Single bed monolith catalytic converter

The three-way converter, unlike the oxidizing type, is capable of reducing HC, CO and NO_x emissions; all at the same time. In theory, it seems impossible to reduce all three pollutants in one system since the reduction of HC and CO requires the addition of oxygen, while the reduction of NO_x calls for the removal of oxygen. In actuality, the three-way system really can reduce all three pollutants, but only if the amount of oxygen in the exhaust system is precisely controlled. Due to this precise oxygen control requirement, the three-way converter system is used only in cars equipped with an oxygen sensor system (1980 Calif. cars and all 1981 and later models).

There are no service procedures required for the catalytic converter, although the converter body should be inspected occasionally for damage. Some models with the V-6 the V-6 engine require a catalyst change at 30,000 mile intervals (consult your Owner's Manual).

PRECAUTIONS

1. Use only unleaded fuel.
2. Avoid prolonged idling; the engine should run no longer than 20 min. at curb idle and no longer than 10 min. at fast idle.
3. Do not disconnect any of the spark plug leads while the engine is running.
4. Make engine compression checks as quickly as possible.

CATALYST TESTING

At the present time there is no known way to reliably test catalytic converter operation in the field. The only reliable test is a 12 hour and 40 min. "soak" test (CVS) which must be done in a laboratory.

An infrared HC/CO tester is not sensitive enough to measure the higher tailpipe emissions from a failing converter. Thus, a bad converter may allow enough emissions to escape so that the car is no longer in compliance with Federal or state standards, but will still not cause the needle on a tester to move off zero.

The chemical reactions which occur inside a catalytic converter generate a great deal of heat. Most converter problems can be traced to fuel or ignition system problems which cause unusually high emissions. As a result of the increased intensity of the chemical reactions, the converter literally burns itself up.

A completely failed converter might cause a tester to show a slight reading. As a result, it is occasionally possible to detect one of these.

As long as you avoid severe overheating and the use of leaded fuels it is reasonably safe to assume that the converter is working properly. If you are in doubt, take the car to a diagnostic center that has a tester.

Oxygen Sensor

OPERATION

◢ **See Figure 36**

An oxygen sensor is used on all 1980 models built for Calif. and on all 1981 and later models. The sensor protrudes into the exhaust stream and monitors the oxygen content of the exhaust gases. The difference between the oxygen content of the exhaust gases and that of the outside air generates a voltage signal to the ECM. The ECM monitors this voltage and, depending upon the value of the signal received, issues a command to adjust for a rich or a lean condition.

No attempt should ever be made to measure the voltage output of the sensor. The current drain of any conventional voltmeter would be such that it would permanently damage the sensor. No jumpers, test leads or any other electrical connections should ever be made to the sensor. Use these tools ONLY on the ECM side of the wiring harness connector AFTER disconnecting it from the sensor.

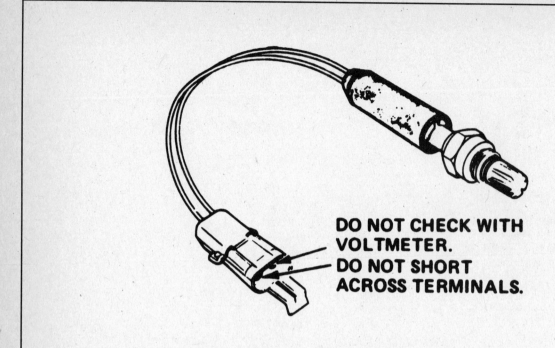

**DO NOT CHECK WITH VOLTMETER.
DO NOT SHORT ACROSS TERMINALS.**

Fig. 36 The oxygen sensor assembly threads into the exhaust manifold

REMOVAL & INSTALLATION

▶ **See Figure 37**

The oxygen sensor must be replaced every 3,000 MILES (4800 km). The sensor may be difficult to remove when the engine temperature is below 120°F (48°C). Excessive removal force may damage the threads in the exhaust manifold or pipe; *follow the removal procedure carefully.*

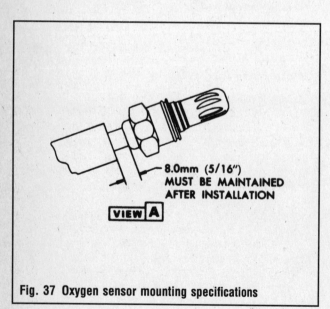

8.0mm (5/16")
**MUST BE MAINTAINED
AFTER INSTALLATION**

VIEW **A**

Fig. 37 Oxygen sensor mounting specifications

1. Locate the oxygen sensor. On the V8 engines, it is on the front of the left side exhaust manifold, just above the point where it connects to the exhaust pipe. On the V6 engines, it is on the inside of the exhaust pipe where it bends toward the back of the car.

➡**On the V6 engine you may find it necessary to raise the front of the car and remove the oxygen sensor from underneath.**

2. Trace the wires leading from the oxygen sensor back to the first connector and then disconnect them (the connector on the V6 engine is attached to a bracket mounted on the right rear of the engine block, while the connector on the V8 engine is attached to a bracket mounted on the top of the left side exhaust manifold).
3. Spray a commercial heat riser solvent onto the sensor threads and allow it to soak in for at least five minutes.
4. Carefully unscrew and remove the sensor.
5. To install, first coat the new sensor's threads with GM anti-seize compound no. 5613695 or the equivalent.

➡**The GM anti-seize compound is NOT a conventional anti-seize paste. The use of a regular paste may electrically insulate the sensor, rendering it useless. The threads MUST be coated with the proper electrically-conductive anti-seize compound.**

6. Installation torque is 30 ft. lbs. (42 Nm). *Do not overtighten.*
7. Reconnect the electrical connector. Be careful not to damage the electrical pigtail. Check the sensor boot for proper fit and installation. Install the air cleaner, if removed.

DIESEL ENGINE EMISSIONS CONTROLS

Crankcase Ventilation

OPERATION

▶ **See Figures 38 and 39**

A Crankcase Depression Regulator Valve (CDRV) is used to regulate (meter) the flow of crankcase gases back into the engine to be burned. The CDRV is designed to limit vacuum in the crankcase as the gases are drawn from the valve covers through the CDRV and into the intake manifold (air crossover).

Fresh air enters the engine through the combination filter, check valve and oil fill cap. The fresh air mixes with blow-by gases and enters both valve covers. The gases pass through a filter installed on the valve covers and are drawn into connecting tubing.

Intake manifold vacuum acts against a spring loaded diaphragm to control the flow of crankcase gases. Higher intake vacuum levels pull the diaphragm closer to the top of the outlet tube. This reduces the amount of gases being drawn from the crankcase and decreases the vacuum level in the crankcase. As the intake vacuum decreases, the spring pushes the diaphragm away from the top of the outlet tube allowing more gases to flow to the intake manifold.

➡**Do not allow any solvent to come in contact with the diaphragm of the Crankcase Depression Regulator Valve because the diaphragm will fail.**

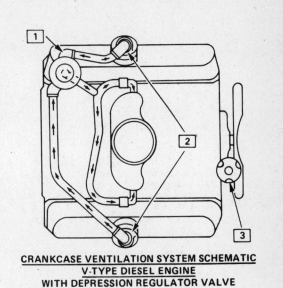

**CRANKCASE VENTILATION SYSTEM SCHEMATIC
V-TYPE DIESEL ENGINE
WITH DEPRESSION REGULATOR VALVE**

1. Crankcase depression regulator
2. Ventilation filter
3. Breather cap

Fig. 38 Schematic of the diesel crankcase ventilation airflow

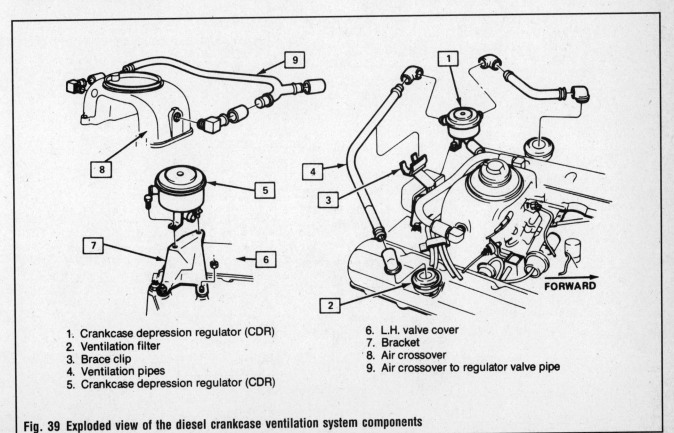

1. Crankcase depression regulator (CDR)
2. Ventilation filter
3. Brace clip
4. Ventilation pipes
5. Crankcase depression regulator (CDR)
6. L.H. valve cover
7. Bracket
8. Air crossover
9. Air crossover to regulator valve pipe

Fig. 39 Exploded view of the diesel crankcase ventilation system components

Exhaust Gas Recirculation (EGR) System

OPERATION

♦ **See Figures 40 and 41**

To lower the formation of nitrogen oxides (NO_x) in the exhaust, it is necessary to reduce combustion temperatures. This is done in the diesel, as in the gasoline engine, by introducing exhaust gases into the cylinders through the EGR valve.

FUNCTIONAL TESTS OF COMPONENTS

Vacuum Regulator Valve (VRV)
♦ **See Figure 42**

The Vacuum Regulator Valve is attached to the side of the injection pump and regulates vacuum in proportion to throttle angle. Vacuum from the vacuum pump is supplied to port A and vacuum at port B is reduced as the throttle is opened. At closed throttle, the vacuum is 15 inches; at half throttle—6 inches; at wide open throttle there is zero vacuum.

EGR System Diagnosis—Diesel Engine

Condition	Possible Causes	Correction
EGR valve will not open. Engine stalls on deceleration engine runs rough on light throttle	Binding or stuck EGR valve. No vacuum to EGR valve. Control valve blocked or air flow restricted.	Replace EGR valve. Replace EGR valve. Check VRV, RVR, solenoid, T.C.C. Operation, Vacuum Pump and connecting hoses.
EGR valve will not close. (Heavy smoke on acceleration).	Binding or stuck EGR valve. Constant high vacuum to EGR valve.	Replace EGR valve. Check VRV, RVR, solenoid, and connecting hoses.
EGR valve opens partially.	Binding EGR valve. Low vacuum at EGR valve.	Replace EGR valve. Check VRV, RVR, solenoid, vacuum pump, and connecting hoses.

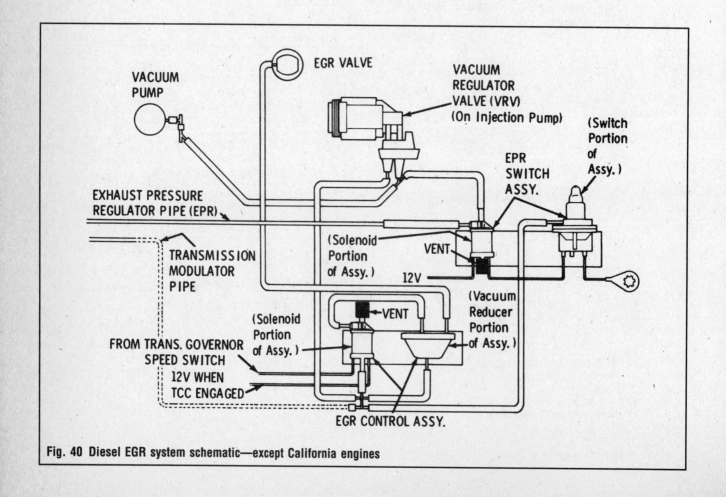

Fig. 40 Diesel EGR system schematic—except California engines

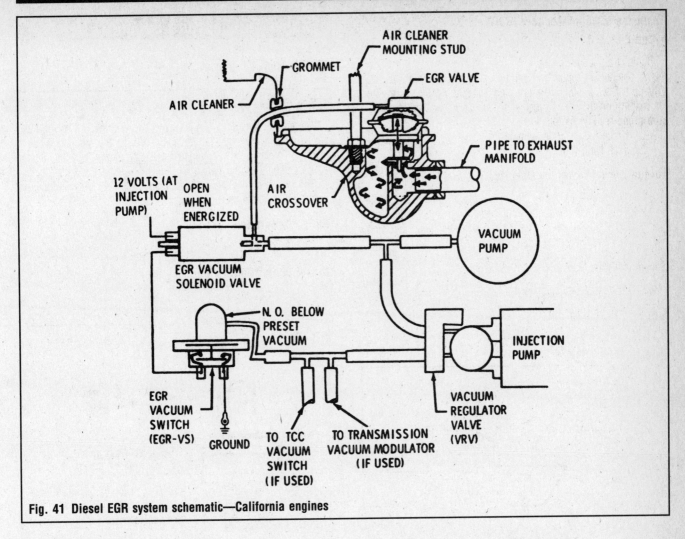

Fig. 41 Diesel EGR system schematic—California engines

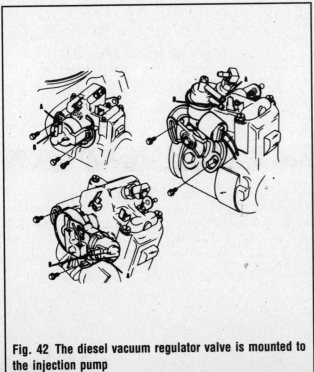

Fig. 42 The diesel vacuum regulator valve is mounted to the injection pump

Exhaust Gas Recirculation (EGR) Valve

◗ **See Figure 43**

Apply vacuum to vacuum port. The valve should be fully open at 10.5 inch and closed below 6 inch.

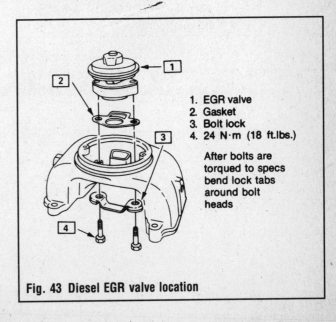

1. EGR valve
2. Gasket
3. Bolt lock
4. 24 N·m (18 ft.lbs.)

After bolts are torqued to specs bend lock tabs around bolt heads

Fig. 43 Diesel EGR valve location

Response Vacuum Reducer (RVR)
♦ **See Figure 44**

Connect a vacuum gauge to the port marked "To EGR valve or T.C.C. solenoid." Connect a hand operated vacuum pump to the VRV port. Draw a 50.66 kPa (15 inch) vacuum on the pump and the reading on the vacuum gauge should be lower than the vacuum pump reading as follows:
- 0.75 inch Except High Altitude
- 2.5 inch High Altitude

Torque Converter Clutch Operated Solenoid

When the torque converter clutch is engaged, an electrical signal energizes the solenoid allowing ports 1 and 2 to be interconnected. When the solenoid is not energized, port 1 is closed and ports 2 and 3 are interconnected.

Solenoid Energized

- Ports 1 and 3 are connected.

Solenoid De-Energized

- Ports 2 and 3 are connected.

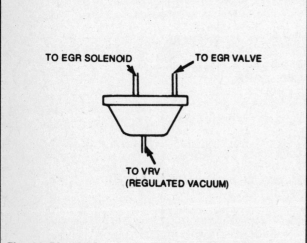

Fig. 44 Diesel EGR system response vacuum reducer—except California engines

Engine Temperature Sensor (ETS)

OPERATION

♦ **See Figure 45**

The engine temperature sensor has two terminals. Twelve volts are applied to one terminal and the wire from the other terminal leads to the fast idle solenoid and Housing Pressure Cold Advance solenoid that is part of the injection pump.

The switch contacts are closed below 125°F. At the calibration point, the contacts are open which turns off the solenoids.

Above Calibration

- Open Circuit.

Below Calibration

- Closed Circuit.

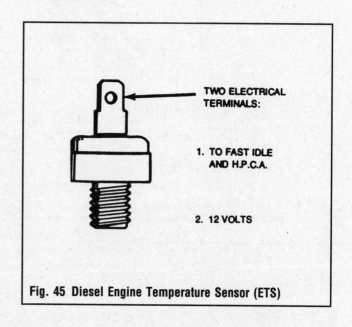

Fig. 45 Diesel Engine Temperature Sensor (ETS)

VACUUM DIAGRAMS

Following are vacuum diagrams for most of the engine and emissions package combinations covered by this manual. Because vacuum circuits will vary based on various engine and vehicle options, always refer first to the vehicle emission control information label, if present. Should the label be missing, or should vehicle be equipped with a different engine from the vehicle's original equipment, refer to the diagrams below for the same or similar configuration.

If you wish to obtain a replacement emissions label, most manufacturers make the labels available for purchase. The labels can usually be ordered from a local dealer.

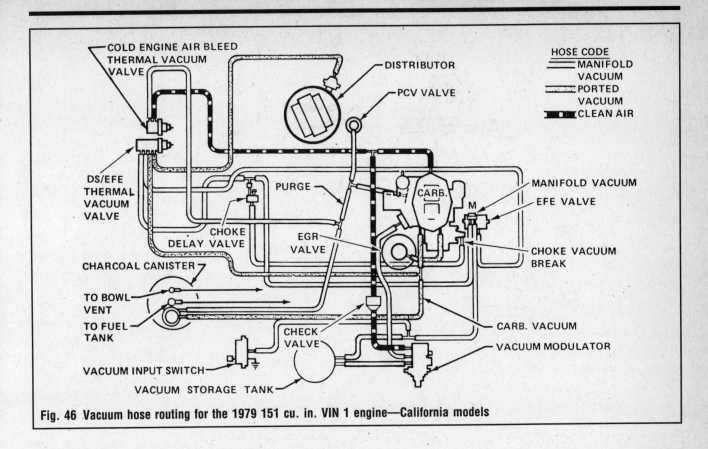

Fig. 46 Vacuum hose routing for the 1979 151 cu. in. VIN 1 engine—California models

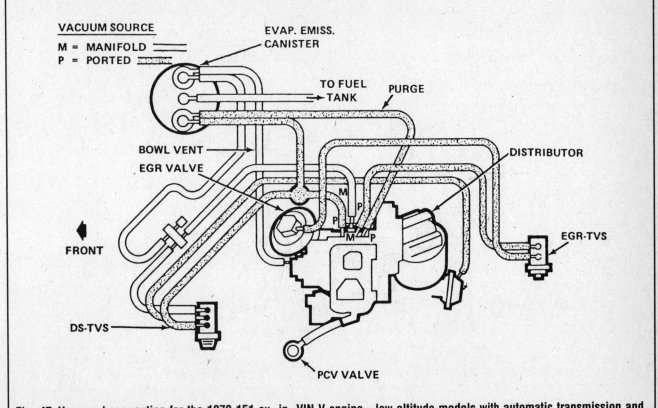

Fig. 47 Vacuum hose routing for the 1979 151 cu. in. VIN V engine—low altitude models with automatic transmission and A/C

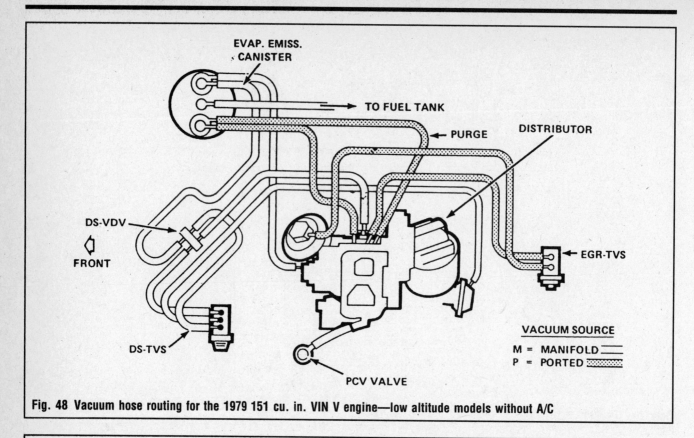

Fig. 48 Vacuum hose routing for the 1979 151 cu. in. VIN V engine—low altitude models without A/C

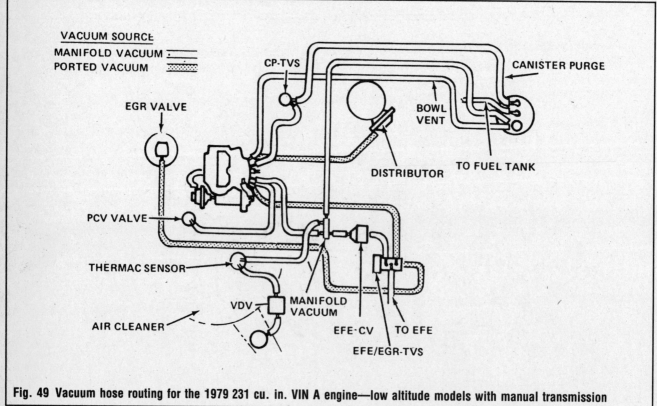

Fig. 49 Vacuum hose routing for the 1979 231 cu. in. VIN A engine—low altitude models with manual transmission

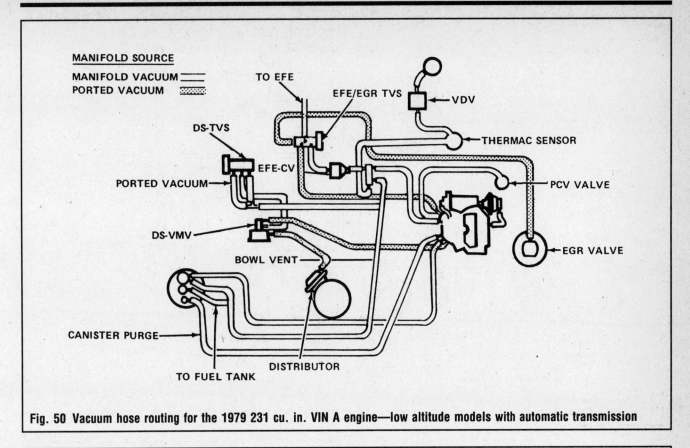

Fig. 50 Vacuum hose routing for the 1979 231 cu. in. VIN A engine—low altitude models with automatic transmission

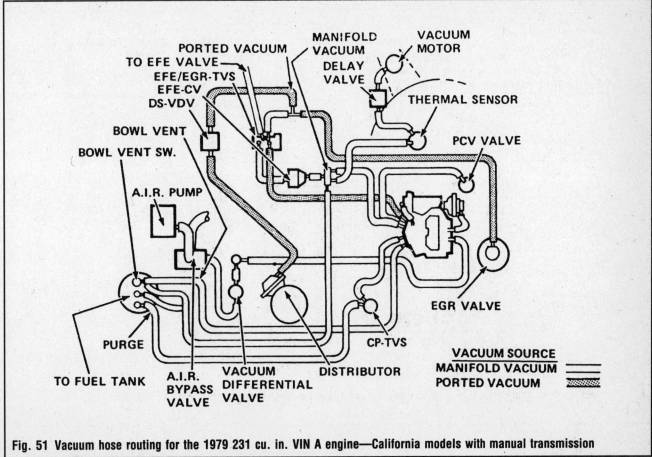

Fig. 51 Vacuum hose routing for the 1979 231 cu. in. VIN A engine—California models with manual transmission

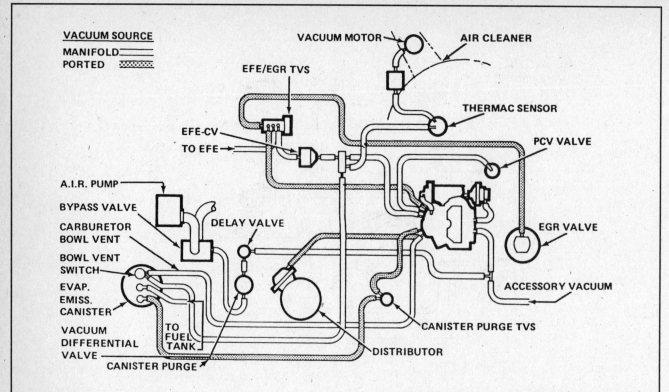

Fig. 52 Vacuum hose routing for the 1979 231 cu. in. VIN A engine—high altitude and California models with automatic transmission

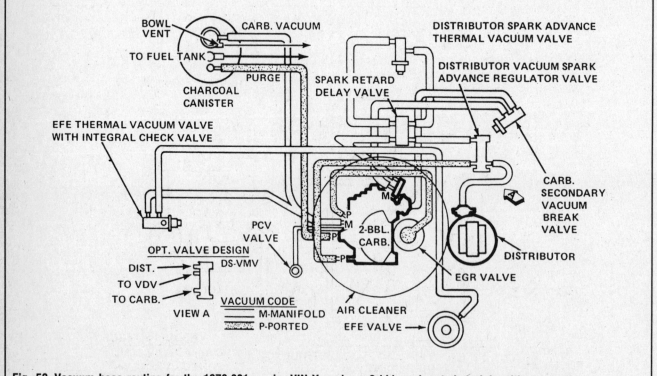

Fig. 53 Vacuum hose routing for the 1979 301 cu. in. VIN Y engine—2-bbl. carbureted models with automatic transmission and A/C

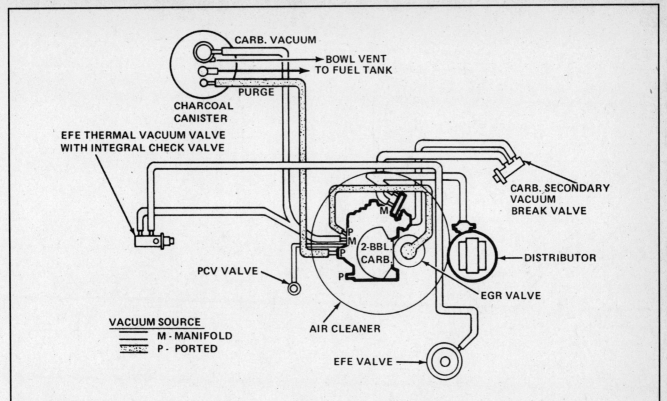

Fig. 54 Vacuum hose routing for the 1979 301 cu. in. VIN Y engine—2-bbl. models with automatic transmission, but without A/C

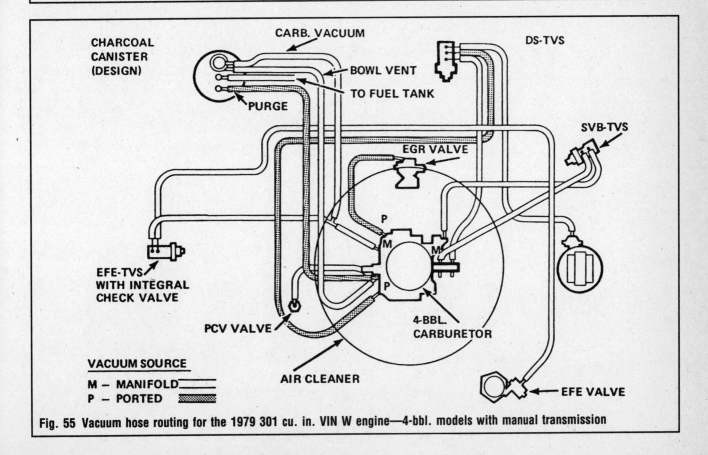

Fig. 55 Vacuum hose routing for the 1979 301 cu. in. VIN W engine—4-bbl. models with manual transmission

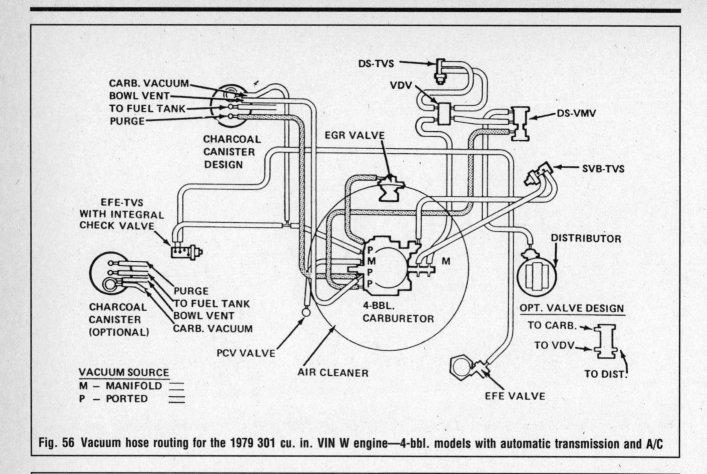

Fig. 56 Vacuum hose routing for the 1979 301 cu. in. VIN W engine—4-bbl. models with automatic transmission and A/C

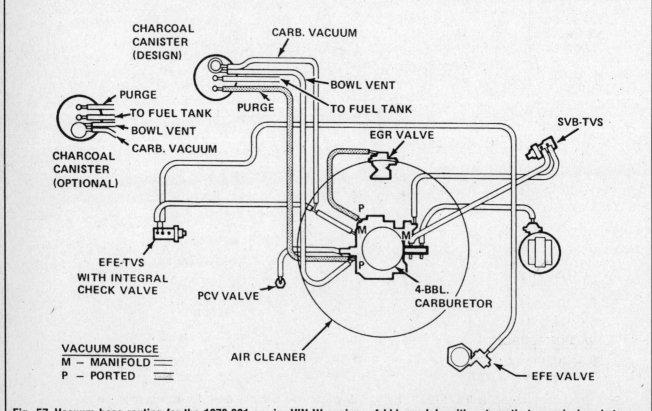

Fig. 57 Vacuum hose routing for the 1979 301 cu. in. VIN W engine—4-bbl. models with automatic transmission, but without A/C

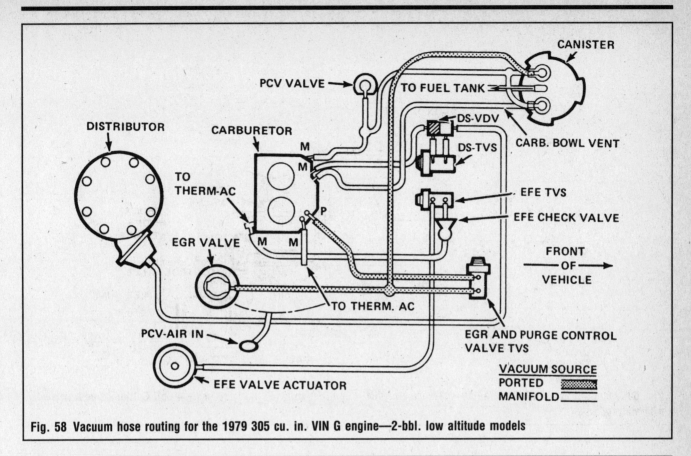

Fig. 58 Vacuum hose routing for the 1979 305 cu. in. VIN G engine—2-bbl. low altitude models

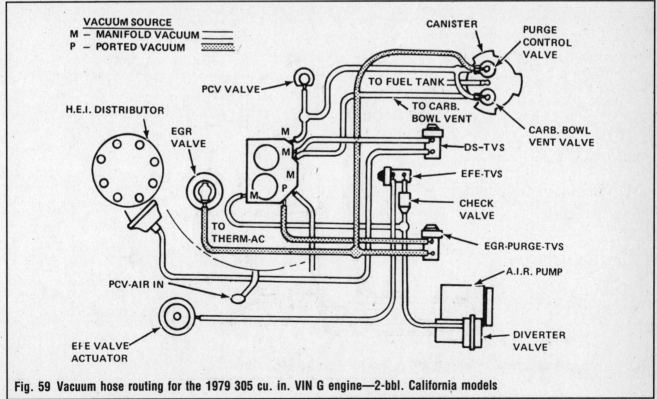

Fig. 59 Vacuum hose routing for the 1979 305 cu. in. VIN G engine—2-bbl. California models

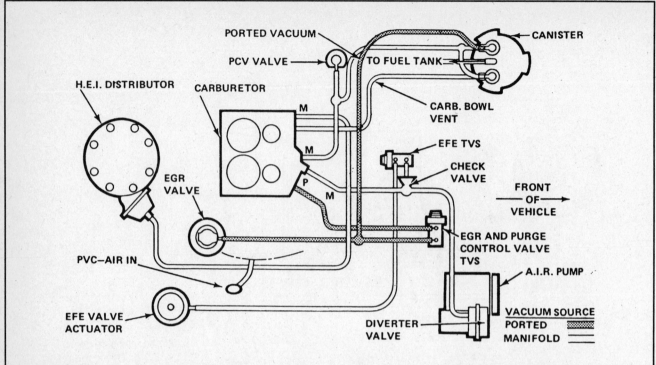

Fig. 60 Vacuum hose routing for the 1979 305 cu. in. VIN H and 350 cu. in. VIN L engines—4-bbl. California and high altitude models

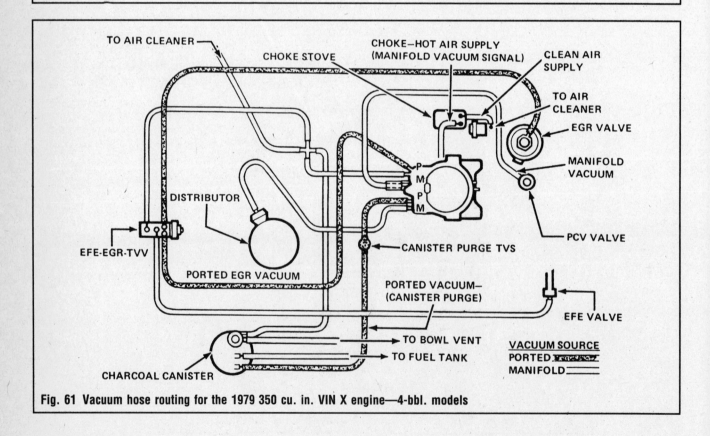

Fig. 61 Vacuum hose routing for the 1979 350 cu. in. VIN X engine—4-bbl. models

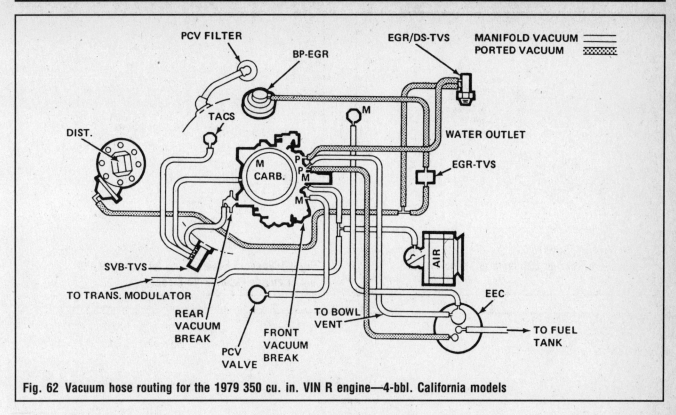

Fig. 62 Vacuum hose routing for the 1979 350 cu. in. VIN R engine—4-bbl. California models

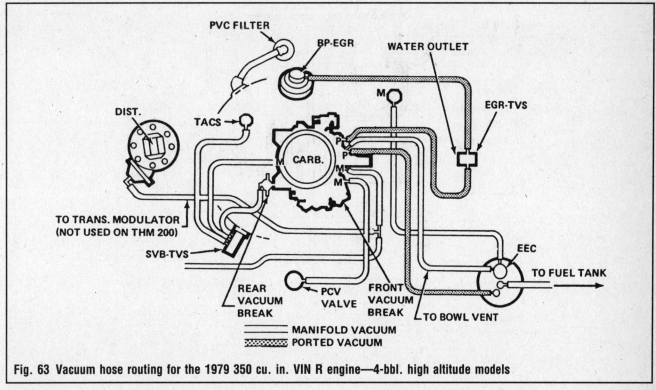

Fig. 63 Vacuum hose routing for the 1979 350 cu. in. VIN R engine—4-bbl. high altitude models

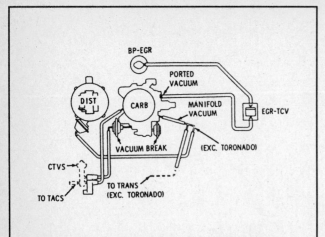

Fig. 64 Vacuum hose routing for the 1979 350 cu. in. VIN R engine—except California and high altitude models

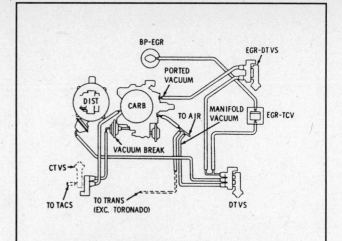

Fig. 65 Vacuum hose routing for the 1979 350 cu. in. VIN R engine—California models

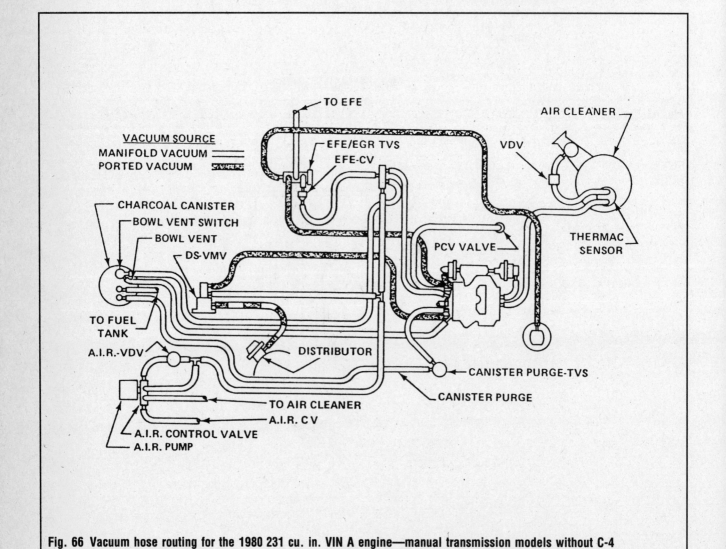

Fig. 66 Vacuum hose routing for the 1980 231 cu. in. VIN A engine—manual transmission models without C-4

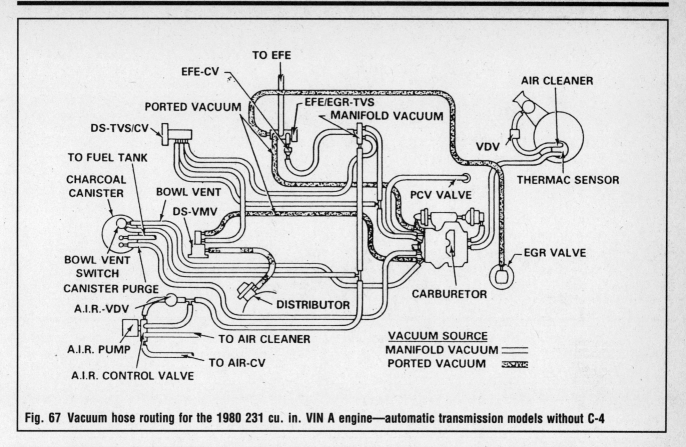

Fig. 67 Vacuum hose routing for the 1980 231 cu. in. VIN A engine—automatic transmission models without C-4

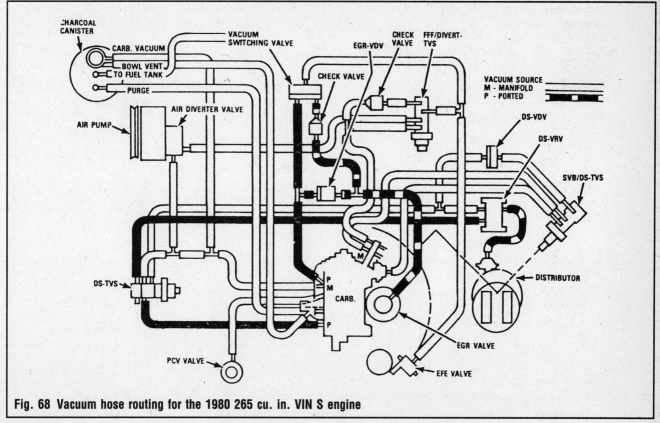

Fig. 68 Vacuum hose routing for the 1980 265 cu. in. VIN S engine

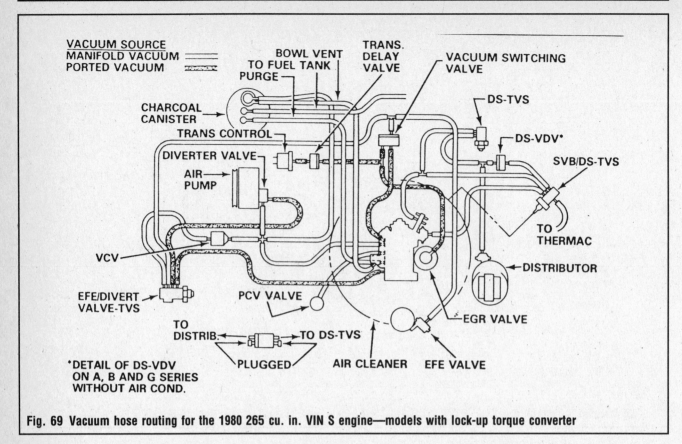

Fig. 69 Vacuum hose routing for the 1980 265 cu. in. VIN S engine—models with lock-up torque converter

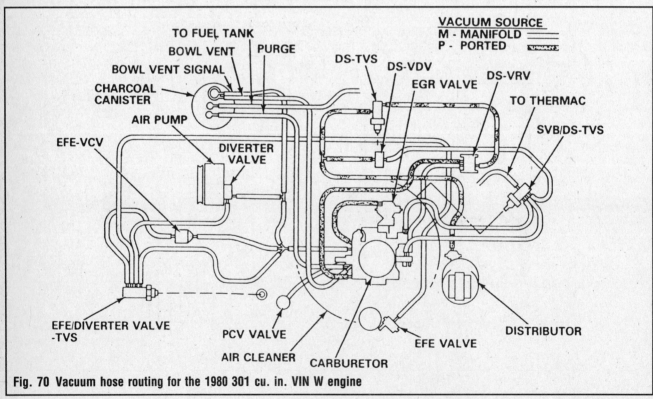

Fig. 70 Vacuum hose routing for the 1980 301 cu. in. VIN W engine

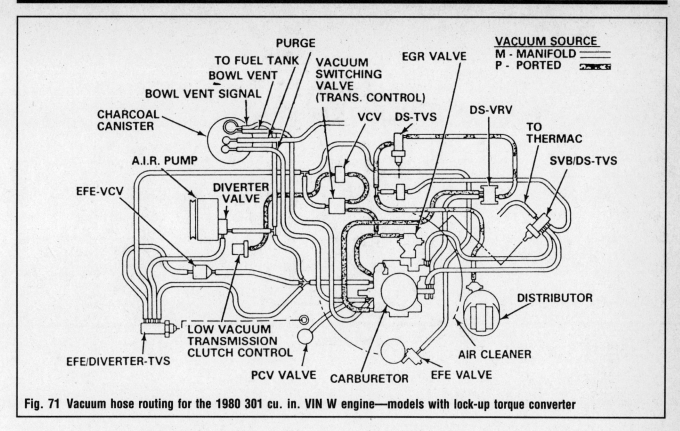

Fig. 71 Vacuum hose routing for the 1980 301 cu. in. VIN W engine—models with lock-up torque converter

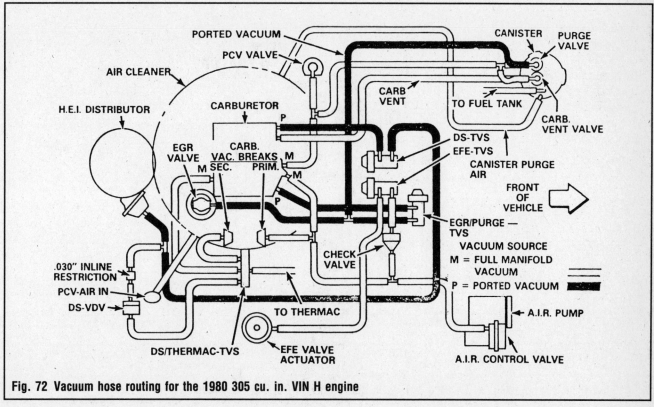

Fig. 72 Vacuum hose routing for the 1980 305 cu. in. VIN H engine

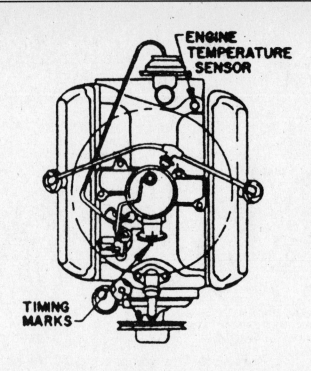

Fig. 73 Vacuum hose routing for the 1980 350 cu. in. diesel engine—low altitude federal models

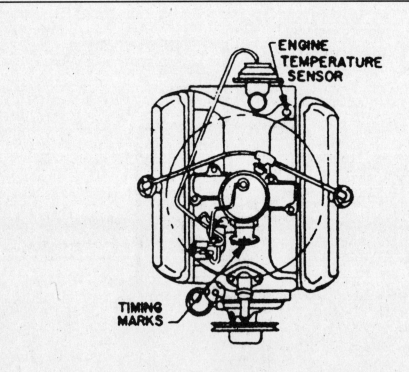

Fig. 74 Vacuum hose routing for the 1980 350 cu. in. diesel engine—California models

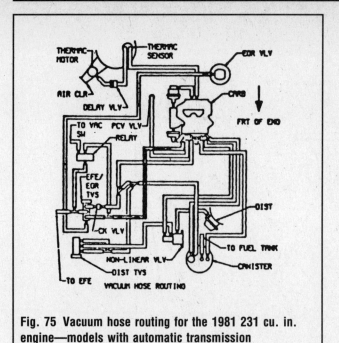

Fig. 75 Vacuum hose routing for the 1981 231 cu. in. engine—models with automatic transmission

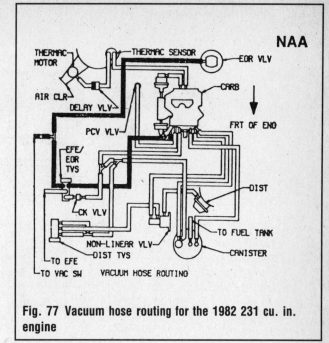

Fig. 77 Vacuum hose routing for the 1982 231 cu. in. engine

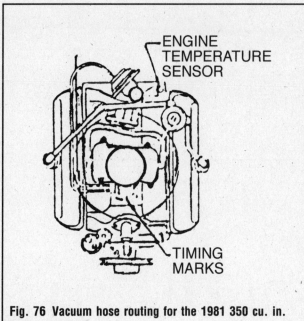
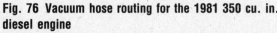

Fig. 76 Vacuum hose routing for the 1981 350 cu. in. diesel engine

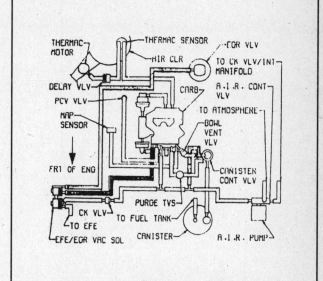

Fig. 78 Vacuum hose routing for the 1983 231 cu. in. engine—2-bbl. California models with automatic transmission

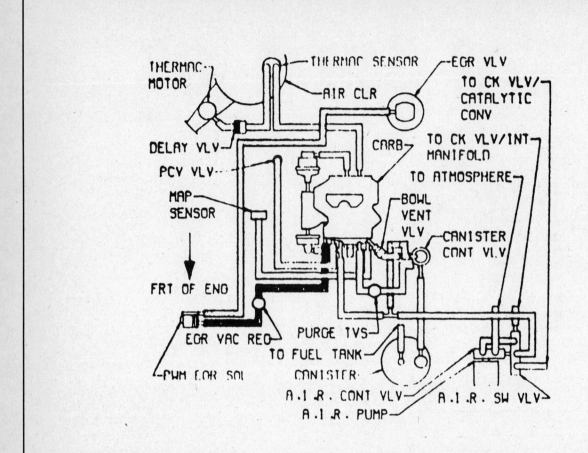

Fig. 79 Vacuum hose routing for the 1983 231 cu. in. engine—2-bbl. federal models with automatic transmission

BASIC FUEL SYSTEM
DIAGNOSIS 5-2
CARBURETED FUEL SYSTEM 5-2
MECHANICAL FUEL PUMP 5-2
  REMOVAL & INSTALLATION 5-2
  TESTING 5-3
CARBURETOR 5-4
  REMOVAL & INSTALLATION 5-4
  ADJUSTMENTS 5-7
  OVERHAUL 5-15
DIESEL ENGINE FUEL
SYSTEM 5-25
FUEL SUPPLY PUMP 5-25
  REMOVAL & INSTALLATION 5-25
  WATER IN FUEL 5-25
  PURGING THE FUEL TANK 5-25
INJECTION PUMP 5-26
  REMOVAL & INSTALLATION 5-26
  ADJUSTMENTS 5-26
INJECTION NOZZLE 5-27
  REMOVAL & INSTALLATION 5-27
INJECTION PUMP ADAPTER AND
  SEAL 5-28
  REMOVAL & INSTALLATION 5-28
FUEL TANK 5-29
TANK ASSEMBLY 5-29
  DRAINING THE TANK 5-29
  REMOVAL & INSTALLATION 5-29
SPECIFICATION CHARTS
MV CARBURETOR
  SPECIFICATIONS 5-17
5210-C AND 6510-C 2-BARREL
  CARBURETOR
  SPECIFICATIONS 5-18
2GC, GE, GV 2-BARREL CARBURETOR
  SPECIFICATIONS 5-19
2MC, M2MC, M2ME, E2MC, E2ME
  2-BARREL CARBURETOR
  SPECIFICATIONS 5-20
2MC, M2MC, M2ME, E2ME
  CARBURETOR
  SPECIFICATIONS 5-21
M4MC, M4ME, E4MC 4-BARREL
  CARBURETOR
  SPECIFICATIONS 5-22
4-BBL CARBURETOR
  SPECIFICATIONS 5-25

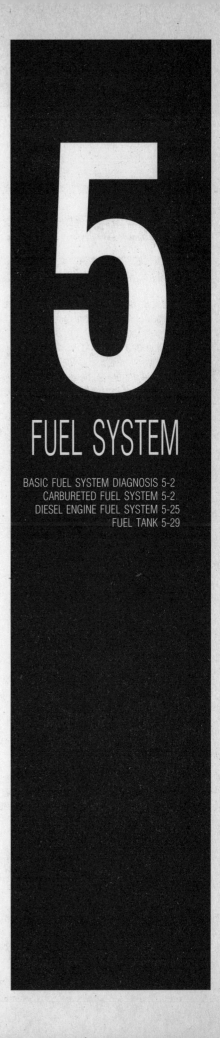

5
FUEL SYSTEM

BASIC FUEL SYSTEM DIAGNOSIS 5-2
CARBURETED FUEL SYSTEM 5-2
DIESEL ENGINE FUEL SYSTEM 5-25
FUEL TANK 5-29

BASIC FUEL SYSTEM DIAGNOSIS

When there is a problem starting or driving a vehicle, two of the most important checks involve the ignition and the fuel systems. The questions most mechanics attempt to answer first, "is there spark?" and "is there fuel?" will often lead to solving most basic problems. For ignition system diagnosis and testing, please refer to the information on engine electrical components and ignition systems found earlier in this manual. If the ignition system checks out (there is spark), then you must determine if the fuel system is operating properly (is there fuel?).

CARBURETED FUEL SYSTEM

Mechanical Fuel Pump

Fuel pumps used on all engines are of the single-action mechanical type. The fuel pump rocker arm is held in constant engagement with the eccentric on the camshaft by the rocker arm spring. As the end of the rocker arm which is in contact with the eccentric moves upward, the fuel link pulls the fuel diaphragm downward. The action of the diaphragm enlarges the fuel chamber, drawing fuel from the tank. Fuel flows to the carburetor only when the pressure in the outlet line is less than the pressure maintained by the diaphragm spring.

The fuel pumps on all engines are not serviceable and must be replaced if defective.

REMOVAL & INSTALLATION

◆ **See Figure 1**

1. Locate the fuel pump on the side of the cylinder block and disconnect the fuel lines.
2. Remove the two pump mounting bolts.

➥**On 305 and 350 Chevrolet-built engines: if the pushrod is to be removed, take out the two adaptor bolts and lockwashers and remove the adaptor and gasket. For installation use heavy grease to hold the pushrod in place. Coat the pipe plug threads or adaptor gasket with sealer if pushrod was removed.**

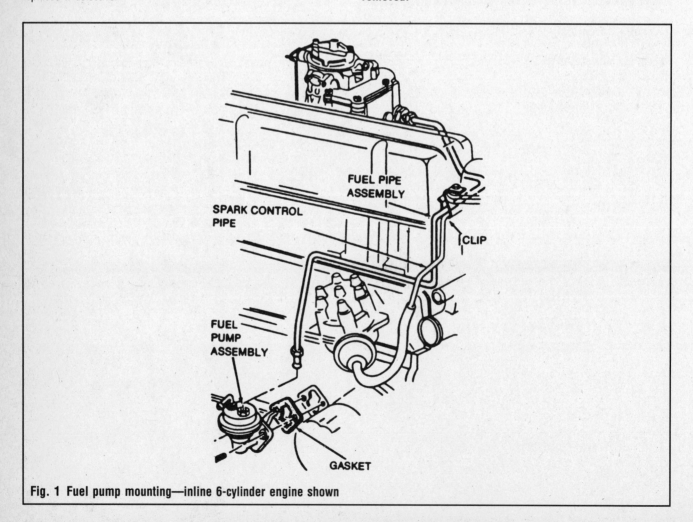

Fig. 1 Fuel pump mounting—inline 6-cylinder engine shown

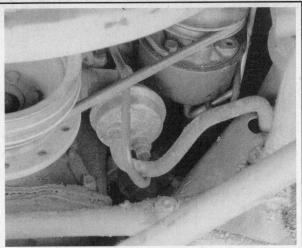

The fuel pump is easily accessible from under the vehicle

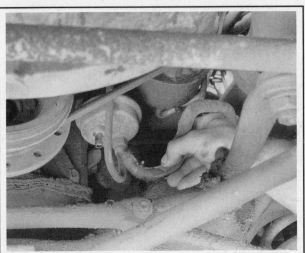

To remove the fuel pump, detach the rubber fuel inlet hose from the pump

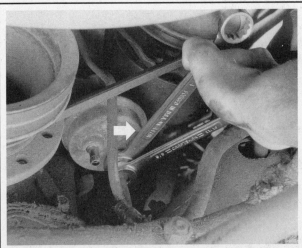

When disconnecting the pump outlet fitting, ALWAYS use a back-up wrench (see arrow)

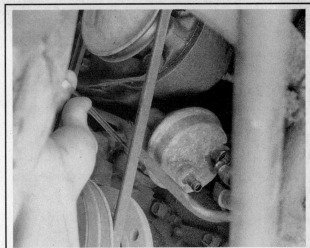

After disconnecting the outlet line, unfasten the retaining bolts, then remove the fuel pump

3. Remove the pump and the gasket.
4. Use a new gasket when installing the pump.
5. Install the fuel lines, start the engine and check for leaks.

TESTING

The fuel line from the tank to the pump is the suction side of the system and the line from the pump to the carburetor is the pressure side of the system. A leak on the pressure side, therefore, would be made apparent by dripping fuel, but a leak on the suction side would not be apparent except for the reduction of the volume of fuel on the pressure side.

1. Tighten any loose line connections and look for bends or kinks.
2. Disconnect the fuel pipe at the carburetor. Disconnect the distributor-to-coil primary wire so that the engine can be cranked without firing. Place a container at the end of the pipe and crank the engine a few revolutions. If little or no gasoline flows from the open end of the pipe, the fuel pipe is clogged or the pump is defective.
3. If fuel flows from the pump in good volume from the pipe at the carburetor, check fuel pressure to be certain that the pump is operating within specified limits as follows:

   a. Attach a fuel pump pressure test gauge to the disconnected end of the pipe;

   b. Run the engine at approximately 450 to 1,000 rpm on the gasoline still remaining in the carburetor bowl. Note the reading on the pressure gauge.

   c. If the pump is operating properly the pressure will be within the specifications listed in the "Tune-Up Specifications" chart found in Chapter 2. The pressure will remain constant between speeds of 450 to 1,000 rpm. If the pressure is too low or too high at different speeds, the pump should be replaced.

➡️**There are no adjustments that can be made on these fuel pumps.**

Carburetor

REMOVAL & INSTALLATION

♦ **See Figures 2 and 3**

1. Remove the air cleaner assembly.
2. Tag and disconnect all vacuum lines, electric wires and fuel lines from the carburetor. Tag and disconnect the throttle linkage.
3. Disconnect the automatic transmission downshift linkage.
4. Disconnect the idle solenoid wiring.
5. Remove the carburetor attaching nuts and remove the carburetor.
6. Installation is in the reverse order of removal. Use a new gasket and fill the float bowl with fuel to ease starting.

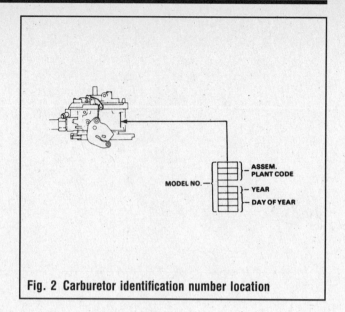

Fig. 2 Carburetor identification number location

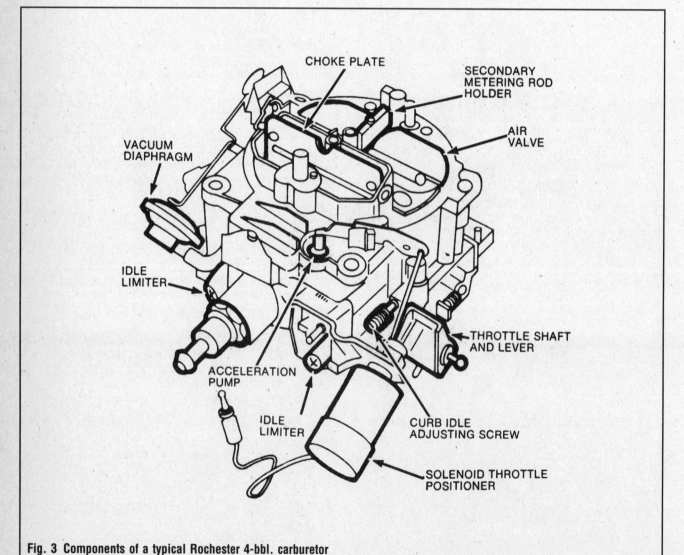

Fig. 3 Components of a typical Rochester 4-bbl. carburetor

1. Fuel line
2. Electrical connector
3. Throttle cable
4. Linkage

The carburetor is mounted to the intake manifold, with various lines attached to it

Remove the small clip retaining the throttle cable . . .

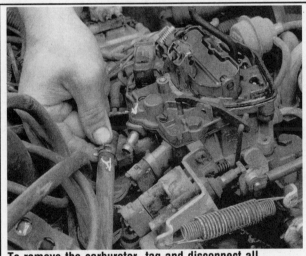

To remove the carburetor, tag and disconnect all necessary fuel and vacuum lines

. . . then detach the throttle cable from the carburetor

Detach the carburetor electrical connections

Use needlenose pliers to remove the clip . . .

. . . then remove the linkage from the clamp

An extension may be helpful to access some of the carburetor mounting bolts

If necessary, detach any remaining electrical connectors

Remove the carburetor from the intake manifold . . .

Remove the carburetor mounting bolts

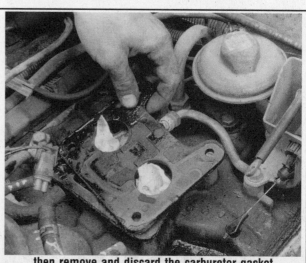

. . . then remove and discard the carburetor gasket. Always use a new gasket during assembly

ADJUSTMENTS

Float Level

MV CARBURETOR

▶ See Figure 4

1. Remove the top of the carburetor if you have not done so already.

2. Hold the float retainer in place and the float arm against the top of the float needle by pushing down on the top of the float arm at the outer end toward the float bowl casting.

3. Using an adjustable T-scale, measure the distance from the top of the float to the float bowl gasket surface. See the specifications chart for the proper measurement.

➡ The float bowl gasket should be removed and the gauge held on the index point of the bowl float for accurate measurement.

4. Adjust the float level by bending the float arm up or down at the float arm junction.

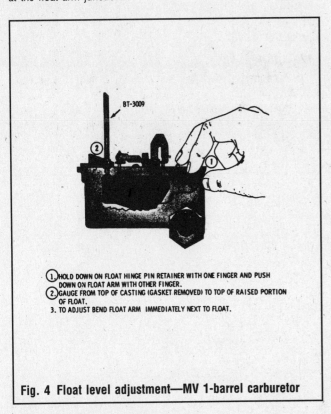

Fig. 4 Float level adjustment—MV 1-barrel carburetor

5210-C AND 6510-C CARBURETORS

▶ See Figure 5

1. With the carburetor air horn inverted, and the float tang resting lightly on the inlet needle, insert the specified gauge between the air horn and the float.

2. Bend the float tang if an adjustment is needed.

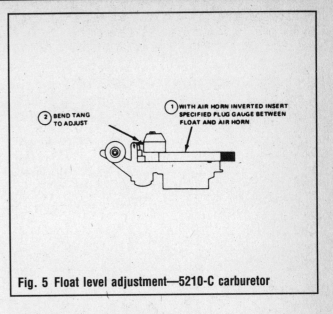

Fig. 5 Float level adjustment—5210-C carburetor

2GC, 2GE AND 2GV CARBURETORS

▶ See Figure 6

1. Remove the air horn assembly from the carburetor.

2. Hold the air horn assembly upside down and measure the distance from the air horn gasket to the lip at the toe of the float. See the chart for the proper measurement.

3. Bend the float arm to adjust the float level to the proper specifications.

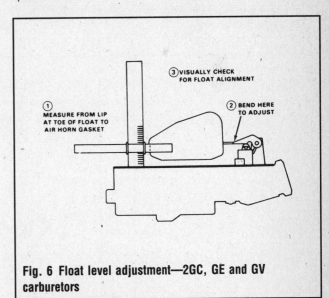

Fig. 6 Float level adjustment—2GC, GE and GV carburetors

2MC CARBURETOR

▶ See Figure 7

1. Remove the air horn assembly from the carburetor. Remove the gasket.

2. Measure the distance from the air horn gasket surface to the

top of the float at the toe (1/16 in. back from the toe on 1974 and 1975 models; 3/16 in. back on 1976 and later models).

3. After making sure the retaining pin is in place, bend the float arm to adjust the float level.

E2MC, E2ME, E4MC AND E4ME CARBURETORS

♦ See Figure 7

1. Remove the air horn.
2. Hold the float retainer in place and lightly push down on the float against the needle.
3. Measure the gap between the casting surface and the top of the float at a point 3/16 inch back from the float toe.

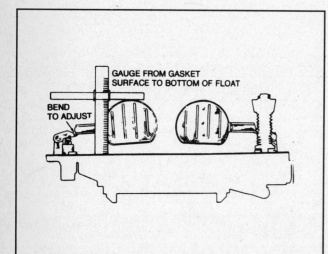

Fig. 7 Float level adjustment—2MC carburetor shown, M2ME and E2ME similar

4. To adjust, remove the float and bend the float arm.
5. On CCC carburetors, if the float level varies more than 1/16 either way, adjust as follows:

    a. Level too high: Hold the float retainer firmly in place and push down on the center of the float body until the correct gap is attained.

    b. Level too low: Lift out the metering rods. Remove the solenoid connector screw. Turn the lean mixture solenoid screw clockwise counting the number of turns until the screw is lightly seated. Then, remove the screw. Lift the solenoid and connector from the float bowl. Remove the float and bend the arm to adjust. Install the float and check the adjustment. Install the mixture screw to the exact number of turns noted earlier. Install all other parts.

M4MC CARBURETOR

♦ See Figure 8

1. With the air horn assembly and gasket removed from the carburetor, measure the distance from the air horn gasket surface to the top of the float at the toe.
2. To adjust the float level, bend the float arm by pushing on the pontoon.
3. After the adjustment, check the float alignment.

Choke Coil Lever

MV CARBURETOR

1. Place the fast idle speed screw on the highest step of the fast idle cam.
2. Hold the choke plate fully closed.
3. Insert a 0.120 in. gauge through the hole in the arm on the choke housing and into the hole in the casting.
4. Bend the link to adjust.

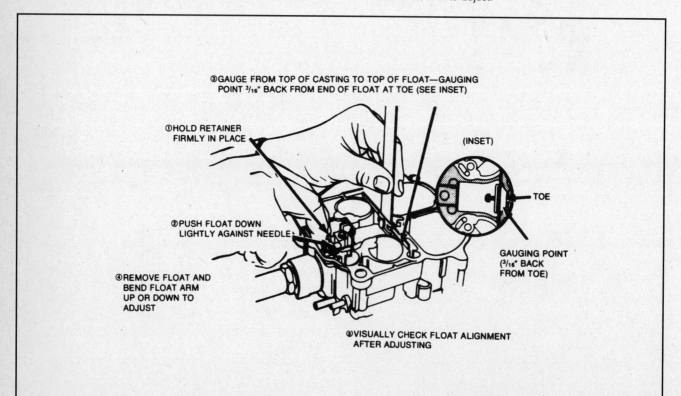

Fig. 8 Float level adjustment—M4MC carburetor

2 AND 4-BBL. CARBURETORS
▶ See Figures 9 and 10

1. Remove the choke cover and thermostatic coil from the choke housing.
2. Push the coil tang counterclockwise until the choke plate is fully closed.
3. Insert a 0.120 in. gauge into the hole in the choke housing. The lower edge of the choke coil lever should just contact the side of the gauge.
4. Bend the choke rod to adjust, if necessary.

Automatic Choke

MV CARBURETOR

1. Place the fast idle cam follower on the high step of the cam.
2. Loosen the three retaining screws and rotate the cover counterclockwise until the choke plate just closes.
3. Align the index mark on the cover with the specified housing mark. Tighten the three screws.

2-BBL. CARBURETORS

1. Place the idle speed screw or follower on the highest step of the fast idle cam.
2. Loosen the choke coil cover retaining screws.
3. Rotate the choke cover counterclockwise until the choke plate just closes.
4. Align the index mark on the choke cover with the specified point on the choke housing.

4-BBL. CARBURETORS

1. Loosen the choke housing cover screws.
2. Place the fast idle cam follower on the highest step of the fast idle cam.

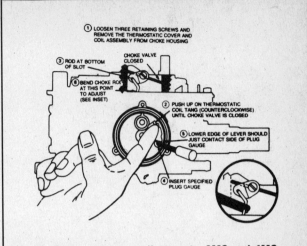

Fig. 10 Choke coil lever adjustment—2MC and 4MC carburetors

3. Rotate the cover and coil assembly counterclockwise until the choke plate just closes.
4. Align the index mark on the cover with the specified index point on the housing.
5. Tighten the retaining screws.

Choke Unloader

MV CARBURETOR
▶ See Figure 11

1. Hold the throttle valve wide open.
2. Hold-down the choke plate with your finger and insert the specified gauge between the upper edge of the choke plate and the airhorn wall.
3. Bend the linkage tang to adjust.

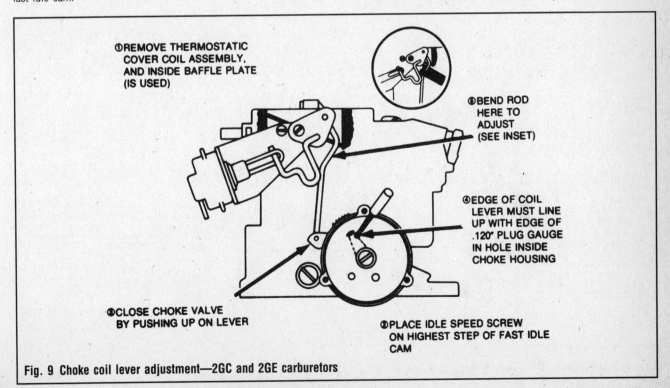

Fig. 9 Choke coil lever adjustment—2GC and 2GE carburetors

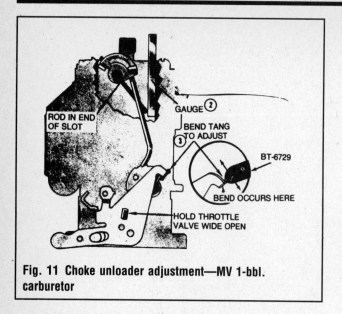

Fig. 11 Choke unloader adjustment—MV 1-bbl. carburetor

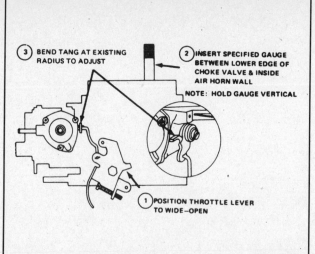

Fig. 12 Choke unloader adjustment—5210-C and 6510-C 2-bbl. carburetors

5210-C AND 6510-C CARBURETORS

▶ See Figure 12

1. Place the throttle in the wide open position.
2. Insert a 0.350 or 0.400 in. gauge (see chart) between the lower edge of the choke valve and the air horn wall.
3. Bend the tang of the choke arm to adjust.

1974–80 2GE, 2GC AND 2MC CARBURETORS

▶ See Figures 13 and 14

1. Hold the throttle plates wide open.
2. Close the choke plate.
3. Bend the unloader tang to obtain the proper clearance between the upper edge of the choke plate and the airhorn wall.

1974–80 4-BBL. CARBURETORS

▶ See Figure 15

1. With the choke plate completely closed, hold the throttle plates wide open.
2. Measure the distance between the upper edge of the choke plate and the airhorn wall.
3. Bend the tang on the fast idle lever to adjust.

1981–83 2 AND 4-BBL. CARBURETORS

The unloader adjustment on these carburetors requires special tools and is quite complicated. Service here is best left to a professional mechanic.

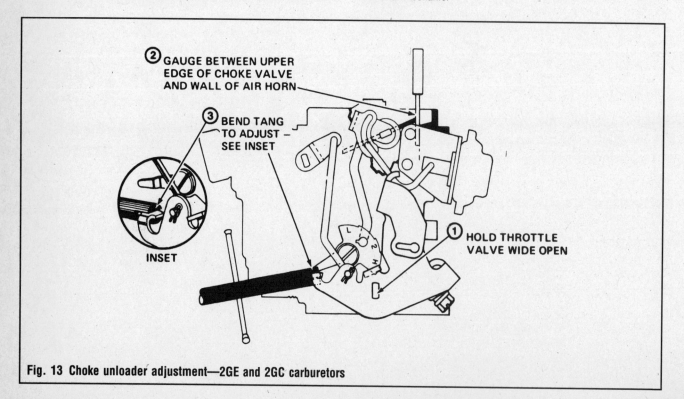

Fig. 13 Choke unloader adjustment—2GE and 2GC carburetors

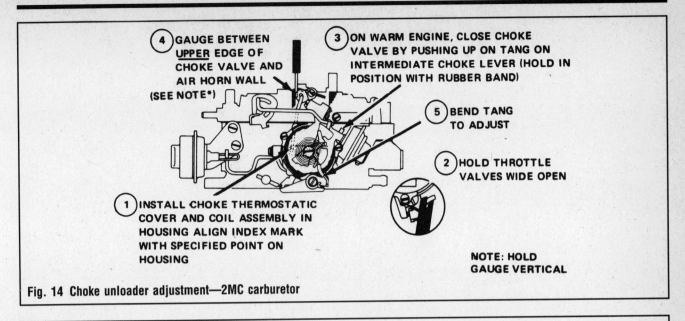

Fig. 14 Choke unloader adjustment—2MC carburetor

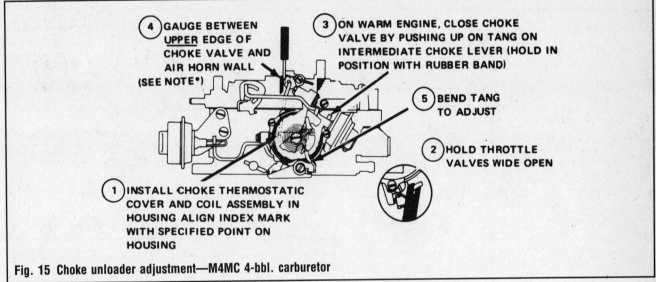

Fig. 15 Choke unloader adjustment—M4MC 4-bbl. carburetor

Vacuum Break

MV CARBURETOR

▶ See Figure 16

1. On vehicles equipped with TAC air cleaners, plug the sensor's vacuum take-off port after removing the air cleaner.

2. Using an external vacuum source, apply vacuum to the vacuum break diaphragm until the plunger is fully seated.

3. After the plunger is seated, push the choke plate fully closed.

5210-C CARBURETOR

▶ See Figure 17

1. Remove the three hex-headed screws and ring which retain the choke cover.

2. Push the diaphragm shaft against the stop. Push the coil lever clockwise.

3. Insert the specified size gauge on the down side of the primary choke plate.

4. Take the slack out of the linkage and turn the adjusting screw with a 5/22 in. Allen wrench.

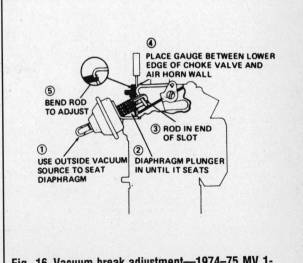

Fig. 16 Vacuum break adjustment—1974–75 MV 1-barrel carburetor

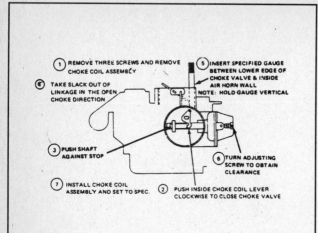

Fig. 17 Vacuum break adjustment—5210-C and 6510-C carburetors

6510-C CARBURETOR

▶ **See Figure 17**

1. Remove the choke coil assembly.
2. Push the choke coil lever clockwise to close the choke valve.
3. Push the choke shaft against its stop.
4. Take the slack out of the linkage, in the open direction.
5. Insert the specified gauge between the lower edge of the choke plate and the air horn wall. Turn the adjusting screw in the diaphragm housing to adjust.

2GC AND 2GE CARBURETORS

▶ **See Figure 18**

1. Remove the air cleaner. Vehicles equipped with TAC air cleaners should have the sensor's vacuum take-off port plugged.

2. Using an external vacuum source, apply vacuum to the vacuum break diaphragm until the plunger is fully seated.
3. When the plunger is seated, push the choke plate toward the closed position. Place the idle speed screw on the high step of the fast idle cam.
4. Holding the choke plate in the closed position, place the specified size gauge between the upper edge of the choke plate and the air horn wall.
5. If the measurement is not correct, bend the vacuum break rod.

2MC CARBURETOR

▶ **See Figures 19 and 20**

1. Place the cam follower on the highest step of the fast idle cam.
2. Seat the vacuum break diaphragm by using an outside vacuum source.

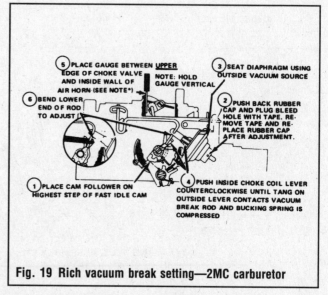

Fig. 19 Rich vacuum break setting—2MC carburetor

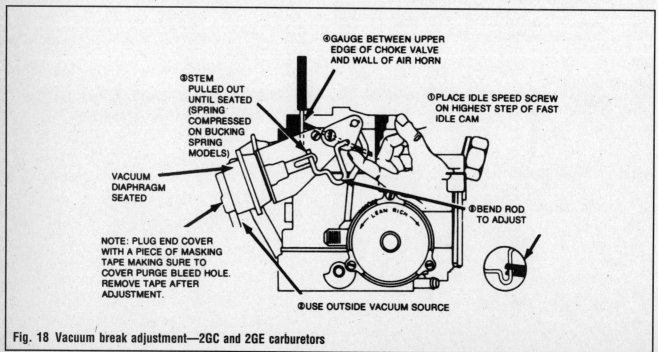

Fig. 18 Vacuum break adjustment—2GC and 2GE carburetors

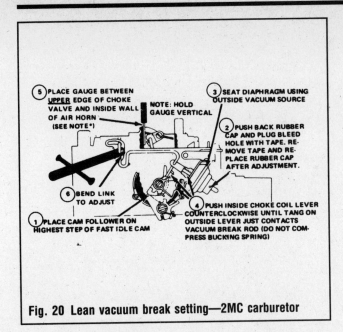

Fig. 20 Lean vacuum break setting—2MC carburetor

3. Remove the choke cover and coil and push up on the coil lever until the tang on the vacuum break lever contacts the tang on the vacuum break plunger stem. Compress the backing spring for rich adjustment only.

4. With the choke rod in the bottom of the slot in the choke lever, measure the distance between the upper edge of the choke plate and the inside wall of the air horn.

5. Bend the link rod at the vacuum break plunger stem to adjust the lean setting. Bend the link rod at the opposite from the diaphragm to adjust the rich setting.

1975–80 4-BBL. CARBURETORS

◆ **See Figures 21 and 22**

1. Place the cam follower lever on the highest step of the fast idle cam.

2. Remove the choke cover and coil assembly from the choke housing.

3. Seat the front vacuum diaphragm using an outside vacuum source.

4. Push up on the inside choke coil lever until the tang on the vacuum break lever contacts the tang on the vacuum break plunger.

5. Place the proper size gauge between the upper edge of the choke plate and the inside of the air horn wall.

6. To adjust, turn the adjustment screw on the vacuum break plunger lever.

7. To adjust the secondary vacuum break, with the choke cover and coil removed, the cam follower on the highest step of the fast idle cam, tape over the bleed hole in the rear vacuum break diaphragm.

8. Seat the rear diaphragm using an outside vacuum source.

9. Close the choke by pushing up on the choke coil lever inside the choke housing. Make sure the choke rod is in the bottom of the slot in the choke lever.

10. Measure between the upper edge of the choke plate and the air horn wall with a wire type gauge.

11. To adjust, bend the vacuum break rod at the first bend near the diphragm.

1981–83 2 AND 4-BBL. CARBURETORS

These carburetors require special tools for adjustment. Service is best left to a professional mechanic.

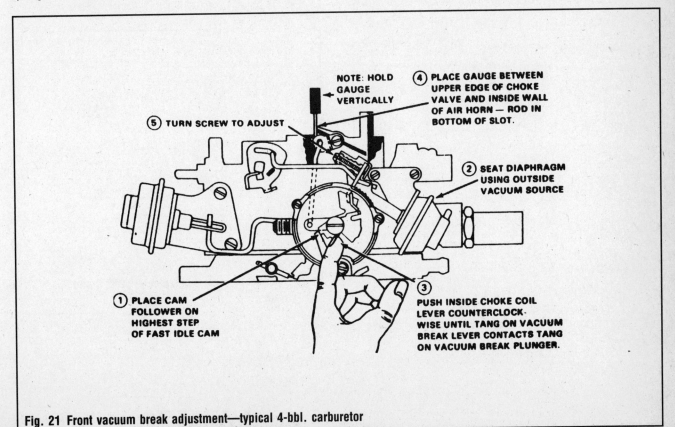

Fig. 21 Front vacuum break adjustment—typical 4-bbl. carburetor

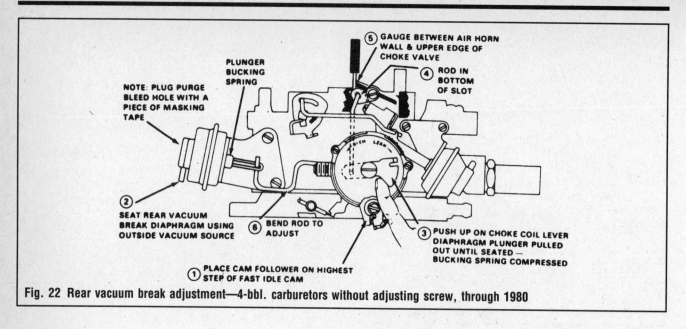

Fig. 22 Rear vacuum break adjustment—4-bbl. carburetors without adjusting screw, through 1980

Fast Idle Cam

MV CARBURETOR

▶ See Figure 23

1. Adjust curb idle speed with solenoid (if equipped). Hold the fast idle speed screw on the second cam step against the shoulder of the high step.
2. Hold the choke plate closed.
3. Measure the distance between the center upper edge of the choke plate and the air horn wall.
4. Bend the linkage rod at the upper angle to adjust the clearance.

the choke plate (between the lower edge of the choke valve and inside the choke wall).
3. If adjustment is necessary, bend the tang (see illustration).

2GC AND 2GE CARBURETORS

1. Turn the idle speed screw in until it just contacts the lower step of the fast idle cam. Then, turn the screw in one full turn.
2. Place the idle speed screw on the second step of the fast idle cam against the shoulder of the high step.
3. Measure the distance between the upper edge of the choke plate and the air horn wall. Push the choke plate closed first.
4. If adjustment is required, bend the choke lever tang.

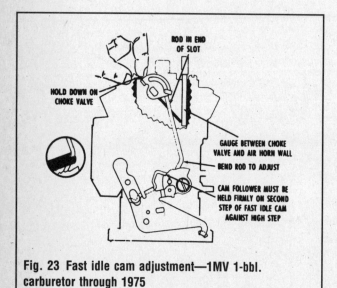

Fig. 23 Fast idle cam adjustment—1MV 1-bbl. carburetor through 1975

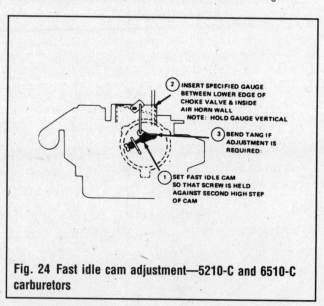

Fig. 24 Fast idle cam adjustment—5210-C and 6510-C carburetors

5210-C AND 6510-C CARBURETORS

▶ See Figure 24

1. Set the fast idle cam so that the screw is held against the second high step of the fast idle cam.
2. Insert the specified drill bit or gauge on the "down" side of

2MC CARBURETORS

▶ See Figure 25

1. Adjust the fast idle speed.
2. Place the cam follower lever on the second step of the fast idle cam, holding it firmly against the shoulder of the high step.
3. Close the choke coil lever inside the choke housing.

4. Gauge between the upper edge of the choke plate and the inside of the air horn wall.

5. Bend the tang on the intermediate choke lever to adjust.

4-BBL. CARBURETORS

♦ See Figure 25

1. Adjust the fast idle and place the cam follower on the second step of the fast idle cam.

2. Close the choke plate by pushing counterclockwise on the external chock lever. On 1975–80 models, remove the coil assembly from the choke housing and push on the choke coil lever.

3. Measure between the upper edge of the choke plate and the air horn wall.

4. To adjust, 1975–80 models, bend the tang on the fast idle cam. Be sure that the tang rests against the cam after bending.

Air Valve Dashpot

4-BBL. CARBURETORS

1. Seat the front vacuum break diaphragm by using an outside vacuum source.

2. The air valves must be closed completely.

3. Measure the clearance between the air valve dashpot and the end of the slot in the air valve lever. The clearance should be 0.050 in.

4. Bend the air valve dashpot rod, if necessary, to adjust.

OVERHAUL

♦ See Figures 26, 27 and 28

Efficient carburetion depends greatly on careful cleaning and inspection during overhaul, since dirt, gum, water, or varnish in or on the carburetor parts are often responsible for poor performance.

Overhaul your carburetor in a clean, dusted free area. Carefully disassemble the carburetor, referring often to the exploded views and directions packaged with the rebuilding kit. Keep all similar and look-alike parts segregated during disassembly and cleaning to avoid accidental interchange during assembly. Make a note of all jet sizes.

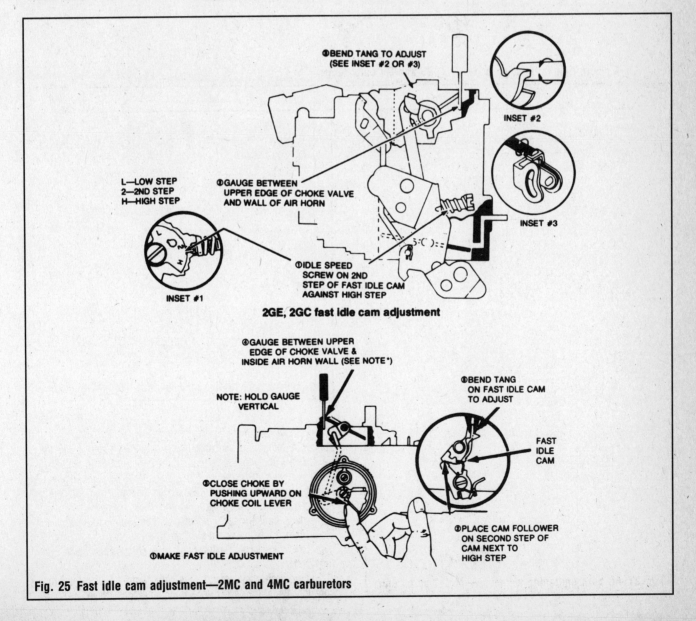

Fig. 25 Fast idle cam adjustment—2MC and 4MC carburetors

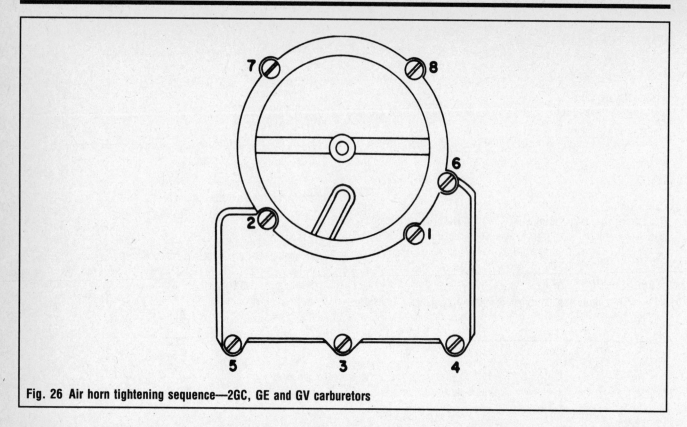

Fig. 26 Air horn tightening sequence—2GC, GE and GV carburetors

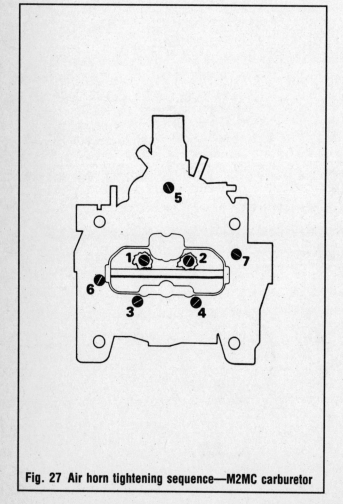

Fig. 27 Air horn tightening sequence—M2MC carburetor

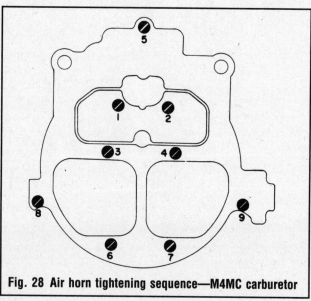

Fig. 28 Air horn tightening sequence—M4MC carburetor

When the carburetor is disassembled, wash all parts (except diaphragms, electric choke units, pump plunger, and any other plastic, leather, fiber, or rubber parts) in clean carburetor solvent. Do not leave parts in the solvent any longer than is necessary to sufficiently loosen the deposits. Excessive cleaning may remove the special finish from the float bowl and choke valve bodies, leaving these parts unfit for service. Rinse all parts in clean solvent and blow them dry with compressed air or allow them to air dry. Wipe clean all cork, plastic, leather, and fiber parts with a clean, lint-free cloth.

Blow out all passages and jets with compressed air and be sure that there are no restrictions or blockages. Never use wire or similar tools to clean jets, fuel passages, or air bleeds. Clean all jets and valves separately to avoid accidental interchange.

Check all parts for wear or damage. If wear or damage is found, replace the defective parts. Especially check the following:

1. Check the float needle and seat for wear. If wear is found, replace the complete assembly.

2. Check the float hinge pin for wear and the float(s) for dents or distortion. Replace the float if fuel has leaked into it.

3. Check the throttle and choke shaft bores for wear or an out-of-round condition. Damage or wear to the throttle arm, shaft, or shaft bore will often require replacement of the throttle body. These parts require a close tolerance of fit; wear may allow air leakage, which could affect starting and idling.

➡ **Throttle shafts and bushings are not included in overhaul kits. They can be purchased separately.**

4. Inspect the idle mixture adjusting needles for burrs or grooves. Any such condition requires replacement of the needle, since you will not be able to obtain a satisfactory idle.

5. Test the accelerator pump check valves. They should pass air one way but not the other. Test for proper seating by blowing and sucking on the valve. Replace the valve as necessary. If the valve is satisfactory, wash the valve again to remove breath moisture.

6. Check the bowl cover for warped surfaces with a straight-edge.

7. Closely inspect the valves and seats for wear and damage, replacing as necessary.

8. After the carburetor is assembled, check the choke valve for freedom of operation.

Carburetor overhaul kits are recommended for each overhaul.

These kits contain all gaskets and new parts to replace those which deteriorate most rapidly. Failure to replace all parts supplied with the kit (especially gaskets) can result in poor performance later.

Some carburetor manufacturers supply overhaul kits of three basic types: minor repair; major repair; and gasket kits. Basically, they contain the following,

Minor Repair Kits:
• All gaskets
• Float needle valve
• All diaphragms
• Spring for the pump diaphragm

Major Repair Kits
• All jets and gaskets
• All diaphragms
• Float needle valve
• Pump ball valve
• Float
• Complete intermediate rod
• Intermediate pump lever
• Some cover hold-down screws and washers

Gasket Kits:
• All gaskets

After cleaning and checking all components, reassemble the carburetor, using new parts and referring to the exploded view. When reassembling, make sure that all screws and jets are tight in their seats, but do not overtighten as the tips will be distorted. Tighten all screws gradually, in rotation. DO NOT tighten needle valves into their seats; needle valve and valve seat damage will occur, along with uneven jetting. *Always use new gaskets.* Be sure to adjust the float level when reassembling.

MV Carburetor Specifications

Year	Carburetor Identification ①	Float Level (in.)	Metering Rod (in.)	Pump Rod	Idle Vent (in.)	Vacuum Break (in.)	Auxiliary Vacuum Break (in.)	Fast Idle Off Car (in.)	Choke Rod (in.)	Choke Unloader (in.)	Fast Idle Speed (rpm)
1974	7044017	23/64	.072	—	—	.350	—	—	.275	0.500	800
	7044014	23/64	.079	—	—	.275	—	—	.230	0.500	600
	7044314	23/64	.073	—	—	.245	—	—	.245	0.500	600
1975	Manual	11/32	0.080	—	—	0.350	0.312	—	0.275	0.275	1800 ②
	Automatic	11/32	0.080	—	—	0.200	0.215	—	0.160	0.275	1800 ②
1976	17056012	11/32	—	—	—	0.140	0.265	—	0.100	.0.265	—
	17056013	11/32	—	—	—	0.165	0.320	—	0.140	0.265	—
	17056014	11/32	—	—	—	0.140	0.265	—	0.100	0.265	—
	17056015	11/32	—	—	—	0.165	0.320	—	0.140	0.265	—
	17056018	11/32	—	—	—	0.140	0.260	—	0.100	0.265	—
	17056314	11/32	—	—	—	0.165	0.320	—	0.135	0.265	—

① The carburetor identification number is stamped on the float bowl, next to the fuel inlet nut
② Preset
③ Low step of cam

5210-C and 6510-C 2-Barrel Carburetor Specifications

Year	Carburetor Identification ①	Float Level (in.)	Air Valve Spring (turn)	Pump Rod (in.)	Primary Vacuum Break (in. or deg.)	Secondary Vacuum Break (in.)	Secondary Opening (in.)	Fast Idle Cam (Choke Rod) (in. or deg.)	Choke Unloader (in.)	Fast Idle Speed (rpm)
1977	458102	.420	—	—	.250	—	—	.085	.350	2500
	458103	.420	—	—	.250	—	—	.085	.350	2500
	458104	.420	—	—	.250	—	—	.085	.350	2500
	458105	.420	—	—	.250	—	—	.085	.350	2500
	458107	.420	—	—	.275	.400	—	.125	.350	2500
	458109	.420	—	—	.275	.400	—	.125	.350	2500
	458110	.420	—	—	.300	.400	—	.120	.350	2500
	458112	.420	—	—	.300	.400	—	.120	.350	2500
	527200	.520	—	—	.275	—	—	.150	.400	2400
	527201	.520	—	—	.300	—	—	.150	.400	2400
	527202	.520	—	—	.275	—	—	.150	.400	2400
	527203	.520	—	—	.300	—	—	.150	.400	2400
	527204	.520	—	—	.275	—	—	.150	.400	2400
	527206	.520	—	—	.275	—	—	.150	.400	2400
1978	10001047	.520	—	—	.325	Not Required	—	.150	.350	2200
	10001049	.520	—	—	.325	Not Required	—	.150	.350	2200
	10004048	.520	—	—	.300	Not Required	—	.150	.350	2400
	10004049	.520	—	—	.300	Not Required	—	.150	.350	2400
1978	10001056	.520	—	—	.325	—	—	.150	.350	2400
6510-C	10001058	.520	—	—	.325	—	—	.150	.350	2400
1979	10008489	.520	—	—	.250	—	—	.150	.350	2400
6510-C	10008490	.520	—	—	.250	—	—	.150	.350	2400
	10008491	.520	—	—	.250	—	—	.150	.350	2400
	10008492	.520	—	—	.250	—	—	.150	.350	2400

Carburetors manufactured by Holley

2GC, GE, GV 2-Barrel Carburetor Specifications

Year	Carburetor Identification ①	Float Level (in.)	Air Valve Spring (turn)	Pump Rod (in.)	Primary Vacuum Break (in. or deg.)	Secondary Vacuum Break (in.)	Secondary Opening (in.)	Fast Idle Cam (Choke Rod) (in. or deg.)	Choke Unloader (in.)	Fast Idle Speed (rpm)
1974	7043060	.670	—	1⁵/₁₆	0.157	—	—	0.085	.180	②
	7043062	.670	—	1⁵/₁₆	0.167	—	—	0.085	.180	②
	7043070	.670	—	1⁵/₁₆	0.157	—	—	0.085	.180	②
	7043071	.670	—	1⁵/₁₆	0.195	—	—	0.085	.180	②
	7043072	.670	—	1⁵/₁₆	0.167	—	—	0.085	.180	②
	7044063	.670	—	1⁵/₁₆	0.157	—	—	0.085	.180	②
	7044066	.670	—	1⁵/₁₆	0.177	—	—	0.085	.180	②
	7044067	.670	—	1⁵/₁₆	0.177	—	—	0.085	.180	②
1975	7045160	⁹/₁₆	1⁷/₃₂	1¹¹/₃₂	0.145	0.265	1 Rich	0.085	0.180	Preset
	7045161	⁹/₁₆	1⁷/₃₂	1¹¹/₃₂	0.145	0.265	1 Rich	0.085	0.180	Preset
1976	Pontiac 400	⁹/₁₆	1⁹/₃₂	1¹¹/₃₂	0.165	0.285	1 Rich	0.085	0.180	—
1977	17057140	¹⁵/₃₂	—	1⁹/₁₆	0.140	0.100	—	0.080	0.325	②
	17057141	⁷/₁₆	—	1¹/₂	0.110	0.110	—	0.080	0.140	②
	17057144	⁷/₁₆	—	1¹⁷/₃₂	0.130	0.130	—	0.080	0.140	②
	17057145	⁷/₁₆	—	1¹/₂	0.110	0.110	—	0.080	0.140	②
	17057146	⁷/₁₆	—	1¹⁷/₃₂	0.110	0.110	—	0.080	0.140	②
	17057147	⁷/₁₆	—	1¹/₂	0.110	0.110	—	0.080	0.140	②
	17057148	⁷/₁₆	—	1¹⁷/₃₂	0.110	0.110	—	0.080	0.140	②
	17057445	⁷/₁₆	—	1¹/₂	0.140	0.140	—	0.080	0.140	②
	17057446	⁷/₁₆	—	1¹/₂	0.130	0.130	—	0.080	0.140	②
	17057447	⁷/₁₆	—	1¹/₂	0.130	0.130	—	0.080	0.140	②
	17057448	⁷/₁₆	—	1¹/₂	0.130	0.130	—	0.080	0.140	②
	17057112	¹⁹/₃₂	—	1²¹/₃₂	—	0.130	—	0.260	0.325	②
	17057113	¹⁹/₃₂	—	1²¹/₃₂	—	0.130	—	0.260	0.325	②
	17057114	¹⁹/₃₂	—	1²¹/₃₂	—	0.130	—	0.260	0.325	②
1978	17058145	⁷/₁₆	—	1¹⁹/₃₂	0.110	0.060	—	0.080	0.160	②
	17058182	⁷/₁₆	—	1¹⁹/₃₂	0.110	0.080	—	0.080	0.140	②
	17058183	⁷/₁₆	—	1¹⁹/₃₂	0.110	0.080	—	0.080	0.140	②
	17058185	⁷/₁₆	—	1¹⁹/₃₂	0.110	0.050	—	0.080	0.140	②
	17058187	⁷/₁₆	—	1¹⁹/₃₂	0.110	0.080	—	0.080	0.140	②
	17058189	⁷/₁₆	—	1¹⁹/₃₂	0.110	0.080	—	0.080	0.140	②
	17058147	⁷/₁₆	—	1¹⁹/₃₂	0.140	0.100	—	0.080	0.140	②
	17058444	⁷/₁₆	—	1¹⁹/₃₂	0.140	0.100	—	0.080	0.140	②
	17058448	⁷/₁₆	—	1¹⁹/₃₂	0.140	0.100	—	0.080	0.140	②
	17058440	⁷/₁₆	—	1¹⁹/₃₂	0.140	0.100	—	0.080	0.140	②
	17058446	⁷/₁₆	—	1⁵/₈	0.140	0.140	—	0.080	0.140	②

① Carburetor identification number is stamped on the float bowl next to the fuel inlet nut
② See underhood sticker

2MC, M2MC, M2ME, E2MC, E2ME 2-Barrel Carburetor Specifications

Year	Carburetor Identification ①	Float Level (in.)	Fast Idle Cam Choke Rod) (deg./in.)	Choke Unloader (deg./in.)	Vacuum Break Lean or Front (deg./in.)	Vacuum Break Rich or Rear (deg./in.)	Pump Rod (in.)	Choke Coil Level (in.)	Automatic Choke (notches)
1977	17057150	$1/8$	.085	0.190	0.160	0.090	$11/32$ ③	0.120	2 Rich
	17057152	$1/8$	.085	0.190	0.160	0.090	$11/32$ ③	0.120	2 Rich
	17057156	$1/8$	.085	0.190	0.160	0.090	$11/32$ ③	0.120	1 Rich
	17057158	$1/8$	.085	0.190	0.160	0.090	$11/32$ ③	0.120	1 Rich
	17057172	$11/32$	.075	0.240	0.135	0.240	$3/8$ ③	0.120	2 Rich
1978	17058150	$3/8$	0.065	0.203	0.203	0.133	$1/4$ ②	0.120	2 Rich
	17058151	$3/8$	0.065	0.203	0.229	0.133	$11/32$ ③	0.120	2 Rich
	17058152	$3/8$	0.065	0.203	0.203	0.133	$1/4$ ②	0.120	2 Rich
	17058154	$3/8$	0.065	0.203	0.146	0.245	$11/32$ ③	0.120	2 Rich
	17058155	$3/8$	0.065	0.203	0.146	0.245	$11/32$ ③	0.120	2 Rich
	17058156	$3/8$	0.065	0.230	0.229	0.133	$11/32$ ③	0.120	2 Rich
	17058158	$3/8$	0.065	0.203	0.229	0.133	$11/32$ ③	0.120	2 Rich
	17058450	$3/8$	0.065	0.203	0.146	0.289	$11/32$ ③	0.120	2 Rich
1979	17059160	$11/32$	0.110	0.195	0.129	0.187	$1/4$ ②	0.120	2 Rich
	17059150	$3/8$	0.071	0.220	0.195	0.129	$1/4$ ②	0.120	2 Rich
	17059151	$3/8$	0.071	0.220	0.243	0.142	$11/32$ ③	0.120	2 Rich
	17059152	$3/8$	0.071	0.220	0.195	0.129	$1/4$ ②	0.120	2 Rich
	17059180	$11/32$	0.039	0.243	0.103	0.090	$1/4$ ②	0.120	2 Rich
	17059190	$11/32$	0.039	0.243	0.103	0.090	$1/4$ ②	0.120	2 Rich
	17059492	$11/32$	0.039	0.277	0.129	0.117	$9/32$ ②	0.120	1 Rich
	17059134	$15/32$	38	38	27	—	$1/4$	0.120	1 Lean
	17059136	$15/32$	38	38	27	—	$1/4$	0.120	1 Lean
	17059193	$13/32$	24.5	35	19	17	$1/4$ ②	0.120	2 Rich
	17059194	$11/32$	24.5	35	19	17	$1/4$ ②	0.120	2 Rich
	17059491	$11/32$	24.5	38	23	21	$9/32$ ②	0.120	1 Lean
1980	17080195	$9/32$	24.5	38	19	38	—	0.120	—
	17080197	$9/32$	24.5	38	19	38	—	0.120	—
	17080495	$5/16$	24.5	38	21	30	—	0.120	—
	17080493	$5/16$	24.5	38	21	30	—	0.120	—
	17080150	$3/8$	14	35	38	27	$11/32$ ③	0.120	—
	17080153	$3/8$	14	35	38	27	$11/32$ ③	0.120	—
	17080152	$3/8$	14	35	38	27	$11/32$ ③	0.120	—
	17080496	$5/16$	24.5	38	21	21	$3/8$	0.120	④
	17080498	$5/16$	24.5	38	21	21	$3/8$	0.120	④
	17080490	$5/16$	24.5	38	21	21	$3/8$	0.120	④
	17080492	$5/16$	24.5	38	21	21	$3/8$	0.120	④
	17080491	$5/16$	24.5	38	21	21	$3/8$	0.120	④

2MC, M2MC, M2ME, E2MC, E2ME 2-Barrel Carburetor Specifications (cont.)

Year	Carburetor Identification ①	Float Level (in.)	Fast Idle Cam Choke Rod) (deg./in.)	Choke Unloader (deg./in.)	Vacuum Break Lean or Front (deg./in.)	Vacuum Break Rich or Rear (deg./in.)	Pump Rod (in.)	Choke Coil Level (in.)	Automatic Choke (notches)
	17080190	9/32	24.5	38	22	20	1/4	0.120	④
	17080191	11/32	24.5	38	18	18	1/4	0.120	④
	17080195	9/32	24.5	38	19	14	1/4	0.120	④
	17080197	9/32	24.5	38	19	14	1/4	0.120	④
	17080192	9/32	24.5	38	22	20	1/4	0.120	④
	17080160	5/16	14.5	37.5	28.5	33.5	1/4	0.120	④
1981	17081191	5/16	24.5°	38°	28°	24°	—	0.120	④
	17081192	3/8	18°	38°	28°	24°	—	0.120	④
	17081994	3/8	18°	38°	28°	24°	—	0.120	④
	17081196	5/16	24.5°	38°	28°	24°	—	0.120	④
	17081197	3/8	18°	38°	28°	24°	—	0.120	④
	17081198	3/8	18°	38°	28°	24°	—	0.120	④
	17081199	3/8	18°	38°	28°	24°	—	0.120	④
	17081150	13/32	14°	35°	24°	36°	—	0.120	④
	17081152	13/32	14°	35°	24°	36°	—	0.120	④
	17080191	11/32	24.5°	38°	18°	18°	1/4	0.120	④
	17081492	9/32	24.5°	38°	17°	19°	1/4	0.120	④
	17081493	9/32	24.5°	38°	17°	19°	1/4	0.120	④
	17081170	13/32	20°	38°	25°	—	1/4	0.120	④
	17081171	13/32	20°	38°	25°	—	1/4	0.120	④
	17081174	9/32	20°	38°	25°	—	1/4	0.120	④
	17081175	9/32	20°	38°	25°	—	1/4	0.120	④
1982	17082130	3/8	20°	38°	27°	—	—	—	—
	17082132	3/8	20°	38°	27°	—	—	—	—
	17082138	3/8	20°	38°	27°	—	—	—	—
	17082140	3/8	20°	38°	27°	—	—	—	—
	17082150	13/32	14°	35°	24°	38°	—	—	—
	17082150	13/32	14°	35°	24°	40°	—	—	—
	17082182	5/16	18°	32°	28°	24°	—	—	—
	17082184	5/16	18°	32°	28°	24°	—	—	—
	17082186	5/16	18°	27°	21°	19°	—	—	—
	17082192	5/16	18°	32°	28°	24°	—	—	—
	17082194	5/16	18°	32°	28°	24°	—	—	—
	17082196	5/16	18°	27°	21°	19°	—	—	—

① The carburetor identification number is stamped on the float bowl, next to the fuel inlet nut.
② Inner hole
③ Outer hole
④ Tamper resistant choke

2MC, M2MC, M2ME, E2ME CARBURETOR SPECIFICATIONS

Year	Carburetor Identification ①	Flat Level (in.)	Choke Rod (in.)	Choke Unloader (in.)	Vacuum Break Lean or Front (deg./in.)	Vacuum Break Rich or Rear (deg./in.)	Pump Rod (in.)	Choke Coil Lever (in.)	Automatic Choke (notches)
'83	17082130, 132	3/8	.110	.243	27/.157	—	②	.120	Fixed
	17083190, 192	5/16	.096	.195	28/.164	24/.136	②	.120	Fixed
	17083193	5/16	.090	.157	23/.129	28/.164	②	.120	Fixed
	17083194	5/16	.090	.220	27/.157	25/.142	②	.120	Fixed

① The carburetor identification number is stamped on the float bowl, next to the fuel inlet nut.
② Not Adjustable

M4MC, M4ME, E4MC 4-Barrel Carburetor Specifications

Year	Carburetor Identification ①	Float Level (in.)	Air Valve Spring (turn)	Pump Rod (in.)	Primary Vacuum Break (in. or deg.)	Secondary Vacuum Break (in. or deg.)	Secondary Opening (in.)	Fast Idle Cam (Choke Rod) in. or deg.)	Choke Unloader (in. or deg.)	Fast Idle Speed (rpm)
1974	7043263	.390	5/8	.410	.290	—	0.070	.205	.310	1500
	7044262	.390	3/8	.410	.260	—	0.070	.205	.310	1500
	7044266	.390	1/2	.410	.260	—	0.070	.205	.310	1500
	7044267	.390	3/8	.410	.260	—	0.070	.205	.310	1500
	7044268	.390	1/2	.410	.260	—	0.070	.205	.310	1500
	7044269	.390	1/2	.410	.290	—	0.070	.205	.310	1500
	7044270	.390	3/4	.410	.290	—	0.070	.205	.310	1500
	7044272	.390	3/8	.315	.290	—	0.070	.205	.310	1500
	7044273	.390	3/4	.410	.290	—	0.070	.205	.310	1500
	7044274	.390	9/16	.315	.290	—	0.070	.205	.310	1500
	7044560	.390	3/8	.410	.260	—	0.070	.205	.310	1500
	7044568	.390	1/2	.410	.260	—	0.070	.205	.310	1500
1975	7045183	3/8	1/8	9/32	0.190	0.140	—	0.135	0.235	②
	7045250	3/8	1/2	9/32	0.250	0.180	—	0.170	0.300	②
	7045483	3/8	1/2	9/32	0.275	0.180	—	0.135	0.235	②
	7045550	3/8	1/2	9/32	0.275	0.180	—	0.135	0.235	②
	7045264	17/32	1/2	9/32	0.150	0.260	—	0.130	0.235	②
	7045184	3/8	3/4	9/32	0.190	0.140	—	0.135	0.235	②
	7045185	3/8	3/4	9/32	0.275	0.140	—	0.135	0.235	②
	7045251	3/8	3/4	9/32	0.190	0.140	—	0.135	0.235	②
	7045244	5/16	3/4	15/32	0.130	0.115	Index	0.095	0.240	1800③
	7045544	5/16	3/4	15/32	0.145	0.130	Index	0.095	0.240	1800③
	7045240	7/16	7/16	9/32	0.135	0.120	Index	0.095	0.240	1800③
	7045548	7/16	7/16	9/32	0.135	0.120	Index	0.095	0.240	1800③
	7045541	7/16	7/16	9/32	0.135	0.120	Index	0.095	0.240	1800③
	7045274	1/2	—	9/32	0.150	0.260	—	0.230	0.230	1800
	7045260	1/2	—	9/32	0.150	0.260	—	0.130	0.230	1800
	7045262	1/2	—	9/32	0.150	0.260	—	0.130	0.230	1800
	7045266	1/2	—	9/32	0.150	0.260	—	0.130	0.230	1800
	7045562	1/2	—	9/32	0.150	0.260	—	0.130	0.230	1800
1976	17056544	5/16	3/4	3/8	0.130	0.130	Index	0.095	0.250	—
	17056244	5/16	3/4	3/8	0.130	0.120	Index	0.095	0.250	—
	17056240	15/32	7/16	9/32	0.135	0.120	Index	0.095	0.250	—
	17056540	15/32	7/16	3/8	0.135	0.120	Index	0.095	0.250	—
	17056250	13/32	1/2	9/32	0.190	0.140	—	0.130	0.230	900④
	17056251	13/32	3/4	9/32	0.190	0.140	—	0.130	0.230	900
	17056253	13/32	1/2	9/32	0.190	0.140	—	0.130	0.230	900④
	17056255	13/32	3/4	9/32	0.190	0.140	—	0.130	0.230	900
	17056256	13/32	3/4	9/32	0.190	0.140	—	0.130	0.230	900

M4MC, M4ME, E4MC 4-Barrel Carburetor Specifications (cont.)

Year	Carburetor Identification ①	Float Level (in.)	Air Valve Spring (turn)	Pump Rod (in.)	Primary Vacuum Break (in. or deg.)	Secondary Vacuum Break (in. or deg.)	Secondary Opening (in.)	Fast Idle Cam (Choke Rod) in. or deg.)	Choke Unloader (in. or deg.)	Fast Idle Speed (rpm)
	17056257	13/32	3/4	9/32	0.190	0.140	—	0.130	0.230	900
	17056550	13/32	1/2	9/32	0.190	0.140	—	0.130	0.230	1000
	17056551	13/32	3/4	9/32	0.190	0.140	—	0.130	0.230	800
	17056553	13/32	1/2	9/32	0.190	0.140	—	0.130	0.230	1000
1977	17057202	15/32	7/8	9/32	0.160	—	—	0.325	0.280	1600 ⑤
	17057204	15/32	7/8	9/32	0.160	—	—	0.325	0.280	1600 ⑤
	1707250	13/32	1/2	9/32	0.135	0.180	—	0.100	0.220	⑦
	1707253	13/32	1/2	9/32	0.135	0.180	—	0.100	0.220	⑦
	1707255	13/32	1/2	9/32	0.135	0.180	—	0.100	0.220	⑦
	1707256	13/32	1/2	9/32	0.135	0.180	—	0.100	0.220	⑦
	1707258	13/32	1/2	9/32	0.135	0.225	—	0.100	0.220	⑦
	1707550	13/32	1/2	9/32	0.135	0.225	—	0.100	0.220	⑦
	1707553	13/32	1/2	9/32	0.135	0.225	—	0.100	0.220	⑦
	17057262	17/32	1/2	3/8	0.150	0.240	—	0.130	0.220	⑦
1978	17058253	13/32	1/2	9/32	0.129	0.183	—	0.096	0.220	⑦
	17058250	13/32	1/2	9/32	0.129	0.183	—	0.096	0.220	⑦
	17058258	13/32	1/2	9/32	0.136	0.230	—	0.103	0.220	⑦
	17058553	13/32	1/2	9/32	0.136	0.230	—	0.103	0.220	⑦
	17058272	15/32	5/8	3/8	0.126	0.195	—	0.071	0.227	⑦
	17058241	5/16	3/4	3/8	0.117	0.103	—	0.096	0.243	⑦
	17058274	17/32	1/2	3/8	0.149	0.260	—	0.129	0.220	⑦
	17058264	17/32	1/2	3/8	0.149	0.260	—	0.129	0.220	⑦
1979	17059253	13/32	1/2	9/32	23	30.5	—	18	35	⑦
	17059250	13/32	1/2	9/32	23	30.5	—	18	35	⑦
	17059251	13/32	1/2	9/32	23	30.5	—	—	35	⑦
	17059258	13/32	1/2	9/32	24	32	—	—	35	⑦
	17059256	13/32	1/2	9/32	24	32	—	—	35	⑦
	17059553	13/32	1/2	9/32	24	36.5	—	19	35	⑦
	1709240	7/32	3/4	9/32	21	21	—	14.5	30	⑦
	1709243	7/32	3/4	9/32	21	21	—	14.5	30	⑦
	1709540	7/32	3/4	9/32	21	23	—	14.5	38	⑦
	1709543	7/32	3/4	9/32	21	23	—	14.5	38	⑦
	1709542	7/32	3/4	9/32	13	13	—	14.5	30	⑦
1980	17080253	13/32	1/2	9/32	26	34	—	17	35	⑦
	17080250	13/32	1/2	9/32	26	34	—	17	35	⑦
	17080252	13/32	1/2	9/32	26	34	—	17	35	⑦
	17080251	13/32	1/2	9/32	26	34	—	17	35	⑦
	17080259	13/32	1/2	9/32	26	34	—	17	35	⑦
	17080260	13/32	1/2	9/32	26	34	—	17	35	⑦

M4MC, M4ME, E4MC 4-Barrel Carburetor Specifications (cont.)

Year	Carburetor Identification ①	Float Level (in.)	Air Valve Spring (turn)	Pump Rod (in.)	Primary Vacuum Break (in. or deg.)	Secondary Vacuum Break (in. or deg.)	Secondary Opening (in.)	Fast Idle Cam (Choke Rod) in. or deg.	Choke Unloader (in. or deg.)	Fast Idle Speed (rpm)
	17080553	15/32	1/2	9/32	25	35	—	17	35	⑦
	17080554	15/32	1/2	9/32	25	34	—	17	35	⑦
	17080272	15/32	5/8	3/8	23	29.5	—	14.5	33	⑦
	17080249	7/16	3/4	9/32	23	20.5	—	18	38	⑦
	17080270	15/32	5/8	3/8	26	34	—	14.5	35	⑦
	17080241	7/16	3/4	9/32	23	20.5	—	18	38	⑦
	17080249	7/16	3/4	9/32	23	20.5	—	18	38	⑦
	17080244	5/16	5/8	9/32	18	14	—	24.5	38	⑦
	17080242	13/32	9/16	9/32	15	18	—	14.5	35	⑦
	17080243	3/16	9/16	9/32	16	16	—	14.5	30	⑦
1981	17081248	3/8	5/8	⑥	28	24	—	24.5	38	⑦
	17081289	13/32	5/8	⑥	28	24	—	24.5	38	⑦
	17081253	15/32	1/2	⑥	25	36	—	14	35	⑦
	17081254	15/32	1/2	⑥	25	36	—	14	35	⑦
1982	17082202	11/32	—	⑥	20	20	—	—	—	⑦
	17082204	11/32	—	⑥	20	20	—	—	—	⑦
	17082244	7/16	—	⑥	32	21	16	—	—	⑦
	17082245	3/8	—	⑥	32	26	26	—	—	⑦
	17082246	3/8	—	⑥	32	26	26	—	—	⑦
	17082247	13/32	—	⑥	38	28	24	—	—	⑦
	17082248	13/32	—	⑥	38	28	24	—	—	⑦
	17082251	15/32	—	⑥	35	25	45	—	—	⑦
	17082253	15/32	—	⑥	35	25	36	—	—	⑦
	17082264	7/16	—	⑥	32	21	16	—	—	⑦
	17082265	3/8	—	⑥	32	26	26	—	—	⑦
	17082266	3/8	—	⑥	32	26	26	—	—	⑦

① Carburetor identification number is stamped on the float bowl next to the fuel inlet nut.
② 900 rpm with fast idle cam follower on lowest step of fast idle cam
③ Trans. in Park with fast idle cam follower on highest step of fast idle cam
④ In Park; 1000 rpm (Park) in California
⑤ In Park
⑥ No pump rod adjustment required on carburetors used with the CCC system.
⑦ See underhood decal

4-BBL CARBURETOR SPECIFICATIONS

Year	Carburetor Identification ①	Float Level (in.)	Air Valve Spring (turn)	Pump Rod (in.)	Primary Vacuum Break (in./deg.)	Secondary Vacuum Break (in./deg.)	Secondary Opening (in.)	Choke Rod (in.)	Choke Unloader (in./deg.)	Fast Idle Speed ② (rpm)
'83	17082265	3/8	5/8	Fixed	0.149/26	0.149/26	①	0.139	0.195	⑯
	17082266	3/8	5/8	Fixed	0.149/26	0.149/26	①	0.139	0.195	⑯
	17082267	3/8	5/8	Fixed	0.149/26	0.149/26	①	0.096	0.195	⑯
	17082268	3/8	5/8	Fixed	0.149/26	0.149/26	①	0.096	0.195	⑯
	17083242	9/32	9/16	Fixed	0.110/20	—	①	0.139	0.243	⑯
	17083244	1/4	9/16	Fixed	0.117/21	0.083/16	①	0.139	0.195	⑯
	17083248	3/8	5/8	Fixed	0.149/26	0.149/26	①	0.139	0.195	⑯
	17083250	7/16	1/2	Fixed	0.157/27	0.271/42	①	0.071	0.220	⑯
	17083253	7/16	1/2	Fixed	0.157/27	0.269/41	①	0.071	0.220	⑯
	17083553	7/16	1/2	Fixed	0.157/27	0.269/41	①	0.071	0.220	⑯

① On highest step.
⑯ See underhood sticker

DIESEL ENGINE FUEL SYSTEM

◆ **See Figure 29**

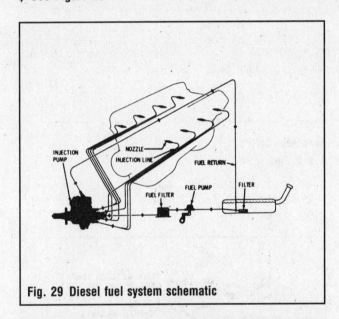

Fig. 29 Diesel fuel system schematic

Fuel Supply Pump

REMOVAL & INSTALLATION

The diesel fuel supply pump is serviced in the same manner as the fuel pump on gasoline engines. Refer to the procedure at the beginning of this section.

WATER IN FUEL

Water is the worst enemy of the diesel fuel injection system. The injection pump, which is designed and constructed to extremely close tolerances, and the injectors can be easily damaged if enough water is forced through them in the fuel. Engine performance will also be drastically affected, and engine damage can occur.

Diesel fuel is much more susceptible than gasoline to water contamination. Diesel-engined cars are equipped with an indicator lamp system that turns on an instrument panel lamp if water (1 to 2½ gallons) is detected in the fuel tank. The lamp will come on for 2 to 5 seconds each time the ignition is turned on, assuring the driver the lamp is working. If there is water in the fuel, the light will come back on after a 15 to 20 second off delay, and then remain on.

PURGING THE FUEL TANK

Cars which have a "Water in Fuel" light may have the water removed from the tank with a siphon pump. The pump hose should be hooked up to the ¼ in. fuel return hose (the smaller of the two hoses) above the rear axle or under the hood near the fuel pump. Siphoning should continue until all water is removed from the tank. Use a clear plastic hose or observe the filter bowl on the siphon pump (if equipped) to determine when clear fuel begins to flow. Be sure to remove the cap on the fuel tank while purging. Replace the cap when finished. Discard the fuel filter and replace with a new filter.

Injection Pump

REMOVAL & INSTALLATION

▶ **See Figure 30**

1. Remove the air cleaner.
2. Remove the filters and pipes from the valve covers and air crossover.
3. Remove the air crossover and cap and intake manifold with screened covers (tool J-26996-1).
4. Disconnect the throttle rod and return spring.
5. Remove the bellcrank.
6. Remove the throttle and transmission cables from the intake manifold brackets.
7. Disconnect the fuel lines from the filter and remove the filter.
8. Disconnect the fuel inlet line at the pump.
9. Remove the rear A/C compressor brace and remove the fuel line.
10. Disconnect the fuel return line from the injection pump.
11. Remove the clamps and pull the fuel return lines from each injection nozzle.
12. Using two wrenches, disconnect the high pressure lines at the nozzles.
13. Remove the three injection pump retaining nuts with tool J-26987 or its equivalent.
14. Remove the pump and cap all lines and nozzles.
To install:
15. Remove the protective caps.
16. Line up the offset tang on the pump driveshaft with the pump driven gear and install the pump.
17. Install, but do not tighten the pump retaining nuts.
18. Connect the high pressure lines at the nozzles.
19. Using two wrenches, tighten the high pressure line nuts to 25 ft. lbs.
20. Connect the fuel return lines to the nozzles and pump.
21. Align the timing mark on the injection pump with the line on the timing mark adaptor and tighten the mounting nuts to 35 ft. lbs.

➡**A ¾ in. open end wrench on the boss at the front of the injection pump will aid in rotating the pump to align the marks.**

22. Adjust the throttle rod:
    a. remove the clip from the cruise control rod and remove the rod from the bellcrank.
    b. loosen the locknut on the throttle rod a few turns, then shorten the rod several turns.
    c. rotate the bellcrank to the full throttle stop, then lengthen the throttle rod until the injection pump lever contacts the injection pump full throttle stop, then release the bellcrank.
    d. tighten the throttle rod locknut.
23. Install the fuel inlet line between the transfer pump and the filter.
24. Install the rear A/C compressor brace.
25. Install the bellcrank and clip.
26. Connect the throttle rod and return spring.
27. Adjust the transmission cable:
    a. push the snap-lock to the disengaged position.
    b. rotate the injection pump lever to the full throttle stop and hold it there.
    c. push in the snap-lock until it is flush.
    d. release the injection pump lever.
28. Start the engine and check for fuel leaks.
29. Remove the screened covers and install the air crossover.
30. Install the tubes in the air flow control valve in the air crossover and install the ventilation filters in the valve covers.
31. Install the air cleaner.
32. Start the engine and allow it to run for two minutes. Stop the engine, let it stand for two minutes, then restart. This permits the air to bleed off within the pump.

ADJUSTMENTS

Slow Idle Speed
▶ **See Figure 31**

1. Run the engine to normal operating temperature.
2. Insert the probe of a magnetic pickup tachometer into the timing indicator hole.

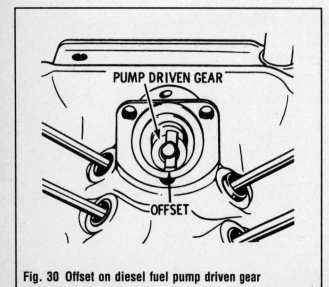

Fig. 30 Offset on diesel fuel pump driven gear

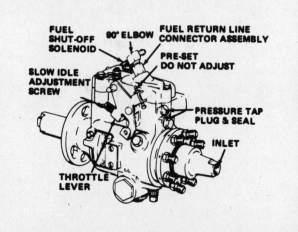

Fig. 31 Diesel injection pump slow idle adjustment screw location

3. Set the parking brake and block the drive wheels.

4. Place the transmission in Drive and turn the A/C Off.

5. Turn the slow idle screw on the injection pump to obtain the idle specification on the emission control label.

Fast Idle Solenoid

1. Set the parking brake and block the drive wheels.

2. Run the engine to normal operating temperature.

3. Place the transmission in Drive, disconnect the compressor clutch wire and turn the A/C On. On cars without A/C, disconnect the solenoid wire, and connect jumper wires to the solenoid terminals. Ground one of the wires and connect the other to a 12 volt power source to activate the solenoid.

4. Adjust the fast idle solenoid plunger to obtain 650 rpm.

Cruise Control Servo Relay Rod

1. Turn the engine off.

2. Adjust the rod to minimum slack, then put the clip in the first free hole closest to the bellcrank, but within the servo bail.

Injection Timing
♦ **See Figure 32**

For the engine to be properly timed, the lines on the top of the injection pump adapter and the flange of the injection pump must be aligned.

1. The engine must be off for resetting the timing.

2. Loosen the three pump retaining nuts with tool J-26987, an injection pump intake manifold wrench, or its equivalent.

3. Align the timing marks and tighten the pump retaining nuts to 35 ft. lbs.

➡**The use of a ¾ in. open end wrench on the boss at the front of the pump will aid in rotating the pump to align the marks.**

4. Adjust the throttle rod. (See Step 22 of the Injection Pump removal and installation procedure.)

Injection Nozzle

REMOVAL & INSTALLATION

Lines Removed
♦ **See Figures 33, 34 and 35**

1. Remove the fuel return line from the nozzle.

2. Remove the nozzle hold-down clamp and spacer using tool J-26952.3. Cap the high pressure line and nozzle tip.

➡**The nozzle tip is highly susceptible to damage and must be protected at all times.**

3. If an old nozzle is to be reinstalled, a new compression seal and carbon stop seal must be installed after removal of the used seals.

4. Remove the caps and install the nozzle, spacer and clamp. Torque to 25 ft. lbs.

5. Replace return line, start the engine and check for leaks.

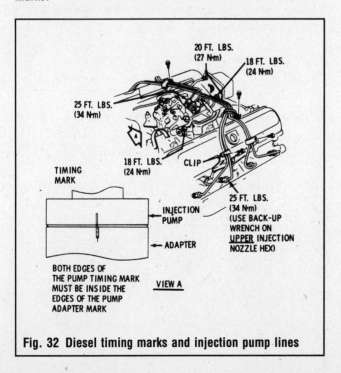

Fig. 32 Diesel timing marks and injection pump lines

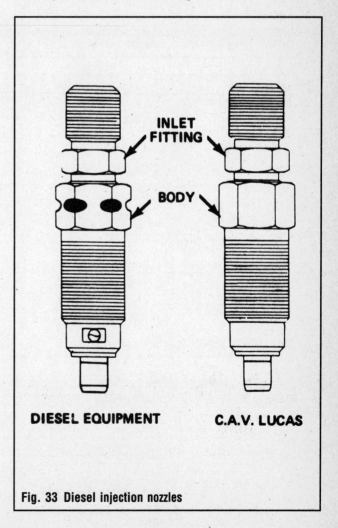

Fig. 33 Diesel injection nozzles

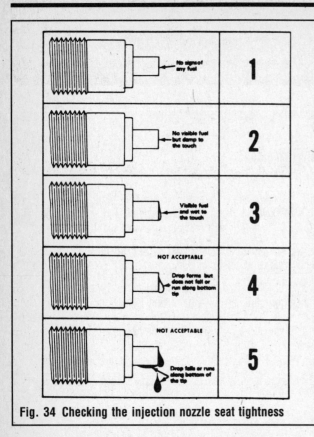

Fig. 34 Checking the injection nozzle seat tightness

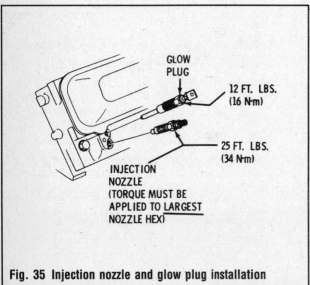

Fig. 35 Injection nozzle and glow plug installation

Injection Pump Adapter and Seal

REMOVAL & INSTALLATION

◆ See Figures 36, 37 and 38

1. Remove injection pump and lines as described earlier.
2. Remove the injection pump adapter.
3. Remove the seal from the adapter.
4. File the timing mark from the adapter. Do not file the mark off the pump.

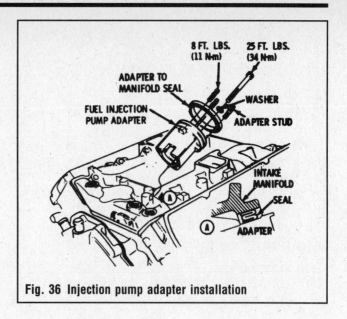

Fig. 36 Injection pump adapter installation

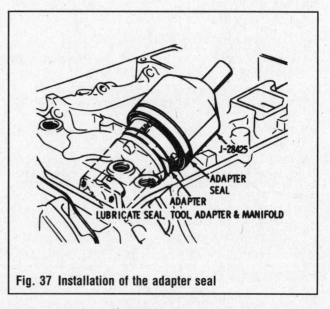

Fig. 37 Installation of the adapter seal

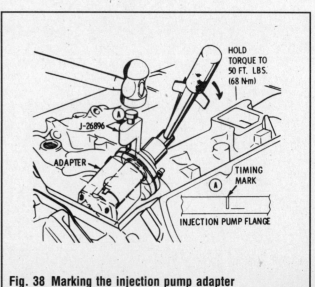

Fig. 38 Marking the injection pump adapter

5. Position the engine at TDC of No. 1 cylinder. Align the mark on the balancer with the zero mark on the indicator. The index is offset to the right when No. 1 is at TDC.

6. Apply a chassis lube to the seal areas. Install, but do not tighten the injection pump.

7. Install the new seal on the adapter using tool J-28425, or its equivalent.

8. Tighten the adapter bolts to 25 ft. lbs.

9. Install timing tool J-26896 into the injection pump adapter. Tighten the tool, toward No. 1 cylinder to 50 ft. lbs. Mark the injection pump adapter. Remove the tool.

10. Install the injection pump.

FUEL TANK

Tank Assembly

DRAINING THE TANK

Gasoline Engines

➡**If the car is to be stored for any extended length of time, the fuel should be drained from the complete system, including carburetor, fuel pump, all fuel lines, and the fuel tank in order to prevent gum formations and poor engine performance.**

1. Have a carbon dioxide fire extinguisher near the work area. Remove the negative battery cable from the battery.

2. Use a hand-operated siphon pump, and follow the manufacturer's instructions for its use. As the fuel tank has a restrictor in the filler neck, connect the drain hose to the main fuel pipe at the fuel pump or at the tank gauge unit. Drain the fuel.

3. Reconnect any removed hoses, lines and cap.

✳✳ CAUTION

Never drain or store gasoline in an open container due to the possibility of fire or explosion. Never siphon gasoline by mouth!

Diesel Engines

1. Remove the fuel tank cap.

2. Connect a siphon pump to the ¼ in. fuel return hose (the smaller of the two hoses) above the rear axle, or under the hood near the fuel pump on the passenger's side of the engine, near the front.

3. Operate the siphon pump until all fuel is removed from the fuel tank. Be sure to reinstall the fuel return hose and the fuel cap.

REMOVAL & INSTALLATION

▸ **See Figures 39 and 40**

1. Drain tank.

2. Disconnect tank unit wire from connector in rear compartment.

3. Remove the ground wire retaining screw from the underbody.

4. Disconnect the hoses from the tank unit.

5. Support the fuel tank and disconnect the two fuel tank retaining straps.

6. Remove the tank from the car.

7. Remove the fuel gauge retaining cam, and remove the tank unit from the tank.

8. Installation is the reverse of removal. On California emissions-equipped cars, center the fuel filler pipe in the opening as required. Always replace the O-ring when the tank unit has been removed.

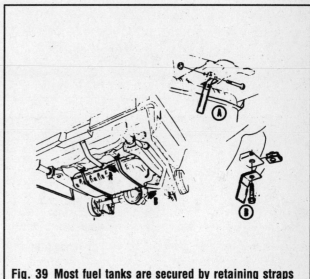

Fig. 39 Most fuel tanks are secured by retaining straps

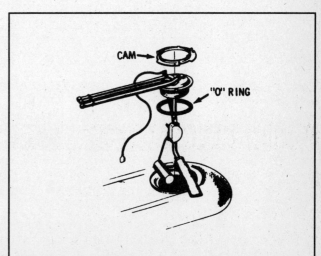

Fig. 40 Typical installation of the fuel gauge unit into the tank

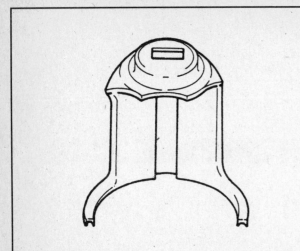

A special tool is usually available to remove or install the fuel pump locking cam

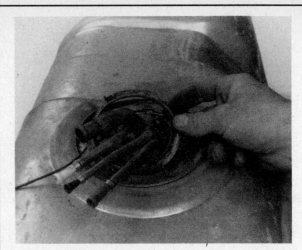

Once the locking cam is released it can be removed to free the fuel pump

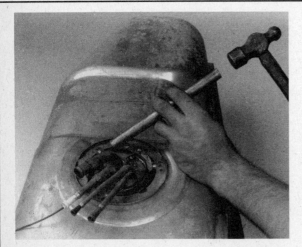

A brass drift and a hammer can be used to loosen the fuel pump locking cam

UNDERSTANDING AND
TROUBLESHOOTING ELECTRICAL
SYSTEMS 6-2
SAFETY PRECAUTIONS 6-2
UNDERSTANDING BASIC
ELECTRICITY 6-2
THE WATER ANALOGY 6-2
CIRCUITS 6-2
AUTOMOTIVE CIRCUITS 6-3
SHORT CIRCUITS 6-3
TROUBLESHOOTING 6-3
BASIC TROUBLESHOOTING
THEORY 6-4
TEST EQUIPMENT 6-4
TESTING 6-6
WIRING HARNESSES 6-8
WIRING REPAIR 6-8
ADD-ON ELECTRICAL
EQUIPMENT 6-10
HEATER 6-12
BLOWER MOTOR 6-12
REMOVAL & INSTALLATION 6-12
HEATER CORE 6-12
REMOVAL & INSTALLATION 6-12
RADIO 6-20
RADIO RECEIVER 6-20
REMOVAL & INSTALLATION 6-20
WINDSHIELD WIPERS 6-24
WINDSHIELD WIPER BLADE AND
ARM 6-24
REMOVAL & INSTALLATION 6-24
WINDSHIELD WIPER MOTOR 6-25
REMOVAL & INSTALLATION 6-25
LINKAGE REPLACEMENT 6-25
INSTRUMENTS AND
SWITCHES 6-27
LIGHT SWITCH 6-27
REPLACEMENT &
INSTALLATION 6-27
WINDSHIELD WIPER SWITCH 6-27
REMOVAL & INSTALLATION 6-27
SPEEDOMETER CABLE 6-28
REMOVAL & INSTALLATION 6-28
INSTRUMENT CLUSTER 6-28
REMOVAL & INSTALLATION 6-28
IGNITION SWITCH 6-32
REMOVAL & INSTALLATION 6-32
SEAT BELT/STARTER INTERLOCK
SYSTEM 6-32
DISABLING THE INTERLOCK
SYSTEM 6-32
LIGHTING 6-32
HEADLIGHTS 6-32
REMOVAL & INSTALLATION 6-32
AIMING 6-32
SIGNAL AND MARKER LIGHTS 6-35
REMOVAL & INSTALLATION 6-35
TRAILER WIRING 6-39
CIRCUIT PROTECTION 6-39
FUSES 6-39

FUSIBLE LINKS 6-42
REPLACEMENT 6-42
CIRCUIT BREAKERS 6-42
FLASHERS 6-42
REPLACEMENT 6-42
WIRING DIAGRAMS 6-44

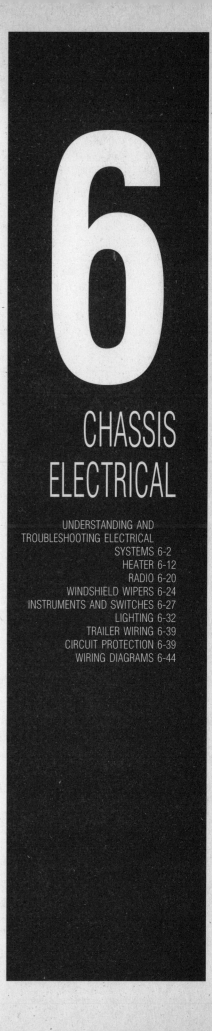

6
CHASSIS
ELECTRICAL

UNDERSTANDING AND
TROUBLESHOOTING ELECTRICAL
SYSTEMS 6-2
HEATER 6-12
RADIO 6-20
WINDSHIELD WIPERS 6-24
INSTRUMENTS AND SWITCHES 6-27
LIGHTING 6-32
TRAILER WIRING 6-39
CIRCUIT PROTECTION 6-39
WIRING DIAGRAMS 6-44

UNDERSTANDING AND TROUBLESHOOTING ELECTRICAL SYSTEMS

Over the years import and domestic manufacturers have incorporated electronic control systems into their production lines. In fact, electronic control systems are so prevalent that all new cars and trucks built today are equipped with at least one on-board computer. These electronic components (with no moving parts) should theoretically last the life of the vehicle, provided that nothing external happens to damage the circuits or memory chips.

While it is true that electronic components should never wear out, in the real world malfunctions do occur. It is also true that any computer-based system is extremely sensitive to electrical voltages and cannot tolerate careless or haphazard testing/service procedures. An inexperienced individual can literally cause major damage looking for a minor problem by using the wrong kind of test equipment or connecting test leads/connectors with the ignition switch **ON**. When selecting test equipment, make sure the manufacturer's instructions state that the tester is compatible with whatever type of system is being serviced. Read all instructions carefully and double check all test points before installing probes or making any test connections.

The following section outlines basic diagnosis techniques for dealing with automotive electrical systems. Along with a general explanation of the various types of test equipment available to aid in servicing modern automotive systems, basic repair techniques for wiring harnesses and connectors are also given. Read the basic information before attempting any repairs or testing. This will provide the background of information necessary to avoid the most common and obvious mistakes that can cost both time and money. Although the replacement and testing procedures are simple in themselves, the systems are not, and unless one has a thorough understanding of all components and their function within a particular system, the logical test sequence these systems demand cannot be followed. Minor malfunctions can make a big difference, so it is important to know how each component affects the operation of the overall system in order to find the ultimate cause of a problem without replacing good components unnecessarily. It is not enough to use the correct test equipment; the test equipment must be used correctly.

Safety Precautions

✳✳ CAUTION

Whenever working on or around any electrical or electronic systems, always observe these general precautions to prevent the possibility of personal injury or damage to electronic components.

• Never install or remove battery cables with the key **ON** or the engine running. Jumper cables should be connected with the key **OFF** to avoid power surges that can damage electronic control units. Engines equipped with computer controlled systems should avoid both giving and getting jump starts due to the possibility of serious damage to components from arcing in the engine compartment if connections are made with the ignition **ON**.

• Always remove the battery cables before charging the battery. Never use a high output charger on an installed battery or attempt to use any type of "hot shot" (24 volt) starting aid.

• Exercise care when inserting test probes into connectors to in-

sure good contact without damaging the connector or spreading the pins. Always probe connectors from the rear (wire) side, NOT the pin side, to avoid accidental shorting of terminals during test procedures.

• Never remove or attach wiring harness connectors with the ignition switch **ON**, especially to an electronic control unit.

• Do not drop any components during service procedures and never apply 12 volts directly to any component (like a solenoid or relay) unless instructed specifically to do so. Some component electrical windings are designed to safely handle only 4 or 5 volts and can be destroyed in seconds if 12 volts are applied directly to the connector.

• Remove the electronic control unit if the vehicle is to be placed in an environment where temperatures exceed approximately 176°F (80°C), such as a paint spray booth or when arc/gas welding near the control unit location.

Understanding Basic Electricity

Understanding the basic theory of electricity makes electrical troubleshooting much easier. Several gauges are used in electrical troubleshooting to see inside the circuit being tested. Without a basic understanding, it will be difficult to understand testing procedures.

THE WATER ANALOGY

Electricity is the flow of electrons—hypothetical particles thought to constitute the basic stuff of electricity. Many people have been taught electrical theory using an analogy with water. In a comparison with water flowing in a pipe, the electrons would be the water. As the flow of water can be measured, the flow of electricity can be measured. The unit of measurement is amperes, frequently abbreviated amps. An ammeter will measure the actual amount of current flowing in the circuit.

Just as the water pressure is measured in units such as pounds per square inch, electrical pressure is measured in volts. When a voltmeter's two probes are placed on two live portions of an electrical circuit with different electrical pressures, current will flow through the voltmeter and produce a reading which indicates the difference in electrical pressure between the two parts of the circuit.

While increasing the voltage in a circuit will increase the flow of current, the actual flow depends not only on voltage, but on the resistance of the circuit. The standard unit for measuring circuit resistance is an ohm, measured by an ohmmeter. The ohmmeter is somewhat similar to an ammeter, but incorporates its own source of power so that a standard voltage is always present.

CIRCUITS

An actual electric circuit consists of four basic parts. These are: the power source, such as a generator or battery; a hot wire, which conducts the electricity under a relatively high voltage to the component supplied by the circuit; the load, such as a lamp, motor, resistor or relay coil; and the ground wire, which carries the current back to the source under very low voltage. In such a circuit the bulk of the resistance exists between the point where the hot wire is connected to the load, and the point where the load is grounded. In an automobile, the vehicle's frame or body, which is made of steel, is used as a part of the ground circuit for many of the electrical devices.

Remember that, in electrical testing, the voltmeter is connected in parallel with the circuit being tested (without disconnecting any wires) and measures the difference in voltage between the locations of the two probes; that the ammeter is connected in series with the load (the circuit is separated at one point and the ammeter inserted so it becomes a part of the circuit); and the ohmmeter is self-powered, so that all the power in the circuit should be off and the portion of the circuit to be measured contacted at either end by one of the probes of the meter.

For any electrical system to operate, it must make a complete circuit. This simply means that the power flow from the battery must make a complete circle. When an electrical component is operating, power flows from the battery to the component, passes through the component causing it to perform it to function (such as lighting a light bulb) and then returns to the battery through the ground of the circuit. This ground is usually (but not always) the metal part of the vehicle on which the electrical component is mounted.

Perhaps the easiest way to visualize this is to think of connecting a light bulb with two wires attached to it to your vehicle's battery. The battery in your vehicle has two posts (negative and positive). If one of the two wires attached to the light bulb was attached to the negative post of the battery and the other wire was attached to the positive post of the battery, you would have a complete circuit. Current from the battery would flow out one post, through the wire attached to it and then to the light bulb, where it would pass through causing it to light. It would then leave the light bulb, travel through the other wire, and return to the other post of the battery.

AUTOMOTIVE CIRCUITS

The normal automotive circuit differs from this simple example in two ways. First, instead of having a return wire from the bulb to the battery, the light bulb return the current to the battery through the chassis of the vehicle. Since the negative battery cable is attached to the chassis and the chassis is made of electrically conductive metal, the chassis of the vehicle can serve as a ground wire to complete the circuit. Secondly, most automotive circuits contain switches to turn components on and off.

Some electrical components which require a large amount of current to operate also have a relay in their circuit. Since these circuits carry a large amount of current, the thickness of the wire in the circuit (gauge size) is also greater. If this large wire were connected from the component to the control switch on the instrument panel, and then back to the component, a voltage drop would occur in the circuit. To prevent this potential drop in voltage, an electromagnetic switch (relay) is used. The large wires in the circuit are connected from the vehicle battery to one side of the relay, and from the opposite side of the relay to the component. The relay is normally open, preventing current from passing through the circuit. An additional, smaller wire is connected from the relay to the control switch for the circuit. When the control

switch is turned on, it grounds the smaller wire from the relay and completes the circuit.

SHORT CIRCUITS

If you were to disconnect the light bulb (from the previous example of a light-bulb being connected to the battery by two wires) from the wires and touch the two wires together (please take our word for this; don't try it), the result will be a shower of sparks. A similar thing happens (on a smaller scale) when the power supply wire to a component or the electrical component itself becomes grounded before the normal ground connection for the circuit. To prevent damage to the system, the fuse for the circuit blows to interrupt the circuit—protecting the components from damage. Because grounding a wire from a power source makes a complete circuit—less the required component to use the power—the phenomenon is called a short circuit. The most common causes of short circuits are: the rubber insulation on a wire breaking or rubbing through to expose the current carrying core of the wire to a metal part of the car, or a shorted switch.

Some electrical systems on the vehicle are protected by a circuit breaker which is, basically, a self-repairing fuse. When either of the described events takes place in a system which is protected by a circuit breaker, the circuit breaker opens the circuit the same way a fuse does. However, when either the short is removed from the circuit or the surge subsides, the circuit breaker resets itself and does not have to be replaced as a fuse does.

Troubleshooting

When diagnosing a specific problem, organized troubleshooting is a must. The complexity of a modern automobile demands that you approach any problem in a logical, organized manner. There are certain troubleshooting techniques that are standard:

1. Establish when the problem occurs. Does the problem appear only under certain conditions? Were there any noises, odors, or other unusual symptoms?

2. Isolate the problem area. To do this, make some simple tests and observations; then eliminate the systems that are working properly. Check for obvious problems such as broken wires, dirty connections or split/disconnected vacuum hoses. Always check the obvious before assuming something complicated is the cause.

3. Test for problems systematically to determine the cause once the problem area is isolated. Are all the components functioning properly? Is there power going to electrical switches and motors? Is there vacuum at vacuum switches and/or actuators? Is there a mechanical problem such as bent linkage or loose mounting screws? Performing careful, systematic checks will often turn up most causes on the first inspection without wasting time checking components that have little or no relationship to the problem.

4. Test all repairs after the work is done to make sure that the problem is fixed. Some causes can be traced to more than one component, so a careful verification of repair work is important in order to pick up additional malfunctions that may cause a problem to reappear or a different problem to arise. A blown fuse, for example, is a simple problem that may require more than another fuse to repair. If you don't look for a problem that caused a fuse to blow, a shorted wire (for example) may go undetected.

Experience has shown that most problems tend to be the result of a fairly simple and obvious cause, such as loose or corroded connectors or air leaks in the intake system. This makes careful inspection of components during testing essential to quick and accurate troubleshooting.

BASIC TROUBLESHOOTING THEORY

Electrical problems generally fall into one of three areas:
• The component that is not functioning is not receiving current.
• The component itself is not functioning.
• The component is not properly grounded.
Problems that fall into the first category are by far the most complicated. It is the current supply system to the component which contains all the switches, relay, fuses, etc.

The electrical system can be checked with a test light and a jumper wire. A test light is a device that looks like a pointed screwdriver with a wire attached to it. It has a light bulb in its handle. A jumper wire is a piece of insulated wire with an alligator clip attached to each end.

If a light bulb is not working, you must follow a systematic plan to determine which of the three causes is the villain.
1. Turn on the switch that controls the inoperable bulb.
2. Disconnect the power supply wire from the bulb.
3. Attach the ground wire to the test light to a good metal ground.
4. Touch the probe end of the test light to the end of the power supply wire that was disconnected from the bulb. If the bulb is receiving current, the test light will go on.

➡**If the bulb is one which works only when the ignition key is turned on (turn signal), make sure the key is turned on.**

If the test light does not go on, then the problem is in the circuit between the battery and the bulb. As mentioned before, this includes all the switches, fuses, and relays in the system. Turn to a wiring diagram and find the bulb on the diagram. Follow the wire that runs back to the battery. The problem is an open circuit between the battery and the bulb. If the fuse is blown and, when replaced, immediately blows again, there is a short circuit in the system which must be located and repaired. If there is a switch in the system, bypass it with a jumper wire. This is done by connecting one end of the jumper wire to the power supply wire into the switch and the other end of the jumper wire to the wire coming out of the switch. If the test light illuminates with the jumper wire installed, the switch or whatever was bypassed is defective.

➡**Never substitute the jumper wire for the bulb, as the bulb is the component required to use the power from the power source.**

5. If the bulb in the test light goes on, then the current is getting to the bulb that is not working in the car. This eliminates the first of the three possible causes. Connect the power supply wire and connect a jumper wire from the bulb to a good metal ground. Do this with the switch which controls the bulb works with jumper wire installed, then it has a bad ground. This is usually caused by the metal area on which the bulb mounts to the vehicle being coated with some type of foreign matter.
6. If neither test located the source of the trouble, then the light bulb itself is defective.
The above test procedure can be applied to any of the compo-

nents of the chassis electrical system by substituting the component that is not working for the light bulb. Remember that for any electrical system to work, all connections must be clean and tight.

TEST EQUIPMENT

➡**Pinpointing the exact cause of trouble in an electrical system can sometimes only be accomplished by the use of special test equipment. The following describes different types of commonly used test equipment and explains how to use them in diagnosis. In addition to the information covered below, the tool manufacturer's instructions booklet (provided with the tester) should be read and clearly understood before attempting any test procedures.**

Jumper Wires

Jumper wires are simple, yet extremely valuable, pieces of test equipment. They are basically test wires which are used to bypass sections of a circuit. The simplest type of jumper wire is a length of multi-strand wire with an alligator clip at each end. Jumper wires are usually fabricated from lengths of standard automotive wire and whatever type of connector (alligator clip, spade connector or pin connector) that is required for the particular vehicle being tested. The well equipped tool box will have several different styles of jumper wires in several different lengths. Some jumper wires are made with three or more terminals coming from a common splice for special purpose testing. In cramped, hard-to-reach areas it is advisable to have insulated boots over the jumper wire terminals in order to prevent accidental grounding, sparks, and possible fire, especially when testing fuel system components.

Jumper wires are used primarily to locate open electrical circuits, on either the ground (−) side of the circuit or on the hot (+) side. If an electrical component fails to operate, connect the jumper wire between the component and a good ground. If the component operates only with the jumper installed, the ground circuit is open. If the ground circuit is good, but the component does not operate, the circuit between the power feed and component may be open. By moving the jumper wire successively back from the lamp toward the power source, you can isolate the area

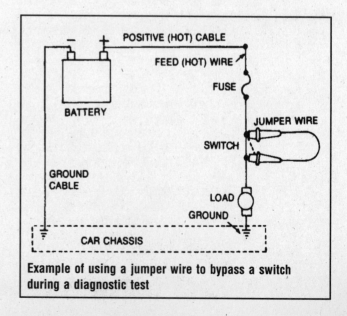

Example of using a jumper wire to bypass a switch during a diagnostic test

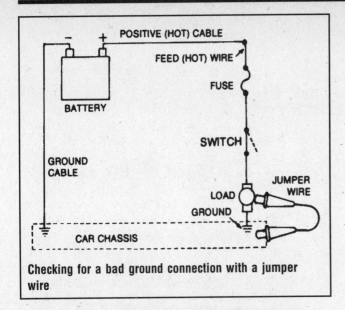

Checking for a bad ground connection with a jumper wire

of the circuit where the open is located. When the component stops functioning, or the power is cut off, the open is in the segment of wire between the jumper and the point previously tested.

You can sometimes connect the jumper wire directly from the battery to the hot terminal of the component, but first make sure the component uses 12 volts in operation. Some electrical components, such as fuel injectors, are designed to operate on about 4 volts and running 12 volts directly to the injector terminals can cause damage.

By inserting an in-line fuse holder between a set of test leads, a fused jumper wire can be used for bypassing open circuits. Use a 5 amp fuse to provide protection against voltage spikes. When in doubt, use a voltmeter to check the voltage input to the component and measure how much voltage is normally being applied.

✳✳ CAUTION

Never use jumpers made from wire that is of lighter gauge than that which is used in the circuit under test. If the jumper wire is of too small a gauge, it may overheat and possibly melt. Never use jumpers to bypass high resistance loads in a circuit. Bypassing resistances, in effect, creates a short circuit. This may, in turn, cause damage and fire. Jumper wires should only be used to bypass lengths of wire.

Unpowered Test Lights

The 12 volt test light is used to check circuits and components while electrical current is flowing through them. It is used for voltage and ground tests. Twelve volt test lights come in different styles but all have three main parts; a ground clip, a probe, and a light. The most commonly used 12 volt test lights have pick-type probes. To use a 12 volt test light, connect the ground clip to a good ground and probe wherever necessary with the pick. The pick should be sharp so that it can be probed into tight spaces.

✳✳ CAUTION

Do not use a test light to probe electronic ignition spark plug or coil wires. Never use a pick-type test light to probe

wiring on computer controlled systems unless specifically instructed to do so. Any wire insulation that is pierced by the test light probe should be taped and sealed with silicone after testing.

Like the jumper wire, the 12 volt test light is used to isolate opens in circuits. But, whereas the jumper wire is used to bypass the open to operate the load, the 12 volt test light is used to locate the presence of voltage in a circuit. If the test light glows, you know that there is power up to that point; if the 12 volt test light does not glow when its probe is inserted into the wire or connector, you know that there is an open circuit (no power). Move the test light in successive steps back toward the power source until the light in the handle does glow. When it glows, the open is between the probe and point which was probed previously.

➡ **The test light does not detect that 12 volts (or any particular amount of voltage) is present; it only detects that some voltage is present. It is advisable before using the test light to touch its terminals across the battery posts to make sure the light is operating properly.**

Self-Powered Test Lights

The self-powered test light usually contains a 1.5 volt penlight battery. One type of self-powered test light is similar in design to the 12 volt unit. This type has both the battery and the light in the handle, along with a pick-type probe tip. The second type has the light toward the open tip, so that the light illuminates the contact point. The self-powered test light is a dual purpose piece of test equipment. It can be used to test for either open or short circuits when power is isolated from the circuit (continuity test). A powered test light should not be used on any computer controlled system or component unless specifically instructed to do so. Many engine sensors can be destroyed by even this small amount of voltage applied directly to the terminals.

Voltmeters

A voltmeter is used to measure voltage at any point in a circuit, or to measure the voltage drop across any part of a circuit. It can also be used to check continuity in a wire or circuit by indicating current flow from one end to the other. Analog voltmeters usually have various scales on the meter dial and a selector switch to allow the selection of different voltages. The voltmeter has a positive and a negative lead. To avoid damage to the meter, always connect the negative lead to the negative (−) side of the circuit (to ground or nearest the ground side of the circuit) and connect the positive lead to the positive (+) side of the circuit (to the power source or the nearest power source). Note that the negative voltmeter lead will always be black and that the positive voltmeter will always be some color other than black (usually red).

Depending on how the voltmeter is connected into the circuit, it has several uses. A voltmeter can be connected either in parallel or in series with a circuit and it has a very high resistance to current flow. When connected in parallel, only a small amount of current will flow through the voltmeter current path; the rest will flow through the normal circuit current path and the circuit will work normally. When the voltmeter is connected in series with a circuit, only a small amount of current can flow through the circuit. The circuit will not work properly, but the voltmeter reading will show if the circuit is complete or not.

Ohmmeters

The ohmmeter is designed to read resistance (which is measured in ohms or Ω) in a circuit or component. Although there are several different styles of ohmmeters, all analog meters will usually have a selector switch which permits the measurement of different ranges of resistance (usually the selector switch allows the multiplication of the meter reading by 10, 100, 1000, and 10,000). A calibration knob allows the meter to be set at zero for accurate measurement. Since all ohmmeters are powered by an internal battery, the ohmmeter can be used as a self-powered test light. When the ohmmeter is connected, current from the ohmmeter flows through the circuit or component being tested. Since the ohmmeter's internal resistance and voltage are known values, the amount of current flow through the meter depends on the resistance of the circuit or component being tested.

The ohmmeter can be used to perform a continuity test for opens or shorts (either by observation of the meter needle or as a self-powered test light), and to read actual resistance in a circuit. It should be noted that the ohmmeter is used to check the resistance of a component or wire while there is no voltage applied to the circuit. Current flow from an outside voltage source (such as the vehicle battery) can damage the ohmmeter, so the circuit or component should be isolated from the vehicle electrical system before any testing is done. Since the ohmmeter uses its own voltage source, either lead can be connected to any test point.

➡ **When checking diodes or other solid state components, the ohmmeter leads can only be connected one way in order to measure current flow in a single direction. Make sure the positive (+) and negative (−) terminal connections are as described in the test procedures to verify the one-way diode operation.**

In using the meter for making continuity checks, do not be concerned with the actual resistance readings. Zero resistance, or any ohm reading, indicates continuity in the circuit. Infinite resistance indicates an open in the circuit. A high resistance reading where there should be none indicates a problem in the circuit. Checks for short circuits are made in the same manner as checks for open circuits except that the circuit must be isolated from both power and normal ground. Infinite resistance indicates no continuity to ground, while zero resistance indicates a dead short to ground.

Ammeters

An ammeter measures the amount of current flowing through a circuit in units called amperes or amps. Amperes are units of electron flow which indicate how fast the electrons are flowing through the circuit. Since Ohms Law dictates that current flow in a circuit is equal to the circuit voltage divided by the total circuit resistance, increasing voltage also increases the current level (amps). Likewise, any decrease in resistance will increase the amount of amps in a circuit. At normal operating voltage, most circuits have a characteristic amount of amperes, called "current draw" which can be measured using an ammeter. By referring to a specified current draw rating, measuring the amperes, and comparing the two values, one can determine what is happening within the circuit to aid in diagnosis. An open circuit, for example, will not allow any current to flow so the ammeter reading will be zero. More current flows through a heavily loaded circuit or when the charging system is operating.

An ammeter is always connected in series with the circuit being tested. All of the current that normally flows through the circuit must also flow through the ammeter; if there is any other path for the current to follow, the ammeter reading will not be accurate. The ammeter itself has very little resistance to current flow and therefore will not affect the circuit, but it will measure current draw only when the circuit is closed and electricity is flowing. Excessive current draw can blow fuses and drain the battery, while a reduced current draw can cause motors to run slowly, lights to dim and other components to not operate properly. The ammeter can help diagnose these conditions by locating the cause of the high or low reading.

Multimeters

Different combinations of test meters can be built into a single unit designed for specific tests. Some of the more common combination test devices are known as Volt/Amp testers, Tach/Dwell meters, or Digital Multimeters. The Volt/Amp tester is used for charging system, starting system or battery tests and consists of a voltmeter, an ammeter and a variable resistance carbon pile. The voltmeter will usually have at least two ranges for use with 6, 12 and/or 24 volt systems. The ammeter also has more than one range for testing various levels of battery loads and starter current draw. The carbon pile can be adjusted to offer different amounts of resistance. The Volt/Amp tester has heavy leads to carry large amounts of current and many later models have an inductive ammeter pickup that clamps around the wire to simplify test connections. On some models, the ammeter also has a zero-center scale to allow testing of charging and starting systems without switching leads or polarity. A digital multimeter is a voltmeter, ammeter and ohmmeter combined in an instrument which gives a digital readout. These are often used when testing solid state circuits because of their high input impedance (usually 10 megohms or more).

The tach/dwell meter that combines a tachometer and a dwell (cam angle) meter is a specialized kind of voltmeter. The tachometer scale is marked to show engine speed in rpm and the dwell scale is marked to show degrees of distributor shaft rotation. In most electronic ignition systems, dwell is determined by the control unit, but the dwell meter can also be used to check the duty cycle (operation) of some electronic engine control systems. Some tach/dwell meters are powered by an internal battery, while others take their power from the vehicle battery in use. The battery powered testers usually require calibration (much like an ohmmeter) before testing.

TESTING

Open Circuits

To use the self-powered test light or a multimeter to check for open circuits, first isolate the circuit from the vehicle's 12 volt power source by disconnecting the battery or wiring harness connector. Connect the test light or ohmmeter ground clip to a good ground and probe sections of the circuit sequentially with the test light. (start from either end of the circuit). If the light is out/or there is infinite resistance, the open is between the probe and the circuit ground. If the light is on/or the meter shows continuity, the open is between the probe and end of the circuit toward the power source.

Short Circuits

By isolating the circuit both from power and from ground, and using a self-powered test light or multimeter, you can check for shorts to ground in the circuit. Isolate the circuit from power and ground. Connect the test light or ohmmeter ground clip to a good ground and probe any easy-to-reach test point in the circuit. If the light comes on or there is continuity, there is a short somewhere in the circuit. To isolate the short, probe a test point at either end of the isolated circuit (the light should be on/there should be continuity). Leave the test light probe engaged and open connectors, switches, remove parts, etc., sequentially, until the light goes out/continuity is broken. When the light goes out, the short is between the last circuit component opened and the previous circuit opened.

➡️**The battery in the test light and does not provide much current. A weak battery may not provide enough power to illuminate the test light even when a complete circuit is made (especially if there are high resistances in the circuit). Always make sure that the test battery is strong. To check the battery, briefly touch the ground clip to the probe; if the light glows brightly the battery is strong enough for testing. Never use a self-powered test light to perform checks for opens or shorts when power is applied to the electrical system under test. The 12 volt vehicle power will quickly burn out the light bulb in the test light.**

Available Voltage Measurement

Set the voltmeter selector switch to the 20V position and connect the meter negative lead to the negative post of the battery. Connect the positive meter lead to the positive post of the battery and turn the ignition switch **ON** to provide a load. Read the voltage on the meter or digital display. A well charged battery should register over 12 volts. If the meter reads below 11.5 volts, the battery power may be insufficient to operate the electrical system properly. This test determines voltage available from the battery and should be the first step in any electrical trouble diagnosis procedure. Many electrical problems, especially on computer controlled systems, can be caused by a low state of charge in the battery. Excessive corrosion at the battery cable terminals can cause a poor contact that will prevent proper charging and full battery current flow.

Normal battery voltage is 12 volts when fully charged. When the battery is supplying current to one or more circuits it is said to be "under load." When everything is off the electrical system is under a "no-load" condition. A fully charged battery may show about 12.5 volts at no load; will drop to 12 volts under medium load; and will drop even lower under heavy load. If the battery is partially discharged the voltage decrease under heavy load may be excessive, even though the battery shows 12 volts or more at no load. When allowed to discharge further, the battery's available voltage under load will decrease more severely. For this reason, it is important that the battery be fully charged during all testing procedures to avoid errors in diagnosis and incorrect test results.

Voltage Drop

When current flows through a resistance, the voltage beyond the resistance is reduced (the larger the current, the greater the reduction in voltage). When no current is flowing, there is no voltage drop because there is no current flow. All points in the circuit which are connected to the power source are at the same voltage as the power source. The total voltage drop always equals the total source voltage. In a long circuit with many connectors, a series of small, unwanted voltage drops due to corrosion at the connectors can add up to a total loss of voltage which impairs the operation of the normal loads in the circuit. The maximum allowable voltage drop under load is critical, especially if there is more than one high resistance problem in a circuit because all voltage drops are cumulative. A small drop is normal due to the resistance of the conductors.

INDIRECT COMPUTATION OF VOLTAGE DROPS

1. Set the voltmeter selector switch to the 20 volt position.
2. Connect the meter negative lead to a good ground.
3. While operating the circuit, probe all loads in the circuit with the positive meter lead and observe the voltage readings. A drop should be noticed after the first load. But, there should be little or no voltage drop before the first load.

DIRECT MEASUREMENT OF VOLTAGE DROPS

1. Set the voltmeter switch to the 20 volt position.
2. Connect the voltmeter negative lead to the ground side of the load to be measured.
3. Connect the positive lead to the positive side of the resistance or load to be measured.
4. Read the voltage drop directly on the 20 volt scale.

Too high a voltage indicates too high a resistance. If, for example, a blower motor runs too slowly, you can determine if perhaps there is too high a resistance in the resistor pack. By taking voltage drop readings in all parts of the circuit, you can isolate the problem. Too low a voltage drop indicates too low a resistance. Take the blower motor for example again. If a blower motor runs too fast in the MED and/or LOW position, the problem might be isolated in the resistor pack by taking voltage drop readings in all parts of the circuit to locate a possibly shorted resistor.

HIGH RESISTANCE TESTING

1. Set the voltmeter selector switch to the 4 volt position.
2. Connect the voltmeter positive lead to the positive post of the battery.
3. Turn on the headlights and heater blower to provide a load.
4. Probe various points in the circuit with the negative voltmeter lead.
5. Read the voltage drop on the 4 volt scale. Some average maximum allowable voltage drops are:
- FUSE PANEL: 0.7 volts
- IGNITION SWITCH: 0.5 volts
- HEADLIGHT SWITCH: 0.7 volts
- IGNITION COIL (+): 0.5 volts
- ANY OTHER LOAD: 1.3 volts

➡️**Voltage drops are all measured while a load is operating; without current flow, there will be no voltage drop.**

Resistance Measurement

The batteries in an ohmmeter will weaken with age and temperature, so the ohmmeter must be calibrated or "zeroed" before taking measurements. To zero the meter, place the selector switch in its lowest range and touch the two ohmmeter leads together. Turn the calibration knob until the meter needle is exactly on zero.

➡All analog (needle) type ohmmeters must be zeroed before use, but some digital ohmmeter models are automatically calibrated when the switch is turned on. Self-calibrating digital ohmmeters do not have an adjusting knob, but its a good idea to check for a zero readout before use by touching the leads together. All computer controlled systems require the use of a digital ohmmeter with at least 10 megohms impedance for testing. Before any test procedures are attempted, make sure the ohmmeter used is compatible with the electrical system or damage to the on-board computer could result.

To measure resistance, first isolate the circuit from the vehicle power source by disconnecting the battery cables or the harness connector. Make sure the key is **OFF** when disconnecting any components or the battery. Where necessary, also isolate at least one side of the circuit to be checked in order to avoid reading parallel resistances. Parallel circuit resistances will always give a lower reading than the actual resistance of either of the branches. When measuring the resistance of parallel circuits, the total resistance will always be lower than the smallest resistance in the circuit. Connect the meter leads to both sides of the circuit (wire or component) and read the actual measured ohms on the meter scale. Make sure the selector switch is set to the proper ohm scale for the circuit being tested to avoid misreading the ohmmeter test value.

※※ WARNING

Never use an ohmmeter with power applied to the circuit. Like the self-powered test light, the ohmmeter is designed to operate on its own power supply. The normal 12 volt automotive electrical system current could damage the meter!

Wiring Harnesses

The average automobile contains about ½ mile of wiring, with hundreds of individual connections. To protect the many wires from damage and to keep them from becoming a confusing tangle, they are organized into bundles, enclosed in plastic or taped together and called wiring harnesses. Different harnesses serve different parts of the vehicle. Individual wires are color coded to help trace them through a harness where sections are hidden from view.

Automotive wiring or circuit conductors can be in any one of three forms:
1. Single strand wire
2. Multi-strand wire
3. Printed circuitry

Single strand wire has a solid metal core and is usually used inside such components as alternators, motors, relays and other devices. Multi-strand wire has a core made of many small strands of wire twisted together into a single conductor. Most of the wiring in an automotive electrical system is made up of multi-strand wire, either as a single conductor or grouped together in a harness. All wiring is color coded on the insulator, either as a solid color or as a colored wire with an identification stripe. A printed circuit is a thin film of copper or other conductor that is printed on an insulator backing. Occasionally, a printed circuit is sandwiched between two sheets of plastic for more protection and flexibility. A complete printed circuit, consisting of conductors, insulat-

ing material and connectors for lamps or other components is called a printed circuit board. Printed circuitry is used in place of individual wires or harnesses in places where space is limited, such as behind instrument panels.

Since automotive electrical systems are very sensitive to changes in resistance, the selection of properly sized wires is critical when systems are repaired. A loose or corroded connection or a replacement wire that is too small for the circuit will add extra resistance and an additional voltage drop to the circuit. A ten percent voltage drop can result in slow or erratic motor operation, for example, even though the circuit is complete. The wire gauge number is an expression of the cross-section area of the conductor. The most common system for expressing wire size is the American Wire Gauge (AWG) system.

Gauge numbers are assigned to conductors of various cross-section areas. As gauge number increases, area decreases and the conductor becomes smaller. A 5 gauge conductor is smaller than a 1 gauge conductor and a 10 gauge is smaller than a 5 gauge. As the cross-section area of a conductor decreases, resistance increases and so does the gauge number. A conductor with a higher gauge number will carry less current than a conductor with a lower gauge number.

➡Gauge wire size refers to the size of the conductor, not the size of the complete wire. It is possible to have two wires of the same gauge with different diameters because one may have thicker insulation than the other.

12 volt automotive electrical systems generally use 10, 12, 14, 16 and 18 gauge wire. Main power distribution circuits and larger accessories usually use 10 and 12 gauge wire. Battery cables are usually 4 or 6 gauge, although 1 and 2 gauge wires are occasionally used. Wire length must also be considered when making repairs to a circuit. As conductor length increases, so does resistance. An 18 gauge wire, for example, can carry a 10 amp load for 10 feet without excessive voltage drop; however if a 15 foot wire is required for the same 10 amp load, it must be a 16 gauge wire.

An electrical schematic shows the electrical current paths when a circuit is operating properly. It is essential to understand how a circuit works before trying to figure out why it doesn't. Schematics break the entire electrical system down into individual circuits and show only one particular circuit. In a schematic, no attempt is made to represent wiring and components as they physically appear on the vehicle; switches and other components are shown as simply as possible. Face views of harness connectors show the cavity or terminal locations in all multi-pin connectors to help locate test points.

If you need to backprobe a connector while it is on the component, the order of the terminals must be mentally reversed. The wire color code can help in this situation, as well as a keyway, lock tab or other reference mark.

WIRING REPAIR

Soldering is a quick, efficient method of joining metals permanently. Everyone who has the occasion to make wiring repairs should know how to solder. Electrical connections that are soldered are far less likely to come apart and will conduct electricity much better than connections that are only "pig-tailed" together. The most popular (and preferred) method of soldering is with an electrical soldering gun. Soldering irons are available in many sizes and wattage ratings. Irons with higher wattage ratings deliver higher temperatures and recover lost heat faster. A small soldering iron rated for no more than 50 watts is recommended, especially on electrical systems where excess heat can damage the components being soldered.

There are three ingredients necessary for successful soldering; proper flux, good solder and sufficient heat. A soldering flux is necessary to clean the metal of tarnish, prepare it for soldering and to enable the solder to spread into tiny crevices. When soldering, always use a rosin core solder which is non-corrosive and will not attract moisture once the job is finished. Other types of flux (acid core) will leave a residue that will attract moisture and cause the wires to corrode. Tin is a unique metal with a low melting point. In a molten state, it dissolves and alloys easily with many metals. Solder is made by mixing tin with lead. The most common proportions are 40/60, 50/50 and 60/40, with the percentage of tin listed first. Low priced solders usually contain less tin, making them very difficult for a beginner to use because more heat is required to melt the solder. A common solder is 40/60 which is well suited for all-around general use, but 60/40 melts easier and is preferred for electrical work.

Soldering Techniques

Successful soldering requires that the metals to be joined be heated to a temperature that will melt the solder, usually 360–460°F (182–238°C). Contrary to popular belief, the purpose of the soldering iron is not to melt the solder itself, but to heat the parts being soldered to a temperature high enough to melt the solder when it is touched to the work. Melting flux-cored solder on the soldering iron will usually destroy the effectiveness of the flux.

➡ **Soldering tips are made of copper for good heat conductivity, but must be "tinned" regularly for quick transference of heat to the project and to prevent the solder from sticking to the iron. To "tin" the iron, simply heat it and touch the flux-cored solder to the tip; the solder will flow over the hot tip. Wipe the excess off with a clean rag, but be careful as the iron will be hot.**

After some use, the tip may become pitted. If so, simply dress the tip smooth with a smooth file and "tin" the tip again. Flux-cored solder will remove oxides but rust, bits of insulation and oil or grease must be removed with a wire brush or emery cloth. For maximum strength in soldered parts, the joint must start off clean and tight. Weak joints will result in gaps too wide for the solder to bridge.

If a separate soldering flux is used, it should be brushed or swabbed on only those areas that are to be soldered. Most solders contain a core of flux and separate fluxing is unnecessary. Hold the work to be soldered firmly. It is best to solder on a wooden board, because a metal vise will only rob the piece to be soldered of heat and make it difficult to melt the solder. Hold the soldering tip with the broadest face against the work to be soldered. Apply solder under the tip close to the work, using enough solder to give a heavy film between the iron and the piece being soldered, while moving slowly and making sure the solder melts properly. Keep the work level or the solder will run to the lowest part and favor the thicker parts, because these require more heat to melt the solder. If the soldering tip overheats (the solder coating on the face of the tip burns up), it should be retinned. Once the soldering is completed, let the soldered joint stand until cool. Tape and seal all soldered wire splices after the repair has cooled.

Wire Harness Connectors

Most connectors in the engine compartment or that are otherwise exposed to the elements are protected against moisture and dirt which could create oxidation and deposits on the terminals.

These special connectors are weather-proof. All repairs require the use of a special terminal and the tool required to service it. This tool is used to remove the pin and sleeve terminals. If removal is attempted with an ordinary pick, there is a good chance that the terminal will be bent or deformed. Unlike standard blade type terminals, these weather-proof terminals cannot be straightened once they are bent. Make certain that the connectors are properly seated and all of the sealing rings are in place when connecting leads. On some models, a hinge-type flap provides a backup or secondary locking feature for the terminals. Most secondary locks are used to improve connector reliability by retaining the terminals if the small terminal lock tangs are not positioned properly.

Molded-on connectors require complete replacement of the connection. This means splicing a new connector assembly into the harness. All splices should be soldered to insure proper contact. Use care when probing the connections or replacing terminals in them as it is possible to short between opposite terminals. If this happens to the wrong terminal pair, it is possible to damage certain components. Always use jumper wires between connectors for circuit checking and never probe through weatherproof seals.

Open circuits are often difficult to locate by sight because corrosion or terminal misalignment are hidden by the connectors. Merely wiggling a connector on a sensor or in the wiring harness may correct the open circuit condition. This should always be considered when an open circuit or a failed sensor is indicated. Intermittent problems may also be caused by oxidized or loose connections. When using a circuit tester for diagnosis, always probe connections from the wire side. Be careful not to damage sealed connectors with test probes.

All wiring harnesses should be replaced with identical parts, using the same gauge wire and connectors. When signal wires are spliced into a harness, use wire with high temperature insulation only. It is seldom necessary to replace a complete harness. If replacement is necessary, pay close attention to insure proper harness routing. Secure the harness with suitable plastic wire clamps to prevent vibrations from causing the harness to wear in spots or contact any hot components.

➡ **Weatherproof connectors cannot be replaced with standard connectors. Instructions are provided with replacement connector and terminal packages. Some wire harnesses have mounting indicators (usually pieces of colored tape) to mark where the harness is to be secured.**

In making wiring repairs, its important that you always replace damaged wires with wiring of the same gauge as the wire being replaced. The heavier the wire, the smaller the gauge number. Wires are color-coded to aid in identification and whenever possible the same color coded wire should be used for replacement. A wire stripping and crimping tool is necessary to install solderless terminal connectors. Test all crimps by pulling on the wires; it should not be possible to pull the wires out of a good crimp.

Wires which are open, exposed or otherwise damaged are repaired by simple splicing. Where possible, if the wiring harness is accessible and the damaged place in the wire can be located, it is best to open the harness and check for all possible damage. In an inaccessible harness, the wire must be bypassed with a new insert, usually taped to the outside of the old harness.

When replacing fusible links, be sure to use fusible link wire, NOT ordinary automotive wire. Make sure the fusible segment is of the same gauge and construction as the one being replaced and double the stripped end when crimping the terminal connector for a good contact. The melted (open) fusible link segment of the wiring harness should be cut off as close to the harness as possible, then a new segment spliced in as described. In the case of a damaged fusible link that feeds two harness wires, the harness connections should be replaced with two fusible link wires so that each circuit will have its own separate protection.

➡**Most of the problems caused in the wiring harness are due to bad ground connections. Always check all vehicle ground connections for corrosion or looseness before performing any power feed checks to eliminate the chance of a bad ground affecting the circuit.**

Hard-Shell Connectors

Unlike molded connectors, the terminal contacts in hard-shell connectors can be replaced. Weatherproof hard-shell connectors with the leads molded into the shell have non-replaceable terminal ends. Replacement usually involves the use of a special terminal removal tool that depresses the locking tangs (barbs) on the connector terminal and allows the connector to be removed from the rear of the shell. The connector shell should be replaced if it shows any evidence of burning, melting, cracks, or breaks. Replace individual terminals that are burnt, corroded, distorted or loose.

➡**The insulation crimp must be tight to prevent the insulation from sliding back on the wire when the wire is pulled. The insulation must be visibly compressed under the crimp tabs, and the ends of the crimp should be turned in for a firm grip on the insulation.**

The wire crimp must be made with all wire strands inside the crimp. The terminal must be fully compressed on the wire strands with the ends of the crimp tabs turned in to make a firm grip on the wire. Check all connections with an ohmmeter to insure a good contact. There should be no measurable resistance between the wire and the terminal when connected.

Fusible Links

The fuse link is a short length of special, Hypalon (high temperature) insulated wire, integral with the engine compartment wiring harness and should not be confused with standard wire. It is several wire gauges smaller than the circuit which it protects. Under no circumstances should a fuse link replacement repair be made using a length of standard wire cut from bulk stock or from another wiring harness.

To repair any blown fuse link use the following procedure:

1. Determine which circuit is damaged, its location and the cause of the open fuse link. If the damaged fuse link is one of three fed by a common No. 10 or 12 gauge feed wire, determine the specific affected circuit.

2. Disconnect the negative battery cable.

3. Cut the damaged fuse link from the wiring harness and discard it. If the fuse link is one of three circuits fed by a single feed wire, cut it out of the harness at each splice end and discard it.

4. Identify and procure the proper fuse link with butt connectors for attaching the fuse link to the harness.

➡**Heat shrink tubing must be slipped over the wire before crimping and soldering the connection.**

5. To repair any fuse link in a 3-link group with one feed:

a. After cutting the open link out of the harness, cut each of the remaining undamaged fuse links close to the feed wire weld.

b. Strip approximately ½ in. (13mm) of insulation from the detached ends of the two good fuse links. Insert two wire ends into one end of a butt connector, then carefully push one stripped end of the replacement fuse link into the same end of the butt connector and crimp all three firmly together.

➡**Care must be taken when fitting the three fuse links into the butt connector as the internal diameter is a snug fit for three wires. Make sure to use a proper crimping tool. Pliers, side cutters, etc. will not apply the proper crimp to retain the wires and withstand a pull test.**

c. After crimping the butt connector to the three fuse links, cut the weld portion from the feed wire and strip approximately ½ in. (13mm) of insulation from the cut end. Insert the stripped end into the open end of the butt connector and crimp very firmly.

d. To attach the remaining end of the replacement fuse link, strip approximately ½ in. (13mm) of insulation from the wire end of the circuit from which the blown fuse link was removed, and firmly crimp a butt connector or equivalent to the stripped wire. Then, insert the end of the replacement link into the other end of the butt connector and crimp firmly.

e. Using rosin core solder with a consistency of 60 percent tin and 40 percent lead, solder the connectors and the wires at the repairs then insulate with electrical tape or heat shrink tubing.

6. To replace any fuse link on a single circuit in a harness, cut out the damaged portion, strip approximately ½ in. (13mm) of insulation from the two wire ends and attach the appropriate replacement fuse link to the stripped wire ends with two proper size butt connectors. Solder the connectors and wires, then insulate.

7. To repair any fuse link which has an eyelet terminal on one end such as the charging circuit, cut off the open fuse link behind the weld, strip approximately ½ in. (13mm) of insulation from the cut end and attach the appropriate new eyelet fuse link to the cut stripped wire with an appropriate size butt connector. Solder the connectors and wires at the repair, then insulate.

8. Connect the negative battery cable to the battery and test the system for proper operation.

➡**Do not mistake a resistor wire for a fuse link. The resistor wire is generally longer and has print stating, "Resistor-don't cut or splice."**

When attaching a single No. 16, 17, 18 or 20 gauge fuse link to a heavy gauge wire, always double the stripped wire end of the fuse link before inserting and crimping it into the butt connector for positive wire retention.

Add-On Electrical Equipment

The electrical system in your vehicle is designed to perform under reasonable operating conditions without interference between components. Before any additional electrical equipment is installed, it is recommended that you consult your dealer or a reputable repair facility that is familiar with the vehicle and its systems.

If the vehicle is equipped with mobile radio equipment and/or

REMOVE EXISTING VINYL TUBE SHIELDING
REINSTALL OVER FUSE LINK BEFORE CRIMPING
FUSE LINK TO WIRE ENDS

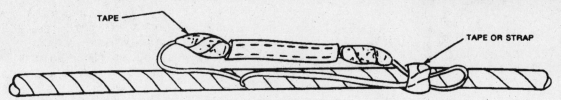

TYPICAL REPAIR USING THE SPECIAL #17 GA. (9.00" LONG-YELLOW) FUSE LINK REQUIRED FOR THE AIR/COND.
CIRCUITS (2) #687E and #261A LOCATED IN THE ENGINE COMPARTMENT

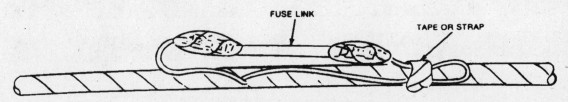

TYPICAL REPAIR FOR ANY IN-LINE FUSE LINK USING THE SPECIFIED GAUGE FUSE LINK FOR THE SPECIFIC CIRCUIT

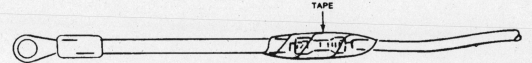

TYPICAL REPAIR USING THE EYELET TERMINAL FUSE LINK OF THE SPECIFIED GAUGE FOR ATTACHMENT TO A CIRCUIT WIRE END

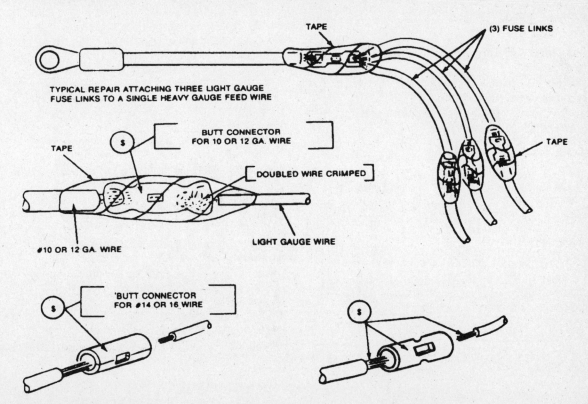

TYPICAL REPAIR ATTACHING THREE LIGHT GAUGE
FUSE LINKS TO A SINGLE HEAVY GAUGE FEED WIRE

FUSIBLE LINK REPAIR PROCEDURE

General fusible link repair—never replace a fusible link with regular wire or a fusible link rated at a higher amperage than the one being replaced

mobile telephone, it may have an effect upon the operation of any on-board computer control modules. Radio Frequency Interference (RFI) from the communications system can be picked up by the vehicle's wiring harnesses and conducted into the control module, giving it the wrong messages at the wrong time. Although well shielded against RFI, the computer should be further protected by taking the following measures:

• Install the antenna as far as possible from the control module. For instance, if the module is located behind the center console area, then the antenna should be mounted at the rear of the vehicle.

• Keep the antenna wiring a minimum of eight inches away from any wiring running to control modules and from the module itself. NEVER wind the antenna wire around any other wiring.

• Mount the equipment as far from the control module as possible. Be very careful during installation not to drill through any wires or short a wire harness with a mounting screw.

• Insure that the electrical feed wire(s) to the equipment are properly and tightly connected. Loose connectors can cause interference.

• Make certain that the equipment is properly grounded to the vehicle. Poor grounding can damage expensive equipment.

HEATER

Blower Motor

REMOVAL & INSTALLATION

▶ **See Figure 1**

Lemans and Grand Am

1. Disconnect the blower motor feed wire and the ground wire.
2. Disconnect the air line from the blower motor case.
3. Remove the blower motor retaining screws and remove the motor.
4. To replace, reverse the removal procedure.

Ventura, Phoenix Through 1979

1. Disconnect the battery.
2. Detach the heater hoses from the clips on the right front fender skirt.
3. Raise the car and remove all fender skirt attaching bolts except those which attach the skirt to the radiator support.
4. Pull down on the skirt and block the skirt out to provide clearance for removal of the blower motor.
5. Disconnect the electrical wiring from the motor.
6. Remove the attaching screws and remove the blower motor. Pry the motor flange gently if the sealer acts as an adhesive.
7. Remove the blower impeller retaining nut and separate the motor from the impeller.
8. To replace, reverse the removal procedure.

Grand Prix through 1976

1. Disconnect the power wire.
2. Remove the motor retaining screws.
3. Remove the motor.
4. To install, reverse the removal procedure.

1977 and Later Grand Prix

1. Disconnect the electrical connections from the blower motor.
2. Remove the blower motor flange screws and remove the motor assembly from the heater case.
3. The installation is in the reverse of the removal procedure.

Heater Core

REMOVAL & INSTALLATION

▶ **See Figures 2, 3 and 4 (pp. 15–16)**

1974–77 GTO, LeMans and Grand Am

WITHOUT AIR CONDITIONING

1. Drain the radiator.
2. Disconnect the heater hoses at the air inlet assembly.
3. Remove nuts from core studs on firewall (under hood). Remove the glove box.

➡ **On 1977 LeMans, remove glove box and door, then remove heater outlet from case. Remove defroster duct screw on all models.**

4. From inside the car, pull the heater assembly from the firewall.
5. Disconnect control cables and wires, then remove heater assembly.
6. To remove core, unhook retaining springs or strips.
7. To install, reverse removal procedure, making sure core is properly sealed during installation.

WITH AIR CONDITIONING

1. Drain the coolant.
2. Disconnect the water hoses at the heater core tubes to prevent spilling coolant during removal.
3. Remove the glove compartment.
4. Remove the cold air duct and heater outlet.
5. Remove the defroster duct attaching screw.
6. Remove the screws and nuts which retain the case to the dash. Remove the blower motor resistor to gain access to the upper retaining nut inside the evaporator case.
7. Move the core and case assembly rearward to free the attaching studs from the cowl and remove the core and case assembly.
8. Disconnect the temperature cable and vacuum hoses from the core and case assembly.

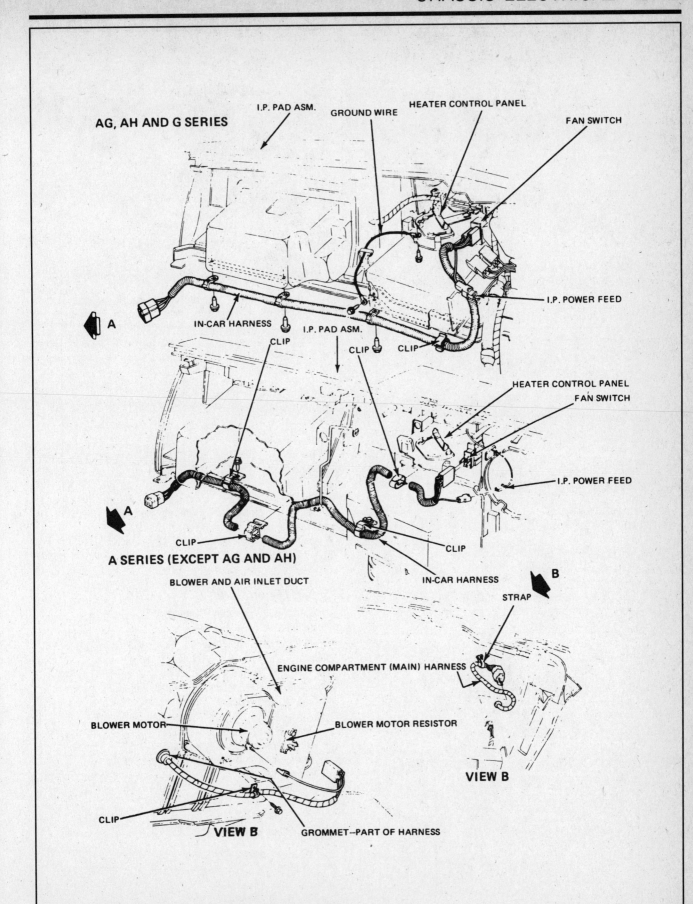

AG, AH AND G SERIES

I.P. PAD ASM.

GROUND WIRE

HEATER CONTROL PANEL

FAN SWITCH

A

IN-CAR HARNESS

I.P. PAD ASM.

CLIP

CLIP

I.P. POWER FEED

CLIP

CLIP

A

A SERIES (EXCEPT AG AND AH)

CLIP

HEATER CONTROL PANEL

FAN SWITCH

I.P. POWER FEED

CLIP

IN-CAR HARNESS

B

STRAP

BLOWER AND AIR INLET DUCT

ENGINE COMPARTMENT (MAIN) HARNESS

BLOWER MOTOR

BLOWER MOTOR RESISTOR

VIEW B

CLIP

VIEW B

GROMMET—PART OF HARNESS

Fig. 1 Heater wire harness routing—LeMans and Grand Prix

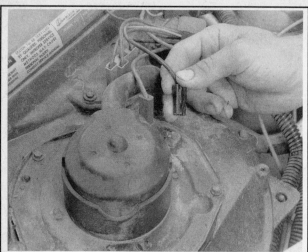

To remove the blower motor, detach the electrical connections

. . . then pull the blower motor up, out of its case

Disconnect the air hose from the blower motor case

Remove the blower motor retaining bolts . . .

9. Remove the core and case assembly from the car.
10. Remove the heater core retaining screws and core.
11. Reverse the above steps for installation.

1978–81 LeMans and Grand Am

WITHOUT AIR CONDITIONING

1. On some vehicles, it may be necessary to remove the lower windshield trim, rubber seals and/or screens for access to the heater core.
2. Disconnect the hoses from the core tubes. Plug them to avoid coolant loss.
3. On the engine side of the firewall, remove the heater core cover from the case.
4. Remove the core bracket and ground screw.
5. Lift out the core.
6. Reverse the procedure for installation.

WITH AIR CONDITIONING

1. Operate the wipers to the up position.
2. Disconnect the hoses at the core tubes.
3. Remove the sealing material and screens from the cooling module.
4. Disconnect all wires from the case.
5. Move the lower windshield reverse molding out of the way.
6. Tape a strip of wood to the lower edge of the glass for protection.
7. Remove the module core cover screws.
8. Cut the cover seal with a knife.
9. Pry the cover off from the side, not from the top.
10. Lift out the core.
11. Installation is the reverse of removal. Use all new sealer when installing.

1975–79 Ventura, Phoenix

1. Disconnect battery.
2. Drain radiator, disconnect heater hoses at core and plug core tubes.
3. Remove nuts from core case studs on firewall.
4. Remove glove box and glove box door.

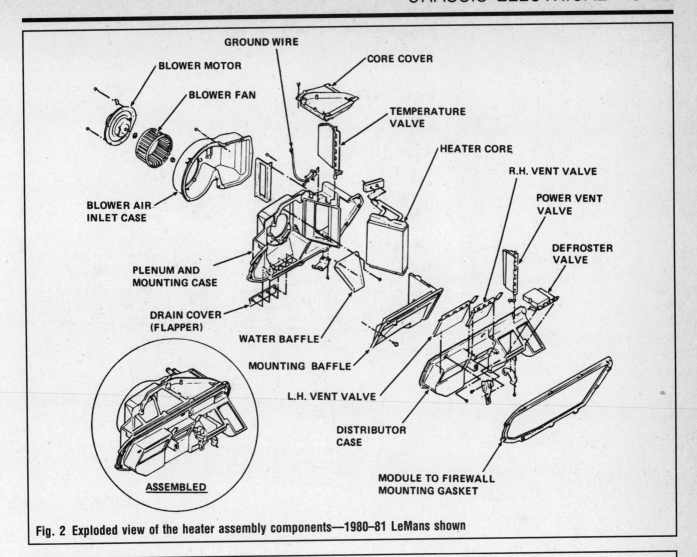

Fig. 2 Exploded view of the heater assembly components—1980–81 LeMans shown

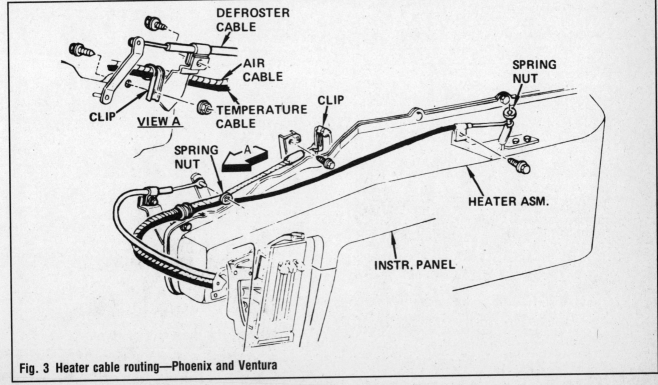

Fig. 3 Heater cable routing—Phoenix and Ventura

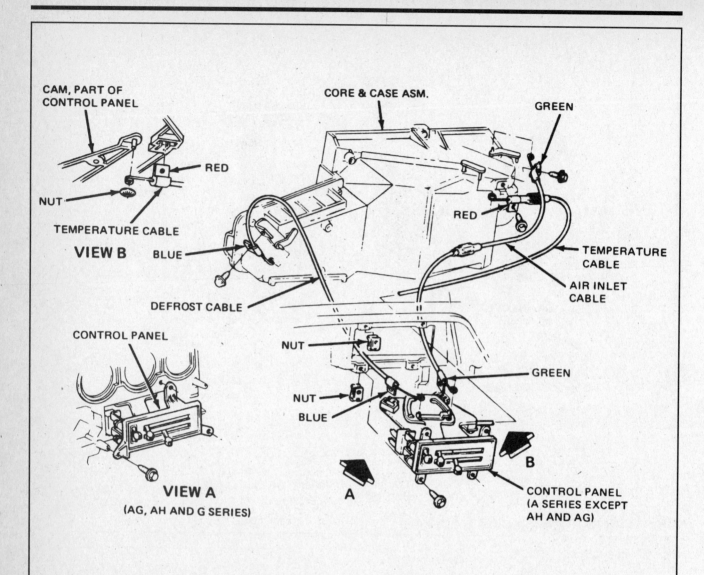

CAM, PART OF
CONTROL PANEL

CORE & CASE ASM.

GREEN

RED

NUT

RED

TEMPERATURE CABLE

TEMPERATURE
CABLE

VIEW B

BLUE

AIR INLET
CABLE

DEFROST CABLE

CONTROL PANEL

NUT

GREEN

NUT

BLUE

VIEW A

(AG, AH AND G SERIES)

A

B

CONTROL PANEL
(A SERIES EXCEPT
AH AND AG)

Fig. 4 Heater control cable and panel mounting—LeMans and Grand Prix

To remove the heater core, unfasten the lower
windshield trim panel screws . . .

. . . then remove the lower windshield trim panel

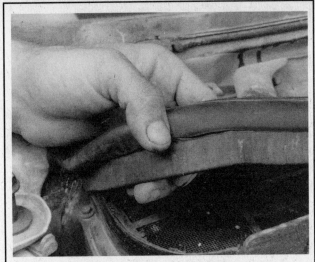

Remove the rubber seal from around the cowl screen

. . . then remove the cowl screen

If necessary, disconnect the windshield washer hose

Unfasten the windshield cowl screen retainers . . .

Unfasten the heater case cover retaining bolts . . .

. . . then remove the heater case cover assembly

. . . then disconnect the heater hoses from the core

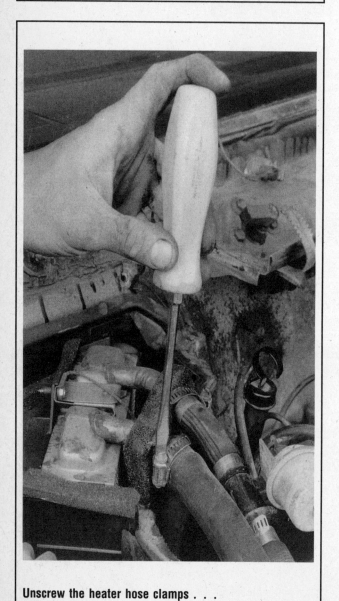

Unscrew the heater hose clamps . . .

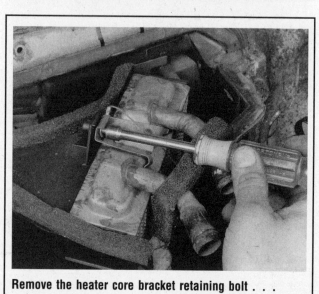

Remove the heater core bracket retaining bolt . . .

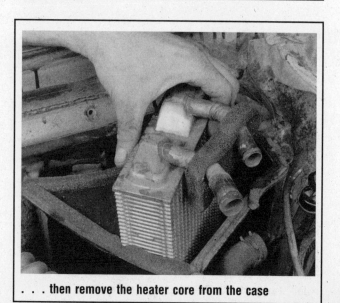

. . . then remove the heater core from the case

5. From inside car, drill out lower right-hand heater case stud with ¼ in. drill.

6. Pull entire heater case, with core, from firewall.

7. Disconnect cables and blower resistor connector, then remove case from car.

8. Remove core from case.

9. To install, reverse removal procedure. Use sealer around core and replace drilled stud with new screw and stamped nut.

Grand Prix through 1976

WITHOUT AIR CONDITIONING

1. Drain the radiator.
2. Disconnect the heater hoses at the air inlet assembly.

➡**The water pump hose goes to the right-hand heater core pipe, the other hose (from rear of right cylinder head) goes to the left-hand heater core pipe.**

3. Remove the nuts from the core studs on the firewall (under hood). Remove the glove compartment.

4. From inside the car, remove the defroster nozzle retaining screw from the heater case and pull the heater assembly from the firewall.

5. Disconnect the control cables, vacuum hoses and wires, then remove the heater assembly.

6. Remove the core.

7. To install, reverse the removal procedure, making sure the core is properly sealed during installation.

WITH AIR CONDITIONING

1. Drain the radiator.
2. Disconnect the heater hoses.
3. Remove the retaining nuts from the core case studs on the engine side of the firewall.
4. Remove the glove box.
5. Remove the defroster duct retaining screw from the heater case and pull the heater assembly from the firewall.
6. Disconnect the heater control cables and wires.
7. Remove the core tube seal and core assembly retaining strips and remove the core.
8. Reverse the steps to install.

1977 Grand Prix

WITHOUT AIR CONDITIONING

1. Disconnect the negative battery terminal.
2. Drain the cooling system, disconnect the heater hoses, and plug the core tubes.
3. Remove the screws and nuts from the heater module on the engine side.
4. Remove the glove box to gain access to, and remove, the defroster duct screw, and the control cables.

5. Loosen the sealer and remove the case assembly and core from inside the vehicle.

6. Installation is the reverse of removal. Use a strip caulk type sealer when installing the case assembly to the firewall.

WITH AIR CONDITIONING

1. Drain the cooling system.
2. Remove the heater hoses and plug the core tubes.
3. Remove the core stud nuts retaining the case to the firewall.
4. Remove the blower motor resistor to gain access to the upper retaining nut inside the evaporator case.
5. Remove the glove box, the cold air duct, and the heater distributor tube.
6. Remove the lower defroster duct tube screw.
7. Remove the core to case retaining screw and pull the assembly from the cowl.
8. Remove the temperature cable and the vacuum hoses from the assembly.
9. Remove the case assembly and remove the core from the case.
10. Installation is in the reverse of removal.

1978–83 Grand Prix

WITHOUT AIR CONDITIONING

1. Disconnect the hoses at the core tubes and position them vertically to prevent coolant loss.
2. Remove the core cover from the module.
3. Remove the core bracket and ground screw.
4. Lift out the core.
5. Installation is the reverse of removal. Replace any damaged sealer.

WITH AIR CONDITIONING

1. Position the wipers in the UP position.
2. Disconnect and unplug the heater hoses.
3. Remove the module top cover seals.
4. Remove the module top screens.
5. Disconnect all electrical connectors.
6. Move the lower windshield reverse molding out of the way.
7. Remove the cowl brackets.
8. Tape a strip of wood to the lower edge of the windshield glass, to protect the glass.
9. Remove the top cover screws.
10. Cut the sealing material along the cowl with a knife.
11. Pry the cover off from the side, not from the top.
12. Remove the core and seal.

Installation is the reverse of removal. Use all new sealing material.

RADIO

Radio Receiver

REMOVAL & INSTALLATION

► **See Figure 5, 6, 7 and 8 (p. 22)**

Ventura and Phoenix Through 1979

1. Disconnect the battery.
2. Remove radio knobs, bezels and hex nuts.
3. Remove support bracket bolt. Remove the Ventura and Phoenix radio sidebrace screw.
4. Disconnect electrical and antenna leads; remove radio from under dash.
5. To install, reverse removal procedure.

LeMans

1. Disconnect the negative battery cable.
2. If necessary, remove the lighter bezel.
3. Remove the upper and lower instrument panel trim plates.
4. Remove the radio knobs and bezels.
5. Remove the two (1976–77) or four (1978–81) front radio retaining screws.
6. Remove the radio from the panel opening, disconnecting the electrical connections and the antenna lead on cars through 1977. For 1978 and later, open glove box door and lower by releasing spring clip. Pull the radio out after loosening rear, right side nut. Disconnect all wiring and remove the radio.

7. To install, reverse the removal procedure. If the radio is to be replaced, remove the bushing from the rear of the radio and install it on the replacement radio.

Grand Am and Grand LeMans

1. Disconnect the battery.
2. Remove the radio knobs and bezels and the retaining hex nut from the right-hand radio tuning shaft.
3. Remove the four retaining screws and the trim plate.
4. Remove the one front retaining screw and the mounting bracket screw.
5. Remove the radio and the mounting bracket from the dash, disconnecting the electrical connections and the antenna lead.
6. To install, reverse the removal procedure.

Grand Prix

1. Disconnect the negative battery terminal.
2. Remove the knobs, bezels, and righthand hex nut from the radio. On 1978 and later models, remove the upper and lower instrument panel trimplates.
3. Remove the four retaining screws and the radio trim plate.
4. Remove the one front retaining screw and the radio mounting bracket retaining screw (below radio). On 1978 and later models, open the glove box and loosen the rear nut at the right side of the radio.
5. Remove the radio and bracket as an assembly; disconnect the radio connections and antenna lead-in while the radio is pulled out.
6. Reverse the steps to install.

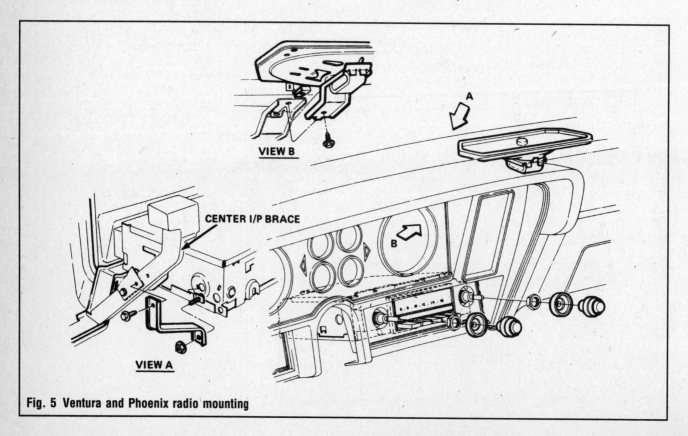

VIEW B

CENTER I/P BRACE

VIEW A

Fig. 5 Ventura and Phoenix radio mounting

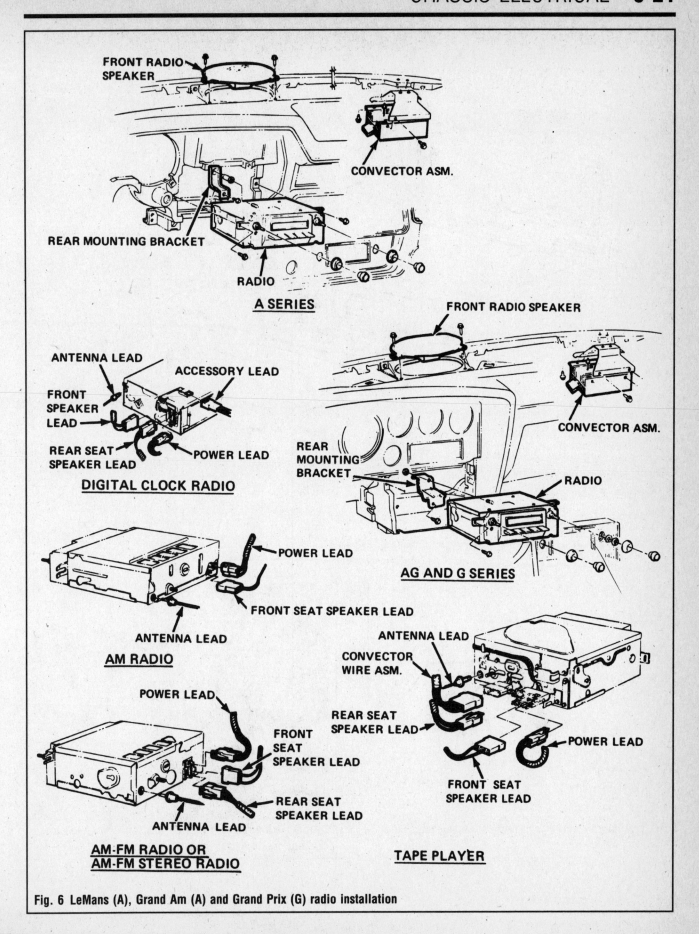

Fig. 6 LeMans (A), Grand Am (A) and Grand Prix (G) radio installation

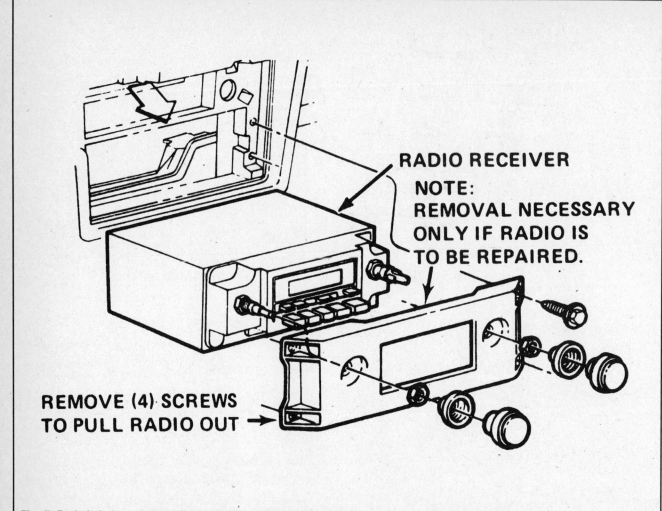

RADIO RECEIVER

NOTE:
REMOVAL NECESSARY
ONLY IF RADIO IS
TO BE REPAIRED.

REMOVE (4) SCREWS
TO PULL RADIO OUT →

Fig. 7 Exploded view of the radio mounting—1978–83 Grand Prix

Fig. 8 It may be necessary to adjust the antenna trim on some vehicles

To remove the radio, it may be necessary to remove the cigarette lighter bezel

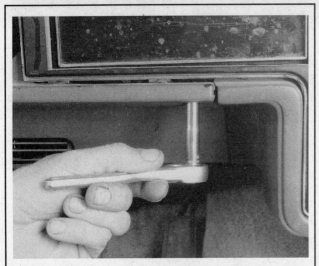

Remove the lower trim panel retaining screws . . .

. . . then pull the trim panel away from the instrument panel

. . . then pull down the lower panel for access to the upper trim panel screws

Remove the radio tuning knobs and bezels

Make sure to remove all of the trim panel retaining screws . . .

Remove the hex nuts from the radio tuning shafts

Remove the radio mounting bracket bolts . . .

Pull the radio from its mounted position . . .

. . . then remove the radio mounting bracket

. . . then detach the connectors and remove the radio from the vehicle

WINDSHIELD WIPERS

Windshield Wiper Blade and Arm

REMOVAL & INSTALLATION

▶ See Figure 9

Please refer to Chapter 1 for information detailing wiper blade replacement.

The wiper arms are attached to the motor drive by a nut, the arm being splined to the drive. An inexpensive wiper arm tool is available to remove the arm from the drive spline (see illustration). You can also use a prytool to carefully separate the arm from the spline.

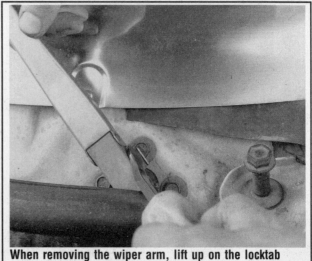

When removing the wiper arm, lift up on the locktab

Fig. 9 A special tool is available to separate the wiper arm from the drive spline

When installing the arm, align the splines and drive tang

Windshield Wiper Motor

REMOVAL & INSTALLATION

▶ **See Figure 10**

1. Remove hoses and wire terminals that are connected to wiper unit.
2. Remove clip or loosen nut that secures wiper crank to wiper linkage arm.

➡ **This clip is under leaf screen on depressed-park (hidden wiper) motors, and accessible only after firewall bolts are removed on some standard motors. On some models, the wiper arm must be removed to facilitate motor removal.**

3. Remove screws that secure wiper motor assembly to firewall, and remove the motor.
4. To install, position wiper assembly on firewall and secure.
5. Connect wire terminals and hoses.
6. Connect wiper crank with wiper linkage arm.

LINKAGE REPLACEMENT

▶ **See Figure 11 (p. 27)**

1. Make sure the wipers are in the fully parked position.
2. Remove the cowl vent screen. On later models, it is necessary to raise the hood.
3. Remove the wiper arm and blade assemblies.
4. Loosen the nuts which attach the transmission drive links to the motor crank arm.
5. Disconnect the transmission drive links from the motor crank arm.
6. Remove the screws which attach the transmission to the body.
7. Remove the transmission and linkage assembly by guiding it through the plenum chamber opening.

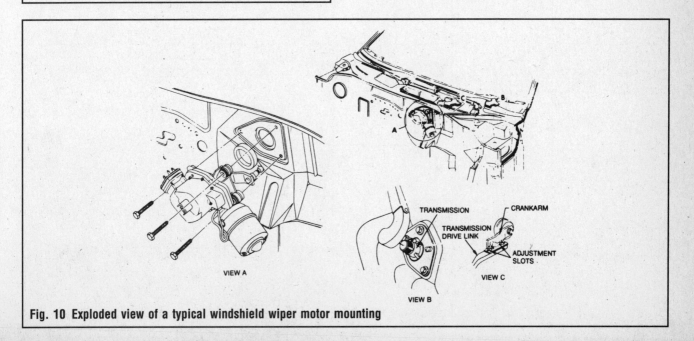

VIEW A

TRANSMISSION

CRANKARM

TRANSMISSION DRIVE LINK

ADJUSTMENT SLOTS

VIEW C

VIEW B

Fig. 10 Exploded view of a typical windshield wiper motor mounting

To remove the windshield wiper motor, tag and disconnect the hoses and lines

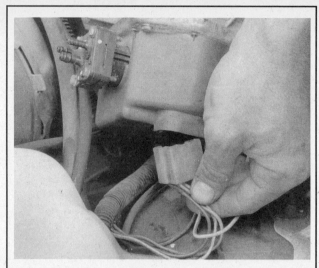

Detach the wiper motor electrical connector

Loosen the nut which attaches the wiper crank to the linkage arm . . .

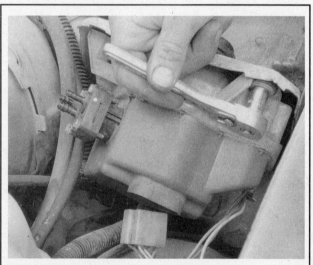

Remove the wiper motor retaining bolts . . .

. . . then separate the wiper crank from the linkage

. . . then remove the wiper motor from the vehicle

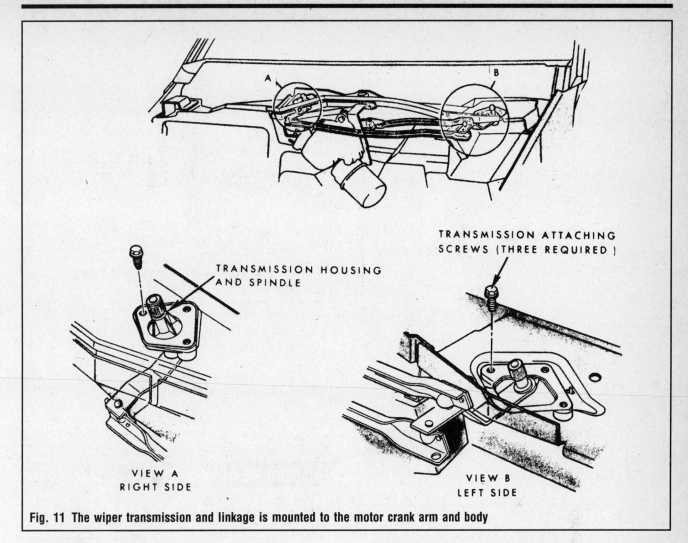

Fig. 11 The wiper transmission and linkage is mounted to the motor crank arm and body

To install:

8. Position the assembly in the plenum chamber through the opening. Loosely install the attaching screws.

9. Install the drive links on the motor crank arm and tighten the attaching nuts.

➡**Wiper motor must be in the park position.**

10. Align the transmissions, and tighten the attaching screws.
11. Reinstall the wiper arms and blades.

INSTRUMENTS AND SWITCHES

Light Switch

REPLACEMENT & INSTALLATION

1. Disconnect the battery.
2. Pull the light switch knob to the "on" position.
3. Reach under the instrument panel and depress the switch shaft retainer, then remove the knob and shaft assembly.

➡**Disconnect the vacuum hose on the vacuum-operated headlamp models.**

4. Remove the retaining ferrule nut.

5. Remove the switch from the instrument panel. Disconnect the multi-plug connector from the switch.

6. Installation is in the reverse order of removal. In checking the lights before installation, the switch must be grounded to test the dome lights on some models.

Windshield Wiper Switch

REMOVAL & INSTALLATION

♦ **See Figure 12**

1. Disconnect the negative battery cable.
2. Remove any necessary trim panels.

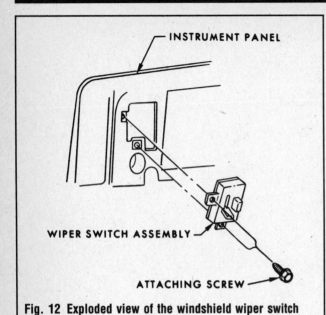

Fig. 12 Exploded view of the windshield wiper switch mounting

3. Unfasten the switch retaining screws.
4. Pull out the switch and detach the electrical connector. Remove the switch from the vehicle.
5. Installation is the reverse of the removal procedure.

Speedometer Cable

REMOVAL & INSTALLATION

◆ **See Figures 13 and 14**

1. Remove the lower A/C duct or lower instrument panel trimplate, if necessary, to gain access.
2. Remove the lower instrument panel trimplates.
3. Reach up behind the speedometer and find where the cable attaches to the speedometer head. Press the retaining clip downward and slide the cable from the head.

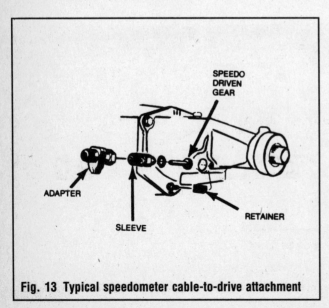

Fig. 13 Typical speedometer cable-to-drive attachment

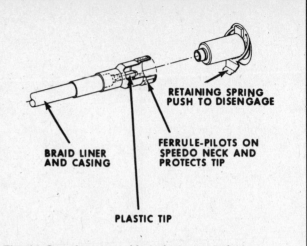

Fig. 14 Speedometer cable-to-instrument cluster attachment

4. Slide the old cable core from the casing. If the core is broken, raise the car and remove the cable retaining clip from the transmission. Pull out the remaining piece of the core.
5. Install in the reverse order of removal.
Before installing, the core should be wiped clean and the casing flushed out with solvent. Before inserting the core into the case, coat the lower two-thirds of the core with a speedometer cable lubricant; *do not lubricate the upper third of the cable.*

Instrument Cluster

REMOVAL & INSTALLATION

◆ **See Figures 15, 16 and 17 (pp. 30–31)**

➡**On some models, individual instruments can be replaced without removing the entire cluster. The procedure below will vary slightly depending on the year of car and models.**

Lemans, Grand Am and Grand Prix

1. Disconnect the battery and remove the lower and upper instrument panel trim plates.
2. On all models except console shift, remove the automatic transmission shift indicator cable.
3. Remove the cluster retaining screws, disconnect the speedometer cable and printed circuit connector (all except Grand Prix) and remove the cluster.
4. Reverse the above procedure for installation.

Ventura, Phoenix

1. Disconnect the battery.
2. Remove the three screws retaining the heater or A/C control panel to the instrument panel carrier.
3. Remove the radio control knobs, bezels and nuts, and remove the radio.
4. Remove the screws at the top and bottom of the carrier securing it to the instrument panel pad and cowl brackets.
5. Disconnect the shift indicator cable at the shift bowl (if au-

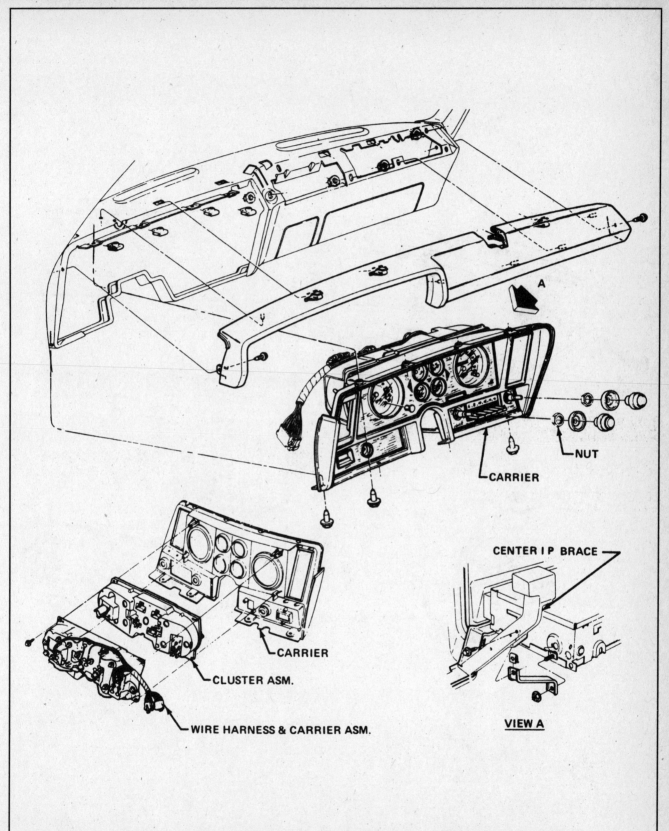

Fig. 15 Ventura and Phoenix instrument panel pad and cluster assembly—1977 vehicle shown, others similar

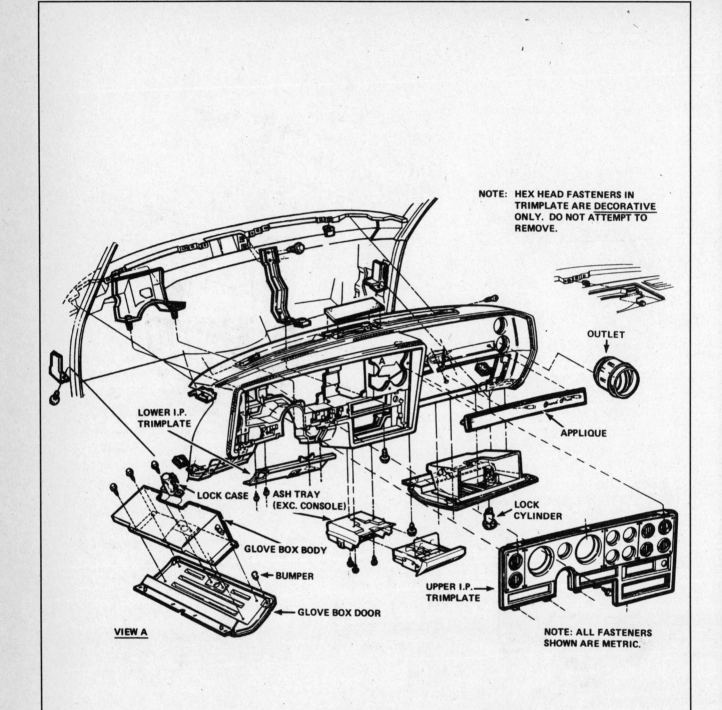

NOTE: HEX HEAD FASTENERS IN TRIMPLATE ARE DECORATIVE ONLY. DO NOT ATTEMPT TO REMOVE.

OUTLET

APPLIQUE

LOWER I.P. TRIMPLATE

LOCK CASE

ASH TRAY (EXC. CONSOLE)

LOCK CYLINDER

GLOVE BOX BODY

BUMPER

GLOVE BOX DOOR

UPPER I.P. TRIMPLATE

VIEW A

NOTE: ALL FASTENERS SHOWN ARE METRIC.

Fig. 16 Exploded view of the instrument panel pad, trim plates and attaching parts—1978 LeMans and Grand Prix

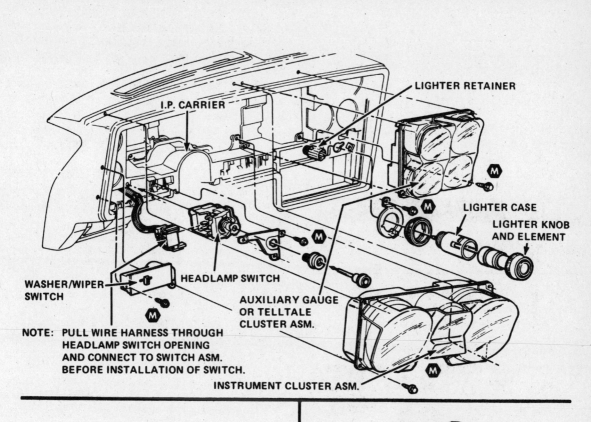

LIGHTER RETAINER

I.P. CARRIER

LIGHTER CASE

LIGHTER KNOB
AND ELEMENT

WASHER/WIPER
SWITCH

HEADLAMP SWITCH

AUXILIARY GAUGE
OR TELLTALE
CLUSTER ASM.

NOTE: PULL WIRE HARNESS THROUGH
HEADLAMP SWITCH OPENING
AND CONNECT TO SWITCH ASM.
BEFORE INSTALLATION OF SWITCH.

INSTRUMENT CLUSTER ASM.

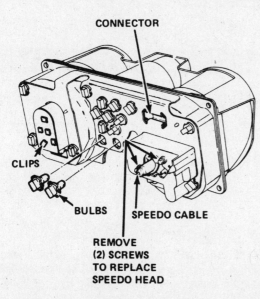

CONNECTOR

CLIPS

BULBS

SPEEDO CABLE

REMOVE
(2) SCREWS
TO REPLACE
SPEEDO HEAD

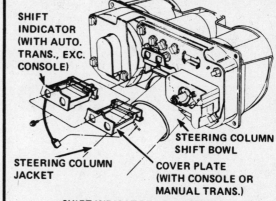

SHIFT
INDICATOR
(WITH AUTO.
TRANS., EXC.
CONSOLE)

STEERING COLUMN
SHIFT BOWL

STEERING COLUMN
JACKET

COVER PLATE
(WITH CONSOLE OR
MANUAL TRANS.)

SHIFT INDICATOR ADJUSTMENT

1. STEERING COLUMN ATTACHMENT SHOULD
   BE COMPLETED.
2. POSITION SHIFT LEVER IN NEUTRAL GATE
   NOTCH.
3. GUIDE CLIP ON EDGE OF SHIFT BOWL TO
   CENTRALLY POSITION POINTER ON "N"
   (NEUTRAL).

NOTE: CARE MUST BE TAKEN TO ASSURE THAT
CABLE RESTS ON BOWL AND NOT ON
COLUMN JACKET.

Fig. 17 LeMans and Grand Prix instrument cluster and related components

tomatic transmission), and remove the two steering column-to-instrument panel nuts.

6. Carefully lower the steering column from the instrument panel and protect it with a shop towel or other padding.

7. Disconnect the speedometer cable from under the dash.

8. Tilt the carrier and cluster assembly forward, disconnect the printed circuit and cluster ground connectors, and all remaining wiring.

9. Place the carrier assembly on a bench. Remove the wire harness and carrier assembly (4 screws) and set it aside. Remove the cluster.

10. Installation is in the reverse order of removal. It is wise to keep all screws and nuts slightly loose when reassembling each sub-assembly, to properly align the components; when you are sure the parts are properly positioned, tighten all fasteners evenly.

Ignition Switch

REMOVAL & INSTALLATION

The ignition switches for all models covered in this guide are incorporated into the steering column lock cylinders. Installation and removal procedures for the switch and lock assembly are covered in Chapter 8.

Seat Belt/Starter Interlock System

The seat belt/starter interlock system was used on 1974 and some 1975 cars. This system prevents the car from being started until the front seat occupants are seated and have fastened their seat belts. If the proper sequence is not followed, the engine will not start. If, after the car is started, the seat belts are unfastened, a warning buzzer and light will be activated.

The shoulder harness and lap belt are permanently fastened together, so that they must both be worn. The shoulder harness uses an inertia-lock reel to allow freedom of movement under normal driving conditions.

In case of system failure, an override switch is located under the hood. This is a "one-start" switch and must be reset each time it is used.

DISABLING THE INTERLOCK SYSTEM

Since the requirement for the interlock system was dropped, the system may be legally disabled. The seat belt warning light is still required.

1. Disconnect the negative battery cable.

2. Locate the interlock harness connector which is on or near the fuse block. The connector has orange, yellow, and green leads running to it.

3. Cut and tape the green lead on the body harness side of the interlock connector.

4. If the car is equipped with heavy-duty cooling and the low coolant warning system, cut the yellow wire behind the connector and tape the ends.

5. If the car is not equipped with heavy-duty cooling and the low coolant warning system, disconnect the buzzer from the fuse panel and remove it.

6. Connect the battery cable. Check the system operation by starting the car with seat belt unfastened.

LIGHTING

Headlights

REMOVAL & INSTALLATION

▶ **See Figure 18**

1. Remove the headlight bezel (outer trim around sealed beam).

2. Remove the sealed beam retainer ring screws and the retainer ring.

3. Lift the sealed beam out and disconnect it from the electrical connector. If the car is equipped with monitor lights, remove the rubber sleeve from the bulb and retain it.

4. To install, connect the sealed beam to the electrical connector, and re-install the monitor light sleeve if equipped. Hold the sealed beam in place and install the retaining ring and screws. Install the headlight bezel and adjust headlight aim.

AIMING

▶ **See Figure 19 (p. 34)**

The headlights must be properly aimed to provide the best, safest road illumination. The lights should be checked for proper aim, and adjusted if necessary, after installing a new sealed beam unit or if the front end sheet metal has been replaced. Certain state and local authorities have requirements for headlight aiming and you should check these before adjusting.

➡**The car's fuel tank should be about half full when adjusting the headlights. Tires should be properly inflated, and if a heavy load is carried in the trunk or in the cargo area of station wagons, it should remain there.**

Horizontal and vertical aiming of each sealed beam unit is provided by two adjusting screws, which move the mounting ring in the body against the tension of the coil spring. There is no adjustment for focus; this is done during headlight manufacturing.

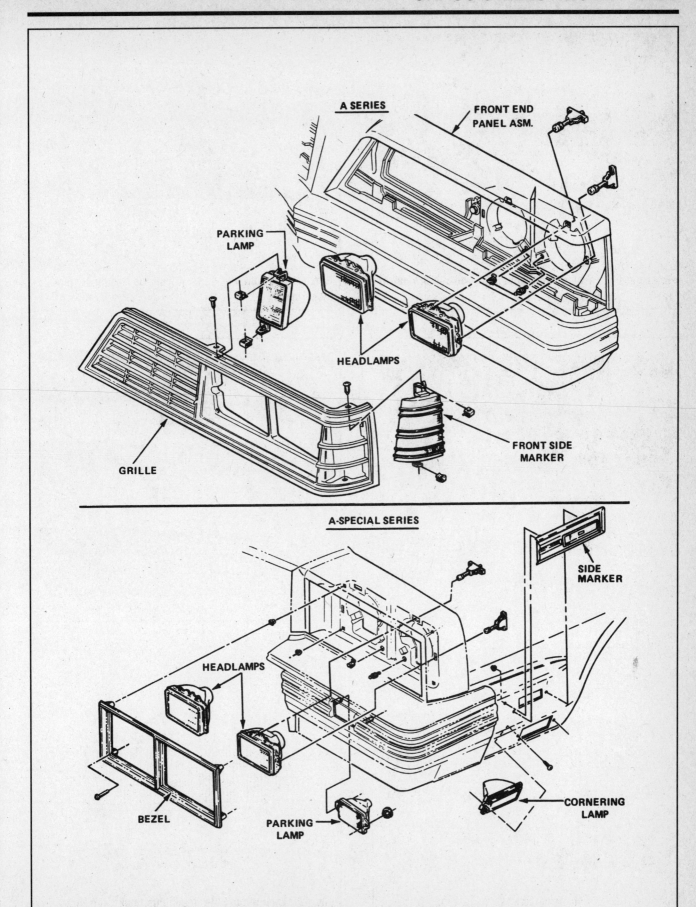

A SERIES

FRONT END
PANEL ASM.

PARKING
LAMP

HEADLAMPS

GRILLE

FRONT SIDE
MARKER

A-SPECIAL SERIES

SIDE
MARKER

HEADLAMPS

BEZEL

PARKING
LAMP

CORNERING
LAMP

Fig. 18 Example of typical headlight and parking light mounting—1981 LeMans and Grand Prix shown

To remove the sealed beam headlight, remove the bezel retaining screws . . .

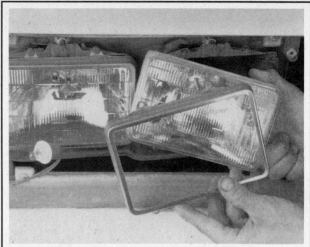

Remove the retaining ring and pull the headlight from its mounting . . .

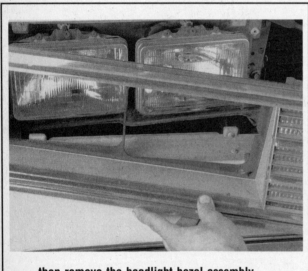

. . . then remove the headlight bezel assembly

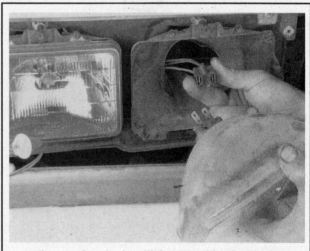

. . . then unplug the headlight assembly electrical connector

Remove the retaining ring screws. Using a magnetic screwdriver can prevent lost screws

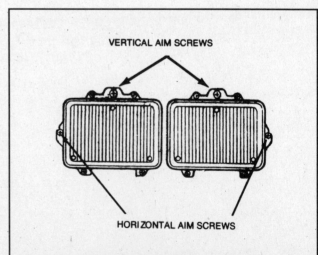

VERTICAL AIM SCREWS

HORIZONTAL AIM SCREWS

Fig. 19 When aiming the headlights, make sure not to confuse the aim screws with the retaining screws

Signal and Marker Lights

REMOVAL & INSTALLATION

Front Turn Signal & Parking Lights

➡This is a general procedure and applies to all models and types covered by this manual. A few steps may need to be slightly altered to comply with your particular vehicle.

1. Disconnect the negative battery cable.
2. To replace the bulb, reach up and in behind the bumper or access the bulb from the engine compartment in front of the radiator, as applicable. You may also access the bulb by removing the light bezel/grille assembly.
3. Twist the lamp socket counterclockwise until it can be pulled backward and out from the housing.
4. Either pull the light bulb from the socket or lightly depress

The parking/turn signal bulb can also be accessed from under the vehicle (see arrow)

To remove the parking/turn signal light, twist and pull the lamp socket from the housing

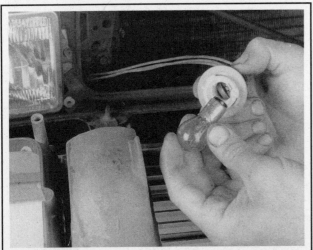

Lightly depress the parking/turn signal bulb and turn it counterclockwise to remove from the socket

the bulb and turn it counterclockwise to release it from the socket, as applicable.

5. Installation is the reverse of the removal procedure. During installation, make sure that the light bulb contacts are clean and free of corrosion.
6. Connect the negative battery cable, then check light operation.

Side Marker Lights

➡This is a general procedure and applies to all models and types covered by this manual. A few steps may need to be slightly altered to comply with your particular vehicle.

1. Disconnect the negative battery cable.
2. Remove the light bezel/grille assembly.
3. Twist the lamp socket counterclockwise until it can be pulled away from the housing.
4. As applicable, carefully pull the light bulb from the socket or lightly depress the bulb and turn it counterclockwise to release it from the socket.

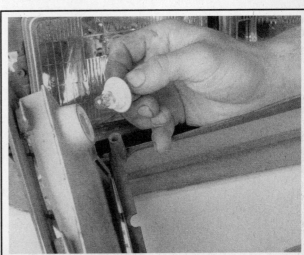

When removing the side marker light, twist the lamp socket to remove it from the housing

5. Installation is the reverse of the removal procedure. During installation, make sure that the light bulb contacts are clean and free of corrosion.

6. Connect the negative battery cable, then check the light operation.

Rear Turn Signal, Brake and Parking Lights

➡**This is a general procedure and applies to all models covered by this manual. A few steps may need to be slightly altered to comply with your particular vehicle.**

1. Disconnect the negative battery cable.

2. Some vehicles are equipped with lenses that are attached with screws accessible from the rear. To remove these, simply unfasten the screws, then remove the lens.

3. On some vehicles, you must open the trunk lid, then twist the socket to release it from the housing.

4. Once the lens is removed or the socket released, as applicable, the bulb can be replaced by carefully pulling it from the

. . . then remove the entire rear light housing/lens assembly

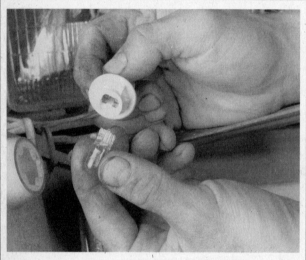

Pull the side marker light bulb from the socket

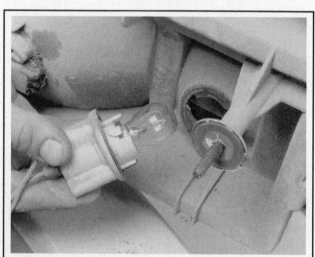

Twist the brake light socket counterclockwise and remove it from the housing . . .

To access the rear exterior light bulb assemblies, unfasten the retaining screws/nuts . . .

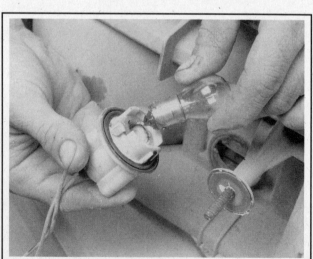

. . . then lightly depress and turn the bulb to remove it from the socket

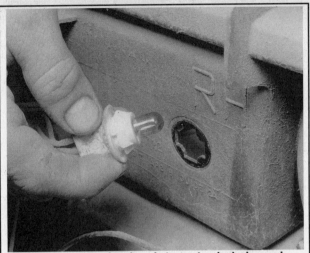

Turn the rear turn signal socket counterclockwise and pull from the housing . . .

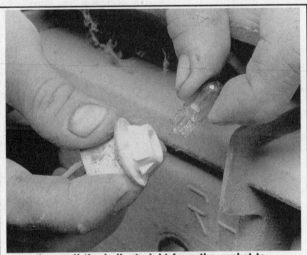

. . . then pull the bulb straight from the socket to remove

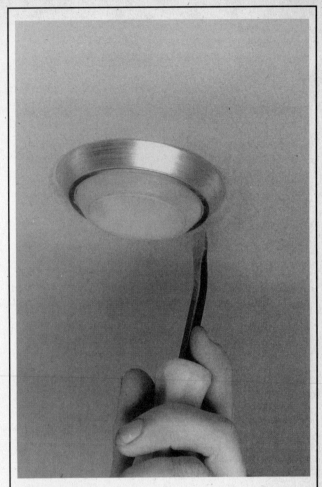

To replace the dome light bulb, you can use a prytool to carefully loosen . . .

socket, or by depressing it, turning it counterclockwise, and removing it from the socket.

5. Installation is the reverse of the removal procedure. During installation, make sure that the light bulb contacts are clean and free of corrosion.

6. Connect the negative battery cable, then check light operation.

Dome Light

1. Disconnect the negative battery cable.
2. Remove the dome light cover by unfastening the retaining screws, or prying the cover off, as applicable.
3. Remove the bulb and replace with a new one.
4. Installation is the reverse of the removal procedure. During installation, make sure that the light bulb contacts are clean and free of corrosion.
5. Connect the negative battery cable, then check light operation.

. . . then remove the dome light lens from the headliner

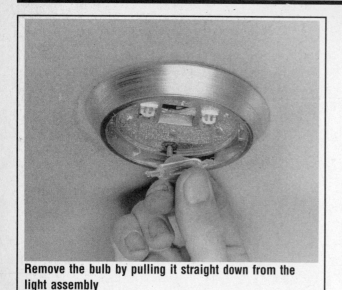
Remove the bulb by pulling it straight down from the light assembly

License Plate Lights

1. Disconnect the negative battery cable.
2. Remove the lamp attaching bolts or screws.
3. Lower the lamp socket, then remove the light bulb.
4. Installation is the reverse of the removal procedure. During installation, make sure that the light bulb contacts are clean and free of corrosion.
5. Connect the negative battery cable, then check light operation.

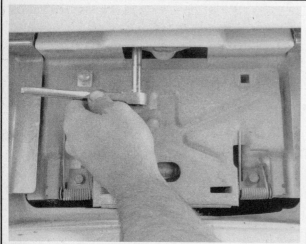
When removing the license plate light bulb, unfasten the lamp attaching bolts

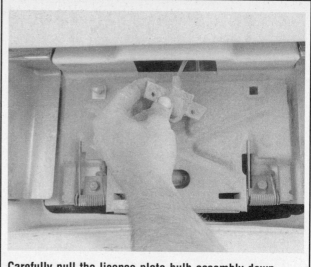
Carefully pull the license plate bulb assembly down

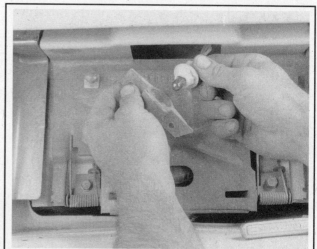
Twist and pull the license plate socket from the housing . . .

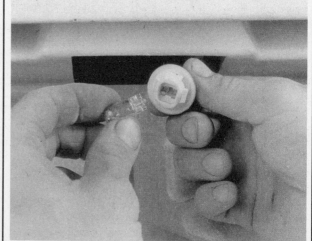
. . . then pull the license plate bulb from the socket to replace it

TRAILER WIRING

Wiring the vehicle for towing is fairly easy. There are a number of good wiring kits available and these should be used, rather than trying to design your own.

All trailers will need brake lights and turn signals as well as tail lights and side marker lights. Most areas require extra marker lights for overwide trailers. Also, most areas have recently required back-up lights for trailers, and most trailer manufacturers have been building trailers with back-up lights for several years.

Additionally, some Class I, most Class II and just about all Class III trailers will have electric brakes. Add to this number an accessories wire, to operate trailer internal equipment or to charge the trailer's battery, and you can have as many as seven wires in the harness.

Determine the equipment on your trailer and buy the wiring kit necessary. The kit will contain all the wires needed, plus a plug adapter set which includes the female plug, mounted on the bumper or hitch, and the male plug, wired into, or plugged into the trailer harness.

When installing the kit, follow the manufacturer's instructions.

The color coding of the wires is usually standard throughout the industry. One point to note: some domestic vehicles, and most imported vehicles, have separate turn signals. On most domestic vehicles, the brake lights and rear turn signals operate with the same bulb. For those vehicles with separate turn signals, you can purchase an isolation unit so that the brake lights won't blink whenever the turn signals are operated, or, you can go to your local electronics supply house and buy four diodes to wire in series with the brake and turn signal bulbs. Diodes will isolate the brake and turn signals. The choice is yours. The isolation units are simple and quick to install, but far more expensive than the diodes. The diodes, however, require more work to install properly, since they require the cutting of each bulb's wire and soldering in place of the diode.

One, final point, the best kits are those with a spring loaded cover on the vehicle mounted socket. This cover prevents dirt and moisture from corroding the terminals. Never let the vehicle socket hang loosely; always mount it securely to the bumper or hitch.

CIRCUIT PROTECTION

Fuses

▶ **See Figures 20, 21, 22 and 23**

The fuse block on all models is located under the left hand side of the instrument panel. All flashers are mounted on the fuse block. Each fuse is marked on the fuse block as to which circuit it is protecting. Some early models also use an in-line 30 amp, fuse for the air conditioning hi-blower, located at the cowl relay and an in-line 10 amp fuse for power antennas.

To determine whether a fuse is blown, remove the suspect fuse and check to see if the element is broken. If so replace the fuse with one of equal amperage value.

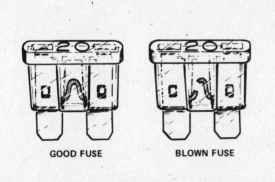

GOOD FUSE   BLOWN FUSE

Fig. 20 The mini-fuses, shown here, are used on 1978–83 vehicles. Earlier vehicles used conventional (cylindrical) fuses

Fuse Color-Coding

Fuse (Amps)	Color Stripe
3	Violet
5	Tan
7.5	Brown
10	Red
20	Clear
25	White

Fig. 21 The fuses range in amperage and are color-coded

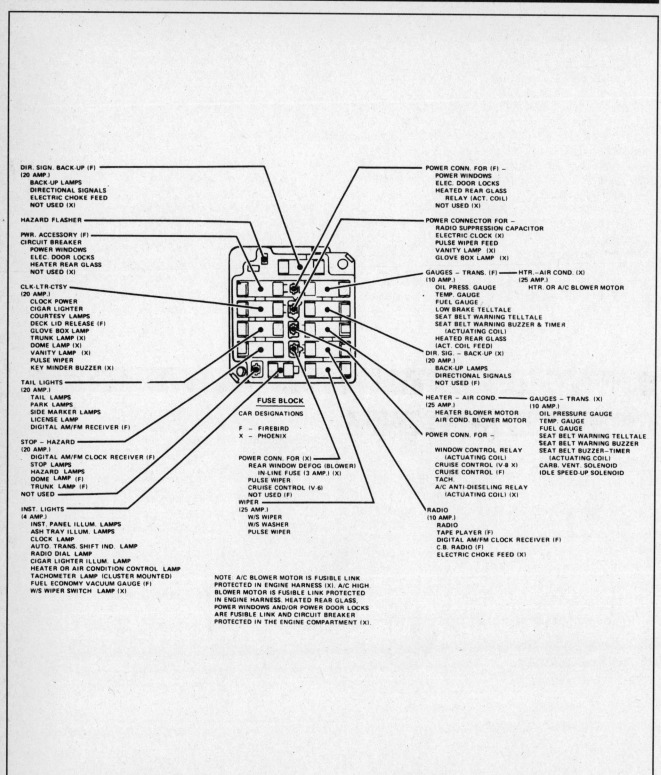

DIR. SIGN. BACK-UP (F)
(20 AMP.)
    BACK-UP LAMPS
    DIRECTIONAL SIGNALS
    ELECTRIC CHOKE FEED
    NOT USED (X)

HAZARD FLASHER

PWR. ACCESSORY (F)
CIRCUIT BREAKER
    POWER WINDOWS
    ELEC. DOOR LOCKS
    HEATER REAR GLASS
    NOT USED (X)

CLK-LTR-CTSY
(20 AMP.)
    CLOCK POWER
    CIGAR LIGHTER
    COURTESY LAMPS
    DECK LID RELEASE (F)
    GLOVE BOX LAMP
    TRUNK LAMP (X)
    DOME LAMP (X)
    VANITY LAMP (X)
    PULSE WIPER
    KEY MINDER BUZZER (X)

TAIL LIGHTS
(20 AMP.)
    TAIL LAMPS
    PARK LAMPS
    SIDE MARKER LAMPS
    LICENSE LAMP
    DIGITAL AM/FM RECEIVER (F)

STOP – HAZARD
(20 AMP.)
    DIGITAL AM/FM CLOCK RECEIVER (F)
    STOP LAMPS
    HAZARD LAMPS
    DOME LAMP (F)
    TRUNK LAMP (F)
NOT USED

INST. LIGHTS
(4 AMP.)
    INST. PANEL ILLUM. LAMPS
    ASH TRAY ILLUM. LAMPS
    CLOCK LAMP
    AUTO. TRANS. SHIFT IND. LAMP
    RADIO DIAL LAMP
    CIGAR LIGHTER ILLUM. LAMP
    HEATER OR AIR CONDITION CONTROL LAMP
    TACHOMETER LAMP (CLUSTER MOUNTED)
    FUEL ECONOMY VACUUM GAUGE (F)
    W/S WIPER SWITCH LAMP (X)

FUSE BLOCK

CAR DESIGNATIONS

F – FIREBIRD
X – PHOENIX

POWER CONN. FOR (X) –
    REAR WINDOW DEFOG (BLOWER)
    IN-LINE FUSE (3 AMP.) (X)
    PULSE WIPER
    CRUISE CONTROL (V-6)
    NOT USED (F)
WIPER
(25 AMP.)
    W/S WIPER
    W/S WASHER
    PULSE WIPER

NOTE: A/C BLOWER MOTOR IS FUSIBLE LINK
PROTECTED IN ENGINE HARNESS (X). A/C HIGH
BLOWER MOTOR IS FUSIBLE LINK PROTECTED
IN ENGINE HARNESS. HEATED REAR GLASS,
POWER WINDOWS AND/OR POWER DOOR LOCKS
ARE FUSIBLE LINK AND CIRCUIT BREAKER
PROTECTED IN THE ENGINE COMPARTMENT (X).

POWER CONN. FOR (F) –
    POWER WINDOWS
    ELEC. DOOR LOCKS
    HEATED REAR GLASS
    RELAY (ACT. COIL)
    NOT USED (X)

POWER CONNECTOR FOR –
    RADIO SUPPRESSION CAPACITOR
    ELECTRIC CLOCK (X)
    PULSE WIPER FEED
    VANITY LAMP (X)
    GLOVE BOX LAMP (X)

GAUGES – TRANS. (F) ——— HTR.–AIR COND. (X)
(10 AMP.)   (25 AMP.)
    OIL PRESS. GAUGE   HTR. OR A/C BLOWER MOTOR
    TEMP. GAUGE
    FUEL GAUGE
    LOW BRAKE TELLTALE
    SEAT BELT WARNING TELLTALE
    SEAT BELT WARNING BUZZER & TIMER
    (ACTUATING COIL)
    HEATED REAR GLASS
    (ACT. COIL FEED)
DIR. SIG. – BACK-UP (X)
(20 AMP.)
    BACK-UP LAMPS
    DIRECTIONAL SIGNALS
    NOT USED (F)

HEATER – AIR COND. ——— GAUGES – TRANS. (X)
(25 AMP.)   (10 AMP.)
    HEATER BLOWER MOTOR   OIL PRESSURE GAUGE
    AIR COND. BLOWER MOTOR   TEMP. GAUGE
POWER CONN. FOR –   FUEL GAUGE
                          SEAT BELT WARNING TELLTALE
    WINDOW CONTROL RELAY   SEAT BELT WARNING BUZZER
    (ACTUATING COIL)   SEAT BELT BUZZER-TIMER
    CRUISE CONTROL (V-8 X)   (ACTUATING COIL)
    CRUISE CONTROL (F)   CARB. VENT. SOLENOID
    TACH.   IDLE SPEED-UP SOLENOID
    A/C ANTI-DIESELING RELAY
    (ACTUATING COIL) (X)

RADIO
(10 AMP.)
    RADIO
    TAPE PLAYER (F)
    DIGITAL AM/FM CLOCK RECEIVER (F)
    C.B. RADIO (F)
    ELECTRIC CHOKE FEED (X)

Fig. 22 Fuse block identification—Phoenix and Ventura

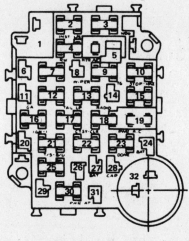

9 - HEATER - AIR COND.
(25 AMP.)
HEATER BLOWER MOTOR
AIR COND. BLOWER MOTOR
IDLE STOP SOLENOID

10 - NOT USED

11 - SEE ITEM NO. 6

12 - NOT USED

13 - WIPER
(25 AMP.)
W/S WIPER
W/S WASHER

14 - CRUISE CONTROL

15 - STOP - HAZARD
(20 AMP.)
STOP LIGHTS
HAZARD LIGHTS
KEY WARNING BUZZER

16 - GAUGES
(20 AMP.)
OIL PRES. GAUGE
TEMP. GAUGE
FUEL GAUGE
LOW BRAKE TELLTALE
SEAT BELT WARNING TELLTALE
SEAT BELT WARNING BUZZER
(ACTUATING COIL FEED)
SEAT BELT BUZZER TIMER
(ACTUATING COIL)
DECK LID RELEASE
TAILGATE UNLOCK (A)

17 - TAIL LIGHTS
(20 AMP.)
TAIL LIGHTS
PARK LIGHTS
CORNERING LIGHTS
SIDE MARKER LIGHTS
LICENSE LAMP

18 - RADIO
(10 AMP.)
RADIO
TAPE PLAYER
TAILGATE AJAR LIGHT (B)

19 - CIRCUIT BREAKER
(30 AMP.)
POWER CONNECTION FOR
ITEM NO. 8 AND 24

20 - SEE ITEM NO. 6

1 - HAZARD FLASHER

2 - INST. LIGHTS
(5 AMP.)
INST. PANEL ILLUM. LIGHTS
ASH TRAY ILLUM. LIGHT
CLOCK LIGHT
AUTO. TRANS. SHIFT
IND. LIGHT
RADIO DIAL LIGHT
CIGAR LIGHTER ILLUM.
HEATER OR AIR COND.
CONTROL LIGHT
FUEL ECONOMY VACUUM
GAUGE LIGHT (B)
W/S WIPER & HEADLAMP SW.
LIGHT

3 - ELECTRIC CHOKE
(20 AMP.)
ELECTRIC CHOKE FEED—
V-6 (A & G)
THROTTLE SOL. (M.T.)—
V-6 (A & G)
NOT USED (B)

4 - NOT USED

5 - PWR. ACSRY.-CIRCUIT BREAKER
(30 AMP.)
POWER WINDOWS
POWER RR WINDOW (STA.
WAGON (B))
ELECTRIC SLIDING SUNROOF

6 - 11 - 20 -
IGN. NO. 1 POWER CONN. FOR —
(GAUGE FUSE)
HEATED RR GLASS RELAY
(ACTUATING COIL)
RADIO SUPPRESSION CAP.
(B-V-6)
PULSE WIPER (A & G)
BLOWER DEFOG (A)

7 - NOT USED

8 - HTD. RR GLASS TIMER

21 - DIR. - SIGN. - BACK-UP
(20 AMP.)
BACK-UP LIGHTS
DIRECTIONAL SIGNALS

22 - CLOCK - LTR. - CTSY.
(20 AMP.)
CLOCK POWER
CIGAR LIGHTER
CTSY. LIGHTS
GLOVE BOX LAMP
PULSE WIPER FEED
POWER ANTENNA
TO HORNS
DIGITAL AM/FM CLOCK
RECEIVER

23 - DOME LAMP
(20 AMP.)
VANITY LIGHT
DOME LAMP
RADIO SUPPRESSION CAPACITOR
TRUNK LIGHT
DOOR COURTESY & WARNING
LAMP (B & G)

24 - POWER CONN. FOR —

ELECTRIC DOOR LOCKS
POWER SEATS

25 - NOT USED

26 - NOT USED

27 - 31 -
POWER CONN. FOR
(CLK-LTR-CTSY FUSE)
PULSE WIPER (B)
POWER ANTENNA
RADIO SUPPRESSION CAP
(A & G)

28 - POWER CONN. FOR —
(DOME LAMP FUSE)
RADIO SUPPRESSION
CAPACITOR
(B-V-8 ONLY)

29 - POWER CONN. FOR—
(RADIO FUSE)
TAILGATE AJAR LAMP (B)

30 - NOT USED

31 - SEE ITEM NO. 27

32 - DIRECTIONAL SIGNAL
FLASHER

CAR DESIGNATIONS

A — LeMANS, GRAND LeMANS,
GRAND AM
G — GRAND PRIX
B — CATALINA
BONNEVILLE

Fig. 23 Fuse block identification—LeMans, Grand LeMans and Grand Prix

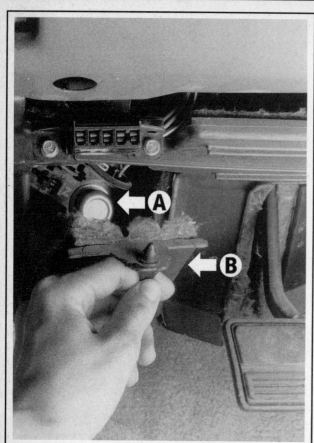

The fuse block (A) is usually concealed by a small cover or trap door (B)

Fusible Links

All models are equipped with fusible links. These links are attached to the lower ends of the main supply wires and connect to the starter solenoid. One of the main wires is a No. 12 red wire which supplies the headlight circuit and the other is a No. 10 red wire which supplies all electrical units except the headlights. The links consist of wire which is several gauges smaller than the supply wires they are connected to and function as additional protection to the wiring. In the event of an overloaded or short circuited condition in that they will melt before the wiring is damaged elsewhere in the circuit. A burned out fusible link would be indicated by: all the electrical accessories dead except the headlights or headlights dead but all other electrical units operative.

REPLACEMENT

⯈ **See Figure 24**

1. Disconnect the battery ground cable.
2. Disconnect the fusible link from the junction block or starter solenoid.
3. Cut the harness directly behind the connector to remove the damaged fusible link.
4. Strip the harness wire approximately ½ in.
5. Connect the new fusible link to the harness wire using a crimp on connector. Solder the connection using resin core solder.
6. Tape all exposed wires with plastic electrical tape.
7. Connect the fusible link to the junction block or starter solenoid and reconnect the battery ground cable.

Circuit Breakers

Circuit breakers are also located in the fuse block. A circuit breaker is an electrical switch which breaks the circuit during an electrical overload. The circuit breaker will remain open until the short or overload condition in the circuit is corrected.

To replace the breaker, pull it out from the fuse block.

Flashers

REPLACEMENT

The turn signal flasher is located under the dash either to the left or right of the steering column on most models. The lower dash panel may have to be removed to gain access to the unit. The hazard flasher is located in the fuse block. On 1980 and later models, both the turn signal flasher and the hazard flasher are located at the lower left hand and the upper right hand corners of the fuse block respectively. Remove these by pulling them from their connectors.

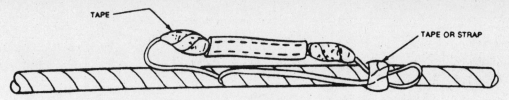

REMOVE EXISTING VINYL TUBE SHIELDING
REINSTALL OVER FUSE LINK BEFORE CRIMPING
FUSE LINK TO WIRE ENDS

TAPE

TAPE OR STRAP

TYPICAL REPAIR USING THE SPECIAL #17 GA (9.00" LONG-YELLOW) FUSE LINK REQUIRED FOR THE AIR/COND
CIRCUITS (2) #687E and #261A LOCATED IN THE ENGINE COMPARTMENT

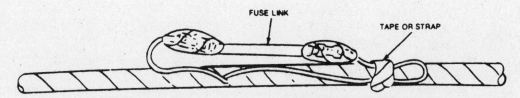

FUSE LINK

TAPE OR STRAP

TYPICAL REPAIR FOR ANY IN-LINE FUSE LINK USING THE SPECIFIED GAUGE FUSE LINK FOR THE SPECIFIC CIRCUIT

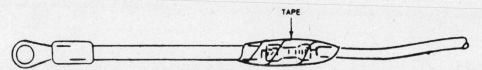

TAPE

TYPICAL REPAIR USING THE EYELET TERMINAL FUSE LINK OF THE SPECIFIED GAUGE FOR ATTACHMENT TO A CIRCUIT WIRE END

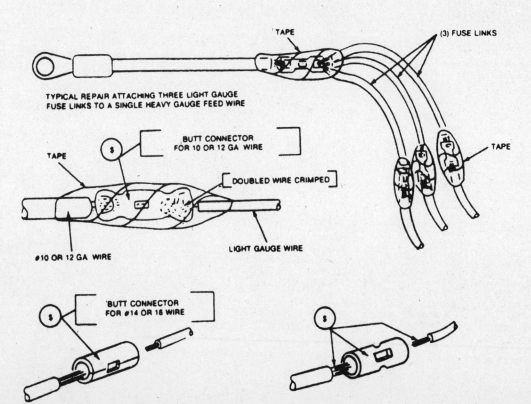

TAPE

(3) FUSE LINKS

TYPICAL REPAIR ATTACHING THREE LIGHT GAUGE
FUSE LINKS TO A SINGLE HEAVY GAUGE FEED WIRE

TAPE

TAPE

BUTT CONNECTOR
FOR 10 OR 12 GA WIRE

DOUBLED WIRE CRIMPED

LIGHT GAUGE WIRE

#10 OR 12 GA WIRE

BUTT CONNECTOR
FOR #14 OR 16 WIRE

Fig. 24 Fusible link repair procedure

WIRING DIAGRAMS

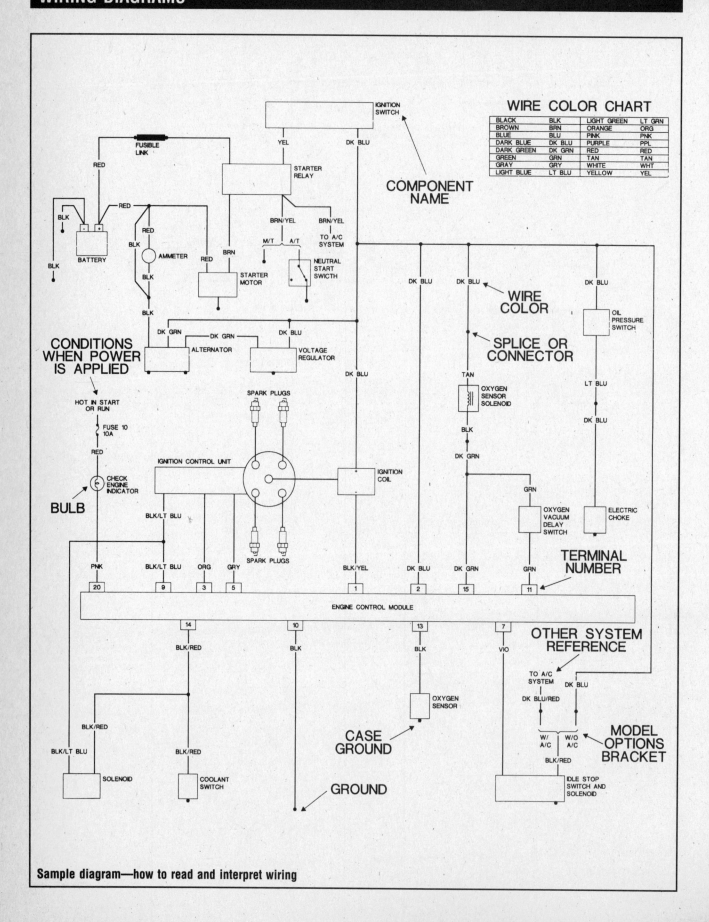

Sample diagram—how to read and interpret wiring

WIRING DIAGRAM SYMBOLS

BATTERY	CONNECTOR OR SPLICE	CIRCUIT BREAKER	CAPACITOR	COIL	DIODE	FUSE	FUSIBLE LINK	GROUND	LED
RESISTOR	SINGLE FILAMENT BULB	DUAL FILAMENT BULB	HEATING ELEMENT	SOLENOID OR COIL	VARIABLE RESISTOR	CRYSTAL	POTENTIOMETER	HORN OR SPEAKER	
ALTERNATOR	DISTRIBUTOR ASSEMBLY	IGNITION COIL	SPARK PLUG	STEPPER MOTOR	HEAT ACTIVATED SWITCH	RELAY			
NORMALLY OPEN SWITCH	NORMALLY CLOSED SWITCH	GANGED SWITCH	3-POSITION SWITCH	REED SWITCH	MOTOR OR ACTUATOR	SPEED SENSOR	JUNCTION BLOCK	MODEL OPTIONS BRACKET	

Common wiring diagram symbols

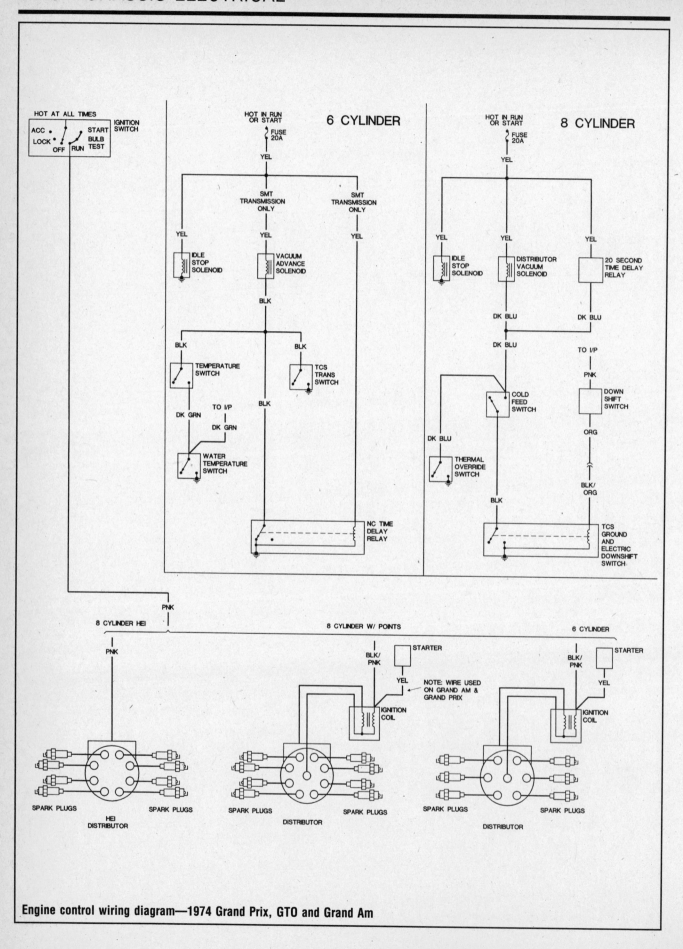

Engine control wiring diagram—1974 Grand Prix, GTO and Grand Am

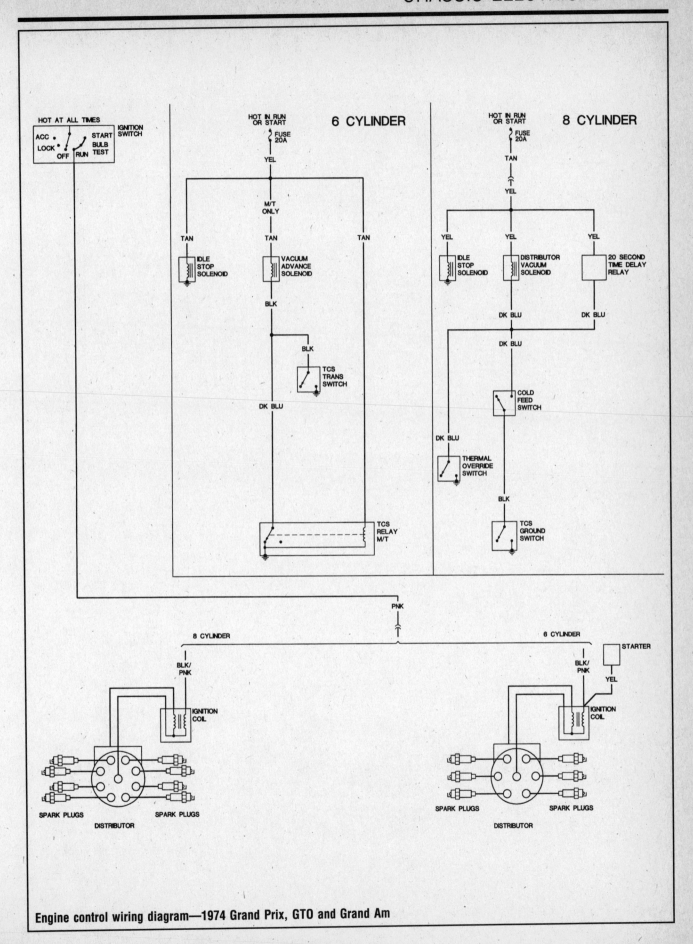

Engine control wiring diagram—1974 Grand Prix, GTO and Grand Am

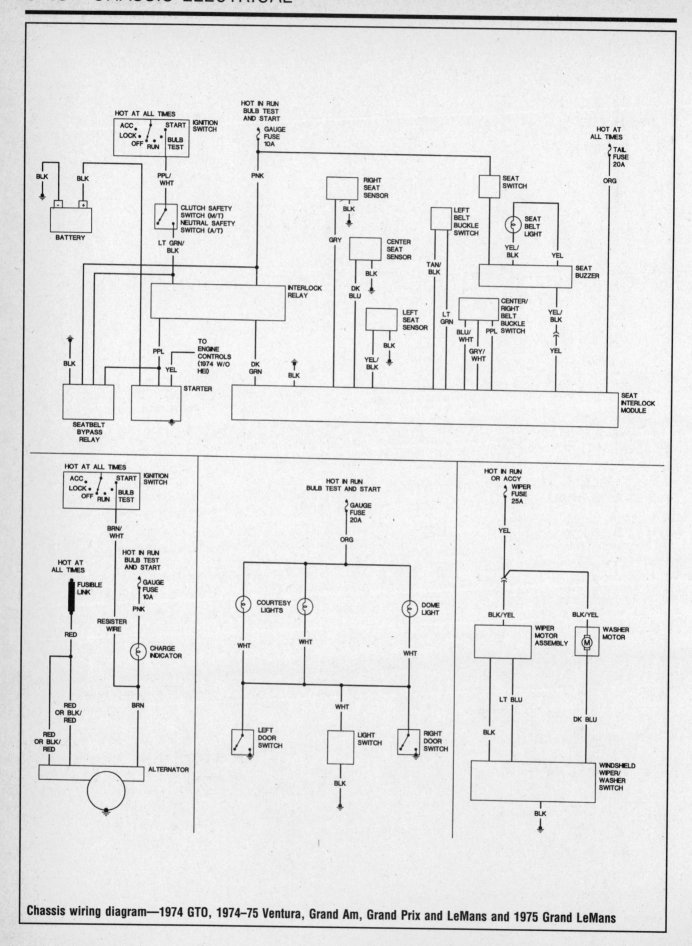

Chassis wiring diagram—1974 GTO, 1974–75 Ventura, Grand Am, Grand Prix and LeMans and 1975 Grand LeMans

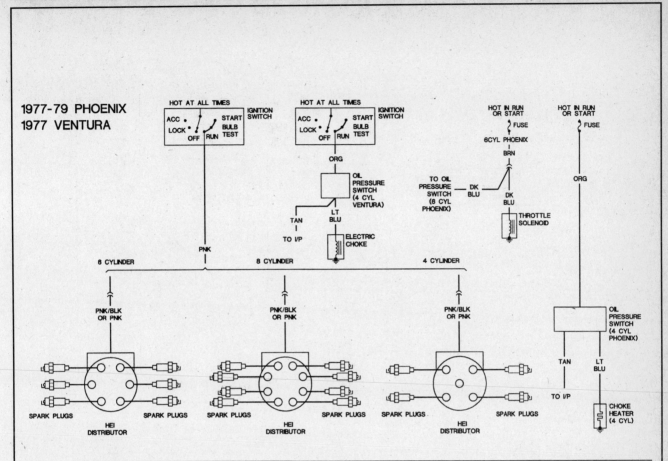

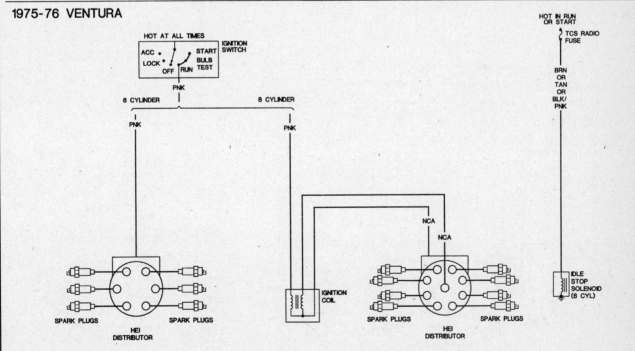

Engine control wiring diagram—1975–77 Ventura and 1977–79 Phoenix

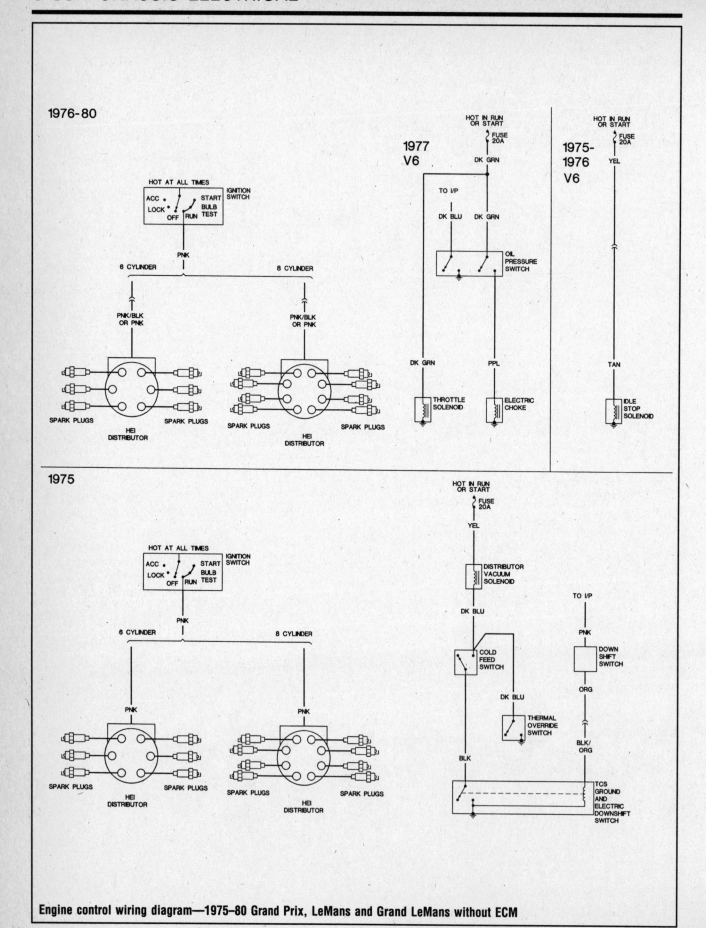

Engine control wiring diagram—1975–80 Grand Prix, LeMans and Grand LeMans without ECM

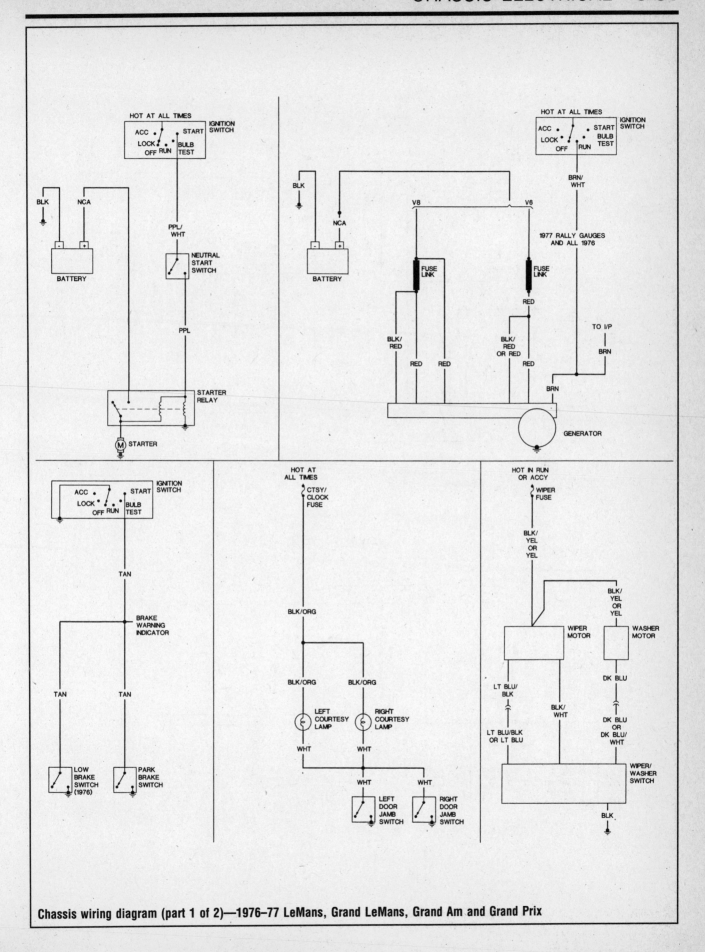

Chassis wiring diagram (part 1 of 2)—1976–77 LeMans, Grand LeMans, Grand Am and Grand Prix

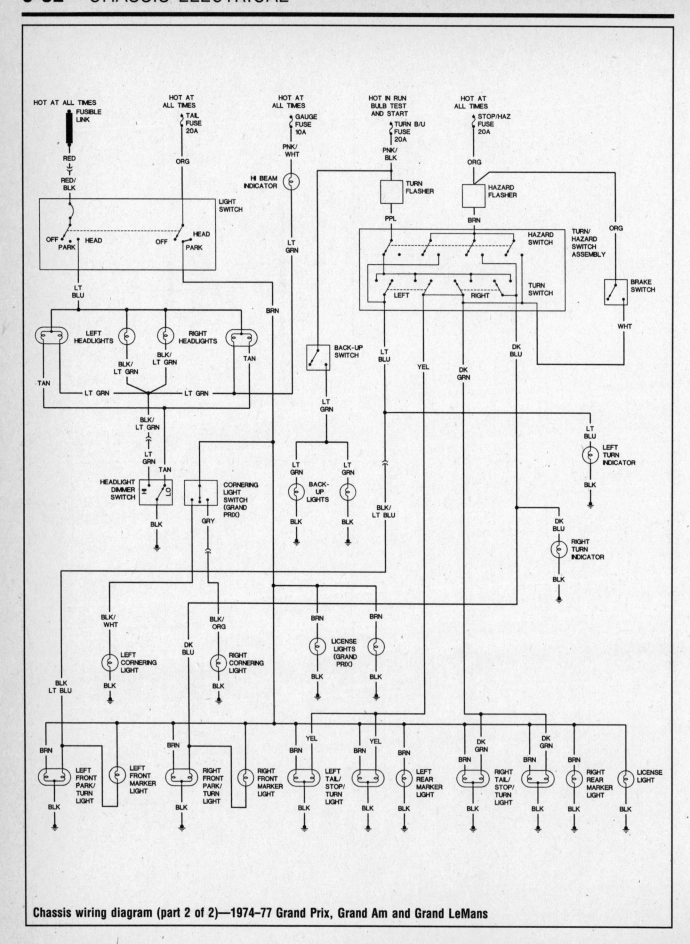

Chassis wiring diagram (part 2 of 2)—1974–77 Grand Prix, Grand Am and Grand LeMans

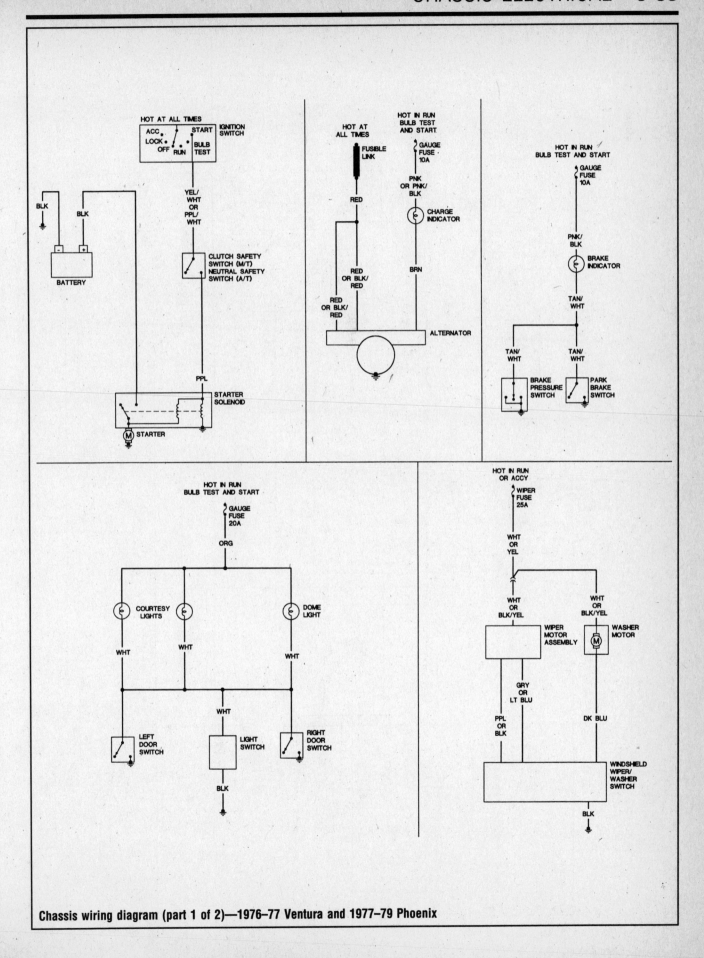

Chassis wiring diagram (part 1 of 2)—1976–77 Ventura and 1977–79 Phoenix

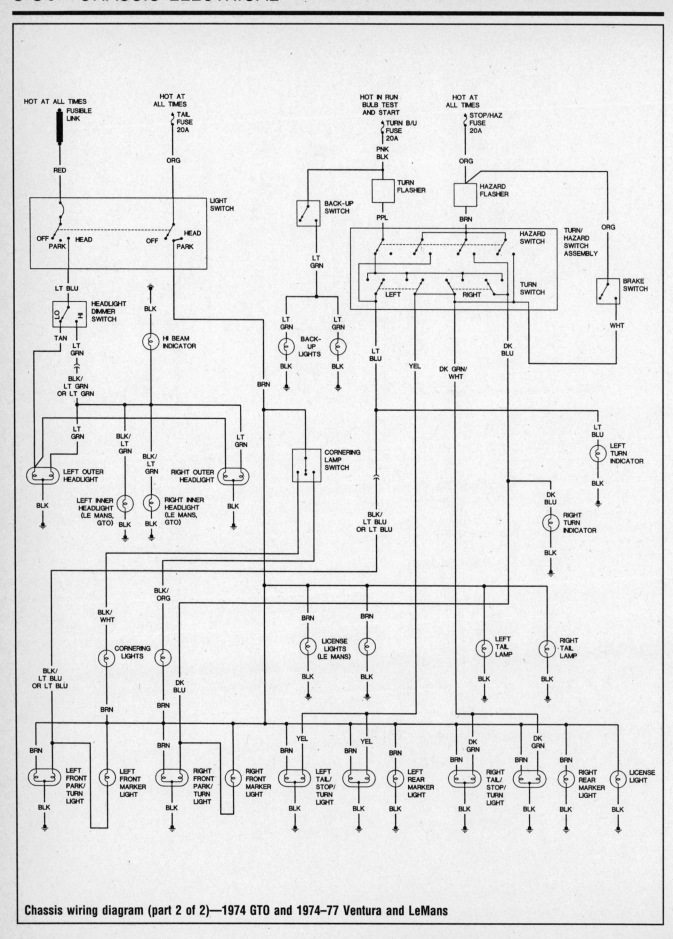

Chassis wiring diagram (part 2 of 2)—1974 GTO and 1974–77 Ventura and LeMans

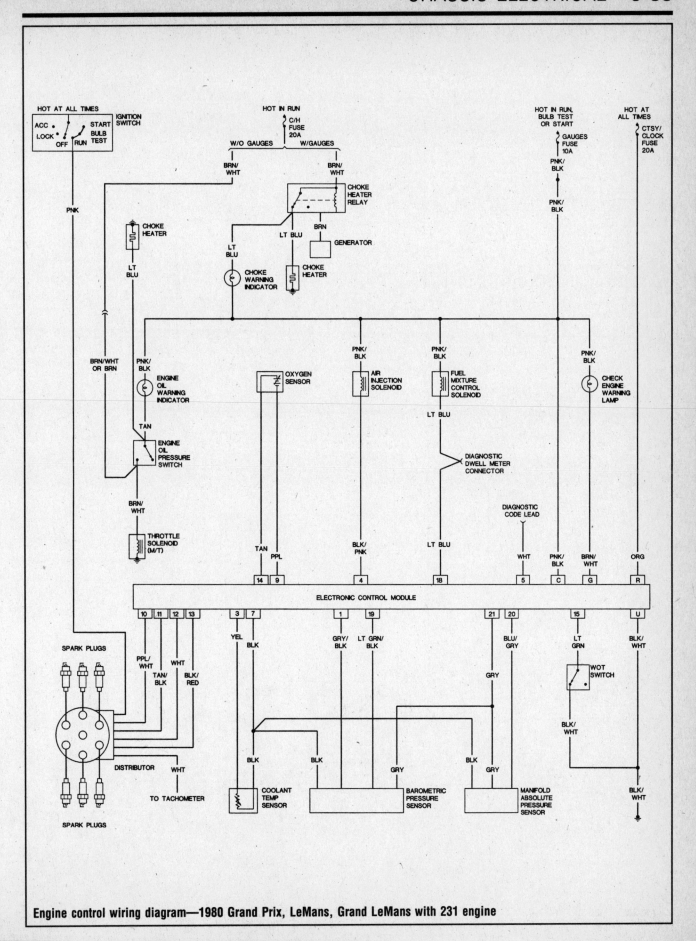

Engine control wiring diagram—1980 Grand Prix, LeMans, Grand LeMans with 231 engine

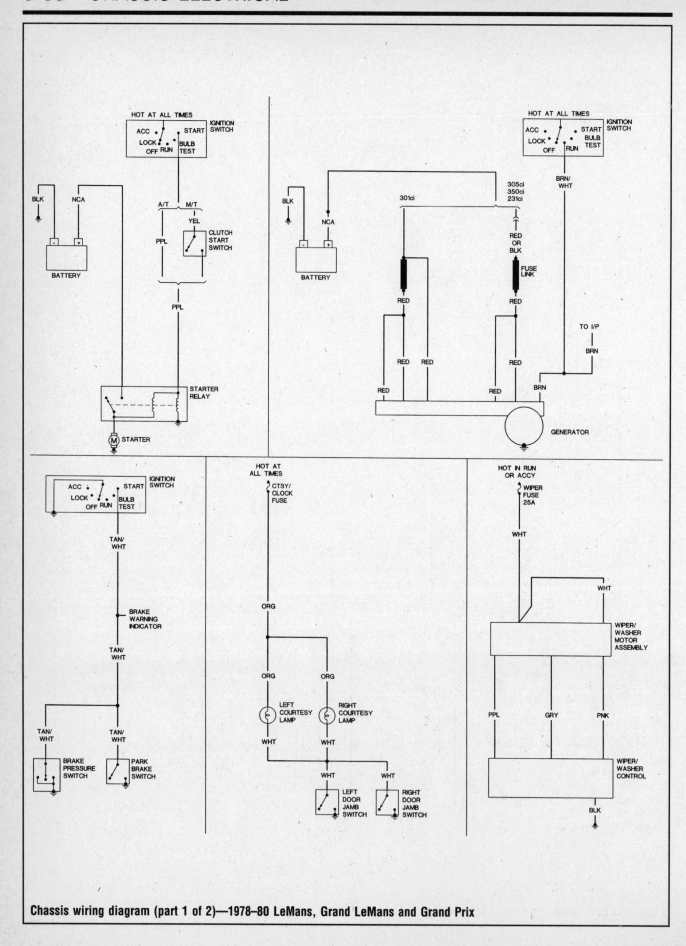

Chassis wiring diagram (part 1 of 2)—1978–80 LeMans, Grand LeMans and Grand Prix

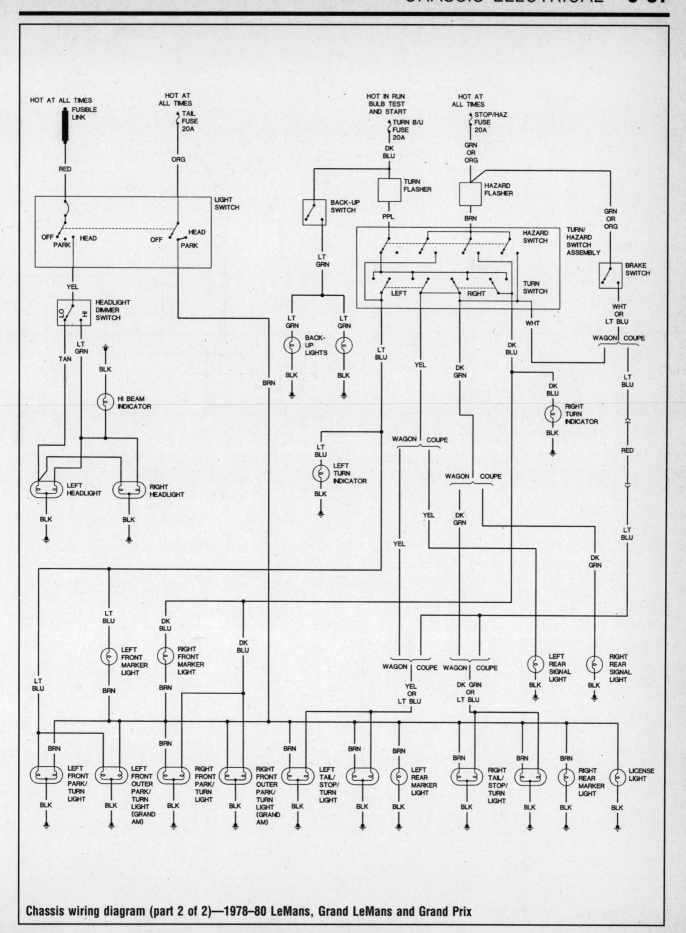

Chassis wiring diagram (part 2 of 2)—1978–80 LeMans, Grand LeMans and Grand Prix

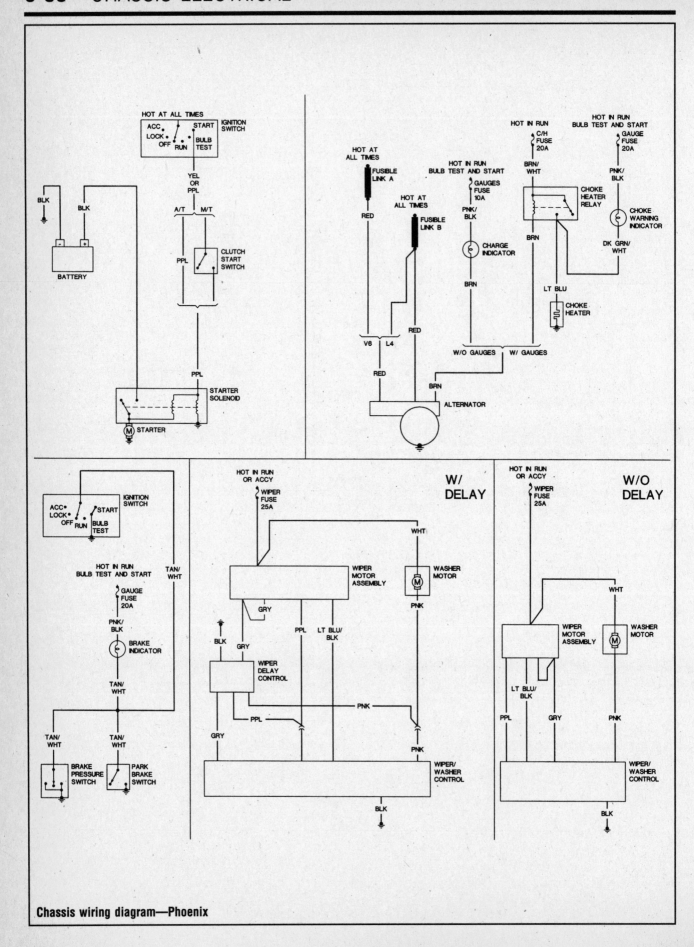

Chassis wiring diagram—Phoenix

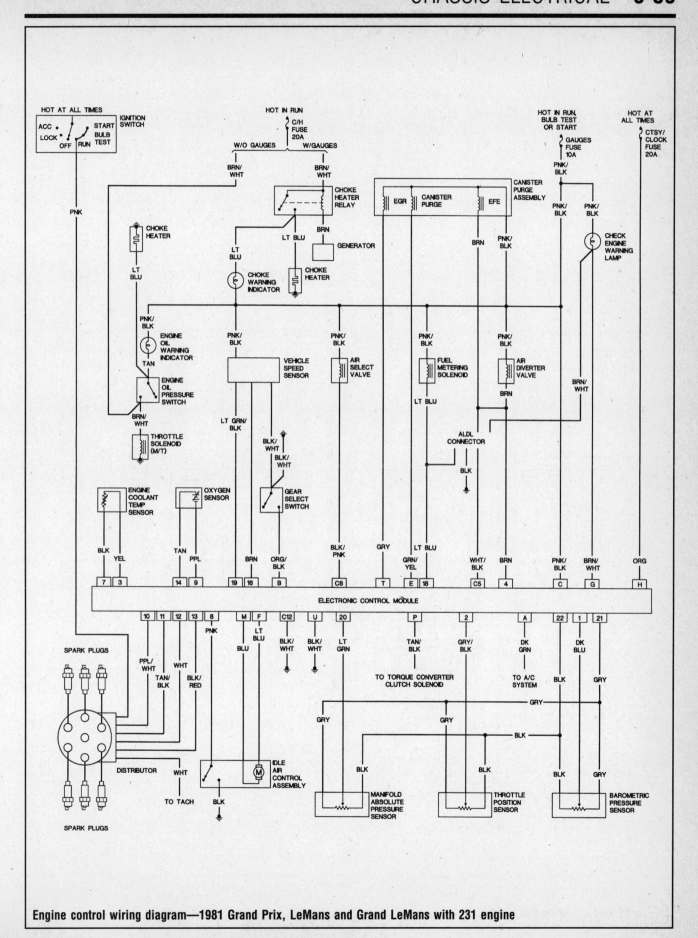

Engine control wiring diagram—1981 Grand Prix, LeMans and Grand LeMans with 231 engine

HOT AT ALL TIMES
IGNITION SWITCH
ACC · START
LOCK · BULB TEST
OFF RUN

HOT IN RUN OR START
CH FUSE 20A
BRN/WHT

HOT IN RUN, BULB TEST OR START
GAUGES FUSE 10A
PNK/BLK

HOT AT ALL TIMES
CTSY/CLOCK FUSE 20A

W/ GAUGES

W/O GAUGES

CHOKE HEATER RELAY

BRN/WHT
THROTTLE SOLENIOD (M/T)

OIL PRESSURE SWITCH

BRN
TO GENERATOR

LT BLU
LT BLU
CHOKE HEATER

CHOKE WARNING INDICATOR
PNK/BLK

TAN
ENGINE OIL WARNING INDICATOR
PNK/BLK

LT BLU
CHOKE HEATER

PNK/BLK
PNK/BLK

CHECK ENGINE WARNING LAMP

W/ GAUGES

W/O GAUGES

PNK/BLK
BRAKE/TORQUE CONVERTER CLUTCH SOLENOID
PNK

PNK/BLK
CANISTER PURGE SOLENOID
DK GRN/YEL

PNK/BLK
VEHICLE SPEED SENSOR
LT GRN/BLK

PNK/BLK
EGR SOLENOID

PNK/BLK
AIR DIVERTER VALVE

PNK/BLK
AIR SELECT VALVE
PNK/BLK

PNK/BLK
FUEL METERING SOLENOID
LT BLU

OXYGEN SENSOR

PPL
AUTOMATIC TRANSMISSION
TORQUE CONVERTER CLUTCH SOLENOID
THIRD GEAR SWITCH

BLK/WHT
BLK/WHT

GEAR SELECT SWITCH

DIAGNOSTIC CONNECTOR
BLK

PPL
ORG

TAN/BLK
BRN
ORG/BLK
GRY
BLK/PNK
LT BLU
PNK/BLK
WHT/BLK
WHT/DK GRN

P H 16 19 H T 4 H 18 G 5 G 9 14 R

ELECTRONIC CONTROL MODULE

10 11 12 13 8 D M A U 12 7 3 2 22 20 21

SPARK PLUGS

PPL/WHT
TAN/BLK
WHT
BLK/RED

LT BLU
DK GRN/WHT
BLK/WHT
BLK
YEL

PNK
BLU
TO A/C SYSTEM

ENGINE COOLANT TEMP SENSOR

DK BLU
BLK
LT GRN
GRY

GRY

VIN W   VIN S
VACUUM FILTER

DISTRIBUTOR

WHT
TO TACHOMETER FILTER

IDLE AIR CONTROL ASSEMBLY
BLK

BLK
LT GRN
GRY

THROTTLE POSITION SENSOR

VACUUM SENSOR

SPARK PLUGS

Engine control wiring diagram—1980–81 LeMans and Grand LeMans and 1981 Grand Prix with 265 engine

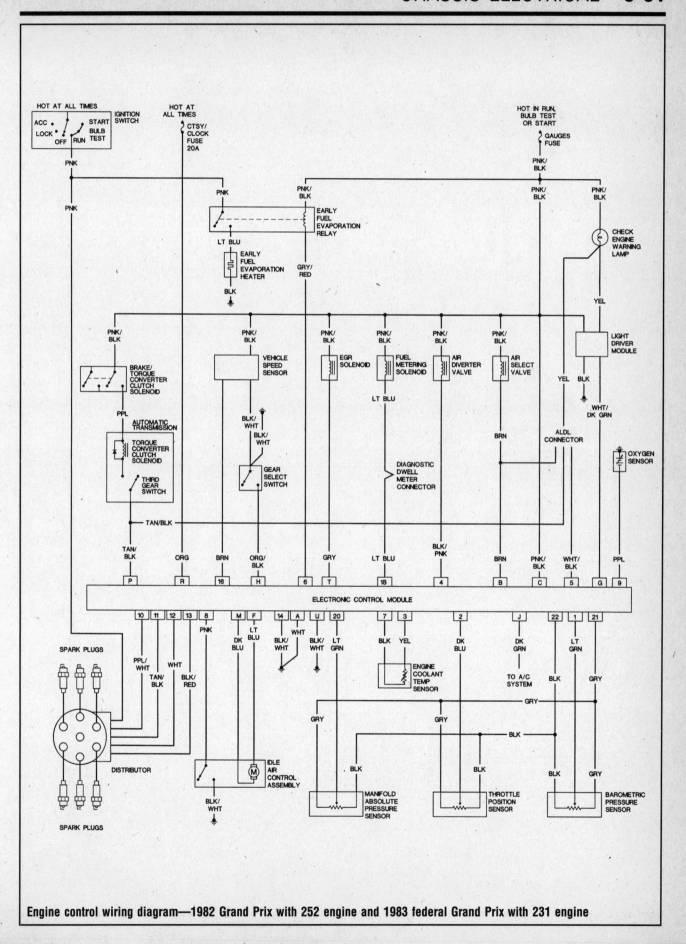

Engine control wiring diagram—1982 Grand Prix with 252 engine and 1983 federal Grand Prix with 231 engine

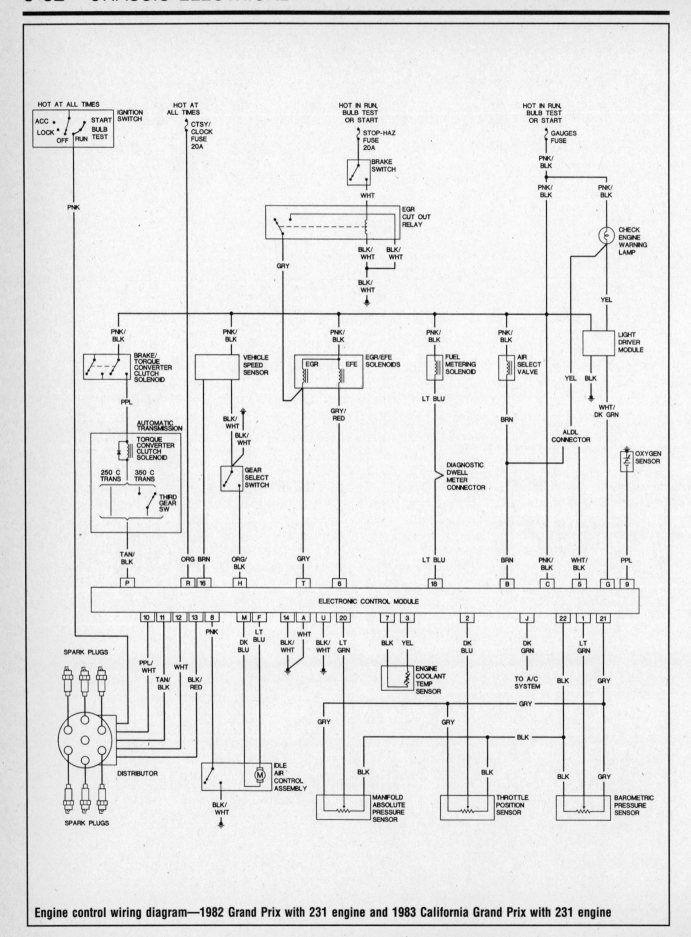

Engine control wiring diagram—1982 Grand Prix with 231 engine and 1983 California Grand Prix with 231 engine

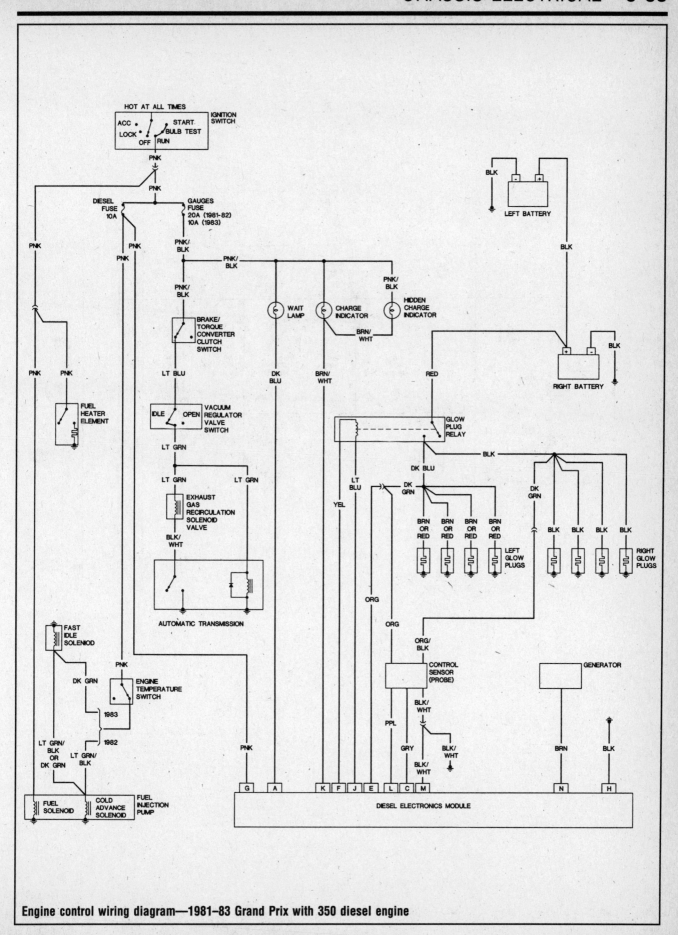

Engine control wiring diagram—1981-83 Grand Prix with 350 diesel engine

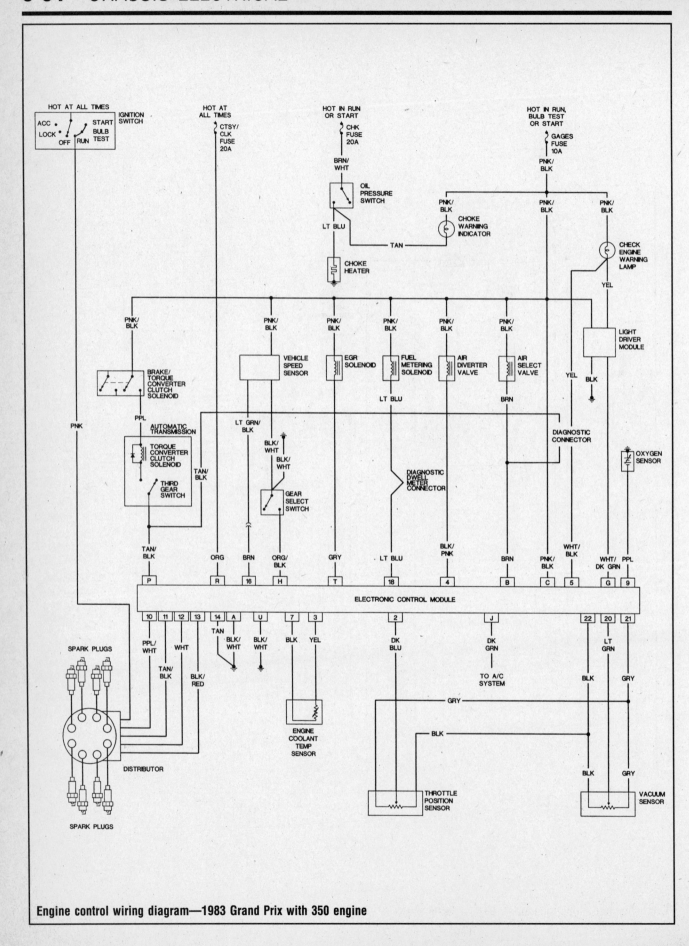

Engine control wiring diagram—1983 Grand Prix with 350 engine

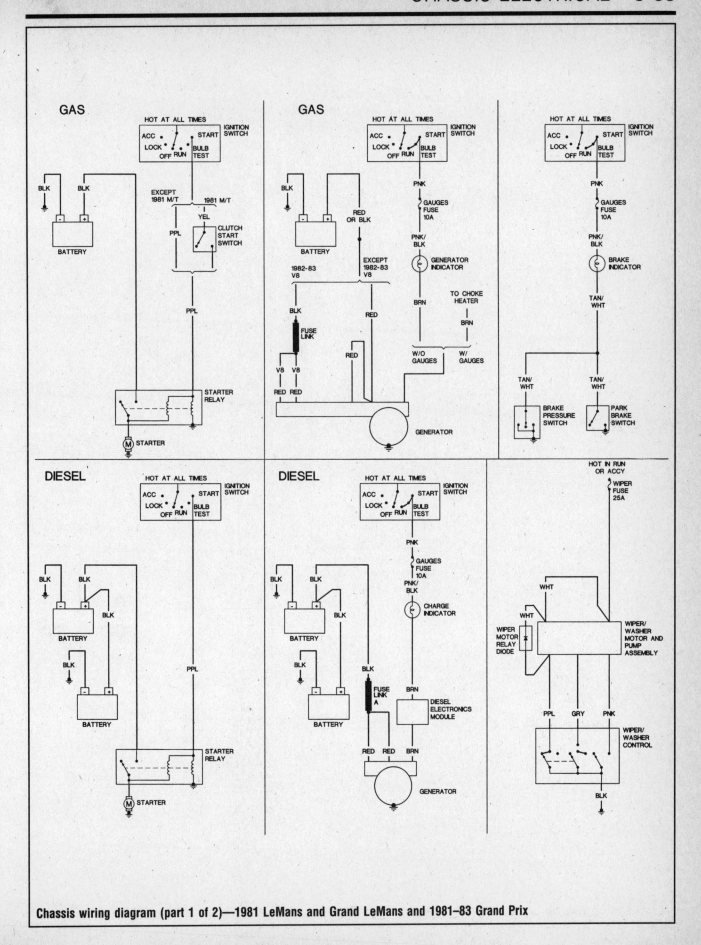

Chassis wiring diagram (part 1 of 2)—1981 LeMans and Grand LeMans and 1981–83 Grand Prix

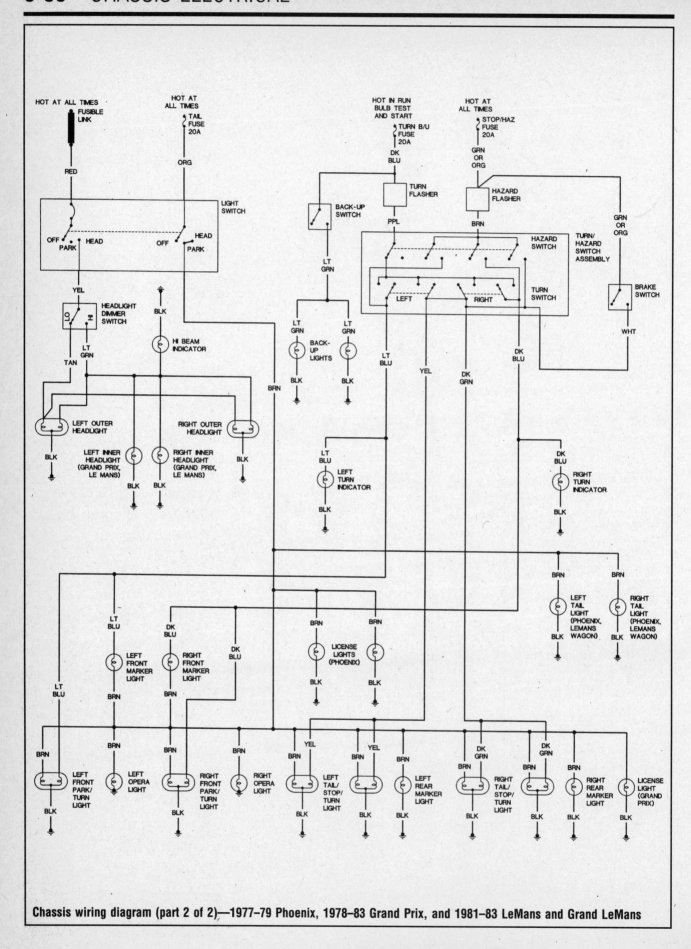

Chassis wiring diagram (part 2 of 2)—1977–79 Phoenix, 1978–83 Grand Prix, and 1981–83 LeMans and Grand LeMans

MANUAL TRANSMISSION 7-2
UNDERSTANDING THE MANUAL
TRANSMISSION 7-2
IDENTIFICATION 7-2
ADJUSTMENT 7-2
LINKAGE 7-2
TRANSMISSION ASSEMBLY 7-6
REMOVAL & INSTALLATION 7-6
CLUTCH 7-7
UNDERSTANDING THE CLUTCH 7-7
ADJUSTMENT 7-7
FREE-PLAY 7-7
DRIVEN DISC AND PRESSURE
PLATE 7-8
REMOVAL & INSTALLATION 7-8
AUTOMATIC TRANSMISSION 7-12
IDENTIFICATION 7-12
FLUID PAN 7-12
REMOVAL & INSTALLATION/FILTER
SERVICE 7-12
ADJUSTMENTS 7-14
SHIFT LINKAGE/CABLE 7-14
DETENT (DOWNSHIFT)
LINKAGE 7-17
ACCELERATOR PEDAL DOWNSHIFT
LINKAGE 7-17
NEUTRAL SAFETY SWITCH 7-18
ADJUSTMENT 7-18
DIESEL ENGINE TRANSMISSION 7-19
ADJUSTMENTS 7-19
TRANSMISSION ASSEMBLY 7-21
REMOVAL & INSTALLATION 7-21
DRIVELINE 7-23
DRIVESHAFT AND U-JOINTS 7-23
REMOVAL & INSTALLATION 7-23
U-JOINT OVERHAUL 7-24
REAR AXLE 7-26
IDENTIFICATION 7-26
AXLE SHAFT AND BEARINGS 7-26
REMOVAL & INSTALLATION 7-28
DETERMINING GEAR RATIO 7-32
SPECIFICATION CHARTS
MANUAL TRANSMISSION I.D.
CHART 7-3

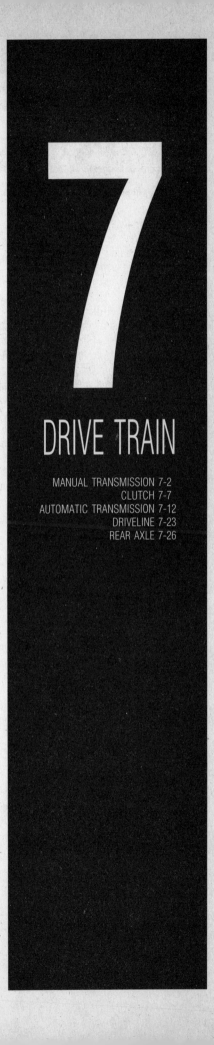

7

DRIVE TRAIN

MANUAL TRANSMISSION 7-2
CLUTCH 7-7
AUTOMATIC TRANSMISSION 7-12
DRIVELINE 7-23
REAR AXLE 7-26

MANUAL TRANSMISSION

Understanding the Manual Transmission

Because of the way an internal combustion engine breathes, it can produce torque (or twisting force) only within a narrow speed range. Most overhead valve pushrod engines must turn at about 2500 rpm to produce their peak torque. Often by 4500 rpm, they are producing so little torque that continued increases in engine speed produce no power increases.

The torque peak on overhead camshaft engines is, generally, much higher, but much narrower.

The manual transmission and clutch are employed to vary the relationship between engine RPM and the speed of the wheels so that adequate power can be produced under all circumstances. The clutch allows engine torque to be applied to the transmission input shaft gradually, due to mechanical slippage. The vehicle can, consequently, be started smoothly from a full stop.

The transmission changes the ratio between the rotating speeds of the engine and the wheels by the use of gears. 4-speed or 5-speed transmissions are most common. The lower gears allow full engine power to be applied to the rear wheels during acceleration at low speeds.

The clutch driveplate is a thin disc, the center of which is splined to the transmission input shaft. Both sides of the disc are covered with a layer of material which is similar to brake lining and which is capable of allowing slippage without roughness or excessive noise.

The clutch cover is bolted to the engine flywheel and incorporates a diaphragm spring which provides the pressure to engage the clutch. The cover also houses the pressure plate. When the clutch pedal is released, the driven disc is sandwiched between the pressure plate and the smooth surface of the flywheel, thus forcing the disc to turn at the same speed as the engine crankshaft.

The transmission contains a mainshaft which passes all the way through the transmission, from the clutch to the driveshaft. This shaft is separated at one point, so that front and rear portions can turn at different speeds.

Power is transmitted by a countershaft in the lower gears and reverse. The gears of the countershaft mesh with gears on the mainshaft, allowing power to be carried from one to the other. Countershaft gears are often integral with that shaft, while several of the mainshaft gears can either rotate independently of the shaft or be locked to it. Shifting from one gear to the next causes one of the gears to be freed from rotating with the shaft and locks another to it. Gears are locked and unlocked by internal dog clutches which slide between the center of the gear and the shaft. The forward gears usually employ synchronizers; friction members which smoothly bring gear and shaft to the same speed before the toothed dog clutches are engaged.

Five different manual transmissions have been available in the mid-size Pontiacs since 1974. The 1974 through 1976 three-speeds and four-speeds were built by Saginaw; the heavy-duty three-speed also available during these years was built by Muncie. Three, four and five speed transmissions have been offered between 1976 and 1979, the former two built by Muncie and the five-speeder a Warner T-50 unit. Three-speed Muncie transmissions were available in these cars until 1981; no manual transmissions have been offered for 1982 or '83.

Identification

Transmission I.D. codes are stamped or painted on the side of the gearbox case, on a flat boss. See the transmission I.D. chart for code information.

Adjustment

LINKAGE

♦ **See Figures 1 thru 7 (pp. 4–5)**

Three Speed Column Shift

1974–77 VEHICLES

1. Place the transmission in reverse.
2. Raise the car and support it with jackstands.
3. Loosen the swivel bolts on the shift rods at the transmission. Make sure the shift rods are free to move in the swivels.
4. Push up on the reverse shift rod until the detent in the column is felt and tighten the swivel bolt for the first/reverse rod.
5. Place the transmission in neutral and insert a 3/16 in. rod through the 2–3 shift lever and into the alignment hole. Tighten the swivel bolt at the transmission.
6. Lower the car. Check the shifter operation. Place the shifter in reverse, and the ignition switch in the **LOCK** position. Make sure the ignition key can be removed and that the steering wheel will not turn.

1978–81 VEHICLES

1. Turn the ignition switch **OFF**.
2. Raise and support the car.
3. Remove the retainer from the shift rods.
4. Place the transmission levers in Neutral.
5. Align the control levers and place a 1/4 inch gauge pin into the levers and brackets, with the shift handle in Neutral.
6. Loosen the nuts on the shift rods and adjust the trunnion and pin assembly on First/Reverse, then tighten the nuts and install the shift rod and retainer.
7. Loosen the shift rod nut and adjust the trunnion and pin assembly on Second/Third, then tighten the nuts and install the shift rod and retainer.
8. Remove the gauge pin from the control lever assembly and check the operation of the control lever. Re-adjust as required.
9. Lower the car.

Three-Speed Floor Shift

1. Place the transmission in reverse, and the ignition switch in the **LOCK** position.
2. Raise the car in the air and support it with jackstands.

Manual Transmission I.D. Chart

Year	Code	Transmission	Car Model	Engine
1974	TM	Saginaw 3 spd.	Le Mans/Ventura	250-6
	TN	Saginaw 3 spd.	Le Mans/Ventura	350-8
	RM	Muncie 3 spd.	Le Mans	350-8
	WC	Saginaw 4 spd.	Le Mans/Ventura	350-8
1975	DC	Saginaw 3 spd.	Le Mans/Ventura	250-6 260-8
1976	DC	Saginaw 3 spd.	Le Mans Ventura	250-6 260-8
	SA	Warner 5 spd.	Le Mans/Ventura	260-8
1977	ZH	Muncie 3 spd.	Le Mans/Ventura	231-6
	SS	Muncie 4 spd.	Ventura	301-8①
	RJ	Warner 5 spd.	Ventura	151-4
1978	UR	Muncie 3 spd.	Ventura/Phoenix	231-6
	RZ	Muncie 3 spd.	Le Mans, Grand Prix	231-6
	SS	Muncie 4 spd.	Ventura/Phoenix	301-8①
	RJ	Warner 5 spd.	Ventura/Phoenix	151-4①
1979	UC	Muncie 3 spd.	Phoenix	231-6
	SA	Muncie 3 spd.	Le Mans/Grand Prix	231-6
	SR	Muncie 4 spd.	Phoenix	305-8
	SB SC	Muncie 4 spd.	Le Mans/Grand Prix	231-6 301-8
1980	Z6	Muncie 3 spd.	Le Mans	231-6
1981	Z6	Muncie 3 spd.	Le Mans	231-6

① Except California

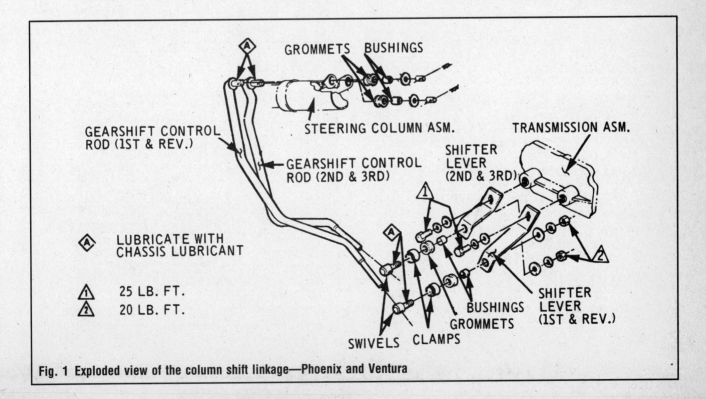

Fig. 1 Exploded view of the column shift linkage—Phoenix and Ventura

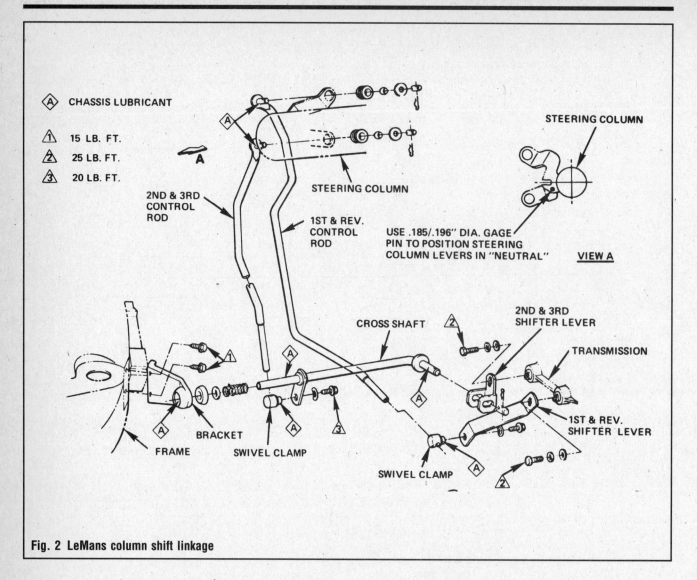

◇ A   CHASSIS LUBRICANT

△1   15 LB. FT.

△2   25 LB. FT.

△3   20 LB. FT.

2ND & 3RD CONTROL ROD

1ST & REV. CONTROL ROD

STEERING COLUMN

STEERING COLUMN

USE .185/.196" DIA. GAGE PIN TO POSITION STEERING COLUMN LEVERS IN "NEUTRAL"   VIEW A

CROSS SHAFT

2ND & 3RD SHIFTER LEVER

TRANSMISSION

1ST & REV. SHIFTER LEVER

FRAME

BRACKET

SWIVEL CLAMP

SWIVEL CLAMP

Fig. 2 LeMans column shift linkage

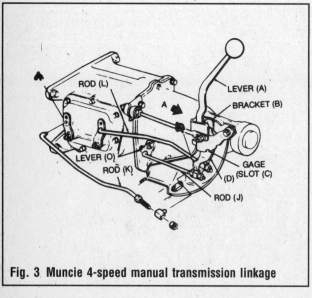

ROD (L)

LEVER (A)

BRACKET (B)

LEVER (O)

ROD (K)

GAGE (D) (SLOT (C))

ROD (J)

Fig. 3 Muncie 4-speed manual transmission linkage

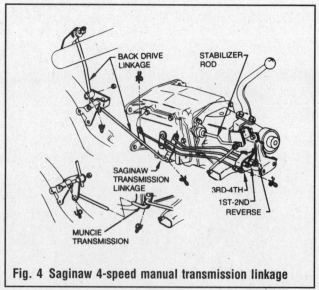

BACK DRIVE LINKAGE

STABILIZER ROD

SAGINAW TRANSMISSION LINKAGE

MUNCIE TRANSMISSION

3RD-4TH

1ST-2ND REVERSE

Fig. 4 Saginaw 4-speed manual transmission linkage

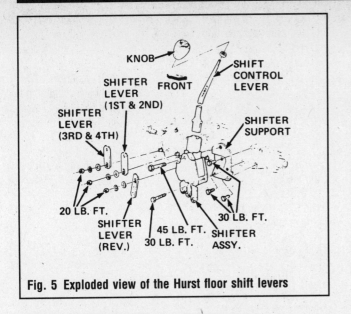

Fig. 5 Exploded view of the Hurst floor shift levers

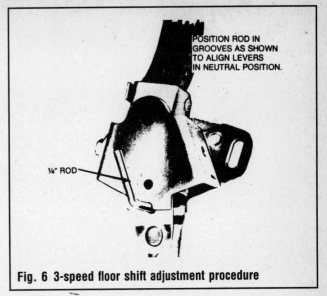

Fig. 6 3-speed floor shift adjustment procedure

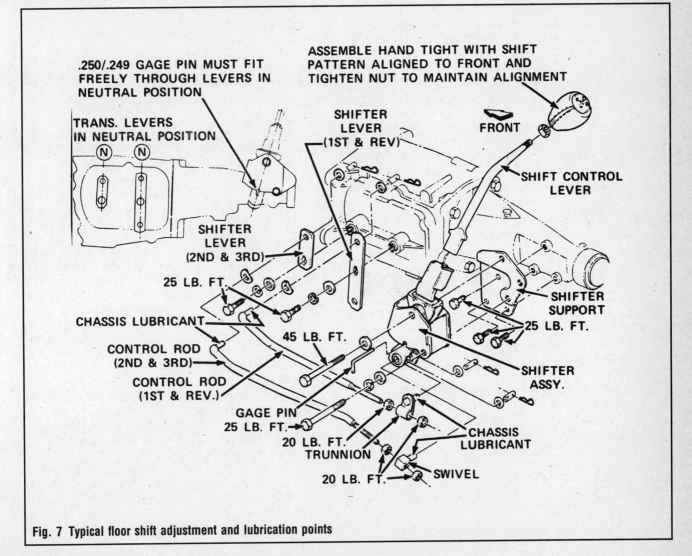

Fig. 7 Typical floor shift adjustment and lubrication points

➡**Do not place the shifter in reverse from below.**

3. Loosen the swivel bolt on the back drive rod at the equalizer. Make sure the rod moves freely in the swivel.

4. Pull down lightly on the back drive rod until a stop is felt. Tighten the swivel bolt.

5. Place the shifter in neutral, and loosen the jam nuts at the shifter assembly.

6. Insert a ¼ in. pin through the shift lever brackets and levers as shown in the illustration. Adjust the swivels to obtain a "free pin" fit at the levers.

7. Tighten the jam nuts.

8. Lower the car and check the shifter operation.

Four-Speed Floor Shift

1974 VEHICLES

The four-speed shift linkage is adjusted in exactly the same manner as the Saginaw three speed floor shift described earlier.

1977–79 VEHICLES

1. Turn the ignition switch to the **OFF** position.
2. Raise and support the car.
3. Loosen the locknuts at the swivels on the shift rods.
4. Set the transmission levers in Neutral.
5. Place the shifter in Neutral.
6. Align the control levers and place a ¼ inch gauge pin into the levers and bracket.
7. Tighten the First/Second shift rod nut against the swivel. Tighten to 10 ft. lbs.
8. Tighten the Third/Fourth shift rod nut against the swivel. Tighten to 10 ft. lbs.
9. Tighten the reverse shift control rod nut to 10 ft. lbs.
10. Remove the gauge pin, check for proper operation of the levers and lower the car.

Five-Speed Floor Shift

The five-speed transmission linkage is internal and cannot be adjusted.

Transmission Assembly

REMOVAL & INSTALLATION

Three-Speed and Four-Speed Transmissions

1. Raise the car in the air and support it with jackstands.
2. Remove the driveshaft.
3. Disconnect the shift linkage. On floor shift models, remove the shift lever from the shifter assembly. The shift lever is retained by a pin and spring clip arrangements. See the illustration for removal.
4. If equipped with Transmission Controlled Spark (TCS), disconnect the TCS switch wire.
5. Support the engine with a jack. Remove the bolts which attach the crossmember to the transmission.

6. Disconnect the parking brake cable, and unbolt the transmission crossmember from the frame. On dual exhaust models, it may be necessary to disconnect the left-hand exhaust pipe at the exhaust manifold to provide clearance.

7. Disconnect the speedometer cable at the transmission.

8. Remove the two top transmission-to-bellhousing bolts and install guide studs in their place. The guide studs may be fabricated from two old transmission bolts by simply cutting the heads off the bolts.

9. Remove the two lower transmission attaching bolts.

10. Carefully slide the transmission rearward and remove it from the car.

To install:

11. Bring the transmission into position with the bellhousing and carefully guide it into the housing.

12. Install the transmission. You may have to turn the input shaft one way or the other to get the splines to mate with the grooves in the clutch hub.

13. Install the transmission attaching bolts.

14. Raise the engine with the jack if necessary, and install the crossmember. Install the exhaust pipe if it was removed.

15. Install the driveshaft. Connect the speedometer cable.

16. Connect the TCS switch wire. Install the shift lever or shift linkage.

17. Install the driveshaft, then carefully lower the vehicle.

Five-Speed Transmission

1. Remove the shift control knob, the shift boot retainer, shift boot, and insulator.

2. Pull back the edge of the carpeting and remove the bolts that attach the shifter assembly and remove the assembly.

3. Raise the car in the air and support it with jackstands.

4. Remove the driveshaft.

5. Disconnect the speedometer cable. Remove the catalytic converter support bracket.

6. Support the engine with a jack and remove the bolts which attach the crossmember to the transmission. Unbolt the crossmember from the frame and remove it from the car.

7. Remove the two upper bolts which attach the transmission to the bellhousing. Install guide pins in their place. These may be made from a pair of old transmission bolts with the heads cut off. Guide pins are necessary to prevent distortion of the clutch plate when the two lower bolts are removed. If no guide pins are available, support the transmission in some way before removing the two lower bolts.

8. Remove the two lower bolts and slide the transmission out of the bellhousing.

9. To install the transmission, bring it into position with the bellhousing and carefully guide it into the housing. It will probably be necessary to turn the input shaft one way or the other to get the splines to mate with the grooves in the clutch hub.

10. Reinstall the crossmember.

11. Install the driveshaft and the speedometer cable. Reinstall the catalytic converter support bracket.

12. Install the shifter.

CLUTCH

Understanding the Clutch

The purpose of the clutch is to disconnect and connect engine power at the transmission. A vehicle at rest requires a lot of engine torque to get all that weight moving. An internal combustion engine does not develop a high starting torque (unlike steam engines) so it must be allowed to operate without any load until it builds up enough torque to move the vehicle. To a point, torque increases with engine rpm. The clutch allows the engine to build up torque by physically disconnecting the engine from the transmission, relieving the engine of any load or resistance.

The transfer of engine power to the transmission (the load) must be smooth and gradual; if it weren't, drive line components would wear out or break quickly. This gradual power transfer is made possible by gradually releasing the clutch pedal. The clutch disc and pressure plate are the connecting link between the engine and transmission. When the clutch pedal is released, the disc and plate contact each other (the clutch is engaged) physically joining the engine and transmission. When the pedal is pushed in, the disc and plate separate (the clutch is disengaged) disconnecting the engine from the transmission.

Most clutch assemblies consists of the flywheel, the clutch disc, the clutch pressure plate, the throw out bearing and fork, the actuating linkage and the pedal. The flywheel and clutch pressure plate (driving members) are connected to the engine crankshaft and rotate with it. The clutch disc is located between the flywheel and pressure plate, and is splined to the transmission shaft. A driving member is one that is attached to the engine and transfers engine power to a driven member (clutch disc) on the transmission shaft. A driving member (pressure plate) rotates (drives) a driven member (clutch disc) on contact and, in so doing, turns the transmission shaft.

There is a circular diaphragm spring within the pressure plate cover (transmission side). In a relaxed state (when the clutch pedal is fully released) this spring is convex; that is, it is dished outward toward the transmission. Pushing in the clutch pedal actuates the attached linkage. Connected to the other end of this is the throw out fork, which hold the throw out bearing. When the clutch pedal is depressed, the clutch linkage pushes the fork and bearing forward to contact the diaphragm spring of the pressure plate. The outer edges of the spring are secured to the pressure plate and are pivoted on rings so that when the center of the spring is compressed by the throw out bearing, the outer edges bow outward and, by so doing, pull the pressure plate in the same direction away from the clutch disc. This action separates the disc from the plate, disengaging the clutch and allowing the transmission to be shifted into another gear. A coil type clutch return spring attached to the clutch pedal arm permits full release of the pedal. Releasing the pedal pulls the throw out bearing away from the diaphragm spring resulting in a reversal of spring position. As bearing pressure is gradually released from the spring center, the outer edges of the spring bow outward, pushing the pressure plate into closer contact with the clutch disc. As the disc and plate move closer together, friction between the two increases and slippage is reduced until, when full spring pressure is applied (by fully releasing the pedal) the speed of the disc and plate are the same. This stops all slipping, creating a direct connection between the plate and disc which results in the transfer of power

from the engine to the transmission. The clutch disc is now rotating with the pressure plate at engine speed and, because it is splined to the transmission shaft, the shaft now turns at the same engine speed.

The clutch is operating properly if:

1. It will stall the engine when released with the vehicle held stationary.

2. The shift lever can be moved freely between 1st and reverse gears when the vehicle is stationary and the clutch disengaged.

A single plate dry disc-type clutch is used on all cars. The clutch pressure plate is of the disc spring type; pressure plate spring pressure forces the clutch driven plate against the flywheel, thereby coupling the engine to the transmission.

The clutch linkage mechanism consists of a clutch release bearing (throwout bearing), and the appropriate linkage to manually connect the bearing release arm to the clutch pedal.

Adjustment

FREE-PLAY

♦ **See Figure 8**

1. Total clutch pedal free-play should be between ¾ in. and 1 in. The free-play is adjusted by means of a threaded rod which rides in the outer end of the throwout bearing arm.

2. To adjust the free-play, first remove the pedal return spring.

3. Loosen the locknut on the equalizer rod (the fork rod in illustration).

4. Adjust the rod length by turning the rod. When the release bearing (throwout bearing) is just *lightly* resting on the fingers of the pressure plate, the adjustment should be just about right.

5. Check the clutch pedal free-play. There should be no more than one inch of free-play before resistance is encountered. If there is too much free-play, the clutch will not engage fully. If

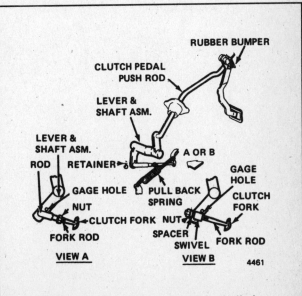

Fig. 8 Clutch pedal free-play (all models similar)

there is too little, the pressure plate will ride against the clutch all the time and the clutch will wear out quickly.

6. Tighten the lock rod nut and install the return spring.

Driven Disc and Pressure Plate

REMOVAL & INSTALLATION

♦ **See Figures 9 and 10**

1. Remove the transmission as previously outlined.
2. Disconnect the clutch return spring and the clutch rod assembly. Remove the throwout bearing.
3. Remove the bell housing. The starter does not have to be removed. The clutch release arm can stay in the housing.
4. Scribe an "X" mark on the flywheel opposite the mark on the pressure plate cover. The marks are there for balance purposes.
5. Remove the pressure plate attaching bolts and remove the pressure plate and clutch assembly.

To install:

6. To install the clutch and pressure plate assembly, you will need a clutch alignment tool or an old input shaft. During installation, be very careful not to get grease on the clutch disc, the flywheel or the pressure plate.
7. Install the clutch disc and pressure plate assembly, being careful to align the "X" marks. Install the attaching bolts loosely.
8. Align the clutch disc using an alignment tool or an old input shaft. Leave the alignment tool in place while you tighten the attaching bolts. (Alignment tools are available at most auto parts jobbers or auto tool dealers).

9. Tighten the attaching bolts; tighten the three bolts marked "L" first. Tighten all the bolts to 30 ft. lbs.
10. Reinstall the bell housing.
11. Install the throwout bearing (release bearing).
12. Install the transmission.

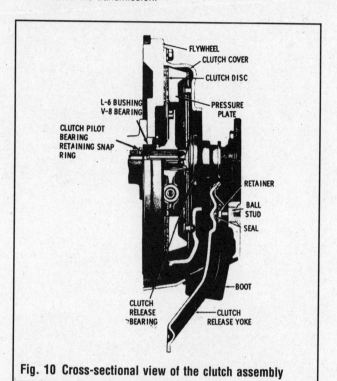

Fig. 10 Cross-sectional view of the clutch assembly

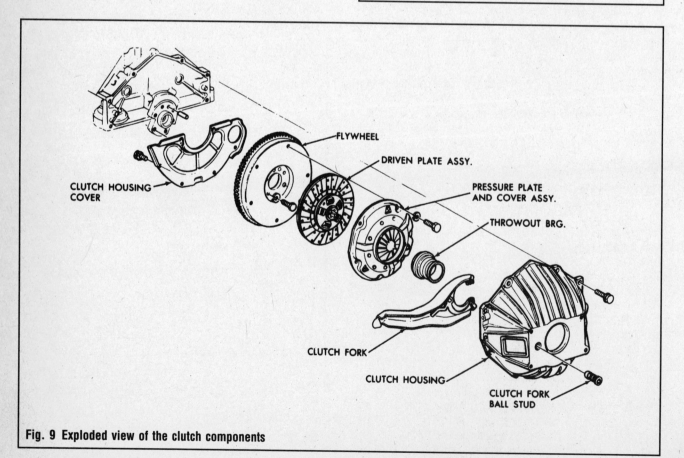

Fig. 9 Exploded view of the clutch components

Loosen and remove the clutch and pressure plate bolts evenly, a little at a time . . .

If necessary, lock the flywheel in place and remove the retaining bolts . . .

. . . then carefully remove the clutch and pressure plate assembly from the flywheel

. . . then remove the flywheel from the crankshaft in order replace it or have it machined

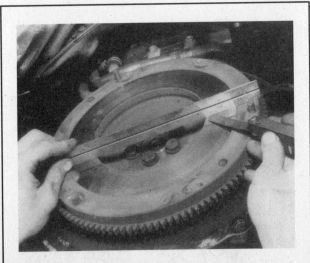

Check across the flywheel surface, it should be flat

Upon installation, it is usually a good idea to apply a thread-locking compound to the flywheel bolts

Check the pressure plate for excessive wear

Clutch plate installed with the arbor in place

Be sure that the flywheel surface is clean, before installing the clutch

Clutch plate and pressure plate installed with the alignment arbor in place

Install a clutch alignment arbor, to align the clutch assembly during installation

Pressure plate-to-flywheel bolt holes should align

You may want to use a thread locking compound on the clutch assembly bolts

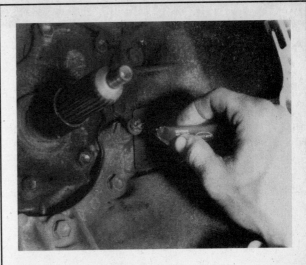

Grease the clutch release fork ball

Install the clutch assembly bolts and tighten in steps, using an X pattern

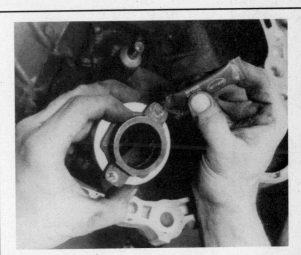

On these style bearings, grease the throwout bearing assembly at the outer contact points . . .

Be sure to use a torque wrench to tighten all bolts

. . . and at the throwout bearing assembly at the inner contact points

AUTOMATIC TRANSMISSION

Identification

♦ **See Figures 11, 12 and 13**

The automatic transmissions covered in this guide are easily identified by the shape of their oil pans. The 1974–76 M-40 pans are similar (irregular-shaped) to the later THM 400, and the M-38 pan (1974–76) is similar to the later THM 350. More transmission identification can be found in the beginning of Chapter 1.

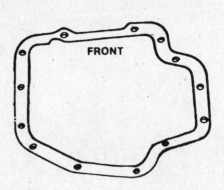

Fig. 13 Automatic transmission fluid pan shape—Turbo Hydra-Matic 400 shown, earlier M-40 similar

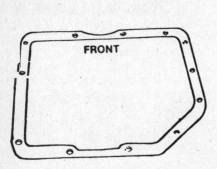

Fig. 11 Automatic transmissions can usually be identified by the shape of their fluid pan—Turbo Hydra-Matic 350 shown, earlier M-38 similar

Fluid Pan

REMOVAL & INSTALLATION/FILTER SERVICE

The fluid should be changed with the transmission warm. A 20 minute drive at highway speeds should accomplish this.

1. Raise and support the vehicle, preferably in a level attitude.
2. With the Turbo Hydra-Matic 350, support the transmission and remove the support crossmember.
3. Place a large pan under the transmission pan. Remove all the front and side pan bolts. Loosen the rear bolts about four turns.

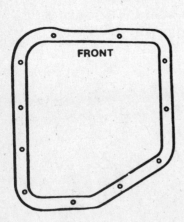

Fig. 12 Turbo Hydra-Matic 200 automatic transmission fluid pan

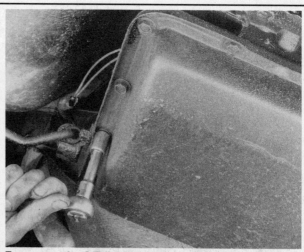

To remove the A/T fluid pan, remove the front and side bolts, then loosen the rear bolts 4 turns each

Carefully pry the pan loose, being careful not to distort the flange

Unfasten the filter-to-body retaining screws . . .

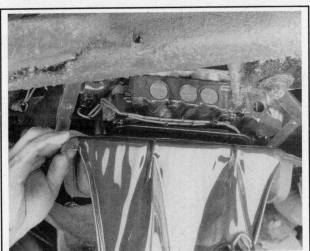

Allow the automatic transmission fluid to drain completely into a suitable container

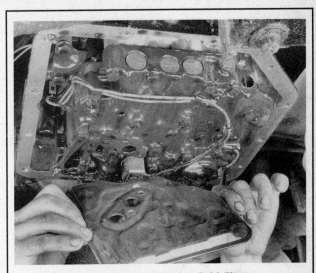

. . . then remove the transmission fluid filter

After all of the fluid has drained, remove the automatic transmission pan

4. Pry the pan loose and let it drain.

5. Remove the pan and gasket. Clean the pan thoroughly with solvent and air dry it. Be very careful not to get any lint from rags in the pan.

➡ It is normal to find a SMALL amount of metal shavings in the pan. An excessive amount of metal shavings indicates transmission damage which must be handled by a professional automatic transmission mechanic.

6. Remove the strainer to valve body screws, the strainer, and the gasket. Most 350 transmissions will have a throw-away filter instead of a strainer. On the 400 transmission, remove the filter retaining bolt, filter, and intake pipe O-ring.

7. If there is a strainer, clean it in solvent and air dry.

To install:

8. Install the new filter or cleaned strainer with a new gasket. Tighten the screws to 12 ft. lbs. On the 400, install a new intake pipe O-ring and a new filter, tightening the retaining bolt to 10 ft. lbs.

9. Install the pan with a new gasket. Tighten the bolts evenly to 12 ft. lbs. (8 for Powerglide and Torque Drive).

10. Lower the car and add the proper amount of DEXRON® or DEXRON® II automatic transmission fluid through the dipstick tube.

11. Start the engine in Park and let it idle. Do not race the engine. Shift into each shift lever position, shift back into Park, and check the fluid level on the dipstick. The level should be ¼ in. below ADD. Be very careful not to overfill. Recheck the level after the car has been driven long enough to thoroughly warm up the transmission. Add fluid as necessary. The level should then be at FULL.

Adjustments

♦ **See Figures 14 thru 20 (pp. 15–17)**

➡**For diesel engines, please refer to the procedures located later in this chapter.**

SHIFT LINKAGE/CABLE

Column Shift

1. Loosen the swivel screw on the shift linkage clamp.
2. Set the lever on the transmission into Neutral by moving it

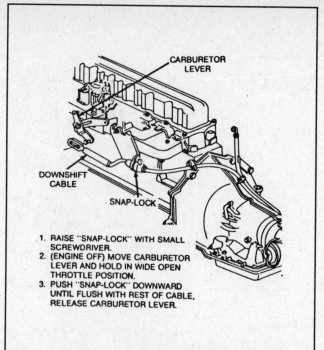

1. RAISE "SNAP-LOCK" WITH SMALL SCREWDRIVER.
2. (ENGINE OFF) MOVE CARBURETOR LEVER AND HOLD IN WIDE OPEN THROTTLE POSITION.
3. PUSH "SNAP-LOCK" DOWNWARD UNTIL FLUSH WITH REST OF CABLE, RELEASE CARBURETOR LEVER.

Fig. 14 Automatic transmission linkage adjustment procedure—250 cu. in. 6-cylinder engine

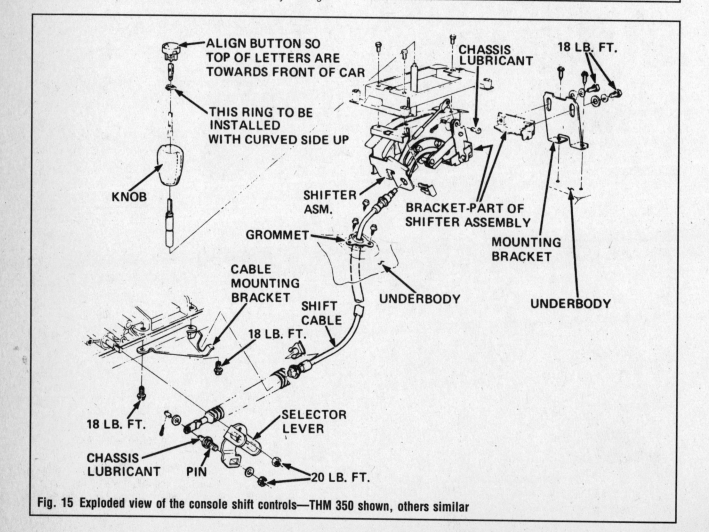

Fig. 15 Exploded view of the console shift controls—THM 350 shown, others similar

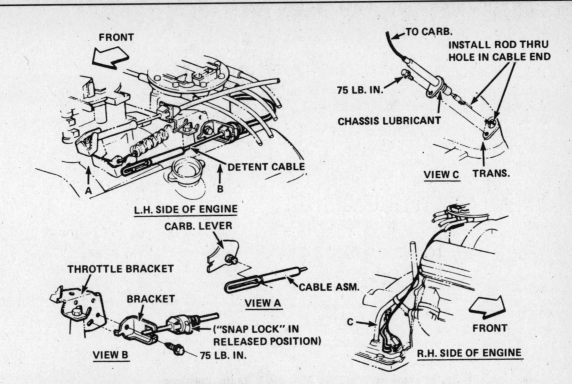

DETENT CONTROL CABLE ADJUSTMENT PROCEDURE
1. AFTER INSTALLATION TO TRANSMISSION, AND CLIP IF SPECIFIED, INSTALL DETENT CONTROL CABLE IN CONTROL CABLE BRACKET WITH "SNAP LOCK" DISENGAGED (DETENT CABLE SHOULD BE FREE TO SLIDE THROUGH "SNAP LOCK" TO ALLOW FOR ADJUSTMENT).
2. INSTALL DETENT CONTROL CABLE TO CARBURETOR LEVER.
3. OPEN CARBURETOR LEVER TO "FULL THROTTLE STOP" AND HOLD IN THIS POSITION.
4. CARBURETOR LEVER <u>MUST BE TIGHT AGAINST FULL THROTTLE STOP</u>, THEN PUSH "SNAP LOCK" UNTIL IT IS FLUSH WITH THE REST OF THE DETENT CABLE FITTING.
5. RELEASE CARBURETOR LEVER.

Fig. 16 Downshift (detent) cable adjustment

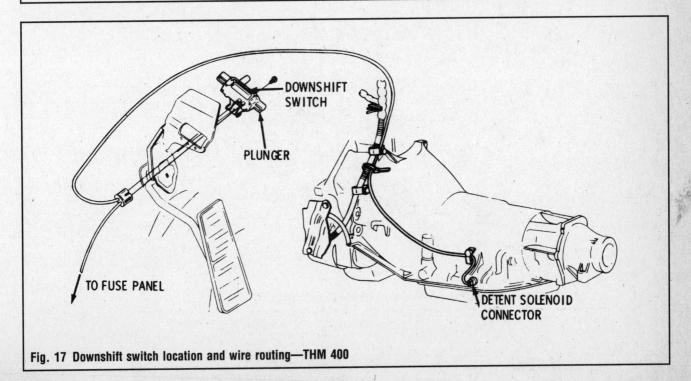

Fig. 17 Downshift switch location and wire routing—THM 400

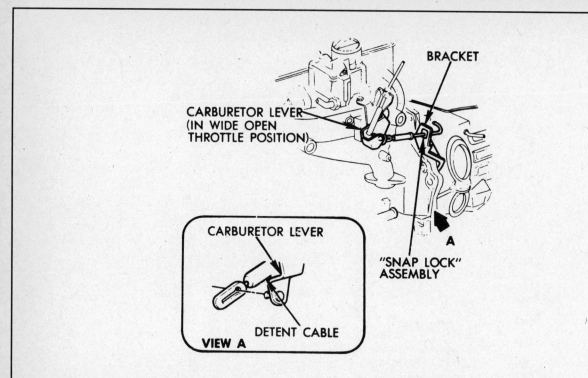

Fig. 18 Downshift detent switch location—THM 200 and 350, and M-38 transmissions

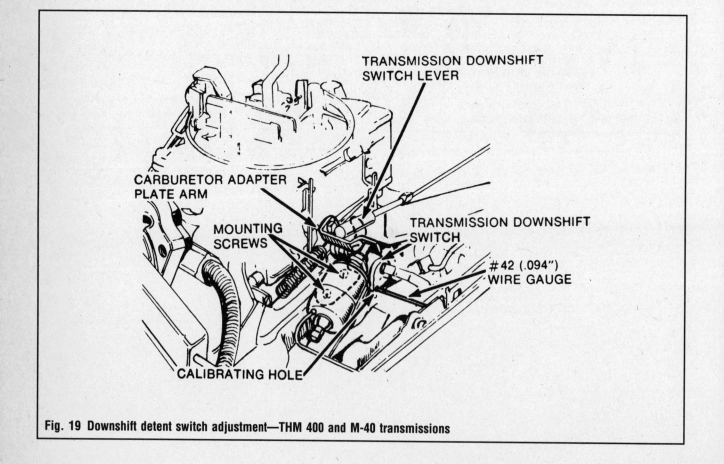

Fig. 19 Downshift detent switch adjustment—THM 400 and M-40 transmissions

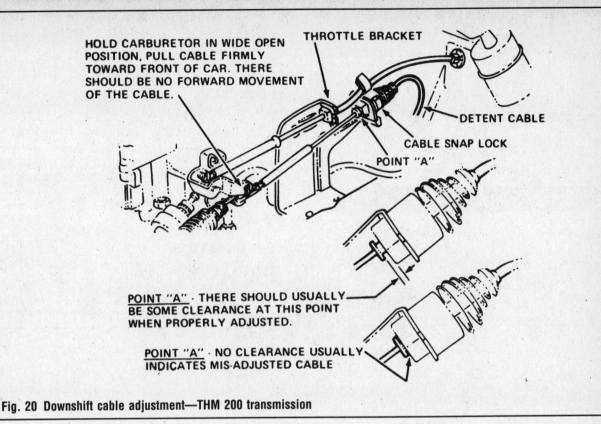

HOLD CARBURETOR IN WIDE OPEN POSITION, PULL CABLE FIRMLY TOWARD FRONT OF CAR. THERE SHOULD BE NO FORWARD MOVEMENT OF THE CABLE.

THROTTLE BRACKET

DETENT CABLE

CABLE SNAP LOCK

POINT "A"

POINT "A" · THERE SHOULD USUALLY BE SOME CLEARANCE AT THIS POINT WHEN PROPERLY ADJUSTED.

POINT "A" · NO CLEARANCE USUALLY INDICATES MIS-ADJUSTED CABLE

Fig. 20 Downshift cable adjustment—THM 200 transmission

counterclockwise to the L1 detent, then clockwise three detent positions to Neutral.

3. Place the transmission selector lever (in the car) in Neutral as determined by the stop in the steering column. DO NOT use the indicator pointer for reference.

4. Tighten the shift linkage screw.

5. Check that the key cannot be removed and that the steering wheel is not locked with the key in Run and the transmission in Reverse. Check that the key can be removed and the transmission linkage is locked when the key is in Lock and the transmission is in Park. *Be sure the car will start only in Park and Neutral.* If it starts in any gear, the neutral start switch must be adjusted. Start the engine and check for proper shifting in all ranges.

Console (Floor) Shift

1. Disconnect the shift cable from the transmission range selector lever (at the transmission) by removing the nut from the pin (see illustration).

2. Set the range selector lever in PARK by rotating the lever clockwise.

3. Set the gearshift lever in the car to PARK.

4. Unlock the ignition switch and rotate the transmission range selector lever counterclockwise two full detent positions (you'll feel it go into each position).

5. Set the gearshift lever in the car to NEUTRAL and move it forward fully against its stop in NEUTRAL.

6. Assemble the shift cable and pin to the range selector at the transmission, allowing the cable to position the pin in the slot of the lever. Tighten the nut to 20 ft. lbs.

DETENT (DOWNSHIFT) LINKAGE

Turbo Hydra-Matic 400

Turbo Hydra-Matic 400 transmissions are equipped with an electrical downshift switch operated by the throttle linkage. The switch is located above the gas pedal.

➡**Perform the adjustment with the engine off.**

1. Push the switch plunger forward until it is flush with the switch housing.

2. Push the accelerator pedal to the wide open position to set the switch (engine off).

3. Road test the car to check the operation of the switch.

Turbo Hydra-Matic 350

Two types of downshift linkage are used on the Turbo 350. On 1974–75 models, the cable adjustment is made at the accelerator pedal. On 1975–76 models, V8's are adjusted at the accelerator pedal, while the 250–6 engine is adjusted at the carburetor. For 1977 and later models, all engines are adjusted at the carburetor.

ACCELERATOR PEDAL DOWNSHIFT LINKAGE

1. Hold the adjustment sleeve in place.
2. Pull the cable as far as possible.

3. Press the accelerator pedal to the wide open position. The cable will adjust.

1974–76 250 6-Cylinder Engines and All 1977–83 Models

1. Raise the "snap-lock" with a small prytool or other tool. See the illustration.

2. With the engine off, hold the carburetor lever in the wide-open position.

3. Push the "snap-lock" downward until it is flush with the rest of the cable, then release the carburetor lever.

Neutral Safety Switch

ADJUSTMENT

The neutral safety switch prevents the engine from being started in any transmission position except Neutral or Park. The switch is located on the upper side of the steering column under the instrument panel on column shift cars and inside the shift console on floor shift models.

Column Shift

♦ See Figure 21

1. Place the shift lever in Neutral.

2. Loosen the switch securing screws. Remove the console first if necessary.

3. Move the switch until you can insert a 0.090 in. gauge pin into the hole in the switch and through to the alignment hole.

4. Tighten the screws and remove the pin.

5. Step on the brake pedal and check to see that the engine will only start in Neutral or Park.

Console Mounted Switch

1. Place the shifter in Park.

2. Remove the center console.

3. Loosen the switch securing screws.

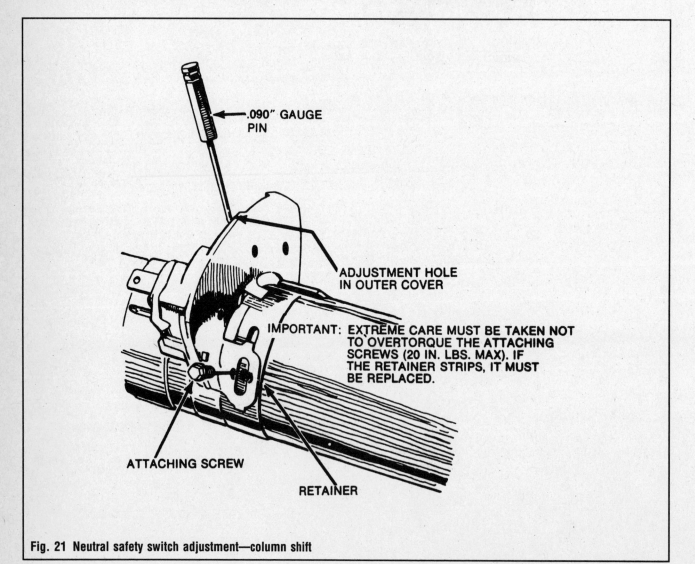

.090" GAUGE PIN

ADJUSTMENT HOLE IN OUTER COVER

IMPORTANT: EXTREME CARE MUST BE TAKEN NOT TO OVERTORQUE THE ATTACHING SCREWS (20 IN. LBS. MAX). IF THE RETAINER STRIPS, IT MUST BE REPLACED.

ATTACHING SCREW

RETAINER

Fig. 21 Neutral safety switch adjustment—column shift

4. Fit a 0.090 in. gauge pin into the outer hole on the switch cover.

5. Move the switch until the gauge pin drops into the alignment hole on the inner slide. Tighten the switch securing screws.

6. Remove the gauge pin. Check to make sure the car will only start in Neutral or Park.

7. Install the center console.

Diesel Engine Transmission

ADJUSTMENTS

Linkage

➡Before making any linkage adjustments, check the injection timing, and adjust if necessary. Also note that these adjustments should be performed together. The vacuum valve adjustment (THM 350's only) on 1979 and later models requires the use of several special tools. If you do not have these tools at your disposal, refer the adjustment to a qualified, professional technician.

Throttle Rod
♦ See Figure 22

1. If equipped with cruise control, remove the clip from the control rod, then remove the rod from the bellcrank.

2. Remove the throttle valve cable (THM 200) or detent cable (THM 350) from the bellcrank.

3. Loosen the locknut on the throttle rod, then shorten the rod several turns.

4. Rotate the bellcrank to the full throttle stop, then lengthen the throttle rod until the injection pump lever contacts the injection pump full throttle stop. Release the bellcrank.

5. Tighten the throttle rod locknut.

6. Connect the throttle valve or detent cable and cruise control rod to the bellcrank. Adjust if necessary.

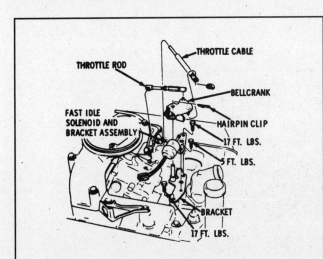

Fig. 22 Exploded view of the throttle linkage on diesel engines

Throttle Valve (TV) or Detent Cable
♦ See Figure 23

Refer to the cable adjustment procedures for gas engines. Adjust according to the style of cable which is used.

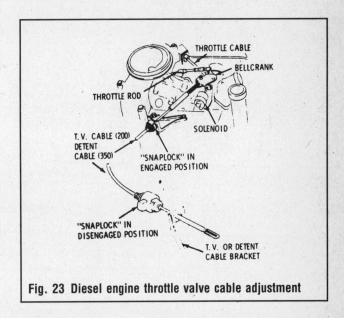

Fig. 23 Diesel engine throttle valve cable adjustment

Transmission Vacuum Valve
♦ See Figures 24, 25, 26 and 27

1979–83 Models

➡A special angle gauge adaptor is needed for this procedure.

1. Remove the air cleaner assembly.

2. Remove the air intake crossover from the intake manifold. Cover the intake manifold passages to prevent foreign material from entering the engine.

3. Disconnect the throttle rod from the injection pump throttle lever.

4. Loosen the transmission vacuum valve-to-injection pump bolts.

5. Mark and disconnect the vacuum lines from the vacuum valve.

6. Attach a carburetor angle gauge adapter (Kent-Moore tool J-26701-15 or its equivalent) to the injection pump throttle lever. Attach the angle gauge (J-26701 or its equivalent) to the gauge adapter.

7. Turn the throttle lever to the wide open throttle position. Set the angle gauge to zero degrees.

8. Center the bubble in the gauge level.

9. Set the angle gauge to one of the following settings, according to the year and type of engine, as shown in the accompanying figure.

10. Attach a vacuum gauge to port 2 and a vacuum source (e.g. hand-held vacuum pump) to port 1 of the vacuum valve (as illustrated).

11. Apply 18–22 in. Hg of vacuum to the valve. Slowly rotate

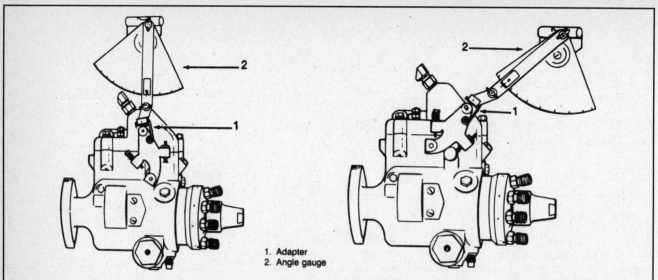

1. Adapter
2. Angle gauge

Fig. 24 Angle gauge mounting (with adapter) for diesel vacuum valve adjustment. The gauge is positioned differently, depending upon the type of throttle lever used

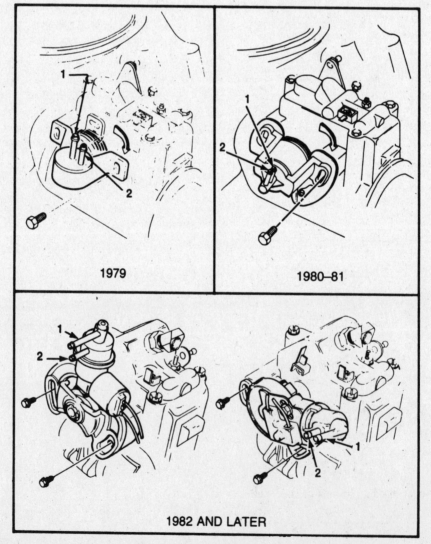

1979

1980–81

1982 AND LATER

Fig. 25 Diesel engine transmission vacuum valve adjustment—1979–83 vehicles

Year	Engine	Setting
1980	V8	49–50°
1981	V8—Calif.	49–50°
1981	V8—non-Calif.	58°
1982	V8	58°
1983	V8	58°

Fig. 26 Specifications for setting the angle gauge

Year	In. Hg.
1979	8½–9
1980	7
1981 Calif.	7–8
1981 non-Calif.	8½–9
1982–83	10½

Fig. 27 Vacuum reading specifications

the valve until the vacuum reading drops to one of the values shown in the accompanying figure.

12. Tighten the vacuum valve retaining bolts.
13. Reconnect the original vacuum lines to the vacuum valve.
14. Remove the angle gauge and adapter.
15. Connect the throttle rod to the throttle lever.
16. Install the air intake crossover, using new gaskets.
17. Install the air cleaner assembly.

Transmission Assembly

REMOVAL & INSTALLATION

◗ **See Figures 28, 29 and 30**

➡**This procedure covers both gasoline and diesel engine vehicles.**

1. Open the hood and place protectors on the fenders. Remove the air cleaner assembly.

2. Disconnect the detent cable at its upper end.
3. Remove the transmission oil dipstick, and the bolt holding the dipstick tube if it is accessable.
4. Jack up the car and safety support it with jackstands.

➡**If a floor pan reinforcement is used, remove it if it interferes with driveshaft removal or installation.**

6. Disconnect the speedometer cable at the transmission.
7. Disconnect the shift linkage at the transmission.
8. Tag and disconnect all electrical leads at the transmission and any clips that hold these leads to the transmission case.
9. Remove the flywheel cover and matchmark the flywheel and torque converter for later assembly.
10. Remove the torque converter-to-flywheel bolts and/or nuts.
11. On gasoline engined cars, disconnect the catalytic converter support bracket.
12. Remove the transmission support-to-transmission mount bolt and transmission support-to-frame bolts, and any insulators (if used).
13. Position a transmission jack under the transmission and raise it slightly.
14. Slide the transmission support rearward.
15. Loosen the transmission enough to gain access to the oil cooler lines and detent cable attachments.
16. Tag and disconnect the oil cooler lines and detent cable. Plug all openings.
17. Support the engine and remove the engine-to-transmission bolts.
18. Disconnect the transmission assembly, being careful not to damage any cables, lines or linkage.
19. Install a C-clamp or torque converter holding tool onto the transmission housing to hold the converter in the housing. Remove the transmission assembly from the car (a hydraulic floor jack is best for this).
20. To install, reverse the removal procedure. When installing the flex plate-to-converter bolts, make sure that the weld nuts on the converter are flush with the flex plate and that the converter ro-

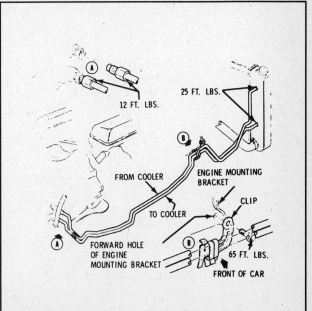

Fig. 28 Transmission oil cooler line mounting—gasoline engines

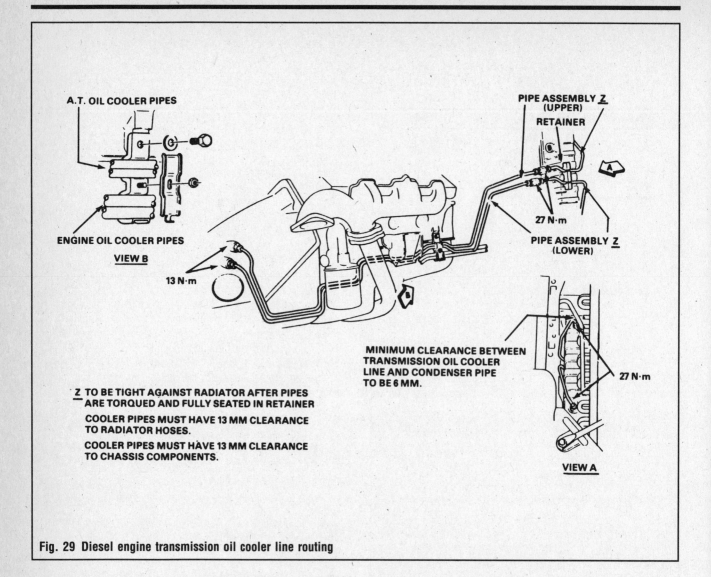

A.T. OIL COOLER PIPES

ENGINE OIL COOLER PIPES

VIEW B

13 N·m

PIPE ASSEMBLY **Z** (UPPER)

RETAINER

27 N·m

PIPE ASSEMBLY **Z** (LOWER)

MINIMUM CLEARANCE BETWEEN TRANSMISSION OIL COOLER LINE AND CONDENSER PIPE TO BE 6 MM.

27 N·m

VIEW A

Z TO BE TIGHT AGAINST RADIATOR AFTER PIPES ARE TORQUED AND FULLY SEATED IN RETAINER

COOLER PIPES MUST HAVE 13 MM CLEARANCE TO RADIATOR HOSES.

COOLER PIPES MUST HAVE 13 MM CLEARANCE TO CHASSIS COMPONENTS.

Fig. 29 Diesel engine transmission oil cooler line routing

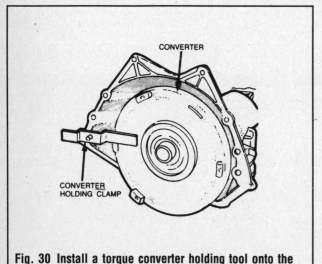

CONVERTER

CONVERTER HOLDING CLAMP

Fig. 30 Install a torque converter holding tool onto the transmission housing to hold the converter in place

tates freely by hand. Hand-start the three bolts and tighten them finger-tight, then torque them evenly.

Install a new oil seal on the oil filler tube before installing the tube. Tighten the flywheel-to-converter bolts to 35 ft. lbs. Tighten the transmission-to-engine bolts to 35 to 40 ft. lbs. Adjust the shift linkage and detent cable following the procedures in this chapter, and check the transmission fluid if the transmission was not drained previously.

DRIVELINE

Driveshaft and U-joints

Mid-size Pontiac driveshafts are of the conventional, open type. Located at either end of the driveshaft is a U-joint or universal joint, which allows the driveshaft to move up and down to match the motion of the rear axle. The front U-joint connects the driveshaft to a slip-jointed yoke. This yoke is internally splined, and allows the driveshaft to move in and out on the transmission splines. The rear U-joint is clamped or bolted to a companion flange fastened to the rear axle drive pinion. The rear U-joint is secured in the yoke in one of two ways. Dana and Cleveland design driveshafts use a conventional type snapring to hold each bearing cup in the yoke. The snapring fits into a groove located in each yoke end, just on top of the bearing cup. A Saginaw design driveshaft secures the U-joints differently. Nylon material is injected through a small hole in the yoke during manufacture, and flows along a circular groove between the U-joint and the yoke creating a non-metallic snapring.

There are two methods of attaching the rear U-joint to the rear axle. One method employs a pair of straps, while the other method is a set of bolted flanges. Bad U-joints, requiring replacement, will produce a clunking sound when the car is put into gear and when the transmission shifts from gear to gear. This is due to worn needle bearings or a scored trunnion end possibly caused by improper lubrication during assembly. U-joints require no periodic maintenance and therefore have no lubrication fittings.

Some driveshafts, generally those in heavy-duty applications, use a damper as part of the slip joint. This vibration damper cannot be serviced separately from the slip joint. If either component goes bad, the two must be replaced as a unit.

REMOVAL & INSTALLATION

Driveshaft
See Figures 31, 32 and 33

1. Raise the vehicle in the air and support it with jackstands.
2. Mark the relationship of the driveshaft to the differential flange so that they can be reassembled in the same position.
3. Disconnect the rear U-joint by removing the U-bolts or retaining straps.
4. To prevent the loss of the needle bearings, tape the bearing caps in place. If you are replacing the U-joint, this is not necessary.
5. Remove the driveshaft from the transmission by sliding it rearward. There will be some oil leakage from the rear of the transmission. It can be contained by placing a small plastic bag over the rear of the transmission and holding it in place with a rubber band.

To install:
6. To install the driveshaft, insert the front yoke into the transmission so that the driveshaft splines mesh with the transmission splines.
7. Using the reference marks made earlier, align the driveshaft with the differential flange and secure it with the U-bolts or retaining straps.

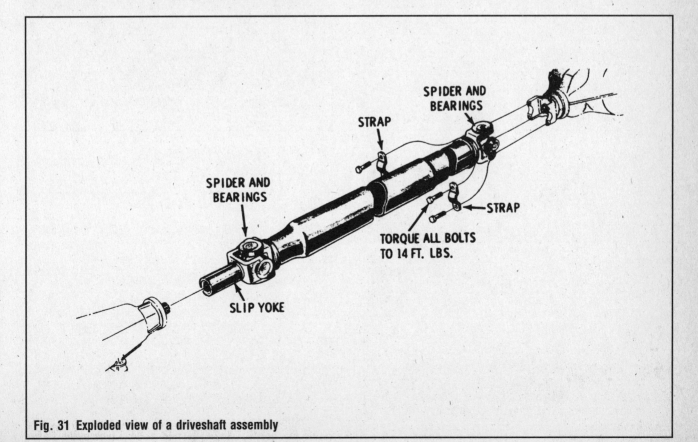

Fig. 31 Exploded view of a driveshaft assembly

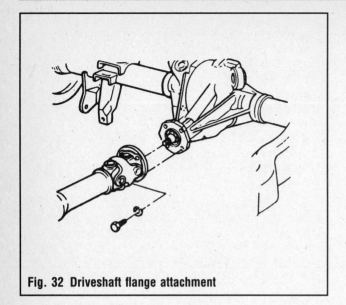

Fig. 32 Driveshaft flange attachment

Remove the strap-type driveshaft retainer . . .

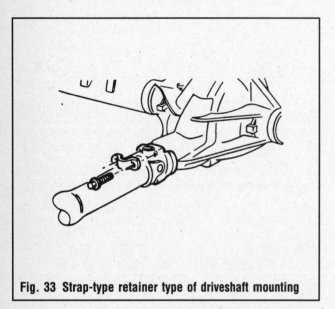

Fig. 33 Strap-type retainer type of driveshaft mounting

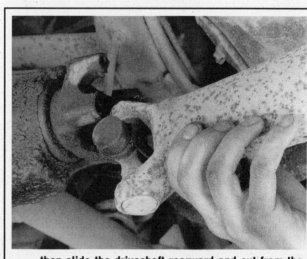

. . . then slide the driveshaft rearward and out from the vehicle

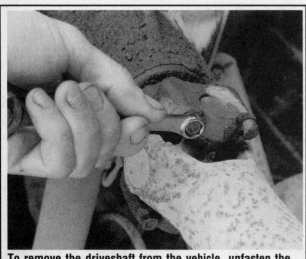

To remove the driveshaft from the vehicle, unfasten the retaining bolts

U-JOINT OVERHAUL

♦ See Figures 34, 35, and 36

➡NEVER clamp a driveshaft in a vise, as the tube is easily dented. Always clamp on one of the yokes, and support the shaft horizontally.

1. Remove the driveshaft as explained above and remove the snaprings from the ends of the bearing cup.

2. After removing the snaprings, place the driveshaft on the floor and place a large diameter socket under one of the bearing cups. Using a hammer and a drift, tap on the bearing opposite this one. This will push the trunion through the yoke enough to force the bearing cup out of the yoke and into the socket. Repeat this procedure for the other bearing cups. If a hammer doesn't loosen the cups, they will have to be pressed out.

➡A Saginaw design driveshaft secures its U-joints in a different manner than the conventional snaprings of the Dana

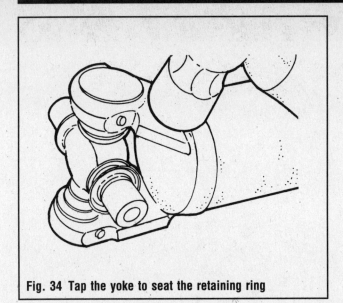

Fig. 34 Tap the yoke to seat the retaining ring

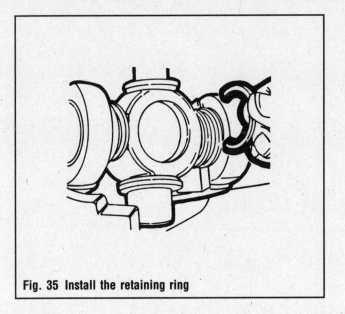

Fig. 35 Install the retaining ring

and Cleveland designs. Nylon material is injected through a small hole in the yoke and flows along a circular groove between the U-joint and the yoke thus creating a synthetic snapring. Disassembly of this Saginaw-type U-joint requires that the joint be pressed from the yoke. If a press is not available, it may be carefully hammered out using the same procedure (Step 2) as the Dana design although it may require more force to break the nylon ring. Either method, press or hammer, will damage the bearing cups and destroy the nylon rings. Replacement kits include new bearing cups and conventional metal snaprings to replace the original nylon type rings.

3. Using solvent, thoroughly clean the entire U-joint assembly. Inspect for excessive wear in the yoke bores and on the four ends of the trunnion. The needle bearings should not be scored, broken, or loose in their cups. Bearing cups may suffer slight distortion during removal and should be replaced.

4. Pack the bearings with chassis lube (lithium base) and completely fill each trunnion end with the same lubricant.

5. Place new dust seals on trunnions with cavity of seal toward end of trunnion. Care must be taken to avoid distortion of the seal. A suitable size socket and a vise can be used to press on the seal.

6. Insert one bearing cup about ¼ of the way into the yoke and place the trunnion into yoke and bearing cup. Install another bearing cup and press both cups in and install the snaprings. Snaprings on the Dana and Cleveland shafts must go on the outside of the yoke while the Saginaw shaft requires that rings go on the inside of the yoke. The gap in the Saginaw ring must face in toward the yoke. Once installed, the trunnion must move freely in yoke.

➡The Saginaw shaft uses two different size bearing cups (the ones with the groove) fit into the driveshaft yoke.

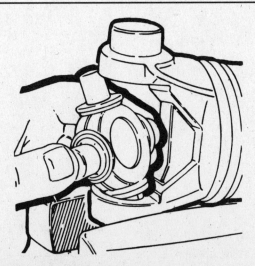

Fig. 36 Partially inserted bearing cap

REAR AXLE

Identification

▶ **See Figure 37**

The rear axle number is located in the right or left axle tube adjacent to the axle carrier (differential). See the "Rear Axle Codes" chart at the end of the chapter for information on determining axle ratio from the letter codes. Anti-slip differentials are identified by a tag attached to the lower right section of the axle cover.

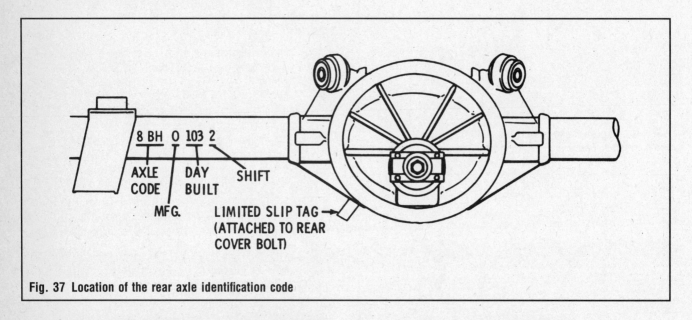

Fig. 37 Location of the rear axle identification code

Axle Shaft and Bearings

▶ **See Figures 38, 39, 40 and 41 (p. 28)**

Two types of axles are used on these models, the C and the non-C type. Axle shafts in the C type are retained by C-shaped locks, which fit grooves at the inner end of the shaft. Axle shafts in the non-C type are retained by the brake backing plate, which is bolted to the axle housing. Bearings in the C type axle consist of an outer race, bearing rollers, and a roller cage retained by snaprings. The non-C type axle uses a unit roller bearing (inner race, rollers, and outer race), which is pressed onto the shaft up to a shoulder. When servicing C or non-C type axles, it is imperative to determine the axle type before attempting any service. Before attempting any service to the drive axle or axle shafts, remove the axle carrier cover and visually determine if the axle shafts are retained by C-shaped locks at the inner end, or by the brake backing plate at the outer end.

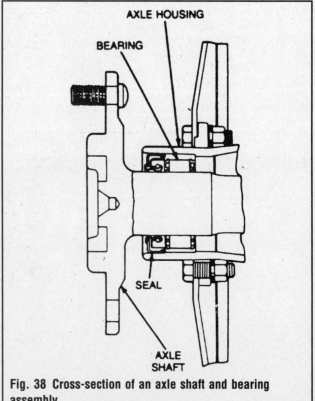

Fig. 38 Cross-section of an axle shaft and bearing assembly

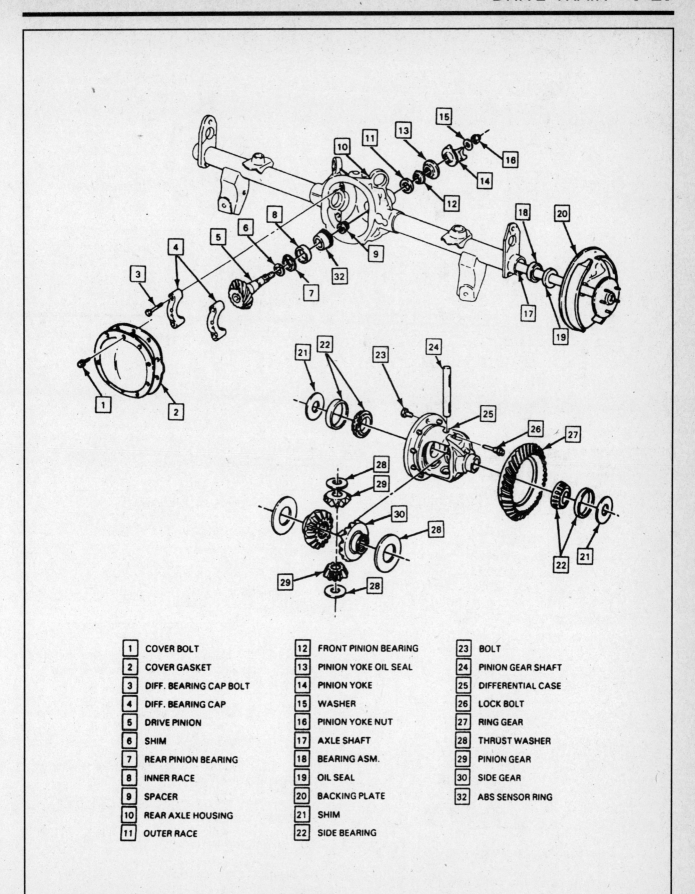

1	COVER BOLT	12	FRONT PINION BEARING	23	BOLT
2	COVER GASKET	13	PINION YOKE OIL SEAL	24	PINION GEAR SHAFT
3	DIFF. BEARING CAP BOLT	14	PINION YOKE	25	DIFFERENTIAL CASE
4	DIFF. BEARING CAP	15	WASHER	26	LOCK BOLT
5	DRIVE PINION	16	PINION YOKE NUT	27	RING GEAR
6	SHIM	17	AXLE SHAFT	28	THRUST WASHER
7	REAR PINION BEARING	18	BEARING ASM.	29	PINION GEAR
8	INNER RACE	19	OIL SEAL	30	SIDE GEAR
9	SPACER	20	BACKING PLATE	32	ABS SENSOR RING
10	REAR AXLE HOUSING	21	SHIM		
11	OUTER RACE	22	SIDE BEARING		

Fig. 39 Exploded view of a standard rear axle assembly

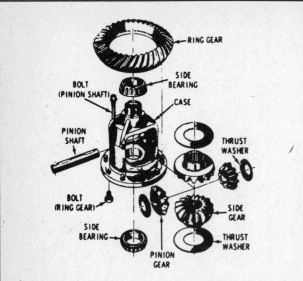

Fig. 40 Exploded view of a conventional differential case assembly

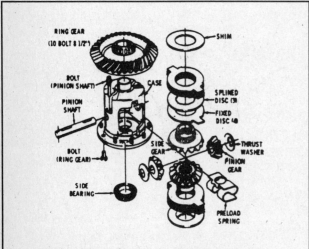

Fig. 41 Exploded view of a disc-type limited slip differential case assembly

REMOVAL & INSTALLATION

Non C-Type

◗ **See Figures 42 and 43**

Design allows for maximum axle shaft end-play of 0.022 in., which can be measured with a dial indicator. If end-play is found to be excessive, the bearing should be replaced. Shimming the bearing is not recommended as this ignores end-play of the bearing itself and could result in improper seating of the bearing.

1. Raise the vehicle, then remove the wheel, tire and brake drum.
2. Remove the nuts holding the retainer plate to the backing plate. Disconnect the brake line.
3. Remove the retainer and install nuts, finger-tight, to prevent the brake backing plate from being dislodged.
4. Pull out the axle shaft and bearing assembly, using a slide hammer.

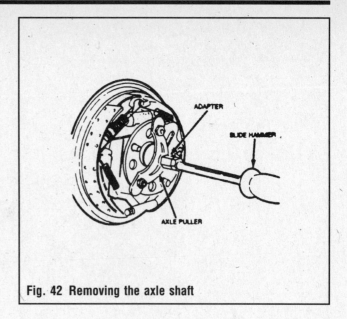

Fig. 42 Removing the axle shaft

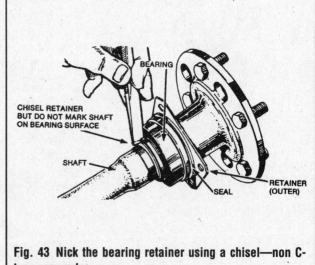

Fig. 43 Nick the bearing retainer using a chisel—non C-type rear axle

5. Using a chisel, nick the bearing retainer in three or four places. The retainer does not have to be cut, merely collapsed sufficiently, to allow the bearing retainer to be slid from the shaft.
6. Press off the bearing and install the new one by pressing it into position.
7. Press on the new retainer.

➡**Do not attempt to press the bearing and the retainer on at the same time.**

8. Assemble the shaft and bearing in the housing being sure that the bearing is seated properly in the housing.
9. Install the retainer, drum, wheel and tire. Bleed the brakes.

C-Type

◗ **See Figures 44, 45, 46 and 47**

1. Raise the vehicle and remove the wheels.
2. Remove the differential cover. Remove the differential pinion shaft lockscrew and the differential pinion shaft.

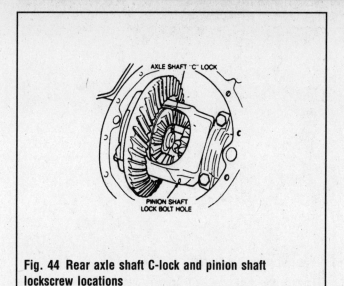

Fig. 44 Rear axle shaft C-lock and pinion shaft lockscrew locations

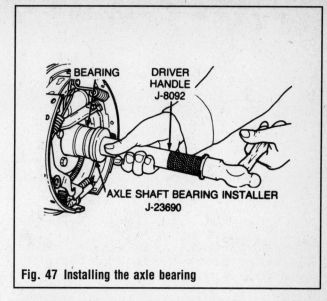

Fig. 47 Installing the axle bearing

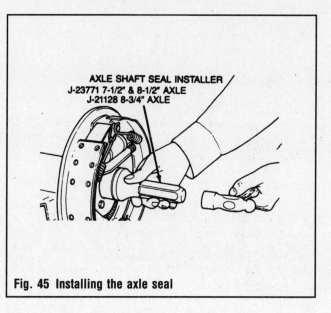

Fig. 45 Installing the axle seal

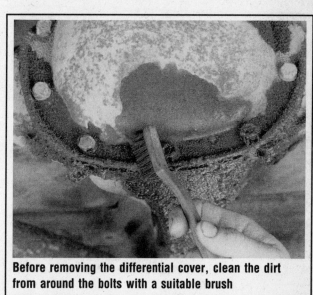

Before removing the differential cover, clean the dirt from around the bolts with a suitable brush

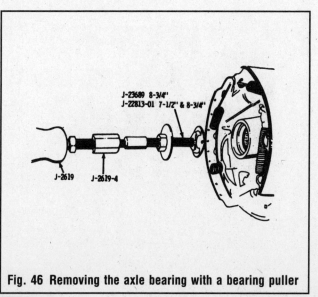

Fig. 46 Removing the axle bearing with a bearing puller

Remove the lower cover retaining bolts . . .

. . . then pry the cover away from the axle housing and allow the fluid to drain completely

Loosen the pinion shaft lockscrew using a wrench

Remove the remaining bolts, then take the cover off the rear axle housing assembly

Remove the lockscrew (see arrow) so the pinion shaft may be withdrawn

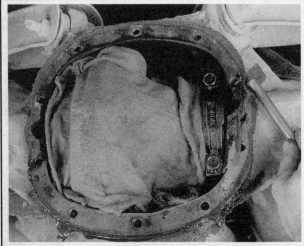

Place a rag over the internal components, then carefully scrape off all the old gasket material

Pull the pinion shaft from the differential in order to access the axle shaft C-lock

If the axle shaft is pushed inward, the C-lock may be removed from the groove

Use a suitable tool to drive the new seal into position

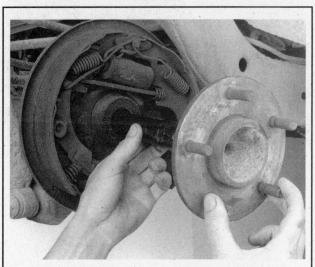

Carefully pull the axle shaft straight out to remove it

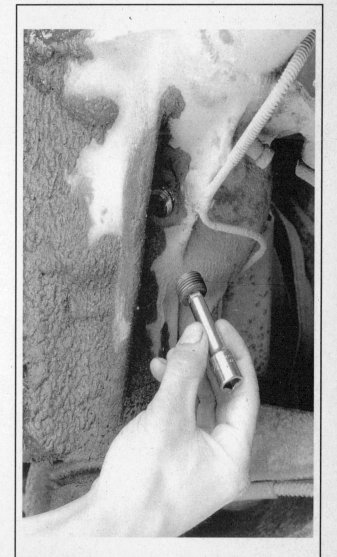

Remove the drain plug, then fill the rear axle with lubricant

A prytool (or the end of the shaft) may be used to dislodge and remove the old bearing seal

3. Push the flanged end of the axle shaft toward the center of the vehicle and remove the "C" lock from the end of the shaft.

4. Remove the axle shaft from the housing, being careful not to damage the oil seal.

5. Remove the oil seal by inserting the button end of the axle shaft behind the steel case of the oil seal. Pry the seal loose from the bore.

6. Seat the legs of the bearing puller behind the bearing. Seat a washer against the bearing and hold it in place with a nut. Use a slide hammer to pull the bearing.

7. Pack the cavity between the seal lips with wheel bearing lubricant and lubricate a new wheel bearing with same.

8. Use a suitable driver and install the bearing until it bottoms against the tube. Install the oil seal.

9. Slide the axle shaft into place. Be sure that the splines on the shaft do not damage the oil seal. Make sure that the splines engage the differential side gear.

10. Install the axle shaft C-lock on the inner end of the axle shaft and push the shaft outward so that the C-lock seats in the differential side gear counterbore.

11. Position the differential pinion shaft through the case and pinions, aligning the hole in the case with the hole for the lockscrew.

12. Use a new gasket and install the carrier cover. Be sure that the gasket surfaces are clean before installing the gasket and cover.

13. Fill the axle with lubricant to the bottom of the filler hole.

14. Install the brake drum and wheels and lower the car. Check for leaks and road test the car.

DETERMINING GEAR RATIO

Determining the axle ratio of any given axle can be a very useful "tool" to the contemporary car owner. Axle ratios are a major factor in a vehicle's fuel mileage, so the car buyer of today should know both what he or she is looking for, and what the salesperson is talking about. Knowledge of axle ratios is also valuable to the owner/mechanic who is shopping through salvage yards for a used axle, who is repairing his or her own rear axle, or who is changing rear axle ratios by changing rear axles.

The rear axle ratio is said to have a certain ratio, say 4.11. It is called a "4.11 rear" although the 4.11 actually means 4.11 to 1 (4.11:1). This means that the driveshaft will turn 4.11 times for every turn of the rear wheels. The number 4.11 is determined by dividing the number of teeth on the pinion gear into the number of teeth on the ring gear. In the case of a 4.11 rear, there could be 9 teeth on the pinion and 37 teeth on the ring gear (37 ÷ 9 = 4.11). This provides a sure way, although troublesome, of determining your rear axle's ratio. The axle must be drained and the rear cover removed to do this, and then the teeth counted.

A much easier method is to jack up the car and safely support it with jackstands, so BOTH rear wheels are off the ground. Block the front wheels, set the parking brake and put the transmission in Neutral. Make a chalk mark on the rear wheel and the driveshaft. Turn the rear wheel one complete revolution and count the number of turns that the driveshaft makes (having an assistant here to count one or the other is helpful). The number of turns the driveshaft makes in one complete revolution of the rear wheel is an approximation of the rear axle ratio.

WHEELS 8-2
  WHEEL ASSEMBLY 8-2
    REMOVAL & INSTALLATION 8-2
    INSPECTION 8-2
  WHEEL LUG STUDS 8-2
    REPLACEMENT 8-2
FRONT SUSPENSION 8-2
  SPRINGS 8-4
    REMOVAL & INSTALLATION 8-4
  SHOCK ABSORBERS 8-4
    TESTING 8-4
    REMOVAL & INSTALLATION 8-4
  UPPER BALL JOINTS 8-5
    INSPECTION 8-5
    REMOVAL & INSTALLATION 8-5
  LOWER BALL JOINTS 8-8
    INSPECTION 8-8
    REMOVAL & INSTALLATION 8-8
  SWAY BAR 8-9
    REMOVAL & INSTALLATION 8-9
  UPPER CONTROL ARM 8-9
    REMOVAL & INSTALLATION 8-9
  LOWER CONTROL ARM 8-10
    REMOVAL & INSTALLATION 8-10
  FRONT END ALIGNMENT 8-11
    CAMBER 8-11
    CASTER 8-11
    STEERING AXIS INCLINATION 8-11
    TOE-IN 8-12
REAR SUSPENSION 8-13
  COIL SPRINGS 8-16
    REMOVAL & INSTALLATION 8-16
  LEAF SPRINGS 8-16
    REMOVAL & INSTALLATION 8-16
  SHOCK ABSORBERS 8-17
    REMOVAL & INSTALLATION 8-17
STEERING 8-20
  STEERING WHEEL 8-20
    REMOVAL & INSTALLATION 8-20
  TURN SIGNAL SWITCH 8-22
    REMOVAL & INSTALLATION 8-22
  IGNITION LOCK CYLINDER 8-23
    REMOVAL & INSTALLATION 8-23
  TIE ROD ENDS 8-24
    REMOVAL & INSTALLATION 8-24
  POWER STEERING GEARBOX 8-27
    REMOVAL & INSTALLATION 8-27
  POWER STEERING PUMP 8-28
    REMOVAL & INSTALLATION 8-28
    BLEEDING 8-28
COMPONENT LOCATIONS
  FRONT SUSPENSION
    COMPONENTS 8-3
  REAR SUSPENSION
    COMPONENTS 8-15
SPECIFICATION CHARTS
  WHEEL ALIGNMENT
    SPECIFICATIONS 8-12

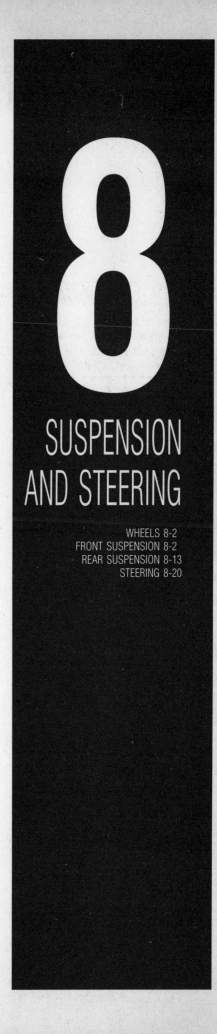

8

SUSPENSION
AND STEERING

WHEELS 8-2
FRONT SUSPENSION 8-2
REAR SUSPENSION 8-13
STEERING 8-20

WHEELS

Wheel Assembly

REMOVAL & INSTALLATION

1. If equipped, remove the hub cap or wheel cover.
2. Loosen, but do not remove the lug nuts.
3. Raise and safely support the vehicle so the tire is clear of the ground.

✳✳ CAUTION

Always use a suitable floor jack for raising the vehicle to be serviced. Never use the jacking device supplied with the vehicle for vehice service. That jacking device is designed for emergency use only to change a flat tire.

4. Remove the lug nuts, then remove the wheel from the vehicle.
To install:
5. Install the wheel.
6. Install the lug nuts, then hand-tighten in a star pattern.
7. Carefully lower the vehicle.
8. Final tighten the lug nuts in a star pattern to 103 ft. lbs. (140 Nm).

INSPECTION

Inspect the tread for abnormal wear, check for nails or other foreign material embedded into the tire. To check for leaks, submerse the wheel assembly into a tub of water and watch for air bubbles.

Wheels must be replaced if they are bent, dented, leak air through welds, have elongated bolt holes, if wheel nuts won't stay tight, or if the wheels are heavily rusted. Replacement wheels must be equivalent to the original equipment wheels in load capacity, diameter, rim width, offset and mounting configuration.

A wheel of improper size may affect wheel bearing lift, brake cooling, speedometer/odometer calibration, vehicle ground clearance and tire clearance to the body and/or chassis.

✳✳ CAUTION

Replacement with used wheels is not recommended as their service history may have included severe treatment or very high mileage and they could fail without warning.

Wheel Lug Studs

REPLACEMENT

1. Raise and safely support the vehicle.
2. Remove the wheel and tire assembly.
3. If removing the front wheel lug stud(s), remove the caliper, rotor and splash shield, as outlined in Section 9 of this manual.
4. If removing the rear wheel lug stud(s), remove the brake drum as outlined in Section 9 of this manual.
5. Install a lug nut on the stud and, using tool J-6627, press the stud from its seat in the hub. Do not damage the wheel mounting surface on the hub flange.
6. Remove the nut and pull the stud out of the hub.
To install:
7. Install a new serrated bolt into the hole in the hub. Rotate the stud slowly to make sure the serrations are aligned with those made by the original bolt.
8. Place four flat washers over the outside end of the stud and thread a standard lug nut with the flat side against the washers. Tighten the lug nut until the stud head seats against the back side of the hub.
9. Remove the lug nut and washers.
10. Install the brake drum, or caliper, rotor and splash shield, as applicable. Refer to Section 9 for details.
11. Install the wheel and tire assembly, then carefully lower the vehicle. Final tighten the lug nuts to 103 ft. lbs. (140 Nm).

FRONT SUSPENSION

◆ **See Figure 1 (p. 4)**

The front suspension is designed to allow each wheel to compensate for changes in the road surface level without appreciably affecting the opposite wheel. Each wheel is independently connected to the frame by a steering knuckle, ball joint assemblies, and upper and lower control arms. The control arms are specifically designed and positioned to allow the steering knuckles to move in a prescribed three dimensional arc. The front wheels are held in proper relationship to each other by two tie rods which are connected to steering arms on the knuckles and to an intermediate rod.

Coil chassis springs are mounted between the spring housings on the frame or front end sheet metal and the lower control arms. Ride control is provided by double, direct acting, shock absorbers mounted inside the coil springs and attached to the lower control arms by bolts and nuts. The upper portion of each shock absorber extends through the upper control arm frame bracket and is secured with two grommets, two grommet retainers, and a nut.

Side roll of the front suspension is controlled by a spring steel stabilizer shaft. It is mounted in rubber bushings which are held to the frame side rails by brackets. The ends of the stabilizer are connected to the lower control arms by link bolts isolated by rubber grommets.

The upper control arm is attached to a cross-shaft through isolating rubber bushings. The cross-shaft, in turn, is bolted to frame brackets.

A ball joint assembly is riveted to the outer end of the upper arm. It is pre-loaded by a rubber spring to insure proper seating of the ball in the socket. The upper ball joint is attached to the steering knuckle by a torque prevailing nut.

The inner ends of the lower control arm have pressed-in bush-

FRONT SUSPENSION COMPONENTS

1. Stabilizer bar
2. Upper control arm
3. Outer tie-rod end
4. Lower ball joint
5. Coil spring
6. Shock absorber
7. Lower control arm
8. Inner tie-rod end

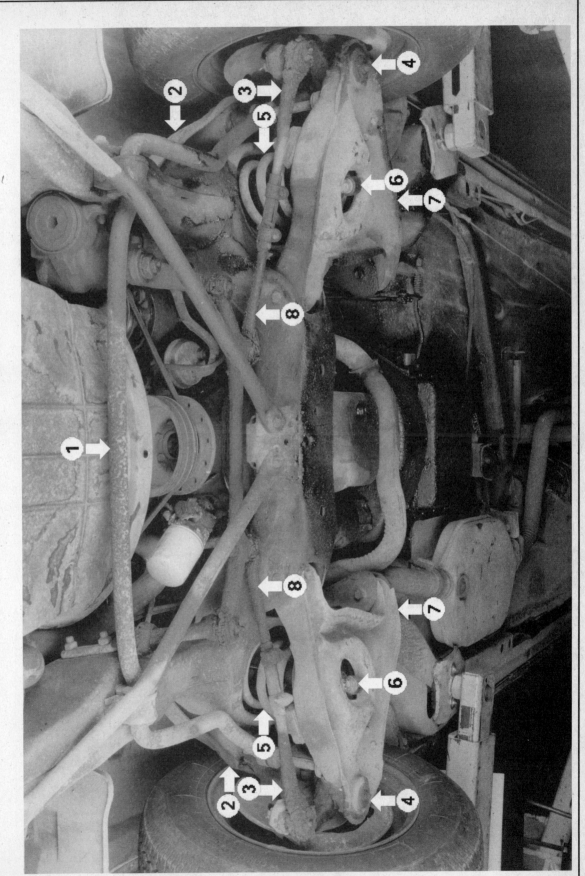

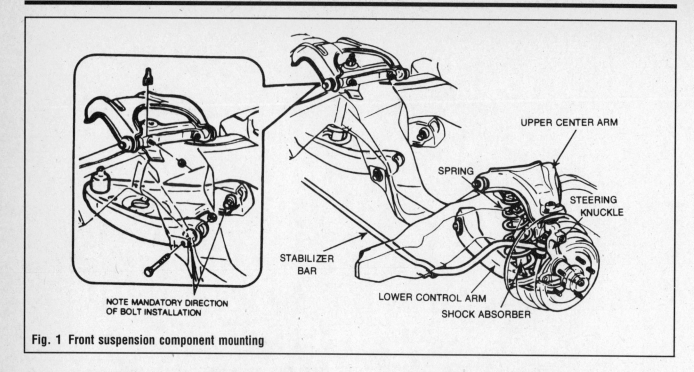

UPPER CENTER ARM

SPRING

STEERING KNUCKLE

STABILIZER BAR

LOWER CONTROL ARM

SHOCK ABSORBER

NOTE MANDATORY DIRECTION OF BOLT INSTALLATION

Fig. 1 Front suspension component mounting

ings. Bolts, passing through the bushings, attach the arm to the frame. The lower ball joint assembly is a press fit in the arm and attaches to the steering knuckle with a torque prevailing nut.

Rubber grease seals are provided at ball socket assemblies to keep dirt and moisture from entering the joint and damaging bearing surfaces.

Springs

REMOVAL & INSTALLATION

⬩ **See Figures 2, 3 and 4**

✳✳ CAUTION

The coil springs are under a considerable amount of tension. Be extremely careful when removing or installing them; they can exert enough force to cause serious injury.

1. Jack up the front end of the car, and support the car at the frame with jackstands so the control arms hang free.
2. Remove the shock absorber. Disconnect the stabilizer bar at the steering knuckle.
3. Support the inner end of the control arm with a floor jack.
4. Raise the jack enough to take the tension off the lower control arm pivot bolts.
5. Chain the spring to the lower control arm.
6. Remove first the rear, then the front pivot bolt.
7. *Cautiously lower the jack until all spring tension is released.*
8. Note the way in which the spring is installed in relation to the drain holes on the control arm and remove it.
To install:
9. Position the spring to the control arm and raise it into place.
10. Install the pivot bolts and tighten the nuts to 100 ft. lbs.

11. Replace the shock absorber and stabilizer bar.
12. Remove the jackstands, then carefully lower the vehicle.

Shock Absorbers

TESTING

Visually inspect the shock absorber. If there is evidence of leakage and the shock absorber is covered with oil, the shock has reached the end of its life and should be replaced.

If there is no sign of excessive leakage (a small amount of weeping is normal) bounce the car at one corner by pressing down on the fender or bumper and releasing. When you have the car bouncing as much as you can, release the fender or bumper. The car should stop bouncing after the first rebound. If the bouncing continues past the center point of the bounce more than once, the shock absorbers are worn and should be replaced.

REMOVAL & INSTALLATION

⬩ **See Figure 5**

1. Raise the car, and with an open end wrench hold the upper stem of the shock absorber from turning. Remove the upper stem retaining nut, retainer and grommet.
2. Remove the two bolts retaining the lower shock absorber pivot to the lower control arm and then pull the shock out through the bottom of the control arm.
To install:
3. With the lower retainer and the rubber grommet in place over the upper stem, install the shock (fully extended) back through the lower control arm.
4. Install the upper grommet, retainer and nut onto the upper stem.

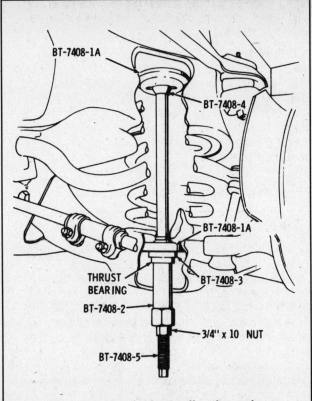

Fig. 2 When removing the front coil spring make sure the lock on the top of the spring compressor is in position whenever the tool is used

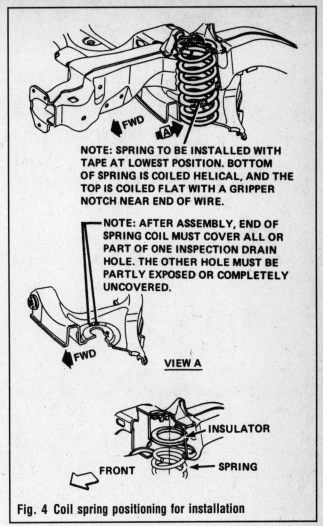

NOTE: SPRING TO BE INSTALLED WITH TAPE AT LOWEST POSITION. BOTTOM OF SPRING IS COILED HELICAL, AND THE TOP IS COILED FLAT WITH A GRIPPER NOTCH NEAR END OF WIRE.

NOTE: AFTER ASSEMBLY, END OF SPRING COIL MUST COVER ALL OR PART OF ONE INSPECTION DRAIN HOLE. THE OTHER HOLE MUST BE PARTLY EXPOSED OR COMPLETELY UNCOVERED.

VIEW A

INSULATOR

FRONT   SPRING

Fig. 4 Coil spring positioning for installation

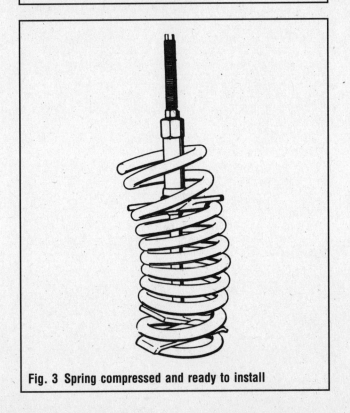

Fig. 3 Spring compressed and ready to install

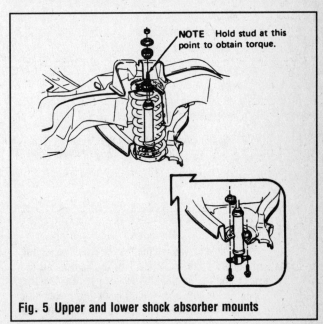

NOTE   Hold stud at this point to obtain torque.

Fig. 5 Upper and lower shock absorber mounts

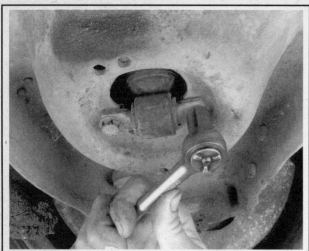

To remove the shock absorber, remove the two lower pivot-to-control arm bolts . . .

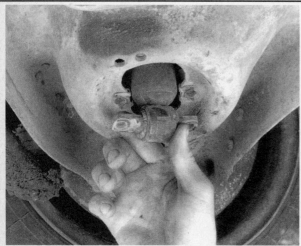

. . . then pull the shock absorber out through the bottom of the lower control arm

5. Hold the upper stem from turning with an open end wrench and then tighten the retaining nut.

6. Reinstall the retainers on the lower end of the shock.

Upper Ball Joints

INSPECTION

▶ See Figure 6

➡Before performing this inspection, make sure the wheel bearings are adjusted correctly and that the control arm bushings are in good condition. All models covered in this guide are equipped with wear indicators on the lower ball joint. As long as the indicator extends below the ball stud seat, replacement is unnecessary; if only the lower ball joint is bad, however, both upper and lower ball joints should be replaced.

1. Raise the car by placing the jack under the lower control arm at the spring seat.

2. Raise the car until there is a 1–2 in clearance under the wheel.

3. Insert a bar under the wheel and pry upward. If the wheel raises more than 1/8 in., the ball joints are worn. Determine whether the upper or lower ball joint is worn by visual inspection while prying on the wheel.

REMOVAL & INSTALLATION

▶ See Figures 7, 8 and 9

1. Raise the vehicle and support securely. Support the lower control arm securely. Remove the tire and wheel.

2. Remove the upper ball stud cotter pin and loosen the ball stud nut *just one turn.*

3. Procure a special tool designed to press out ball joints. These tools are available at most automotive parts stores. Locate the tool between the upper and lower ball joints and press the joints out of the steering knuckle. Remove the tool.

4. Remove the ball joint stud nut, and separate the joint from the steering knuckle. Lift the upper arm up and place a block of wood between the frame and the arm to support it.

5. With the control arm in the raised position, drill a hole 1/4 in. deep into each rivet. Use a 1/8 in. drill bit.

6. Use a 1/2 in. drill bit and drill off the heads of each rivet.

7. Punch out the rivets using a small punch and then remove the ball joint.

To install:

8. Install the new ball joint using fasteners that meet GM specifications. Bolts should come in from the bottom with the nuts going on top. Torque to 10 ft. lbs.

9. Turn the ball stud cotter pin hole to the fore and aft position. Remove the block of wood from between the upper control arm and frame.

10. Clean and inspect the steering knuckle hole. Replace the steering knuckle if any out of roundness is noted.

11. Insert the ball stud into the steering knuckle, and install and tighten the stud nut to 60 ft. lbs. Install a new cotter pin. *If nut must be turned to align cotter pin holes, tighten it further. Do not back off!*

12. Install a lube fitting, and fill the joint with fresh grease.

13. Remove the lower control arm support (jack, etc.) and lower the car.

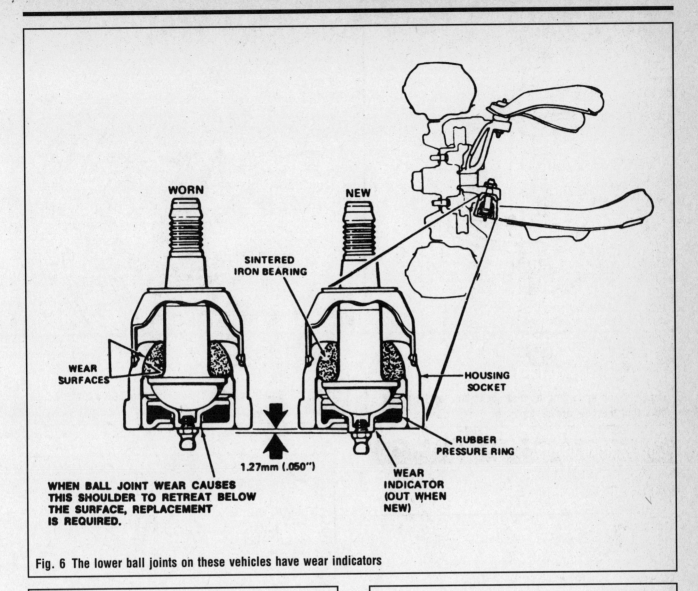

WORN

NEW

SINTERED
IRON BEARING

WEAR
SURFACES

HOUSING
SOCKET

1.27mm (.050")

RUBBER
PRESSURE RING

WHEN BALL JOINT WEAR CAUSES
THIS SHOULDER TO RETREAT BELOW
THE SURFACE, REPLACEMENT
IS REQUIRED.

WEAR
INDICATOR
(OUT WHEN
NEW)

Fig. 6 The lower ball joints on these vehicles have wear indicators

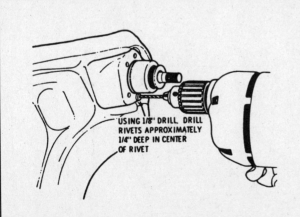

USING 1/8" DRILL DRILL
RIVETS APPROXIMATELY
1/4" DEEP IN CENTER
OF RIVET

Fig. 7 With the control arm in the raised position, first
use a 1/8 in. bit to drill a hole 1/4 in. deep into each
rivet . . .

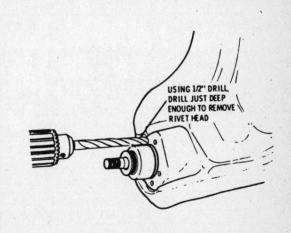

USING 1/2" DRILL
DRILL JUST DEEP
ENOUGH TO REMOVE
RIVET HEAD

Fig. 8 . . . then use a 1/2 in. bit to drill the heads off
each rivet

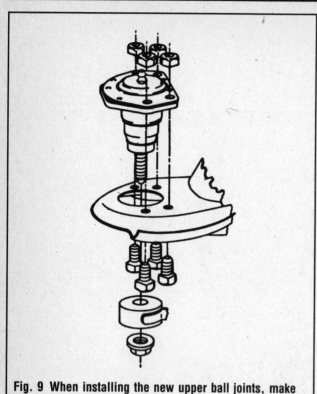

Fig. 9 When installing the new upper ball joints, make sure that the nuts are on top

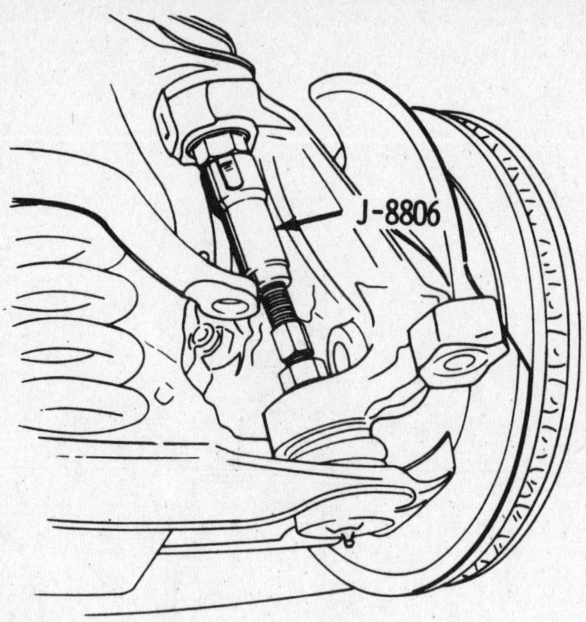

Lower Ball Joints

INSPECTION

Please refer to the procedure, under Upper Ball Joints for lower ball joint inspection.

REMOVAL & INSTALLATION

▶ **See Figures 10, 11 and 12**

1. Raise the vehicle and support it securely. Support the lower control arm with a jack.
2. Remove the lower ball stud cotter pin, and loosen the ball stud nut just one turn.
3. Install a special tool designed for such work between the two ball studs, and press the stud downward in the steering knuckle. Then, remove the stud nut.
4. Pull the tire outward and at the same time upward, with your hands on the bottom (of the tire), to free the steering knuckle from the ball stud. Then, remove the wheel.
5. Lift up on the upper control arm and place a block of wood between it and the frame. Be careful not to put any tension on the brake hose in doing this.
6. Press the ball joint out of the lower control arm with a tool made for that purpose. You may have to disconnect the tie rod at the steering knuckle to do this.

To install:

7. Position the new ball joint, with the vent in the rubber boot

Fig. 10 Use a suitable tool to disconnect the lower ball joint

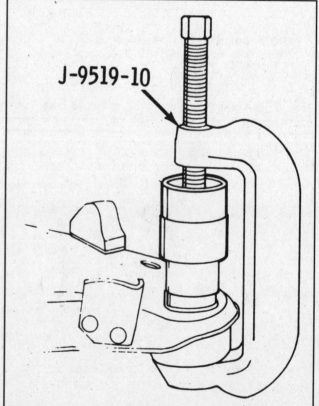

Fig. 11 Press the lower ball joint out of the lower control arm

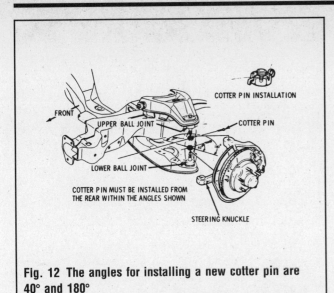

Fig. 12 The angles for installing a new cotter pin are 40° and 180°

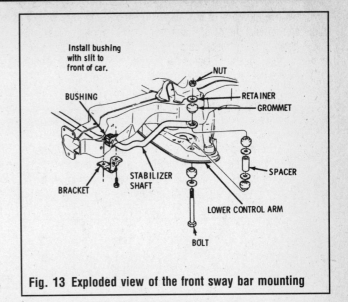

Fig. 13 Exploded view of the front sway bar mounting

facing inward, onto the lower control arm. Press the joint fully into the control arm with a tool designed for this.

8. Turn the ball stud cotter pin hole so it is fore and aft.

➡ **Cotter pins on Le Mans series and Grand Prix must be installed from the rear as shown in the illustration.**

9. Remove the block of wood holding the upper control arm out of the way, and inspect the tapered hole in the steering knuckle. Remove any dirt from the hole. If the hole is out of round or there is other noticeable damage, replace the entire steering knuckle.

Sway Bar

REMOVAL & INSTALLATION

◆ **See Figure 13**

1. Jack up the front end of the car and safely support it with jackstands.

2. Disconnect each side of the sway bar linkage by removing the nut from the link bolt. Pull the bolt from the linkage and remove the retainers, grommets and spacer.

3. Remove the bracket-to-frame or body bolts on both sides of the car and remove the sway bar, rubber bushings and brackets.

4. To install, reverse the removal procedure. Make sure the rubber bushings are installed squarely in the bracket with the slit in the bushings facing the front of the car. Tighten the sway bar link nuts to 13 ft. lbs.

Upper Control Arm

REMOVAL & INSTALLATION

◆ **See Figure 14**

1. Raise the vehicle on a hoist.
2. Support the outer end of the lower control arm with a jack.

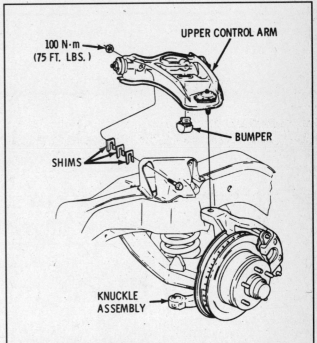

Fig. 14 When installing the upper control arm, make sure the shaft-to-frame bolts are installed in the same position as they were removed

✳✳ CAUTION

Leave the jack in place during removal and installation, in order to keep the spring and control arm positioned.

3. Remove the wheel.
4. Separate the upper ball joint from the steering knuckle as described earlier under "Upper Ball Joint Replacement."
5. Remove the control arm shaft-to-frame nuts.

➡ **Tape the shims together and identify them so that they can be installed in the positions from which they were removed.**

6. Remove the bolts which attach the control arm shaft to the frame and remove the control arm. Note the positions of the bolts.

7. Install in the reverse order of removal. Make sure that the shaft-to-frame bolts are installed in the same position they were in before removal and that the shims are in their original positions.

8. Use free running nuts (not locknuts) to pull serrated bolts through the frame. Then install the locknuts. Tighten the thinner shim pack first.

9. After the car has been lowered to the ground, bounce the front end to center the bushings and then tighten the bushing collar bolts to 45 ft. lbs. Tighten the shaft-to-frame bolts to 90 ft. lbs. The control arm shaft nuts are tightened to 75 ft. lbs.

Lower Control Arm

REMOVAL & INSTALLATION

▶ **See Figure 15**

1. Remove the spring as described earlier in this section.
2. Remove the ball stud from the steering knuckle as described earlier in this section.
3. Remove the control arm pivot bolts and the control arm.
4. To install, reverse the above procedure. If any bolts are to be replaced, do so with bolts of equal strength and quality.

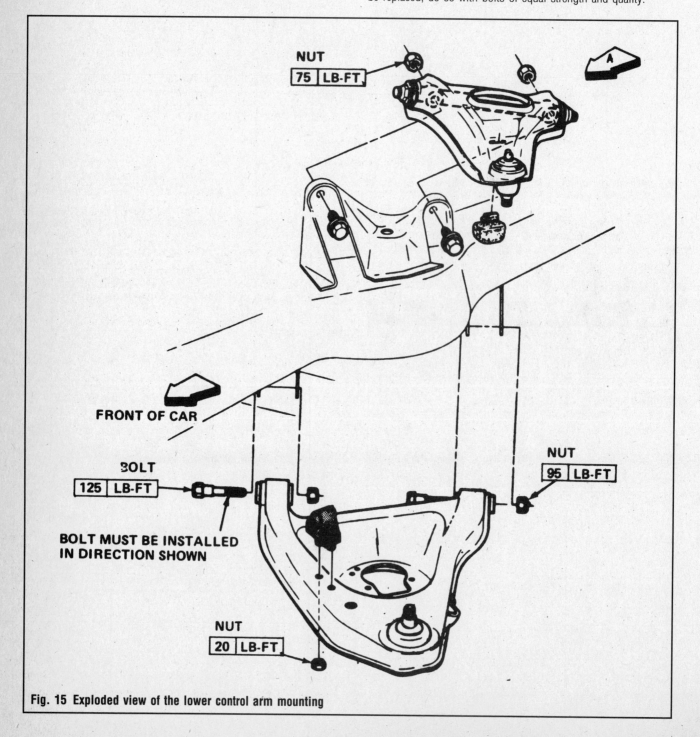

NUT 75 LB-FT

FRONT OF CAR

BOLT 125 LB-FT

BOLT MUST BE INSTALLED IN DIRECTION SHOWN

NUT 95 LB-FT

NUT 20 LB-FT

Fig. 15 Exploded view of the lower control arm mounting

Front End Alignment

▶ **See Figures 16 and 17**

➡ **The procedure for checking and adjusting front wheel alignment requires specialized equipment and professional skills. The following descriptions and adjustment procedures are for general references only.**

Front wheel alignment is the position of the front wheels relative to each other and to the vehicle. It is determined, and must be maintained to provide safe, accurate steering with minimum tire wear. Many factors are involved in wheel alignment and adjustments are provided to return those that might change due to normal wear to their original value. The factors which determine wheel alignment are dependent on one another; therefore, when one of the factors is adjusted, the others must be adjusted to compensate. Descriptions of these factors and their affects on the car are provided below.

➡ **Do not attempt to check and adjust the front wheel alignment without first making a thorough inspection of the front suspension components.**

CAMBER

Camber angle is the number of degrees that the centerline of the wheel is inclined from the vertical. Camber reduces loading of the outer wheel bearing and improves the tire contact patch while cornering.

CASTER

Caster angle is the number of degrees that a line drawn through the steering knuckle pivots is inclined from the vertical, toward the front or rear of the car. Caster improves directional sta-

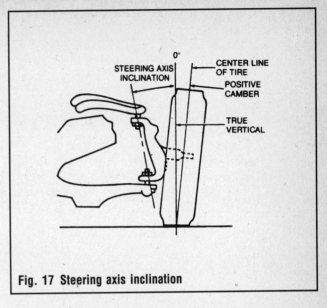

Fig. 17 Steering axis inclination

bility and decreases susceptibility to crosswinds or road surface deviations.

STEERING AXIS INCLINATION

Steering axis inclination is the number of degrees that a line drawn through the steering knuckle pivots is inclined to the vertical, when viewed from the front of the car. This, in combination with caster, is responsible for directional stability and self-centering of the steering. As the steering knuckle swings from lock to lock, the spindle generates an arc, the high point being the straight-ahead position of the wheel. Due to this arc, as the wheel turns, the front of the car is raised. The weight of the car acts against this lift and attempts to return the spindle to the high point of the arc, resulting in self-centering, when the steering wheel is released, and straight-line stability.

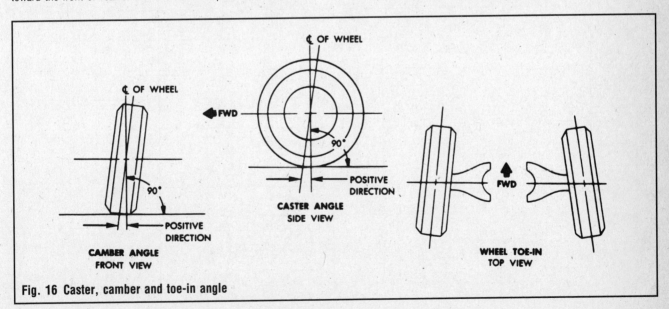

Fig. 16 Caster, camber and toe-in angle

TOE-IN

Toe-in is the difference of the distance between the centers of the front and rear of the front wheels. It is most commonly measured in inches, but is occasionally referred to as an angle between the wheels. Toe-in is necessary to compensate for the tendency of the wheels to deflect rearward while in motion. Due to this tendency, the wheels of a vehicle, with properly adjusted toe-in, are traveling straight forward when the vehicle itself is traveling straight forward, resulting in directional stability and minimum tire wear.

Wheel Alignment Specifications

Year	Model/ Steering Type	Caster Range (deg)	Caster Pref Setting (deg)	Camber Range (deg)	Camber Pref Setting (deg)	Toe-in (In.)	Steering Axis Inclin. (deg.)	Wheel Pivot Ratio (deg.) Inner Wheel	Wheel Pivot Ratio (deg.) Outer Wheel
1974	Le Mans, Grand Am MAN/PWR	①	②	③	④	0 to $^1/_8$	10.35	20	22
	Grand Prix PWR.	$2^1/_2$P to $3^1/_2$P	3P	L: $^1/_2$P to $1^1/_2$P R: 0 to 1P	L-1P R-$^1/_2$P	0 to $^1/_8$	10.35	20	LT:$19^3/_{16}$ RT:$18^{13}/_{16}$
	Ventura	0 to 1P	$^1/_2$P	$^1/_4$N to $^3/_4$P	$^1/_4$P	$^1/_8$P to $^1/_4$P	10.85	20	$18^1/_2$
1975	Le Mans MAN.	$^1/_2$P to $1^1/_2$P	1P	L-$^1/_2$P to $1^1/_2$P R-0 to 1P	L-1P R-$^1/_2$P	0 to $^1/_8$	10.35	20	LT:$19^3/_{16}$ RT:$18^{13}/_{16}$
	Le Mans, Grand Am PWR.	$1^1/_2$P to $2^1/_2$P	2P	L-$^1/_2$P to $1^1/_2$P R-0 to 1P	L-1P R-$^1/_2$P	0 to $^1/_8$	10.35	20	LT:$19^3/_{16}$ RT:$18^{13}/_{16}$
	Grand Prix PWR.	$2^1/_2$P to $3^1/_2$P	3P	L-$^1/_2$P to $1^1/_2$P R-0 to 1 P	L-1P R-$^1/_2$P	0 to $^1/_8$	10.35	20	LT:$19^3/_{16}$ RT:$18^{13}/_{16}$
	Ventura MAN.	$1^1/_2$N to $^1/_2$N	1N	$^1/_4$P to $1^1/_4$P	$^3/_4$P	0 to $^1/_8$	10.85	20	$18^1/_2$
	Ventura PWR.	$^1/_2$P to $1^1/_2$P	1P	$^1/_4$P to $1^1/_4$P	$^3/_4$P	0 to $^1/_8$	10.85	20	$18^1/_2$
1976	Le Mans MAN.	$^1/_2$P to $1^1/_2$P	1P	L-$^1/_2$P to $1^1/_2$P R-0 to 1P	L-1P R-$^1/_2$P	0 to $^1/_8$	10.35	20	LT:$19^3/_{16}$ RT:$18^{13}/_{16}$
	Le Mans, Grand Am, PWR.	$1^1/_2$P to $2^1/_2$P	2P	L-$^1/_2$P to $1^1/_2$P R-0 to 1P	L-1P R-$^1/_2$P	0 to $^1/_8$	10.35	20	LT:$19^3/_{16}$ RT:$18^{13}/_{16}$
	Grand Prix PWR.	$2^1/_2$P to $3^1/_2$P	3P	L-$^1/_2$P to $1^1/_2$P R-0 to 1P	L-1P R-$^1/_2$P	0 to $^1/_8$	10.35	20	LT:$19^3/_{16}$ RT:$18^{13}/_{16}$
	Ventura MAN.	$1^1/_2$N to $^1/_2$N	1N	$^1/_4$P to $1^1/_4$P	$^3/_4$P	0 to $^1/_8$	10	20	$18^1/_2$
	Ventura PWR.	$^1/_2$P to $1^1/_2$P	1P	$^1/_4$P to $1^1/_4$P	$^3/_4$P	0 to $^1/_8$	10	20	$18^1/_2$
1977	Le Mans MAN.	$^1/_2$P to $1^1/_2$P	1P	L-$^1/_2$P to $1^1/_2$P R-0 to 1P	L-1P R-$^1/_2$P	0 to $^1/_8$	10.35	—	—
	Le Mans⑤ PWR.	$1^1/_2$P to $2^1/_2$P	2P	L-$^1/_2$P to $1^1/_2$P R-0 to 1P	L-1P R-$^1/_2$P	0 to $^1/_8$	10.35	—	—
	Le Mans⑥ PWR.	$^1/_2$P to $1^1/_2$P	1P	L-$^1/_2$P to $1^1/_2$P R-0 to 1P	L-1P R-$^1/_2$P	0 to $^1/_8$	10.35	—	—
	Grand Prix PWR.	$4^1/_2$P to $5^1/_2$P	5P	L-$^1/_2$P to $1^1/_2$P R-0 to 1P	L-1P R-$^1/_2$P	0 to $^1/_8$	10.35	—	—
	Ventura MAN.	$1^1/_2$N to $^1/_2$N	1N	$^3/_{10}$P to $1^3/_{10}$P	$^4/_5$P	0 to $^1/_8$	10	—	—
	Ventura PWR.	$^1/_2$P to $1^1/_2$P	1P	$^3/_{10}$P to $1^3/_{10}$P	$^4/_5$P	0 to $^1/_8$	10	—	—
1978	Le Mans MAN.	$^1/_2$P to $1^1/_2$P	1P	0 to 1P	$^1/_2$P	$^1/_{16}$ to $^3/_{16}$	8	—	—
	Le Mans, Grand Prix PWR.	$2^1/_2$P to $3^1/_2$P	3P	0 to 1P	$^1/_2$P	$^1/_{16}$ to $^3/_{16}$	8	—	—
	Phoenix MAN.	$1^1/_2$N to $^1/_2$N	1N	$^3/_{10}$P	$^4/_5$P	$^1/_{16}$ to $^3/_{16}$	10	—	—
	Phoenix PWR.	$^1/_2$P to $1^1/_2$P	1P	$^3/_{10}$P to $1^3/_{10}$P	$^4/_5$P	$^1/_{16}$ to $^3/_{16}$	10	—	—

Wheel Alignment Specifications (cont.)

Year	Model/ Steering Type	Caster Range (deg)	Pref Setting (deg)	Camber Range (deg)	Pref Setting (deg)	Toe-in (in.)	Steering Axis Inclin. (deg.)	Wheel Pivot Ratio (deg.) Inner Wheel	Outer Wheel
1979	Le Mans MAN.	1/2P to 1³/₁₆P	1P	0 to 1P	1/2P	1/16 to 3/16	8	—	—
	Le Mans, Grand Prix PWR.	2¹/₂P to 3¹/₂P	3P	0 to 1P	1/2P	1/16 to 3/16	8	—	—
	Phoenix MAN.	1¹/₂N to 1/2P	1N	1/2P to 1¹/₂P	1P	1/16 to 3/16	10	—	—
	Phoenix PWR.	1/2P to 1¹/₂P	1P	1/2P to 1¹/₂P	1P	1/16 to 3/16	10	—	—
1980–81	Le Mans MAN.	1/2P to 1¹/₂P	1P	0 to 1P	1/2P	1/16 to 3/16	8	—	—
	Le Mans PWR.	2¹/₂P to 3¹/₂P	3P	0 to 1P	1/2P	1/16 to 3/16	8	—	—
	Grand Prix MAN.	0 to 2 P	1P	5/16P to 1⁵/₁₆P	1/8P	1/16 to 1/4	8	—	—
	Grand Prix PWR.	2 to 4P	3P	5/16P to 1⁵/₁₆P	1/8P	1/16 to 1/4	8	—	—
1982–83	Grand Prix MAN.	1/2P to 1¹/₂P	1P	0 to 1P	1/2P	1/16 to 3/16	—	—	—
	Grand Prix PWR.	2¹/₂P to 3¹/₂P	3P	0 to 1P	1/2P	1/16 to 3/16	—	—	—

MAN-Manual   LH-Left Hand   L-Left   LT-Left turn   ③ LH: 1/2P to 1¹/₂P
PWR-Power   RH-Right Hand   R-Right   RT-Right turn   RH: 0 to 1P
① Manual steering—1¹/₂N to 1/2N   ④ LH: 1P
   Power steering—1/2P to 1/2P   RH: 1/2P
② Manual steering—1N   ⑤ Radial tires
   Power steering—0   ⑥ Belted bias-ply tires

REAR SUSPENSION

▶ See Figures 18, 19 and 20

A four-link, coil spring rear suspension is used on all mid-size Pontiacs except for the Ventura/Phoenix series. The axle housing of the four-link suspension is connected to the frame by two upper and lower control arms with rubber bushings at each end of the arm. The control arms oppose torque reaction on acceleration and braking, and maintain the axle relationship to the frame.

Two coil springs support the weight of the car in the rear. They are retained between spring seats in the frame and brackets welded to the axle housing. A rubber insulator is used on the upper side. Shock absorbers are mounted on brackets between the axle housing and the frame. A stabilizer bar is optional equipment, being used on cars with the GT package or RTS (Radial Tuned Suspension).

Leaf-spring rear suspension is used on the Ventura and Phoenix models. Staggered shock absorbers (one mounted in front and one mounted behind the axle to reduce spring twist or "wrap-up" during acceleration) are connected between the lower spring seats and the underbody floor pan. Leaf springs are rubber-mounted at the axle and underbody side rail. A stabilizer bar is fitted to the GTO series and other models with the special suspension option.

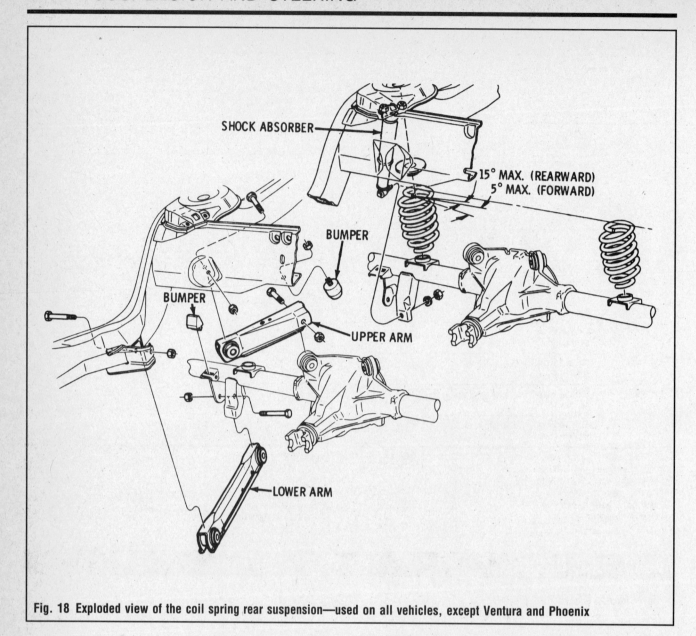

SHOCK ABSORBER

15° MAX. (REARWARD)
5° MAX. (FORWARD)

BUMPER

BUMPER

UPPER ARM

LOWER ARM

Fig. 18 Exploded view of the coil spring rear suspension—used on all vehicles, except Ventura and Phoenix

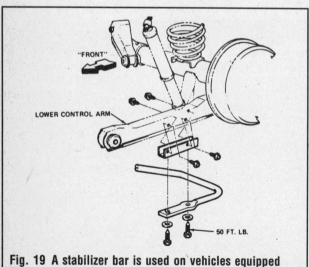

"FRONT"

LOWER CONTROL ARM

50 FT. LB.

Fig. 19 A stabilizer bar is used on vehicles equipped with the optional Radial Tuned Suspension (RTS)

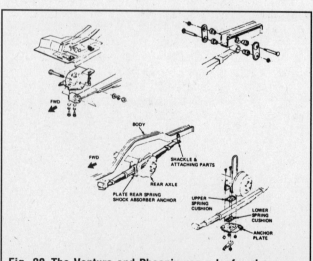

FWD

BODY

FWD

SHACKLE & ATTACHING PARTS

REAR AXLE

PLATE REAR SPRING
SHOCK ABSORBER ANCHOR

UPPER SPRING CUSHION

LOWER SPRING CUSHION

ANCHOR PLATE

Fig. 20 The Ventura and Phoenix use a leaf spring rear suspension

REAR SUSPENSION COMPONENTS

1. Rear axle (differential) housing cover
2. Upper control arm
3. Coil spring
4. Shock absorber
5. Rear axle
6. Lower control arm

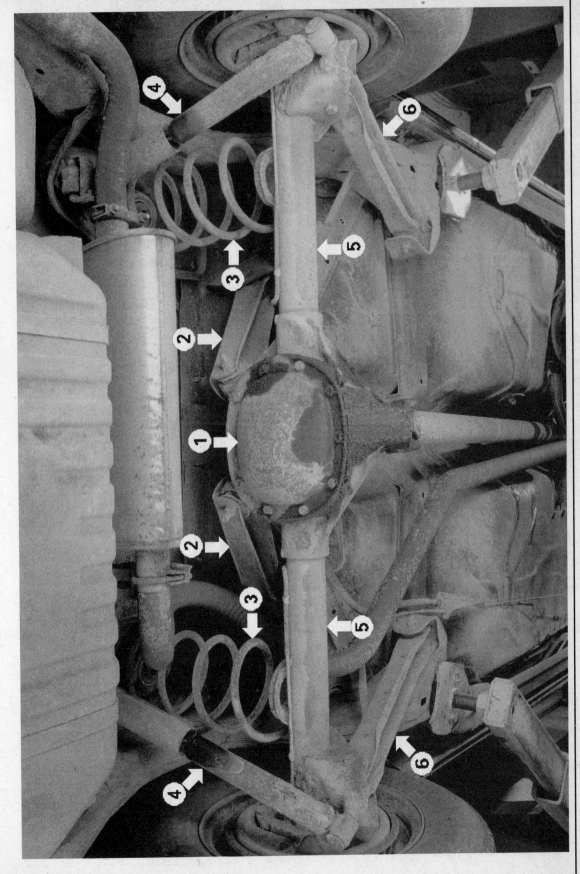

Coil Springs

REMOVAL & INSTALLATION

Except Ventura and Phoenix
♦ See Figure 21

1974–77 VEHICLES

✳✳ CAUTION

When removing the rear coil springs without the aid of a spring compressor, be very careful the spring does not fly out and strike someone. If a spring compressor is available, use it. The following procedure does not use a spring compressor. However, if the axle housing is lowered slowly, the spring should come out without incident.

1. Jack up the rear of the car on the axle housing and support it safely on the frame rails with jackstands. Do not lower the jack yet.
2. Disconnect the brake line at the axle housing.
3. Disconnect the upper control arms at the axle housing.
4. Remove the shock absorber at its lower mount.
5. *Lower the jack slowly.* Do not allow the rear brake hose to become kinked or stretched.
6. Remove the coil spring.

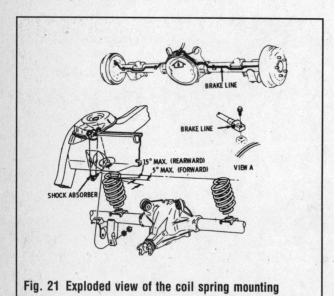

Fig. 21 Exploded view of the coil spring mounting

To install:
7. Mount the coil spring in place.
8. Jack up the rear axle until you are able to connect the shock at its lower mount.
9. Install the upper control arm bolts at the axle housing and torque to 95 ft. lbs.
10. Connect the brake line at the axle housing. Bleed the brakes.
11. Remove the jack stands and lower the car.

1978–83 VEHICLES

1. Jack up the rear of the car at the axle housing and place jack stands under the frame. *Do not lower the jack.*
2. Disconnect the brake line at the axle housing and at the differential housing.
3. Disconnect the upper control arms at the differential housing.
4. Remove the shock absorber lower mount and lower the jack. Be careful not to stretch the brake hose.
5. Remove the spring.
6. Installation is the reverse of removal.

Leaf Springs

REMOVAL & INSTALLATION

Ventura and Phoenix
♦ See Figures 22 and 23

1. Jack up the rear axle housing and safely support the rear end of the car with jackstands placed under the rear frame rails (ahead of the forward rear spring shackles). *Do not lower the jack yet.*

➡ **If removing the right-hand spring, loosen the tailpipe and resonator assembly.**

2. Remove the lower shock absorber nut and move the shock out of the bracket. Compress the shock out of the way.
3. Lower the jack until the springs are completely relaxed. The jack must remain underneath the axle housing for support until the spring is completely removed.

➡ **Do not stretch the brake hose.**

4. Remove the bolts from the rear spring shackles.
5. Remove the four U-bolt attaching nuts. Remove the spacers, which will be reused during installation.
6. Remove the NUT ONLY from the front shackle bolt, and

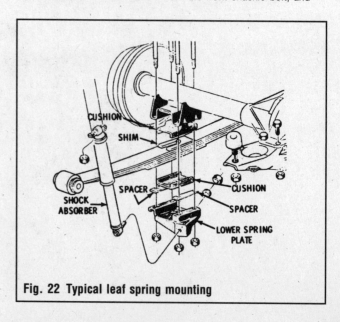

Fig. 22 Typical leaf spring mounting

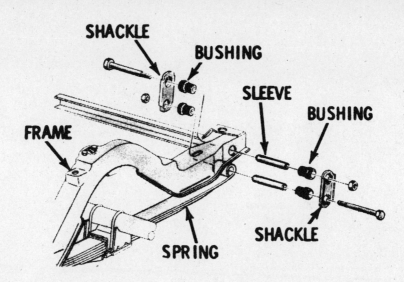

Fig. 23 Exploded view of the leaf spring shackles

while holding the spring up, remove the bolt from the shackle. Remove the spring from the car.

→**Before installation, make sure that any parts, including bolts and nuts, that are replaced with parts of equal strength and quality. Rated nuts and bolts must be replaced with parts of equal rating.**

To install:

7. Install the sleeves and bushing halves in the rear shackle (if removed) and loosely install the shackle bolt and nut.

✳✳ CAUTION

Do not tighten the shackle nuts until the weight of the car is on the springs.

8. Place the upper spring cushion pad on the spring so the cushion is indexed on the spring center locating bolt head.

9. Lower the axle housing onto the spring, keeping the jack underneath the housing.

10. Place the lower spring cushion pad on the spring and the shock absorber anchor plate with the dimple on the cushion indexed in the hole in the plate.

11. Position the spring and shock absorber anchor plate to the spring, with the nut of the spring center locating bolt indexed in the dimple of the lower spring cushion pad.

12. Install the lower spring plate, then loosely install the U-bolt nuts.

13. Raise the jack slightly, and install the shim spacers.

14. Lower the axle housing onto the spring, and tighten the U-bolt nuts to 50 ft. lbs. Install the shock absorber lower end stud into the spring plate, and tighten the shock lower end stud nut to 65 ft. lbs. Make sure the shock stud does not rotate while the nut is tightened.

15. Raise the car so the weight of the car is on the springs.

Tighten the spring front bolt nut to 60 ft. lbs., and the rear shackle nut to 105 ft. lbs.

16. Remove the jack stands and lower the car.

Shock Absorbers

REMOVAL & INSTALLATION

→**Examine the shock absorbers following the "Testing" procedure given for front shocks.**

Except Superlift System

◆ **See Figure 24**

1. Jack up the rear end of the car and support it with jackstands. Support the rear axle with a hydraulic jack to prevent stretching the brake hose.

2. Remove the nut from the lower end stud of the shock. Tap the shock free from the bracket.

3. Disconnect the shock at the top by removing the bolts, nuts and lockwashers. Remove the shock from the car.

→**Shock absorbers are often difficult to remove from their mounting points due to age (rust, etc). A liberal application of penetrating oil around the bushings and bolts before removing any nuts is recommended.**

Superlift Shock Absorbers

LEMANS SERIES, GRAND AM AND GRAND PRIX

◆ **See Figures 25 and 26 (p. 19)**

The Superlift shock system is an air-assist leveling device consisting of a neoprene boot and an air cylinder, built around a hy-

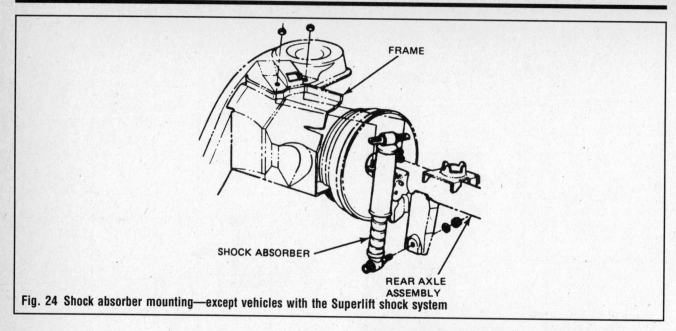

Fig. 24 Shock absorber mounting—except vehicles with the Superlift shock system

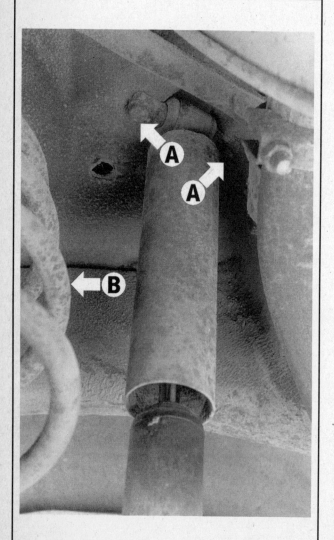

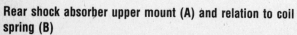
Rear shock absorber upper mount (A) and relation to coil spring (B)

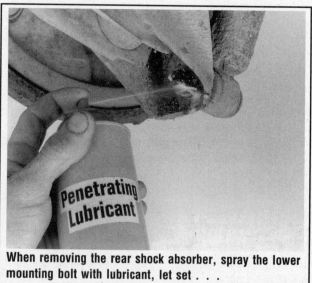
When removing the rear shock absorber, spray the lower mounting bolt with lubricant, let set . . .

. . . then remove the lower shock retaining bolt

Superlift System
Air Pressure Leak Tests

A. Broken or cracked line

A. Inflate system to approximately 90 psi. and inspect the lines for evidence of escaping air.

B. Loose connections or leaking valve core.

B. Apply a solution of soap and water to all connections and the valve core. If air bubbles appear, a leak exists.

C. Fill valve leaking.

C. Detach the valve assembly from the car with air pressure retained inside the valve and immerse the assembly in water. If air bubbles appear, a leak exists.

D. Superlift shocks leaking.

D. Remove Superlifts from car and immerse in water with air pressure applied to Superlift. If air bubbles appear, shock unit is leaking and should be replaced.

Fig. 25 Use this chart to test the Superlift shock system for malfunctioning

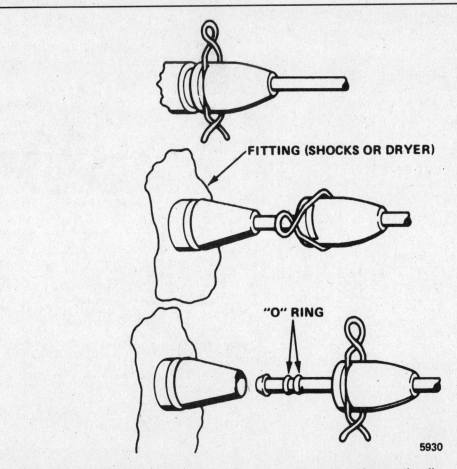

FITTING (SHOCKS OR DRYER)

"O" RING

5930

Fig. 26 When disconnecting the Superlift air line clip, be careful as not to damage the clip

draulic shock absorber. Depending on the load carried in the car, the Superlift system can be adjusted to maintain a level ride by increasing air pressure (a valve is located in the rear bumper or trunk area on models so equipped).

The Superlift shocks are removed from the car in the same manner as conventional rear shocks, except that the air line is disconnected from the Superlift before the shock unit is removed from the car. Also, to prevent damage to the neoprene boot on the Superlift unit, do not rotate the free end of the shock (when disconnected from the car) when the opposite end is still attached. Note the air line clip illustration when removing the air line.

If you suspect an air leak in the system, consult the chart above for the appropriate test procedures.

STEERING

Steering Wheel

REMOVAL & INSTALLATION

Non-Tilt Wheels
▶ **See Figure 27**

1. Disconnect the negative battery cable.
2. Remove the center pad assembly, either by removing the screws or by gently prying the pad off. Lift up on the pad and disconnect the horn wire by pushing in on the insulator and turning counterclockwise.
3. If no factory marks are visible, matchmark the steering wheel to the shaft.
4. Remove the steering wheel nut retainer and attaching nut. Using a puller, remove the steering wheel.
To install:
5. Align the marks on the wheel hub to the marks on the steering shaft.
6. Install the steering wheel, retainer and nut, and tighten the nut to 30 ft. lbs.

➡When the mark on the steering-wheel hub and the steering shaft are lined up, the wheel spokes should be horizontal as the car is driven straight ahead. If they are not horizontal it may be necessary to adjust the tie rod ends until the steering wheel is properly aligned.

7. Install the horn wire in the cam tower, push in and turn clockwise. Align the pad assembly into position and either press into place or install the screws. Connect the negative battery cable.

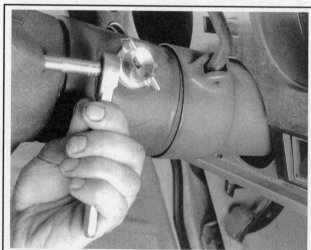

To remove the steering wheel, unfasten the horn pad screws/bolts . . .

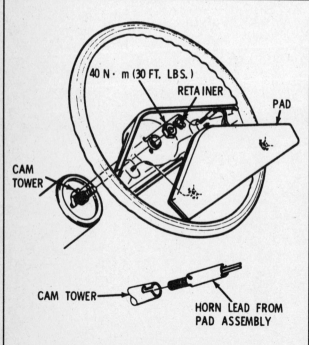

Fig. 27 Exploded view of the deluxe steering wheel and pad assembly

. . . then lift the horn pad up, off the steering wheel assembly

Detach the horn electrical connector

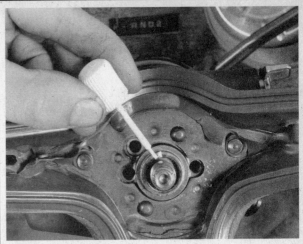

Matchmark the position of the steering shaft to the wheel, in order to assure proper installation

On some vehicles, you must remove a retaining circlip

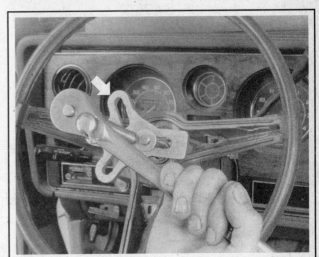

Attach a suitable steering wheel puller (see arrow) to the steering wheel . . .

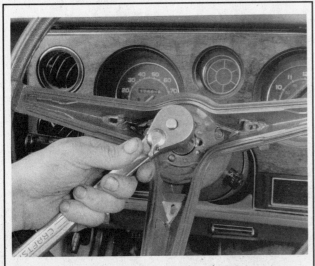

Loosen and remove the steering wheel retaining nut

. . . and use the puller to separate the steering wheel from the shaft

Tilt and Telescope Wheels

♦ **See Figures 28 and 29**

1. Remove the negative battery cable.
2. Remove the pad assembly by either removing the screws or prying the pad off. Disconnect the bayonet-type connector at the horn wire by pushing in and turning counter-clockwise.
3. Push the locking lever counterclockwise until the full release position is obtained.
4. Scribe a mark on the plate assembly where the two attaching screws attach the plate assembly to the locking lever. Remove the two screws.
5. Unscrew the plate assembly and remove.

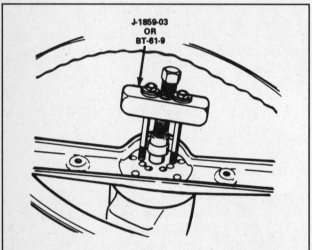

Fig. 28 You must use a suitable puller to remove the steering wheel from the shaft

6. Remove the steering wheel nut retainer and nut. Using a puller, remove the wheel.

To install:

7. Install a 5/16 in. × 18 set screw into the upper shaft at the full extended position and lock.
8. Install the steering wheel, aligning the scribe mark on the hub with the slash mark on the end of the shaft. Make sure that the unattached end of the horn upper contact assembly is seated flush against the top of the horn contact assembly.
9. Install the nut on the upper steering shaft, along with the nut retainer. Torque to 30 ft. lbs.
10. Remove the set screw installed earlier.
11. Install the plate assembly and tighten finger-tight.
12. Position the locking lever in the vertical position and move the lever counterclockwise until the holes in the plate align with the holes in the lever. Install the attaching screws.
13. Align the pad assembly with the holes in the steering wheel and install the retaining screws. Connect the negative battery cable. Check to see that the locking lever securely locks the wheel travel and that the wheel travel is free in the unlocked position.

Turn Signal Switch

REMOVAL & INSTALLATION

♦ **See Figures 30 and 31**

Except Tilt and Telescopic Column

1. Disconnect the negative battery cable.
2. Remove the steering wheel as described earlier.

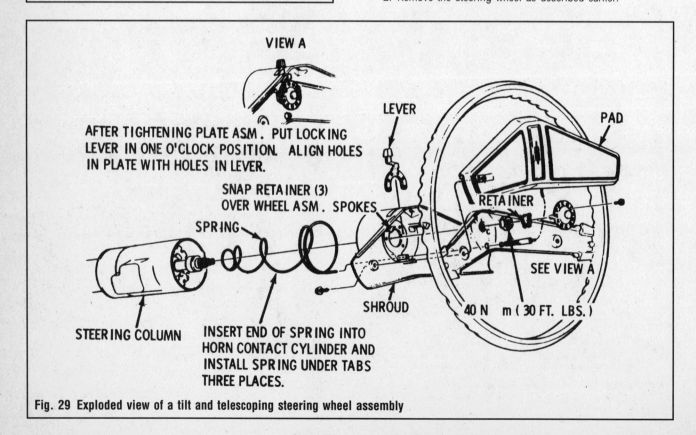

Fig. 29 Exploded view of a tilt and telescoping steering wheel assembly

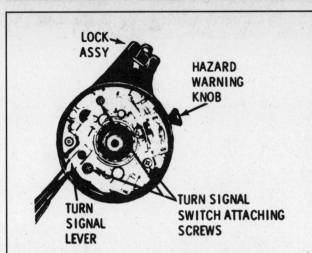

Fig. 30 The turn signal switch is secured with three retaining screws

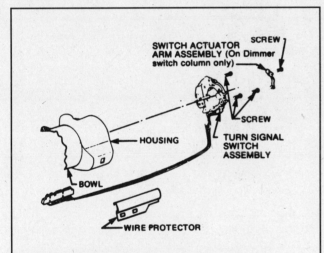

Fig. 31 Exploded view of the turn signal switch mounting—standard column shown, tilt column similar

3. Remove the covers from the steering column shaft. The plastic keepers under the cover are not necessary for installation.

4. Depress the lockplate and remove the snapring from the shaft. Remove the lock-plate and the cancelling cam.

5. Remove the upper bearing preload spring.

6. Place the turn signal lever in the right turn position, then remove the turn signal lever attaching screw and the lever. On 1978 and later models with the dimmer switch in the turn signal lever, remove the actuator arm screw and the arm.

7. Push in on the hazard warning knob, then remove the screw and the hazard warning knob.

8. Remove the three turn signal switch attaching screws.

9. Remove the lower trim panel and then disconnect the turn signal connector from the wiring harness. Lift the connector from the mounting bracket on the right side of the jacket.

10. Remove the four bolts which attach the bracket assembly to the jacket.

11. Loosen the screw holding the shift indicator needle and disconnect the clip from the link.

12. Remove the two nuts from the column support bracket while holding the column in position. Remove the bracket assembly and wire protector from the wiring, then loosely install the bracket-to-support column.

13. Tape the turn signal wires at the connector, then carefully pull the turn signal switch and wiring from the top end of the column.

14. To install, reverse the removal procedure. Use a new snapring. If the cover screws are to be replaced, make sure the replacement screws are the same size.

Models with Tilt and Telescopic Column

✳✳ WARNING

All elements of energy-absorbing (telescopic) steering columns are very sensitive to damage. Do not strike any part of the column (nuts, bolts, etc.) as this could ruin the entire assembly.

1. Disconnect the negative battery cable.
2. Remove the steering wheel as outlined earlier.
3. Remove the cover from the steering column shaft.
4. Press down on the lockplate and pry the snapring from the shaft.
5. Remove the lockplate and the canceling cam.
6. Remove the upper bearing preload spring.
7. Remove the turn signal lever and the hazard flasher knob.
8. Lift up on the tilt lever and position the housing in its central position.
9. Remove the switch attaching screws.
10. Remove the lower trim cap from the instrument panel and disconnect the turn signal connector from the wiring harness.
11. Remove the four bolts which secure the bracket assembly to the jacket.
12. Loosen the screw that holds the shift indicator needle and disconnect the clip from the link.
13. Remove the two nuts from the column support bracket while holding the column in position. Remove the bracket assembly and wire protector from the wiring, then loosely install the support column bracket.
14. Tape the turn signal wires at the connector to keep them fit and parallel.
15. Carefully remove the turn signal switch and wiring from the column.
16. To install, reverse the removal procedure, using a new snapring.

Ignition Lock Cylinder

REMOVAL & INSTALLATION

▶ **See Figure 32 and 33**

1. Disconnect the negative battery cable.
2. Remove the steering wheel.
3. On models equipped with a tilt and telescope column, pry up the three tabs on the plastic lock cover. On other models, remove the three screws.

4. Depress the steering wheel lock plate and pry the snapring from the shaft.

5. Remove the lock plate, cancelling cam, and upper bearing spring.

6. Remove the turn signal lever. Push the hazard warning knob in and unscrew the knob.

7. Remove the turn signal switch screws and pull the switch up out of the way.

8. Turn the ignition key to the **RUN** position.

9. Insert a long thin screwdriver into the slot in the upper bearing housing and depress the release tab while pulling the cylinder from the column.

To install:

10. Insert a new lock cylinder into the column after aligning the key on the cylinder with the keyway in the column.

11. Press inward on the cylinder while turning it clockwise.

12. The rest of the installation is in the reverse order of removal.

13. Connect the negative battery cable.

Tie Rod Ends

REMOVAL & INSTALLATION

◆ **See Figures 34, 35 and 36 (p. 27)**

1. Remove the cotter pins and nuts from the tie-rod end studs.

2. Tap on the steering arm near the tie-rod end (use another hammer as backing) and pull down on the tie-rod, if necessary, to free it.

3. Remove the inner stud in the same manner as the outer.

4. Loosen the clamp bolts and unscrew the ends if they are being replaced.

5. Lubricate the tie-rod end threads with chassis grease if they were removed. Install each end assembly an equal distance from the sleeve.

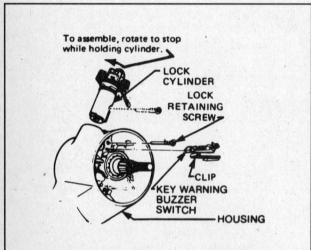

Fig. 32 View of the ignition lock cylinder—standard column shown

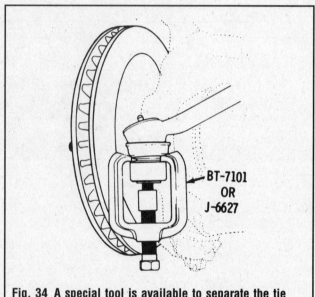

Fig. 34 A special tool is available to separate the tie rod end

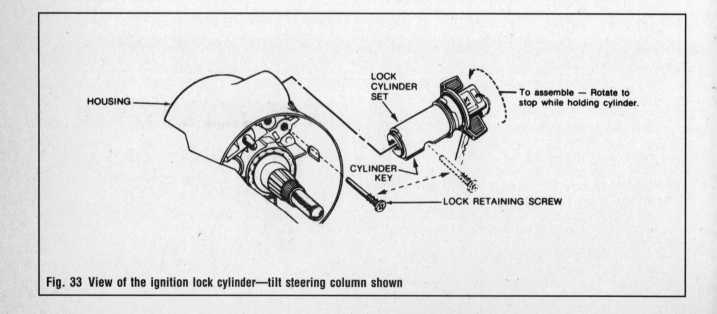

Fig. 33 View of the ignition lock cylinder—tilt steering column shown

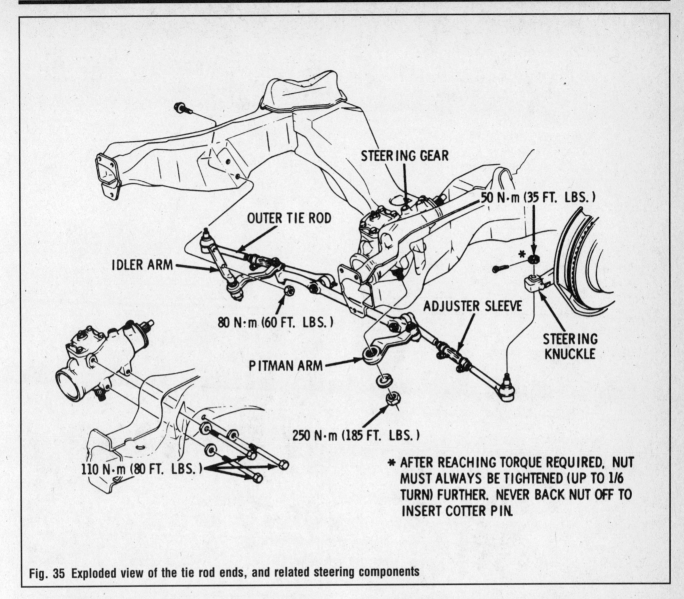

STEERING GEAR

OUTER TIE ROD

IDLER ARM

50 N·m (35 FT. LBS.)

*

ADJUSTER SLEEVE

80 N·m (60 FT. LBS.)

STEERING KNUCKLE

PITMAN ARM

250 N·m (185 FT. LBS.)

110 N·m (80 FT. LBS.)

* AFTER REACHING TORQUE REQUIRED, NUT MUST ALWAYS BE TIGHTENED (UP TO 1/6 TURN) FURTHER. NEVER BACK NUT OFF TO INSERT COTTER PIN.

Fig. 35 Exploded view of the tie rod ends, and related steering components

Before beginning removal, matchmark the installed position of the tie-rod end

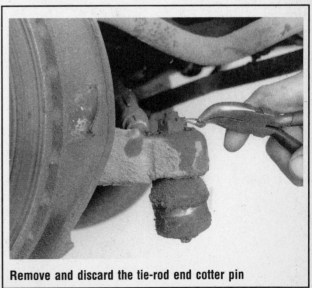

Remove and discard the tie-rod end cotter pin

Use a ratchet to loosen and remove the nut from the tie-rod end stud

. . . then use it to free the tie-rod end from the steering knuckle

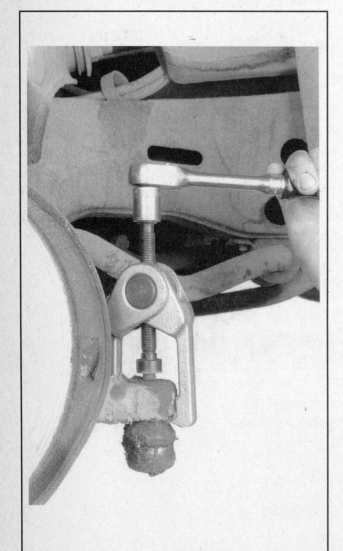

If you have access to one, attach a puller to the tie-rod end . . .

Loosen the tie-rod end clamp bolts . . .

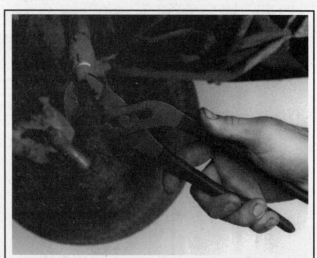

. . . then unscrew the tie-rod end to remove it from the vehicle

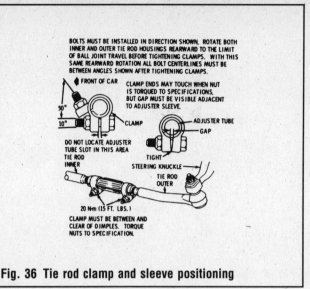

Fig. 36 Tie rod clamp and sleeve positioning

6. Ensure that the tie-rod end stud threads and nut are clean. Install new seals and install the studs into the steering arms and relay rod.

7. Install the stud nuts. Tighten the inner and outer end nuts to 35 ft. lbs. Install *new* cotter pins.

8. Have a reputable repair shop check and adjust the toe-in if necessary.

➡**Before tightening the sleeve clamps, ensure that the clamps are positioned so that adjusting sleeve slot is covered by the clamp. Never back nut off to insert cotter pin; always tighten it until the pin can fit through the castellations.**

Power Steering Gearbox

REMOVAL & INSTALLATION

◆ **See Figure 37**

1. Remove the coupling shield from the steering shaft.

2. Disconnect the hoses from the gearbox and cap or plug the hose fittings.

3. Jack up the front end of the car and support it with jackstands.

4. Remove the pitman shaft nut, then disconnect the pitman shaft using a puller (it is a press-fit).

5. Remove the three bolts attaching the gearbox to the frame side rail and remove the gearbox.

➡**If the mounting threads are stripped, do not repair; replace the housing.**

6. Before installing the gearbox, apply a sodium fiber grease to the gearbox mounting pads to prevent squeaks between the gear housing and the frame. Note that the flat on the gearbox lower shaft must index with the flat in the coupling flange and make sure there is a minimum of .040 in. clearance between the coupling hub and the steering gearbox upper seal.

7. Reverse the removal procedure for installation. Before tightening the gearbox-to-frame bolts, shift the gearbox as necessary to place it in the same place as the steering shaft so that the flexible coupling is not distorted. Tighten the gearbox-to-frame bolts to 80 ft. lbs., and the pitman shaft nut to 185 ft. lbs.

8. After connecting the hoses to the pump add GM Power Steering Fluid or an equivalent to bring the fluid level to the full COLD mark. Bleed the system by running the engine at idle for

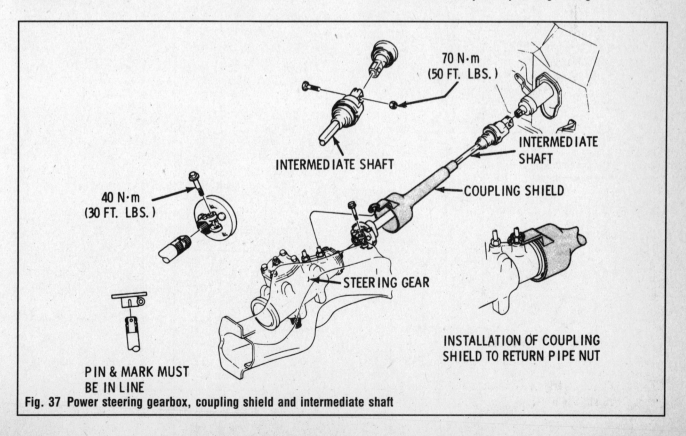

Fig. 37 Power steering gearbox, coupling shield and intermediate shaft

30 secones then at a fast idle for one minute BEFORE turning the steering wheel. Then, with the engine still running, turn the steering wheel through its full travel two or three times. Recheck the oil level and top up if necessary.

Power Steering Pump

REMOVAL & INSTALLATION

♦ **See Figures 38, 39 and 40**

1. Disconnect the negative battery cable.
2. Detach the hoses from the pump and tape the openings shut to prevent leakage.
3. Remove the pump drive belt.
4. Remove the retaining bolts, and any necessary braces, then remove the pump.
5. If a new pump is being installed and the pulley is being transferred, a puller is necessary to remove the pulley.

To install:

6. Position a new pump and secure with the retaining bolts and/or braces.
7. Attach the hoses to the pump, then tighten the hose fittings to 20 ft. lbs. (27 Nm). Fill the power steering pump reservoir with the proper type and amount of fluid, then turn the pump backward (counterclockwise as viewed from the front) until bubbles no longer appear in the reservoir.
8. Install the pump drive belt.
9. Any time the pump is removed, air must be bled from the system upon reinstallation. Bleed the system as outlined later in this section.

BLEEDING

1. Fill the pump reservoir to the proper level. See Section 1 for fluid recommendations. Turn the engine ON. Turn the steering wheel fully to the left and right without hitting the stops, until the power steering fluid reaches normal operating temperature (165-175°), then stop the engine.

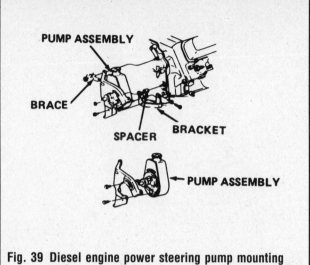

Fig. 39 Diesel engine power steering pump mounting

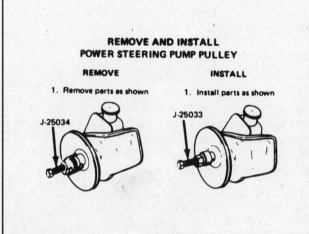

Fig. 40 Use a puller to remove the power steering pump pulley

2. Raise the front of the vehicle off the ground and safely support it on jackstands. Failure to raise the front end off the ground could cause flat spots to be worn into the tires during the bleeding procedure.
3. Turn the wheels to the full left position and add power steering fluid to the COLD mark on the dipstick, if necessary.
4. Bleed the system by turning the wheels, with the engine running, from side to side without hitting hard against the stops. Maintain the fluid level at the COLD mark on the dipstick. Fluid with air in it will have a milky appearance. Air must be eliminated from the fluid before normal steering action can be obtained. Continue turning the wheels back and forth until all of the air is bled from the system.
5. Return the wheels to the center position and operate the engine for an additional 2-3 minutes, then stop the engine.
6. Road test the car to make sure the steering functions normally and is free of noise. Check the fluid level. Add fluid to the HOT mark, if necessary.

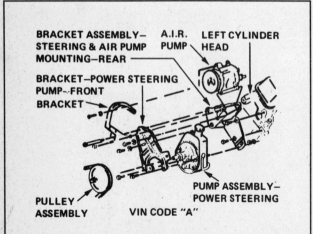

Fig. 38 Power steering pump mounting—231 V6 engine shown, V8 slightly different

BRAKE OPERATING SYSTEM 9-2
BASIC OPERATING PRINCIPLES 9-2
  DISC BRAKES 9-2
  DRUM BRAKES 9-3
ADJUSTMENTS 9-3
  FRONT BRAKES 9-3
  REAR DRUM BRAKE SHOES 9-3
MASTER CYLINDER 9-3
  REMOVAL & INSTALLATION 9-3
  OVERHAUL 9-5
POWER BOOSTER 9-6
  REMOVAL & INSTALLATION 9-6
HYDRO-BOOST II BRAKE
  BOOSTER 9-6
  HYDRO-BOOST SYSTEM
    CHECKS 9-6
  HYDRO-BOOST TESTS 9-7
  HYDRO-BOOST SYSTEM
    BLEEDING 9-7
  HYDRO-BOOST
    TROUBLESHOOTING 9-7
  OVERHAUL 9-7
  REMOVAL & INSTALLATION 9-8
COMBINATION VALVE 9-9
  REMOVAL & INSTALLATION 9-11
BRAKE BLEEDING 9-11
  MANUAL BLEEDING 9-11
FRONT DISC BRAKES 9-12
DISC BRAKE PADS 9-12
  INSPECTION 9-12
  REMOVAL & INSTALLATION 9-14
DISC BRAKE CALIPERS 9-16
  REMOVAL, INSTALLATION &
    OVERHAUL 9-16
BRAKE DISC (ROTOR) 9-18
  REMOVAL & INSTALLATION 9-18
  INSPECTION 9-19
WHEEL BEARINGS 9-20
  ADJUSTMENT 9-20
  REMOVAL, PACKING &
    INSTALLATION 9-20
REAR DRUM BRAKES 9-24
BRAKE DRUM 9-25
  REPLACEMENT 9-25
  DRUM INSPECTION 9-25
BRAKE SHOES 9-25
  REMOVAL & INSTALLATION 9-25
WHEEL CYLINDERS 9-28
  REMOVAL & INSTALLATION 9-28
  OVERHAUL 9-29
PARKING BRAKE 9-29
ADJUSTMENT 9-29
COMPONENT LOCATIONS
REAR DRUM BRAKE
  COMPONENTS 9-24
SPECIFICATION CHARTS
BRAKE SPECIFICATIONS 9-30

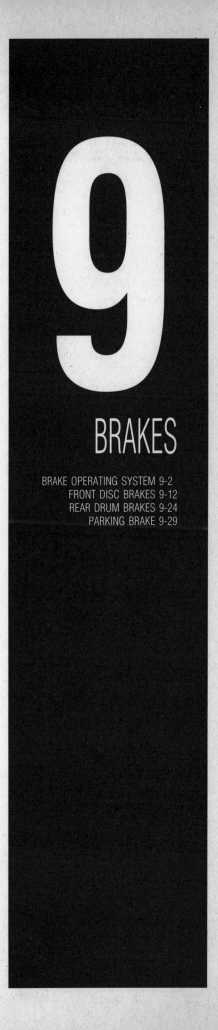

9

BRAKES

BRAKE OPERATING SYSTEM 9-2
FRONT DISC BRAKES 9-12
REAR DRUM BRAKES 9-24
PARKING BRAKE 9-29

BRAKE OPERATING SYSTEM

Basic Operating Principles

Hydraulic systems are used to actuate the brakes of all modern automobiles. The system transports the power required to force the frictional surfaces of the braking system together from the pedal to the individual brake units at each wheel. A hydraulic system is used for two reasons.

First, fluid under pressure can be carried to all parts of an automobile by small pipes and flexible hoses without taking up a significant amount of room or posing routing problems.

Second, a great mechanical advantage can be given to the brake pedal end of the system, and the foot pressure required to actuate the brakes can be reduced by making the surface area of the master cylinder pistons smaller than that of any of the pistons in the wheel cylinders or calipers.

The master cylinder consists of a fluid reservoir along with a double cylinder and piston assembly. Double type master cylinders are designed to separate the front and rear braking systems hydraulically in case of a leak. The master cylinder coverts mechanical motion from the pedal into hydraulic pressure within the lines. This pressure is translated back into mechanical motion at the wheels by either the wheel cylinder (drum brakes) or the caliper (disc brakes).

Steel lines carry the brake fluid to a point on the vehicle's frame near each of the vehicle's wheels. The fluid is then carried to the calipers and wheel cylinders by flexible tubes in order to allow for suspension and steering movements.

In drum brake systems, each wheel cylinder contains two pistons, one at either end, which push outward in opposite directions and force the brake shoe into contact with the drum.

In disc brake systems, the cylinders are part of the calipers. At least one cylinder in each caliper is used to force the brake pads against the disc.

All pistons employ some type of seal, usually made of rubber, to minimize fluid leakage. A rubber dust boot seals the outer end of the cylinder against dust and dirt. The boot fits around the outer end of the piston on disc brake calipers, and around the brake actuating rod on wheel cylinders.

The hydraulic system operates as follows: When at rest, the entire system, from the piston(s) in the master cylinder to those in the wheel cylinders or calipers, is full of brake fluid. Upon application of the brake pedal, fluid trapped in front of the master cylinder piston(s) is forced through the lines to the wheel cylinders. Here, it forces the pistons outward, in the case of drum brakes, and inward toward the disc, in the case of disc brakes. The motion of the pistons is opposed by return springs mounted outside the cylinders in drum brakes, and by spring seals, in disc brakes.

Upon release of the brake pedal, a spring located inside the master cylinder immediately returns the master cylinder pistons to the normal position. The pistons contain check valves and the master cylinder has compensating ports drilled in it. These are uncovered as the pistons reach their normal position. The piston check valves allow fluid to flow toward the wheel cylinders or calipers as the pistons withdraw. Then, as the return springs force the brake pads or shoes into the released position, the excess fluid reservoir through the compensating ports. It is during the time the pedal is in the released position that any fluid that has leaked out of the system will be replaced through the compensating ports.

Dual circuit master cylinders employ two pistons, located one behind the other, in the same cylinder. The primary piston is actuated directly by mechanical linkage from the brake pedal through the power booster. The secondary piston is actuated by fluid trapped between the two pistons. If a leak develops in front of the secondary piston, it moves forward until it bottoms against the front of the master cylinder, and the fluid trapped between the pistons will operate the rear brakes. If the rear brakes develop a leak, the primary piston will move forward until direct contact with the secondary piston takes place, and it will force the secondary piston to actuate the front brakes. In either case, the brake pedal moves farther when the brakes are applied, and less braking power is available.

All dual circuit systems use a switch to warn the driver when only half of the brake system is operational. This switch is usually located in a valve body which is mounted on the firewall or the frame below the master cylinder. A hydraulic piston receives pressure from both circuits, each circuit's pressure being applied to one end of the piston. When the pressures are in balance, the piston remains stationary. When one circuit has a leak, however, the greater pressure in that circuit during application of the brakes will push the piston to one side, closing the switch and activating the brake warning light.

In disc brake systems, this valve body also contains a metering valve and, in some cases, a proportioning valve. The metering valve keeps pressure from traveling to the disc brakes on the front wheels until the brake shoes on the rear wheels have contacted the drums, ensuring that the front brakes will never be used alone. The proportioning valve controls the pressure to the rear brakes to lessen the chance of rear wheel lock-up during very hard braking.

Warning lights may be tested by depressing the brake pedal and holding it while opening one of the wheel cylinder bleeder screws. If this does not cause the light to go on, substitute a new lamp, make continuity checks, and, finally, replace the switch as necessary.

The hydraulic system may be checked for leaks by applying pressure to the pedal gradually and steadily. If the pedal sinks very slowly to the floor, the system has a leak. This is not to be confused with a springy or spongy feel due to the compression of air within the lines. If the system leaks, there will be a gradual change in the position of the pedal with a constant pressure.

Check for leaks along all lines and at wheel cylinders. If no external leaks are apparent, the problem is inside the master cylinder.

DISC BRAKES

Instead of the traditional expanding brakes that press outward against a circular drum, disc brake systems utilize a disc (rotor) with brake pads positioned on either side of it. An easily-seen analogy is the hand brake arrangement on a bicycle. The pads squeeze onto the rim of the bike wheel, slowing its motion. Automobile disc brakes use the identical principle but apply the braking effort to a separate disc instead of the wheel.

The disc (rotor) is a casting, usually equipped with cooling fins between the two braking surfaces. This enables air to circulate between the braking surfaces making them less sensitive to heat buildup and more resistant to fade. Dirt and water do not drastically affect braking action since contaminants are thrown off by the centrifugal action of the rotor or scraped off the by the pads. Also, the equal clamping action of the two brake pads tends to ensure uniform, straight line stops. Disc brakes are inherently self-adjusting. There are three general types of disc brake:

1. A fixed caliper.
2. A floating caliper.
3. A sliding caliper.

The fixed caliper design uses two pistons mounted on either side of the rotor (in each side of the caliper). The caliper is mounted rigidly and does not move.

The sliding and floating designs are quite similar. In fact, these two types are often lumped together. In both designs, the pad on the inside of the rotor is moved into contact with the rotor by hydraulic force. The caliper, which is not held in a fixed position, moves slightly, bringing the outside pad into contact with the rotor. There are various methods of attaching floating calipers. Some pivot at the bottom or top, and some slide on mounting bolts. In any event, the end result is the same.

DRUM BRAKES

Drum brakes employ two brake shoes mounted on a stationary backing plate. These shoes are positioned inside a circular drum which rotates with the wheel assembly. The shoes are held in place by springs. This allows them to slide toward the drums (when they are applied) while keeping the linings and drums in alignment. The shoes are actuated by a wheel cylinder which is mounted at the top of the backing plate. When the brakes are applied, hydraulic pressure forces the wheel cylinder's actuating links outward. Since these links bear directly against the top of the brake shoes, the tops of the shoes are then forced against the inner side of the drum. This action forces the bottoms of the two shoes to contact the brake drum by rotating the entire assembly slightly (known as servo action). When pressure within the wheel cylinder is relaxed, return springs pull the shoes back away from the drum.

Most modern drum brakes are designed to self-adjust themselves during application when the vehicle is moving in reverse. This motion causes both shoes to rotate very slightly with the drum, rocking an adjusting lever, thereby causing rotation of the adjusting screw. Some drum brake systems are designed to self-adjust during application whenever the brakes are applied. This on-board adjustment system reduces the need for maintenance adjustments and keeps both the brake function and pedal feel satisfactory.

Adjustments

FRONT BRAKES

There is no adjustment provision on hydraulic disc brakes; they are inherently self-adjusting.

REAR DRUM BRAKE SHOES

◆ See Figure 1

➡ **Drum brakes are self-adjusting, but provision is made for manual adjustment as follows:**

1. Jack up the rear of the car and support it with jackstands.
2. The inner sides of the brake backing plates have a lanced area, oblong in shape. Knock this area out with a punch—you will have to remove the brake drum to clean out any metal pieces that will be deposited by the punch, and you will have to purchase rubber plugs at a GM dealer to plug the punched holes now in the backing plates. Many cars will already have the holes punched and plugs installed.

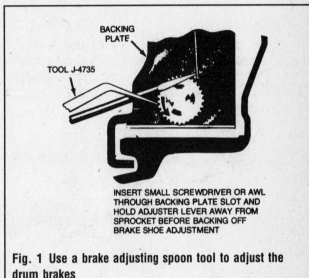

INSERT SMALL SCREWDRIVER OR AWL THROUGH BACKING PLATE SLOT AND HOLD ADJUSTER LEVER AWAY FROM SPROCKET BEFORE BACKING OFF BRAKE SHOE ADJUSTMENT

Fig. 1 Use a brake adjusting spoon tool to adjust the drum brakes

3. Insert a brake adjusting spoon into the hole, along with a small screwdriver to hold the adjuster lever away from the sprocket. Turn the star-shaped adjusting screw inside the drum with the spoon, until the wheel can *just* be turned by hand. Do this to both wheels until there is equal drag on each wheel.
4. Back off each adjusting screw about 25 notches. If you still hear and feel the brake shoes dragging slightly when you turn the wheels by hand, back off another one or two notches. If there is still excess drag on the drums, the parking brake cables could be excessively tight.
5. Install the rubber plugs into the adjusting holes. Check the parking brake adjustment.

Master Cylinder

REMOVAL & INSTALLATION

◆ See Figures 2 and 3

On power brake-equipped models, the master cylinder can be removed without removing the power vacuum cylinder from the car.

1. Use a clean syringe to remove as much fluid from the master cylinder as possible.
2. Clean the area around the master cylinder.

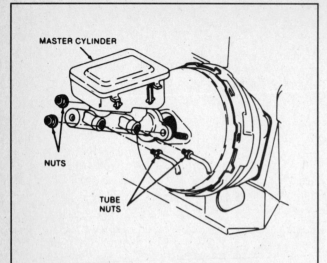

Fig. 2 On vehicles equipped with power brakes, the master cylinder is mounted to the power brake booster

To remove the master cylinder, drain as much fluid as possible from the reservoir using a syringe

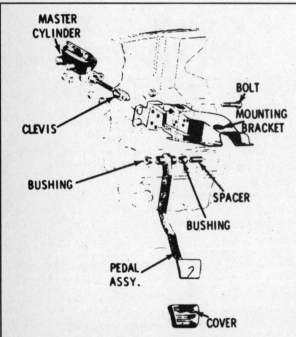

Fig. 3 The master cylinder is mounted directly to the firewall on vehicles without power brakes

Use a flare-end wrench (see arrow) to disconnect the brake fluid lines from the master cylinder

3. Disconnect the hydraulic lines at the master cylinder. Plug or tape the ends of the lines to prevent dirt from entering and to prevent fluid from leaking out.

4. Remove the master cylinder attaching nuts and remove the master cylinder.

5. Installation is the reverse of the removal procedure. Bleed the brake system, as outlined later in this section.

✳✳ WARNING

Be careful to keep brake fluid away from all body paint—the fluid acts like paint remover, and a few drops will quickly bubble any paint with which it comes in contact.

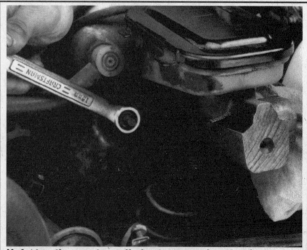

Unfasten the master cylinder-to-power booster (or firewall on manual brakes) retaining nuts . . .

. . . then remove master cylinder from the vehicle

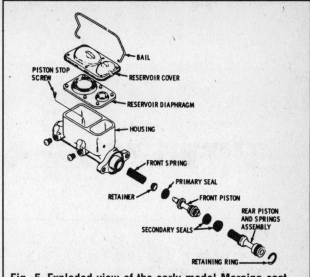

Fig. 5 Exploded view of the early model Moraine cast iron master cylinder with integral reservoir

OVERHAUL

♦ **See Figures 4 and 5**

The models covered in this guide are equipped with either Moraine or Bendix master cylinders. The rebuilding kits may differ slightly, but the procedures are the same. Follow the instructions that come with each particular kit.

➡ **Overhaul procedures for power brake master cylinders and manual master cylinders is the same.**

1. Remove the master cylinder from the car.
2. Remove the mounting gasket and boot, and the main cover, and purge the unit of its fluid.
3. Secure the cylinder in a vise and remove the pushrod retainer and secondary piston stop bolt found inside the forward reservoir.

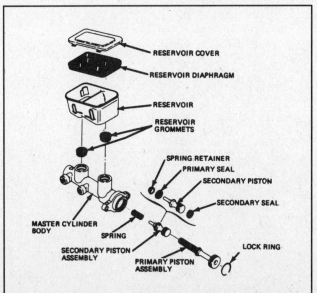

Fig. 4 Exploded view of the master cylinder—late model vehicles with plastic, removable reservoir

4. Compress the retaining ring and extract it along with the primary piston assembly.
5. Blow compressed air into the piston stop screw hole to force the secondary piston, spring, and retainer from the bore of the cylinder. An alternative method is to use hooked wire to snag and extract the secondary piston.
6. Check the brass tube fitting inserts and if they are damaged, remove them. Leave undamaged inserts in place.
7. If replacement is necessary, thread a 6-3 × ⅝ in. self-tapping screw into the insert. Hook the end of the screw with a claw hammer and pry the insert free.
8. An alternative way to remove the inserts is to first drill the outlet holes to ¹³/₆₄ in. and thread them with a ¼ in.-20 tap. Position a thick washer over the hole to serve as a spacer, and then thread a ¼ in.-20 × ¾ in. hex head bolt into the insert and tighten the bolt until the insert is freed.
9. Use denatured alcohol and compressed air to clean the parts. Slight rust may be removed with crocus cloth. *Never use petroleum-based solvents to clean brake parts.*
10. Replace the brass tube inserts by positioning them in their holes and threading a brake line tube nut into the outlet hole. Turn down the nut until the insert is seated.
11. Check the piston assemblies for correct identification and, when satisfied, position the replacement secondary seals in the twin grooves of the secondary piston.
12. The outside seal is correctly placed when its lips face the flat end of the piston.
13. Slip the primary seal and its protector over the end of the secondary piston opposite the secondary seals. The flat side of this seal should face the piston's compensating hole flange.
14. Replace the primary piston assembly with assembled pieces in the overhaul kit.
15. Moisten the cylinder bore and the secondary piston's inner and outer seals with brake fluid. Assemble the secondary piston spring to its retainer and position them over the end of the primary seal.
16. Insert the combined spring and piston assembly into the cylinder and use a small wooden dowel or pencil to seat the spring against the end of the bore.

17. Moisten the primary piston seals with brake fluid and push it, pushrod receptacle end out, into the cylinder.

18. Keep the piston pushed in and snap the retaining ring into place.

19. Relax the pressure on the pistons and allow them to seek their static positions.

20. Replace the secondary piston stop screw and torque it to 25–40 inch lbs.

21. Replace the reservoir diaphragm and cover.

Power Booster

REMOVAL & INSTALLATION

♦ **See Figure 6**

1. Disconnect the booster pushrod from the brake pedal arm by removing the retaining clip, and sliding the eyelet end of the pushrod off of the pin on the brake arm.

2. Disconnect the master cylinder from the booster.

3. Remove the attaching nuts and remove the booster from the firewall.

4. Installation is the reverse of removal. Tighten the booster-to-firewall attaching nuts to 22–33 ft. lbs.

Hydro-Boost II Brake Booster

The Hydro-Boost II system is a hydraulically-operated power brake booster bolted to the back of the dual master cylinder on 1980 and later diesel engined cars. The Hydro-Boost differs from typical vacuum-type brake boosters in that its source of power is hydraulic; the power steering pump provides the hydraulic fluid pressure (the pump operates both the Hydro-Boost and the power steering gear). Therefore, the Hydro-Boost unit is part of both the steering and braking sub-systems of the car and problems or malfunctions in one system may affect the operation of the other.

HYDRO-BOOST SYSTEM CHECKS

1. A defective Hydro-Boost cannot cause any of the following conditions:
   a. Noisy brakes
   b. Fading pedal
   c. Pulling brakes

If any of these occur, check elsewhere in the brake system.

2. Check the fluid level in the master cylinder. It should be within ¼ in. of the top. If it isn't, add only DOT-3 or DOT-4 brake fluid until the correct level is reached.

3. Check the fluid level in the power steering pump. The engine should be at normal running temperature and stopped. The level should register on the pump dipstick. Add power steering fluid to bring the reservoir level up to the correct level. Low fluid level will result in both poor steering and stopping ability.

✳✳ CAUTION

The brake hydraulic system uses brake fluid only, while the power steering and Hydro-Boost systems use power steering fluid only. Don't mix the two.

4. Check the power steering pump belt tension, and inspect all of the power steering/Hydro-Boost hoses for kinks or leaks.

5. Check and adjust the engine idle speed, as necessary.

6. Check the power steering pump fluid for bubbles. If air bubbles are present in the fluid, bleed the system:
   a. Fill the power steering pump reservoir to specifications with the engine at normal operating temperature.
   b. With the engine running, rotate the steering wheel

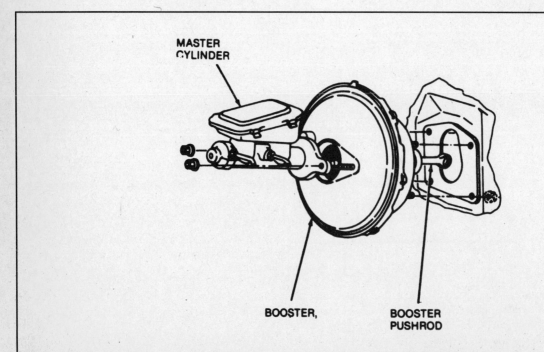

MASTER CYLINDER

BOOSTER,

BOOSTER PUSHROD

Fig. 6 View of the power brake booster mounting

through its normal travel 3 or 4 times, without holding the wheel against the stops.

c. Check the fluid level again.

7. If the problem still exists, go on to the Hydro-Boost test sections and troubleshooting.

HYDRO-BOOST TESTS

Functional Test

1. Check the brake system for leaks or low fluid level. Correct as necessary.

2. Place the transmission in Neutral and stop the engine. Apply the brakes 4 or 5 times to empty the accumulator.

3. Keep the pedal depressed with moderate (25–40 lbs.) pressure and start the engine.

4. The brake pedal should fall slightly and then push back up against your foot. If no movement is felt, the Hydro-Boost system is not working.

Accumulator Leak Test

1. Run the engine at normal idle. Turn the steering wheel against one of the stops; hold it there for no longer than 5 seconds. Center the steering wheel and stop the engine.

2. Keep applying the brakes until a "hard" pedal is obtained. There should be a minimum of 1 power-assisted brake application when pedal pressure of 20–25 lbs. is applied.

3. Start the engine and allow it to idle. Rotate the steering wheel against the stop. Listen for a light "hissing" sound; this is the accumulator being charged. Center the steering wheel and stop the engine.

4. Wait one hour and apply the brakes without starting the engine. As in step 2, there should be at least 1 stop with power assist. If not, the accumulator is defective and must be replaced.

HYDRO-BOOST SYSTEM BLEEDING

The system should be bled whenever the booster is removed and installed.

1. Fill the power steering pump until the fluid level is at the base of the pump reservoir neck. Disconnect the battery lead from the distributor.

➡ **Remove the electrical lead to the fuel solenoid terminal on the injection pump before cranking the engine.**

2. Jack up the front of the car, turn the wheels all the way to the left, and crank the engine for a few seconds.

3. Check steering pump fluid level. If necessary, add fluid to the "Add" mark on the dipstick.

4. Lower the car, connect the battery lead, and start the engine. Check fluid level and add fluid to the "Add" mark if necessary.

With the engine running, turn the wheels from side to side to bleed air from the system. Make sure that the fluid level stays above the internal pump casting.

5. The Hydro-Boost system should now be fully bled. If the fluid is foaming after bleeding, stop the engine, let the system set for one hour, then repeat the second part of Step 4.

The preceding procedures should be effective in removing excess air from the system, however sometimes air may still remain trapped. When this happens the booster may make a "gulping" noise when the brake is applied. Lightly pumping the brake pedal with the engine running should cause this noise to disappear. After the noise stops, check the pump fluid level and add as necessary.

HYDRO-BOOST TROUBLESHOOTING

HIGH PEDAL AND STEERING EFFORT (IDLE)
1. Loose/broken power steering pump belt
2. Low power steering fluid level
3. Leaking hoses or fittings
4. Low idle speed
5. Hose restriction
6. Defective power steering pump

HIGH PEDAL EFFORT (IDLE)
1. Binding pedal/linkage
2. Fluid contamination
3. Defective Hydro-Boost unit

POOR PEDAL RETURN
1. Binding pedal linkage
2. Restricted booster return line
3. Internal return system restriction

PEDAL CHATTER/PULSATION
1. Power steering pump drivebelt slipping
2. Low power steering fluid level
3. Defective power steering pump
4. Defective Hydro-Boost unit

BRAKES OVERSENSITIVE
1. Binding pedal/linkage
2. Defective Hydro-Boost unit

NOISE
1. Low power steering fluid level
2. Air in the power steering fluid
3. Loose power steering pump drivebelt
4. Hose restrictions

OVERHAUL

◆ **See Figure 7**

GM Hydro-Boost II units may be rebuilt. Kits are available through auto parts jobbers and Pontiac dealers.

➡ **Have a drain pan ready to catch and discard leaking fluid during disassembly.**

Use the accompanying illustrations to overhaul the Hydro-Boost system. If replacing the power piston/accumulator, dispose of the old one as shown.

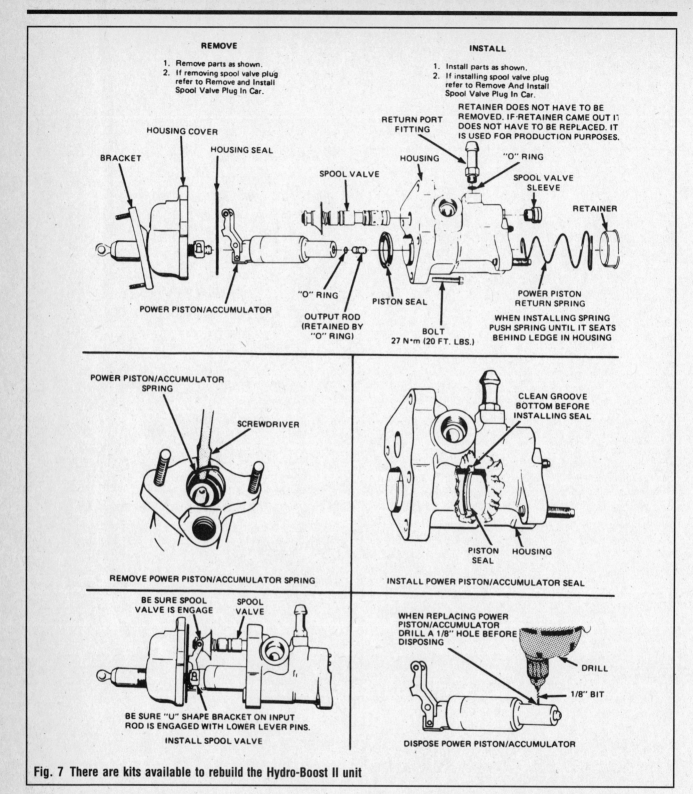

REMOVE
1. Remove parts as shown.
2. If removing spool valve plug refer to Remove and Install Spool Valve Plug In Car.

INSTALL
1. Install parts as shown.
2. If installing spool valve plug refer to Remove And Install Spool Valve Plug In Car.

RETAINER DOES NOT HAVE TO BE REMOVED. IF RETAINER CAME OUT IT DOES NOT HAVE TO BE REPLACED. IT IS USED FOR PRODUCTION PURPOSES.

BRACKET
HOUSING COVER
HOUSING SEAL
SPOOL VALVE
HOUSING
RETURN PORT FITTING
"O" RING
SPOOL VALVE SLEEVE
RETAINER
POWER PISTON/ACCUMULATOR
"O" RING
OUTPUT ROD (RETAINED BY "O" RING)
PISTON SEAL
BOLT 27 N•m (20 FT. LBS.)
POWER PISTON RETURN SPRING
WHEN INSTALLING SPRING PUSH SPRING UNTIL IT SEATS BEHIND LEDGE IN HOUSING

POWER PISTON/ACCUMULATOR SPRING
SCREWDRIVER
REMOVE POWER PISTON/ACCUMULATOR SPRING

CLEAN GROOVE BOTTOM BEFORE INSTALLING SEAL
PISTON SEAL
HOUSING
INSTALL POWER PISTON/ACCUMULATOR SEAL

BE SURE SPOOL VALVE IS ENGAGE
SPOOL VALVE
BE SURE "U" SHAPE BRACKET ON INPUT ROD IS ENGAGED WITH LOWER LEVER PINS.
INSTALL SPOOL VALVE

WHEN REPLACING POWER PISTON/ACCUMULATOR DRILL A 1/8" HOLE BEFORE DISPOSING
DRILL
1/8" BIT
DISPOSE POWER PISTON/ACCUMULATOR

Fig. 7 There are kits available to rebuild the Hydro-Boost II unit

REMOVAL & INSTALLATION

Spool Valve Plug and Seal
▶ See Figure 8

1. Turn the engine off and pump the brake pedal 4 or 5 times to deplete the accumulator inside the boost unit.
2. Remove the master cylinder from the booster unit with the brake lines attached. Fasten the master cylinder out of the way with tape or wire.
3. Push the spool valve plug in and use a small prytool to carefully remove the retaining ring.
4. Remove the spool valve plug and the O-ring.
5. Installation is the reverse of removal. Bleed the system upon installation, following the above bleeding instructions.

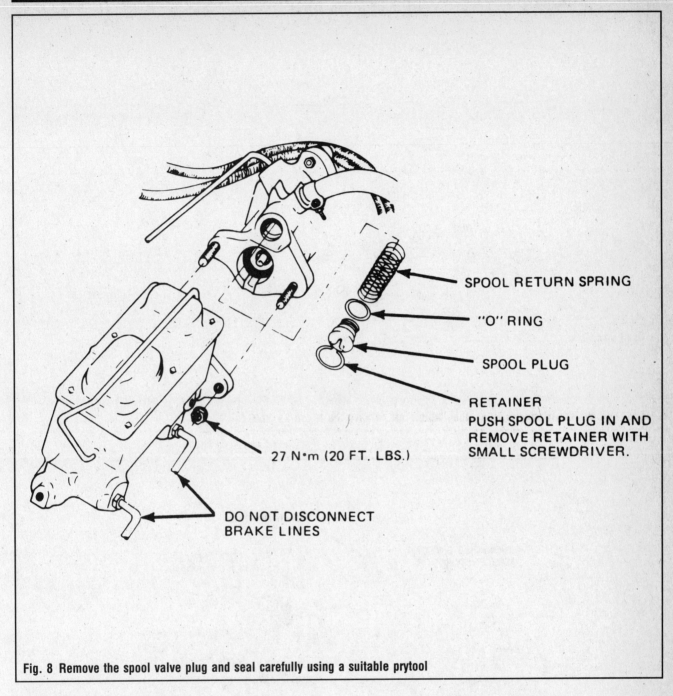

SPOOL RETURN SPRING

"O" RING

SPOOL PLUG

RETAINER
PUSH SPOOL PLUG IN AND
REMOVE RETAINER WITH
SMALL SCREWDRIVER.

27 N•m (20 FT. LBS.)

DO NOT DISCONNECT
BRAKE LINES

Fig. 8 Remove the spool valve plug and seal carefully using a suitable prytool

Hydro-Boost II Unit
▶ See Figure 9

✳✳ WARNING

Power steering fluid and brake fluid cannot be mixed. If brake seals contact the steering fluid or steering seals contact brake fluid, damage will result.

1. Turn the engine **OFF** and pump the brake pedal 4 or 5 times to deplect the accumulator inside the unit.
2. Remove the two nuts from the master cylinder, and remove the cylinder keeping the brake lines attached. Secure the master cylinder out of the way.
3. Remove the three hydraulic lines from the booster.
4. Remove the booster unit from the firewall.
5. To install, reverse the removal procedure. Bleed the Hydro-Boost system.

Combination Valve
▶ See Figure 10

The combination valve used on the mid-size Pontiacs is a three-function valve. It serves as a metering valve, balance valve, and brake warning switch. There are two different valves, one manufactured by Bendix and one manufactured by Kelsey-Hayes. Both valves serve the same function and differ only in minor details. In any case, all combination valves are non-adjustable and must be replaced if they are found to be defective.

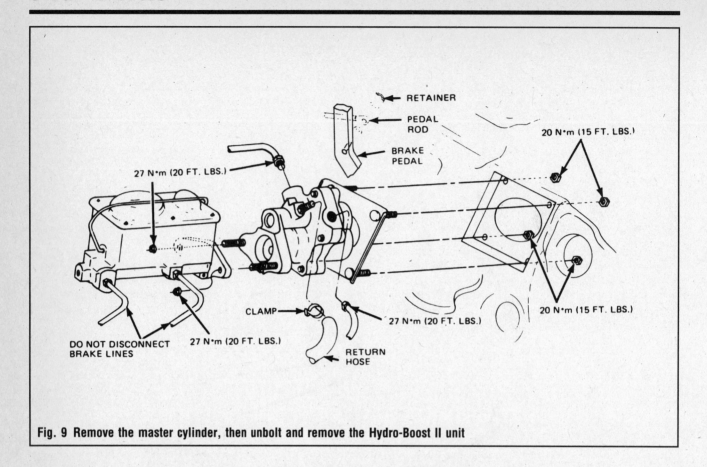

Fig. 9 Remove the master cylinder, then unbolt and remove the Hydro-Boost II unit

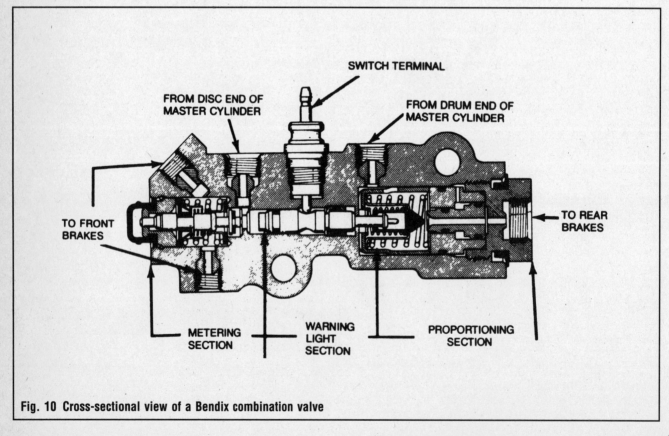

Fig. 10 Cross-sectional view of a Bendix combination valve

REMOVAL & INSTALLATION

♦ **See Figure 11**

1. Disconnect all the brake lines at the valve. Plug the lines to prevent contamination and loss of fluid.
2. Disconnect the warning switch wiring connector from the valve switch terminal.
3. Remove the attaching bolts and remove the valve.
4. Install the valve in the reverse order of removal.
5. Bleed the entire brake system after valve installation.

Brake Bleeding

The hydraulic brake system must be bled any time one of the lines is disconnected or any time air enters the system. If the brake pedal feels spongy upon application, and goes almost to the floor but regains height when pumped, air has entered the system. It must be bled out. Check for leaks that would have allowed the entry of air and repair them before bleeding the system. The correct bleeding sequence is: right rear wheel cylinder, left rear, right front, and left front. If the master cylinder is equipped with bleeder valves, bleed them first then go to the wheel cylinder nearest the master cylinder (left front) followed by the right front, left rear, and right rear.

MANUAL BLEEDING

♦ **See Figure 12**

This method of bleeding requires two people, one to depress the brake pedal and the other to open the bleeder screws.

1. Clean the top of the master cylinder, remove the cover and fill the reservoirs with clean fluid. To prevent squirting fluid, replace the cover.

➡**On cars with front disc brakes, it will be necessary to hold in the metering valve pin during the bleeding procedure. The metering valve is located beneath the master cylinder and the pin is situated under the rubber boot on the end of the valve housing. This may be taped in or held by an assistant.**

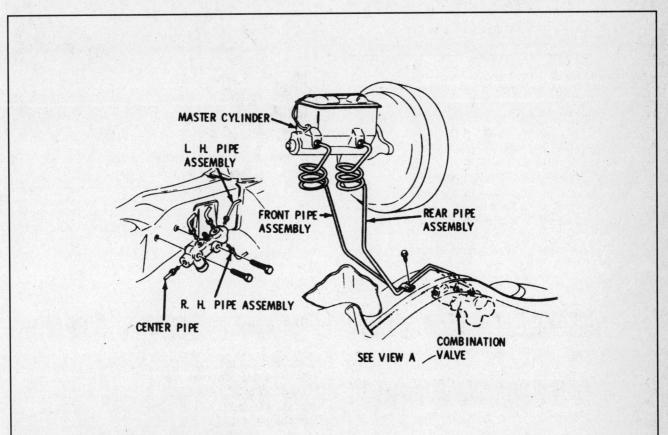

Fig. 11 Typical combination valve mounting

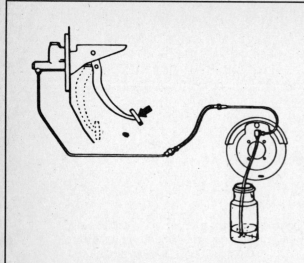

Fig. 12 Have an assistant gently pump the brake pedal while your bleed each wheel

✳✳ CAUTION

Never reuse brake fluid which has been bled from the system.

2. Fill the master cylinder with brake fluid.

3. Install a box-end wrench on the bleeder screw on the right rear wheel.

4. Attach a length of small diameter, clear vinyl tubing to the bleeder screw. Submerge the other end of the rubber tubing in a glass jar partially filled with clean brake fluid. Make sure the rubber tube fits on the bleeder screw snugly or you may be squirted with brake fluid when the bleederscrew is opened.

5. Have your friend slowly depress the brake pedal. As this is done, open the bleeder screw half a turn and allow the fluid to run through the tube. Close the bleeder screw, then return the brake pedal to its fully released position.

6. Repeat this procedure until no bubbles appear in the jar. Refill the master cylinder.

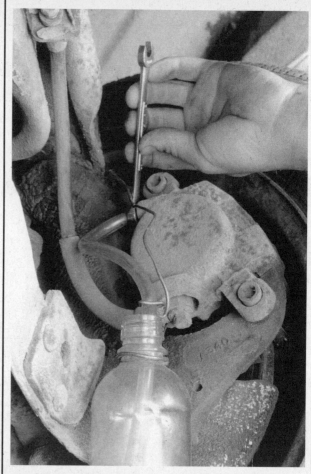

To bleed the front disc brakes, submerge the hose in brake fluid then open the bleeder valve

7. Repeat this procedure on the left rear, right front, and left front wheels, in that order. Periodically refill the master cylinder so it does not run dry.

8. If the brake warning light is on, depress the brake pedal firmly. If there is no air in the system, the light will go out.

FRONT DISC BRAKES

♦ See Figure 13

Disc Brake Pads

INSPECTION

♦ See Figures 14, 15 and 16

Brake pads should be inspected once a year or at 7,500 miles, whichever occurs first. Check both ends of the outboard shoe, looking in at each end of the caliper; then check the lining thickness on the inboard shoe, looking down through the inspection hole. Lining should be more than .020″ thick above the rivet (so that the lining is thicker than the metal backing). Keep in mind that any applicable state inspection standards that are more stringent take precedence. All four pads must be replaced if one shows excessive wear.

➡**All 1979 and later models have a wear indicator that makes a noise when the linings wear to a degree where replacement is necessary. The spring clip is an integral part of the inboard shoe and lining. When the brake pad reaches a certain degree of wear, the clip will contact the rotor and produce a warning noise.**

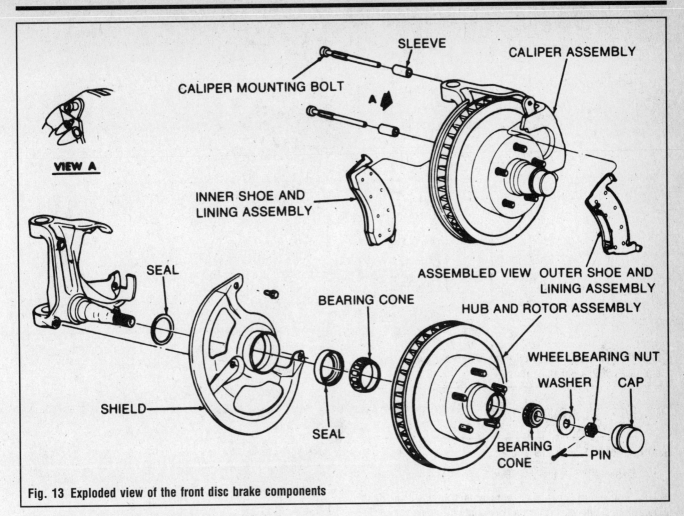

Fig. 13 Exploded view of the front disc brake components

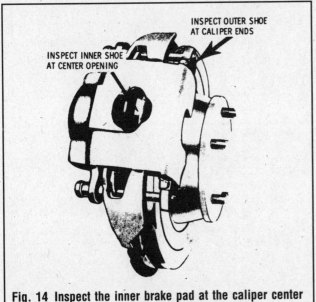

Fig. 14 Inspect the inner brake pad at the caliper center opening, and the outer pad at the caliper ends

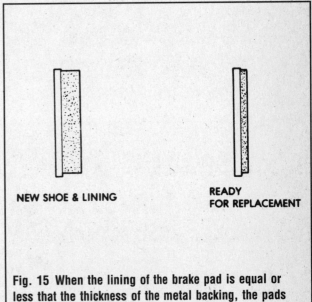

Fig. 15 When the lining of the brake pad is equal or less that the thickness of the metal backing, the pads must be replaced

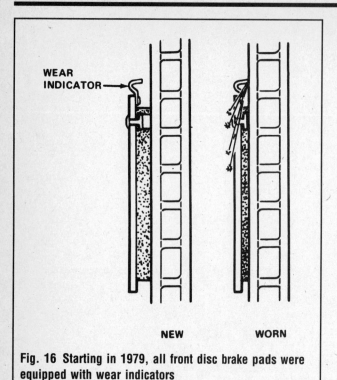

WEAR INDICATOR →

NEW   WORN

Fig. 16 Starting in 1979, all front disc brake pads were equipped with wear indicators

REMOVAL & INSTALLATION

▶ **See Figures 17, 18, 19 and 20**

1. Siphon off ⅔ of the brake fluid from the master cylinder.

➡ **The insertion of the thicker replacement pads will push the caliper piston back into its bore and will cause a full master cylinder to overflow.**

2. Jack the car up and support it with jackstands. Remove the wheel(s).

3. Install a C-clamp on the caliper so that the solid side of the clamp rests against the back of the caliper and the screw end rests against the metal part of the outboard pad.

To remove the brake pads, bottom out the caliper piston is its bore, using a large C-clamp

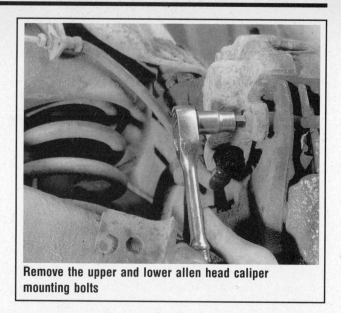

Remove the upper and lower allen head caliper mounting bolts

Lift the caliper up and off of the rotor

With the caliper suspended from the body with a piece of wire, remove the outboard brake pad

Remove the inboard pad from the caliper

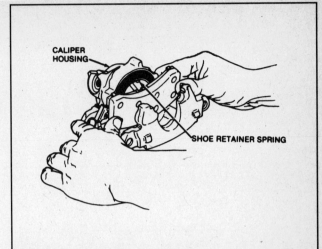

Fig. 18 Install the inboard brake pad into the caliper housing

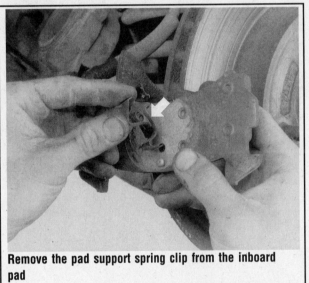

Remove the pad support spring clip from the inboard pad

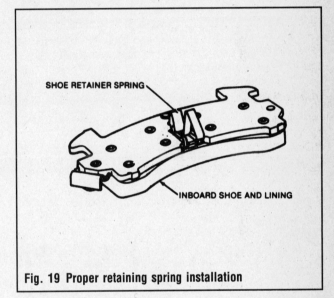

Fig. 19 Proper retaining spring installation

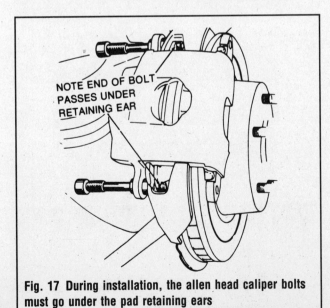

Fig. 17 During installation, the allen head caliper bolts must go under the pad retaining ears

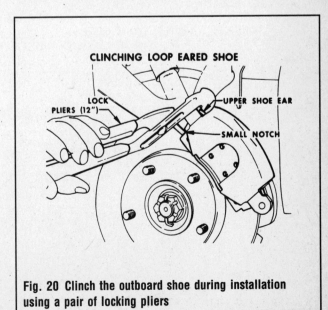

Fig. 20 Clinch the outboard shoe during installation using a pair of locking pliers

4. Tighten the clamp until the caliper moves enough to bottom the piston in its bore. Remove the clamp.

5. Remove the two allen head caliper mounting bolts enough to allow the caliper to be pulled off the disc.

6. Place the caliper where it won't be supported by the brake hose (hang it by a wire hook from the frame). Remove the outboard and inboard pads.

7. Remove the pad support spring clip from the inboard pad.

8. Remove the two bolt ear sleeves and the four rubber bushings from the ears.

To install:

9. Brake pads should be replaced when they are worn to within 1/32 in. of the rivet heads.

10. Check the inside of the caliper for leakage and the condition of the piston dust boot.

11. Lubricate the two new sleeves and four bushings with a silicone spray.

12. Install the bushings in each caliper ear. Install the two sleeves in the two inboard ears.

13. Install the pad support spring clip and the old pad into the center of the piston. You will then push this pad down to get the piston flat against the caliper. This part of the job is a hassle and requires an assistant. While the assistant holds the caliper and loosens the bleeder valve to relieve pressure, you get a prybar and try to force the old pad in to make the piston flush with the caliper surface. When it is flush, close the bleeder valve so that no air gets into the system.

➡**On models with wear sensors, make sure the wear sensor is toward the rear of the caliper.**

14. Position the outboard shoe with the ears of the shoes over the caliper ears and the tab at the bottom engaged in the caliper cutout notch.

15. With the two shoes in position, place the caliper over the brake disc and align the holes in the caliper with those of the mounting bracket.

✳✳ CAUTION

Make certain that the brake hose is not twisted or kinked.

16. Install the mounting bracket bolts through the sleeves in the inboard caliper ears and through the mounting bracket, making sure that the ends of the bolts pass under the retaining ears on the inboard shoe.

17. Tighten the bolts into the bracket and tighten to 35 ft. lbs. Bend over the outer pad ears.

18. Install the front wheel and lower the car.

19. Add fluid to the master cylinder reservoirs so that they are 1/4 in. from the top.

20. Test the brake pedal by pumping it to obtain a "hard" pedal. Check the fluid level again and add fluid as necessary. Do not move the vehicle until a "hard" pedal is obtained. Bleed the brakes if necessary.

Disc Brake Calipers

REMOVAL, INSTALLATION & OVERHAUL

▶ **See Figures 21, 22 and 23**

1. Perform the removal steps for pad replacement.
2. Disconnect the brake hose and plug the line.
3. Remove the U-shaped retainer from the fitting.
4. Pull the hose from the frame bracket and remove the caliper with the hose attached.
5. Clean the outside of the caliper with denatured alcohol.
6. Remove the brake hose and discard the copper gasket.
7. Remove the brake fluid from the caliper.
8. Place clean rags inside the caliper opening to catch the piston when it is released.
9. Apply compressed air to the caliper fluid inlet hole and force the piston out of its bore. *Do not blow the piston out*, but use just enough pressure to ease it out.

✳✳ CAUTION

Do not place your fingers in front of the piston in an attempt to catch it while applying compressed air; serious injury could result.

10. Use a suitable prytool to pry the boot out of the caliper. Avoid scratching the bore.
11. Remove the piston seal from its groove in the caliper bore. *Do not use a metal tool of any type for this operation.*
12. Blow out all passages in the caliper and bleeder valve. Clean the piston and piston bore with fresh brake fluid.
13. Examine the piston for scoring, scratches or corrosion. If any of these conditions exist the piston must be replaced, as it is plated and cannot be refinished.
14. Examine the bore for the same defects. Light rough spots may be removed by rotating crocus cloth, using finger pressure, in the bore. *Do not polish with an in-and-out motion or use any other abrasive.*
15. Lubricate the piston bore and the new rubber parts with *fresh brake fluid*. Position the seal in the piston bore groove.
16. Lubricate the piston with brake fluid and assemble the boot into the piston groove so that the fold faces the open end of the piston.
17. Insert the piston into the bore, taking care not to unseat the seal.
18. Force the piston to the bottom of the bore. (This will require a force of 50–100 lbs). Seat the boot lip around the caliper counterbore. Proper seating of the boot is very important for sealing out contaminants.
19. Install the brake hose into the caliper using a new copper gasket.
20. Lubricate the new sleeves and rubber bushings. Install the bushings in the caliper ears. Install the sleeves so that the end toward the disc pad is flush with the machined surface.

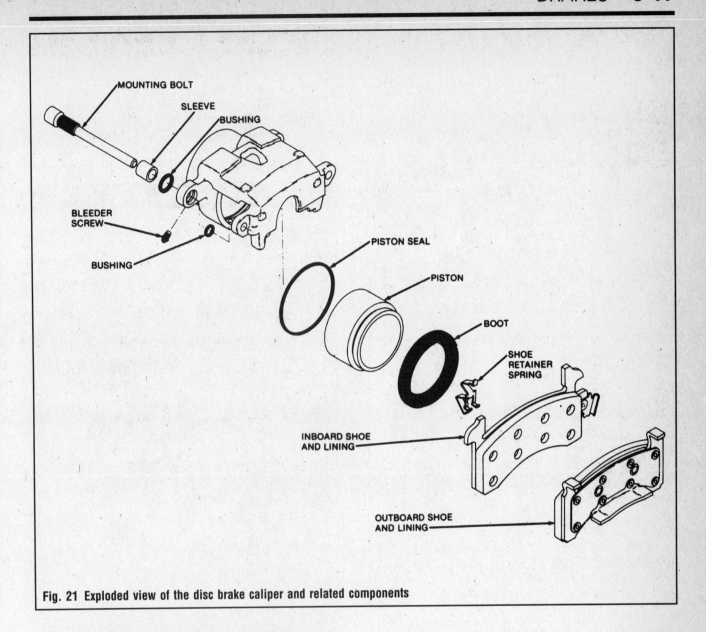

Fig. 21 Exploded view of the disc brake caliper and related components

To remove the caliper, use a C-clamp to compress the piston in the caliper bore

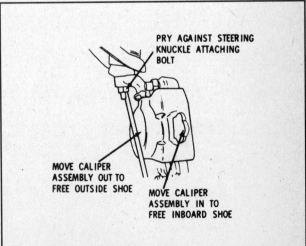

Fig. 22 The piston can also be compressed in its bore by prying on the caliper as shown

Disconnect and plug the brake hose from the rear of the caliper

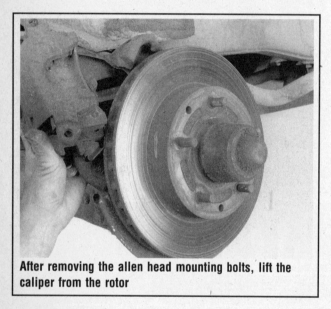

After removing the allen head mounting bolts, lift the caliper from the rotor

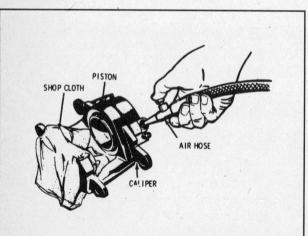

Fig. 23 Use compressed air to force the piston out of the caliper. Make sure to keep your fingers out of the way!

➡Lubrication of the sleeves and bushings is essential to ensure the proper operation of the sliding caliper design.

21. Install the shoe support spring in the piston.

22. Install the disc pads in the caliper and remount the caliper on the hub. (See "Disc Brake Pad Removal and Installation.")

23. Reconnect the brake hose to the steel brake line. Install the retainer clip. Bleed the brakes (see "Brake Bleeding").

24. Replace the wheels, check the brake fluid level, check the brake pedal travel, and road-test the vehicle.

Brake Disc (Rotor)

REMOVAL & INSTALLATION

1. Raise the car, support it with jackstands, and remove the wheel and tire assembly.

2. Remove the brake caliper as outlined earlier in this section.

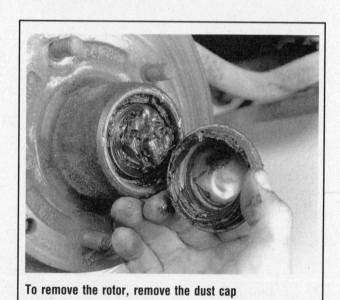

To remove the rotor, remove the dust cap

Use needle-nose pliers to remove the cotter pin from the spindle. Discard the cotter pin

Remove the castellated nut . . .

. . . then pull the rotor assembly off the wheel spindle

. . . then remove the washer

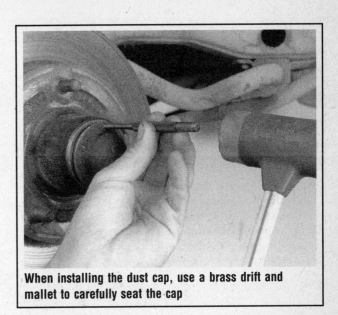

When installing the dust cap, use a brass drift and mallet to carefully seat the cap

3. Remove the dust cap and remove the wheel bearing nut after removing the cotter pin.

4. Remove the wheel bearing, hub, and disc assembly from the spindle.

5. Installation is in the reverse order of removal. Adjust the wheel bearing as outlined in this chapter.

INSPECTION

▶ **See Figure 24**

1. Check the disc for any obvious defects such as excessive rust, chipping, or deep scoring. Light scoring is normal on disc brakes.

2. Make sure there is no wheel bearing play and then check the disc for runout as follows:

3. Install a dial indicator on the caliper so that its feeler will contact the disc about one inch below its outer edge.

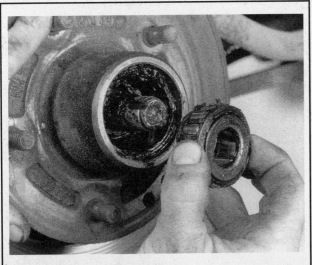

Remove the outer wheel bearing . . .

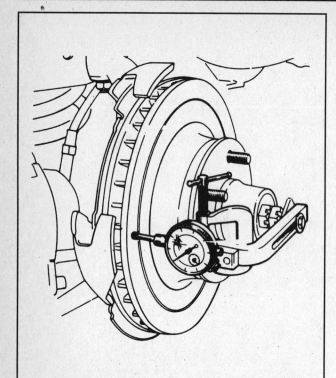

Fig. 24 Use a dial indicator to check brake rotor (disc) runout

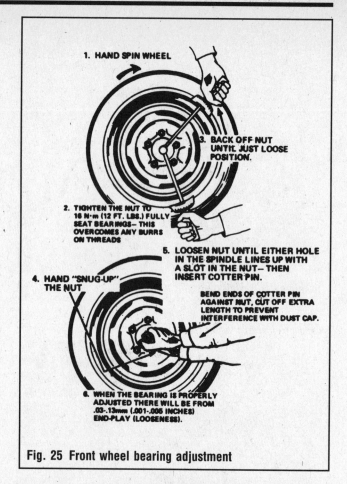

Fig. 25 Front wheel bearing adjustment

4. Turn the disc and observe the runout reading. If the reading exceeds 0.002 in., the disc should be replaced.

➡ **All brake rotors (discs) have a minimum thickness dimension cast into them, on the hub between the lugs. This is the minimum wear dimension and not a refinish dimension. Do not reuse a brake rotor that will not meet specifications. Refinishing of brake rotors can be handled at machine shops equipped for brake work.**

Wheel Bearings

Properly adjusted bearings have a slightly loose feeling. Wheel bearings must never be preloaded. Preloading will damage the bearings and eventually the spindles. If the bearings are too loose, they should be cleaned, inspected, and then adjusted.

Hold the tire at the top and bottom and move the wheel in and out of the spindle. If the movement is greater than 0.005 in., the bearings are too loose.

ADJUSTMENT

◆ See Figure 25

1. Raise and support the car by the lower control arm.
2. Remove the hub cap, then remove the dust cap from the hub.
3. Remove the cotter pin and spindle nut.
4. Spin the wheel forward by hand. Tighten the nut until snug to fully seat the bearings.

5. Back off the nut ¼–½ turn until it is just loose, then tighten it finger-tight.
6. Loosen the nut until either hole in the spindle lines up with a slot in the nut and then insert the cotter pin. This may appear to be too loose, but it is the correct adjustment. The spindle nut should not be even finger-tight.
7. Proper adjustment creates 0.001–0.005 in. of end-play.

REMOVAL, PACKING & INSTALLATION

◆ See Figure 26

✳✳ CAUTION

Some brake pads contain asbestos, which has been determined to be a cancer causing agent. Never clean the brake surfaces with compressed air! Avoid inhaling any dust from any brake surface! When cleaning brake surfaces, use a commercially available brake cleaning fluid.

1. Raise and support the vehicle safely using jackstands. Remove the wheel and tire assembly.
2. On disc brake cars, remove the hub and disc as an assembly. Remove the caliper mounting bolts and wire the caliper out of the way.

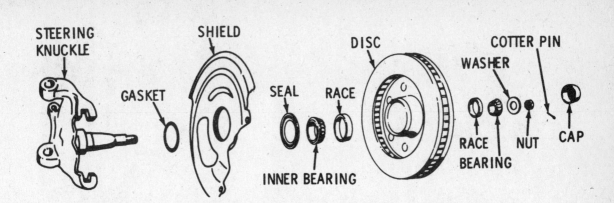

Fig. 26 Exploded view of the wheel bearings and related components

Pry the dust cap from the hub taking care not to distort or damage its flange

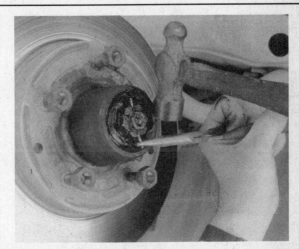

If difficulty is encountered, gently tap on the pliers with a hammer to help free the cotter pin

Once the bent ends are cut, grasp the cotter pin and pull or pry it free of the spindle

Loosen and remove the castellated nut from the spindle

Remove the washer from the spindle

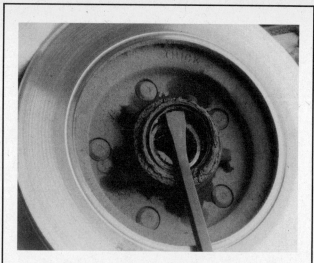

Use a small prytool to remove the old inner bearing seal

With the nut and washer out of the way, the outer bearings may be removed from the hub

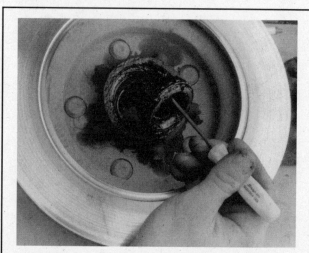

With the seal removed, the inner bearing may be withdrawn from the hub

Pull the hub and inner bearing assembly from the spindle

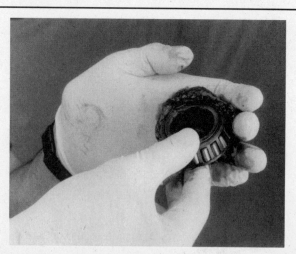

Thoroughly pack the bearing with fresh, high temperature wheel-bearing grease before installation

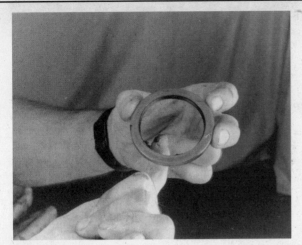

Apply a thin coat of fresh grease to the new inner bearing seal lip

After the bearings are adjusted, install the dust cap by gently tapping on the flange—DO NOT damage the cap by hammering on the center

4. Clean all the parts in solvent, air dry them, and check them for excessive wear or damage.

5. To replace the outer or inner bearing race, first knock out the old race with a hammer and a brass drift. New races must be installed squarely and evenly to avoid damage. Use a short piece of two-by-four or something similar.

✳✳ WARNING

Never use old bearing parts with new parts. If the old bearing is damaged, the entire bearing assembly will have to be replaced including the outer race.

6. Pack the bearings with wheel bearing grease. It is important that the bearings be fully packed, and not simply coated with lubricant. It is a good idea to wear plastic protective gloves while packing. Immerse the bearing completely in the lubricant and work the grease into the bearing with your hand.

7. Lightly grease the steering spindle and the inside of the hub.

8. Place the inner bearing in the hub race and install a new grease seal.

9. Install the hub and rotor assembly (or hub and drum assembly) on the spindle.

10. Install the outer wheel bearing. Adjust the wheel bearing as outlined earlier.

11. Reinstall the caliper assembly on disc brake models.

12. Install the dust cap, wheel and tire assembly, and lower the car.

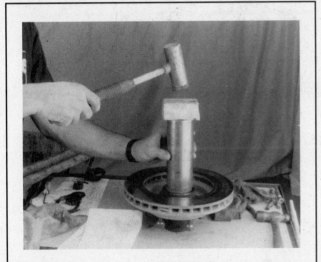

Use a suitably sized driver to install the inner bearing seal to the hub

3. Remove the outer bearing from the hub. The inner bearing assembly will remain in the hub and may be removed after prying out the inner seal. Discard the seal.

✳✳ CAUTION

If using compressed air to dry the bearings. DO NOT allow the bearing to turn without lubrication.

REAR DRUM BRAKES

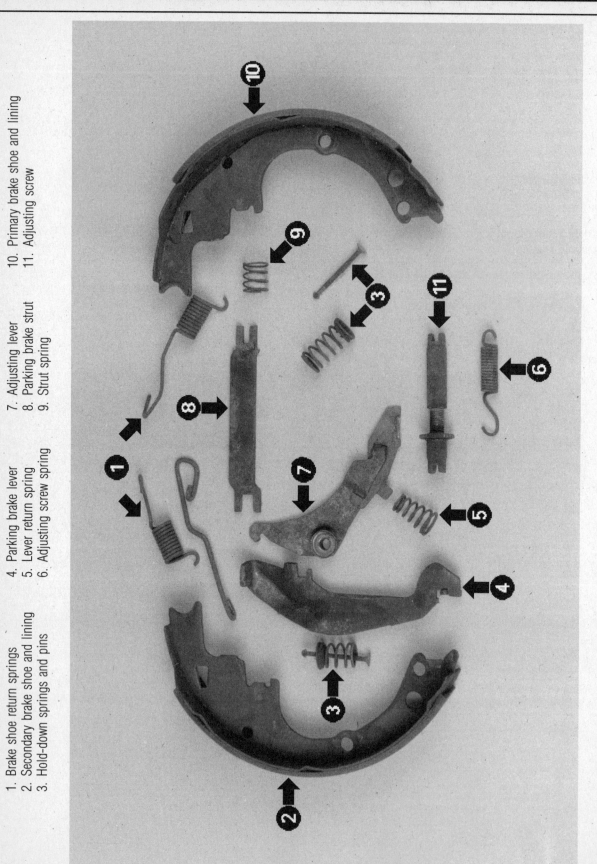

REAR DRUM BRAKE COMPONENTS

1. Brake shoe return springs
2. Secondary brake shoe and lining
3. Hold-down springs and pins
4. Parking brake lever
5. Lever return spring
6. Adjusting screw spring
7. Adjusting lever
8. Parking brake strut
9. Strut spring
10. Primary brake shoe and lining
11. Adjusting screw

Brake Drum

REPLACEMENT

1. Raise and support the car.
2. Remove the wheel or wheels.
3. Pull the brake drum off. It may be necessary to gently tap the rear edges of the drum to start it off the studs.
4. If extreme resistance to removal is encountered, it will be necessary to retract the adjusting screw. Knock out the access hole in the brake drum and turn the adjuster to retract the linings away from the drum.
5. Install a replacement hole cover before reinstalling drum.
6. Install the drums in the same position on the hub as removed. Adjust front wheel bearings as described at the end of this chapter.

DRUM INSPECTION

1. Check the drums for any cracks, scores, grooves, or an out-of-round condition. Replace if cracked. Slight scores can be removed with fine emery cloth while extensive scoring requires turning the drum on a lathe.
2. Never have a drum turned more than 0.060 in.

Brake Shoes

REMOVAL & INSTALLATION

▶ **See Figure 27**

1. Raise the car and support it on jackstands.
2. Slacken the parking brake cable.

To remove the brake drum, remove the wheel and tire, then pull the drum from the axle

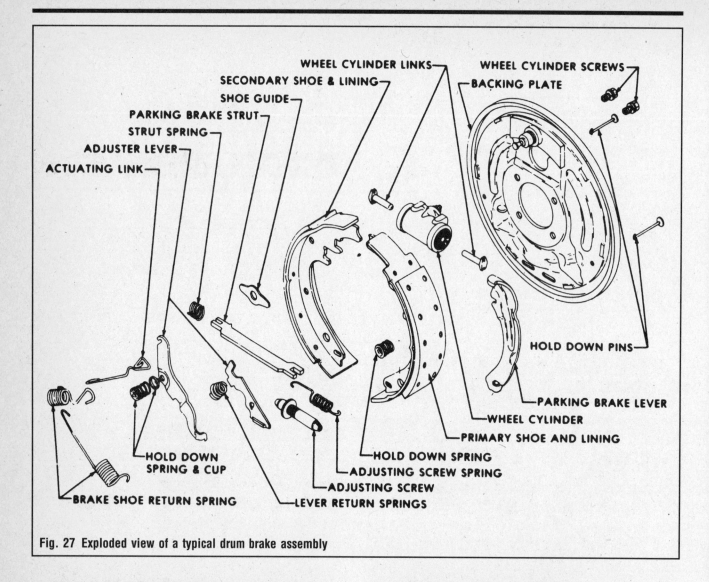

WHEEL CYLINDER LINKS

SECONDARY SHOE & LINING

SHOE GUIDE

PARKING BRAKE STRUT

STRUT SPRING

ADJUSTER LEVER

ACTUATING LINK

WHEEL CYLINDER SCREWS

BACKING PLATE

HOLD DOWN PINS

PARKING BRAKE LEVER

WHEEL CYLINDER

PRIMARY SHOE AND LINING

HOLD DOWN SPRING

ADJUSTING SCREW SPRING

ADJUSTING SCREW

LEVER RETURN SPRINGS

HOLD DOWN SPRING & CUP

BRAKE SHOE RETURN SPRING

Fig. 27 Exploded view of a typical drum brake assembly

When removing the drum brakes, work on one side, leaving the other side for reference

Before removal, clean the brake components using a commercially available spray cleaner

For drum brake shoe removal, special tools are available . . .

Use the special tool to push in and turn the hold-down spring to disengage it . . .

. . . to unhook and remove the return springs

. . . then remove the hold-down spring and the pin from the rear of the brake backing plate

Remove the left side return spring

Remove the parking brake strut and spring

After removing the pawl and lever return spring, the rear wheel shoes can be pulled off

Detach the secondary shoe from the parking brake lever . . .

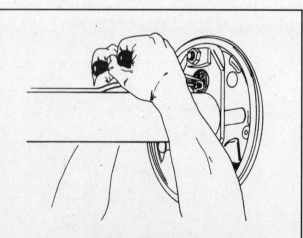

. . . then use pliers to detach the rear cable from the parking brake lever

3. Remove the rear wheel and brake drum. The front wheel and drum may be removed as a unit by removing the spindle nut and cotter pin.

4. Free the brake shoe return springs, actuator pull-back spring, hold-down pins and springs, and actuator assembly.

➡ **Special tools available from auto supply stores will ease removal of the spring and anchor pin, but the job may still be done with common hand tools.**

5. Disconnect the parking brake lever from the secondary shoe and remove the shoe. The shoes may be removed together.

To install:

6. Clean and inspect all brake parts.

7. Check the wheel cylinders for seal condition and leaking.

8. Repack wheel bearings and replace the seals.

9. Inspect the replacement shoes for nicks or burrs, lubricate the backing plate contact points, brake cable and levers, and adjusting screws and then assemble.

10. Make sure that the right and left-hand adjusting screws are not mixed. You can prevent this by working on one side at a time. This will also provide you with a reference for reassembly. The star wheel should be nearest to the secondary shoe when correctly installed.

11. To install, reverse the removal procedure. When completed, make an initial adjustment as previously described.

➡ **Maintenance procedures for the metallic lining option are the same as those for standard linings. Do not substitute these linings in standard drums, unless they have been honed to a 20 micro-inch finish and equipped with special heat-resistant springs.**

Wheel Cylinders

REMOVAL & INSTALLATION

♦ **See Figure 28**

1. Remove the brake drum as described above.

2. Clean all dirt away from around the brake line connection, and disconnect the brake line.

Fig. 28 The wheel cylinder may be secured to the backing plate with bolts or, as shown here, a circlip which is removed using two awls

3. Remove the wheel cylinder from the backing plate.
To install:
4. Install the wheel cylinder onto the backing plate.
5. Connect the brake pipe. Tighten the connection to 100 in. lbs.
6. Install brake shoes, drum, and wheel, and flush and bleed brakes.

OVERHAUL

▶ **See Figure 29**

As is the case with master cylinders, overhaul kits for wheel cylinders are readily available. When rebuilding and installing wheel cylinders, avoid getting any contaminants into the system. Always install clean, new high-quality brake fluid. If dirty or improper fluid has been used, it will be necessary to drain the entire system, flush the system with proper brake fluid, replace all rubber components, refill, and bleed the system.
1. Remove the rubber boots from the cylinder ends with pliers. Discard the boots.
2. Remove and discard the pistons and cups.
3. Wash the cylinder and metal parts in denatured alcohol or clean brake fluid.

✳✳ WARNING

Never use a mineral-based solvent such as gasoline, kerosene, or paint thinner for cleaning purposes. These solvents will swell rubber components and quickly deteriorate them.

4. Allow the parts to air dry or use compressed air. Do not use rags for cleaning since lint will remain in the cylinder bore.

PARKING BRAKE

All models are equipped with a foot-operated, ratchet-type parking brake. A cable assembly connects this pedal to an intermediate cable by means of an equalizer. Adjustment is made at the equalizer. The intermediate cable connects with two rear cables and each of these cables enters a rear wheel.

ADJUSTMENT

▶ **See Figure 30**

The need for parking brake adjustment is indicated if parking brake pedal travel is more than 15 "clicks" under heavy foot pressure.
1. Depress the parking brake pedal exactly two ratchet clicks.
2. Jack up the car and safely support it with jackstands.
3. Tighten the adjusting nut until the left rear wheel can just be turned rearward using two hands, but is locked when forward rotation is attempted.
4. With the mechanism totally disengaged, the rear wheels should turn freely in either direction with no brake drag.

➡**It is very important that the parking brake cables are not adjusted too tightly, causing brake drag.**

5. Remove the jackstands and lower the car.

5. Inspect the piston and replace it if it shows scratches.
6. Lubricate the cylinder bore and counterbore with clean brake fluid.
7. Install the rubber cups (flat side out) and then the pistons (flat side in).
8. Insert new boots into the counterbores by hand. Do not lubricate the boots.
9. Install the wheel cylinder to the backing plate and connect all pushrods and springs. Connect the brake line, install the brake drum, and bleed the brakes.

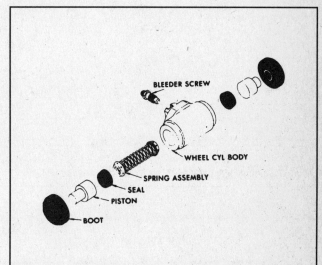
Fig. 29 Exploded view of the wheel cylinder assembly

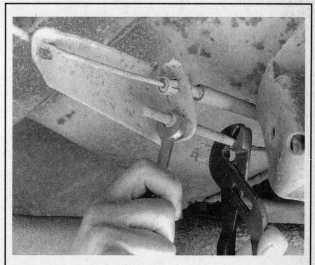
Parking brake cable adjustment

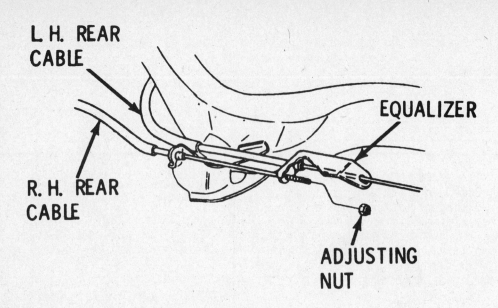

Fig. 30 Location of the parking brake equalizer and adjusting nut

Brake Specifications
All measurements given are (in.) unless noted

Year	Model	Lug Nut Torque (ft. lbs.)	Master Cylinder Bore	Brake Disc		Minimum Pad Thickness	Brake Drum		Minimum Lining Thickness	
				Minimum Thickness	Maximum Run-Out	Front	Max Machine O/S	Max Wear Limit	Front	Rear
1974	All	80①	1.125④	.965	.004	.125	.030③	9.560⑤	②	②
1975	All	80①	1.125④	.965	.004	.125	.030③	9.560⑤	⑥	⑥
1976	All	80①	1.125⑦	.965	.004	.125	.030③	9.560⑤	⑧	⑧
1977	All	80①	1.125⑦	.980	.004	⑨	.030③	9.560⑤	⑧	⑧
1978	All	80①	1.125⑦	.980	.004	⑨	.030③	9.560⑤	⑧	⑧
1979	All	80①	1.125⑦	.980	.004	⑨	.030③	9.560⑤	⑧	⑧
1980	All	80①	1.125⑦	.980	.004	⑨	.030③	9.560⑤	⑧	⑧
1981	All	80①	1.125⑦	.980	.005	⑨	.030③	9.560⑤	⑧	⑧
1982–83	All	80①	1.125⑦	.980	.005	⑨	.030③	9.560⑤	⑧	⑧

① 90 ft. lbs. w/cast aluminum wheels
② Primary .196, secondary .265
③ Turning down the drum .030 increases overall inside diameter .060 in.
④ Power brakes; w/manual brakes 1.000
⑤ Le Mans wagon and Grand Prix 11.060 in.; 1980 and later Grand Prix 11.090
⑥ Le Mans: Primary .230
　　　　　Secondary .300
　Grand Prix,
　Le Mans wagon: Primary .250
　　　　　　Secondary .290
　Ventura: Primary .200
　　　　　Secondary .200
⑦ Power brakes; Le Mans manual brakes .937
　　　　　Ventura manual brakes 1.000
⑧ Le Mans, Primary .232
　Grand Prix: Secondary .230
⑨ To within .020 in. of rivet at either end of shoe

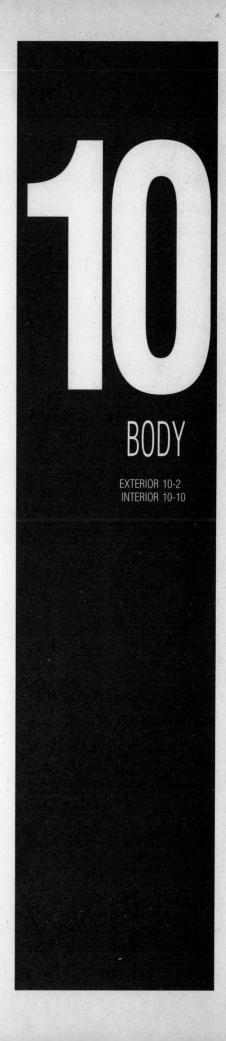

10

BODY

EXTERIOR 10-2
INTERIOR 10-10

EXTERIOR 10-2
 DOORS 10-2
  REMOVAL & INSTALLATION 10-2
  ADJUSTMENT 10-3
 HOOD 10-4
  REMOVAL & INSTALLATION 10-4
  ALIGNMENT 10-5
 TRUNK LID 10-6
  REMOVAL & INSTALLATION 10-6
  ALIGNMENT 10-6
 BUMPERS 10-7
  REMOVAL & INSTALLATION 10-7
 GRILLE 10-8
  REMOVAL & INSTALLATION 10-8
 OUTSIDE MIRRORS 10-8
  REMOVAL & INSTALLATION 10-8
 ANTENNA 10-9
  REMOVAL & INSTALLATION 10-9
INTERIOR 10-10
 FRONT DOOR PANELS 10-10
  REMOVAL & INSTALLATION 10-10
 REAR DOOR PANELS 10-14
  REMOVAL & INSTALLATION 10-14
 DOOR LOCKS 10-14
  REMOVAL & INSTALLATION 10-14
 DOOR GLASS 10-16
  REMOVAL & INSTALLATION 10-16
  ADJUSTMENT 10-17
 FRONT DOOR REGULATOR 10-18
  REMOVAL & INSTALLATION 10-18
 ELECTRIC WINDOW MOTOR 10-18
  REMOVAL & INSTALLATION 10-18
 WINDSHIELD 10-18
  REMOVAL 10-18
  INSTALLATION 10-19
 REAR WINDOW GLASS 10-21
  REMOVAL 10-21
  INSTALLATION 10-21
 STATIONARY GLASS 10-23
  REMOVAL & INSTALLATION 10-23
 REAR DOOR VENT WINDOW 10-23
  REMOVAL & INSTALLATION 10-23
 INSIDE REAR VIEW MIRROR 10-24
  REPLACEMENT 10-24
 SEATS 10-25
  REMOVAL & INSTALLATION 10-25
 SEAT BELT SYSTEMS 10-25
  REMOVAL & INSTALLATION 10-25
 POWER SEAT MOTOR 10-25
  REMOVAL & INSTALLATION 10-25

EXTERIOR

Doors

REMOVAL & INSTALLATION

▶ **See Figures 1 and 2**

When removing the door, it is easier to remove the hinges with the door because the door side hinges are very accessible.

➡**All factory installed door hardware attaching screws contain an epoxy thread-locking compound to ensure that the torque setting will be maintained. Service replacement screws may not contain a thread-locking compound. Such screws must be treated with No. 1052279 Loctite® 75 or equivalent. The adhesive is placed on the fastener prior to installation.**

1. Disconnect the negative battery cable. Mark the position of the door hinges-to-body to make the installation easier.
2. If equipped with power operated components, remove the

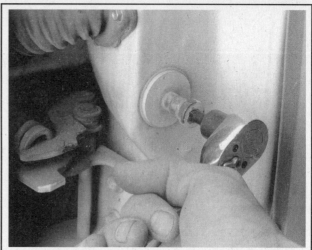

To adjust the door, first matchmark, then remove the door lock striker

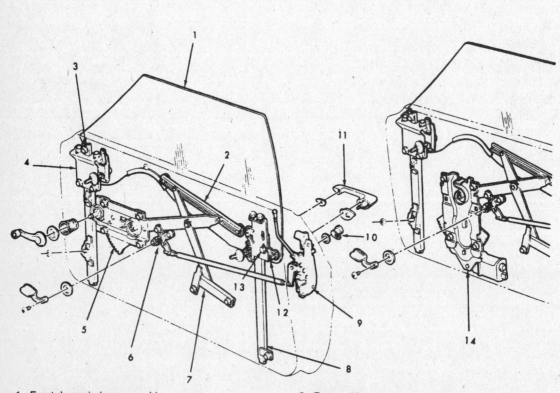

1. Front door window assembly
2. Lower sash channel cam
3. Window front upper stop
4. Front guide
5. Window regulator—manual
6. Door lock remote control
7. Inner panel cam

8. Rear guide
9. Door lock
10. Door lock cylinder
11. Door outside handle
12. Window rear upper stop (on window)
13. Window rear upper stop (on guide)
14. Window regulator—electric

Fig. 1 Front door assembly and related components—early model vehicles without ventilator

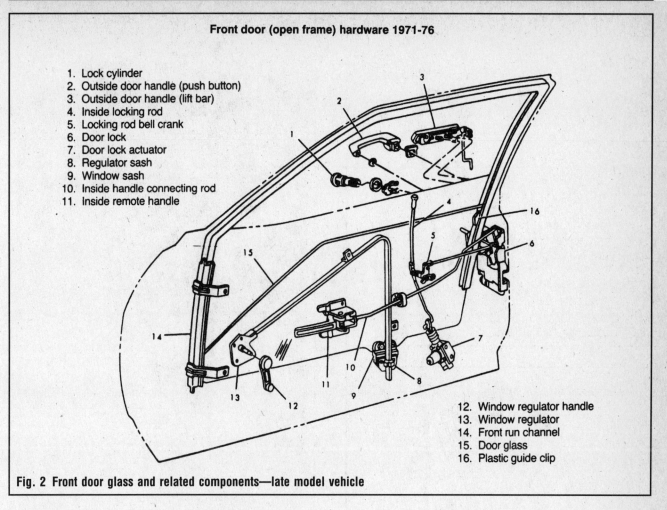

Front door (open frame) hardware 1971-76

1. Lock cylinder
2. Outside door handle (push button)
3. Outside door handle (lift bar)
4. Inside locking rod
5. Locking rod bell crank
6. Door lock
7. Door lock actuator
8. Regulator sash
9. Window sash
10. Inside handle connecting rod
11. Inside remote handle

12. Window regulator handle
13. Window regulator
14. Front run channel
15. Door glass
16. Plastic guide clip

Fig. 2 Front door glass and related components—late model vehicle

trim panel and detach the inner panel water deflector enough to disconnect the wiring harness from the components. Separate and remove the rubber conduit and the wiring harness from the door.

3. Using an assistant (to support the door), remove the upper and lower hinge-to-body bolts. Remove the door from the vehicle.

4. To install, reverse the removal procedures. Tighten the hinge-to-body bolt to 15–21 ft. lbs.

ADJUSTMENT

▶ **See Figures 3, 4 and 5**

The door adjustments are made possible through the use of floating anchor plates in the door and the body hinge pillars.

1. Remove the door lock striker from the body and allow the door to hang freely on its hinges.

2. Using a door hinge alignment tool, loosen the door hinge-to-body pillar bolts.

3. Using the tool attachments, adjust the door up/down and fore/aft.

➡**If a rearward adjustment is made, it may be necessary to replace the jamb switch.**

4. At the door hinge pillar attachments, adjust the door in and out.

5. After adjusting the door, tighten the door hinge-to-body pillar to 15–21 ft. lbs.

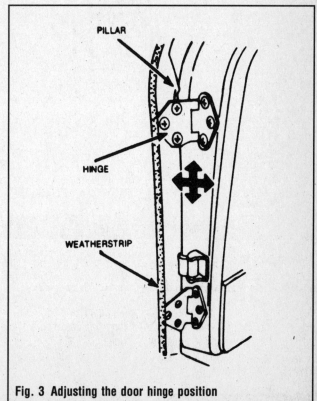

Fig. 3 Adjusting the door hinge position

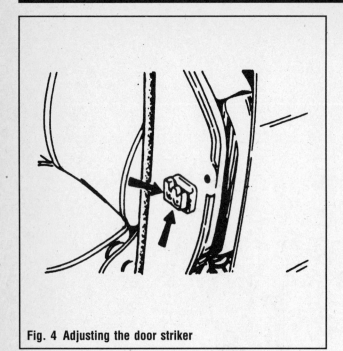

Fig. 4 Adjusting the door striker

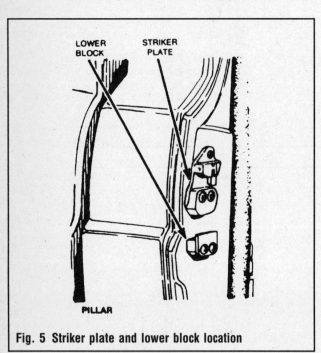

Fig. 5 Striker plate and lower block location

Hood

REMOVAL & INSTALLATION

1. Disconnect the negative battery cable. Using a scratch awl or a marker, scribe the hinge onto the hood. If equipped with a hood light, disconnect the electrical connector.
2. Using an assistant to support the hood, remove the hinge-to-hood bolts. Remove the hood.

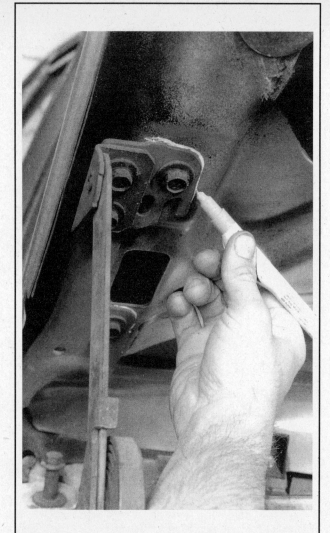

Before removing the hood, matchmark the position of the hood hinge . . .

. . . then support the hood and remove the hood-to-hinge mounting bolts

3. To install, reverse the removal procedures. Check the hood alignment with the hood latch.

ALIGNMENT

♦ **See Figures 6, 7, 8, 9 and 10**

➡ **When aligning the hood and the latch, align the hood (first), then the latch (second).**

Hood

The hood hinge-to-body mount is slotted to provide forward and rearward movement. Adjust the hood so that it is flush with the body sheet metal.
1. Using a scratch awl, scribe the hinge outline onto the hood.
2. Loosen the appropriate screws and shift the hood into proper alignment with the vehicles sheet metal.

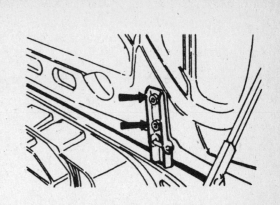

Fig. 8 Loosen the hinge bolts to permit fore, aft and horizontal adjustment

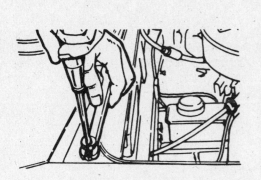

Fig. 6 The hood is adjusted vertically by stop screws at the front and/or rear position

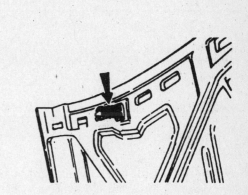

Fig. 9 The hood striker can be adjusted for proper lock engagement

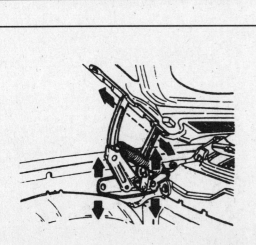

Fig. 7 The height of the hood at the rear is adjusted by loosening the hinge-to-body bolts and moving the hood up and down

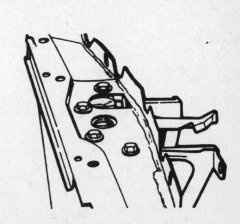

Fig. 10 The hood latch can also be repositioned slightly to give more positive lock engagement

✳✳ CAUTION

Make sure that the rear of the hood is properly positioned at the cowl seal; proper sealing will restrict fumes from the engine compartment from being pulled through the cowl vent.

3. After adjustment, tighten the appropriate screws.

Latch

The hood latch assembly is mounted on a plate with elongated holes, which allow horizontal adjustment.

Striker

The striker, on the hood, adjusts laterally to align with the hood latch assembly.

Trunk Lid

REMOVAL & INSTALLATION

▶ **See Figures 11 and 12**

1. Disconnect the negative battery cable. Open the trunk lid and place protective coverings over the rear fenders to protect the paint from damage.

2. Mark the location of the hinge-to-trunk lid bolts and disconnect the electrical connections and wiring from the lid, if equipped.

3. Using an assistant to support the lid, remove the hinge-to-lid bolts and the lid from the vehicle.

➡**Some later vehicles use gas cushioned shock type assemblies to aid in supporting the trunk lid assembly. Remove the retaining clips and remove the shock assemblies from the trunk lid before removing the hinge retaining bolts.**

4. To install, reverse the removal procedures. Adjust the position of the trunk lid to the body. Rear compartment torque rods are adjustable to increase or decrease operating effort. To increase

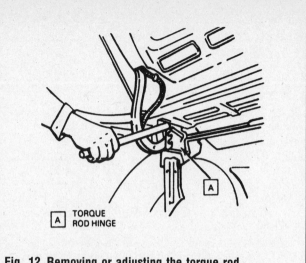

Fig. 12 Removing or adjusting the torque rod

A TORQUE ROD HINGE

the amount of effort needed to raise the rear compartment lid or to decrease the amount of effort to close the lid, reposition the end of the rod to a lower torque rod adjusting notch. To decrease the amount of effort needed to raise the rear compartment lid or to increase the amount of effort to close the lid, reposition the end of the rod to a higher torque rod adjusting notch. Refer to the illustration. Prop the trunk lid in full-open position to keep lid from falling when torque rods are disengaged from the torque rod bracket.

ALIGNMENT

Trunk Lid

▶ **See Figure 13**

The trunk lid can be aligned slightly by loosening the hinge-to-lid bolts and shifting the lid into position.

➡**When adjusting the hinge/latch-to-body positions, be sure to use alignment marks as reference points.**

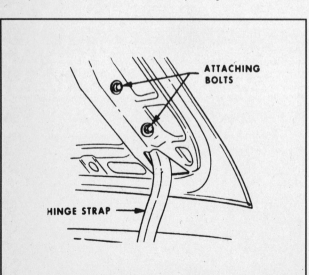

ATTACHING BOLTS

HINGE STRAP ➡

Fig. 11 Location of the trunk lid-to-hinge mounting bolts

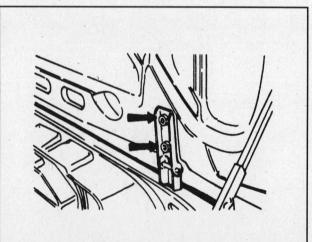

Fig. 13 Loosen the hinge bolts to permit fore-and-aft and horizontal adjustment

Bumpers

REMOVAL & INSTALLATION

Front

▶ **See Figure 14**

1. Disconnect the negative battery cable. Raise and support the vehicle safely.

2. Properly support the bumper. As required, disconnect all the necessary electrical connections at the turn signal assemblies and the cornering light housings.

3. On the vehicles without the energy absorber type bumper, remove the bolts from the frame and remove the bumper.

4. On vehicles equipped with the energy absorber type bumper, remove the bolts from the reinforcement to the energy absorber (each side) and remove the bumper assembly.

5. Installation is the reverse of the removal procedure.

Rear

1. Disconnect the negative battery cable. Raise and support the vehicle safely.

2. Properly support the bumper. As required, disconnect all the necessary electrical connections at the tail light assembly housings.

3. On the vehicles without the energy absorber type bumper, remove the bolts from the frame and remove the bumper.

4. On vehicles equipped with the energy absorber type bumper, remove the bolts from the reinforcement to the energy absorber (each side) and remove the bumper assembly.

5. Installation is the reverse of the removal procedure.

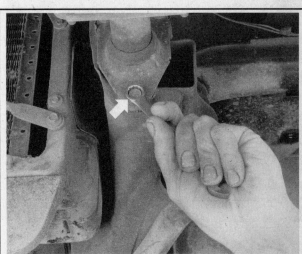

To remove the front bumper, unfasten the reinforcement-to-energy absorber bolts

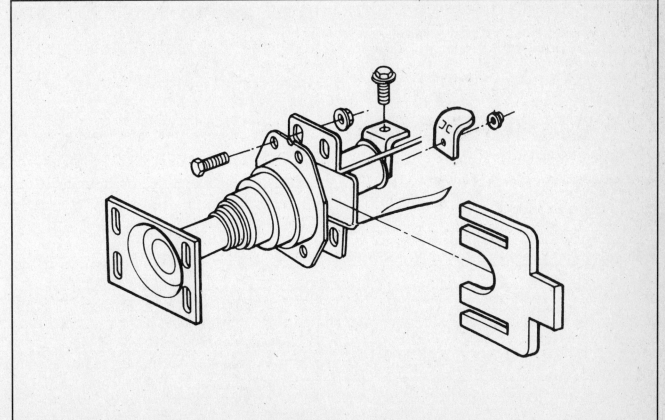

Fig. 14 Some vehicles use an energy absorbing front bumper

You can remove the rear bumper by supporting it, then removing the retaining bolts

Grille

REMOVAL & INSTALLATION

1. Disconnect the negative battery cable. As required, open the hood.
2. Remove the sheet metal screws that retain the grille assembly to its mounting.
3. On some vehicles, the headlight trim rings may have to be removed before the grille assembly can be removed from the vehicle.
4. Remove the grille assembly from the vehicle.
5. Installation is the reverse of the removal procedure.

Outside Mirrors

♦ See Figures 15, 16, 17 and 18

➡The mirror glass may be replaced by placing a piece of tape over the glass then breaking the mirror face. Adhesive back mirror faces are available.

REMOVAL & INSTALLATION

Standard Mirror

1. Remove the door trim panel.
2. Remove the mirror base to door outer panel stud nuts and remove the mirror from the door.
3. Install the base gasket and reverse the above to install.

Manual Remote Mirror

LEFT SIDE

1. Remove the door trim panel and detach the remote control lever. Peel back the insulator and water deflector to gain access to the mirror cable.
2. Detach the cable from any retaining tabs in the door.

3. Remove the attaching nuts and remove the mirror and cable assembly from the door.
4. Install the base gasket, then reverse the above to install.

RIGHT SIDE

1. Remove the door trim panel and detach the remote control lever. Peel back the insulator and water deflector to gain access to the mirror cable.
2. On models, with the instrument panel mounted control, remove the set screw from the control knob.
3. Remove the shroud side finishing panel as follows:
   a. Remove the sill plate screws and sill plate.
   b. Remove the litter container if so equipped.

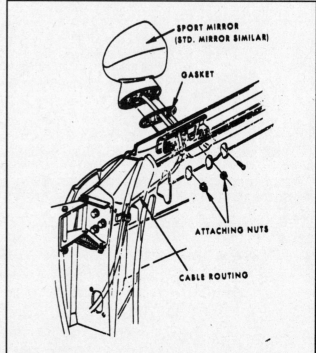

Fig. 15 View of a typical right door's outside mirror mounting

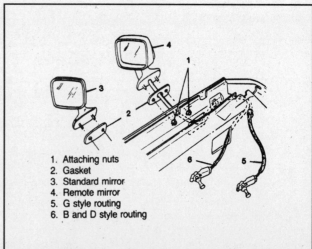

1. Attaching nuts
2. Gasket
3. Standard mirror
4. Remote mirror
5. G style routing
6. B and D style routing

Fig. 16 View of a typical left door's outside mirror installation

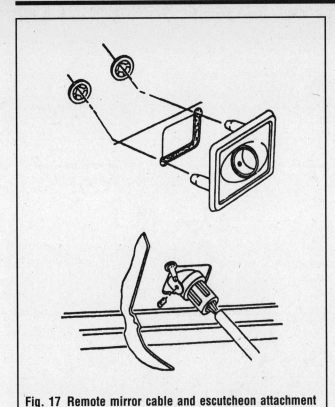

Fig. 17 Remote mirror cable and escutcheon attachment

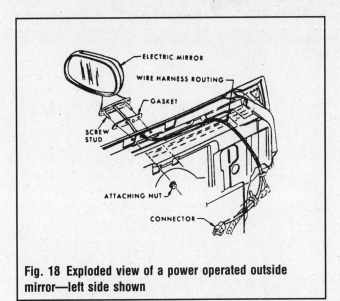

Fig. 18 Exploded view of a power operated outside mirror—left side shown

c. Remove the screw retaining the hinge pillar pinch-weld upper finishing lace.

d. Grasp the shroud finishing panel at the forward edge toward the dash panel and pull inward to disengage the plastic retaining clip, and slide the panel rearward.

4. Feed the remote cable through the shroud and rubber conduit between the door and pillar and detach the cable from any retaining tabs in the door.

5. Remove the attaching nuts and remove the mirror and cable assembly from the door.

6. Reverse the above to install. Make sure the remote mirror operates properly before installing the trim.

Power Operated Mirror

1. Remove the door trim panel and disconnect the wire harness at the connector. Peel back the insulator pad and water deflector enough to gain access to the wire harness.

2. Detach the harness from any retaining tabs in the door.

3. Remove the attaching nuts and remove the mirror and harness assembly from the door.

4. Reverse the above to install. Make sure mirror operates correctly before installing the door panel.

Antenna

REMOVAL & INSTALLATION

Manual Type
▶ **See Figure 19**

1. Unscrew the mast from the top of the fender.

2. Unscrew the nut and the bezel from the top of the fender.

3. On later vehicles it may be necessary to remove a bolt/screw which retains the base of the antenna under the fender. This bolt/screw is accessible under the hood.

4. Disconnect the antenna lead from the antenna. On some later vehicles the antenna lead may even plug into another lead under the hood.

5. Reach under the fender and remove the antenna base.

6. When installing the antenna to the fender make sure the retaining nut is tight. A loose antenna or one that does not make good contact at the fender can cause radio interference.

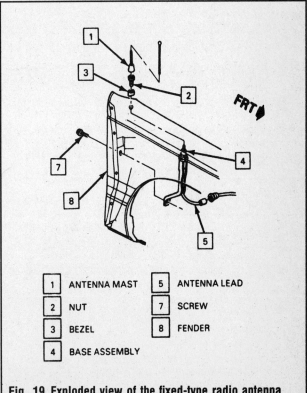

1	ANTENNA MAST	5	ANTENNA LEAD
2	NUT	7	SCREW
3	BEZEL	8	FENDER
4	BASE ASSEMBLY		

Fig. 19 Exploded view of the fixed-type radio antenna mounting

Power Type

♦ See Figure 20

➡The power antenna relay is located under the dash area in the convenience center.

1. Lower the antenna by turning off the radio or the ignition.

➡If the mast has failed in the UP position, and the mast or entire assembly is being replaced, the mast may be cut off to facilitate removal.

2. Disconnect the negative battery cable.

3. Remove the fender skirt attaching screws except those to the battery tray and radiator support.

➡On some vehicles there is an access plate which may reduce the amount of fender skirt bolts that have to be removed.

4. Pull down on the rear edge of the skirt and block with a 2″ × 4″ block of wood.

5. Remove the motor bracket attaching screws. Disconnect the motor electrical connections. Disconnect the antenna lead in wire. Remove the motor from the vehicle.

6. Reverse the above service procedures to install the assembly. Be sure the antenna mast is in the fully retracted position before installation.

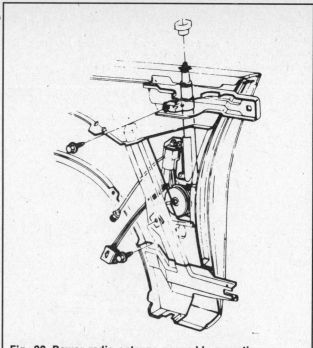

Fig. 20 Power radio antenna assembly mounting

INTERIOR

Front Door Panels

REMOVAL & INSTALLATION

♦ See Figures 21, 22, 23 and 24

1. Disconnect the negative battery cable. Remove the door handles and the locking knob from the inside of the doors. If equipped with remote control mirrors, remove the remote mirror escutcheon, then disengage the end of the mirror control cable from the escutcheon.

➡If equipped with door pull handles, remove the screws through the handle into the door inner panel.

2. Use a special tool to remove the spring clip, then remove the window regulator crank handle.

3. If equipped with a switch cover plate in the door armrest, remove the cover plate screws, then disconnect the switches and the cigar lighter, if equipped from the electrical harness.

4. If equipped with an integral armrest, remove the screws inserted through the pull cup into the armrest hanger support. If equipped with an armrest applied after the door trim installation, remove the armrest-to-inner panel screws.

5. If equipped with two-piece trim panels, disengage the retainer clips from the front and the rear of the upper trim panel, using tool No. BT-7323A, then lift the upper door trim and slide it slightly rearward to disengage it from the door inner panel at the beltline.

➡If equipped with electric switches in the door trim panel, disconnect the electrical connectors from the switch assembly.

6. Along the upper edge of the lower trim panel, remove the mounting screws. At the lower edge of the panel, insert tool No. BT-7323A between the inner panel and the trim panel, then disengage the retaining clips from around the outer perimeter. To remove the lower panel, push the panel down and outward to disengage it from the door.

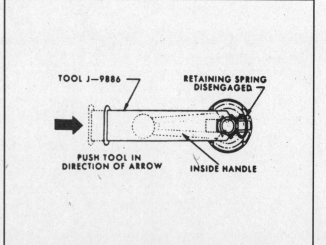

TOOL J—9886

RETAINING SPRING DISENGAGED

PUSH TOOL IN DIRECTION OF ARROW

INSIDE HANDLE

Fig. 21 A special tool must be used to remove the spring clip from the inside door handle

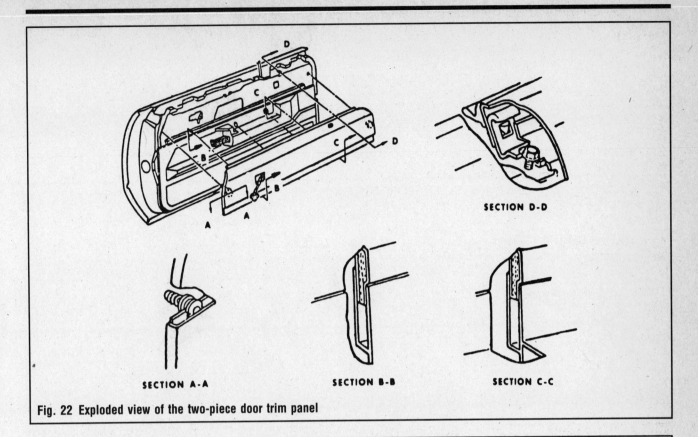

SECTION D-D

SECTION A-A   SECTION B-B   SECTION C-C

Fig. 22 Exploded view of the two-piece door trim panel

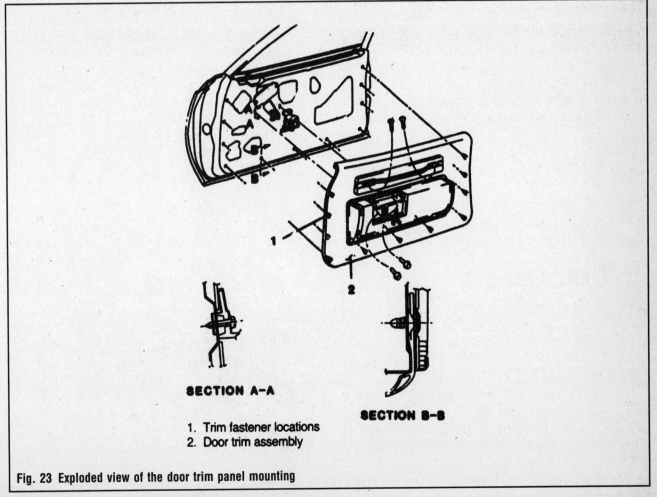

SECTION A-A

SECTION B-B

1. Trim fastener locations
2. Door trim assembly

Fig. 23 Exploded view of the door trim panel mounting

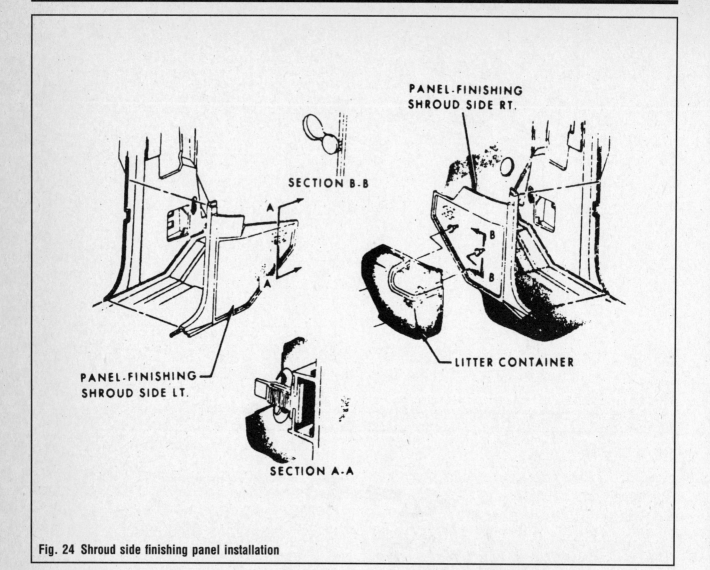

Fig. 24 Shroud side finishing panel installation

To remove the door panel, insert the special tool behind the window regulator handle . . .

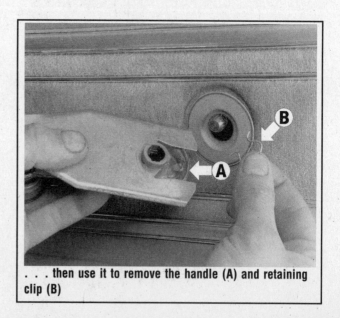

. . . then use it to remove the handle (A) and retaining clip (B)

Remove the door armrest retaining screws . . .

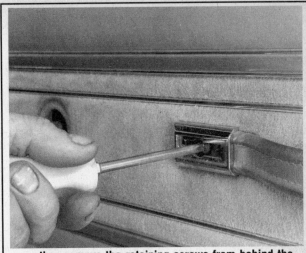

. . . then remove the retaining screws from behind the trim covers

. . . then remove the armrest from the door panel

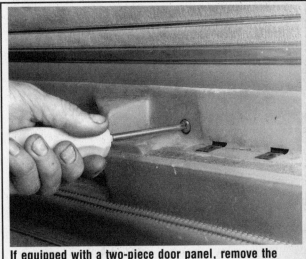

If equipped with a two-piece door panel, remove the lower panel retaining screws . . .

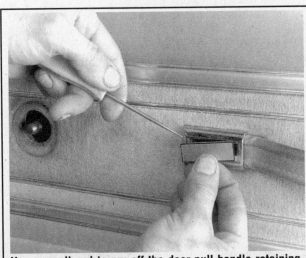

Use a small awl to pry off the door pull handle retaining screw covers . . .

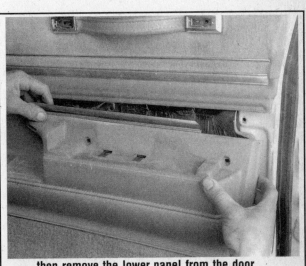

. . . then remove the lower panel from the door assembly

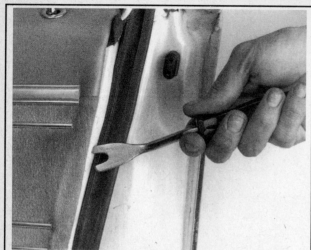

You can use a trim panel removal tool to pry the upper door panel retainers apart . . .

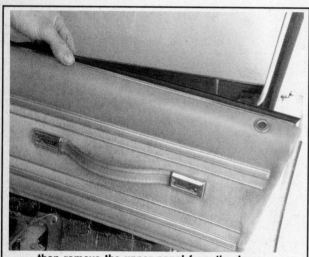

. . . then remove the upper panel from the door assembly

➡If equipped with courtesy lights, disconnect the wiring harness.

7. If equipped with an insulator pad glued to the door inner panel, remove the pad with a putty knife by separating it from the inner panel.

8. To install, reverse the removal service removal procedures.

Rear Door Panels

REMOVAL & INSTALLATION

1. Disconnect the negative battery cable. Remove the door handles and the locking knob from the inside of the doors. If equipped with a switch cover plate in the door armrest, remove the cover plate screws, then disconnect the switch from the electrical harness.

➡If equipped with door pull handles, remove the screws through the handle into the door inner panel.

2. If equipped with an integral armrest, remove the screws inserted through the pull cup into the armrest hanger support. If equipped with an armrest applied after the door trim installation, remove the armrest-to-inner panel screws.

3. If equipped with two-piece trim panels, disengage the retainer clips from the front and the rear of the upper trim panel, using tool No. BT-7323A, then lift the upper door trim and slide it slightly rearward to disengage it from the door inner panel at the beltline.

4. Along the upper edge of the lower trim panel, remove the mounting screws. At the lower edge of the panel, insert tool No. BT-7323A between the inner panel and the trim panel, then disengage the retaining clips from around the outer perimeter. To remove the lower panel, push the panel down and outward to disengage it from the door.

➡If equipped with courtesy lights, disconnect the wiring harness.

5. If equipped with an insulator pad glued to the door inner panel, remove the pad (with a putty knife) by separating it from the inner panel.

6. To install, reverse the service removal procedures.

Door Locks

The door locks use a fork bolt lock design, which includes a safety interlock feature. The door is securely closed when the door lock fork bolt engages the striker bolt.

REMOVAL & INSTALLATION

◆ See Figures 25, 26 and 27

➡Never attempt to make repairs to the lock actuator assembly, replace the assembly.

1. Disconnect the negative battery cable. Remove the door trim, then detach the insulator pad, if equipped and the inner panel water deflector enough to access the door lock.

2. Disconnect the electrical connector from the actuator assembly. If equipped with vacuum operated power locks, disconnect the vacuum line from the actuator assembly.

3. Remove the electric lock actuator by performing the following procedures:

   a. Using a center punch, drive the center pins out of pop rivets.

   b. Using a ¼ in. drill bit, drill the heads off of the pop rivets.

   c. Disconnect the lock actuator connecting rod and remove the lock actuator through the access hole.

➡On some vehicles, it may be necessary to remove the inside handle, the lock and the connecting rod as a unit.

4. Installation is the reverse of the removal procedure. When attaching the power door lock actuator to the door, use ¼ in. x ½ in. pop rivets or nuts and bolts.

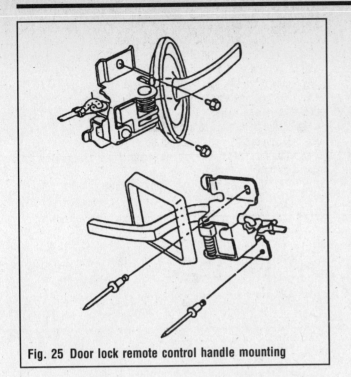

Fig. 25 Door lock remote control handle mounting

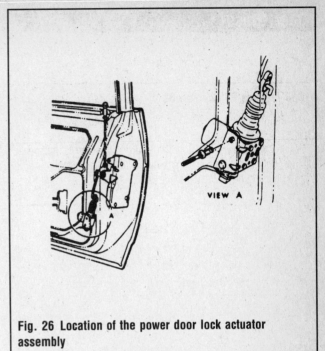

Fig. 26 Location of the power door lock actuator assembly

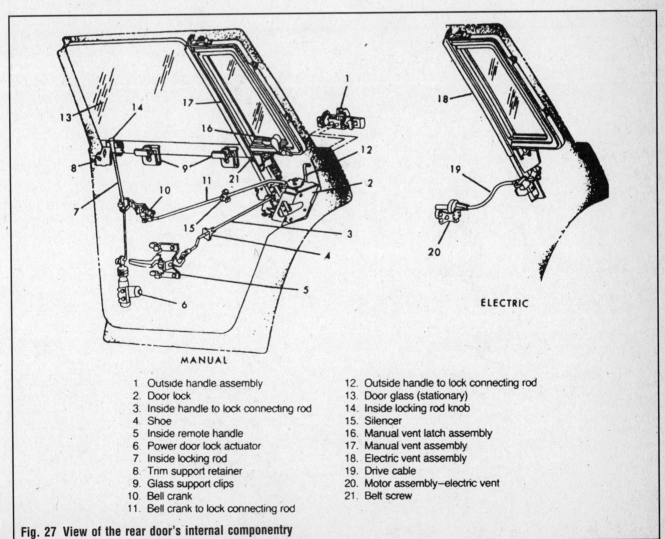

MANUAL

ELECTRIC

1. Outside handle assembly
2. Door lock
3. Inside handle to lock connecting rod
4. Shoe
5. Inside remote handle
6. Power door lock actuator
7. Inside locking rod
8. Trim support retainer
9. Glass support clips
10. Bell crank
11. Bell crank to lock connecting rod
12. Outside handle to lock connecting rod
13. Door glass (stationary)
14. Inside locking rod knob
15. Silencer
16. Manual vent latch assembly
17. Manual vent assembly
18. Electric vent assembly
19. Drive cable
20. Motor assembly—electric vent
21. Belt screw

Fig. 27 View of the rear door's internal componentry

Door Glass

REMOVAL & INSTALLATION

◆ **See Figures 28, 29 and 30**

1. Remove the door trim panel(s) as outlined earlier in this section.

2. With the glass in the half raised position (on coupe), or full up position (on sedan), mark the location of the mounting screws, then remove the following components:

a. The front belt stabilizer and trim retainer.
b. The rear belt stabilizer and pin assembly.
c. The front up-travel stop (on the glass).
d. The rear up-travel stop (on the glass).

3. Remove the vertical guide upper and lower screws, then disengage the guide assembly from the roller and lay in the bottom of the door.

4. Position the glass to expose the lower sash channel cam nuts, then remove the nuts through the inner panel access hole.

5. While supporting the glass, separate it from the lower sash channel cam.

6. Raise the glass slowly and slide it rearward.

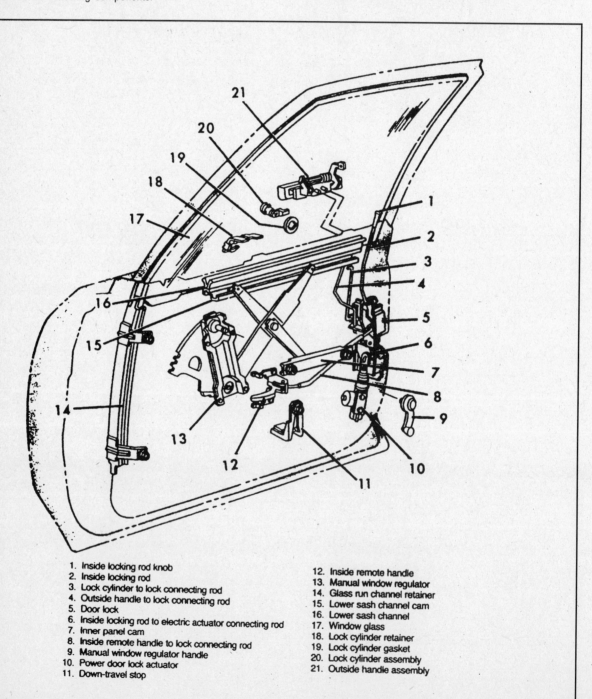

1. Inside locking rod knob
2. Inside locking rod
3. Lock cylinder to lock connecting rod
4. Outside handle to lock connecting rod
5. Door lock
6. Inside locking rod to electric actuator connecting rod
7. Inner panel cam
8. Inside remote handle to lock connecting rod
9. Manual window regulator handle
10. Power door lock actuator
11. Down-travel stop
12. Inside remote handle
13. Manual window regulator
14. Glass run channel retainer
15. Lower sash channel cam
16. Lower sash channel
17. Window glass
18. Lock cylinder retainer
19. Lock cylinder gasket
20. Lock cylinder assembly
21. Outside handle assembly

Fig. 28 View of the front door's internal componentry

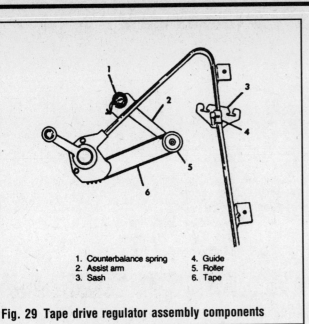

Fig. 29 Tape drive regulator assembly components

1. Counterbalance spring	4. Guide
2. Assist arm	5. Roller
3. Sash	6. Tape

7. Tilt the top of the glass inboard until the front up-step roller clears the front loading hole at the inner panel belt reinforcement.

8. Rotate the glass rearward 45°, then raise it slowly to clear the glass attaching screws through the belt loading holes.

To install:

9. Install the glass and engage it in the lower sash channel cam, fasten the nuts.

10. Engage the slide assembly to the roller and fasten the vertical guide upper and lower screws.

11. Install the components removed in Step 2.

12. Install the trim panel(s) and tighten the hardware fasteners to 90–125 inch lbs. (10–14 Nm)

ADJUSTMENT

1. Remove the door panel(s) as outlined earlier.

2. To rotate the window, loosen the front and rear up-stops, adjust the inner panel cam and the up-stops, then tighten the screws.

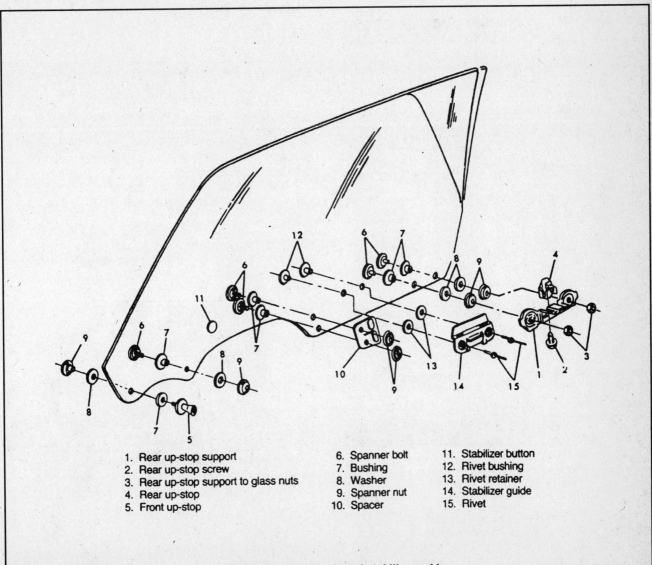

1. Rear up-stop support	6. Spanner bolt	11. Stabilizer button
2. Rear up-stop screw	7. Bushing	12. Rivet bushing
3. Rear up-stop support to glass nuts	8. Washer	13. Rivet retainer
4. Rear up-stop	9. Spanner nut	14. Stabilizer guide
5. Front up-stop	10. Spacer	15. Rivet

Fig. 30 Exploded view of the door glass assembly—note the riveted stabilizer guide

3. To adjust the window's upper inboard and outboard edge, perform the following procedures:

a. Position the window in the partially down position.

b. Loosen the vertical guide upper support (lower) screws, which are accessible through the inner panel access holes.

c. Loosen the pin assembly screws, the rear up-stop screw and the front belt stabilizer screw.

d. Adjust the vertical guide upper support and pin assembly (in or out) as required, then tighten the screws. Adjust and tighten the other components.

➡**When adjusting the glass, make sure it remains inboard of the blow-out clip, when cycled.**

4. If the window is too far forward or rearward, position the window partially down, loosen the vertical guide (upper and lower) screws, then adjust as required.

5. If the window is too high or low in its UP position, adjust the front and rear up travel stop.

6. If the window is too high or low in its DOWN position, adjust the down travel stop.

7. If the window binds during the up and down operations, adjust the front and/or rear belt stabilizer pin assemblies.

Front Door Regulator

REMOVAL & INSTALLATION

◆ See Figures 28, 29 and 30

1. Remove the door panel(s) as outlined earlier.

2. Prop the window in the half raised position (on coupe), full up position (on sedan), by inserting rubber wedges between the window and the inner panel (at the belt) at the front and rear of the window.

➡**If rubber stops are not available, remove the window.**

3. Mark (locate) and remove the inner panel cam and the vertical guide screws. Remove the vertical guide through the large access hole.

4. Using a center punch and ¼ in. drill bit, drive out the center pins and drill out the rivets of the regulator.

5. Remove the lower sash channel cam-to-glass rear nut, then slide the regulator rearward and disengage the rollers from the lower sash channel cam.

6. Remove the regulator through the largest inner panel access hole.

7. To install, reverse the removal procedure. Use ¼-20 x ½ in. nuts to mount the regulator.

Electric Window Motor

REMOVAL & INSTALLATION

1. Remove the door panel(s) as outlined earlier.

2. Prop the window in the half raised position (on coupe), full up position (on sedan), by inserting rubber wedges between the window and the inner panel (at the belt) at the front and rear of the window.

➡**If rubber stops are not available, remove the window.**

3. Mark (locate) and remove the inner panel cam and the vertical guide screws. Remove the vertical guide through the large access hole. Disconnect the electrical connector from the window regulator motor.

4. Using a center punch and ¼ in. drill bit, drive out the center pins and drill out the rivets of the regulator.

5. Remove the lower sash channel cam-to-glass rear nut, then slide the regulator rearward and disengage the rollers from the lower sash channel cam.

6. Remove the regulator and motor through the largest inner panel access hole.

To install:

7. Install the motor and install the regulator.

8. Use ¼-20 x ½ in. nuts to mount the regulator.

9. Install the window as described earlier.

Windshield

➡**The bonded windshield requires special tools and expertise. We recommend that replacement procedures be left to professional installers.**

REMOVAL

◆ See Figure 31

1. Place protective coverings over the hood.

2. Remove the windshield wiper arms and windshield trim.

3. If equipped with a radio antenna built into the windshield, disconnect the antenna's lead from the lower end of the windshield and tape the lead onto the outer surface of the windshield to protect it from damage.

4. Using a utility knife and the edge of the windshield as a guide, cut through the adhesive material around the entire perimeter.

5. Using a Hot Knife tool No. J-24709-1 and a cold knife, completely cut through the urethane adhesive.

6. With the help of an assistant, remove the windshield from the vehicle.

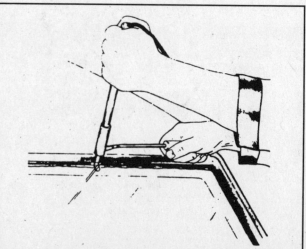

Fig. 31 Use an electric cutting tool to cut the window seal

7. If reinstalling the windshield, perform the following procedures:

a. Place the windshield onto a protective bench or holding fixture.

b. Using a razor blade or a sharp scraper, remove the excessive adhesive from the perimeter of the windshield.

c. Using denatured alcohol or lacquer thinner with a cloth, remove all traces of the adhesive from the perimeter of the windshield.

INSTALLATION

◗ **See Figures 32, 33, 34 and 35**

Seal Intact

This method is used when no other adhesive materials are used in the installation procedures. When using a new windshield for installation, do not use kerosene or gasoline as a solvent, for a film is left which will prevent adhesion of the sealing material. When using a volatile cleaner, avoid contacting the plastic laminate material (around the edge of the glass) for discoloration and/ or deterioration may occur.

1. To prepare the windshield frame for glass installation, perform the following procedures:

a. Using a sharp scraper or a chisel, clean the excess sealing material from the windshield frame.

➡**It is not necessary to remove all traces of the original material; there should be no mounds or loose pieces remaining. If, while removing the old material, the metal surface has been exposed, cover the area with black primer.**

b. Inspect the reveal molding retaining clip(s); if the upper end of the clip(s) are bent (more than 1/16 in.) away from the body metal, replace the clip(s).

➡**When using weatherstrip adhesive, apply enough material to obtain a water tight seal beneath the spacer; DO NOT allow the material to squeeze out excessively.**

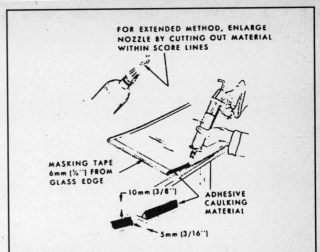

Fig. 33 Applying adhesive to a windshield whose seal is not intact

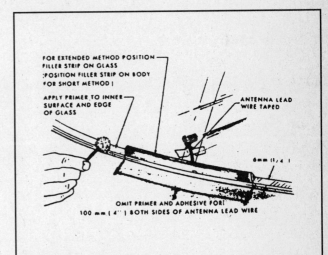

Fig. 34 Preparing an embedded antenna windshield for installation—seal not intact

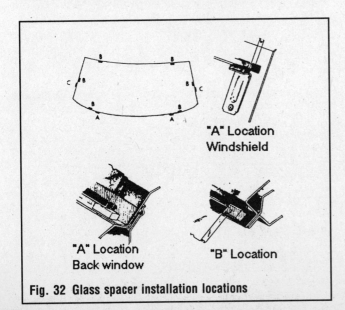

"A" Location Windshield

"A" Location Back window

"B" Location

Fig. 32 Glass spacer installation locations

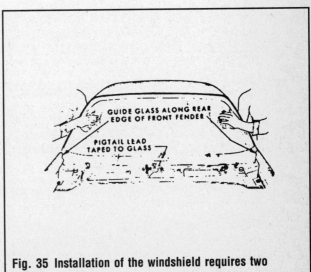

Fig. 35 Installation of the windshield requires two people

c. Cement the flat rubber spacers to the window opening at the pinchweld flanges; locate the spacers so that they are equally spaced around the perimeter of the windshield.

d. Reinstall the metal supports at the lower edge of the windshield glass.

2. Using an assistant, lift the glass into the window opening; the windshield can be positioned without the use of suction cups. Check the position of the glass, it should not overlap the pinchweld flange (around the entire perimeter) by more than ³⁄₁₆ in. The overlap across the top of the windshield can be corrected by readjusting the lower metal support spacers.

3. Check the relationship of the glass to the contour of the body. The gap between the glass and the pinchweld frame should be between ⅛–¼ in. If there is difficulty in maintaining this distance, perform one of the following correction methods:

a. Reposition the flat spacers.

b. Apply excessive amounts of adhesive caulking material to the wide gaps.

c. Try another windshield.

d. Rework the pinchweld flange.

4. After the final adjustments have been made, apply pieces of masking tape over the edges of the glass and the body, then slit the tape between the glass and the body. Remove the glass from the opening.

➡**The tape will be used for alignment of the glass upon installation and will aid in the clean up operation.**

5. If desired, apply masking to the inboard edge of the windshield; the tape should be placed ¼ in. (from the outer edge) around the top and sides (not the bottom) of the glass.

6. Using alcohol and a clean cloth, clean the inner perimeter of the glass and allow it to air dry.

7. Using the Urethane Adhesive Kit No. 9636067 (two primers are provided), apply primer using the following procedures:

a. Apply the clear primer around the entire perimeter of the glass. Allow the primer to dry for 5 minutes.

b. If refinishing or painting operations are needed for any portions of the glass opening apply the black primer to these portions. Allow the primer to dry for 5 minutes.

8. Using a caulking gun and an adhesive cartridge, apply a smooth continuous bead ⅜ in. wide around the entire perimeter of the glass.

9. Reposition the glass to the window opening using the tape as the installation guide. Apply light hand pressure to the glass to ensure a bond to the body opening. Using a small brush or a flat bladed tool, paddle the bonding material around the edge of the glass to ensure a water tight seal.

10. Using a soft, warm water spray, allow the water to spill over the edges of the glass to detect water leaks. If a water leak is encountered, paddle additional material around the leak.

11. Cement rubber spacers between the right and left sides of the windshield and the frame to keep the glass centered during the installation procedures.

➡**After the windshield installation, the vehicle must remain at room temperature for 6 hours.**

12. Install the windshield molding strips. Remove the masking tape from the inner perimeter of the windshield; pull the tape toward the center.

13. Complete the installation by replacing all of the removed parts.

Seal Not Intact

This method is used in conjunction with unknown adhesive materials such as butyl strips. When using a new windshield for installation, do not use kerosene or gasoline as a solvent, for a film is left which will prevent adhesion of the sealing material. When using a volatile cleaner, avoid contacting the plastic laminate material (around the edge of the glass) for discoloration and/or deterioration may occur.

1. To prepare the windshield frame for glass installation, perform the following procedures:

a. Using a sharp scraper or a chisel, clean the excess sealing material from the windshield frame.

➡**If using Butyl tape or unknown material to install the windshield, it is necessary to remove all traces of the original material. If using a Urethane sealing material, it is not necessary to remove all traces of the original material; there should be no mounds or loose pieces remaining. If while removing the old material, the metal surface has been exposed, cover the area with black primer.**

b. Inspect the reveal molding retaining clip(s); if the upper end of the clip(s) is bent (more than ¹⁄₁₆ in.) away from the body metal, replace the clip(s).

➡**If using weatherstrip adhesive, apply enough material to obtain a water tight seal beneath the spacer; DO NOT allow the material to squeeze out excessively. Weatherstrip material is not compatible with other replacement adhesives; leaks may develop where the two dissimilar materials are joined.**

c. Cement the flat rubber spacers to the window opening at the pinchweld flanges; locate the spacers so that they are equally spaced around the perimeter of the windshield.

d. Reinstall the metal supports at the lower edge of the windshield glass.

2. Using an assistant, lift the glass into the window opening; the windshield can be positioned without the use of suction cups. Check the position of the glass, it should not overlap the pinchweld flange (around the entire perimeter) by more than ³⁄₁₆ in. The overlap across the top of the windshield can be corrected by readjusting the lower metal support spacers.

3. Check the relationship of the glass to the contour of the body. The gap between the glass and the pinchweld frame should be between ⅛–¼ in. If there is difficulty in maintaining this distance, perform one of the following correction methods:

a. Reposition the flat spacers.

b. Apply excessive amounts of adhesive caulking material to the wide gaps.

c. Try another windshield.

d. Rework the pinchweld flange.

4. After the final adjustments have been made, apply pieces of masking tape over the edges of the glass and the body, then slit the tape between the glass and the body. Remove the glass from the opening.

➡**The tape will be used for alignment of the glass upon installation and will aid in the clean up operation.**

5. If desired, apply masking to the inboard edge of the windshield; the tape should be placed ¼ in. (from the outer edge) around the top and sides (not the bottom) of the glass.

6. If equipped with an embedded antenna, apply an 8 in. bu-

tyl filler strip to the bottom inner center surface of the windshield. If not equipped with an embedded windshield antenna the butyl strip is not necessary.

7. Using alcohol and a clean cloth, clean the inner perimeter of the glass and allow it to air dry.

8. Using the Urethane Adhesive Kit No. 9636067 (two primers are provided), apply primer using the following procedures:

a. If equipped with an embedded windshield antenna, apply the clear primer around the entire perimeter (except at the location of the filler strip); If not equipped with an embedded windshield antenna, apply the clear primer around the entire perimeter of the glass. Allow the primer to dry for 5 minutes.

b. If refinishing or painting operations are needed for any portions of the glass opening apply the black primer to these portions. Allow the primer to dry for 5 minutes.

9. Using a caulking gun and an adhesive cartridge, apply a smooth continuous bead ⅜ in. wide around the entire perimeter of the glass.

10. Reposition the glass to the window opening using the tape as the installation guide. Apply light hand pressure to the glass to ensure a bond to the body opening. Using a small brush or a flat bladed tool, paddle the bonding material around the edge of the glass to ensure a water tight seal.

➡**If equipped with an embedded antenna, paddle additional material at the edges of the butyl strip; avoid the area near the antenna pigtail.**

11. Using a soft, warm water spray, allow the water to spill over the edges of the glass to detect water leaks. If a water leak is encountered, paddle additional material around the leak.

12. Cement rubber spacers between the right and left sides of the windshield and the frame, to keep the glass centered during the installation procedures.

13. Install the windshield molding strips. Remove the masking tape from the inner perimeter of the windshield; pull the tape toward the center.

14. Complete the installation by replacing all of the removed parts.

➡**After the windshield installation, the vehicle must remain at room temperature for 6 hours.**

Rear Window Glass

➡**The bonded rear window requires special tools and procedures.**

REMOVAL

1. Place protective coverings over the trunk.
2. Remove the trim and molding from around the glass.
3. If equipped with a rear window electric grid defogger (built into the glass) disconnect the wiring harness connectors from the glass and tape the leads onto the outer surface of the window to protect it from damage.
4. Using a utility knife and the edge of a window as a guide, cut through the adhesive material around the entire perimeter.
5. Using a hot knife tool No. J-24709-1 and a cold knife, completely cut through the urethane adhesive.
6. With the help of an assistant, remove the window from the vehicle.

7. If reinstalling the window, perform the following procedures:

a. Place the window onto a protective bench or holding fixture.

b. Using a razor blade or a sharp scraper, remove the excessive adhesive from the perimeter of the window.

c. Using denatured alcohol or lacquer thinner with a cloth, remove all traces of the adhesive from the perimeter of the window.

INSTALLATION

Seal Intact

This method is used when no other adhesive materials are used in the installation procedures. When using a new window for installation, do not use kerosene or gasoline as a solvent, for a film is left which will prevent adhesion of the sealing material. When using a volatile cleaner, avoid contacting the plastic laminate material (around the edge of the glass) for discoloration and/or deterioration may occur.

1. To prepare the window frame for glass installation, perform the following procedures:

a. Using a sharp scraper or a chisel, clean the excess sealing material from the window frame.

➡**It is not necessary to remove all traces of the original material; there should be no mounds or loose pieces remaining. If while removing the old material, the metal surface has been exposed, cover the area with black primer.**

b. Inspect the reveal molding retaining clip(s); if the upper end of the clip(s) is bent (more than ¹⁄₁₆ in.) away from the body metal, replace the clip(s).

➡**When using weatherstrip adhesive, apply enough material to obtain a water tight seal beneath the spacer; DO NOT allow the material to squeeze out excessively.**

c. Cement the flat rubber spacers to the window opening at the pinchweld flanges; locate the spacers so that they are equally spaced around the perimeter of the window.

d. Reinstall the metal supports at the lower edge of the windshield glass.

2. Using an assistant, lift the glass into the window opening; the windshield can be positioned without the use of suction cups. Check the position of the glass, it should not overlap the pinchweld flange (around the entire perimeter) by more than ¹⁄₁₆ in. The overlap across the top of the window can be corrected by readjusting the lower metal support spacers.

3. Check the relationship of the glass to the contour of the body. The gap between the glass and the pinchweld frame should be between ⅛–¼ in. If there is difficulty in maintaining this distance, perform one of the following correction methods:

a. Reposition the flat spacers.

b. Apply excessive amounts of adhesive caulking material to the wide gaps.

c. Try another window.

d. Rework the pinchweld flange.

4. After the final adjustments have been made, apply pieces of masking tape over the edges of the glass and the body, then slit the tape between the glass and the body. Remove the glass from the opening.

➡**The tape will be used for alignment of the glass upon installation and will aid in the clean up operation.**

5. If desired, apply masking to the inboard edge of the window; the tape should be placed ¼ in. (from the outer edge) around the top and sides (NOT the bottom) of the glass.

6. Using alcohol and a clean cloth, clean the inner perimeter of the glass and allow it to air dry.

7. Using the Urethane Adhesive Kit No. 9636067 (two primers are provided), apply primer using the following procedures:

a. Apply the clear primer around the entire perimeter of the glass. Allow the primer to dry for 5 minutes.

b. If refinishing or painting operations are needed for any portions of the glass opening, apply the black primer to these portions. Allow the primer to dry for 5 minutes.

8. Using a caulking gun and an adhesive cartridge, apply a smooth continuous bead ⅜ in. wide around the entire perimeter of the glass.

9. Reposition the glass to the window opening using the tape as the installation guide. Apply light hand pressure to the glass to ensure a bond to the body opening. Using a small brush or a flat bladed tool, paddle the bonding material around the edge of the glass to ensure a water tight seal.

10. Using a soft, warm water spray, allow the water to spill over the edges of the glass to detect water leaks. If a water leak is encountered, paddle additional material around the leak.

11. Cement rubber spacers between the right and left sides of the window and the frame to keep the glass centered during the installation procedures.

12. Install the window molding strips. Remove the masking tape from the inner perimeter of the window; pull the tape toward the center.

➡ **After the window installation, the vehicle must remain at room temperature for 6 hours.**

13. Complete the installation by replacing all of the removed parts.

Seal Not Intact

This method is used in conjunction with unknown adhesive materials such as butyl strips. When using a new window for installation, do not use kerosene or gasoline as a solvent, for a film is left which will prevent adhesion of the sealing material. When using a volatile cleaner, avoid contacting the plastic laminate material (around the edge of the glass) for discoloration and/or deterioration may occur.

1. To prepare the window frame for glass installation, perform the following procedures:

a. Using a sharp scraper or a chisel, clean the excess sealing material from the windshield frame.

➡ **If using butyl tape or unknown material to install the window, it is necessary to remove all traces of the original material. If using a urethane sealing material, it is not necessary to remove all traces of the original material; there should be no mounds or loose pieces remaining. If while removing the old material, the metal surface has been exposed, cover the area with black primer.**

b. Inspect the reveal molding retaining clip(s); if the upper end of the clip(s) is bent (more than 1/16 in.) away from the body metal, replace the clip(s).

➡ **If using weatherstrip adhesive, apply enough material to obtain a water tight seal beneath the spacer; DO NOT allow the material to squeeze out excessively. Weatherstrip mate-** rial is not compatible with other replacement adhesives; leaks may develop where the two dissimilar materials are joined.

c. Cement the flat rubber spacers to the window opening at the pinchweld flanges; locate the spacers so that they are equally spaced around the perimeter of the window.

d. Reinstall the metal supports at the lower edge of the window glass.

2. Using an assistant, lift the glass into the window opening; the window can be positioned without the use of suction cups. Check the position of the glass, it should not overlap the pinchweld flange (around the entire perimeter) by more than 3/16 in. The overlap across the top of the window can be corrected by re-adjusting the lower metal support spacers.

3. Check the relationship of the glass to the contour of the body. The gap between the glass and the pinchweld frame should be between ⅛–¼ in. If there is difficulty in maintaining this distance, perform one of the following correction methods:

a. Reposition the flat spacers.

b. Apply excessive amounts of adhesive caulking material to the wide gaps.

c. Try another window.

d. Rework the pinchweld flange.

4. After the final adjustments have been made, apply pieces of masking tape over the edges of the glass and the body, then slit the tape between the glass and the body. Remove the glass from the opening.

➡ **The tape will be used for alignment of the glass upon installation and will aid in the clean up operation.**

5. If desired, apply masking to the inboard edge of the window; the tape should be placed ¼ in. (from the outer edge) around the top and sides (NOT the bottom) of the glass.

6. If equipped with an electric defogger, apply an 8 in. butyl filler strip to the bottom inner center surface of the glass. If not equipped with an electric defogger, the butyl strip is not necessary.

7. Using alcohol and a clean cloth, clean the inner perimeter of the glass and allow it to air dry.

8. Using the Urethane Adhesive Kit No. 9636067 (two primers are provided), apply primer using the following procedures:

a. If equipped with a defogger, apply the clear primer around the entire perimeter (except at the location of the filler strip); if not equipped with a defogger, apply the clear primer around the entire perimeter of the glass. Allow the primer to dry for 5 minutes.

b. If refinishing or painting operations are needed for any portions of the glass opening apply the black primer to these portions. Allow the primer to dry for 5 minutes. Apply the clear primer around the entire perimeter of the glass. Allow the primer to dry for 5 minutes.

c. If refinishing or painting operations are needed for any portions of the glass opening apply the black primer to these portions. Allow the primer to dry for 5 minutes.

9. Using a caulking gun and an adhesive cartridge, apply a smooth continuous bead ⅜ in, wide around the entire perimeter of the glass.

10. Reposition the glass to the window opening using the tape as the installation guide. Apply light hand pressure to the glass to ensure a bond to the body opening. Using a small brush or a flat bladed tool, paddle the bonding material around the edge of the glass to ensure a water tight seal.

→If equipped with an electric defogger, paddle additional material at the edges of the butyl strip; avoid the area near the electrical harness.

11. Using a soft, warm water spray, allow the water to spill over the edges of the glass to detect water leaks. If a water leak is encountered, paddle additional material around the leak.

12. Cement rubber spacers between the right and left sides of the window and the frame to keep the glass centered during the installation procedures.

13. Install the window molding strips. Remove the masking tape from the inner perimeter of the window; pull the tape toward the center.

14. Complete the installation by replacing all of the removed parts.

→After the window installation, the vehicle must remain at room temperature.

Stationary Glass

REMOVAL & INSTALLATION

Some rear door windows are a frameless, solid, safety plate glass window which is retained by two beltline support clips; the window remains in a fixed position.

1. Remove the rear door panel as outlined earlier.

2. Remove the beltline support clips and the trim support retainer.

3. With the use of suction cups, slide the glass down and remove it from the inboard side of the door.

4. To install, lubricate the glass channel with silicone spray or liquid soap, then reverse the removal procedures.

Rear Door Vent Window

The rear doors have a movable vent window which can be either manual or electrically operated. The window is held in place by mounting screws in the upper door frame and the door belt return flange.

The manual vent window has a latch handle which locks or opens the window.

The electric vent window is operated by an electric motor and a drive cable assembly. It is controlled by a master switch on the left front armrest or on a switch on the rear door trim panel.

REMOVAL & INSTALLATION

◆ **See Figures 36 and 37**

Manual

1. Remove the rear door glass as outlined earlier.
2. Remove the frame and the belt mounting screws, then pull

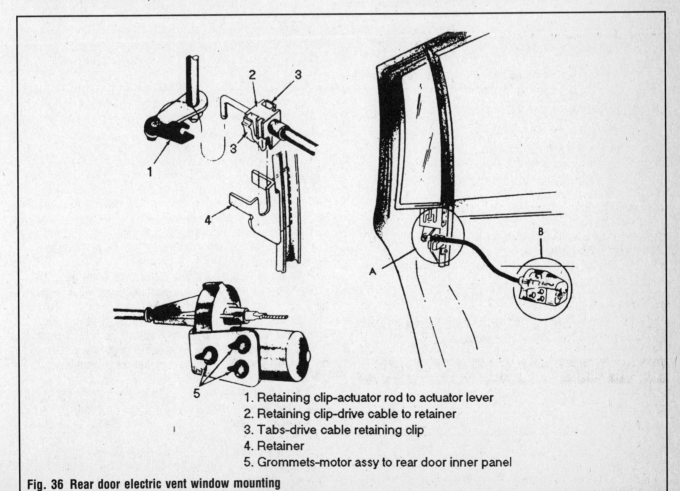

1. Retaining clip-actuator rod to actuator lever
2. Retaining clip-drive cable to retainer
3. Tabs-drive cable retaining clip
4. Retainer
5. Grommets-motor assy to rear door inner panel

Fig. 36 Rear door electric vent window mounting

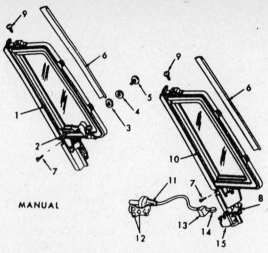

1. Manual vent window assembly
2. Manual latch handle
3. Washer (inboard of glass)
4. Spacer (outboard of glass)
5. Support screw
6. Reveal molding
7. Belt attaching screw
8. Actuator lever
9. Upper frame attaching screw
10. Electric vent window assembly
11. Electric actuator assembly
12. Grommets—motor assembly to rear door inner panel
13. Retaining clip—drive cable to retainer
14. Retaining clip—actuator rod to actuator lever
15. Retainer

Fig. 37 Exploded view of the rear door vent window hardware

the top of the vent assembly forward and remove it from the inside of the door.

3. To install, lubricate the glass channel with silicone spray or liquid soap, then reverse the removal procedures.

Electric

1. Remove the rear door glass as outlined earlier.

2. Disconnect the actuator rod-to-actuator lever plastic clip, by rotating the clip inward with a suitable tool.

3. To remove the drive cable plastic retaining clip, depress the tabs and push up.

4. Remove the upper frame screws and the belt screw.

5. Pull the top of the vent assembly forward and remove it from the inside of the door.

6. To install, lubricate the glass channel with silicone spray or liquid soap, then reverse the removal procedures.

Inside Rear View Mirror

REPLACEMENT

Headliner Mounted

On some vehicles, the rear view mirror is attached to the headliner moulding by two screws.

1. Remove the two attaching screws.
2. Remove the mirror assembly.
3. To install, reverse the removal procedures.

Windshield Mounted

On most vehicles the rear view mirror is attached to a support which is secured to the windshield glass. A service replacement windshield glass has the support bonded to the glass assembly. To install a detached mirror support or install a new part, use the following procedures to complete the service.

1. Locate the support position at the center of the glass 22 in. (557mm) from the bottom of the glass to the bottom of the support.

2. Circle the location on the outside of the glass with a wax pencil or crayon. Draw a large circle around the support circle.

3. Clean the area within the circle with household cleaner and dry with a clean towel. Repeat the procedures using rubbing alcohol.

4. Sand the bonding surface of the support with fine grit (320–360) emery cloth or sandpaper. If the original support is being used, remove the old adhesive with rubbing alcohol and a clean towel.

5. Apply the adhesive as outlined in the kit instructions.

6. Position the support to the marked location with the rounded end UP.

7. Press the support to the glass for 30–60 seconds. Exces-

sive adhesive can be removed after five minutes with rubbing alcohol.

✳✳ CAUTION

DO NOT apply excessive pressure to the windshield glass. The glass may break, causing personal injury.

Seats

REMOVAL & INSTALLATION

Manual and Power

FRONT

1. Disconnect the negative battery cable.
2. Operate the front seat to the full forward position.
3. Remove the screws, rear support covers and adjuster hold-down nuts.
4. Remove the seat belt cover.
5. Operate the seat to the full rearward position.
6. Remove the screws, front support covers and adjuster hold-down nuts.
7. Remove the seat belt anchor bolt using a Torx® socket J 29843-9.
8. Disconnect and electrical connections to the seat.
9. Before removing the seat, place paint protection over the trim to prevent damage.
10. With an assistant, remove the seat assembly with adjusters attached.

To install:

11. With an assistant, install the seat assembly onto the mounting studs.
12. Connect all electrical connections and seat belts. Tighten the seat belt anchor to 31 ft. lbs. (42 Nm).
13. Install and tighten the front nuts to 22 ft. lbs. (30 Nm). Install the support covers.
14. Move the seat to the full forward position.
15. Install the seat belt cover, rear nuts and torque to 22 ft. lbs. (30 Nm).
16. Install the support covers, connect the negative battery cable and check operation.

Rear

SEAT BOTTOM

1. The seat bottom is held in place by dome stops located on the floor pan. The dome stops hook over the frame wires on the seatbottom.
2. To disengage, push the lower front edge of the seatbottom rearward, lift up and pull forward to disengage the dome stops.

To install:

3. Slide the bottom rearward, press down and pull forward. The frame wire in the bottom should slide into the dome stops.

SEATBACK

1. Remove the two retaining bolts in the lower corners.
2. Lift the rear seatback off the hooks on the seat panel.

3. Hang the seatback over the hooks on the panel and install the two bolts.

Seat Belt Systems

REMOVAL & INSTALLATION

Lap Belts and Floor Attachments

1. For the front seats, move the seat forward. For the rear and third seats remove the seat cushion.
2. Disconnect the electrical connector on the driver's belt.
3. Remove the anchor bolt cover and remove the anchor bolt using tool J 29843-9 or its equivalent.
4. Remove the safety belt and sleeve.
5. Installation is the reverse of removal. Tighten the anchor bolt to 31 ft. lbs. (42 Nm).

Shoulder Belts

FRONT SEATS

1. Remove the guide cover and remove the guide anchor bolt using tool J 29843-9 or its equivalent.
2. Remove the center upper and lower pillar panel. Refer to appropriate procedure in this section.
3. Remove the retractor anchor bolt using tool J 29843-9 or its equivalent and remove the retractor.
4. Remove the safety belt anchor bolt using tool J 29843-9 or its equivalent.
5. Remove the safety belt from the center pillar trim panels.
6. Installation is the reverse of removal. Torque all anchor bolts to 31 ft. lbs. (42 Nm).

REAR SEAT

1. Remove the seat cushion. Refer to the appropriate procedure in this section.
2. Remove the lap belt retractor anchor bolt using tool J 29843-9 or its equivalent.
3. Remove the shoulder belt retractor cover and remove the anchor bolt using tool J 29843-9 or its equivalent.
4. Remove the safety belt with the shoulder belt retractor and lap belt retractor from the vehicle.
5. Installation is the reverse of removal. Torque all anchor bolts to 31 ft. lbs. (42 Nm).

Power Seat Motor

REMOVAL & INSTALLATION

◆ See Figure 38

Two-Way Power Seats

1. If the seat will move, shift it to a position near the middle of its travel.
2. Remove the nuts that attach the seat adjuster to the floor and then tilt the seat rearward for access.

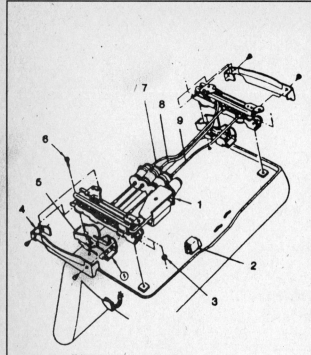

1. Transmission assembly
2. Seat relay
3. Nut
4. Adjuster track lower cover
5. Adjuster track upper cover
6. Adjuster-to-seat frame attaching bolts
7. Horizontal drive cable
8. Rear vertical drive cable
9. Front vertical drive cable

Fig. 38 Six-way power seat adjuster components

3. On the full width seat, disconnect both power cables at the motor.

4. Disconnect the wiring harness at the motor.

5. Remove the screws that secure the motor support to the seat frame. Remove the motor with the support attached. Then, remove the screws that attach the motor to the support bracket and remove the motor from the bracket.

To install:

6. Install the motor and fasten the screws that attach the motor to the support bracket.

7. Connect the wiring harness and both power cables at the motor.

8. Fasten the nuts which attach the seat adjuster to the floor.

9. Make sure you test the motor for proper operation to the extremes of travel in both directions.

Six-Way Power Seat Permanent Magnet Motor

1. Unbolt the seat from the floor of the vehicle. Place it upside down in a location where the upholstery is protected from dirt.

2. Disconnect the wires going to the motor at the motor control relay.

3. Remove the two mounting screws that attach the motor mounting support to the seat. Remove the three screws attaching the transmission to the motor.

4. Now, move the motor outboard or away from the transmission far enough to disengage it from the rubber coupling that connects it to the transmission, and remove it.

To install:

5. Install the motor to transmission attaching screws and fasten the two mounting screws that attach the motor mounting support to the seat.

➡**When installing the motor, make sure that the rubber coupling is properly engaged at the motor and transmission.**

6. Connect the motor control relay wires and install the seat.

7. Check the motor for proper operation to the extremes of travel in both directions.

GLOSSARY

AIR/FUEL RATIO: The ratio of air-to-gasoline by weight in the fuel mixture drawn into the engine.

AIR INJECTION: One method of reducing harmful exhaust emissions by injecting air into each of the exhaust ports of an engine. The fresh air entering the hot exhaust manifold causes any remaining fuel to be burned before it can exit the tailpipe.

ALTERNATOR: A device used for converting mechanical energy into electrical energy.

AMMETER: An instrument, calibrated in amperes, used to measure the flow of an electrical current in a circuit. Ammeters are always connected in series with the circuit being tested.

AMPERE: The rate of flow of electrical current present when one volt of electrical pressure is applied against one ohm of electrical resistance.

ANALOG COMPUTER: Any microprocessor that uses similar (analogous) electrical signals to make its calculations.

ARMATURE: A laminated, soft iron core wrapped by a wire that converts electrical energy to mechanical energy as in a motor or relay. When rotated in a magnetic field, it changes mechanical energy into electrical energy as in a generator.

ATMOSPHERIC PRESSURE: The pressure on the Earth's surface caused by the weight of the air in the atmosphere. At sea level, this pressure is 14.7 psi at 32°F (101 kPa at 0°C).

ATOMIZATION: The breaking down of a liquid into a fine mist that can be suspended in air.

AXIAL PLAY: Movement parallel to a shaft or bearing bore.

BACKFIRE: The sudden combustion of gases in the intake or exhaust system that results in a loud explosion.

BACKLASH: The clearance or play between two parts, such as meshed gears.

BACKPRESSURE: Restrictions in the exhaust system that slow the exit of exhaust gases from the combustion chamber.

BAKELITE: A heat resistant, plastic insulator material commonly used in printed circuit boards and transistorized components.

BALL BEARING: A bearing made up of hardened inner and outer races between which hardened steel balls roll.

BALLAST RESISTOR: A resistor in the primary ignition circuit that lowers voltage after the engine is started to reduce wear on ignition components.

BEARING: A friction reducing, supportive device usually located between a stationary part and a moving part.

BIMETAL TEMPERATURE SENSOR: Any sensor or switch made of two dissimilar types of metal that bend when heated or cooled due to the different expansion rates of the alloys. These types of sensors usually function as an on/off switch.

BLOWBY: Combustion gases, composed of water vapor and unburned fuel, that leak past the piston rings into the crankcase during normal engine operation. These gases are removed by the PCV system to prevent the buildup of harmful acids in the crankcase.

BRAKE PAD: A brake shoe and lining assembly used with disc brakes.

BRAKE SHOE: The backing for the brake lining. The term is, however, usually applied to the assembly of the brake backing and lining.

BUSHING: A liner, usually removable, for a bearing; an anti-friction liner used in place of a bearing.

CALIPER: A hydraulically activated device in a disc brake system, which is mounted straddling the brake rotor (disc). The caliper contains at least one piston and two brake pads. Hydraulic pressure on the piston(s) forces the pads against the rotor.

CAMSHAFT: A shaft in the engine on which are the lobes (cams) which operate the valves. The camshaft is driven by the crankshaft, via a belt, chain or gears, at one half the crankshaft speed.

CAPACITOR: A device which stores an electrical charge.

CARBON MONOXIDE (CO): A colorless, odorless gas given off as a normal byproduct of combustion. It is poisonous and extremely dangerous in confined areas, building up slowly to toxic levels without warning if adequate ventilation is not available.

CARBURETOR: A device, usually mounted on the intake manifold of an engine, which mixes the air and fuel in the proper proportion to allow even combustion.

CATALYTIC CONVERTER: A device installed in the exhaust system, like a muffler, that converts harmful byproducts of combustion into carbon dioxide and water vapor by means of a heat-producing chemical reaction.

CENTRIFUGAL ADVANCE: A mechanical method of advancing the spark timing by using flyweights in the distributor that react to centrifugal force generated by the distributor shaft rotation.

CHECK VALVE: Any one-way valve installed to permit the flow of air, fuel or vacuum in one direction only.

CHOKE: A device, usually a moveable valve, placed in the intake path of a carburetor to restrict the flow of air.

CIRCUIT: Any unbroken path through which an electrical current can flow. Also used to describe fuel flow in some instances.

CIRCUIT BREAKER: A switch which protects an electrical circuit from overload by opening the circuit when the current flow exceeds a predetermined level. Some circuit breakers must be reset manually, while most reset automatically.

COIL (IGNITION): A transformer in the ignition circuit which steps up the voltage provided to the spark plugs.

COMBINATION MANIFOLD: An assembly which includes both the intake and exhaust manifolds in one casting.

COMBINATION VALVE: A device used in some fuel systems that routes fuel vapors to a charcoal storage canister instead of venting them into the atmosphere. The valve relieves fuel tank pressure and allows fresh air into the tank as the fuel level drops to prevent a vapor lock situation.

COMPRESSION RATIO: The comparison of the total volume of the cylinder and combustion chamber with the piston at BDC and the piston at TDC.

CONDENSER: 1. An electrical device which acts to store an electrical charge, preventing voltage surges. 2. A radiator-like device in the air conditioning system in which refrigerant gas condenses into a liquid, giving off heat.

CONDUCTOR: Any material through which an electrical current can be transmitted easily.

CONTINUITY: Continuous or complete circuit. Can be checked with an ohmmeter.

COUNTERSHAFT: An intermediate shaft which is rotated by a mainshaft and transmits, in turn, that rotation to a working part.

CRANKCASE: The lower part of an engine in which the crankshaft and related parts operate.

CRANKSHAFT: The main driving shaft of an engine which receives reciprocating motion from the pistons and converts it to rotary motion.

CYLINDER: In an engine, the round hole in the engine block in which the piston(s) ride.

CYLINDER BLOCK: The main structural member of an engine in which is found the cylinders, crankshaft and other principal parts.

CYLINDER HEAD: The detachable portion of the engine, usually fastened to the top of the cylinder block and containing all or most of the combustion chambers. On overhead valve engines, it contains the valves and their operating parts. On overhead cam engines, it contains the camshaft as well.

DEAD CENTER: The extreme top or bottom of the piston stroke.

DETONATION: An unwanted explosion of the air/fuel mixture in the combustion chamber caused by excess heat and compression, advanced timing, or an overly lean mixture. Also referred to as "ping".

DIAPHRAGM: A thin, flexible wall separating two cavities, such as in a vacuum advance unit.

DIESELING: A condition in which hot spots in the combustion chamber cause the engine to run on after the key is turned off.

DIFFERENTIAL: A geared assembly which allows the transmission of motion between drive axles, giving one axle the ability to turn faster than the other.

DIODE: An electrical device that will allow current to flow in one direction only.

DISC BRAKE: A hydraulic braking assembly consisting of a brake disc, or rotor, mounted on an axle, and a caliper assembly containing, usually two brake pads which are activated by hydraulic pressure. The pads are forced against the sides of the disc, creating friction which slows the vehicle.

DISTRIBUTOR: A mechanically driven device on an engine which is responsible for electrically firing the spark plug at a predetermined point of the piston stroke.

DOWEL PIN: A pin, inserted in mating holes in two different parts allowing those parts to maintain a fixed relationship.

DRUM BRAKE: A braking system which consists of two brake shoes and one or two wheel cylinders, mounted on a fixed backing plate, and a brake drum, mounted on an axle, which revolves around the assembly.

DWELL: The rate, measured in degrees of shaft rotation, at which an electrical circuit cycles on and off.

ELECTRONIC CONTROL UNIT (ECU): Ignition module, module, amplifier or igniter. See Module for definition.

ELECTRONIC IGNITION: A system in which the timing and firing of the spark plugs is controlled by an electronic control unit, usually called a module. These systems have no points or condenser.

END-PLAY: The measured amount of axial movement in a shaft.

ENGINE: A device that converts heat into mechanical energy.

EXHAUST MANIFOLD: A set of cast passages or pipes which conduct exhaust gases from the engine.

FEELER GAUGE: A blade, usually metal, of precisely predetermined thickness, used to measure the clearance between two parts.

FIRING ORDER: The order in which combustion occurs in the cylinders of an engine. Also the order in which spark is distributed to the plugs by the distributor.

FLOODING: The presence of too much fuel in the intake manifold and combustion chamber which prevents the air/fuel mixture from firing, thereby causing a no-start situation.

FLYWHEEL: A disc shaped part bolted to the rear end of the crankshaft. Around the outer perimeter is affixed the ring gear. The starter drive engages the ring gear, turning the flywheel, which rotates the crankshaft, imparting the initial starting motion to the engine.

FOOT POUND (ft. lbs. or sometimes, ft.lb.): The amount of energy or work needed to raise an item weighing one pound, a distance of one foot.

FUSE: A protective device in a circuit which prevents circuit overload by breaking the circuit when a specific amperage is present. The device is constructed around a strip or wire of a lower amperage rating than the circuit it is designed to protect. When an amperage higher than that stamped on the fuse is present in the circuit, the strip or wire melts, opening the circuit.

GEAR RATIO: The ratio between the number of teeth on meshing gears.

GENERATOR: A device which converts mechanical energy into electrical energy.

HEAT RANGE: The measure of a spark plug's ability to dissipate heat from its firing end. The higher the heat range, the hotter the plug fires.

HUB: The center part of a wheel or gear.

HYDROCARBON (HC): Any chemical compound made up of hydrogen and carbon. A major pollutant formed by the engine as a byproduct of combustion.

HYDROMETER: An instrument used to measure the specific gravity of a solution.

INCH POUND (inch lbs.; sometimes in.lb. or in. lbs.): One twelfth of a foot pound.

INDUCTION: A means of transferring electrical energy in the form of a magnetic field. Principle used in the ignition coil to increase voltage.

INJECTOR: A device which receives metered fuel under relatively low pressure and is activated to inject the fuel into the engine under relatively high pressure at a predetermined time.

INPUT SHAFT: The shaft to which torque is applied, usually carrying the driving gear or gears.

INTAKE MANIFOLD: A casting of passages or pipes used to conduct air or a fuel/air mixture to the cylinders.

JOURNAL: The bearing surface within which a shaft operates.

KEY: A small block usually fitted in a notch between a shaft and a hub to prevent slippage of the two parts.

MANIFOLD: A casting of passages or set of pipes which connect the cylinders to an inlet or outlet source.

MANIFOLD VACUUM: Low pressure in an engine intake manifold formed just below the throttle plates. Manifold vacuum is highest at idle and drops under acceleration.

MASTER CYLINDER: The primary fluid pressurizing device in a hydraulic system. In automotive use, it is found in brake and hydraulic clutch systems and is pedal activated, either directly or, in a power brake system, through the power booster.

MODULE: Electronic control unit, amplifier or igniter of solid state or integrated design which controls the current flow in the ignition primary circuit based on input from the pick-up coil. When the module opens the primary circuit, high secondary voltage is induced in the coil.

NEEDLE BEARING: A bearing which consists of a number (usually a large number) of long, thin rollers.

OHM: (Ω) The unit used to measure the resistance of conductor-to-electrical flow. One ohm is the amount of resistance that limits current flow to one ampere in a circuit with one volt of pressure.

OHMMETER: An instrument used for measuring the resistance, in ohms, in an electrical circuit.

OUTPUT SHAFT: The shaft which transmits torque from a device, such as a transmission.

OVERDRIVE: A gear assembly which produces more shaft revolutions than that transmitted to it.

OVERHEAD CAMSHAFT (OHC): An engine configuration in which the camshaft is mounted on top of the cylinder head and operates the valve either directly or by means of rocker arms.

OVERHEAD VALVE (OHV): An engine configuration in which all of the valves are located in the cylinder head and the camshaft is located in the cylinder block. The camshaft operates the valves via lifters and pushrods.

OXIDES OF NITROGEN (NOx): Chemical compounds of nitrogen produced as a byproduct of combustion. They combine with hydrocarbons to produce smog.

OXYGEN SENSOR: Used with the feedback system to sense the presence of oxygen in the exhaust gas and signal the computer which can reference the voltage signal to an air/fuel ratio.

PINION: The smaller of two meshing gears.

PISTON RING: An open-ended ring which fits into a groove on the outer diameter of the piston. Its chief function is to form a seal between the piston and cylinder wall. Most automotive pistons have three rings: two for compression sealing; one for oil sealing.

PRELOAD: A predetermined load placed on a bearing during assembly or by adjustment.

PRIMARY CIRCUIT: The low voltage side of the ignition system which consists of the ignition switch, ballast resistor or resistance wire, bypass, coil, electronic control unit and pick-up coil as well as the connecting wires and harnesses.

PRESS FIT: The mating of two parts under pressure, due to the inner diameter of one being smaller than the outer diameter of the other, or vice versa; an interference fit.

RACE: The surface on the inner or outer ring of a bearing on which the balls, needles or rollers move.

REGULATOR: A device which maintains the amperage and/or voltage levels of a circuit at predetermined values.

RELAY: A switch which automatically opens and/or closes a circuit.

RESISTANCE: The opposition to the flow of current through a circuit or electrical device, and is measured in ohms. Resistance is equal to the voltage divided by the amperage.

RESISTOR: A device, usually made of wire, which offers a preset amount of resistance in an electrical circuit.

RING GEAR: The name given to a ring-shaped gear attached to a differential case, or affixed to a flywheel or as part of a planetary gear set.

ROLLER BEARING: A bearing made up of hardened inner and outer races between which hardened steel rollers move.

ROTOR: 1. The disc-shaped part of a disc brake assembly, upon which the brake pads bear; also called, brake disc. 2. The device mounted atop the distributor shaft, which passes current to the distributor cap tower contacts.

SECONDARY CIRCUIT: The high voltage side of the ignition system, usually above 20,000 volts. The secondary includes the ignition coil, coil wire, distributor cap and rotor, spark plug wires and spark plugs.

SENDING UNIT: A mechanical, electrical, hydraulic or electromagnetic device which transmits information to a gauge.

SENSOR: Any device designed to measure engine operating conditions or ambient pressures and temperatures. Usually electronic in nature and designed to send a voltage signal to an on-board computer, some sensors may operate as a simple on/off switch or they may provide a variable voltage signal (like a potentiometer) as conditions or measured parameters change.

SHIM: Spacers of precise, predetermined thickness used between parts to establish a proper working relationship.

SLAVE CYLINDER: In automotive use, a device in the hydraulic clutch system which is activated by hydraulic force, disengaging the clutch.

SOLENOID: A coil used to produce a magnetic field, the effect of which is to produce work.

SPARK PLUG: A device screwed into the combustion chamber of a spark ignition engine. The basic construction is a conductive core inside of a ceramic insulator, mounted in an outer conductive base. An electrical charge from the spark plug wire travels along the conductive core and jumps a preset air gap to a grounding point or points at the end of the conductive base. The resultant spark ignites the fuel/air mixture in the combustion chamber.

SPLINES: Ridges machined or cast onto the outer diameter of a shaft or inner diameter of a bore to enable parts to mate without rotation.

TACHOMETER: A device used to measure the rotary speed of an engine, shaft, gear, etc., usually in rotations per minute.

THERMOSTAT: A valve, located in the cooling system of an engine, which is closed when cold and opens gradually in response to engine heating, controlling the temperature of the coolant and rate of coolant flow.

TOP DEAD CENTER (TDC): The point at which the piston reaches the top of its travel on the compression stroke.

TORQUE: The twisting force applied to an object.

TORQUE CONVERTER: A turbine used to transmit power from a driving member to a driven member via hydraulic action, providing changes in drive ratio and torque. In automotive use, it links the driveplate at the rear of the engine to the automatic transmission.

TRANSDUCER: A device used to change a force into an electrical signal.

TRANSISTOR: A semi-conductor component which can be actuated by a small voltage to perform an electrical switching function.

TUNE-UP: A regular maintenance function, usually associated with the replacement and adjustment of parts and components in the electrical and fuel systems of a vehicle for the purpose of attaining optimum performance.

TURBOCHARGER: An exhaust driven pump which compresses intake air and forces it into the combustion chambers at higher than atmospheric pressures. The increased air pressure allows more fuel to be burned and results in increased horsepower being produced.

VACUUM ADVANCE: A device which advances the ignition timing in response to increased engine vacuum.

VACUUM GAUGE: An instrument used to measure the presence of vacuum in a chamber.

VALVE: A device which control the pressure, direction of flow or rate of flow of a liquid or gas.

VALVE CLEARANCE: The measured gap between the end of the valve stem and the rocker arm, cam lobe or follower that activates the valve.

VISCOSITY: The rating of a liquid's internal resistance to flow.

VOLTMETER: An instrument used for measuring electrical force in units called volts. Voltmeters are always connected parallel with the circuit being tested.

WHEEL CYLINDER: Found in the automotive drum brake assembly, it is a device, actuated by hydraulic pressure, which, through internal pistons, pushes the brake shoes outward against the drums.

ADD-ON ELECTRICAL EQUIPMENT   6-10
ADJUSTMENT (CLUTCH)   7-7
   FREE-PLAY   7-7
ADJUSTMENT (MANUAL TRANSMISSION)   7-2
   LINKAGE   7-2
ADJUSTMENTS (AUTOMATIC TRANSMISSION)   7-14
   ACCELERATOR PEDAL DOWNSHIFT LINKAGE   7-17
   DETENT (DOWNSHIFT) LINKAGE   7-17
   SHIFT LINKAGE/CABLE   7-14
ADJUSTMENTS (BRAKE OPERATING SYSTEM)   9-3
   FRONT BRAKES   9-3
   REAR DRUM BRAKE SHOES   9-3
AIR CLEANER   1-20
   REMOVAL & INSTALLATION   1-20
AIR CONDITIONING   1-31
   DISCHARGING, EVACUATING & CHARGING   1-33
   GENERAL SERVICING PROCEDURES   1-32
   SAFETY PRECAUTIONS   1-31
   SYSTEM INSPECTION   1-33
AIR INJECTION REACTOR (AIR) SYSTEM   4-10
   COMPONENT REMOVAL & INSTALLATION   4-12
   OPERATION   4-10
   SERVICE   4-12
AIR MANAGEMENT SYSTEM   4-13
   OPERATION   4-13
   REMOVAL & INSTALLATION   4-14
AIR POLLUTION   4-2
ALTERNATOR   3-10
   ALTERNATOR PRECAUTIONS   3-10
   REMOVAL & INSTALLATION   3-11
   TESTING   3-13
ANTENNA   10-9
   REMOVAL & INSTALLATION   10-9
ANTI-DIESELING SOLENOID   4-14
   OPERATION   4-14
AUTOMATIC TRANSMISSION   7-12
AUTOMATIC TRANSMISSION (FLUIDS AND LUBRICANTS)   1-48
   DRAIN, REFILL & FILTER SERVICE   1-49
   LEVEL CHECK & FLUID RECOMMENDATIONS   1-48
AUTOMOTIVE EMISSIONS   4-3
AUTOMOTIVE POLLUTANTS   4-2
   HEAT TRANSFER   4-3
   TEMPERATURE INVERSION   4-2
AVOIDING THE MOST COMMON MISTAKES   1-2
AVOIDING TROUBLE   1-2
AXLE SHAFT AND BEARINGS   7-26
   DETERMINING GEAR RATIO   7-32
   REMOVAL & INSTALLATION   7-28
BASIC FUEL SYSTEM DIAGNOSIS   5-2
BASIC OPERATING PRINCIPLES   9-2
   DISC BRAKES   9-2
   DRUM BRAKES   9-3
BATTERY (ENGINE ELECTRICAL)   3-19
   REMOVAL & INSTALLATION   3-19
BATTERY (ROUTINE MAINTENANCE)   1-24
   BATTERY FLUID   1-24
   CABLES   1-26
   CHARGING   1-27
   GENERAL MAINTENANCE   1-24
   REPLACEMENT   1-27
BATTERY AND STARTER SPECIFICATIONS   3-20
BATTERY, STARTING AND CHARGING SYSTEMS   3-4
   BASIC OPERATING PRINCIPLES   3-4
BELTS   1-27
   CHECKING TENSION & ADJUSTING   1-28
   INSPECTION   1-27
   REMOVAL & INSTALLATION   1-29
BLOCK HEATER   3-84
   REMOVAL & INSTALLATION   3-84
BLOWER MOTOR   6-12
   REMOVAL & INSTALLATION   6-12

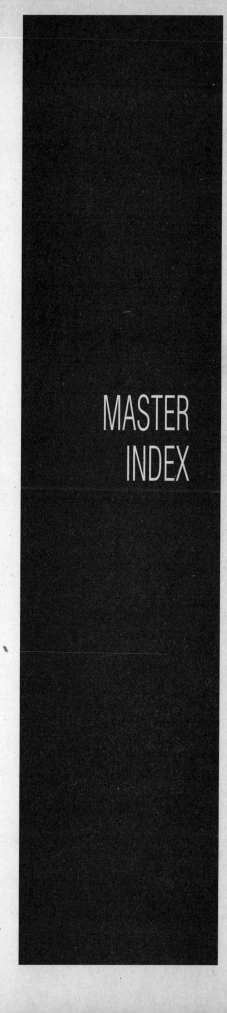

MASTER

INDEX

BODY LUBRICATION 1-57
   DOOR HINGES 1-57
   HOOD LATCH & HINGES 1-57
BOLTS, NUTS AND OTHER THREADED RETAINERS 1-8
BRAKE BLEEDING 9-11
   MANUAL BLEEDING 9-11
BRAKE DISC (ROTOR) 9-18
   INSPECTION 9-19
   REMOVAL & INSTALLATION 9-18
BRAKE DRUM 9-25
   DRUM INSPECTION 9-25
   REPLACEMENT 9-25
BRAKE MASTER CYLINDER 1-54
   LEVEL CHECK & FLUID RECOMMENDATIONS 1-54
BRAKE OPERATING SYSTEM 9-2
BRAKE SHOES 9-25
   REMOVAL & INSTALLATION 9-25
BRAKE SPECIFICATIONS 9-30
BREAKER POINTS AND CONDENSER 2-9
   DWELL ADJUSTMENT 2-12
   REMOVAL & INSTALLATION 2-9
BUMPERS 10-7
   REMOVAL & INSTALLATION 10-7
CAMSHAFT 3-64
   INSPECTION 3-65
   REMOVAL & INSTALLATION 3-64
CAMSHAFT BEARINGS 3-66
   REMOVAL & INSTALLATION 3-66
CAMSHAFT SPECIFICATIONS 3-32
CAPACITIES CHART 1-67
CARBURETED ENGINES 2-22
   FAST IDLE 2-31
   IDLE SPEED & MIXTURE 2-22
CARBURETED FUEL SYSTEM 5-2
CARBURETOR 5-4
   ADJUSTMENTS 5-7
   OVERHAUL 5-15
   REMOVAL & INSTALLATION 5-4
CATALYTIC CONVERTER 4-28
   CATALYST TESTING 4-29
   OPERATION 4-28
   PRECAUTIONS 4-29
CHASSIS GREASING 1-55
   AUTOMATIC TRANSMISSION LINKAGE 1-57
   FRONT SUSPENSION 1-55
   PARKING BRAKE LINKAGE 1-56
   STEERING LINKAGE 1-56
CHECKING ENGINE COMPRESSION 3-23
CIRCUIT BREAKERS 6-42
CIRCUIT PROTECTION 6-39
CLUTCH 7-7
COIL SPRINGS 8-16
   REMOVAL & INSTALLATION 8-16
COMBINATION VALVE 9-9
   REMOVAL & INSTALLATION 9-11
COMPONENT LOCATIONS
   FRONT SUSPENSION COMPONENTS 8-3
   HEI DISTRIBUTOR COMPONENTS 3-8
   MAINTENANCE COMPONENT LOCATIONS—231 V6 1-19
   REAR DRUM BRAKE COMPONENTS 9-24
   REAR SUSPENSION COMPONENTS 8-15
COMPUTER COMMAND CONTROL (CCC) SYSTEM 4-20
   ACTIVATING THE TROUBLE CODE 4-25
   BASIC TROUBLESHOOTING 4-23
COMPUTER CONTROLLED CATALYTIC CONVERTER (C-4)
   SYSTEM 4-19
   OPERATION 4-19
CONTROLLED COMBUSTION SYSTEM 4-18

   OPERATION 4-18
   SERVICE 4-19
COOLING 1-58
   ENGINE 1-58
   TRANSMISSION 1-59
COOLING SYSTEM 1-50
   CHECK THE RADIATOR CAP 1-53
   CLEAN THE RADIATOR OF DEBRIS 1-53
   DRAINING, FLUSHING & TESTING THE COOLING SYSTEM 1-52
   LEVEL CHECK & FLUID RECOMMENDATIONS 1-50
CRANKCASE DEPRESSION REGULATOR AND FLOW CONTROL
   VALVE 1-21
   SERVICING 1-21
CRANKCASE EMISSIONS 4-5
CRANKCASE VENTILATION 4-31
   OPERATION 4-31
CRANKSHAFT AND CONNECTING ROD SPECIFICATIONS 3-29
CRANKSHAFT AND MAIN BEARINGS 3-75
   CHECKING CLEARANCE 3-76
   CRANKSHAFT END-PLAY & INSTALLATION 3-77
   MAIN BEARING INSPECTION & REPLACEMENT 3-76
   MAIN BEARING REPLACEMENT 3-76
   REMOVAL 3-75
CYLINDER HEAD 3-43
   CHECKING FOR HEAD WARPAGE 3-48
   CLEANING & INSPECTION 3-47
   REMOVAL & INSTALLATION 3-43
DESCRIPTION AND OPERATION 2-12
   HEI SYSTEM PRECAUTIONS 2-13
DESIGN 3-24
DIESEL ENGINE EMISSIONS CONTROLS 4-31
DIESEL ENGINE FUEL SYSTEM 5-25
DIESEL ENGINE PRECAUTIONS 2-2
DIESEL ENGINE TRANSMISSION 7-19
   ADJUSTMENTS 7-19
DIESEL FUEL INJECTION 2-31
   IDLE SPEED ADJUSTMENT 2-31
DIESEL INJECTION TIMING 2-21
   DIESEL ENGINES 2-21
DIESEL MAINTENANCE INTERVALS 1-66
DISC BRAKE CALIPERS 9-16
   REMOVAL, INSTALLATION & OVERHAUL 9-16
DISC BRAKE PADS 9-12
   INSPECTION 9-12
   REMOVAL & INSTALLATION 9-14
DISTRIBUTOR 3-5
   REMOVAL & INSTALLATION 3-5
DISTRIBUTOR COMPONENTS TESTING 2-14
DO'S 1-7
DON'TS 1-8
DOOR GLASS 10-16
   ADJUSTMENT 10-17
   REMOVAL & INSTALLATION 10-16
DOOR LOCKS 10-14
   REMOVAL & INSTALLATION 10-14
DOORS 10-2
   ADJUSTMENT 10-3
   REMOVAL & INSTALLATION 10-2
DRIVELINE 7-23
DRIVEN DISC AND PRESSURE PLATE 7-8
   REMOVAL & INSTALLATION 7-8
DRIVESHAFT AND U-JOINTS 7-23
   REMOVAL & INSTALLATION 7-23
   U-JOINT OVERHAUL 7-24
EARLY FUEL EVAPORATION (EFE) SYSTEM 4-14
   OPERATION 4-14
   REMOVAL & INSTALLATION 4-15
EGR SYSTEM DIAGNOSIS—DIESEL ENGINE 4-32

ELECTRIC WINDOW MOTOR 10-18
   REMOVAL & INSTALLATION 10-18
ELECTRONIC SPARK CONTROL (ESC) 4-27
ELECTRONIC SPARK TIMING (EST) 4-27
ENGINE (ENGINE MECHANICAL) 3-33
   REMOVAL & INSTALLATION 3-33
ENGINE (FLUIDS AND LUBRICANTS) 1-45
   LEVEL CHECK 1-45
   OIL & FILTER CHANGE 1-46
ENGINE CORE PLUGS (FREEZE PLUGS) 3-83
   REMOVAL & INSTALLATION 3-83
ENGINE ELECTRICAL 3-2
ENGINE IDENTIFICATION CODES 1-16
ENGINE MECHANICAL 3-22
ENGINE MECHANICAL PROBLEMS 3-93
ENGINE OIL AND FUEL RECOMMENDATIONS 1-42
   FUEL 1-44
   OIL 1-43
   SYNTHETIC OIL 1-44
ENGINE OVERHAUL TIPS 3-22
   INSPECTION TECHNIQUES 3-22
   OVERHAUL TIPS 3-22
   REPAIRING DAMAGED THREADS 3-22
   TOOLS 3-22
ENGINE PERFORMANCE 3-96
ENGINE TEMPERATURE SENSOR (ETS) 4-34
   OPERATION 4-34
ENGLISH TO METRIC CONVERSION CHARTS 1-70
EVAPORATIVE CANISTER 1-22
   SERVICING 1-22
EVAPORATIVE EMISSION CONTROL SYSTEM 4-7
   OPERATION 4-7
   SERVICE 4-9
EVAPORATIVE EMISSION CONTROLS 4-5
EVAPORATIVE EMISSIONS 4-5
EXHAUST EMISSION CONTROLS 4-9
EXHAUST GAS RECIRCULATION (EGR) SYSTEM (DIESEL) 4-32
   FUNCTIONAL TESTS OF COMPONENTS 4-32
   OPERATION 4-32
EXHAUST GAS RECIRCULATION (EGR) SYSTEM (GASOLINE) 4-16
   EGR VALVE CLEANING 4-18
   OPERATION 4-16
   REMOVAL & INSTALLATION 4-16
EXHAUST GASES 4-3
   CARBON MONOXIDE 4-4
   HYDROCARBONS 4-3
   NITROGEN 4-4
   OXIDES OF SULFUR 4-4
   PARTICULATE MATTER 4-4
EXHAUST MANIFOLD 3-42
   REMOVAL & INSTALLATION 3-42
EXHAUST SYSTEM 3-90
EXTERIOR 10-2
FASTENERS, MEASUREMENTS AND CONVERSIONS 1-8
5210-C AND 6510-C 2-BARREL CARBURETOR SPECIFICATIONS 5-18
4-BBL CARBURETOR SPECIFICATIONS 5-25
FIRING ORDERS 2-8
FLASHERS 6-42
   REPLACEMENT 6-42
FLUID DISPOSAL 1-42
FLUID PAN 7-12
   REMOVAL & INSTALLATION/FILTER SERVICE 7-12
FLUIDS AND LUBRICANTS 1-42
FLYWHEEL AND RING GEAR 3-83
   REMOVAL & INSTALLATION 3-83
FRONT DISC BRAKES 9-12
FRONT DOOR PANELS 10-10
   REMOVAL & INSTALLATION 10-10

FRONT DOOR REGULATOR 10-18
   REMOVAL & INSTALLATION 10-18
FRONT END ALIGNMENT 8-11
   CAMBER 8-11
   CASTER 8-11
   STEERING AXIS INCLINATION 8-11
   TOE-IN 8-12
FRONT SUSPENSION 8-2
FRONT SUSPENSION COMPONENTS 8-3
FUEL FILTER 1-22
   REMOVAL & INSTALLATION 1-22
FUEL SUPPLY PUMP 5-25
   PURGING THE FUEL TANK 5-25
   REMOVAL & INSTALLATION 5-25
   WATER IN FUEL 5-25
FUEL TANK 5-29
FUSES 6-39
FUSIBLE LINKS 6-42
   REPLACEMENT 6-42
GASOLINE ENGINE TUNE-UP SPECIFICATIONS 2-33
GASOLINE ENGINES 2-20
   INSPECTION & ADJUSTMENT 2-20
GENERAL ENGINE SPECIFICATIONS 3-25
GENERAL INFORMATION (EXHAUST SYSTEM) 3-90
   COMPONENT REPLACEMENT 3-91
   SPECIAL TOOLS 3-91
GENERAL INFORMATION (IDLE SPEED AND MIXTURE
   ADJUSTMENTS) 2-22
GENERAL RECOMMENDATIONS 1-58
GRAND PRIX DIESEL TUNE-UP SPECIFICATIONS 2-36
GRILLE 10-8
   REMOVAL & INSTALLATION 10-8
HANDLING A TRAILER 1-59
HEADLIGHTS 6-32
   AIMING 6-32
   REMOVAL & INSTALLATION 6-32
HEATER 6-12
HEATER CORE 6-12
   REMOVAL & INSTALLATION 6-12
HEI DISTRIBUTOR COMPONENTS 3-8
HEI SYSTEM MAINTENANCE 2-15
   COMPONENT REPLACEMENT 2-15
HIGH ENERGY IGNITION (HEI) SYSTEM 2-12
HITCH (TONGUE) WEIGHT 1-58
HOOD 10-4
   ALIGNMENT 10-5
   REMOVAL & INSTALLATION 10-4
HOSES 1-30
   INSPECTION 1-30
   REMOVAL & INSTALLATION 1-30
HOW TO BUY A USED VEHICLE 1-62
HOW TO USE THIS BOOK 1-2
HYDRO-BOOST II BRAKE BOOSTER 9-6
   HYDRO-BOOST SYSTEM BLEEDING 9-7
   HYDRO-BOOST SYSTEM CHECKS 9-6
   HYDRO-BOOST TESTS 9-7
   HYDRO-BOOST TROUBLESHOOTING 9-7
   OVERHAUL 9-7
   REMOVAL & INSTALLATION 9-8
IDENTIFICATION (AUTOMATIC TRANSMISSION) 7-12
IDENTIFICATION (MANUAL TRANSMISSION) 7-2
IDENTIFICATION (REAR AXLE) 7-26
IDLE SPEED AND MIXTURE ADJUSTMENTS 2-22
IDLE SPEED CONTROL (ISC) 4-27
   V6 ENGINES 4-27
IGNITION LOCK CYLINDER 8-23
   REMOVAL & INSTALLATION 8-23
IGNITION SWITCH 6-32

REMOVAL & INSTALLATION 6-32
IGNITION TIMING 2-20
INDUSTRIAL POLLUTANTS 4-2
INJECTION NOZZLE 5-27
  REMOVAL & INSTALLATION 5-27
INJECTION PUMP 5-26
  ADJUSTMENTS 5-26
  REMOVAL & INSTALLATION 5-26
INJECTION PUMP ADAPTER AND SEAL 5-28
  REMOVAL & INSTALLATION 5-28
INSIDE REAR VIEW MIRROR 10-24
  REPLACEMENT 10-24
INSTRUMENT CLUSTER 6-28
  REMOVAL & INSTALLATION 6-28
INSTRUMENTS AND SWITCHES 6-27
INTAKE MANIFOLD 3-38
  REMOVAL & INSTALLATION 3-38
INTERIOR 10-10
JACKING 1-60
JACKING PRECAUTIONS 1-62
JUMP STARTING A DEAD BATTERY 1-59
JUMP STARTING PRECAUTIONS 1-59
JUMP STARTING PROCEDURE 1-60
LEAF SPRINGS 8-16
  REMOVAL & INSTALLATION 8-16
LIGHT SWITCH 6-27
  REPLACEMENT & INSTALLATION 6-27
LIGHTING 6-32
LOWER BALL JOINTS 8-8
  INSPECTION 8-8
  REMOVAL & INSTALLATION 8-8
LOWER CONTROL ARM 8-10
  REMOVAL & INSTALLATION 8-10
MAINTENANCE COMPONENT LOCATIONS—231 V6 1-19
MAINTENANCE OR REPAIR? 1-2
MANUAL TRANSMISSION 7-2
MANUAL TRANSMISSION (FLUIDS AND LUBRICANTS) 1-48
  DRAIN & REFILL 1-48
  FLUID RECOMMENDATIONS 1-48
  LEVEL CHECK 1-48
MANUAL TRANSMISSION I.D. CHART 7-3
MASTER CYLINDER 9-3
  OVERHAUL 9-5
  REMOVAL & INSTALLATION 9-3
MECHANICAL FUEL PUMP 5-2
  REMOVAL & INSTALLATION 5-2
  TESTING 5-3
M4MC, M4ME, E4MC 4-BARREL CARBURETOR SPECIFICATIONS 5-22
MIXTURE CONTROL SOLENOID (M/C) 4-26
MV CARBURETOR SPECIFICATIONS 5-17
NATURAL POLLUTANTS 4-2
NEUTRAL SAFETY SWITCH 7-18
  ADJUSTMENT 7-18
1974–76 MAINTENANCE INTERVALS—GASOLINE-ENGINED
  CARS 1-64
1977 AND LATER MAINTENANCE INTERVALS—GASOLINE-ENGINED
  CARS 1-65
OIL PAN 3-78
  REMOVAL & INSTALLATION 3-78
OIL PUMP 3-78
  OVERHAUL 3-79
  REMOVAL & INSTALLATION 3-78
OUTSIDE MIRRORS 10-8
  REMOVAL & INSTALLATION 10-8
OXYGEN SENSOR 4-29
  OPERATION 4-29
  REMOVAL & INSTALLATION 4-30
PARKING BRAKE 9-29

ADJUSTMENT 9-29
PISTON AND RING SPECIFICATIONS 3-30
PISTONS AND CONNECTING RODS 3-66
  ASSEMBLY & INSTALLATION 3-74
  CLEANING & INSPECTION 3-69
  CONNECTING ROD BEARINGS 3-73
  PISTON RING END-GAP 3-71
  PISTON RING SIDE CLEARANCE CHECK & INSTALLATION 3-71
  REMOVAL 3-66
POINT TYPE IGNITION 2-9
POSITIVE CRANKCASE VENTILATION (PCV) VALVE 1-20
  REMOVAL & INSTALLATION 1-21
POSITIVE CRANKCASE VENTILATION SYSTEM 4-6
  OPERATION 4-6
  PCV VALVE SERVICE 4-6
  REMOVAL & INSTALLATION 4-7
POWER BOOSTER 9-6
  REMOVAL & INSTALLATION 9-6
POWER SEAT MOTOR 10-25
  REMOVAL & INSTALLATION 10-25
POWER STEERING GEARBOX 8-27
  REMOVAL & INSTALLATION 8-27
POWER STEERING PUMP (STEERING) 8-28
  BLEEDING 8-28
  REMOVAL & INSTALLATION 8-28
POWER STEERING PUMP (FLUIDS AND LUBRICANTS) 1-54
  LEVEL CHECK & FLUID RECOMMENDATIONS 1-54
RADIATOR 3-87
  REMOVAL & INSTALLATION 3-87
RADIO 6-20
RADIO RECEIVER 6-20
  REMOVAL & INSTALLATION 6-20
REAR AXLE 7-26
REAR AXLE (FLUIDS AND LUBRICANTS) 1-49
  DRAIN & REFILL 1-50
  LEVEL CHECK & FLUID RECOMMENDATIONS 1-49
REAR DOOR PANELS 10-14
  REMOVAL & INSTALLATION 10-14
REAR DOOR VENT WINDOW 10-23
  REMOVAL & INSTALLATION 10-23
REAR DRUM BRAKE COMPONENTS 9-24
REAR DRUM BRAKES 9-24
REAR MAIN OIL SEAL 3-80
  REMOVAL & INSTALLATION 3-80
REAR SUSPENSION 8-13
REAR SUSPENSION COMPONENTS 8-15
REAR WINDOW GLASS 10-21
  INSTALLATION 10-21
  REMOVAL 10-21
RECOMMENDED LUBRICANTS 1-43
ROCKER ARMS 3-36
  REMOVAL & INSTALLATION 3-36
ROUTINE MAINTENANCE 1-19
SAFETY PRECAUTIONS 6-2
SEAT BELT/STARTER INTERLOCK SYSTEM 6-32
  DISABLING THE INTERLOCK SYSTEM 6-32
SEAT BELT SYSTEMS 10-25
  REMOVAL & INSTALLATION 10-25
SEATS 10-25
  REMOVAL & INSTALLATION 10-25
SERIAL NUMBER IDENTIFICATION 1-14
SERVICING YOUR VEHICLE SAFELY 1-7
SHOCK ABSORBERS (FRONT SUSPENSION) 8-4
  REMOVAL & INSTALLATION 8-4
  TESTING 8-4
SHOCK ABSORBERS (REAR SUSPENSION) 8-17
  REMOVAL & INSTALLATION 8-17
SIGNAL AND MARKER LIGHTS 6-35

REMOVAL & INSTALLATION   6-35
SPARK PLUGS   2-2
   CHECKING & REPLACING SPARK PLUG WIRES   2-7
   INSPECTION & GAPPING   2-4
   REMOVAL & INSTALLATION   2-3
   SPARK PLUG HEAT RANGE   2-2
SPECIAL TOOLS   1-6
SPECIFICATION CHARTS
  BATTERY AND STARTER SPECIFICATIONS   3-20
  BRAKE SPECIFICATIONS   9-30
  CAMSHAFT SPECIFICATIONS   3-32
  CAPACITIES CHART   1-67
  CRANKSHAFT AND CONNECTING ROD SPECIFICATIONS   3-29
  DIESEL MAINTENANCE INTERVALS   1-66
  EGR SYSTEM DIAGNOSIS—DIESEL ENGINE   4-32
  ENGINE IDENTIFICATION CODES   1-16
  ENGLISH TO METRIC CONVERSION CHARTS   1-70
  5210-C AND 6510-C 2-BARREL CARBURETOR SPECIFICATIONS   5-18
  4-BBL CARBURETOR SPECIFICATIONS   5-25
  GASOLINE ENGINE TUNE-UP SPECIFICATIONS   2-33
  GENERAL ENGINE SPECIFICATIONS   3-25
  GRAND PRIX DIESEL TUNE-UP SPECIFICATIONS   2-36
  MANUAL TRANSMISSION I.D. CHART   7-3
  M4MC, M4ME, E4MC 4-BARREL CARBURETOR SPECIFICATIONS   5-22
  MV CARBURETOR SPECIFICATIONS   5-17
  1974–76 MAINTENANCE INTERVALS—GASOLINE-ENGINED CARS   1-64
  1977 AND LATER MAINTENANCE INTERVALS—GASOLINE-ENGINED CARS   1-65
  PISTON AND RING SPECIFICATIONS   3-30
  RECOMMENDED LUBRICANTS   1-43
  STANDARD TORQUE SPECIFICATIONS AND FASTENER MARKINGS   1-10
  TORQUE SPECIFICATIONS   3-31
  2GC, GE, GV 2-BARREL CARBURETOR SPECIFICATIONS   5-19
  2MC, M2MC, M2ME, E2MC, E2ME 2-BARREL CARBURETOR SPECIFICATIONS   5-20
  2MC, M2MC, M2ME, E2ME CARBURETOR SPECIFICATIONS   5-21
  VALVE SPECIFICATIONS   3-27
  WHEEL ALIGNMENT SPECIFICATIONS   8-12
SPEEDOMETER CABLE   6-28
   REMOVAL & INSTALLATION   6-28
SPRINGS   8-4
   REMOVAL & INSTALLATION   8-4
STANDARD AND METRIC MEASUREMENTS   1-12
STANDARD TORQUE SPECIFICATIONS AND FASTENER MARKINGS   1-10
STARTER   3-14
   REMOVAL & INSTALLATION   3-14
   SHIMMING THE STARTER   3-16
   STARTER OVERHAUL   3-17
STATIONARY GLASS   10-23
   REMOVAL & INSTALLATION   10-23
STEERING   8-20
STEERING WHEEL   8-20
   REMOVAL & INSTALLATION   8-20
SWAY BAR   8-9
   REMOVAL & INSTALLATION   8-9
TACHOMETER HOOKUP   2-19
   GASOLINE ENGINES (HEI SYSTEM)   2-19
TANK ASSEMBLY   5-29
   DRAINING THE TANK   5-29
   REMOVAL & INSTALLATION   5-29
THERMOSTAT   3-86
   REMOVAL & INSTALLATION   3-86
THERMOSTATIC AIR CLEANER (THERMAC)   4-9

OPERATION   4-9
   SYSTEM CHECKS   4-10
THROTTLE POSITION SENSOR (TPS)   4-27
TIE ROD ENDS   8-24
   REMOVAL & INSTALLATION   8-24
TIMING CHAIN   3-61
   REMOVAL & INSTALLATION   3-61
TIMING CHAIN COVER AND FRONT OIL SEAL   3-56
   REMOVAL & INSTALLATION   3-56
TIMING GEARS   3-64
   REMOVAL & INSTALLATION   3-64
TIPS   1-62
   ROAD TEST CHECKLIST   1-63
   USED VEHICLE CHECKLIST   1-62
TIRES AND WHEELS   1-38
   CARE OF SPECIAL WHEELS   1-41
   INFLATION & INSPECTION   1-39
   TIRE DESIGN   1-39
   TIRE ROTATION   1-38
   TIRE STORAGE   1-39
TOOLS AND EQUIPMENT   1-3
TORQUE   1-9
   TORQUE ANGLE METERS   1-12
   TORQUE WRENCHES   1-11
TORQUE SPECIFICATIONS   3-31
TRAILER TOWING   1-58
TRAILER WEIGHT   1-58
TRAILER WIRING   6-39
TRANSMISSION   1-17
   AUTOMATIC TRANSMISSIONS   1-17
   MANUAL TRANSMISSIONS   1-17
TRANSMISSION ASSEMBLY (AUTOMATIC TRANSMISSION)   7-21
   REMOVAL & INSTALLATION   7-21
TRANSMISSION ASSEMBLY (MANUAL TRANSMISSION)   7-6
   REMOVAL & INSTALLATION   7-6
TRANSMISSION CONVERTER CLUTCH (TCC)   4-28
TROUBLE CODE IDENTIFICATION CHART   4-24
TROUBLESHOOTING   6-3
   BASIC TROUBLESHOOTING THEORY   6-4
   TEST EQUIPMENT   6-4
   TESTING   6-6
TROUBLESHOOTING CHARTS
  ENGINE MECHANICAL PROBLEMS   3-93
  ENGINE PERFORMANCE   3-96
  TROUBLE CODE IDENTIFICATION CHART   4-24
TROUBLESHOOTING THE HEI SYSTEM   2-14
   ENGINE FAILS TO START   2-14
   ENGINE RUNS, BUT RUNS ROUGH OR CUTS OUT   2-14
TRUNK LID   10-6
   ALIGNMENT   10-6
   REMOVAL & INSTALLATION   10-6
TUNE-UP PROCEDURES   2-2
TURN SIGNAL SWITCH   8-22
2GC, GE, GV 2-BARREL CARBURETOR SPECIFICATIONS   5-19
2MC, M2MC, M2ME, E2MC, E2ME 2-BARREL CARBURETOR SPECIFICATIONS   5-20
2MC, M2MC, M2ME, E2ME CARBURETOR SPECIFICATIONS   5-21
   REMOVAL & INSTALLATION   8-22
UNDERSTANDING AND TROUBLESHOOTING ELECTRICAL SYSTEMS   6-2
UNDERSTANDING BASIC ELECTRICITY   6-2
   AUTOMOTIVE CIRCUITS   6-3
   CIRCUITS   6-2
   SHORT CIRCUITS   6-3
   THE WATER ANALOGY   6-2
UNDERSTANDING ELECTRICITY   3-2
   BASIC CIRCUITS   3-2
   TROUBLESHOOTING   3-3

UNDERSTANDING THE CLUTCH 7-7
UNDERSTANDING THE MANUAL TRANSMISSION 7-2
UPPER BALL JOINTS 8-5
    INSPECTION 8-5
    REMOVAL & INSTALLATION 8-5
UPPER CONTROL ARM 8-9
    REMOVAL & INSTALLATION 8-9
VACUUM DIAGRAMS 4-34
VALVE COVER 3-35
    REMOVAL & INSTALLATION 3-35
VALVE LASH 2-21
VALVE LIFTERS 3-55
    REMOVAL & INSTALLATION 3-55
VALVE SPECIFICATIONS 3-27
VALVES, SPRINGS AND GUIDES 3-48
    INSPECTION 3-50
    LAPPING THE VALVES 3-51
    REMOVAL 3-48
    VALVE ADJUSTMENT 3-54
    VALVE GUIDES 3-52
    VALVE INSTALLATION 3-53
    VALVE SPRINGS 3-53
VEHICLE 1-14
    ENGINE 1-15
VEHICLE EMISSION CONTROL INFORMATION LABEL 1-17
VOLTAGE REGULATOR 3-14
WATER PUMP 3-84
    REMOVAL & INSTALLATION 3-84
WHEEL ALIGNMENT SPECIFICATIONS 8-12
WHEEL ASSEMBLY 8-2

    INSPECTION 8-2
    REMOVAL & INSTALLATION 8-2
WHEEL BEARINGS (FLUIDS AND LUBRICANTS) 1-58
    REMOVAL, PACKING & INSTALLATION 1-58
WHEEL BEARINGS (FRONT DISC BRAKES) 9-20
    ADJUSTMENT 9-20
    REMOVAL, PACKING & INSTALLATION 9-20
WHEEL CYLINDERS 9-28
    OVERHAUL 9-29
    REMOVAL & INSTALLATION 9-28
WHEEL LUG STUDS 8-2
    REPLACEMENT 8-2
WHEELS 8-2
WHERE TO BEGIN 1-2
WINDSHIELD 10-18
    INSTALLATION 10-19
    REMOVAL 10-18
WINDSHIELD WIPER BLADE AND ARM 6-24
    REMOVAL & INSTALLATION 6-24
WINDSHIELD WIPER MOTOR 6-25
    LINKAGE REPLACEMENT 6-25
    REMOVAL & INSTALLATION 6-25
WINDSHIELD WIPER SWITCH 6-27
    REMOVAL & INSTALLATION 6-27
WINDSHIELD WIPERS 6-24
WINDSHIELD WIPERS (ROUTINE MAINTENANCE) 1-34
    ELEMENT (REFILL) CARE & REPLACEMENT 1-34
WIRING DIAGRAMS 6-44
WIRING HARNESSES 6-8
    WIRING REPAIR 6-8